A Companion [illegible] Philosophy of Action

Blackwell Companions to Philosophy

This outstanding student reference series offers a comprehensive and authoritative survey of philosophy as a whole. Written by today's leading philosophers, each volume provides lucid and engaging coverage of the key figures, terms, topics, and problems of the field. Taken together, the volumes provide the ideal basis for course use, representing an unparalleled work of reference for students and specialists alike.

Already published in the series:

1. A Companion to Business Ethics
   Edited by Robert E. Frederick
2. A Companion to the Philosophy of Science
   Edited by W. H. Newton-Smith
3. A Companion to Environmental Philosophy
   Edited by Dale Jamieson
4. A Companion to Analytic Philosophy
   Edited by A. P. Martinich and David Sosa
5. A Companion to Genethics
   Edited by Justine Burley and John Harris
6. A Companion to Philosophical Logic
   Edited by Dale Jacquette
7. A Companion to Early Modern Philosophy
   Edited by Steven Nadler
8. A Companion to Philosophy in the Middle Ages
   Edited by Jorge J. E. Gracia and Timothy B. Noone
9. A Companion to African-American Philosophy
   Edited by Tommy L. Lott and John P. Pittman
10. A Companion to Applied Ethics
    Edited by R. G. Frey and Christopher Heath Wellman
11. A Companion to the Philosophy of Education
    Edited by Randall Curren
12. A Companion to African Philosophy
    Edited by Kwasi Wiredu
13. A Companion to Heidegger
    Edited by Hubert L. Dreyfus and Mark A. Wrathall
14. A Companion to Rationalism
    Edited by Alan Nelson
15. A Companion to Pragmatism
    Edited by John R. Shook and Joseph Margolis
16. A Companion to Ancient Philosophy
    Edited by Mary Louise Gill and Pierre Pellegrin
17. A Companion to Nietzsche
    Edited by Keith Ansell Pearson
18. A Companion to Socrates
    Edited by Sara Ahbel-Rappe and Rachana Kamtekar
19. A Companion to Phenomenology and Existentialism
    Edited by Hubert L. Dreyfus and Mark A. Wrathall
20. A Companion to Kant
    Edited by Graham Bird
21. A Companion to Plato
    Edited by Hugh H. Benson
22. A Companion to Descartes
    Edited by Janet Broughton and John Carriero
23. A Companion to the Philosophy of Biology
    Edited by Sahotra Sarkar and Anya Plutynski
24. A Companion to Hume
    Edited by Elizabeth S. Radcliffe
25. A Companion to the Philosophy of History and Historiography
    Edited by Aviezer Tucker
26. A Companion to Aristotle
    Edited by Georgios Anagnostopoulos
27. A Companion to the Philosophy of Technology
    Edited by Jan-Kyrre Berg Olsen Friis, Stig Andur Pedersen, and Vincent F. Hendricks
28. A Companion to Latin American Philosophy
    Edited by Susana Nuccetelli, Ofelia Schutte, and Otávio Bueno
29. A Companion to the Philosophy of Literature
    Edited by Garry L. Hagberg and Walter Jost
30. A Companion to the Philosophy of Action
    Edited by Timothy O'Connor and Constantine Sandis
31. A Companion to Relativism
    Edited by Steven D. Hales
32. A Companion to Hegel
    Edited by Stephen Houlgate and Michael Baur
33. A Companion to Schopenhauer
    Edited by Bart Vandenabeele

A Companion to the Philosophy of Action

Edited by

Timothy O'Connor and Constantine Sandis

A John Wiley & Sons, Ltd., Publication

This paperback edition first published 2013

Edition history: Blackwell Publishing Ltd (hardback, 2010)

Blackwell Publishing was acquired by John Wiley & Sons in February 2007. Blackwell's publishing program has been merged with Wiley's global Scientific, Technical, and Medical business to form Wiley-Blackwell.

Registered Office
John Wiley & Sons Ltd, The Atrium, Southern Gate, Chichester, West Sussex, PO19 8SQ, United Kingdom

Editorial Offices
350 Main Street, Malden, MA 02148-5020, USA
9600 Garsington Road, Oxford, OX4 2DQ, UK
The Atrium, Southern Gate, Chichester, West Sussex, PO19 8SQ, UK

For details of our global editorial offices, for customer services, and for information about how to apply for permission to reuse the copyright material in this book please see our website at www.wiley.com/wiley-blackwell.

Library of Congress Cataloging-in-Publication Data

A companion to the philosophy of action / edited by Timothy O'Connor and Constantine Sandis.
p. cm. – (Blackwell companions to philosophy)
Includes bibliographical references and index.
ISBN 978-1-4051-8735-0 (hardcover : alk. paper); ISBN 978-1-1183-4632-7 (pbk.)
1. Act (Philosophy) I. O'Connor, Timothy, 1965– II. Sandis, Constantine, 1976–
B105.A35C65 2010
128'.4–dc22

2009053164

A catalogue record for this book is available from the British Library.

Cover image: Making corn stacks, fresco from tomb of Menna, Thebes, Egypt, © 1400–1390 BC, 18th dynasty. Photo © The Art Archive / Gianni Dagli Orti.
Cover design by Workhaus.

Set in 10/12.5pt Photina by Toppan Best-set Premedia Limited

1 2013

This paperback edition is dedicated to the memory of two wonderful contributors:

Paul Hoffman and Fred Stoutland

Contents

List of Illustrations

Notes on Contributors

Kieran Allen is Senior Lecturer in the School of Sociology in University College Dublin. He has lectured extensively on Weber and has written *Max Weber: A Critical Introduction* (London: Pluto Press, 2004). His latest book was on *Ireland's Economic Crash* (Dublin: Liffey Press, 2009).

Maria Alvarez is Lecturer in Philosophy at the University of Southampton, UK. She has published widely on actions, reasons, and their relation. Her book, *Kinds of Reasons: An Essay in the Philosophy of Action*, will be published by Oxford University Press in 2010.

Kent Bach, Professor Emeritus of Philosophy at San Francisco State University, was educated at Harvard College and University of California, Berkeley. He has written extensively in philosophy of language, theory of knowledge, and philosophy of mind. His books include *Thought and Reference* (Oxford University Press, 1987; expanded edition 1994) and, with Robert M. Harnish, *Linguistic Communication and Speech Acts* (MIT Press, 1979).

Annette Baier is currently Associate in Philosophy at the University of Otago, from which she first graduated. She has published on Hume, ethics, and philosophy of mind. Her most recent book is *Death and Character: Further Reflections on Hume*. She has books forthcoming on *Hume on Justice* (Harvard University Press) and on *How We Live* (Oxford University Press).

Marc Bekoff is Professor Emeritus of Ecology and Evolutionary Biology at the University of Colorado, Boulder. His latest books are *Animals at Play: Rules of the Game* (a kid's book) and *Wild Justice: The Moral Lives of Animals* (written with Jessica Pierce). Marc's homepage is http://literati.net/Bekoff.

Stephen Boulter is Senior Lecturer in Philosophy at Oxford Brookes University. Prior to taking up his current post he was Gifford Research Fellow in the Department of Philosophy at the University of Glasgow in 1998–1999. He is the author of *The Rediscovery of Common Sense Philosophy* (Palgrave Macmillan, 2007) and is currently working on a book on medieval philosophy.

John Broome is White's Professor of Moral Philosophy at the University of Oxford. He is the author of *The Microeconomics of Capitalism* (1983), *Weighing Goods* (1991), *Counting the Cost of Global Warming* (1992), *Ethics Out of Economics* (1999) and *Weighing Lives* (2004).

Randolph Clarke is Professor of Philosophy at Florida State University. He is the author of *Libertarian Accounts of Free Will* (Oxford University Press, 2003) and many articles on agency, free will, and moral responsibility.

Ursula Coope is Tutorial Fellow of Corpus Christi College and Professor of Ancient Philosophy at Oxford University. She is the author of *Time for Aristotle* (Oxford University Press, 2005) and of papers on Aristotle's *Physics* and his philosophy of action. She is currently writing about the development of the concept of the will in ancient philosophy.

Wayne A. Davis is Professor of Philosophy at Georgetown University. His publications focus on philosophy of language and philosophy of mind, and include *Implicature* (Cambridge University Press, 1996), *Meaning, Expression and Thought* (Cambridge University Press, 2003), and *Nondescriptive Meaning and Expression* (Oxford University Press, 2005).

Sabine Döring is Professor of Philosophy at Eberhard-Karls-Universität Tübingen. Her publications include 'Explaining action by emotion,' *Philosophical Quarterly*, 53 (2003), 'Seeing what to do: Affective perception and rational motivation,' *Dialectica* 61 (2007), and 'Why be emotional?' in Peter Goldie (ed.), *Oxford Handbook of the Philosophy of Emotion* (Oxford University Press, 2009). She is also (together with Rainer Reisenzein) editor of *Perspectives on Emotional Experience*, a special issue of *Emotion Review: Journal of the International Society for Research on Emotion*, 1(3) (2009).

Fred Dretske is Senior Research Scholar at Duke University and Professor Emeritus at Stanford and at the University of Wisconsin. His publications include *Seeing and Knowing* (1969), *Knowledge and the Flow of Information* (1981), *Explaining Behavior* (1988), and *Naturalizing the Mind* (1995).

R. A. Duff has taught philosophy at the University of Stirling since 1970. He works on the philosophy of criminal law, especially on penal theory and on the principles and structures of criminal liability. He has published *Trials and Punishments* (1986); *Intention, Agency and Criminal Responsibility* (1990); *Criminal Attempts* (1996); *Punishment, Communication and Community* (2001); and *Answering for Crime* (2007).

Naomi Eilan is Professor of Philosophy at the University of Warwick and director of the interdisciplinary Consciousness and Self-Consciousness Research Centre. She has published papers in the philosophy of mind and has edited several interdisciplinary volumes, including *Agency and Self Awareness* with Johannes Roessler (Oxford University Press, 2003).

Laura W. Ekstrom holds an AB in Philosophy from Stanford University and a PhD from the University of Arizona. She is Associate Professor of Philosophy at the College of William and Mary, Williamson, VA. She is the author of *Free Will: A Philosophical Study* (Westview Press, 1999), and editor of *Agency and Responsibility: Essays on the*

Metaphysics of Freedom (Westview Press, 2000). She has published articles in metaphysics, ethics, and the philosophy of religion.

Stephen Everson has taught at the Universities of Oxford; Cambridge; and Michigan, Ann Arbor. He is currently Lecturer in Philosophy at the University of York. Everson has published on various topics in ancient philosophy, ethics, and the philosophy of action, and he is the author of *Aristotle on Perception* (Oxford University Press, 1999).

John Martin Fischer got his BA and MA in philosophy at Stanford University in 1975 and his PhD from Cornell in 1982. He has taught at Yale University, visited at UCLA and Santa Clara Unversity, and is currently Distinguished Professor and Chair of the Department of Philosophy at the University of California, Riverside, where he holds a UC President's Chair. His books include *The Metaphysics of Free Will* (Blackwell, 1994), *Responsibility and Control: A Theory of Moral Responsibility* (co-authored with Mark Ravizza, Cambridge University Press, 1998); *My Way: Essays on Moral Responsibility* (Oxford University Press,2006) *Four Views on Free Will* (co-authored with Pereboom, Kane, and Vargas, Blackwell, 2007); and *Our Stories: Essays on Life, Death, and Free Will* (Oxford University Press, 2009).

Elisa Freschi works in the fields of linguistics, epistemology, and deontic logic, both western and Indian. After a *laurea* degree (BA and MA) in Sanskrit and a BA in western philosophy, she completed her PhD dissertation on Indian philosophy at Università Sapienza in Rome, Italy, where she is currently Research Fellow.

Margaret Gilbert is Melden Chair of Moral Philosophy at the University of California at Irvine. Her books include On *Social Facts* (1989), *Living Together* (1996), *Sociality and Responsibility* (2000), *Marcher Ensemble* (2003), and *A Theory of Political Obligation* (2006).

Hans-Johann Glock is Professor of Philosophy at the University of Zürich and Visiting Professor at the University of Reading. His publications include: as author, *A Wittgenstein Dictionary* (Blackwell, 1996) and *Quine and Davidson on Language, Thought and Reality* (Cambridge University Press, 2003); as editor, *Strawson and Kant* (Oxford University Press, 2003), *What is Analytic Philosophy?* (Cambridge University Press, 2008), *La Mente de los Animales: Problemas Conceptuales* (KRK Ediciones, 2009), and (edited with John Hyman) *Wittgenstein and Analytic Philosophy* (Oxford University Press, 2009).

Mitchell Green is Horace W. Goldsmith Distinguished Teaching Professor of Philosophy, University of Virginia. He is author of *Self-Expression* (Oxford University Press, 2007) and co-editor of *Moore's Paradox: New Essays on Belief, Rationality and the First Person* (Oxford University Press, 2007).

Adrian Haddock is Lecturer in Philosophy at the University of Stirling. He has published essays on action, knowledge, and idealism. He is, with Alan Millar and Duncan Pritchard, one of the authors of *The Nature and Value of Knowledge: Three Investigations* (Oxford University Press, forthcoming).

Edward Harcourt is University Lecturer in Philosophy at Oxford University and a Fellow of Keble College. His papers, on subjects which include metaethics, moral psychology and Wittgenstein, have appeared in various leading journals.

John Heil is Honorary Research Associate at Monash University and Professor of Philosophy at Washington University in St Louis. He works on issues in metaphysics and the philosophy of mind. His most recent books include *From An Ontological Point of View* (Oxford 2003) and *Philosophy of Mind: A Guide and Anthology* (Oxford, 2004).

Paul Hoffman is Professor of Philosophy at the University of California, Riverside. His *Essays on Descartes* were published in 2009 by Oxford University Press.

Jennifer Hornsby has been Professor of Philosophy at Birkbeck, University of London, since 1995, and is now also a co-director of the Centre for the Study of Mind in Nature in Oslo. Her main interests are in philosophy of action, mind, language, and feminist philosophy.

Rosalind Hursthouse is Professor of Philosophy at the University of Auckland, New Zealand. She is the author of *On Virtue Ethics* (1999) and of various articles in the same area, including some on Aristotle.

T. H. Irwin is Professor of Ancient Philosophy at the University of Oxford and a Fellow of Keble College. From 1975 to 2006 he taught at Cornell University. He is the author of: *Plato's Gorgias* (translation and notes), Clarendon Plato Series (Oxford University Press, 1979); *Aristotle's Nicomachean Ethics* (translation and notes), (Hackett Publishing Co., 2nd edn 1999); *Aristotle's First Principles* (Oxford University Press, 1988); *Classical Thought*, Oxford University Press, 1989; *Plato's Ethics* (Oxford University Press, 1995); *The Development of Ethics*, 3 vols (Oxford University Press, 2007–9).

Ben Jeffares is currently a Marsden Post-Doctoral Fellow at Victoria University of Wellington, New Zealand. He is working (with Kim Sterelny) on a project entitled 'Human uniqueness: A bio-cultural synthesis' and has published numerous articles in evolutionary psychology.

Brian Leiter is John P. Wilson Professor of Law and Director of the Center for Law, Philosophy and Human Values at the University of Chicago. He is author of *Nietzsche on Morality* (2002) and co-editor of *Nietzsche's Daybreak* (1997), *Nietzsche* (2001), and *Nietzsche and Morality* (2007).

Neil Levy is Principal Research Fellow at the Centre for Applied Philosophy and Public Ethics, University of Melbourne, and Director of Research at the Oxford Centre for Neuroethics.

Daniel Little is Professor of Philosophy and Chancellor at the University of Michigan–Dearborn. He is the author of six books, more recently *Microfoundations, Method and Causation: On the Philosophy of the Social Sciences* (Transaction Publishers 1998) and *The Paradox of Wealth and Poverty: Mapping the Ethical Dilemmas of Global Development* (Westview Press, 2003). His current book, *History's Pathways*, will appear with Springer in 2010.

E. J. Lowe has been Professor of Philosophy at Durham University, UK, since 1995. Books include *Kinds of Being* (Blackwell, 1989), *Subjects of Experience* (Cambridge University Press, 1996), *The Possibility of Metaphysics* (Oxford University Press, 1998), *The Four-Category Ontology* (Oxford University Press, 2006), *Personal Agency* (Oxford University Press, 2008), and *More Kinds of Being* (Wiley-Blackwell, 2009).

Kirk Ludwig is Professor of Philosophy at the University of Florida. He is co-author, with Ernie Lepore, of *Donald Davidson's Truth-Theoretic Semantics* (Oxford University Press, 2007) and of *Donald Davidson: Meaning, Truth, Language and Reality* (Oxford University Press, 2005), and editor of *Donald Davidson* (Cambridge University Press, 2003). He has published numerous articles in the philosophy of mind, language and action.

Bertram F. Malle was born and educated in Graz, Austria, before coming to the United States in 1990. He received his PhD at Stanford University in 1994 and joined the University of Oregon Psychology Department the same year. Since 2008 he is Professor of Psychology at Brown University. Malle's research focuses on social cognition and the folk theory of the mind, exploring such issues as intentionality judgments, mental state inferences, behavior explanations, and moral sentiments. His publications include *How the Mind Explains Behavior: Folk Explanations, Meaning, and Social Interaction* (MIT Press, 2004). He has edited, with S. D. Hodges, *Other Minds: How Humans Bridge the Divide Between Self and Other* (New York: Guilford Press, 2005).

Alfred R. Mele is William H. and Lucyle T. Werkmeister Professor of Philosophy at Florida State University. He is author of *Irrationality* (1987), *Springs of Action* (1992), *Autonomous Agents* (1995), *Self-Deception Unmasked* (2001), *Motivation and Agency* (2003), *Free Will and Luck* (2006), and *Effective Intentions* (2009). He has also edited and co-edited several volumes: *The Philosophy of Action* (1997), *Mental Causation* (1993), *The Oxford Handbook of Rationality* (2004), and *Rationality and the Good* (2007).

Elijah Millgram is E. E. Ericksen Professor of Philosophy at the University of Utah. He is the author of *Practical Induction* (Harvard University Press, 1997), *Ethics Done Right* (Cambridge University Press, 2005), and *Hard Truths* (Wiley-Blackwell, 2009).

Katherine J. Morris is a Fellow in Philosophy at Mansfield College, Oxford. Her books include *Descartes' Dualism*, co-authored with Gordon Baker (Routledge, 1996) and *Sartre* (Blackwell, 2008, Great Minds series). She has published widely on Descartes, Wittgenstein, Sartre, and Merleau-Ponty and will be bringing out a book on Merleau-Ponty next year as part of Continuum's 'Starting With' series. She also co-edits a series of books from Oxford University Press under the general title 'International Perspectives in Philosophy and Psychiatry.'

Eddy Nahmias is Associate Professor in the Philosophy Department and at the Neuroscience Institute at Georgia State University. He specializes in philosophy of mind and cognitive science, free will, moral psychology, and experimental philosophy. He is co-editing the volume *Moral Psychology: Classic and Contemporary Readings* (Wiley-Blackwell) and writing the book *Rediscovering Free Will* (Oxford University Press), which examines scientific research relevant to free will and moral responsibility.

Timothy O'Connor is Professor of Philosophy and a member of the Cognitive Sciences Program at Indiana University. He is the author of two books, *Persons and Causes: The Metaphysics of Free Will* (2000) and *Theism and Ultimate Explanation: The Necessary Shape of Contingency* (2008) and editor of four other volumes treating topics in philosophy of mind and action theory.

David S. Oderberg is Professor of Philosophy at the University of Reading and has published widely on metaphysics, ethics, and other subjects. Among his ethics publications are the companion volumes *Moral Theory* and *Applied Ethics* (Blackwell, 2000).

Philip Pettit teaches political theory and philosophy at Princeton, where he is L. S. Rockefeller University Professor of Politics and Human Values. His forthcoming books include: *The Conversational Imperative: Communication, Commitment and the Moral Point of View*, which is the text of his Blackwell/Brown Lectures in Philosophy, 2009; and *Group Agency: the Possibility, Design and Status of Corporate Agents*, co-authored with Christian List.

Avital Pilpel is Philosophy Lecturer at the University of Haifa, the Interdisciplinary Center in Herzliya, and Beit Berl's Teacher College (Kfar Saba, Israel). His PhD deals with belief change in scientific explanations, under Prof. Isaac Levi (Columbia University). His main interest is rational belief change in science. He also investigates rational belief change in other fields, from economics to medicine.

Thomas Pink is Professor of Philosophy at King's College London. He is the author of *Free Will: A Very Short Introduction* (2004) and other books and papers on mind and ethics. He is preparing a two-volume work, *The Ethics of Action*, on action and normativity, and Hobbes' *Dialogues Concerning Liberty, Necessity and Chance* for the Clarendon edition of the works of Hobbes.

Bill Pollard is an Honorary Research Fellow at the University of Edinburgh. He has taught at the universities of Durham, York, Warwick and Edinburgh in the UK, and Dartmouth College, USA. He has published a range of articles on habits and is author of *Habits in Action* (VDM, 2008).

Joëlle Proust is a philosopher of mind working at the Institut Jean-Nicod (Paris) as Director of Research in CNRS. She works in the field of the theory of the will and, more specifically, on the connection between mental action and metacognition, understood as the practical capacity to predict or evaluate the cognitive adequacy of one's mental states.

Michael Quante is Professor of Practical Philosophy in the Department of Philosophy at the Westfälische Wilhelms-University in Münster and has previously been Professor of Practical and Modern Philosophy in the Department of Philosophy at the University of Cologne (2005–2009) and Professor for Philosophy of Law and Social Philosophy at the University Duisburg-Essen (2004–2005). He is associated editor of the journal *Ethical Theory and Moral Practice*. His books include *Hegel's Concept of Action* (Cambridge University Press, 2004; original German publication 1993), *Personales Leben und menschlicher Tod* (Suhrkamp, 2002), *Person* (De Gruyter, 2007), *Karl Marx: Ökonomisch-Philosophische Manuskripte* (Suhrkamp, 2009). He also co-edited with Dean Moyar *Hegel's Phenomenology of Spirit* (Cambridge University Press, 2008).

Soran Reader is Reader in Philosophy at Durham University. She runs the Centre for Ethical Philosophy, which explores philosophical issues from the patients' perspective. She developed and continues to extend a needs-based ethics. She studies violence to provide arguments for pacifism, and works on philosophical bases for issues in feminism.

Johannes Roessler is Associate Professor in the Department of Philosophy at Warwick University. He works on issues in epistemology and the philosophy of mind. He is co-editor of two interdisciplinary collections, *Agency and Self-Awareness. Issues in Philosophy and Psychology* (2003) and *Joint Attention: Communication and Other Minds* (2005).

David-Hillel Ruben has a BA in Philosophy from Dartmouth College (USA) and a PhD from Harvard University. He is Director of New York University in London and Professor of Philosophy at Birkbeck, University of London. He is the author of, among other books, *Action and Its Explanation* (Oxford University Press, 2003), *Explaining Explanation* (Routledge, 1990), and *The Metaphysics of the Social World* (Routledge, 1985).

Constantine Sandis is Senior Lecturer in Philosophy at Oxford Brookes University and New York University in London. He is author of *The Things We Do and Why We Do Them* (Palgrave Macmillan, 2012), as well as editor of *New Essays on the Explanation of Action* (Palgrave Macmillan, 2009) and co-editor, with Arto Laitinen, of *Hegel on Action* (Palgrave Macmillan, 2010). Constantine is currently working on *An Introduction to the Philosophy of Action* for Wiley-Blackwell.

Severin Schroeder is Lecturer in Philosophy at the University of Reading. He is the author of three books on the philosophy of Wittgenstein: a monograph on the private language argument, *Das Privatsprachen-Argument* (Schöningh, 1998); *Wittgenstein: The Way Out of the Fly-Bottle* (Polity, 2006); and *Wittgenstein lesen* (Frommann-Holzboog, 2009). He is editor of *Wittgenstein and Contemporary Philosophy of Mind* (Palgrave Macmillan, 2001), and *Philosophy of Literature* (Wiley-Blackwell, 2010).

Timothy Schroeder graduated from Stanford University and is now Associate Professor of Philosophy at Ohio State. He works on the philosophy of mind and moral psychology and has written a book – *Three Faces of Desire* – which unites philosophical and scientific evidence in pursuit of the nature of desire.

G. F. Schueler is Professor of Philosophy and Chair of the Philosophy Department at the University of Delaware. He is author of *Desire* (MIT Press, 1995) and *Reasons and Purposes* (Oxford University Press, 2003), and he has written numerous essays in ethics and philosophy of action.

Scott Sehon is Professor of Philosophy at Bowdoin College. He has published a number of articles on philosophy of action and a book entitled *Teleological Realism: Mind, Agency, and Explanation* (MIT Press, 2005).

Michael Smith is McCosh Professor of Philosophy at Princeton University. He is author of *The Moral Problem* (1994); *Ethics and the A Priori: Selected Essays on Moral Psychology and Meta-Ethics* (2004); and, together with Frank Jackson and Philip Pettit, co-author of *Mind, Morality and Explanation: Selected Collaborations* (2004).

Kim Sterelny works on evolutionary theory, particularly the evolution of cognition, culture and behavior. More specifically, he has worked on the evolution of inheritance systems (especially the evolutionary role of non-genetic inheritance), on the relation between ecology and evolution, and on the relation between microevolution over short periods in local populations and large-scale patterns and processes. His most recent books are *Dawkins versus Gould* (2nd edn, 2007), and *Thought in a Hostile World* (2003), and a monograph on the nature of biodiversity co-authored with James Maclaurin. He is currently working with Brett Calcott on the evolution of complexity and with Ben Jeffares on the evolutionary roots of human cooperation.

Ralf Stoecker is Professor of Philosophy (particularly applied ethics) at the University of Potsdam, Germany. Stoecker studied philosophy in Hamburg, Heidelberg, and Bielefeld, writing a dissertation on the topic of events (*Was sind Ereignisse?* Berlin and New York 1992) and a Habilitation on the brain death debate and its moral and metaphysical bearings (*Der Hirntod*, Freiburg 1999). His areas of specialization are applied ethics, philosophy of personhood, and action theory. Since the 1990s Stoecker has published papers on various aspects of human action in order to establish a non-standard account of agency, which combines Davidson's insights with those of Ryle and Wittgenstein. He is editor of *Reflecting Davidson: Donald Davidson Responding to an International Forum of Philosophers* (De Gruyer, 1993).

Tom Stoneham is Professor of Philosophy at the University of York. He is author of *Berkeley's World* (Oxford University Press, 2002) and has written several articles on idealism in the early modern period as well as papers on philosophy of mind, time, and modality. He is currently working on the imagination and dreams, reflections in mirrors, and the rationalist epistemology of Edward Herbert.

Rowland Stout is based at University College Dublin. His most recent books include Action (Acumen, 2005) and The Inner Life of a Rational Agent (Edinburgh, 2006).

Frederick Stoutland is Professor of Philosophy Emeritus at St Olaf College, Minnesota and was until recently Permanent Visiting Professor of Philosophy at Uppsala University (Sweden). He has published papers on philosophy of action and related topics and has edited *Philosophical Probings: Essays on von Wright's Later Work*. Further publication details may be found at http://www.filosofi.uu.se/personal/Fredst.htm.

Bart Streumer is Lecturer in Philosophy at the University of Reading. He has published articles on the nature of reasoning and on the relation between 'ought' and 'can,' and is currently working on a book-length defense of an error theory about normative judgments.

Matthew Stuart is Associate Professor of Philosophy at Bowdoin College. He has published articles in the *Philosophical Review* and *Journal of the History of Philosophy* and is currently working on a book about Locke's metaphysics. He is also editor of Wiley-Blackwell's forthcoming *Companion to Locke*.

Nassim N. Taleb is Distinguished Professor at New York University's Polytechnic Institute and the author of *The Black Swan: The Impact of the Highly Improbable* (Penguin, 2007).

Julia Tanney is Senior Lecturer at the University of Kent and has published numerous articles on philosophy of mind, rules, reason, action theory, and self-knowledge. She has contributed commentaries on Gilbert Ryle for several publications as well as writing a critical study for the Routledge 60th anniversary edition of *The Concept of Mind* and for Payot's French re-publication of *La Notion d'esprit*. Tanney has also written introductions to the new edition of Ryle's *Collected Papers*, Vols 1–2, and the entry on Ryle for the *Stanford Encyclopedia of Philosophy*.

Roger Teichmann is Philosophy Lecturer at St Hilda's College, Oxford. His book *The Philosophy of Elizabeth Anscombe* was published by Oxford University Press in 2008.

Sergio Tenenbaum is Associate Professor of Philosophy at the University of Toronto. He is the author of *Appearances of the Good* (Cambridge University Press, 2007) and of various articles on ethics, moral psychology, and Kant's ethics.

Christine J. Thomas is Associate Professor of Philosophy at Dartmouth College. She is the author of a number of articles on Plato's metaphysics, epistemology, and philosophy of language. Recent publications include 'Speaking of something: Plato's *Sophist* and Plato's Beard' (*Canadian Journal of Philosophy*, 2008), and 'Inquiry without Names in Plato's *Cratylus* (*Journal of the History of Philosophy*, 2008).

Eric Watkins is Professor of Philosophy at the University of California, San Diego. He has received fellowships from the Fulbright Foundation, the National Endowment for the Humanities, the National Science Foundation, and the Alexander von Humboldt Foundation. He has published several dozen articles on Kant as well as a book, *Kant and the Metaphysics of Causality* (Cambridge University Press, 2005), which was awarded the Book Prize in 2005 from the *Journal of the History of Philosophy*.

Bernard Weiner received his PhD from the University of Michigan in 1963 and is Distinguished Professor of Psychology at the University of California, Los Angeles. He was awarded the Donald Campbell Award for research in social psychology and the E. L. Thorndike Research Award for Career Achievement in educational psychology. Weiner's book publications include *Judgments of Responsibility* (Guilford, 1995) and *Social Motivation, Justice, and the Moral Emotions* (Erlbaum, 2006).

Thomas Williams is Professor of Catholic Studies and Professor of Philosophy at the University of South Florida. He is editor of *The Cambridge Companion to Duns Scotus* (2003) and co-author, with Sandra Visser, of *Anselm* (2009).

Hong Yu Wong is Jacobsen Research Fellow at the Institute of Philosophy and at Birkbeck College, University of London. He has written articles in metaphysics and in philosophy of mind and action.

Gideon Yaffe is Associate Professor of Philosophy and Law at the University of Southern California. He is author of a number of articles which apply philosophy of action to the criminal law, including 'Conditional intent and *mens rea*' (*Legal Theory*, 2004), 'Trying, acting and attempted crimes' (*Law and Philosophy*, 2008), and 'Excusing mistakes of law' (*Philosophers Imprint*, 2009).

Anna C. Zielinska is Lecturer in Philosophy at the University of Grenoble. She works on theories of action, moral philosophy, philosophy of language, and on Kotarbinski, Wittgenstein, and Ricœur. She is the editor of the forthcoming *Textes-Clés* on metaethics for Librairie Vrin.

Michael J. Zimmerman is Professor of Philosophy at the University of North Carolina at Greensboro. He is the author of books and articles on the theory of action, moral responsibility, moral obligation, and intrinsic value.

Preface to the Paperback Edition

In collaboration with many contributors, we have taken the opportunity of a paperback edition to correct errors in typography, dating, and grammar. The rest of the content remains unaltered, including a regrettable distortion of chronology in the ordering of the essays on Hegel and Nietzsche. This edition is dedicated to the memory of two wonderful contributors, Paul Hoffman and Fred Stoutland: requiescant in pace.

Constantine Sandis and Timothy O'Connor, January 2012

Acknowledgments

Volumes of this form and size are large collaborative efforts. Accordingly, we owe thanks to a great many people. First and foremost, to all the contributors for taking the time to write their chapters, often revising them in the light of comments and making helpful editorial suggestions of their own. Indeed a number of the contributors (too many to name) steered us towards entry topics that we had originally neglected to commission. Special thanks are due to Al Mele and Tom Pink for agreeing to write additional entries at late notice, and to Cengage Learning for granting us permission to use a modified version of Mele's article on 'Intention.' Ralf Stoecker discovered the book's cover image, representing the collective action of wheat threshing during the ancient Egyptian grain harvest. The picture is from a wall painting in the tomb of Menna, Luxor.

We would also like to thank the three anonymous referees who sent helpful comments at a very early stage of the project and collectively influenced its shape. Nick Bellorini at Wiley-Blackwell has been supportive and enthusiastic from the start, offering much advice and encouragement along the way. Likewise Liz Cremona, Barbara Duke, Annette Abel and Ben Thatcher patiently guided us through production. Finally, thanks to Leah Morin and Manuela Tecusan for all their hard work on copy-editing and proofs, and to Robert Vinten for so readily taking on the challenging task of the index.

Constantine Sandis and Timothy O'Connor
September 2009

Introduction

This book aims to offer an overview of the various issues and debates that permeate the philosophy of action and its explanation. It is structured in such a way that it can be read straight through, though it will no doubt be primarily used as a work of reference. To this end, the themed table of contents, cross-references, and index should help the reader to forge alternate pathways through the subject.

The volume divides into four sections. Part I, entitled 'Acts and Actions,' introduces various ontological and conceptual issues concerning the nature of action, its relation to events (not least the movements of our bodies), and our descriptions of them. Some of the chapters elucidate various competing conceptions of the nature of action. Others focus on specific types (or categories) of acts and actions, such as speech acts, collective action, habitual actions, Cambridge actions, and negative acts. Part II, 'Agency and Causation,' surveys philosophical thought centred around the production, purpose, and explanation of action. Topics discussed there include motivation, causal deviancy, and deliberation. Some of the chapters focus explicitly on explanation and causal antecedents, from volition to the explanatory roles of consciousness and emotion. Others are more directly concerned with issues relating to agency and control – for instance mental acts, practical reasoning, strength and weakness of will, addiction and compulsion, bodily awareness, and agential knowledge and causation.Part III, 'Action in Special Contexts,' brings together a number of key ideas and doctrines within the context of (a) normative psychology and (b) nature and science, construed broadly. These chapters also serve to highlight the importance and relevance of action theory both to philosophy as a whole and to neighbouring disciplines. Discussion begins with traditional questions concerning rationality, moral judgment, free will, autonomy, and responsibility, before addressing the wider role of action in ethics and law – from virtue ethics to criminal liability. The chapters concerned with nature and science range over a wide range of disciplines – as diverse as folk psychology, cognitive ethology, evolutionary psychology, history, and social science. Issues discussed here include animal action, scientific challenges to free will, and socio-economic prediction. The final section of the book – Part IV: 'Prominent Figures' – surveys the relevant work of a wide (though by no means exhaustive) range of influential thinkers who have written about action, from Plato to Paul Ricœur. The chapters gathered here should constitute a good starting point for those working within the history of ideas. Many demonstrate, further, the role that action theory can play within a large philosophical system. Although the Indian philosophers discussed in chapter 52 are writing after the rise of Hellenistic philosophy, we chose to open the section with this chapter as the Vedas and Upanishads in which the ideas of classical Indian philosophy originate were composed centuries before Plato. We have also chosen not to include chapters on any living philosophers for reasons of space and, more importantly, because their views are expressed or described throughout this volume as a whole.

While we have tried our best to capture as vast and varied a terrain as possible, volumes of this kind are bound to be selective, even when their theme is as focused as that of philosophy of action. Numerous topics, philosophers, and methodologies that have not been allocated a specific chapter are nonetheless covered across the volume (experimental philosophy of action is a case in point). We hope that readers will use the index to locate their permeating influence.

Constantine Sandis and Timothy O'Connor

Part I

Acts and Actions

1

Action Theory and Ontology

E. J. LOWE

Any comprehensive theory of action should have something to say about the ontology of actions. It should address such questions as the following. What *are* actions, if indeed they are anything at all? – for we shouldn't just *assume* that actions exist. Are they, for instance, a species of *events*? If so, then what are *events*, and what makes actions special among events? How are actions *individuated* and – if this is a different question – what are their *identity conditions*? Must every action have an *agent* (or agents) and, if so, what sort of thing can be an agent, and in virtue of what features can it be said to perform, or engage in, actions? In this chapter I shall say something about all of these questions.

What are Actions?

One obvious way to address this question is to look at action *sentences* and examine their apparent ontological implications. A typical action sentence would be 'John opened the door.' Here John is represented as having performed a certain type of action – opening a door – and thus is represented as having been the agent of a token action of that type. (I take it that the type/token distinction is too familiar to need further elaboration here.) By implication, this token action occurred at some specific time in the past. Extrapolating from this kind of example, we may venture to say that token actions are particular occurrences of certain action types, each possessing an agent (or agents) and a particular time of occurrence. In answer to the question 'But do we really need to include token actions in our ontology?' the following line of argument, due originally to Donald Davidson (1967), may be advanced. Action sentences such as 'John opened the door' can be *adverbially modified* in indefinitely many ways. For instance we can expand this sentence into one such as: 'John opened the door at 1.00 p.m. on Monday, slowly and cautiously, by pushing it [...]' When we ask what *logical form* this expanded action sentence has, it is plausible to answer that it involves *existential quantification over token actions*, so that it is logically equivalent to something like this:

$(\exists a)$(a was a door-opening and John was the agent of a and a occurred at 1.00 p.m. on Monday and a was slow and a was cautious and a was done by pushing ...).

Taking this to be the logical form of our expanded action sentence, we can easily explain, for example, why it entails our original action sentence, 'John opened the door': it does so simply because a conjunction entails each of its conjuncts. However, if we then accept, in addition, W. V. Quine's (1969) criterion of ontological commitment – encapsulated in his famous dictum 'to be is to be the value of a variable' – we may conclude that action sentences like these are implicitly committed to the existence of *token actions*, as the items quantified over by such sentences when their underlying logical form is made explicit (see chapter 6).

Of course, Quine's criterion of ontological commitment is by no means uncontroversial and, in any case, even if it tells us that we are ontologically committed to token actions, it still doesn't really tell us what these items *are*. The usual presumption, however, of those who follow this line of argument is that actions are *events*, even if not all events are actions: that is, they form a *sub*-class of events. This is because it seems natural to describe events in general, as well as actions in particular, as being individual occurrences that possess a particular time of occurrence. On this view, what is distinctive about actions is that they always have *agents* and also, perhaps – at least according to philosophers such as Davidson (1971) – that they are always *intentional* under some description of them. By contrast, it seems that there are many events, such as the explosion of a supernova in the Andromeda galaxy or the spontaneous decay of a radium atom, that have *no* agent and are not intentional under *any* description of them.

Suppose we agree, at least provisionally, that actions are events, although this has been disputed by some – for instance Kent Bach (1980). It then remains to be asked what *events* are. Two views on this issue are particularly dominant at present. One is Davidson's own view, which is that events constitute a basic and irreducible ontological category of particulars, equally fundamental with that of physical *objects* (things such as John, or a radium atom). The other is Jaegwon Kim's (1976) view that events are *property exemplifications*: more precisely, that an event is the exemplification of a property by an object at a time. On this latter view, each token event may be represented by an ordered triple of an object, a property, and a time, of the form $\langle o, P, t \rangle$. So for example John's token action of opening the door, assuming it to be an event, may be represented by the ordered triple ⟨John, door-opening, 1.00 p.m. on Monday⟩. According to this view, events do not constitute a *fundamental* ontological category of particulars, since they may always be analyzed in terms of items which belong to other categories: the categories of *objects*, *properties*, and *times*. It might be objected to the Kimian view that it fails to register the fact that events are *changes* and conflates them with *states* – a state being a condition which does not involve change. In reply, however, it might be urged that the distinction between changes and states is, at best, superficial and sometimes difficult to adjudicate upon: for instance, is uniform motion in a straight line (inertial motion) a *state* of the moving object or a *change* in it?

How should we decide between the Davidsonian and the Kimian views of events, presuming that we should adopt one of them? The Kimian view might seem to be ontologically more extravagant because, while it analyzes events in terms of objects, properties and times, it still leaves us with at least these *three* basic ontological categories, whereas the Davidsonian view is apparently committed only to *two*: objects and events. On the other hand, Occam's razor only enjoins us not to multiply entities (and, by implication, fundamental *categories* of entities) *beyond necessity* – and it may be argued that we need to include *properties* in our ontology in any case, for all sorts of explanatory purposes (for instance, to give adequate accounts of *causation* and causal *laws*).

Before leaving this issue, however, I want to revisit the question of whether actions really are a sub-class of events. In some cases this assumption seems unproblematic, but in others not. Suppose, for instance, that we attribute to John the action of having killed Mary by shooting her. Suppose also, to make matters interesting, that, although John shot Mary on Monday, she did not die until Wednesday, by which time John had already committed suicide in an act of remorse, say on Tuesday. If John's action of killing Mary was an *event*, then what was its time of occurrence? If we say that it occurred on Monday, then we are implying, counterintuitively, that John killed Mary two days before she died. On the other hand, if we say that it occurred on Wednesday, when Mary died, we are implying, equally counterintuitively, that John killed Mary a day after he himself died. The source of the difficulty might be traced to this: intuitively, for John to kill Mary is for John to cause Mary's death, so that in this kind of case an action is an agent's *causing* of an event. The event which is caused – in this case, Mary's death – may quite unproblematically have a time of occurrence (in this case, it was on Wednesday). But what about the *causing*: does *that* plausibly have a time of occurrence? Take another example, which does not involve agents, but simply the causing of one event by another: the case of an explosion causing the collapse of a bridge. The explosion has a time of occurrence, as does the collapse of the bridge (even if these events are, each of them, spread out over a *period* of time, rather than being momentary). But does the explosion's *causing* the collapse have a time of occurrence? Indeed, is *it* an event, in addition to the explosion and the collapse themselves? It is not so clear, I suggest, that the correct answer to either of these questions is 'Yes.' If causings, quite generally, are not events and at least some actions are causings, then not all actions are events, even if some are. We might have to conclude, on this basis, that actions don't constitute a unified category of entities at all – not even a sub-category of some other category.

What Are the Identity Conditions of Actions?

The foregoing discussion feeds directly into another important ontological question concerning actions that was raised at the beginning of this chapter. How are actions *individuated* and – if this is a different question – what are their *identity conditions?* Since the issue of action individuation is a leading theme of chapter 2, I can afford to be fairly brief here as far as this question is concerned. The word 'individuate' has two importantly different senses: a *cognitive* one and a *metaphysical* one. In the cognitive sense, individuation is the singling out of some entity in thought. In the metaphysical sense, it is a mind-independent determination relation between entities. It is in the former sense, for instance, that the police witness may be said to have individuated the perpetrator of the crime at an identity parade. It is in the latter sense, however, that we may say, for example, that a set is individuated by its members: for it is the members of a set, and they alone, that determine *which* set it is – they fix its identity. Since we are concerned in this chapter only with the ontology of action, we shall consider here the individuation of actions only in the metaphysical sense of the word 'individuation.'

What, then – if anything – determines *which* action a given action is (assuming that we are still talking here exclusively about *token* actions)? On the Kimian view of events and actions, the answer seems straightforward enough: a certain *object*, *property*, and *time* always jointly determine this, for an action just *is* the exemplification of a certain property by a certain object at a certain time. This also provides us, immediately, with a *criterion of identity* for token actions, in the following form: If *a* and *b* are token actions, then *a* is identical with *b* if and only if *a* and *b* are exemplifications of the same property by the same object at the same time. However, on the Davidsonian view, no such easy answer is forthcoming. Davidson himself (1969) originally proposed a *causal* criterion of identity for events – and hence for actions – along these lines: If *e* and *f* are token events (or actions), then *e* is identical with *f* if and only if *e* and *f* have the *same causes and effects*. But it was soon pointed out that this criterion seems problematic, because it appears to be implicitly circular, at least on the assumption that all causation is causation by and of events. For then to say that *e* and *f* have the same causes and effects is just to say that the same events cause *e* and *f* and the same events are caused by *e* and *f*. Yet the criterion is supposed to tell us under what conditions events are the same or different, and so it shouldn't just presume that, where the causes and effects of *e* and *f* are concerned, this can be regarded as being already settled.

Even if this problem can be overcome, the Davidsonian criterion of identity for events and actions raises another contentious issue: namely whether a criterion of identity for events tells us how events are *individuated*, in the metaphysical sense of 'individuate.' It is not clear that it necessarily does so. For an account of what individuates an entity *x* is supposed to tell us what determines *which* entity of its type *x* is: and it should presumably tell us this even with regard to *counterfactual* circumstances in which *x* may be supposed to exist, not just with regard to its *actual* circumstances. Now, this appears to imply that, if we consider Davidson's criterion of identity for events as telling us what individuates an event – namely, its causes and effects – then we must assume that an event always has the *same* causes and effects in all counterfactual circumstances in which it may be supposed to exist. And yet this assumption is highly counterintuitive. One readily imagines for example that, although *John*'s shooting Mary was actually one of the causes of Mary's death, her death – that very event – could instead have been caused by, say, *Peter*'s shooting Mary in exactly the same way at the same time. This being so, Davidson's criterion of identity for events and actions, even if it serves to distinguish a given token action from any other token action in the *actual* world, does not serve to identify it in other possible worlds: that is to say, it does not serve as a principle of *transworld identity* for events, and hence as a principle of individuation in the metaphysical sense. By contrast, Kim's criterion of identity for events fairly clearly does serve this further purpose, because it is plausible to say that a given property exemplification couldn't have been an exemplification by a different object of a different property at a different time – in short, that a Kimian event's constituent object, property, and time are all *essential* to it, unlike an event's causes and effects. This may be considered to be another advantage of the Kimian view over the Davidsonian one.

Agents and their Powers

So far I have said very little about the ontological status of the *agents* of actions, but it should be evident that I have been taking these at least to be individual objects of some kind (individual substances, in an older terminology) and, moreover, objects possessing mental as well as purely physical properties, human persons providing a paradigm. However, in everyday and scientific language we often find the term 'agent' applied also to inanimate objects. For instance, in chemistry various chemical compounds are commonly described as being 'agents' and 'reagents.' In this broader sense of 'agent,' an agent is just something that does something – acts in a certain way – and often does so *to* something else – something which, on that account, is often described as a 'patient' in respect of the action being performed. As a corollary to this, the agent and the patient are commonly described as possessing, respectively, an *active* and a corresponding *passive* power (or 'liability'), the agent's action and the patient's reaction constituting the manifestation or exercise of their respective powers on the particular occasion of action.

Clearly some powers and liabilities are *causal* in character: for example, a drop of water's power to dissolve salt is causal in character, because any manifestation or exercise of the power actually consists in the drop of water causing some salt to dissolve on a particular occasion. In the case of human agents, some powers are clearly *mental* in character. Thus John Locke (1975) held the human will to be such a power, volitions (or 'acts of will') constituting its manifestations or exercises on particular occasions (see chapter 60). But, although Lockean volitions are clearly supposed to be capable of having *effects* such as motions of the agent's body, it does not seem that the will, as conceived by Locke, should be thought of as being a causal power in the way that water's power to dissolve salt should be. This is because Locke appears to have supposed, as seems intuitively correct, that the will could be exercised without giving rise to any further effect, as in the case of a person afflicted by paralysis who wills to move his or her body in a certain way but fails to bring about any such motion.

Some theorists of action, however, suppose human and other intelligent agents to possess distinctive *agent-causal* powers. According to one version of this view, a human agent possesses an agent-causal power to cause particular intentional or volitional states in him or herself, with these states then normally playing a contributory causal role in the generation of bodily activity in the agent. Such an agent-causal power, according to these theorists, should not be assimilated to the 'active' causal powers of inanimate substances, such as water's power to dissolve salt. This is basically because, whereas water exercises this power *by acting in a certain way* on some salt so as to bring about its dissolution, a human agent is not, according to these theorists, to be thought of as acting in any way so as to bring about a certain intentional or volitional state in him or herself. Rather, the agent him or herself is supposed to be the (or at least a) cause of the state in question in a direct and irreducible sense, which does not implicate any further action on his or her part. This is the classical doctrine of agent causation, which raises a host of interesting and difficult metaphysical and ontological issues peculiar to itself (see chapter 28).

Setting aside these doctrinal differences between action theorists, we may inquire now into the ontological status of powers and their manifestations. Both seem to be categorizable as *properties* of agents, at least in a relatively broad sense of the word 'property.' Thus *solubility* in water would seem to be a property of salt, as would its actual *dissolving* in water on some occasion. And the same would seem to apply in the case of human agents. John may have a power to close a door and exercise this power on a particular occasion by actually closing one: both the power and his exercising of it seem to qualify as properties of John. However, in recent years, metaphysicians working on the ontology of properties have been keen to emphasize the distinction between properties conceived as *universals* and properties conceived as *particulars* – the latter commonly referred to as 'tropes' or 'modes,' and often described as 'abstract particulars.' Now, when we were discussing earlier the Kimian view of events as property exemplifications, it is evident that it was properties conceived as universals that were at issue. Indeed Kim's view was developed before the modern resurgence of interest in trope theory. Simple examples of tropes would be the particular or individual redness of a certain red apple, or the particular or individual roundness of a certain round ball. However, once we have the ontological resources of trope theory at our disposal, the ontology of action requires some significant re-thinking. For it is natural to categorize both the powers of individual objects, and their manifestations or exercises on particular occasions, as particular properties or tropes, if we think of them as properties at all. And this has important implications for the individuation of actions and their identity conditions.

If an agent's action on a given occasion is to be regarded as trope or mode of the agent that constitutes a particular manifestation or exercise of one of the agent's powers, then we can replace the Kimian account of action individuation by a somewhat similar but importantly different one. On this view, since actions are tropes or modes, they are individuated in the same way in which tropes or modes quite generally are. One common view, thus, is that a trope or mode is individuated simply by its *object* (the thing whose particular property it is) together with its *time of existence*. For example, on this view, it is just *this apple* and *the present time* that, jointly, determine *which* redness the present redness of this apple is. We need no longer invoke – as on the Kimian view – a new (albeit non-fundamental) category of property exemplifications to house token actions, defining the latter as exemplifications of certain universals by certain objects at certain times. Instead we can just say that token actions are, quite simply, a sub-class of *particular* properties – tropes or modes – distinguished (at least) by the fact that they are also manifestations or exercises of another sub-class of particular properties, namely, powers. Indeed, on this approach, it is no longer apparent that we need to include in our ontology a distinctive category of events as such, of which actions are supposedly a sub-category. Tropes or modes seem to do all the ontological work that events were formerly called upon to perform. To be sure, this still leaves us with certain apparent problems on our hands, such as that posed earlier by the question of *when*, precisely, John's killing of Mary should be supposed to have taken place: for tropes, no less than events, seem to be items that are necessarily datable, at least if we are talking about the tropes of objects which themselves exist in time. But these are probably problems for anyone's ontology of action.

See also: BASIC ACTIONS AND INDIVIDUATION (2); BODILY MOVEMENTS (4); ADVERBS OF ACTION AND LOGICAL FORM (6); PLURALISM ABOUT ACTION (12); VOLITION AND THE WILL (13); AGENT CAUSATION (28); LOCKE (60); DAVIDSON (73).

References

Bach, K. (1980). Actions are not events. *Mind*, 89, 114–120.

Davidson, D. (1967). The logical form of action sentences. In N. Rescher (ed.), *The Logic of Decision and Action*. Pittsburgh, PA: University of Pittsburgh Press, 81–95.

Davidson, D. (1969). The individuation of events. In N. Rescher (ed.), *Essays in Honor of Carl G. Hempel*. Dordrecht: D. Reidel, 216–234.

Davidson, D. (1971). Agency. In R. Binkley, R. Bronaugh and A. Marras (eds), *Agent, Action, and Reason*. Toronto: University of Toronto Press, 3–25.

Kim, J. (1976). Events as property exemplifications. In M. Brand and D. Walton (eds), *Action Theory*. Dordrecht: D. Reidel, 159–177.

Locke, J. (1975). *An Essay Concerning Human Understanding* [1690], edited by P. H. Nidditch. Oxford: Oxford University Press.

Quine, W. V. (1969). Existence and quantification. In W. V. Quine, *Ontological Relativity and Other Essays*. New York: Columbia University Press, 91–113.

Further reading

Campbell, K. (1990). *Abstract Particulars*. Oxford: Blackwell.

Davidson, D. (1980). *Essays on Actions and Events*. Oxford: Oxford University Press.

Kim, J. (1993). *Supervenience and Mind: Selected Philosophical Essays*. Cambridge: Cambridge University Press.

Lowe, E. J. (2003). Individuation. In M. J. Loux and D. W. Zimmerman (eds), *The Oxford Handbook of Metaphysics*. Oxford: Oxford University Press, 75–95.

Lowe, E. J. (2008). *Personal Agency: The Metaphysics of Mind and Action*. Oxford: Oxford University Press.

Molnar, G. (2003). *Powers: A Study in Metaphysics*. Oxford: Oxford University Press.

O'Connor, T. (2000). *Persons and Causes: The Metaphysics of Free Will*. New York: Oxford University Press.

Thomson, J. J. (1971). The time of a killing. *Journal of Philosophy*, 68, 115–132.

2

Basic Actions and Individuation

CONSTANTINE SANDIS

Basic Actions

Its theoretical roots can be traced at least as far back as Aristotle (*Physics* 256^{a}6–8; compare *The Bhagavad Gītā*, Ch. IV, lines 16ff.). However, the phrase 'basic action' was only introduced in 1963, by A. C. Danto, in his paper 'What we can do.' The notions employed there, he tells us (1963: 435), were 'defended in a companion paper, 'Basic actions,' to be published subsequently [1965].' The two papers quickly gave rise to a substantial body of critical commentary that would drastically influence the shape of Danto's own subsequent formulations and beget a host of related concepts – such as those of *primitive* actions (Davidson 1971) and *simple* actions (Martin 1972).[1]

Danto's overall aim throughout his writings on basic actions is to identify the point at which the regress of things we can do comes to an end and agency thereby begins (and arguably freedom and moral responsibility with it, too; but contrast Prichard 1949b: 11 and Chisholm 1966 to Frankfurt 1969). So employed, basic actions play a foundational role similar to that of basic beliefs in epistemology, atomic propositions in the philosophy of language, and sense data in the theory of perception[2] (for complications, see Danto 1963: 436 and 1973: 1–27). As Annette Baier has skeptically put it, the search for basic action is a hunt for the most manageable and, through rash induction, also the most minimal cases of action (1971: 161).

That we can locate the most minimal kind of action is entailed by Danto's following claims, which form a central part of his program:

[i] If there are any actions at all, there are basic actions.
[ii] There are basic actions.
[iii] Not every action is a basic action. (1965: 142; cf. 1963: 436)

As Stoutland (1968: 467) remarks, [i] is true on pain of infinite regress (assuming the coherence of Danto's notion of a basic action) and [ii] is jointly entailed by [i] and the contingent fact that there are actions of one kind or another (compare Baier 1971: 163). [iii] is defended in Danto's 'first'paper, of 1963, which argues that there are some things which we can only do non-basically. However, the truth of [iii], as well as that of any answer to the question of what the starting point of agency turns out to be, is crucially dependent upon which definition of 'basic action' we plug in; without an account of what it *is* for an action to be basic, we have no firm conception of what agency consists in.

The nature of basic actions is the focus of Danto's 'second' paper, of 1965. A person's basic actions, Danto tells us there, are those which she 'cannot be said to have caused to happen' (1965: 141–142). Not, at any rate, by doing anything *first* (1965: 142).[3] On these definitions, however, it is arguable that *almost all* actions count as basic. Stoutland (1968), for example, maintains that it is a mistake to think that we typically cause our *actions*, as opposed to their intrinsic results and/or consequences (for these technical notions, see chapter 72). He thus comes to deny that all non-basic actions are cases of someone causing the occurrence of an *action* (in any way). After all, if I cause my right arm to move by pushing it with my left hand, the movement of my right arm hardly qualifies as an action. Moreover, *some* non-basic actions, such as that of honouring someone, are arguably not cases of causing *anything* to happen (Stoutland 1968: 474; see Candlish 1984 for the view that an action is basic *if and only if* it has no result).

Danto's own example of a paradigmatic basic action is that of moving an arm 'without having to do anything to cause it to move' (1965: 144). Yet, as Alvin Goldman has remarked, this is to confuse *causation* with *causal generation* (which he further distinguishes from conventional generation, simple generation, and augmentation generation; 1970: 23–29). It doesn't help matters that Danto further conflates *what* one does with the *event* of one's doing it (see Danto 1973: 39 for example).[4]

On some views, moreover, my moving my arm – that is, Danto's example of a basic action – just *is* my directly (yet perhaps nonetheless causally) bringing about its movement (von Wright 1963: 35ff. and Alvarez and Hyman 1998; see also chapter 72). John Locke (1975: 2.21.5ff.), Thomas Reid (1969: 50), H. A. Prichard (1949a), and H. McCann (1972 and 1974) have all argued that such causation occurs indirectly, *through* (more basic) volitions, which we cause at will (see chapter 62 for questions of regress). It has also been argued that one may *cause* one's causing one's arm to move *by* causing its movement (Chisholm 1979: 371–372; see also chapter 71), and even that we typically cause our own actions – conceived of this time as a bodily movements – without doing anything else (Taylor 1966: 111–112). If so, then almost all of our actions would match Danto's criteria for being basic. The relative merits and demerits of such competing conceptions of agent causation must naturally influence any account of basic action (see chapter 28; also O'Connor 2000: 43–60).

Danto frequently defines basic actions in terms of a causal independence from other things we might *do*. Yet these include the *mental* acts of thinking, intending, deliberating, deciding, and the like, which, on some accounts, are all prime candidates for being causes of simple actions such as that of moving an arm. Danto thus rejects the view that bodily actions are the results of more basic *mental acts* of will (1965: 148), explicitly rebutting all theories which push action back into the mind through inner volitions or any other kind of purported mental acts or undertakings (whose presumed causality he rejects on the ground that this would constitute a form of telekinesis: 1963: 438). In doing so, he purposely denies the force traditionally ascribed to arguments from error and/or illusion (compare to Dancy 1995). This tactfully leaves both dualism and causal theories of action unscathed, Danto consistently maintaining that (a) the basic/non-basic distinction is reproduced in the world of mental acts (1965: 148)[5] and (b) basic bodily actions may be caused by their mental antecedents so long as the latter do not qualify as acts of any kind (1965: 142).

The aforementioned complications have led philosophers such as Chisholm and Stoutland to redefine basic action in a manner which circumvents questions of causality:

> In our terms, 'A is performed by the agent as a basic act' could be defined as: the agent succeeds in making A happen, and there is no B, other than A, which he undertook to make happen with an end to making A happen. (Chisholm 1964: 617, n.7)
>
> [A] basic action of M is an action M does *not* perform *by* performing some other action. (Stoutland 1968: 467, emphasis in the original)

In later works (1969, 1973 and 1979) Danto came to mirror Stoutland's model (Chisholm's being too teleological for his purposes), explaining that, 'through a series of invitations to present my views, the idea has undergone, under the fire of criticisms, considerable modification' (1973: xi). His resulting definitions replace all causal and temporal talk with the notion of *mediation,* thus eliminating some of the aforementioned difficulties:

> An action α is a *basic action* of an agent *m* only if (i) *m* performs x; and (ii) there is no action β, distinct from α, and such that *m* performs α by performing β. (1969: 66)
>
> [I]n the theory of action are cases in which a man *m* does something *through* some other thing that he does. He moves a stone, say, by pushing against it, and the stone is thus moved by him through the application of mechanical force. [...] Actions we do but not *through* any distinct thing which will also do [...] I shall call basic, and mediated ones are accordingly non-basic. (1973: 3 and 28, emphasis in the original)

The shift from 'no distinct action' (1969) to 'no other thing he does' (1973) is motivated by concerns about things we do (from trying to omitting) which would not obviously qualify as actions. Indeed Danto's 1973 set of basic actions is considerably smaller than his 1966 one, effectively limiting paradigm cases to simple bodily movements (see Danto 1973: 78 and 1979: 484–485). It is also noteworthy that, while Danto takes the 'by' and 'through' qualifications to be equivalent in all relevant instances, one may easily construct counterexamples that cut both ways: I might annoy you *by* citing Wittgenstein or merely *through* my citing him (for instance if *in* doing so I win the argument); cases which may, but need not, coincide.

The problem of specifying what we mean by 'basic' remains even after we have settled for a specific causal, teleological, or mediational relation. Annette Baier illustrates this in her list of several ways of doing one thing *by* doing another, thus dividing actions into at least eight kinds of basicness: causally basic, instrumentally basic, conventionally (or expressively) basic, ontologically (including spatially and/or temporally) basic, logically basic, genetically basic, ease basic, and isolation basic (1971: 168–169). She might have also added epistemically basic (what is the most basic action we *set out* to do?), and there are doubtlessly further kinds besides. Indeed Baier later introduces culture-relative and agent-relative senses of basic competence (1972, developed further in 1976 and subsequently discussed in 1985: 4–5).

Baier concludes that 'the intuitive concept of basic action depended on a failure to separate these questions, and will not survive the clear recognition of their variety and distinctness' (1971: 170). Complex disjunctive formulae that match our basic (and challenge our non-basic) intuitions, strengethened *ad infinitum* by ingenious responses to innovative counterexamples, could no doubt be provided. But what would we have gained? Pace Danto's claim that we all intuitively know 'which actions are basic ones' (Danto 1965: 145; retracted in Danto 1979: 472), there are multitudes of equally legitimate conceptions of what counts as basic. An important upshot of all this is that we are not entitled to reject Danto's definitions on the mere ground that they either include or exclude actions which we would intuitively wish to classify as either basic or non-basic (as indeed numerous critics have done, for instance Brand 1968 and Goldman 1970: 24).

Even upon stipulating a definition of basic action, the multitude of competing theoretical stances on the nature of action, causation, and volition outlined above ensures that no example is uncontroversial. Moreover, any search for basic actions requires a method of action individuation. This brings us to the vexed question of whether the difference between basic and non-basic action is one of *kind*, *degree*, or mere *description*.

Action Individuation

Whichever sort of basicness we have in mind, it is tempting to think of qualifying actions as token members of the class of appropriately basic actions (see Danto 1973: 28).[6] So understood, basicness is an *absolute* property (such as that of being saturated), not a *relative* one (like tallness). Such a conception nonetheless allows for varying *degrees* of approximation: if I poison the inhabitants by replenishing the water supply, doing the latter by operating the pump which in turn I do by moving my arm in a particular way, my act of operating the pump may be seen as less basic than that of moving my arm but more so than that of replenishing the water supply (which may seem less basic than my act of poisoning the inhabitants).

But now a question arises with regard to how many actions I have actually performed here. In Elizabeth Anscombe's words:

> Are we to say that the man who (intentionally) moves his arm, operates the pump, replenishes the water supply, poisons the inhabitants, is performing *four* actions? Or only one? [...] moving his arm up and down with his fingers round the pump handle *is*, in these circumstances, operating the pump; and, in these circumstances, it *is* replenishing the house water-supply; and, in these circumstances, it *is* poisoning the household. So there is one action with four descriptions, each dependent on wider circumstances, and each related to the next as description of means to end. (Anscombe 1957, § 26, pp. 45–46)

Irving Thalberg (1977: 85) has labeled those who side with Anscombe 'reductive unifiers.' According to these reductionists, being basic is a matter of description, not kind. The most influential of them, Donald Davidson, maintains that *all* actions are basic under some description, since, strictly speaking, all we ever do is move our bodies: the rest is up to nature (Davidson 1971). By contrast, 'pluralists' or 'multipliers' such as Goldman (1970) and Thomson (1971) claim that each of the above descriptions picks out a different action, and that only one of them (at most) is basic.

Thalberg's own position, non-reductive ('ni'-saying) unification, rejects the very choice between identity and independence in favor of a part–whole relation. On this view (developed in collaboration with Vivian M. Veil), the event of my replenishing the water supply *includes* – but is not identical to – the event of my operating the pump (Weil and Thalberg 1981; cf. Lowe 2003), and is consequently not basic under any description. *Mutatis mutandis*, basic actions may contain (ontologically more basic) elements that are not themselves actions (Weil and Thalberg 1974). Whether or not any two mereologically related events are *numerically* distinct is a moot point. Jennifer Hornsby (1979: 195–196), for example, rejects the labels 'unifiers' and 'multipliers' in favor of 'identifiers' and 'differentiators,' on the grounds that the former pair serves to conflate identity criteria with enumerative criteria which do not obviously apply to action. On Hornsby's conception of what is under dispute, Weil and Thalberg side with the differentiators; however, their *reason* for differentiating as they do has as little to do with numerical distinctness as it does with ontological independence.

We should, on any of the above views, be wary of equating the question 'How many events occurred?' with that of 'How many *things* did I do?'; for we may legitimately speak of one event of my doing several things (see also chapter 1). This is not to deny that we may offer multiple descriptions of one and the same action: Oedipus does not kill Laius *and* his father (though it is true that he strikes Laius and that he kills his father). In addition to such Rylean conjunction tests, we may also apply spatio-temporal criteria to individuation. Suppose that Bob Marley shot the Sheriff at time t^1, but that the Sheriff only died at a later time t^3, before which – at time t^2 – Marley recorded his famous song. Did Marley kill the Sheriff before or after recording his song (he certainly didn't do it during it)? It would be as implausible to claim (with differentiators such as Goldmam 1970 and Thomson 1971) that Marley did not kill the Sheriff until t^3 – after he had left the scene of the crime and was back in the recording studio – as it would be to follow identifiers such as Davidson (1969) and Hornsby (1979) in maintaining that he killed the Sheriff at t^1 – that is, before the Sheriff died (but see chapter 11 for Cambridge actions).

It is often objected (for instance by Bennett 1973) that the implausibility of the latter claim is not (genuinely) ontological but (merely) a linguistic oddity. We do not call a woman a mother before she has any children, yet we may, after the birth or adoption of her first child, legitimately speak of what this 'mother' did before she had any children. Similarly (or so the argument goes), while we cannot at t^1 (while the sheriff was still alive) truthfully *say* that Marley killed the Sheriff, at t^2 (when the sheriff is dead) it becomes perfectly acceptable to talk of Marley 'killing' him at t^1 (before he died). But, if anything, the analogy proves the opposite, for in the former case we do not at t^2 imply that she was already a mother at t^1 any more than we can plausibly state at t^2 that Marley killed the Sheriff at t^1. Legitimate talk at t^2 of a killer's life before t^1 (when his first victim died) does not license the inference – no matter when one makes it – that the said person was already a killer then (see also Ginet 1982: 60 and Mackie 1997).

All such difficulties vanish, however, once we distinguish between the *cause* of the Sheriff's death, namely the shooting, and the logically related yet distinct *causing* of his death, namely the killing (see Lowe 1981 and Weintraub 2003; though cf. Hornsby 1982). While it is, *pace* Weintraub, legitimate to call both these things 'events' of people acting, it would be absurd to think of the causing of an event as something which could itself be brought about (O'Connor 2000: 52–55 and 61). Causings, like all other events, may nonetheless be located temporally; we simply cannot do it here in as fine-grained a manner as we can with the shooting. To *insist* on a more precise temporal location is as silly as insisting that the killing must have also had a spatial location which is smaller than, say, that of a bread tin (Sorensen: 1985, Dretske 1988: 20–21, Sandis 2006: 181; compare Wittgenstein 1953, § 71; Dennett 1978 commits the parallel fallacy of thinking that *spatial* imprecision with regard to the location of persons is philosophically problematic). If Marley shot the Sherriff in March 1973 (before recording his song about it in April 1973), and if the Sheriff (unlike the deputy) did not die until November 1973 (after the hit record was released), then we can truthfully and informatively say that Marley killed the Sheriff in 1973. Needless to say, the location of any given event at a certain minute, hour, day, week, month, season, year, decade, century, or millennium does not imply that it must have been occurring continually throughout that period (consider cricket matches, for example).[7]

See also: ACTION THEORY AND ONTOLOGY (1); BODILY MOVEMENTS (4); SPEECH ACTS (8); CAMBRIDGE ACTIONS (11); VOLITION AND THE WILL (13); INTENTION (14); MENTAL ACTS (27); AGENT CAUSATION (28); BODILY AWARENESS AND BODILY ACTION (29); DELIBERATION AND DECISION (32); INDIAN PHILOSOPHERS (52); REID (62); CHISHOLM (71); VON WRIGHT (72); ANSCOMBE (74).

Notes

1 Danto's much anthologized early papers continue to receive the greater degree of commentary despite the fact that much of the debate is superseded by his later work.

2 Although Danto also takes his view to have certain theological consequences (see Danto 1963: 438 and 445, and 1965: 142).

3 Danto's phrasing suggests that he sees no conceptual space for the possibility of one's either (i) causing an action *directly* or (ii) causing an action by doing something that is simultaneous with it.

4 See Sandis (2012) for a critique of this conflation and its influence on theories of behavioral explanation.

5 Indeed Danto takes it that his view vindicates Descartes: 'Among the things I take Descartes to have meant when he said that we are not in our bodies the way a pilot is in a ship, is that we do not always do things, as pilots must with ships, by causing them to happen' (1965: 148).

6 Accordingly, the abovementioned definitions may be viewed as attempts to isolate, through the specification of necessary and sufficient conditions, a suitable *type* or *kind*, which they all instantiate (albeit one that cannot be identified through generic action descriptions; cf. Danto 1965: 146).

7 Many thanks to Annette Baier, David Dolby, Arto Laitinen, Elizabeth Sandis, and Fred Stoutland for helpful comments.

References

Alvarez, M. and Hyman, J. (1998). Agents and their actions. *Philosophy*, 73, 218–245.
Anscombe, G. E. M. (1957). *Intention*. Oxford: Blackwell.
Aristotle (1934). *Physics*, Books V–VIII, edited by P. H. Wicksteed and F. M. Cornford. Cambridge, MA: Harvard University Press (Loeb Classical Library).
The Bhagavad Gītā, edited by W. V. Johnson, 1995. Oxford: Oxford University Press.
Baier, A. (1971). The search for basic actions. *American Philosophical Quarterly*, 8 (2), 161–170.
Baier, A. (1972). Ways and means. *Canadian Journal of Philosophy*, 1, 275–293.
Baier, A. (1976). Mixing memory and desire. *American Philosophical Quarterly*, 13 (3), 213–220. Reprinted in Baier 1985: 8–21.
Baier, A. (1985). *Postures of the Mind: Essays on Mind and Morals*. London: Methuen.
Bennett, J. (1973). Shooting, Killing and Dying. *Canadian Journal of Philosophy*, 2, 315–323.
Brand, M. (1968). Danto on basic actions. *Nous*, 2 (2), 187–190.
Candlish, S. (1984). Inner and outer basic action. *Proceedings of the Aristotelian Society*, NS 84, 83–102.
Chisholm, R. M. (1964). The descriptive element in the concept of action. *Journal of Philosophy*, 90, 613–624.
Chisholm, R. M. (1966). Freedom and action. In K. Lehrer (ed.), *Freedom and Determinism*, New York: Random House, 11–44.
Chisholm, R. M. (1979). Objects and persons: Revisions and replies. In E. Sosa (ed.), *Essays on the Philosophy of Roderick Chisholm*. Amsterdam: Rodopi, 317–288.
Danto, A. C. (1963). What we can do. In S. Morgenbesser (ed.), *Symposium: Human Action (= Journal of Philosophy)*, 60 (15), 435–445.
Danto, A. C. (1965). Basic actions. *American Philosophical Quarterly*, 2, 141–148.
Danto, A. C. (1969). Complex events. *Philosophy and Phenomenological Research*, 30 (1), 66–77.
Danto, A. C. (1973). *Analytic Philosophy of Action*. Cambridge: Cambridge University Press.
Danto, A. C. (1979). Basic actions and basic concepts. *Review of Metaphysics*, 32 (3), 471–485.
Dancy, J. (1995). Arguments from illusion. *Philosophical Quarterly*, 45 (181), 421–438.
Davidson, D. (1969). The individuation of events. In N. Rescher (ed.), *Essays in Honour of Carl. G. Hempel*, Dordrecht: R. Reidel, 216–234. [Reprinted in Davidson 1980, 163–180.]
Davidson, D. (1971). Agency. In R. Binkley, R. Bronaugh, and A. Marras (eds), *Agent, Action and Reason*, Toronto: University of Toronto Press, 3–37. [Reprinted in Davidson 1980, 43–61.]
Davidson, D. (1980). *Essays on Actions and Events*. Oxford: Oxford University Press.
Dennett, D. (1978). Where am I? In D. Dennet, *Brainstorms: Philosophical Essays on Mind and Psychology*, Cambridge, MA: MIT Press, 310–323.
Dretske, F. (1988). *Explaining Behavior*. Cambridge, MA: MIT Press.
Frankfurt, H. G. (1969). Alternate possibilities and moral responsibility. *Journal of Philosophy*, 66 (23), 829–839.
Ginet, C. (1982). *On Action*. Cambridge: Cambridge University Press.
Goldman, A. I. (1970). *A Theory of Human Action*. Princeton, NJ: Princeton University Press.
Hornsby, J. (1979). Actions and identities. *Analysis*, 39 (4), 195–201.
Hornsby, J. (1982). Reply to Lowe on actions. *Analysis*, 42 (3), 152–153.
Locke, J. (1975). *An Essay Concerning Human Understanding*, edited by P. Nidditch. Oxford: Oxford University Press. [Cited by book, chapter, and section.]
Lowe, E. J. (1981). 'All actions occur inside the body.' *Analysis*, 41 (3), 126–129.
Lowe, E. J. (2003). Individuation. In M. J. Loux and D. W. Zimmerman (eds), *The Oxford Handbook of Metaphysics*. Oxford: Oxford University Press, 75–95.

Mackie, D. (1997). The individuation of actions. *The Philosophical Quarterly*, 47 (186), 38–54.
Martin, J. R. (1972) Basic actions and simple actions. *American Philosophical Quarterly*, 9 (1), 59–68.
McCann, H. (1972). Is raising one's arm a basic action? *Journal of Philosophy*, 64 (9): 235–249.
McCann, H. (1974). Volition and basic action. *Philosophical Review*, 83, 451–473.
O'Connor, T. (2000). *Persons and Causes: The Metaphysics of Free Will*. Oxford: Oxford University Press.
Prichard, H. A. (1949a). Acting, willing, desiring [1938]. In Prichard (1949b), 187–198.
Prichard, H. A. (1949b). *Moral obligation*, edited by W. D. Ross, Oxford: Clarendon Press.
Reid, T. (1969). *Essays on the Active Powers of the Human Mind* [1788; original title: *Essay on the Active Powers of Man*], edited by B. A. Brody. Cambridge, MA: MIT Press.
Sandis, C. (2006) 'When did the killing occur? Donald Davidson on action individuation. *Daimon. Revista de Filosofía*, 37, 179–183.
Sandis, C. (2012). *The Things We Do and Why We Do Them*. Basingstoke: Palgrave Macmillan.
Sorensen, R. A. (1985). Self-deception and scattered events. *Mind*, 94 (373), 64–69.
Stoutland, F. (1968). Basic actions and causality. *Journal of Philosophy*, 65 (16), 467–475.
Taylor, R. (1966). *Action and Purpose*. New Jersey: Prentice Hall.
Irving Thalberg (1977). *Perception, Emotion, and Action: A Component Approach*. Oxford: Blackwell.
Thompson, M. (2008). *Life and Action*. Cambridge, MA: Harvard University Press.
Thomson, J. J. (1971). The time of a killing. *Journal of Philosophy*, 68, 115–132.
Weil, V.M. and Thalberg, I. (1974), The elements of basic action, *Philosophia*, 4 (1), 111–138.
Weil, V. M. and Thalberg, I. (1981). Basic and non-basic actions: 'same' or 'different'? *Analysis*, 41 (1), 12–17.
von Wright, G. H. (1963). *Norm and Action*. London: Routledge and Kegan Paul.
Weintraub, R. 2003. 'The time of a killing.' *Analysis*, 63 (3), 178–182.
Wittgenstein, L. (1953). *Philosophical Investigations*, translated by G. E. M. Anscombe. Oxford: Blackwell.

Further reading

Baier, A. (1970). Act and intent. *Journal of Philosophy*, 67 (9), 649–659.
Dretske, F. (2009). What must actions be for reasons to explain them? In C. Sandis (ed.), 13–21.
Goldman, A. I. (1971). The individuation of action. *Journal of Philosophy*, 68, 761–774.
Hornsby, J. (1980). *Actions*. London: Routledge and Kegan Paul.
Hornsby, J. (1981). Reply to Weil and Thalberg. *Analysis*, 41 (1), 18–21.
Hornsby, J. (1983). Events that are causings: A response to Lowe. *Analysis*, 43 (3), 141–142.
Lowe, E. J. (1983). Reply to Hornsby on Actions. *Analysis*, 43 (3), 140–141.
Sandis, C. (2009) (ed.), *New Essays on the Explanation of Action*. Basingstoke: Palgrave Macmillan.
Thalberg, I. (1971). Singling out actions, their properties, and components. *Journal of Philosophy*, 68, 781–786.
Thomson, J. J. (1971). Individuating actions. *Journal of Philosophy*, 68, 774–781.
Thomson, J. J. (1977). *Acts and Other Events*. Ithaca, NY: Cornell University Press.

3

Trying to Act

JENNIFER HORNSBY

Introduction

Many say that *trying* is a ubiquitous feature of human agency: they claim that we try to do everything we intentionally do. The claim might seem to have a special significance when it is taken to embrace bodily agency. For if someone tries to move her body whenever she moves her body, then it might seem that bodily agency should be understood as some sort of amalgam of 'mental' (trying) and 'physical' (bodily movement). In what follows I shall suggest that the claim about *trying*'s ubiquity can be made to be very plausible. But I shall argue that it lacks the significance which has sometimes been accorded to it. So far from leading us to find a strictly 'mental' component in bodily action, recognizing the ubiquity of *trying* can encourage us to appreciate that a person's involvement in her actions – in her causing what she does – extends into the world beyond her body.

The Extent of Trying

Everyone will agree that one can try to do something but fail to do it. And it is clear enough that one may try to do something and actually do it: we are sometimes successful in our attempts. What is much less obvious is that we have tried to do something *whenever* we have succeeded in doing it. But a case can be made for this (and is made in Armstrong 1973, O'Shaughnessy 1973, and Hornsby 1980.)[1]

A mismatch between what someone tries to do and what she actually does is found in various circumstances. Consider just these three examples.

- [i] Someone tries to unlock a door, wrongly supposing that the key in her hand is the key to its lock.
- [ii] Someone tries to buy a ticket; she calls the ticket office, but isn't surprised to discover that there are actually no longer any tickets available.
- [iii] Someone manifestly makes a great effort to lift a block in order to demonstrate that it is impossibly heavy to lift; she says to her companion, who had thought that the block was made of polystyrene: 'See, I can't lift it.'

In this last example, the agent will think of herself as trying to lift the block. For *try to lift the block* is exactly what she has a reason to do, wanting to demonstrate how very heavy the block actually is. Again in example [ii], the agent is likely to think of herself as trying to act: insofar as she is uncertain that she'll succeed in buying tickets, she won't think of herself as actually doing it. Only in case [i] will the agent *not* think of herself as trying: at least up to the point at which she realizes she has the wrong key, she will think of herself as being in the process of unlocking the door. Unless someone is cognizant of a possibility of failure, or of an actual failure, the idea of themself as trying to do something usually doesn't enter into their thoughts. This might lead one to suppose that, in order for an agent to have tried to Φ, she must either have taken there to have been some sort of difficulty about Φ-ing, or have found that in the event she failed to Φ.

This cannot be right, however. For the judgment that an agent is trying to act in some way may be made by an onlooker irrespective of whether the agent thinks that she may fail, and irrespective of whether there is any real possibility of her failing. So in example [i], for instance, an onlooker who had not foreseen any problem about unlocking the door could say, when it was revealed that the person had the wrong key, that they had known all along that the person would try to unlock it. And if we change the example, so that the person actually holds the key to the door, but the onlooker supposes that she has taken out a different key, then, when there proves to be no problem about unlocking the door, the unlooker has no need to withdraw the claim that the person tried to unlock it. It seems, then, that when an agent is intentionally Φ-ing, doubts or difficulties about her succeeding do not bear on the question of whether she is trying to Φ; they bear rather upon whether there could be any point in thinking of her as trying to Φ, and upon whether it would be appropriate to say that she is trying to Φ.

In order to see that 'try to' applies in many cases where we wouldn't think to apply it, it helps to see that learning what a person is trying to do is one way to come to know something about the person's reasons for acting. Often enough, someone who is asked 'Why are you Φ-ing?,' if she is Φ-ing as a means of Ψ-ing may say any of 'I want to Ψ' or 'I intend to Ψ' or 'I am trying to Ψ' or 'I am Ψ-ing' (Thompson 2008: 97–100). So, when one is told that some agent is trying to Ψ, one may be alerted, not to something that requires especial effort or in which the agent is unlikely to succeed, but to something which the agent has a reason to do, yet is not visibly doing now. (Thompson focuses on cases where Φ-ing is a means, or part of a means, of Ψ-ing; but 'I am trying to Ψ' can be apt also in cases where one's Φ-ing counts conventionally as one's Ψ-ing, and where Φ-ing is a species of Ψ-ing.)

Schroeder (2001) has argued against the idea that we always try to do what we intentionally do. He says (among other things) that it implies that every action is possibly a failure. But there is no such implication if 'A tries to do something' is taken to mean (roughly) 'A does what she can to do the thing.' If *to try to Φ* is *to do what one can to Φ*, then someone who tried to Φ, and who in the event was able to Φ, is someone who Φ-ed. The fact that she tried to Φ would not show that it was possible that she had not been able to Φ, and thus possible that she had failed. (Compare: where it is possibly the case that *p* by virtue of the fact that it is actually the case that *p*, its being possible that *p* cannot amount to its being *merely* possible that *p*.)

Here is a pair of stories which help to confirm the idea that to *try* to Φ is to *do what one can* to Φ. Imagine Adrian walking to the office one morning. When he is half-way there he finds that the street is cordoned off: there is a bomb scare, and he is told that the campus is inaccessible. He tried to get to the office, but he had to turn back. In the second story, things are the same to the half-way point. But now there is no bomb scare; it is rather that Adrian decides that he would be better off going to the library on the other side of town, so he turns round and walks in the opposite direction. Even here, Adrian was trying to get to the office until he turned back. But in this case he did not try to get to the office. (Compare: someone may have *been crossing* the street, although they did not *cross* the street, having been knocked over by a bus, as it might be.) The stories help to confirm the idea that to *try* to Φ is to *do what one can* to Φ, inasmuch as Adrian did what he could to get to the office in the first version, but not in the second, where he could have continued his journey. The stories may also assist in showing that people can be trying to do very much more than anyone would ordinarily be inclined to say that they were trying to do.[2]

Trying to Move the Body

Wittgenstein said: 'When I raise my arm, I do not usually *try* to raise it' (1953, § 622). Thus Wittgenstein rejected the claim about the ubiquity of trying which I've just attempted to make plausible. It might be thought that we have to follow him in rejecting the claim if we are to take the point Wittgenstein was making when he said that he didn't usually try to raise his arm. Wittgenstein had just asked (§ 621): 'What is left over when I subtract the fact that my arm went up from the fact that I raised my arm?' His point (arguably) was that the difference between the action of my raising my arm and my arm's going up is not to be accounted for by reference to some mental state or occurrence which is present when I raise my arm intentionally but would be absent if my arm went up without my raising it. (There are different interpretations of Wittgenstein. But others might want to make the point I here interpret him as making.)

What we shall see in the present section is that Wittgenstein's point can be well taken even by someone who disagrees with him about whether one usually tries to move one's body. This will involve us in looking at a recent account of agency in which a prominent role is given to *trying to*, and in comparing this account with some different ones.

We may assume that Wittgenstein was opposed to a traditional dualistic conception of bodily action – to volitionism. Volitionism conceives of bodily action as involving a causal connection between a volition (or an 'act of will') and a bodily movement. One alternative to volitionism is an account which Snowdon (2001) has called the 'trying theory,' which holds that actions are those events of trying to move the body which cause movements of the body. (Snowdon gives this label to an account defended in Hornsby 1980, especially ch. 3; but that account is retracted here.) The theory would seem to be in Wittgenstein's target area inasmuch as it requires the claim about the ubiquity of trying, which he denied. Still, the trying theory appears to be an improvement on traditional volitionism for three reasons.

In the first place, the theory makes use of a familiar word: it has no need to posit volitions, or acts of will, or items of any sort introduced for a special theoretical purpose. Secondly, the theory avoids a vicious regress to which many volitionists fall prey. Many volitionists took volitions to distinguish 'mere bodily movements' from the voluntary movements which are actions, saying that only the latter are caused by volitions. But if an event's being a voluntary action required its being caused by a volition, then for each volition there would need to be another, and then another (for this regress argument, see Ryle 1949, ch. 3). Thirdly, the trying theory rejects the dualist assumptions of the volitionists, who thought that there must be an event in the mind (a 'mental' one) and an event in the body (a 'physical' one) if there is to be a bodily action. Certainly the trying theory states a necessary condition for action by making use of a piece of psychological vocabulary (the word 'try'). But the theory will not label as 'mental' a person's trying to do something. For, according to the theory, when someone succeeds in doing something, her trying to do the thing *is* her action of doing it, and it must then be every bit as 'physical' as the action itself.

When the trying theory is rested in the identification of events of trying to with actions, it appears to capitalize on the Davidsonian view of agency, according to which actions are redescribable particulars (see Davidson 1971). Davidson maintained that to describe an event as an action is usually to describe it in terms of an effect it has. One may then want to say that to describe an event as someone's trying to do something is usually to describe it in terms of some *intended* effect, and that someone succeeds in doing what she tries to do if her action causes what she intends it to cause. But Davidson, for his part, would need to make an exception for *trying to move the body* if he accepted this view. The exception is needed because Davidson takes bodily movement descriptions of actions to be effect-free descriptions: he holds that a person's moving a bit of her body just *is* a movement of that bit of her body.

Well, an advocate of the trying theory sees no basis for the exception that Davidson makes here. When Davidson identifies a person's moving her body with her body's moving, he fails to follow through with treating verbs of action like 'move' and 'raise' always as causative verbs. The trying theorist says that, if 'her raising the flag' describes an action in terms of an effect it has, then so does 'her raising her arm.' Given that the same causative verb 'raise' occurs both in 'raise the flag' and in 'raise one's arm' and the same causative verb 'move' occurs both in 'move the boulder' and in 'move one's leg,' it seems that, when some part of some person's body moves in a case of intentional agency, the person's moving her body is not only her trying to move it but also (by Davidson's lights) an event which *causes* its movement.

We are now well placed to see why the trying theory should have been thought by many to be objectionable. The events that cause our bodies to move are signals in the motor system, contractions of muscles, and the like. Such events occur inside our bodies. It is no wonder then that the trying theorist has sometimes been thought to treat actions as 'mental.' For she must now accept that actions are events inside us. This has struck people as absurd. Human actions must be accessible, and immediately sensible, from the point of view from which we see human beings at work in the world. And from that point of view, we surely don't come upon events inside people's bodies (see for example Steward 2000, Haddock 2005.)

The apparently absurd conclusion here, that actions are events internal to bodies, is reached when someone's moving her body is treated as a *cause* of a movement of their body. We have seen that, for the particular case of moving one's body, Davidson gave up on the event-causal element which he discerned to be generally present in verbs like 'move'; but he acknowledged the naturalness of saying that someone who has raised her arm has *made* it go up (Davidson 1987, at p. 102 in the 2004 reprint), so that he allowed a seemingly causal character even here. Davidson's own reason for saying that making the arm go up must be identified with, rather than be said to be the cause of, the arm's going up was that he wanted to avoid a regress. (If A's making happen what happens were always an event causally prior to what happens, then, in order for A to make something happen, A would need to make making-what-happens happen, and to make making-what-happens-happen happen, and so on.) Evidently Davidson relies upon an assumption – in which the trying theorist follows him – that someone's making something happen, or their causing something, is always to be spelled out as a matter of a causal relation obtaining between two events: between an action and its effect.

The assumption can, and I think should, be rejected. When it is allowed that causal work is done by an agent who raises her arm, there is no need to suppose that her raising her arm stands to her arm's going up in an event causal relation. Consider the process in which a person is participating so long as she is raising her arm. The relation between this process (her causing her arm to go up) and the state of affairs in which it results (her arm's being up) is not the relation that obtains between two events when one causes the other. So long as a person is raising something, or moving something, it would seem that *she, the agent*, not any event, is the subject of a causal relation (see Lowe 1981).

When a causal role is granted to agents, 'A caused X' cannot be understood as equivalent to 'A's action caused X' (which is how Davidson understands it, save in the special case where a regress otherwise would threaten). But then the trying theory, which treats events of trying to move the body as causes of bodily movements, must be rejected along with its absurd consequence.

So we can say that, even if trying to Φ is a necessary condition of intentionally Φ-ing, still trying to Φ does not introduce any causal element into intentionally Φ-ing. And this means that the idea of *trying* does not belong in any analysis, or interesting account, of intentionally Φ-ing. Wittgenstein's 'What is left over?' question then appears to be misplaced (as I take it Wittgenstein thought that it was). Indeed one might now trade on the ubiquity of 'trying' as a way of seeing that Wittgenstein's question is out of place. The movements of the body that are involved in intentional bodily actions (which are redescribable using 'try to') may be thought to differ essentially from movements of the body that are not so involved (which cannot be described as events of anyone's trying to do anything).[3]

I have used the claim about the ubiquity of trying – the claim that we try to do whatever we intentionally do – to put into question an account of human agency like Davidson's. But the underlying disagreement with Davidson has been about the causality that agency involves. So there could be an argument against a Davidsonian account in which the ubiquity claim played no part. Still, the main point here has been that the ubiquity claim can be freed from the trying theory, into which it is embedded.[4]

When it is freed from that, it may be thought to tell us little more than that an agent is always trying to do various things when she intentionally causes things, or makes things happen – when, having reason to bring about this or that, she exercises her capacities as a bodily agent.

Trying and Intending

My suggestion has been that an examination of the trying theory may lead us to abandon the assumption that actions are usually described in terms of their event-causal effects. Abandoning this assumption does not mean giving up on the general idea of actions as occurrences that are apt to be brought under various descriptions. So we might still say that to describe something as a person's trying to do something is *usually* to describe it in terms of something *intended* by that person. What I want to draw attention to, in closing, is the fact that 'usually' here marks an important qualification: we may try to do something without either intending to do it or doing it intentionally.

For the most part, we do not *intend* to try to do what we intentionally do. Even if someone's Φ-ing intentionally is their trying to Φ, still what is usually intended is to Φ, not to try to Φ. This will explain why, as we saw, agents very often have no thoughts of themselves as *trying*. But they may have such thoughts. A case in point is example [iii] in the opening section above. The person who tried to lift a block in order to show that it was impossibly heavy to lift did not intend to lift it, presumably: if she had been wrong about the weight of the block, so that actually she did lift it when she did what she could to lift it, then she would not have lifted it intentionally. What she intended to do was only to try to lift the block.

Sometimes, then, we may have a reason to try to do something that we have no reason to do. And sometimes, also, when we recognize a difficulty about doing something, we may devise a plan incorporating alternative means, so that we can be ready to try each of the alternatives (for more on this, see Holton 2008). The fact that we can find ourselves with reasons precisely to try to do something represents an extension of the powers we have as agents. In being able to reason practically and think about what we may try to do, we may devise new means to our ends.

See also: ACTION THEORY AND ONTOLOGY (1); BASIC ACTIONS AND INDIVIDUATION (2); BODILY MOVEMENTS (4); THE CAUSAL THEORY OF ACTION (5); VOLITION AND THE WILL (13); INTENTION (14); PRACTICAL REASONING (31); ACTION AND CRIMINAL RESPONSIBILITY (42); RYLE (69); DAVIDSON (73).

Notes

1 Many of the arguments rely on an idea of Grice (first employed in his 1961 paper) to the effect that the use of a word can carry a conversational implicature which is not a semantic implication, so that what may be said using the word can be misleading without being false.

2 It might seem that a crucial question is begged when it is said that Adrian was trying to get to the office in the first version of the story. But it will be very hard to deny this when it is acknowledged that in that version he did try to get there but was prevented by the cordon. For if he has not yet tried to get to the office when he sets out, but has tried to get there when he is turned back, then must he not have been trying to get there in the interval?

3 One might here reach a disjunctive conception of bodily movements: see chapter 4.

4 Those who hold that we don't try to move our bodies whenever we move them intentionally might still endorse a restricted version of the claim about the ubiquity of trying. For instance they might say that (1) the ubiquity claim should be restricted to such things as we do as we have a *means* of doing, and (2) in the ordinary case when one moves a bit of the body directly – say, one simply raises an arm – no *means* are employed. I shan't atempt here to settle the question whether this is right. But I note that there would certainly seems to be cases – such as that of a person who has recently suffered, or recently recovered from, local paralysis – in which it is correct to describe someone as trying to move a bit of her body. These cases need to be considered in the context of a general appreciation of how 'try to' works once it is allowed that someone's moving her body should not be treated as a *cause* of a movement of her body.

References

Armstrong, D. M. (1973). Acting and Trying, *Philosophical Papers*, 2, 1–15. [Reprinted in D. M. Armstrong (1981), *The Nature of Mind*. Brighton: Harvester Press, 1–15.]

Davidson, D. (1971). Agency. In R. Binkley, R. Bronaugh, and A. Marras (eds), *Agent, Action and Reason*, Toronto: University of Toronto Press, 4–25. [Reprinted in D. Davidson (1980), *Essays on Actions and Events*, Oxford: Oxford University Press.]

Davidson, D. (1987). Problems in the explanation of action. In P. Pettit, R. Sylvan and J. Norman (eds.), *Metaphysics and Morality: Essays in Hour of J. J. C. Smart*, Oxford: Blackwell, 35–49. [Reprinted in D. Davidson (2004), *Problems of Rationality*, Oxford: Oxford University Press.]

Grice, H. P. (1961). The causal theory of perception. *Proceedings of the Aristotelian Society*, Suppl. 35, 121–153.

Haddock, A. (2005). At one with our actions, but at two with our bodies. *Philosophical Explorations*, 8, 152–172.

Hornsby, J. (1980). *Actions*. London: Routledge and Kegan Paul.

Holton, R. (2008). Partial belief, partial intention. *Mind*, 117, 27–58.

Lowe, E. J. (1981). 'All actions occur inside the body.' *Analysis*, 41, 126–129.

O'Shaughnessy, B. (1973). Trying (as the mental 'pineal gland'). *Journal of Philosophy*, 70, 365–386.

Ryle, G. (1949). *The Concept of Mind*. London: Hutchinson.

Schroeder, S. (2001). The Concept of Trying. *Philosophical Investigations*, 24, 213–227.

Snowdon, P. (2001). Acting, trying and rewiring. In D. Egonson, J. Josefson, B. Petterson, and T. Ronnow-Rasmussen (eds), *Exploring Practical Philosophy*, Burlington, VT: Ashgate Publishing Company, 1–16.

Steward, H. (2000). Do actions occur inside the body? *Mind and Society*, 1, 107–125.

Thompson, M. (2008). Naïve action theory. In M. Thompson, *Life and Action: Elementary Structures of Practice and Practical Thought*, Cambridge, MA: Harvard University Press, 85–146.

Wittgenstein, L. (1953) *Philosophical Investigations*, translated by G. E. M. Anscombe. Oxford: Blackwell.

Further reading

Adams, F. (1991). He doesn't really want to try. *Analysis*, 51, 109–112.
Adams, F. (1995). Trying: You've got to believe. *Philosophical Research*, 20, 149–161.
Hornsby, J. (1995). Reasons for trying. *Philosophical Research*, 20, 525–539.
Jones, O. R. (1983). Trying. *Mind*, 92, 368–385.
McCann, H. (1974). Trying, paralysis and volitions. *Review of Metaphysics*, 28, 423–442.
Mele, A. (1989). She intends to try. *Philosophical Studies*, 55, 101–106.
Mele, A. (1990). He wants to try. *Analysis*, 50, 251–253.
Mele, A. (1991). He wants to try again: A Rejoinder. *Analysis*, 51, 225–228.
Smith, M. (1983). Actions, attempts and internal events. *Analysis*, 43, 142–146.

4

Bodily Movements

ADRIAN HADDOCK

Introductory

Intentional bodily actions involve bodily movements. If I move my body, then my body moves. So it seems to be true that, if there is an action in which I move my body with a certain intention, then there is an event in which my body moves – viz. a movement of my body. When philosophers of action have reflected on apparent truths like this they have tended to be concerned with the relation between events of this sort and actions. They have not tended to be concerned with the nature of these events, often taking a certain conception of their nature for granted.

But there are at least two different ways of understanding the nature of bodily movements.

The first does not accord any deep significance to the fact that my body can move even if I do not move my body. If I move my body with the intention of doing something, then the movement of my body intrinsically involves my intention of doing this thing. However, if my body moves but I do not move my body with the intention of doing something, then the movement of my body does not intrinsically involve my intention of doing this thing. In this picture, movements of the body which are involved in intentional bodily actions differ intrinsically from movements of the body which are not so involved. We might, following Hornsby (1997), call movements of the former sort agentive movements, or A-movements, and movements of the latter sort mere movements, or M-movements.

The second way of understanding the nature of bodily movements does accord deep significance to the fact that my body can move even if I do not move my body. Even if I move my body with the intention of doing something, the movement of my body does not intrinsically involve my intention of doing this thing; it is just like the movement of my body in a case in which my body moves but I do not move my body with the intention of doing something. In this picture, there is no intrinsic difference between the movements of the body which are involved in intentional bodily actions and the movements of the body which are not. As we might put it, in this picture, all bodily movements are M-movements.

We might think of the first way of understanding the nature of bodily movements as a disjunctive conception of these movements, because of its claim that bodily movements are *either* A-movements *or* M-movements (see Haddock and Macpherson 2008).

And we might think of the second way as a unitary or non-disjunctive conception of bodily movements, because of its claim that all bodily movements are M-movements.

It is this non-disjunctive conception of bodily movements that philosophers of action have tended to take for granted; the disjunctive conception is rarely even considered as a possibility. Whether philosophers of action think of intentional bodily actions as being identical to, or merely as involving, bodily movements caused by either beliefs and desires (Smith 1998), or by intentions (Velleman 2000), or by 'tryings' (Hornsby 1980), or even directly by the agents themselves (Alvarez and Hyman 1998), the non-disjunctive conception is almost invariably assumed. But this assumption has started to come under pressure, with various advantages – not merely for the philosophy of action, but for the philosophy of mind more generally – being claimed for the disjunctive conception (Haddock 2005; Hornsby 1997; Ruben 2003). Of the three main putative advantages, one is epistemic, one is ontological, and one is phenomenological. I will consider each putative advantage in turn.

The Epistemic Advantage

Philosophical worries about knowledge of 'other minds' can stem from the thought that, even though one can directly observe another's bodily movements, one cannot directly observe what is going on in their mind. Knowledge putatively acquired otherwise than by direct observation is assumed to be problematic. The disjunctive conception might be thought to prevent these worries from arising by conceiving of certain directly observable bodily movements as intrinsically mind-involving (Haddock 2005). The hope seems to be that this will enable us to say that, when one directly observes a movement of this sort, one thereby directly observes the intention it intrinsically involves.

However, to know by direct observation that S's body is moving (where S appears to be a person) it is not sufficient to observe the event which is a movement of S's body. One must know that the event one observes is a movement of S's body. Similar considerations apply to knowing that S has a certain intention. So, merely conceiving of some movements as A-movements is, at least, not sufficient for blocking the present worry. It can also seem unnecessary. Coming to know that an event is a movement which intrinsically involves a certain intention is coming to know a fact about a directly observable bodily movement. But – on at least some conceptions of action – coming to know that an event is S's action of moving her body with a certain intention would also be coming to know a fact about a directly observable bodily movement (Velleman 2000). It is not clear that coming to know the latter is any more epistemologically problematic than coming to know the former, given that both are cases of coming to know a fact about a directly observable event. And it is far from clear that coming to know the latter requires the intention to figure in the event intrinsically, rather than in its aetiology.

We might think that one way of coming to know that something is so is by seeing that it is so, where seeing that such-and-such is so is understood as a distinctive mode of perceptual access to the world. So we might think that one can come to know that S is moving her body with the intention of signalling by seeing that she is moving her body with the intention of signaling. A natural response to this thought is that, if seeing that something is so is a mode of distinctively *perceptual* access to the world, then what we see to be so must not itself concern, or be about, any object which we cannot directly observe. So, whereas we can see that S's body is moving because we can directly observe S and we can directly observe the movement of S's body, we cannot see that S is moving her body with a certain intention, because we cannot directly observe S's intention. The hope might be that the disjunctive conception affords a response to this response, by making the intention intrinsic to the directly observable bodily movement. But why should something intrinsic to something directly observable itself be directly observable? It seems to be intrinsic to Michael Dummett's book *Frege: Philosophy of Language* (Dummett 1981) that it contains the expression 'second-level function' (or a suitable translation thereof); but it is evidently possible to observe this book directly without observing this expression (or its translation); perhaps the book is closed, or open on a page on which this expression does not appear. We might try to deal with this objection by making use of the idea that those bodily movements which intrinsically involve intentions *express* the intentions which they intrinsically involve. The hope would be that this idea will enable us to say that the intentions themselves are directly observable. But, even if this hope can be fulfilled, if the putative epistemic advantage is to be an advantage of the disjunctive conception in particular, it will need to be the case that bodily movements can only express those intentions which they intrinsically involve, and cannot express those intentions which they merely have in their aetiology. And it is not clear that this is the case.

The Ontological Advantage

The putative ontological advantage promises to be the most consequential. The prominent causal closure argument against non-reductive conceptions of the psychological can seem to be undermined by a disjunctive conception of bodily movement. According to one natural way of spelling out this argument, bodily movements have sufficient physical causes, because they are physical effects, and because physical effects have sufficient physical causes. So, if psychological causes are distinct from physical causes, it seems that bodily movements cannot have psychological causes, on pain of widespread over-determination. The disjunctive conception can seem to enable us to avoid this conclusion, by undermining the assumption that bodily movements are physical effects. M-movements are physical effects. But not all bodily movements are M-movements. Some are A-movements, and they are not physical but psychological effects, because they intrinsically involve intentions. The conclusion, that bodily movements cannot have psychological causes, no longer follows.

Whether the disjunctive conception succeeds in blocking the causal closure argument is moot, however. If physical effects have sufficient physical causes, and psychological causes are distinct from physical causes, it seems that A-movements cannot have physical effects, on pain of widespread over-determination. The problem which the argument generates seems merely to have been pushed downstream. It can now be tempting to flirt with the claim that the effects of A-movements are themselves A-effects, because they essentially involve the intentions which are intrinsic to their causes. But if this gets serious, it seems that an imperialism of the psychological will result. Reality will seem to consist almost entirely of A-effects. Perhaps this imperialism can be resisted by insisting that, whenever there is an A-movement, there is also an M-movement; as Hornsby puts it, '[w]e have to allow a picture in which there are movements of two different sorts when there are actions' (1997: 107). Perhaps, then, the disjunctive conception will no longer seem to generate imperialism, because we will be able to insist that, whenever there is an A-effect, there is also an M-effect.

But problems will remain. The disjunctive conception promises to enable us to hold on to the non-reductive conception in the face of the causal closure argument, without either disputing that physical effects have sufficient physical causes or countenancing widespread over-determination. But, even if it does not actually countenance widespread over-determination, it is not clear that it avoids a worry which countenancing it seems to generate. Imagine that I move my arm. It looks as if, on the disjunctive conception, there will be an A-movement describable as 'my arm's moving,' and an M-movement describable in the same words. Indeed, it looks as if, whenever there is an A-movement so describable there will be an M-movement so describable. But this co-incidence looks like sheer coincidence, given that the aetiology of the M-movement contains nothing psychological (because over-determination is foreclosed).

Perhaps this worry turns on there being an exact match between the identifying descriptions of the different kinds of movements. Perhaps we can say that, whenever there is an A-movement so describable, there is an M-movement describable *either* like so, *or* like so, *or* like so, *or* like so ... (We might attempt to defend this suggestion by noting that 'my arm's moving' is a description from commonsense psychology, whereas descriptions of M-movements, properly so called, must be couched in the language of physics, whose greater fineness of grain ensures that for every A-movement there is one out of potentially many different M-movements.) Whereas in the previous picture the merely physical aetiology of the M-movement would have to ensure that precisely the right M-movement occurs, in the new picture it need only ensure that one out of a suitable range of M-movements occurs. Some slack is cut, and thereby, it is hoped, the sense of sheer coincidence is removed.

However, even once this slack has been cut, it can still seem coincidental that one M-movement in precisely this range occurs, given that nothing psychological causes there to be such a movement. It is not clear to me that the disjunctive conception can satisfactorily respond to this worry.

The Phenomenological Advantage

The putative phenomenological advantage seems to be the most obvious, and the most promising. What it is supposed to be an advantage over is nicely captured by John McDowell (1994: 90-1) when he speaks of a

> style of thinking [which] gives spontaneity a role in bodily action only in the guise of inner items, pictured as initiating bodily goings-on from within, and taken on that ground to be recognizable as intentions or volitions.

In this picture,

> Our powers as agents withdraw inwards, and our bodies with the powers whose seat they are – which seem to be different powers, since their actualisations are not doings of ours but at best effects of such doings – take on the aspect of alien objects. It comes to seem that what we do, even in those actions that we think of as bodily, is at best to direct our wills, as it were from a distance, at changes of state in those alien objects. And this is surely not a satisfactory picture of our active relation to our bodies. (McDowell 1994: 91)

An example of this style of thinking will help to make McDowell's point vivid: Hornsby's 1980 account of bodily action. (It is worth noting that Hornsby now wishes to distance herself from certain aspects of this account; see chapter 3.)

I can try to do something which involves moving my body without actually doing it, because my body does not move. In such a case there is an event, my trying to do the thing in question, which fails to have as one of its effects a movement of my body. By contrast, if I succeed in doing the thing intentionally, then my trying to do the thing in question has a movement of my body as one of its (numerous) effects. In such a case my action of doing the thing intentionally just is my trying to do the thing in question.

Here my bodily movements are pictured as merely the events initiated by my doings, which are located – as Hornsby (1980) puts it – 'inside the body.' There is a sense in which, in Hornsby's picture, I can direct my will at more things than these movements, because I can try to do move than my body. But it remains the case that the events which are my doings are themselves merely causally related to my bodily movements, which now seem to be no more intimately related to the actualizations of my agentive powers than the movements of objects beyond my self.

The disjunctive conception seems to enable us to deny that bodily movements must be merely the effects of our doings. It seems to enable us to identify our doings with our bodily movements. Such an identification would be very odd in the context of Hornsby's account, in which events of our trying to do things are cases of 'spontaneity in action' (McDowell 1994: 91, n. 5), and our bodily movements are passive occurrences; it would be as if we were merely extending the title 'our doings,' by a kind of courtesy, to goings-on which are really the mere effects of our doings. But, in the context of the disjunctive conception, where there is no volition or intention to which the candidate for identification is merely causally related, there is no such oddity. The candidate is rather a bodily occurrence which intrinsically involves an intention I am in the process of executing. And that seems a fine candidate for the title of an event in which I move my body with the intention of doing something; what we have been calling an intentional bodily action. (It is worth noting that the assumption that actions are events effectively ensures that many, perhaps most, exercises of intentional agency are not actions, because they are not events; see Hornsby 2004 and Thompson 2008. It remains the case that there will be actions in most cases in which intentional agency is exercised.)

This advantage is not merely phenomenological. It seems to support 'a proper understanding of the self as a bodily presence in the world' (McDowell 1994: 91, n. 5) by avoiding at least one guise of the idea that we can separate the self from the bodily presence in the world which the human animal is. I have spoken of the movements of my body. But, in the kind of picture which the disjunctive conception opposes, it would be possible to treat my body as no more mine than my tea cup, or my DVD player – in that, just like these things, my body is something to which I am only externally related. One way to give substance to this idea of an external relation is to say that none of the powers whose actualizations are movements of my body are my powers, but they are merely powers of my body. This is part of what it is for me to be only externally related to my body. If at least one of the powers whose actualizations are movements of my body is a power of mine, there would not be this external relation. And this is just what we have when we identify intentional bodily actions with bodily movements along the lines of the disjunctive conception. In at least some cases, the movements of my body, in the shape of my A-movements, are, just as such, actualizations of my power to execute intentions. This is not what we have in Hornsby's 1980 picture; there the movements of my body are not actualizations of my power to execute intentions. That power's actualizations are confined to events which are always distinct from my bodily movements. In showing us how to give up this picture, and replace it with one in which 'certain bodily goings-on *are* our spontaneity in action, not just effects of it' (McDowell 1994: 91, n. 5), the disjunctive conception offers a more satisfying depiction of our active bodily life.

See also: ACTION THEORY AND ONTOLOGY (1); BASIC ACTIONS AND INDIVIDUATION (2); TRYING TO ACT (3); BODILY AWARENESS AND BODILY ACTION (29); AGENTS' KNOWLEDGE (30); DAVIDSON (73).

References

Alvarez, M. and Hyman, J. (1998). Agents and their actions. *Philosophy*, 73, 218–245.

Dummett, M. (1981). *Frege: Philosophy of Language*. London: Duckworth.

Haddock, A. (2005). At one with our actions, but at two with our bodies: Hornsby's account of action. *Philosophical Explorations*, 8, 157–172.

Haddock, A. and Macpherson, F. (eds) (2008). *Disjunctivism: Perception, Action, Knowledge*. Oxford: Oxford University Press.

Hornsby, J. (1980). *Actions*. London: Routledge and Kegan Paul.

Hornsby, J. (1997). *Simple Mindedness: In Defense of Naive Naturalism in the Philosophy of Mind*. Cambridge, MA: Harvard University Press.

Hornsby, J. (2004). Agency and actions. In J. Hyman and H. Steward (eds), *Agency and Action*, Cambridge: Cambridge University Press, 1–23.

McDowell, J. (1994). *Mind and World*. Cambridge, MA: Harvard University Press.

Ruben, D.-H. (2003). *Action and its Explanation*. Oxford: Clarendon Press.

Smith, M. (1998). The possibility of philosophy of action. In J. Bransen and S. Cuypers (eds), *Human Action, Deliberation and Causation*. Dordecht: Kluwer, 17–41.

Thompson, M. (2008). *Life and Action: Elementary Structures of Practice and Practical Thought*. Cambridge, MA: Harvard University Press.

Velleman, J. D. (2000). *The Possibility of Practical Reason*. Oxford: Oxford University Press.

5

The Causal Theory of Action

WAYNE A. DAVIS

The phrase 'causal theory of action' may refer to any of a number of theses that account for what it is for an agent to do something, or to do something in a particular way, in terms of a causal condition.

Action

If you move your leg, your leg has to move. But your leg can move without your moving your leg. What else is required for you to move your leg? What else, beside the light coming on, is involved in your turning on the light? When the branches of a tree are waving in the wind, why isn't the tree waving its branches? How does this tree differ from a mechanical tree that is waving its branches? The basic principle common to all causal theories is that *the agent performs an action only if an appropriate internal state of the agent causes a particular result in a certain way*. Thus you moved your leg only if your leg moved as a result of some internal state you are in, such as having an activated motor cortex or a desire to move the leg. You turned on the light only if the light came on as a result of some neural and/or mental state you were in. The tree cannot wave its branches because it does not have states capable of causing its branches to wave. The mechanical tree does have such states – perhaps a computer chip that controls a motor. Different ways of moving your leg correspond to different causal processes. Moving your leg through your leg muscles differs in this way from moving it with your hand.[1] Voluntary action (for example moving your leg normally) differs from involuntary action (such as coughing, sneezing, blushing) both in the neural pathways involved and in the initiating state. It is possible, though, for your leg to move as a result of internal states without it being the case that you did anything. A surgeon may have wired you up in such a way that activity in your visual cortex resulting from your seeing a rose activates a pulley that moves your leg. So the initiating state must produce the result in a specific way, not by a 'wayward' or 'deviant' causal chain.

Intentional vs Unintentional Action

What is the difference between intentionally turning on a light and unintentionally turning it on? In both cases you have to turn on the light, so the light has to come on as a result of some appropriate internal state. Causal theories account for this distinction in terms of the presence or absence of a specific mental cause. Your action was intentional only if the initiating cause was the desire or intention to turn on the light. If you turned on the light unintentionally, then the light came on because you wanted to do something else instead, such as turn on the fan. So the causal theory says that *whether an action was intentional depends on whether it was caused by a particular internal state, a desire or intention to perform that action*. The desire to turn on the light must cause the light to come on in the right way for the action to be intentional.[2] If the desire to turn on the light results in you flipping the fan switch by mistake, which unbeknownst to you was wired up to the light, you will not have turned on the light intentionally. A robot or computer can turn on a light, but cannot do so intentionally or unintentionally because it has no mental states at all.[3]

A causal theorist might seek to provide a *semantic analysis*. The goal then would be a non-circular definition of '*S* did *A* intentionally' in which the *definiens* is synonymous with the *definiendum*. This project seems unlikely to succeed. As Fodor (1975: 124–56) observed, most syntactically unstructured expressions of natural languages, especially those of interest to philosophers, cannot be defined in this way.[4] One problem facing any causal analysis for action terminology is that of specifying the right sort of causal chain without circularity. We know that an action is intentional if it is caused by an intention in some ways, but not others. But we do not yet know enough to specify the appropriate ways without using the term 'intentional' (Wilson 1989, chs 9–10). And, given what we do know, it seems clear that we will not be able to specify the appropriate ways without using neurophysiological terminology. A specification in neurophysiological terms would be a valuable scientific definition of intentional action, but not a semantic analysis. Any *definiens* containing neurophysiological terminology will not be *synonymous* with '*S* did *A* intentionally.' The failure of that causal theory as a semantic analysis does not undermine its success in shedding light on what it is to act intentionally. 'Water is H_2O' is not a semantic analysis of 'water,' but it does tell us what water is.

Agent causation

There is a distinction between agent causation and event or state causation. R. Taylor (1966: 111) and Chisholm (1976) objected that, when you move your leg, it is not your desires that cause your leg to move, but *you*. The causal theorist agrees that you cause your leg to move, but rejects the idea that there is any incompatibility between causation by you and causation by your internal states. Indeed, the causal theorist maintains that *what it is for an agent to cause something* is for an appropriate state of (or event involving) the agent to cause it (Goldman 1970: 83ff.). This is true even for inanimate agents: a remote control device cannot cause a light to come on unless activity of the device causes the light to come on. A tree does not cause its branches to wave because no internal state causes the branches to wave.

Reviving this charge, Hornsby (2004: 2) says that the 'standard' causal theory 'leaves agents out' because it is 'event-based.' Velleman (1992) and Bratman (2001) object that the agent does not *do* anything on such theories, but is merely an arena in which mental and physical events take place. Agents are not left out, though, when the relevant events consist of the agent's being in certain states. What the causal theory offers is an account of what it is for an agent to do something. The agent plays an active part in moving her leg because it is *her* internal states that cause it to move. She controls her leg movements in virtue of them being controlled by *her* intentions. How could an agent do anything if the way she was had no effect on anything? How could an agent do anything intentionally if her intentions and plans were ineffective? The causal theorist need not, however, say that any internal state 'plays the role of the agent,' as Velleman does. Agents act because their states have effects; but states are not agents. Velleman's and Bratman's real concern, however, was to provide a causal theory of a specific kind of agency: the 'full-blown' agency that produces 'autonomous' action.

Autonomous Action

Frankfurt (1971) observed that a heroin addict may shoot up intentionally, while regarding the desire to do so as an alien force. Indeed, the addict may have tried hard to give up the habit, only to succumb to it after all. This may seem to show the inadequacy of the causal theory, given that the addict's desire for heroin does cause him to take it. All the example really shows, however, is that the causal conditions for intentional action are not sufficient for more specific types of action. The addict did cause the heroin to enter his body. If we say that the heroin addict's action lacks 'autonomy,' then we can observe that an autonomous action requires more than being caused by a desire or intention to perform that action. The causal theorist can require that the autonomous agent desire that his first-order desire be effective (Frankfurt 1971); or believe that what he desires is right and good (Watson 1975); or decide without reservation to act on the desire (Frankfurt 1976); or desire to act in accordance with justifying reasons (Velleman 1992); or consciously act under their influence (Hornsby 2004); or identify with the desire or decision by deciding to treat it as reason-giving or justificatory in practical reasoning and planning while being satisfied with that decision and acting on it (Bratman 1999); or all of the above.

Action for Reasons

If you wanted a glass of milk and believed that there was milk in the cooler, then you *had a reason to* open the cooler – namely to get the milk. Yet that may not have been *your reason for* opening the cooler. You may have opened it to get a beer. What is the difference between having a reason to do something and doing it for that reason? What is it to act for a reason? The causal theory of reasons maintains that an agent does something for a reason only if the action results from a certain belief and desire (Davidson 1963). Your reason for opening the cooler was to get milk only if you opened it because you wanted to get milk and believed that you would get milk if you opened the cooler. When asked why he left his wife, a man may say that he wanted his wife to have more freedom and believed that she would if he left her. If he did genuinely want and believe those things, then giving her more freedom was a reason he had for leaving her. But, unless he left her because of that belief and desire, his response was a mere rationalization. He did not give the reason for which he left her if in fact he gave no thought to her wellbeing. The causal theory also explains why the mechanical tree did not wave its branches for a reason, even though *there was a reason why* it waved its branches: the cause of the branch waving was not a mental state. The reasons for which something was done entail that there were specific kinds of reasons why it was done.

Causal theories are not concerned with the normative question of what makes a reason good or justifying. *The reasons for doing something* (normative reasons) differ from both *your reasons for doing it* (motivating reasons) and *the reasons why you did it* (causal reasons). The reasons for eating low-fat food, or for contributing to charity, must be true; they *justify* those actions without necessarily causing, or even motivating, them. The reasons for which we act need not be good reasons, or even truths. No causal analysis of normative reasons is plausible.

The causal theory can provide an illuminating account of the similarities and differences between two kinds of motivating reasons. We imagined above that your reason for opening the cooler was *to get beer*. But it is just as true that your reason for opening the cooler was *that there is beer inside*. These reasons are different but complementary. The former reason entails that you wanted to get beer and believed that you would if you opened the cooler. The latter entails that you believed that there was beer inside and wanted to open it if there was. In general, the distinction can be characterized by something like the following conditions (Davis 2005a, § V):

[i] *A's reason for Φ-ing was that p only if A Φ-ed as a result of believing that p and desiring to Φ if p.*

[ii] *A's reason for Φ-ing was to Ψ only if A Φ-ed as a result of wanting to Ψ and of believing that he would Ψ if he Φ-ed.*[5]

The causal theory thus maintains that agents act for reasons only if an interrelated complex of beliefs and desires causes their action. These two conditions do not tell the whole story. As we have mentioned before, the mental states must cause the action in the right way. One additional link in the chain is the occurrent desire to Φ (Davis 2005a, § IV). If your reason for wanting to open the cooler was to get beer, then it occurred to you to open it. Moreover, you opened it because you wanted (intended) to open it, and you wanted to open it because you wanted to get beer and believed you would get beer if you opened it. In general, your reasons for *Φ-ing* are your reasons for *wanting to Φ*. Agents act for reasons only when their action results from practical reasoning of a certain sort. The details of the causal conditions may also need some adjustment. The agent might need to have intentions and not just desires, and may not need beliefs as opposed to some weaker cognitive attitude.

One virtue of the causal theory of reasons is that it provides a simple account of why we can explain a person's actions by citing the reasons for which he did them, and why citing the reasons he had for doing them may not be sufficient to explain them. On the causal theory, explanation by reasons is a type of causal explanation. The fact that your reason for opening the cooler was to get a beer explains why you opened the cooler because it entails that your desire to get a beer caused you to open it. There are not two competing explanations here, as Dancy (2005) charged, but one described in different terms. The causal theory also explains why attributions of reasons for action imply certain counterfactual claims. Just as the claim that Kennedy died because Oswald shot him implies that Kennedy would not have died if Oswald had not shot him (unless there were independent back-up teams), so, if your reason for opening the cooler was to get a beer, we can infer that, if you had not had that reason, you would not have opened the cooler (unless you had independent reasons for opening it). The causal theory also explains why 'A's reason for Φing was to Ψ' and 'A's reason for Ψing was to Φ' are incompatible, given the asymmetry of causation. Finally, the theory explains why there is no mystery about a reason being explanatory but false, or directed to the future. Your reason for opening the cooler may have been false (there was no beer inside) or future-directed (to get a beer), but what explains your action is your real, present beliefs and desires with those objects.

In addition to the explanatory power of the causal theory, direct support for it can be obtained by applying standard experimental methods. Subjects could be told for example that they will receive a $10 reward if they ring a bell once when the light is red, twice when the light is green. The experimenter can manipulate the subjects' beliefs about the light by randomly changing the light from red to green. Then the observation that the subjects ring the bell once when the light is red and twice when it is green would confirm the fact that the belief that the light is red or green, together with the reward-induced desire to ring the bell once or twice when the light is red or green, caused the subjects to ring the bell once or twice. Mill's method of difference is employed.

Adherents as well as opponents of the causal theory of reasons have taken it to claim that *reasons are causes*.[6] This may be acceptable as a slogan or first approximation, but it is neither true nor entailed by the theory. The reasons why an agent does something are causes, but the reasons for which an agent does something are not, even though they tell us what the causes are.[7] Thus one of your reasons for opening the cooler was to get beer. 'To get beer' is not the name of an event or state, and so could not refer to a cause. According to the causal theory, what caused you to open the cooler was your desire to get beer. Similarly, if you suffer from paranoid delusions, your reason for escaping to the wilderness may be that everyone is out to get you. This does not identify a state that caused your action. The cause was your believing that. That you believe everyone to be out to get you is not your reason for escaping, although it might be your reason for seeking psychiatric help (in which case the cause is the state of believing that you have that belief). Your reason in these cases was the *object* of the cause, not the cause itself.

Some reject the causal theory on the grounds that free and responsible action is incompatible with determinism (Ginet 2002: 387, 397). But the causal theory is neutral on this big issue. Principles like [i] and [ii] are compatible with the claim that, when you act for a reason, the beliefs and desires which cause actions are themselves uncaused, or caused by other uncaused mental states.

Dancy (2005) suggests that the connection between belief, desire and action is non-empirical, because it is *rational* and therefore *normative*. But we noted that an agent's reason for doing something may be irrational or a bad reason for doing it. Thus Hitler's reason for exterminating the Jews was that they were contaminating the pure Aryan blood. This reason was false, and would not have justified such a monstrous action even if it had been true. A person whose reason for holding a baby under water for ten minutes is to determine whether it is a witch is being irrational. Hornsby's (1997) observation that reason explanations are distinctive because they rely on a rational pattern in the attitudes of agents is acceptable if it means only that conditions like [i] and [ii] hold, or that people do things for a purpose (Sehon 2005), and carries no endorsement of the agent's reasons.

Many have argued that the causal theory is erroneous because the connection between the beliefs, desires and actions is *necessary* (Melden 1961: 114; von Wright 1971: 94ff.; Stoutland 1999: 198; Dancy 2005). However, it is far from necessary that, if you want to turn on the light and believe that you will turn on the light if you flip the switch, then you will flip the switch. We cannot know that this is true of you, for example, unless we know that you are not paralyzed, and that you do not have the additional belief that you will receive a nasty shock if you flip the switch. This response feeds the contrary objection that causes must be connected to their effects by universal laws, whereas no such laws connect beliefs and desires to actions (Hart and Honoré 1959). But few, if any, causal statements entail laws that connect cause and effect this directly. There is no doubt that flipping a switch sometimes causes a light to go on, and that this is true because of the laws of nature. But 'Whenever the switch is flipped, the light will go on' is not a law of nature (Davidson 1963: 38).

The *causal exclusion* argument, originally presented by C. Taylor (1964) and Malcolm (1968), has recently been developed as an objection to mental causation generally by Kim (1989). The premise of the argument is physicalism, according to which the actions of physical objects can be completely explained in terms of physical causes and laws. If human action can be completely explained by physical causes, as successes in neurophysiology suggest, then how can they be caused by mental states like beliefs and desires? This objection is serious for theories that take mental states to be independent of physical states. But the evidence for physicalism is evidence that your beliefs and desires are not independent of your neurophysiological states. There is no problem at all if, as the evidence for physicalism suggests, mental states *are* physical. For in that case your beliefs and desires are part of the complete neurophysiological explanation of your action. If it should turn out, however, that our beliefs, desires, and intentions are causally ineffective, it would seem to follow that it is an illusion to think that we act intentionally or for reasons. There is no more reason to think that we act for reasons than there is to think that our mental states influence our actions.

This review of objections and replies has focused on the causal theory of reasons, but similar issues arise with other causal theories.[8]

See also: ACTION THEORY AND ONTOLOGY (1); INTENTION (14); REASONS AND CAUSES (17); DEVIANT CAUSAL CHAINS (21); MENTAL CAUSATION AND EPIPHENOMENALISM (23); AGENT CAUSATION (28); MOTIVATIONAL STRENGTH (33); FREE WILL AND DETERMINISM (38); RESPONSIBILITY AND AUTONOMY (39); INTENTIONAL ACTION IN FOLK PSYCHOLOGY (45); DAVIDSON (73).

Notes

1 See Wilson (1989: 82ff.); Mele (1992); Sehon (1998). Note that nothing in the given causal condition requires that actions are, or entail, bodily movements (Hornsby 2004: 4ff., 20).
2 Davidson (1963); Goldman (1970: 61–63); Harman (1976); Mele (1997).
3 Many reserve the term 'action' for things done intentionally (e.g. Hornsby 1997: 285). For objections to the simple analysis of intentional action, and for replies, see Bratman (1987) and Mele (1997). For a recent and more sophisticated causal theory, see Setiya (2003).
4 See also Lyons (1977, § 9.9); Chierchia and McConnell-Ginet (1990: 350–366); Davis (2005b, §13.1).
5 Expressions with similar truth conditions are: *A φ-ed with the intention of ψing*; *A φ-ed in order to ψ*; and *A's purpose (or goal) in φ-ing was to φ*. Condition [ii] holds, I should note, only if 'want' is interpreted in its 'volitive' rather than 'appetitive' sense (Davis 1984; 2005a, § III).
6 See e.g. Velleman (1992); Schueler (1995); Dancy (2000: 15); Stoutland (2001: 910–912); Hornsby (2004: 2). When adherents like Davidson (1963: 686) and Smith (1987: 36–38) say that reasons are causes, they are referring to the reasons why, not to the reasons for which, the agent acted.
7 Hornsby (1997); Setiya (2003: 347); Davis (2005a). Note that, in sentences like 'Given that John was driving twenty-five miles over the speed limit, the police had cause to give him a ticket,' 'cause' does mean 'reason.'
8 I thank Jeff Engelhardt, Matt McAdam, and Facundo Alonso for help on this essay.

References

Bratman, M. (1987). *Intentions, Plans, and Practical Reason*. Cambridge, MA: Harvard University Press.

Bratman, M. (1999). Identification, decision, and treating as a reason. In M. Bratman (ed.), *Faces of Intention: Selected Essays on Intention and Agency*, Cambridge, MA: Cambridge University Press, 185–206.

Bratman, M. (2001). Two problems about human agency. *Proceedings of the Aristotelian Society*, 101, 309–326.

Chierchia, G. and McConnell-Ginet, S. (1990). *Meaning and Grammar: An Introduction to Semantics*. Cambridge, MA: MIT Press.

Chisholm, R. M. (1976). *Person and Object*. La Salle, IL: Open Court.

Dancy, J. (2000). *Practical Reality*. Oxford: Oxford University Press.

Dancy, J. (2005). Two ways of explaining actions. In J. Hyman and H. Steward (eds), *Agency and Action*. Cambridge: Cambridge University Press, 25–42.

Davidson, D. (1963). Actions, reasons, and causes. *Journal of Philosophy*, 60, 685–700. [Reprinted in A. Mele (ed.), (1997).]

Davis, W. A. (1984). The two senses of desire. *Philosophical Studies*, 45, 181–195.

Davis, W. A. (2005a). Reasons and psychological causes. *Philosophical Studies*, 122, 51–101.

Davis, W. A. (2005b). *Nondescriptive Meaning and Reference*. Oxford: Oxford University Press.

Fodor, J. A. (1975). *The Language of Thought*. New York: Thomas Y. Crowell.

Frankfurt, H. (1971). Freedom of the will and the concept of a person. *Journal of Philosophy*, 68, 5–20.

Frankfurt, H. (1976). Identification and externality. In A. Rorty (ed.), *The Identities of Persons*. Berkeley, CA: University of California Press, 239–252.

Ginet, C. (2002). Reasons explanations of action: Causalist versus noncausalist accounts. In R. Kane (ed.), *The Oxford Handbook of Free Will*. Oxford: Oxford University Press, 386–405.
Goldman, A. (1970). *A Theory of Human Action*. Englewood Cliffs, NJ: Prentice-Hall.
Harman, G. (1976). Practical reasoning. *Review of Metaphysics*, 79, 431–463. [Reprinted in A. Mele (ed.), (1997), 149–177.]
Hart, H. L. A. and Honoré, A. M. (1959). *Causation and the Law*. Oxford: Oxford University Press.
Hornsby, J. (1997). Agency and causal explanation [1993]. In Mele (ed.), 283–307.
Hornsby, J. (2004). Agency and action. In J. Hyman and H. Steward (eds), *Agency and Action*. Cambridge: Cambridge University Press, 1–23.
Kim, J. (1989). Mechanism, purpose, and explanatory exclusion. *Philosophical Perspectives*, 3, 77–108.
Lyons, J. (1977). *Semantics*. Cambridge: Cambridge University Press.
Malcolm, N. (1968). The conceivability of mechanism. *Philosophical Review*, 77, 45–72.
Melden, A. I. (1961). *Free Action*. London: Routledge and Kegan Paul.
Mele, A. (1992). *The Springs of Action*. New York: Oxford University Press.
Mele, A. (1997). Introduction. In Mele (ed.), 2–26.
Mele, A. (ed.) (1997). *The Philosophy of Action*. Oxford: Oxford University Press.
Schueler, G. F. (1995). *Desire: Its Role in Practical Reason and the Explanation of Action*. Cambridge, MA: MIT Press.
Sehon, S. (1998). Deviant causal chains and the irreducibility of telelogical explanation. *Pacific Philosophical Quarterly*, 78, 195–213.
Sehon, S. (2005). *Teleological Realism: Mind, Agency, and Explanation*. Cambridge, MA: MIT Press.
Setiya, K. (2003). Explaining action. *The Philosophical Review*, 112, 339–393.
Smith, M. (1987). The Humean theory of motivation. *Mind*, 96, 36–61.
Stoutland, F. (1999). Intentionalists and Davidson on rational explanation. In G. Meggle (ed.), *Actions, Norms, Values*. Berlin: Walter DeGruyter, 191–208.
Stoutland, F. (2001). Responsive action and the belief–desire model. *Grazer-Philosophische-Studien*, 61, 83–106.
Taylor, C. (1964). *Explanation of Behavior*. London: Routledge and Kegan Paul.
Taylor, R. (1966). *Action and Purpose*. Upper Saddle River, NJ: Prentice-Hall.
Velleman, J. D. (1992). What happens when one acts? *Mind*, 101, 461–481.
von Wright, G. H. (1971). *Explanation and Understanding*. Ithaca, NY: Cornell University Press.
Watson, G. (1975). Free agency. *Journal of Philosophy*, 72, 205–20.
Wilson, G. M. (1989). *The Intentionality of Human Action*. Stanford, CA: Stanford University Press.

Further reading

Anscombe, G. E. M. (1963). *Intention*. Ithaca, NY: Cornell University Press.
Audi, R. (1993). *Action, Intention, and Reason*. Ithaca, NY: Cornell University Press.
Bishop, J. (1989). *Natural Agency: An Essay on the Causal Theory of Action*. Cambridge: Cambridge University Press.
Dretske, F. (1988). *Explaining Behavior: Reasons in a World of Causes*. Cambridge, MA: MIT Press.
Frankfurt, H. (1988). *The Importance of What We Care About*. Cambridge: Cambridge University Press.
Heil, J. and Mele, A. (eds) (1993). *Mental Causation*. Oxford: Clarendon Press.
Ginet, C. (1990). *On Action*. Cambridge: Cambridge University Press.
O'Connor, T. J. (ed.) (1995). *Agents, Causes, and Events*. Oxford: Oxford University Press.
Petroski, P. (2000). *Causing Actions*. New York: Oxford University Press.

6

Adverbs of Action and Logical Form

KIRK LUDWIG

Adverbs modify verbs ('He cut the roast *carefully*'), adjectives ('A *very* tall man sat down in front of me'), other adverbs ('He cut the roast *very* carefully'), and sentences ('*Fortunately*, he cut the roast with a knife'). This chapter focuses on adverbial modification of verbs, and specifically action verbs, that is, verbs that express agency – though many of the lessons extend to sentences with event verbs generally. Adverbs and adverbial phrases are traditionally classified under the headings of manner ('carefully'), place ('in the kitchen'), time ('at midnight'), frequency ('often'), and degree ('very'). The problem of adverbials lies in understanding their systematic contribution to the truth conditions of the sentences in which they appear. The solution sheds light on the logical form of action sentences with and without adverbials.

An account of the logical form of a sentence aims to make clear the role of its semantically primitive expressions in fixing the sentence's interpretive truth conditions and, in so doing, to account for all of the entailment relations the sentence stands in toward other sentences in virtue of its logico-semantic form. This is typically done by providing a regimented paraphrase of the sentence that makes clearer the logico-semantic contribution of each expression. For example, the logical form of 'The red ball is under the bed' may be represented as '[The x: x is red and x is a ball][the y: y is a bed] (x is under y).' Thus, the definite descriptions are represented as functioning as restricted quantifiers, and the adjective 'red' is represented as contributing a predicate conjunct to the nominal restriction on the variable in the first definite description.

[1] entails each of the sentences obtained from it by deleting any of the adverbials in brackets or any combination of them; and each of those sentences in turn entails each sentence got from it by deleting any remaining adverbials or combination of them – though not vice versa. This is sometimes called 'modifier drop entailment.' [1] and [2] together entail [3], though [1] alone does not. [3] in turn entails [1].

[1] He cut the roast [carefully] [with a knife] [in his dressing gown] [at midnight] [in the kitchen].

[2] He cut the roast only once.

[3] His cutting of the roast was done carefully, with a knife, in his dressing gown, at midnight, in the kitchen.

These are formal entailments because we recognize their validity in virtue of the pattern of categories of terms in them. That we recognize their validity in virtue of the pattern of categories of terms in them rules out taking each of the sentences derived from [1] by deleting some combination of the adverbials as involving a verb with a different number of argument places, for then the entailments would depend on the meaning of the verb and not on the form of the sentence. In addition, the suggestion that we take each sentence derived from [1] by deleting some combination of adverbials as involving a verb with a different number of argument places would require an infinity of verbs of differing polyadicity, as there is no end to the number of adverbials one can add to a sentence (Kenney 1963, ch. 7). These would plausibly have to be learned independently, since verbs with a distinct number of argument places differ in meaning. The suggestion entails then that to master a natural language like English one has to learn an infinite number of verbs independently. It therefore violates a widely accepted constraint on meaning theories for natural languages, namely, that, on pain of their not being learnable by finite beings like us, natural languages should be represented as having a finite number of semantical primitives (Davidson 1966).

The standard solution to the problem of the semantic contribution of adverbs of action is the event analysis – the *locus classicus* is Davidson's paper 'The logical form of action sentences' (1967), though he is anticipated by Ramsey (1927: 37; for some dissenting views, which champion an operator approach, see Clark 1970; Montague 1974; Rennie 1971; Schwartz 1975; Fulton 1979; Cresswell 1979; Clark 1986). The event analysis treats action verbs as introducing an implicit or hidden quantifier over events, and adverbials as introducing predicates of them. This is strongly suggested by the fact that [3], which contains a description of an event, entails [1] and is entailed by [1] in conjunction with [2], as well as by the fact that adverbs are typically derived from adjectives, which function in logical form as predicates. (In some languages, for example in Dutch and in German, adjectives and adverbs have the same form.) On Davidson's original proposal, [1] would be analyzed as in [1′], where '*e*' is a variable for events (we treat 'careful' as relating an agent to an event, since no event is careful considered in itself).

[1′] (∃*e*)(cut(*e*, he, the roast) and careful(*e*, he) and with(*e*, a knife) and in(*e*, his dressing gown) and at(*e*, midnight) and in(*e*, the kitchen)).

This analysis captures all the entailments from [1] to any sentence derived from it by deleting one or more of the adverbials. [1′] represents these entailments as a matter of conjunction elimination in the scope of an existential quantifier. This analysis also explains why [3] entails [1], and [1] and [2] together entail [3], whose analysis can be represented as in [3′].

[3′] [The *e*: cutting(*e*, he, the roast)](careful(*e*, he) and with(*e*, a knife) and in(*e*, his dressing gown) and at(*e*, midnight) and in(*e*, the kitchen)).

The two-place predicates relating the event to a 'participant' are called case or thematic (or theta-/Θ-) roles (Fillmore 1968).

In a comment on Davidson's 1967 paper, Hector-Neri Castañeda (1967) suggested separating out, in addition, the case roles of the subject and object terms and treating them as separate relational predicates of the event, in order to capture entailments such as those between [4] and [5] and [4] and [6] (for discussion and development, see Bennett 1988; Carlson 1984; Parsons 1980, 1985, 1990; Dowty 1989; Schein 1993). The subject is the agent of the event and the object is its patient, what the agent acts on. When we separate out these case roles, we must take into account that action sentences like [1] and [4] imply that the subject is the sole relevant agent of the event expressed. We will use 'agent(e, x)' to express the relation of x's being an agent of x and write 'the-agent(e, x)' to express 'agent(e, x) and (only $y = x$)(agent(e, y)).' We would then analyze [4] as in [4′], where 'patient(e, x)' expresses a relation between the event and its object, i.e., being the object in which the event is a change. [5] and [6] would be analyzed as in [5′] and [6′], which show how [5] and [6] follow from [4] on the proposed analysis.

[4] He flew the spaceship.
[4′] (∃e)(the-agent(e, he) and flying(e) and patient(e, the spaceship)).
[5] He did something.
[5′] (∃e)(the-agent(e, he)).
[6] The spaceship flew.
[6′] (∃e)(flying(e) and patient(e, the spaceship)).

On this suggestion, we would analyze [1] as in [1″].

[1″] (∃e)(the-agent(e, he) and cutting(e) and patient(e, the roast) and careful(e, he) and with(e, a knife) and in(e, his dressing gown) and at(e, midnight) and in(e, the kitchen)).

On the analysis represented in [1″], [1] entails each sentence derived from it by deleting any combination of adverbials; and together with [2] it entails [3], and likewise [3] entails [1], with the nominal restriction in the noun phrase reinterpreted as 'the-agent(e, he) and patient(e, the roast) and cutting(e).'

A remark is in order about the use of 'cutting(e)' in [1″] to express the event type brought about by the agent that could have come about independently. Not all transitive action verbs in English have an intransitive counterpart in which the object of the first appears as the subject of the second. Verbs that do, like 'fly,' 'melt,' 'break,' 'combine,' 'move,' are called alternating ambitransitive verbs; the intransitive forms, which (unlike the passive forms, for example, 'was melted') strip out the implication of agency, are anticausative or inchoative verbs (the argument structure alternation is often called 'inchoative/causative' alternation). Generalizing the treatment of [4] to action verbs generally commits us to a predicate in logical form which may not have an explicit English counterpart. In favor of this is that [1] like [4] entails [5], an entailment captured by [1″]. For action sentences like [1], whose main verb is not an alternating ambitransitive, we use the gerund to express the consequent event type in logical form.

The analysis so far has ignored tense. Davidson among others suggested that quantification over events suffices to handle tense, the utterance of the sentence serving as a reference point for the event time. Thus 'He cut the roast' may be rendered as in [7], where '*u*' is an indexical that refers, in the context of an utterance of [7], to that utterance of [7] itself, and '<' means 'is earlier than.'

[7] [$\exists e$: $e < u$](the-agent(e, he) and cutting(e) and patient(e, the roast)).

What I say in asserting 'He cut the roast,' though, could have been true in a world in which I did not utter that sentence: but not if it involves a reference to my utterance of it, as the proposed analysis requires. The natural alternative is to treat tense as introducing a quantifier over times, so that 'He cut the roast' may be rendered as in [7′], where 't^*' is an indexical that refers to the time of the utterance (roughly, 'now').

[7′] [$\exists t$: $t < t^*$]($\exists e$)(the-agent(e, t, he) and cutting(e) and patient(e, the roast)).

We interpret 'the-agent(e, t, x)' here as 'agent(e, t, x) and (only $y = x$)($\exists$t′)(agent(e, t', y)).' We include a separate quantifier over time intervals for the clause that secures uniqueness because, as we will see, this time indexes to the primitive action of the agent, and we want to exclude contributions of the relevant sort by any other agent at any other time. As explained below, the need to discover more structure in the agency relation than we have so far motivates including the temporal variable in the agency predicate but not in the event predicate. With a temporal variable to modify as well as an event variable, we can revisit [1″] to see whether it makes better sense to treat some of the adverbials as modifying the time rather than the event. Plausibly the temporal adverbial modifies the time; 'in his dressing gown' is more naturally treated as a relation between time, agent, and dressing gown, as in [1‴].

[1‴] [$\exists t$: $t < t^*$]($\exists e$)(the-agent(e, t, he) and cutting(e) and patient(e, the roast) and careful(e, he) and with(e, a knife) and in(t, he, his dressing gown) and at(t, midnight) and in(e, the kitchen)).

The analysis in [1‴] creates a problem in connection with the view that the same action may be redescribed in terms of various of its effects, which was first noted in an unpublished paper by John Wallace (reported in Parsons 1980). Suppose that I move my finger, flip a switch, turn on the light, illuminate the room, and alert a prowler. According to Anscombe (1957), I have done one thing which I have described in five ways (the example is from Davidson 1963, who follows Anscombe). What I did was move my finger. That is the only thing I did but *not by doing anything else*; it was my only primitive action. The other action sentences redescribe my primitive action in terms of its consequences. Suppose we identify an agent's actions with the events which render action sentences about him true. Consider [8] and [9] (the example is from Pietroski 2000), together with analyses patterned after [1‴] in [8′] and [9′], but suppressing tense for the moment.

[8] Booth pulled the trigger with his finger.
[8′] ($\exists e$)(the-agent(e, Booth) and pulling(e) and patient(e, the trigger) and with(e, his finger)).

[8″] the-agent(ε, Booth) and pulling(ε) and patient(ε, the trigger) and with(ε, his finger).

[9] Booth shot Lincoln with a gun.

[9′] (∃*e*)(the-agent(*e*, Booth) and shooting(*e*) and patient(*e*, Lincoln) and with(*e*, a gun)).

[9″] the-agent(ε, Booth) and shooting(ε) and patient(ε, Lincoln) and with(ε, a gun).

Suppose [8] and [9] are about Booth on the night of his assassination of Lincoln. He did one thing that made both of these sentences true. Let that be designated by 'ε'. Then we have [8″] and [9″], if we assume that the variable '*e*' in [8′] and [9′] takes the agent's actions as values. From [8″] and [9″] we can infer [10] and [11], and in turn [10′] and [11′], which are false.

[10] the-agent(ε, Booth) and pulling(ε) and patient(ε, the trigger) and *with(ε, a gun)*.

[10′] Booth pulled the trigger with a gun.

[11] the-agent(ε, Booth) and shooting(ε) and patient(ε, Lincoln) and *with(ε, his finger)*.

[11′] Booth shot Lincoln with his finger.

Davidson (1985) proposed resolving this problem by introducing a second quantifier over events, which would bind an event variable that represented a primitive action of the agent, which bears an appropriate relation to the consequent event (see also Lombard 1985; Vendler 1984). We can represent this in [9‴], now taking into account tense (we use 'agent' in the sense of 'primitive agent of'; 'the-(agent(f, t, x) and by(f, e))' abbreviates 'agent(f, t, x) and by(f, e) and (only $y = x$)($\exists t'$)($\exists f'$)(agent(f', t', y) and by(f', e))'.

[9‴] [$\exists t$: $t < t^*$]($\exists e$)($\exists f$)(the-(agent(f, t, Booth) and by(f, e)) and shooting(e) and patient(e, Lincoln) and with(e, a gun)).

Now we can say that there is one thing Booth did, move his finger, and there were various consequences of it: the trigger pulling was done with his finger but the shooting, which is distinct, was done with a gun.

We represent the event time as that of the primitive action and not as that of the consequent event. Why? Suppose I put poison in someone's curry powder on Monday and I die on Tuesday. He makes curry on Saturday and dies that evening. When did I kill him? It is clear that what I did to kill him occurred on Monday, not on Saturday, that is, I killed him on Monday, though he did not die until Saturday. (In *Hamlet*, Laertes says, 'I am justly kill'd with mine own treachery' while he still lives; for he *has done* something that *will* bring about his death.)

We represent the relation between primitive action and consequent event with 'by(x, y).' This is a determinable. Different action verbs select different determinate relations. Thus we have so far underspecified the action verb's contribution. One can be an agent of an event in a variety of ways. One can be an agent of an event by being a primitive agent of it (as when I move my finger), by doing something that causes it (as when I break a window by throwing a brick at it), by doing something that contains it (as when I contract my forearm muscles by clenching my fist), or by doing something that partially or wholly constitutes it (as when I play chess by moving pieces intentionally in accordance with the rules). Many action verbs like 'kill' require that something we do contribute causally to a consequent event (in this case, a death) without being mediated (primarily) by another's agency. For example: If I hire an assassin to kill a rival and he does it, I *cause* the death of my rival, and so I am an agent of it, but I did not *kill* him. Similarly, if I direct someone to cut the roast, I cause it to be cut, but I do not cut it myself. These verbs require that we *directly contribute to* the consequent event. Thus, 'by(f, e)' in [9‴] should be subscripted to indicate the specific relation the action verb requires between the primitive action and the consequent event, for example, in the present case, to indicate directly contributing, we would write '$\text{by}_{DC}(f, e)$' – *mutatis mutandis* for other action verbs and modes of agency.

Introducing a second quantifier helps with sentences such as [12], where 'by' relates two events, a striking of Lincoln by a projectile and Lincoln's death, as illustrated in [12′].

[12] Booth killed Lincoln by shooting him.

[12′] $[\exists t{:}\ t < t^*](\exists e)(\exists f)(\text{the-}(\text{agent}(f, t, \text{Booth}) \text{ and } \text{by}_{DC}(f, e)) \text{ and death}(e) \text{ and patient}(e, \text{Lincoln}) \text{ and } (\exists e')(\text{by}_{DC}(f, e') \text{ and shooting}(e') \text{ and patient}(e', \text{Lincoln}) \text{ and by}(e', e)))$.

In light of the second quantifier, we may also revisit the role of 'carefully' in [1], which is more plausibly treated as relating agents to primitive actions rather than consequent events.

From the standpoint of the event analysis, someone's *actions* must either be the events of which she is a primitive agent or both her primitive actions and the things that they bring about. Once we are clear about the underlying structure of agency, however, it is obvious that what we say reflects a choice about word use rather than a dispute about what goes on when we act. So-called negative actions – remaining silent, for example – which seem to present a problem for the analysis, may be brought into the fold by treating sentences attributing them as introducing a state rather than an event quantifier.

Adverbs, like 'slowly,' which have comparative and superlative forms ('more slowly,' 'slowest'), require separate treatment. If we analyze [13] as in [13′], and the subject's crossing of the Channel was her swimming of the Channel, then we can infer [14].

[13] She crossed the Channel slowly.

[13′] $[\exists t{:}\ t < t^*](\exists e)(\exists f)(\text{the-}(\text{agent}(f, t, \text{she}) \text{ and } \text{by}_{DC}(f, e)) \text{ and crossing}(e) \text{ and patient}(e, \text{the Channel}) \text{ and slow}(e))$.

[14] She swam the Channel slowly.

But a slow crossing of the Channel may be a fast swimming of it. This shows that the contribution of 'slowly' is relative to a class determined by the verb it modifies. This is very clear for the superlative forms. The slowest crossing may be the fastest swimming, if the Channel has been swum only once. A crossing is slowest if it is slower than all other Channel crossings; a crossing is slow if it is slower than most crossings. Thus the analysis of [13] should yield [13″].

[13″] [∃*t*: *t* < *t**](∃*e*)(∃*f*)(the-(agent(*f*, *t*, she) and by_{DC}(*f*, *e*)) and crossing(*e*) and patient(*e*, the Channel) and [most *e*′: *e*′ is a Channel crossing](*e* is slower than *e*′))

Adverbs of action expressing attitudes toward what is done, such as 'intentionally,' 'deliberately,' 'willingly,' 'reluctantly,' and the like, are of special interest. 'Intentionally,' for example, creates a partially intensional context. [15] entails [16]; and one can intersubstitute in the subject position on the basis of sameness of reference *salva veritate* (without risking change of truth value). But one cannot intersubstitute *salva veritate* in the object position, given sameness of reference or denotation, nor can one replace *salva veritate* the main verb with another verb that would, if 'intentionally' were deleted, otherwise yield a true sentence. Even if the roast is the king's venison, one cannot infer, from his cutting the roast intentionally, that he cut the king's venison intentionally. Similarly, even if in cutting the roast he offended the king, one cannot infer, from his cutting the roast intentionally, that he offended the king intentionally.

[15] He cut the roast intentionally.
[16] He cut the roast.

This has suggested to some that 'intentionally' is a sentential adverb, which, like 'allegedly' or 'fortunately,' modifies the whole sentence and is properly treated as a sentential operator, as in [15′].

[15′] It was intentional of him that he cut the roast.

However, this hardly makes clear the logical form of [15]. Why does it follow from this that he cut the roast? The adverb 'intentionally' is derived from the adjective 'intentional,' which is derived from the noun 'intention,' which is derived from the verb 'intend.' Assume what is sometimes called 'the Simple View': that one successfully carries out an intention to cut the roast if and only if one cuts the roast intentionally. (Some philosophers deny the right to left direction – we shall return to this shortly.) This suggests that you cut the roast intentionally if and only if you cut the roast and did it with the intention of so doing, where the 'so' picks up the content of the first clause – that is, you cut the roast and did it with the intention that it be a cutting of the roast. The pronoun of cross-reference 'it' in the second clause clearly picks out the action introduced by the verb in the first. The intention, then, is directed at what the agent does when he acts. Putting this together, we have [15″].

[15″] [∃*t*: *t* < *t**](∃*e*)(∃*f*)(the-(agent(*f*, *t*, he) and by_{DC}(*f*, *e*)) and cutting(*e*) and patient(*e*, the roast) and intends(*t*, he, that (∃*e*)(the-(agent(*f*, *t*, he) and by_{DC}(*f*, *e*)) and cutting(*e*) and patient(*e*, the roast))).

The quantifier binding the variable 'f' for the agent's primitive action in the first clause also binds, in the content clause, the corresponding position in the agency relation; the quantifier that binds the temporal argument place in the agency relation in the first clause also binds the temporal argument position in 'intends' and in the agency relation in its content clause. 'Intentionally' is thus treated as introducing a predicate not of the consequence event but of the agent, his primitive action, and the time at which he performs it. This corresponds to the fact that to cut the roast (to do something, F) intentionally one must have an intention directed at what one is doing at the time as a cutting of the roast (as an F-ing). It is not enough that one have an intention directed generally toward an action of the type one is in fact performing. One may have such an intention, and it may even cause the thing intended, though one doesn't do it intentionally. I intend at t to strike fear into my enemy by clenching my fist. This recalls to me my anger at him, which causes me to clench my fist, which strikes fear into him. Yet I do not strike fear into my enemy intentionally, because the intention to do so by clenching my fist was not directed at the fist clenching that struck fear into him. The rejection of the simple view can be easily incorporated into this picture by adding a disjunct within the last conjunct in [15″] which expresses what further attitudes toward the relevant content (foreseen and undesired, for example) license the adverb 'intentionally.' On this account, one performs an action intentionally (unintentionally) under a 'description,' for example, 'cutting the roast,' if and only if the last conjunct in [15″] is made true (false) by the event.

How does the event analysis project to plural action sentences? [18] differs from [17] solely in the number of the pronoun in the subject position.

[17] I insulted the host.
[18] We insulted the host.

As the referent of the subject term in [17] is the agent of the event expressed, so it seems we should treat the referent of the subject term in [18] as the agent of the event expressed. This would commit us to saying that we *as such* (the group consisting of us) are the agent of the insulting. However, [18] is ambiguous between a distributive and a collective reading. On the distributive reading, it is made true, for example, by my insulting the host before dinner and your insulting him afterwards. On the collective reading, it would be made true, for example, by our deliberately talking in our host's presence as if he were not there. Here we do it together. The distributive reading requires that we interpret the subject position as involving, in logical form, a restricted quantifier over members of the group picked out by 'We,' as in [18′], which, with the event analysis of the matrix, gives us [18d] (expanding the abbreviation that secures uniqueness).

[18′] [Each x of us](x insulted the host).
[18d] [Each x of us][$\exists t$: $t < t^*$]($\exists \boldsymbol{e}$)($\exists f$)(agent(f, t, x) and by$_{DC}$(f, e) and (only $y = x$) ($\exists t'$)($\exists f'$)(agent(f', t', y) and by(f', e)) and insulting(e) and patient(e, the host)).
[18c] ($\exists \boldsymbol{e}$)[Each x of us][$\exists t$: $t < t^*$]($\exists f$)(agent(f, t, x) and by$_{DC}$(f, e) and (only y: y is one of us)($\exists t'$)($\exists f'$)(agent(f', t', y) and by$_{DC}$(f', e)) and insulting(e) and patient(e, the host)).

The collective reading is now obtained simply by giving the event quantifier wide scope, as in [18c], and by making a corresponding adjustment to the requirement of uniqueness of agency, to ensure that only members of the group are among the relevant agents of the event. We do something together, then, when we (and only we) are all agents, in the relevant way, via our various individual actions, of a single event. The distributive/collective ambiguity of plural action sentences thus emerges as a scope ambiguity and we can see that plural action sentences do not commit us to group agents per se (for further discussion see Landman 2000; Lasersohn 1989, 1995; Ludwig 2007; Schein 1993, 2002; for discussion of a variety of advanced topics in event semantics see Higginbotham et al. 2000).

See also: ACTION THEORY AND ONTOLOGY (1); BASIC ACTIONS AND INDIVIDUATION (2); THE CAUSAL THEORY OF ACTION (5); COLLECTIVE ACTION (9); REFRAINING, OMITTING, AND NEGATIVE ACTS (7); AGENT CAUSATION (28); DAVIDSON (73); ANSCOMBE (74).

References

Anscombe, G. E. M. (1957). *Intention*. Oxford: Blackwell.

Bennett, J. (1988). *Events and their Names*. Oxford: Clarendon Press.

Carlson, G. (1984). Thematic roles and their role in semantic interpretation. *Linguistics*, 22, 259–279.

Casteñeda, H.-N. (1967). Comments on Donald Davidson's 'The logical form of action sentences.' In N. Rescher (ed.), *The Logic of Decision and Action*. Pittsburgh: University of Pittsburgh Press, 104–112.

Clark, R. (1970). Concerning the logica of predicate modifiers. *Nous* 4, 311–335.

Clark, R. (1986). Predication and paronymous modifers. *Notre Dame Journal of Formal Logic*, 27, 376–392.

Cresswell, M. J. (1979). Interval semantics for some event expressions. In R. Bäuerle, U. Egli, and A. von Stechow (eds), *Semantics from Different Points of View*. Berlin: Springer-Verlag, 90–116.

Davidson, D. (1963). Actions, reasons, and causes. *The Journal of Philosophy*, 60, 685–699.

Davidson, D. (1966). Theories of meaning and learnable languages. In Y. Bar-Hillel (ed.), *Proceedings of the 1964 International Congress for Logic, Methodology and Philosophy of Science*. Amsterdam: North Holland Publishing Co., 383–394.

Davidson, D. (1967). The logical form of action sentences. In N. Rescher (ed.), *The Logic of Decision and Action*. Pittsburgh: University of Pittsburgh Press, 81–95.

Davidson, D. (1985). Adverbs of action. In B. Vermazen and M. Hintikka (eds), *Essays On Davidson*. Oxford: Clarendon Press, 230–241.

Dowty, D. R. (1989). On the semantic content of the notion of 'thematic role.' In G. Chierchia, B. H. Partee, and R. Turner (eds), *Properties, Types and Meaning*. Dordretcht: Kluwer Academic Publishers, 69–129.

Fillmore, C. J. (1968). The case for case. In E. Bach and R. T. Harms (eds), *Universals in Linguistic Theory*. New York: Holt, Rinehart, and Winston, 1–88.

Fulton, J. (1979). An intensional logic of predicates. *Notre Dame Journal of Formal Logic*, 34, 607–620.

Higginbotham, J., F. Pianesi, and A. C. Varzi, eds. (2000). *Speaking of Events*. New York: Oxford University Press.

Kenney, A. (1963). *Action, Emotion and Will*. London: Routledge.

Landman, F. (2000). *Events and Plurality: The Jerusalem Lectures*. Dordretch: Kluwer Academic Publishers.

Lasersohn, P. (1989). On the readings of plural noun phrases. *Linguistic Inquiry*, 20, 130–134.

Lasersohn, P. (1995). *Plurality, Conjunction and Events*. Dordretch: Kluwer Academic Publishers.

Lombard, L. (1985). How not to flip the prowler: Transitive verbs of action and the identity of actions. In E. Lepore and B. McLaughlin (eds), *Actions and Events: Perspectives on the Philosophy of Donald Davidson*. Oxford: Blackwell, 268–281.

Ludwig, K. (2007). Collective intentional behavior from the standpoint of semantics. *Nous*, 41, 355–393.

Montague, R. (1974). English as a formal language. In R. Thomason, ed., *Formal Philosophy*. New Haven: Yale University Press, 188–221.

Parsons, T. (1980). Modifiers and quantifiers in natural language. *Canadian Journal of Philosophy*, 6, 29–60.

Parsons, T. (1985). Underlying events in the logical analysis of English. In E. LePore and B. McLaughlin (eds), *Actions and Events: Perspectives on the Philosophy of Donald Davidson*. Oxford: Blackwell, 235–267.

Parsons, T. (1990). *Events in the Semantics of English: A Study in Subatomic Semantics*. Cambridge, MA: MIT Press.

Pietroski, P. M. (2000). *Causing Actions*. Oxford: Oxford University Press.

Ramsey, F. (1927). Facts and propositions. *Proceedings of the Aristotelian Society* (Suppl. 71927), 153–170.

Rennie, M. K. (1971). Completeness of the logic of predicate modifiers. *Logique et Analyse*, 55, 627–643.

Schein, B. (1993). *Plurals and Events*. Cambridge, MA: MIT Press.

Schein, B. (2002). Events and the semantic content of thematic relations. In G. Preyer and G. Peter (eds), *Logical Form and Language*. Oxford: Clarendon Press, 261–344.

Schwartz, T. (1975). The logic of modifiers. *Journal of Philosophical Logic*, 4, 361–380.

Vendler, Z. (1984). Agency and causation. *Midwest Studies in Philosophy: Causation and Causal Theories*, 9, 371–384.

7

Refraining, Omitting, and Negative Acts

KENT BACH

Action theory has been primarily concerned with the question of what it is to do something, along with such subsidiary questions as what is to do something intentionally and what it is to do one thing by doing another. It has tended to neglect the question of what it is to fail to do something. As we will see, there are different ways in which one can not merely not do something, but fail to do it.

Just consider that at any given moment, including this one, there are countless things you are not doing but very few things (if any) you are failing to do. I bet that at this moment you are not standing on your head or playing a clarinet, much less rescuing someone from a burning skyscraper. Obviously, there is not much point in asking what it is not to do any of the countless things that you could conceivably be doing, and not just because you lack the ability or the opportunity to do most of them. You might not have had the ability to play a clarinet or the opportunity to rescue someone from a burning skyscraper right now, but you could have easily scratched your head or wiggled your right index finger just then. Even though you probably didn't do either one, you didn't *fail* to scratch your head or wiggle your finger, certainly not if you didn't even consider doing them. On the other hand, now that I've mentioned them and implicitly raised the possibility of doing them, the situation is rather different. If you don't scratch your head or wiggle your right index finger *now*, you have refrained from doing these things. But change the example. Suppose you intended but have forgotten that you were to call your spouse just about now. Even though you hadn't considered (until I mentioned it) that you were to have made this call, in which case you can't be said to have refrained from making it, still you failed to make it. These examples illustrate that there are different ways of failing to do something.

A little reflection should reveal that there are least four ways of not only not doing something but of failing to do it: (trying and) *not succeeding, refraining, omitting*, and (some cases of) *allowing*. I don't know if these exhaust the possibilities, but they seem to comprise the main cases, not that they are mutually exclusive. In the following section we will distinguish them and then, in the next two sections, look further at refraining and omitting. We will consider not only what they involve but also whether there can be *acts* of refraining or omitting. In the final section, we will take up the question of whether in any interesting sense there are negative acts of any sort, that is, *acts* of not doing something, as opposed to failures to do something.

Ways of Failing to Do Something

Perhaps the most obvious way to fail *to* do something is to fail *at* doing it, to try but not succeed. There are different possible reasons for failing in this way, depending on whether the failure is due to lack of ability, inadequate effort, faulty execution, insufficient information, deficient resources, or lack of cooperation from other people or from nature. Trying and failing is a worthy subject but, except insofar as it can involve refraining or omitting, it falls outside the scope of this chapter.

To refrain from doing something is, at least at a first approximation, to consider doing it but deciding not to, and thereby not doing it or not even trying to. It seems to follow that refraining must be intentional. Indeed it might seem that all cases of refraining are intentional omissions, but it turns out that only some are.

An omission is a failure to do, or even attempt to do, something that in one way or another one is 'supposed to do,' for instance leaving out a step in a procedure or not fulfilling a responsibility. Omissions can be unintentional, as when one forgets to do something, or intentional. Intentional omissions can be refrainings, but not all are, since one can omit doing something that one *previously* decided against doing. Conversely, not all refrainings are intentional omissions, since one can refrain from doing something that is not something one is supposed to do. In that case there is nothing to omit. And unintentional omissions are not refrainings, for one can fail to do something that one is supposed to do without considering doing it, much less deciding not to do it.

Finally, there is the case of allowing. Ethicists have spilt much ink debating the moral and metaphysical differences between doing and allowing, as in the morbidly popular case of killing vs letting die. Whereas doing in this context means making something happen, allowing is standardly understood as failing to prevent something from happening. I say 'standardly' because some cases of allowing involve removing or disabling an obstacle to the event in question (there is also allowing in the irrelevant sense of granting permission). Contrast, for example, allowing your cat to go outside by opening the back door with allowing her to go outside by not closing the door. The first, allowing by enabling, is an act; the second, allowing by failing to prevent, is not an act. And not just any instance of not preventing an event counts as allowing the event to happen, for then each of us would be allowing all the countless things that are going on right now. There are three ways of allowing an event to occur by failing to prevent it (and not merely by not preventing it): trying but not succeeding at preventing it, refraining from preventing it, and omitting to prevent it. These are cases of the three kinds of failing we have already identified.

In what follows we will refrain from and omit discussing trying and failing. And, since instances of allowing are, as just observed, cases of one of the other kinds of failing (leaving aside allowing by enabling), we will not take up allowing any further either (it has received plenty of attention in the literature on doing and allowing). Our focus will be on refraining and omitting. One question to ask is whether, despite there being ways of failing to do something, failings are nonetheless actions of a sort. Later we will also touch on the question of whether there are such things as negative acts, that is, on whether any instances of not doing something can themselves be cases of doing something (else).

Refraining

What is it that distinguishes refraining from other ways of failing to do something? For starters, it seems that, unlike trying and not succeeding and unlike (unintentionally) omitting to do something, when one refrains from doing something one *decides* not to do it. It might even seem that *any* case of deciding not to do something counts as refraining from doing it. That can't be right, though, if only because deciding now not to do something later is not refraining, either now or later (one might fail to refrain later, or just change one's mind about not doing it).

Having the ability and the opportunity to do something seems necessary for refraining from doing it. For example, if you enter a room and decide not to turn on the light, you don't refrain from turning it on if you can't reach the light switch or if the light bulb is burned out. That is because the light would not have gone on even if you had tried to turn it on. The most that your decision can explain is that you refrained from *trying* to turn on the light. Is it also necessary, as O. H. Green has suggested (1980: 189), for one to be aware that one has the ability and the opportunity? That seems doubtful, although something weaker might be required, namely for one not to think that one lacks the ability and the opportunity. (The analogous point applies to Patricia Milanich's suggestion (1984: 65) that thinking that one can do something is necessary for refraining from doing it: not thinking that one can't do it seems to suffice.) Actually having the ability and the opportunity is necessary. That's why most of us can't refrain from lifting a grand piano, even if we are under the mistaken impression that we can lift it.

Not only does deciding not to do something while having the ability and the opportunity to do it seem necessary for refraining from doing it, but it seems that, as Robert Moore has suggested, 'it is because of this decision' that one does not perform the action (1979: 415) or, we should add, even attempt to do it. That is, one's decision not to do it must have some connection with one's not doing it; the latter must be explained by one's decision rather than by anything else. But just what could that connection amount to? Obviously, it cannot mean (in above example) that your decision not to turn on the light led you to do something more than make the decision. No action is required. And it can't mean that the decision prevented you from turning on the light, for the decision doesn't deprive you of the ability and opportunity to do it and, indeed, you could have immediately changed your mind and turned on the light after all. Could it mean that the decision caused you not to turn on the light? Matters get delicate here, since it is not clear that not doing something can be caused. After all, there was no event of not turning on the light to be caused – to prevent an event from occurring is not to cause the event of its non-occurrence – and it seems that the absence of an event cannot have a cause (here I am siding with Phil Dowe 2004 in his debate with Jonathan Schaffer 2004 on the case against negative causation).

Moore himself does not explicitly consider and reject these possible readings of his connection condition, and his own is clearly weaker: 'the decision not to [turn on the light] is a necessary condition' of your not doing it (1979: 416). He points out why this is not a sufficient condition for refraining. Suppose you are at a concert and, feeling a cough coming on, you stifle it. Although you have resisted the cough, you have not refrained from coughing. That is because the coughing would not have been done intentionally. Rather, you prevented yourself from (unintentionally) coughing. In contrast, if a burglar were about to cough in order to signal his accomplice to follow him but, upon hearing a voice, decided not to (so as not to give himself away), he would have refrained from coughing. In that case, not only would he have coughed had he not decided not to, but he would have done so because of the decision to do so.

This contrast suggests the following necessary condition on refraining: an agent refrains from doing a certain thing only if, had she not decided not to do it, she would have decided to do it and would have done it (or at least tried to do it) because of that decision. This formulation aims to capture the key role of deciding in refraining: in circumstances in which the agent can refrain from performing a certain action, deciding not to perform it is the alternative to deciding to perform it and, therefore, insofar as the agent would have carried out the decision to perform it had he so decided, the decision he actually made explains why he does not perform it.

But is this condition really necessary? It says that, in order for deciding not to do something to count as refraining from doing it, the agent would have decided to do it, had he not decided not to. To be sure, under the circumstances his options were to do it or not to do it, but this does not mean that he had to make a decision one way or the other. Had he not decided not to do it, perhaps he would not have made up his mind before the opportunity to do it had passed. Although not making up his mind was not one of his *options*, still it was a possible alternative to his deciding either way. But if he could have failed to make up his mind instead of deciding to perform the action, it would not be the case that, if he had not decided not to perform it, he would have decided to perform it. This suggests that Moore's original condition, that deciding not to perform the action is necessary for his not performing it, is too strong. However, one might reply that, if the agent does not perform the action because he has not decided one way or the other, he has not *refrained* from doing it but has merely missed the opportunity to do it – he has *omitted* doing it by failing to decide to do it when the opportunity was there.

Is there any special motivational condition on refraining? In particular, does refraining from doing something require that one should have at least some inclination to do it? That may be necessary for *forbearing*, but it seems too strong a requirement on refraining in general – unless the mere fact that one considers performing the action counts as a minimal inclination to do it. But that trivializes the suggestion. Clearly one can decline an unwelcome invitation or refuse to obey an unreasonable order without having any inclination to perform the act in question. However, there are a couple of special cases in which, as with forbearing, the agent does have an inclination, indeed a strong one. These involve repeated or protracted refraining, as in *abstaining* from an action that one has the nasty habit of repeatedly engaging in or in *forswearing* some tempting activity.

Beyond deciding not to do something, is refraining itself an action? Refraining from doing one thing can involve doing something else, but Myles Brand has maintained that 'refraining is itself a kind of action' (1971: 46). He bases this on the claim that refraining from doing one thing requires doing something else to prevent it (ibid., p. 49), but even that is not true. To be sure, in cases where the temptation to do something is very strong, it may take more than a decision to keep oneself from yielding. For example, if you discover a pint of irresistible marble fudge ice cream in the freezer, in order to keep from eating it you might have to throw it out. However, once you throw it out you are no longer in a position to eat it – the opportunity is gone along with the ice cream. So you can no longer refrain from eating it. But, before you threw it out, your decision, not some action, was what kept you from eating it. Throwing it out was the means by which you ensured that your decision would not be reversed, but it was not itself an act of refraining.

Omitting

Omitting to do something is not simply not doing it. If it were, then we would each be omitting to do innumerable things at every moment. That is absurd. What, then, is required for not doing something to count as an omission?

As the ordinary use of the term implies, omitting is leaving something out, and in this sense we commonly speak of omitting something or someone. But we also speak of omitting to do something, and that is our concern here. There are different reasons why not doing something can count as an omission, but they all seem to be cases of failing to do something that one is, in a conveniently broad and vague sense, 'supposed to do.' One obvious case is neglecting to execute a step in a procedure, for instance not cleaning a surface before painting it or not adding baking soda to a batch of batter. Equally obvious is the case of not fulfilling a duty or responsibility, for example not showing up for work or not scrubbing before performing surgery. But even the case of not fulfilling a mere expectation can count as omitting, as when one doesn't greet a neighbor walking by. It could be an intentional omission, a snubbing, or just a case of being preoccupied. Finally, there is the case of failing to carry out a prior intention. If you plan to call someone when you get home and then forget, that's an omission.

So there are various kinds of reasons for which one can be 'supposed to do' something. Since they are all normative in one way or another, what counts as an omission is itself partly a normative matter. That is, there is no norm-independent fact of the matter as to whether someone has omitted doing something rather than has merely not done it. If it is unclear whether someone was supposed to do something that they didn't do, then it is unclear whether or not they omitted doing it, especially if it didn't even occur to them to do it.

Omissions can be intentional or unintentional or, as Patricia Smith (1990) puts it, 'conscious' or 'unconscious.' She reminds us of the familiar legal doctrine that omissions can be negligent even without being conscious. One can omit doing something intentionally or out of ignorance, forgetting, distraction, or carelessness. Take the case of not discharging a duty. A lifeguard is responsible for rescuing swimmers in jeopardy.

Failing to rescue a swimmer could be intentional, say if the lifeguard sees the struggling swimmer but would rather not miss the rest of the music he is listening to. Or he could fail to rescue the swimmer because, having become engaged in a conversation, he gets distracted. Or, due to the heat, he could carelessly allow himself to nod off, not waking up until it's too late. Notice that an omission can be culpable even if it is not intentional.

Are omissions actions? We do sometimes speak of acts of omission. Unintentional omissions certainly don't seem to be actions. To be sure, we sometimes speak of them as being causes. We might say, for example, that Jack's inadvertent failure to turn off his cell phone caused the concert to be disturbed, but it seems more accurate to say that the phone's ringing is what caused the disturbance. John's omission is part of the full causal explanation of the disturbance, but it is not itself a cause. But what if John had intentionally failed to turn off his cell phone, precisely in order to disturb the concert? He would certainly be causally responsible for the disturbance, insofar as his omission is part of its causal explanation, and there is a kind of counterfactual dependence between the disturbance and the omission. But all this doesn't make the omission itself a cause. To be sure, some have argued that omissions can be causes (see Thomson 2003 and McGrath 2005), but even if they can be, it doesn't follow that they are actions (this is evident from the causal asymmetry that Carolina Sartorio (2005) has identified between actions and omissions).

Negative Acts: Inaction as Action?

We have not found reason to suppose that refrainings or omittings are actions. Of course, they can 'occur' during in the course of performing an action. For example, in deliberately driving through a red light, a reckless driver refrains from stopping; a careless driver, not seeing the light until it is too late, neglects to stop. But this does not mean that driving through the red light is itself an act of refraining from stopping or of omitting to stop. But perhaps there are other cases of not doing something that are more plausible candidates for being actions. In addressing this issue, we need to make sure we don't trivialize it. Any action is, after all, a case of not doing something else, but that doesn't make it an *act* of not doing something else. For example, if I select one in an assortment of hors d'oeuvres, I have thereby not taken any of the others. My taking a bacon-wrapped scallop rather than a crabmeat-stuffed mushroom is a case of not taking the mushroom, but that doesn't make it an *act* of not taking the mushroom. Saying that it is would trivialize the claim that some cases of not doing something are acts.

Bruce Vermazen (1985) thinks that there are genuinely 'negative acts.' Using the device of a hyphen to contrast, for example, 'not-moving' with merely not moving, he offers the example of resisting being pushed. By staying put, one can correctly be described as performing an act of not-moving. So-called human statues have turned not-moving into an art form of sorts. In maintaining a particular pose for many minutes, they perform the negative act of not-budging. But what does this show? Keeping oneself from moving is not merely refraining from moving, but actively preventing oneself from moving. So it is a positive action. It just goes to show that physical action does not always involve motion (see Brand 1971: 50).

Vermazen gives the example of refraining from taking an hors d'oeuvre. He has in mind not merely resisting the temptation to take one by exercising will power, as we colloquially say. He imagines keeping oneself from taking one by twiddling the buttons on one's shirt. The twiddling, he suggests, is also the negative act of not taking an hors d'oeuvre. He argues for this on the grounds that the twiddling is the means of not-taking – one not-takes by twiddling. Moreover, there aren't two acts, the act of twiddling and the act of not-taking. However, it doesn't follow that there is only one act, the twiddling, that is also an act of not-taking. Twiddling the buttons keeps one from taking an hors d'oeuvre, but it is not itself also an act of not-taking. If anything is identical with the not-taking, it is the refraining; but that is not an act. However, doing something as a *means to* not doing something else is not itself a *way of* not-doing that other thing.

A different kind of case to consider is that of resisting a physical urge, such as the urge to cough or laugh (I don't mean the case of refraining from voluntarily coughing or laughing). Resisting the urge just seems to be a case of preventing the cough or laugh from occurring. This, like any act of prevention, is a positive action, even though the result is negative.

We have not found convincing examples of negative acts in any interesting sense. Some acts are acts of standing fast, which Vermazen would describe as not-moving; but physical action does not require movement. Standing fast is keeping one's body from moving, and that is a positive action, like preventing an outcome of any other sort, be it the release of a physical urge or the dropping of a heavy object. And an act performed in order not to do something else is not itself the act of not-doing that other thing, and is certainly not itself the act of refraining from doing that other thing. If anything is equivalent to not-doing the other thing, it is the refraining; but refrainings aren't acts. And neither are omissions.

See also: ACTION THEORY AND ONTOLOGY (1); PLURALISM ABOUT ACTION (12); INTENTION (14); THE DOCTRINE OF DOUBLE EFFECT (41).

References

Brand, M. (1971). The language of not doing. *American Philosophical Quarterly*, 8, 45–53.

Dowe, P. (2004). Causes are physically connected to their effects: Why preventers and omissions are not causes. In C. Hitchcock (ed.), *Contemporary Debates in Philosophy of Science*. Oxford: Blackwell, 189–196.

Green, O. H. (1980). Killing and letting die. *American Philosophical Quarterly*, 17, 195–204.

McGrath, S. (2005). Causation by omission: A dilemma. *Philosophical Studies*, 123, 125–48.

Milanich, P. G. (1984). Allowing, refraining, and failing: The structure of omissions, *Philosophical Studies*, 45, 57–67.

Moore, R. E. (1979). Refraining. *Philosophical Studies*, 36, 407–424.

Sartorio, C. (2005). A new asymmetry between actions and omissions. *Nous*, 39, 460–482.

Schaffer, J. (2004). Causes need not be physically connected to their effects: The case for negative causation. In C. Hitchcock (ed.), *Contemporary Debates in Philosophy of Science*. Oxford: Blackwell, 197–215.

Smith (Milanich), P. G. (1990). Contemplating failure: The importance of unconscious omission. *Philosophical Studies*, 59, 159–176.

Thomson, J. J. (2003). Causation: Omissions. *Philosophy and Phenomenological Research*, 66, 81–103.

Vermazen, B. (1985). Negative acts. In B. Vermazen and M. Hintikka (eds), *Essays on Davidson, Actions and Events*. Oxford: Oxford University Press. 93–104.

8

Speech Acts

MITCHELL S. GREEN

Introduction

Speech acts are a topic in the philosophy of language as well as in the distinct but overlapping field of pragmatics. This latter field is explored not just by philosophers, but also by linguists and experimental psychologists (Noveck and Sperber 2006). Speech acts have also gained the attention of literary theorists (Fish 1976; Gorman 1999), computer scientists (Cohen and Perrault 2003), and legal theorists (Hornsby and Langton 1998).

Nineteenth-century analyses of language before Gottlob Frege and Bertrand Russell tended to approach meaning atomistically: theorists would try to discern the meaning of words in isolation from their sentential environment, often with mixed results. Frege and Russell demonstrated the power of a more holistic approach, stressing the contribution of a word to the entire sentence in which it occurs. Thus for, say, Mill, the primary locus of meaning is the word, whereas for Frege and Russell meaning's primary locus is the sentence. Mid-twentieth-century thinkers like J. L. Austin extended this line of thought by urging that meaning is even more fruitfully studied in the context of the sorts of act that such sentences are used to perform. Austin's student Searle enshrined this idea with the dictum that the unit of meaning is the speech act (1969: 16).

Searle's dictum, together with the assumption that speech acts are kinds of act, encourages the conclusion that the philosophy of language is a branch of the theory of action (ibid., p. 17). If that is correct, a discussion of speech acts has a home in the larger treatment of action. Nevertheless, speech acts have distinctive features setting them apart from actions more generally. To see why, we do well to distinguish, first of all, speech acts from acts of speech.

Speech Acts, Acts of Speech, and Performatives

The phrase 'speech act' refers to a certain subset of the set of all acts that can be performed by, or in, saying that you are doing so. I can promise to meet you tomorrow for lunch by saying, 'I promise to meet you tomorrow for lunch,' whereas I cannot tie my shoes or throw a ball by, or in, saying 'I tie these shoes' ('I throw this ball'). These latter sentences can be uttered *simultaneously* with tying a shoe or throwing a ball, but in no sense does the utterance constitute the act it describes. By contrast, one's saying 'I promise' under the right conditions constitutes a promise.

The reason why 'speech act' refers only to a *subset* of the set of all acts that can be performed by, or in, saying that you are doing so is that some other acts meet this latter condition without being speech acts. My saying 'I am speaking' constitutes my speaking; but, as the phrase 'speech act' is normally used, speaking is not a speech act. This may sound counterintuitive, yet speech acts are by definition socially significant acts, often governed by conventions and always governed by norms. Exercising my post-laryngitis voice in the shower by uttering a few words of a favorite poem is not a speech act, because in saying those words I don't commit myself to their truth; testing a microphone – as Ronald Reagan once did, in preparing for a news conference – with the words, 'The bombing of Russia begins in five minutes,' is not a speech act because, thankfully, there was no question of Reagan's meaning what he said. He was not, for instance, committing himself to the truth of what he said; nor was he issuing an order. By contrast, in speech acts we undertake a commitment such that we, for instance, stand to be right or wrong about what we say.

Acts of speech are not, per se, speech acts. Moreover, speech acts do not even require that anyone be speaking or in some other way producing words. A nod or a hand-wave can count as an agreement or an invitation, respectively.

Speech acts are also distinct from performatives. 'Performative' is best used to refer to those sentences or utterances that make explicit the illocutionary force of the act in which they occur. Instead of asserting that it will rain by using the words 'It's going to rain,' I might make explicit the nature of my act by saying, 'I assert that it's going to rain.' This may help my addressees to determine whether I am professing knowledge about tomorrow's weather, or instead expressing hope or idly conjecturing about it. Help to determine, but not guarantee the result: the last quoted sentence could be uttered as a guess or hypothesis, and in neither case would it be reasonable to take the speaker to present herself as knowing about the coming weather.

Let Φ be a verb phrase in the active voice and present tense naming a speech act, and let p be a proposition: then (and only then) 'I Φ that p' is a *performative sentence*. By contrast, a *performative utterance* is any utterance in which a performative sentence is used according to its conventional meaning in such a way as to perform the speech act it describes. Clearly not all speech acts are, or require the use of, performative sentences or utterances; whereas all performative utterances (but not all performative sentences) are, by definition, also speech acts.

In addition to the standard first person singular form, we sometimes use performatives in the first person plural, as in 'We Φ that p,' where that sentence is uttered by a group – such as a legislative body empowered to appoint, demote, declare war, or excommunicate. In cases of this sort, the institution in question is often more appropriately named: 'The Trustees of Company M hereby appoint Ms Jones as its new Treasurer.' Notice that such an utterance is not reducible to any conjunction of performative utterances of the 'I appoint' form, since it may well be that no individual, not even a trustee, is empowered to appoint anyone to such a post. By contrast, some first person plural cases do seem reducible in just this way: 'We protest the recent detentions of civilians,' uttered by a spokesperson for a group of picketers, might really be the summing up of many individual acts of protest.

We have seen that it is distinctive of speech acts that they can be performed by saying that one is doing so. It is also distinctive of them that they can be undone in this way. That is, once done, I cannot undo a punch, or the fact that I uttered certain words. The most I can do is apologize, or make amends in some other way. However, I can retract or rescind promises, compliments, and appointments. This is not to say that I can now make it the case that yesterday's appointment was not made. Rather, I can now nullify its consequences, so that the person who yesterday became my appointee as treasurer no longer holds this position. Similarly, if you are the person to whom I made a promise last week, I can, with your consent, nullify it. As before, it is still the case that I made a promise, but now I am no longer committed to doing what I promised to do. Here too, then, speech acts exhibit properties not typically observed among acts of speech.

Acts and Their Contents

Common sense generally distinguishes between acts and their consequences: the throwing of the ball caused the breaking of the window, and the writing of the letter caused the insulting of the addressee. However, speech acts are widely held to exhibit a different dichotomy, namely between their *force* and their *content*. Consider the utterance of 'You will not eat all of that cake.' This might be meant as a prediction, as an order, or perhaps even as a threat. Which of these possibilities obtains will determine the force of that utterance. No matter the utterance's force, though, the content stays the same, namely the state of affairs of the addressee's not eating all of the cake.[1]

A speech act's force underdetermines its content; for, just from the fact that someone has made an assertion or a promise, we cannot infer what they have asserted or promised to do. Content also underdetermines force. Given the conventional meaning of the words a speaker utters, together with such contextually determined aspects of content as the extension of indexical terms like 'I' and 'here,' the utterance of a meaningful phrase or expression will generally express a content. That content, however, leaves underdetermined what act is being performed: it does not tell us for instance whether the speaker is making an assertion, a request, or a command. This point is easy to miss in the case of indicative sentences: the utterance of an indicative sentence does not constitute an assertion. This is so even for 'I assert that it will rain tomorrow,' which one might utter in the course of testing a microphone. In such a case no assertion is made. In fact, not even the utterance of an indicative sentence in a speech act constitutes an assertion. I might instead utter that sentence as a *guess* rather than as an assertion.[2]

Neither force nor content, then, determines the other, and a full description of a speech act requires adverting to both. However, many factors are relevant to a person's speech act: the decibel level at which they speak, their intonation, the direction of their gaze, their facial expression. Why should we, in our construal of speech acts, focus on force and content to the exclusion of these other factors?

One reason is that our evaluative concepts of *liability* and *credit* depend a great deal more on force and content than they do on other, more peripheral speech behaviors. Said contemptuously or solemnly, a promise is a promise and, in holding a person to the dictum that 'your word is your bond,' we pay attention to whether they issued a promise and what precisely the nature of that promise was. We pay comparatively little attention to the look on their face when they made that promise, or (if we are adults) to whether they were crossing their fingers behind their back. Again, if a person makes a wild guess about tomorrow's stock market and turns out to have been right, we tend to give them less credit than if they had made that prediction on the basis of evidence. These two types of prediction correspond respectively to the forces of guessing and asserting (or at least conjecturing). As such, sensitivity to the force and content of a person's utterances tends to be driven by such normative concerns as a speaker's status, trustworthiness, and deservingness of credit.

Speech Acts, What is Said, and Speaker Meaning

Although the notion has been the subject of considerable controversy in recent years, everyday discourse employs a reasonably clear notion of what is said. When I utter, 'There are four apples in the bowl,' I say there are four apples in the bowl. When I utter, 'There are four apples in the bowl, and three in the basket,' I say, *inter alia*, that there are three apples in the basket, and not (or not just) that there are three in the basket. Elided material continues to be part of what is said. However, much of what we convey by means of our utterances is not. For instance, in saying that there are four apples in the bowl in response to your remark 'I'm hungry!' I may be indicating or suggesting that they are yours for the taking. However, I do not say that they are yours for the taking. So too, if you ask where Susan is and I reply, 'Somewhere in South Africa,' I suggest but do not say that I'm in no position to be more informative about Susan's whereabouts.

In these last two examples, which are cases of what is known as conversational implicature, what is conveyed is no part of what is being said. Nor, generally, is the illocutionary force of what one says. If I make a prediction about tomorrow's rain with the words, 'It will rain,' I may have said what I did with the force of an assertion, but I have not *said that* I was asserting that it would rain. On the other hand, if I predict rain with the words, 'I predict it will rain tomorrow,' I not only say that it will rain tomorrow, I also say that I predict it will.

How does this relate to speaker meaning? Grice (1989) distinguished between two senses of 'mean.' One sense is exemplified by remarks such as 'Those clouds mean rain' and 'Those spots mean measles.' The notion of meaning in play in such cases Grice dubs 'natural meaning..' Grice suggests that we may distinguish this sense of 'mean' from another sense, more relevant to communication, exemplified by such utterances as:

> In saying 'You make a better door than a window,' Hortense meant that you should move.

And

> In gesticulating that way, Salvatore means that there's mud over there.

Grice used the phrase 'non-natural meaning' for this sense of 'mean,' and in more recent literature this jargon has been replaced with the phrase 'speaker meaning.' After distinguishing between natural and (what we shall heretofore call) speaker meaning, Grice characterizes the latter as involving the performance of an action with an intention of producing a belief in an audience by means, at least in part, of the audience's recognition of that intention. This is a so-called 'reflexive communicative intention.'

While most researchers concerned with the topic agree on the existence of the phenomenon of speaker meaning as distinct from natural meaning, Grice's own analysis of this phenomenon is controversial (Vlach 1981, Davis 1992). Regardless of its proper elucidation, however, it seems clear that speaker meaning comprises illocutionary force. That there is water underground is part of what I – the speaker – mean when I say 'There's water underground.' But it is also part of that meaning whether I am asserting, conjecturing, or just guessing that there's water underground. This is why it can be reasonable to ask of someone uttering the sentence just quoted: did they mean it as a statement? (and so on). Thus, although illocutionary force is not naturally construed as part of *what* a speaker means, it nevertheless characterizes *how* the speaker meant it.

Misfires, Abuses, and How Saying Makes It So

Integral to his first systematic presentation of speech acts was Austin's treatment of what he called *infelicities*, which are ways in which a speech act might fail to occur ideally. Infelicities divide into two major kinds: *misfires* and *abuses*. In a misfire, the act one purports to perform does not occur at all. I can only name the newly constructed building 'Aristotle Hall' if I am duly empowered to do so; I can only excommunicate someone from a religious organization if I am an authority within that organization, and so forth. If these conditions are not met, then the act misfires in that no speech act of naming or excommunicating occurs. Instead, all that occurs is an act of speech. Moreover, some speech acts require audience 'uptake' for their performance. I cannot bet with you unless you accept my bet; I cannot make you a promise unless you accept it, and so on – for many (but not all) speech acts. As with the earlier cases, when there is no uptake, there is an act of speech but no speech act.

Austin isolates another form of infelicity in addition to misfires, namely *abuses*. When I make a promise, I give others reason to expect its fulfillment. I can exploit this fact with a lying promise, which I make with no intention of keeping. So too, when I lie I make an assertion without believing what I say. In both these cases, I do perform a speech act – there is no misfire – and that is why, in spite of my insincerity, I am committed to doing what I promised to do, or to being right or wrong about what I asserted.

These points about speech act infelicities are useful background for grasping how, in speech acts, 'saying can make it so.' First of all, there are some fairly trivial ways in which an utterance can make itself true. For instance, in uttering the words, 'I am uttering words,' I make it the case that I am uttering words. So, too, Kaplan's example of 'I am here now' (Kaplan 1979) is, arguably, knowable a priori, in spite of expressing a proposition that is, at best, contingently true. However, speech acts are validated only in part by an associated utterance; conditions the absence of which would produce misfires must be in place as well, lest there be a mere act of speech.

Some authors have noticed an analogy between these facts about speech acts and moves in games. Unless I am a member of one of the competing teams, my carrying a football over a goal line won't count as a touchdown. However, if I am a player, the ball is in play, no fouls have been called and so on, my carrying the ball over the end zone counts as a touchdown. It has been suggested that, similarly, my pronouncing a couple man and wife counts as their becoming betrothed if the appropriate conditions are in place (Searle 1969: 50–3).

This 'counting as' locution, and the analogy with games that supports its applicability to speech acts, suggest a view of them as essentially conventional affairs. Austin, for instance, held that all speech acts depend for their occurrence on what we might call extra-semantic conventions: Austin's view is that the study of speech acts unearths another layer of convention in addition to the those imbuing our words with meaning – a layer without which we could express propositions, but perform few if any socially significant acts with their aid.

This position, which we may call 'force conventionalism,' has been challenged. Strawson (1964) remarks that, while there are conventional means for entreaty, it is doubtful that the only way to make an entreaty is by such conventional means. Why can't I entreat you by laying bare my need – more exactly, by making that need *overt?* Overtness here is a matter not only of making my need open to view, but also of making my intention of so opening it to view, itself open to view.

McDowell develops this though, contending that

> Speech acts are publications of intentions; the primary aim of a speech act is to produce an object – the speech act itself – that is perceptible publicly, and in particular to the audience, embodying an intention whose content is precisely a recognizable performance of that very speech act. Recognition by an audience that such an intention has been made public in this way leaves nothing further needing to happen for the intention to be fulfilled. (1998: 41)

McDowell may here be suggesting that in, for instance, an assertion of p, what is perceptible is an act embodying an intention to assert that p. Until we know more about the institution of assertion, however, it will be unclear whether this proposal offers an alternative to force conventionalism. One proposal aimed at this question is as follows. An intention to assert that p is an intention to commit oneself to *knowing* p to be so; an intention, by contrast, to guess that p is merely an intention to commit oneself to p's being so, and so on. Enumeration of the different commitments characteristic of various speech acts provides the basis, so this suggestion goes, for a view of speech acts not requiring that they depend on extra-semantic conventions (Green 2007, 2009).

Illocutions, Perlocutions, and Implicature

Austin's original term, which has since been replaced by 'speech act,' was 'illocution.' In addition to these, he also recognized those acts or effects that are characteristic consequences of speech acts. A 'perlocutionary effect' of promising is the audience's forming the belief or intention that you will perform the promised act; a perlocutionary effect of asserting that p is my audience's belief that p. Construed teleologically, speech acts aim at effects such as these. However, this teleology is not so integral to the speech act's viability as to pertain to its felicity conditions. An assertion can be felicitous, for instance, even if you don't believe what I say. Austin also denies that perlocutions are a species of speech acts: I cannot persuade you by, or in, saying that I do so (Austin 1962: 118–20).

Speech acts are also to be distinguished from implicature, both conventional and conversational. For the conventional case, consider that mastery of 'but' requires appreciating that it is used to convey a contrast or tension between the two conjuncts it conjoins. However, when one says, 'He was a philosopher, but well dressed,' one does not assert (or perform any other speech act whose content is) that there is a tension between these two properties. For the conversational case, consider that when you say less than might have been expected given such background conversational factors as what is common knowledge and what are the accepted standards of precision, your interlocutors may well take you to be conveying more, but not asserting more than that. In answer to the question 'What time is it?' one might in a given case be expected to answer to within ten minutes accuracy; if one replies with 'It's after four,' one may for that reason convey that one has no more exact information. However, in so answering, one doesn't assert that this is the most one can say.[3]

Direct and Indirect Speech Acts

Sometimes a speech act can be performed by virtue of the performance of another one. For instance, my remark that you are standing on my foot is normally taken as, in addition, a demand that you move; my question whether you can pass the salt is normally taken as a request that you do so. These are examples of so-called 'indirect speech acts' (Searle 1975).

Indirect speech acts are less common than might first appear. In asking whether you intend to quit smoking, I might be suggesting that you quit. However, while the embattled smoker might jump to this interpretation, we do well to consider what evidence would mandate it. After all, while I probably would not have asked whether you intended to quit smoking unless I hoped you would quit, I can evince such a hope without suggesting anything. Similarly, the advertiser who tells us that Miracle Cream reversed hair loss in Bob, Mike, and Fred probably hopes that I will believe it will reverse my own hair loss. That does not show that he is indirectly *asserting* that it will. Whether he is depends, it would seem, on whether he can be accused of being a liar if in fact he does not believe that Miracle Cream will staunch my hair loss.

Whether, in addition to a given speech act, I am also performing an indirect speech act would seem to depend on my intentions. My question whether you can pass the salt is also a request that you do so only if I intend to be so understood. My remark that Miracle Cream helped Bob, Mike and Fred is also an assertion that it will help you only if I intend to be so committed. What is more, these intentions must be feasibly discernible to one's audience. Even if, in remarking on the fine weather, I intend as well to request that you pass the salt, I have not done so. I need to make that intention manifest in some way.

How might I do this? One way is by inference to the best explanation. All else being equal, the best explanation of my asking whether you can pass the salt is that I mean to be requesting that you do so. All else equal, the best explanation of my remarking that you are standing on my foot, particularly if I use a stentorian tone of voice, is that I mean to be demanding that you desist. By contrast, it is doubtful that the best explanation of my asking whether you intend to quit smoking is my intention to suggest that you do so. Another explanation at least as plausible is my hope that you do so.[4]

These considerations suggest that indirect speech acts, if they do occur, can be explained within the framework of conversational implicature – that process by which we mean more than we say, but in a way which is not due exclusively to the conventional meanings of our words. Conversational implicature, too, depends both upon communicative intentions and upon the availability of inference to the best explanation (Grice 1989). The study of speech acts is in this respect intertwined with the study of conversation.

See also: ACTION THEORY AND ONTOLOGY (1); PLURALISM ABOUT ACTION (12); INTENTION (14); INDIAN PHILOSOPHERS (52); RICŒUR (75).

Notes

1 Similar points apply to the contents of non-indicative sentences. The question 'Where's Mary?' expresses a content that can be expressed in non-interrogative speech acts, as in 'No one wonders where Mary is'; so too for imperatives.
2 Guesses, by the way, are not a special kind of assertion. After all, it is appropriate to reply to an assertion with the challenge: 'How do you know?' On the other hand, that would be an inappropriate reply to a guess. If guesses were a species of assertion, that challenge would always be appropriate.
3 Lewis (1979) suggests of a notion of 'conversational score,' in which such factors as common knowledge and standards of precision are used a parameters for explaining many pragmatic phenomena.
4 Bertolet (1994) develops an even more skeptical position, arguing that any alleged case of an indirect speech act can be construed just as an indication, by means of contextual clues, of the speaker's intentional state – hope, desire, and so on, as the case may be. Postulation of a further speech act beyond what has been (relatively) explicitly performed is explanatorily unmotivated.

References

Austin, J. L. (1962). *How to Do Things with Words*, 2nd edn, edited by J. O. Urmson and M. Sbisá. Cambridge, MA: Harvard University Press.
Bertolet, R. (1994). Are there indirect speech acts? In S. Tsohatzidis (ed.), *Foundations of Speech Act Theory: Philosophical and Linguistic Perspectives*. London: Routledge, 335–349.
Cohen, P., and Perrault, R. (2003) Elements of a plan-based theory of speech acts. In M.-P. Huget (ed.), *Communication in Multi-Agent Systems*. Dordrecht: Springer, 1–36.

Davis, W. (1992). Speaker meaning. *Linguistics and Philosophy*, 15, 223–253.
Fish, S. (1976). How to do things with Austin and Searle: Speech act theory and literary criticism. *Modern Language Notes*, 91, 983–1025.
Gorman, D. (1999). The use and abuse of speech-act theory in criticism. *Poetics Today*, 20, 93–119.
Green, M. (2007). *Self-Expression*. Oxford: Oxford University Press.
Green, M. (2009). Speech acts, the handicap principle and the expression of psychological states. *Mind and Language*, 24, 139–163.
Grice, H. P. (1989). Meaning [1957]. In H. P. Grice, *Studies in the Way of Words*. Cambridge, MA: Harvard University Press, 213–223.
Hornsby, J., and Langton, R. (1998). Free speech and illocution. *Legal Theory*, 4, 21–37.
Kaplan, D. (1979). On the logic of demonstratives. *Journal of Philosophical Logic*, 8, 81–98.
Lewis, D. (1979). Scorekeeping in a language game. *Journal of Philosophical Logic*, 8, 339–359.
McDowell, J. (1998). Meaning, communication, and knowledge [1980]. In J. McDowell, *Meaning, Knowledge and Reality*. Cambridge, MA: Harvard University Press, 29–50.
Noveck, I., and Sperber, D. (2006). *Experimental Pragmatics*. London: Palgrave Macmillan.
Searle, J. (1969). *Speech Acts: An Essay in the Philosophy of Language*. Cambridge: Cambridge University Press.
Searle, J. (1975). A taxonomy of illocutionary acts. In K. Gunderson (ed), *Language, Mind and Knowledge*. Minneapolis, MN: University of Minnesota Press, 344–369.
Strawson, P. (1964). Intention and convention in speech acts. *Philosophical Review*, 73, 439–60.
Vlach, F. (1981). Speaker meaning. *Linguistics and Philosophy*, 4, 359–391.

Further reading

Alston, W. (2000). *Illocutionary Acts and Sentence Meaning*. Ithaca, NY: Cornell University Press.
Anscombe, G. E. M. (1963). *Intention*, 2nd edn. Ithaca, NY: Cornell University Press.
Armstrong, D. (1971). Meaning and communication. *Philosophical Review*, 80, 427–447.
Clark, H. (1996). *Using Language*. Cambridge: Cambridge University Press.
Bach, K., and Harnish, R. (1979). *Linguistic Communication and Speech Acts*. Cambridge, MA: MIT Press.
Brandom, R. (1983). Asserting. *Nous*, 17, 637–650.
Frege, G. (1984). The thought: A logical inquiry. Trans. A. Quinton and M. Quinton, *Mind*, 1956; 65: 289–311.
Recanati, F. (1987). *Meaning and Force: the Pragmatics of Performative Utterances*. Cambridge: Cambridge University Press.
Searle, J. (1979). Indirect speech acts. In J. Searle, *Expression and Meaning: Studies in the Theory of Speech Acts*. Cambridge: Cambridge University Press, 30–57.
Searle, J., and D. Vanderveken (1985). *Foundations of Illocutionary Logic*. Cambridge: Cambridge University Press.
Tsohatzidis, S. L. (ed.) (1994). *Foundations of Speech act Theory: Philosophical and Linguistic Perspectives*. London: Routledge.
Vanderveken, D. (1990). *Meaning and Speech Acts*, Vols 12. Cambridge: Cambridge University Press.

9

Collective Action

MARGARET GILBERT

Introduction

The phrase 'collective action' is ambiguous. It may refer to little more than a situation in which several people independently perform a particular action. Or it may refer to a situation in which people act within what has come to be known as a 'collective action problem,' where the 'payoff' to each depends on what is done by the others. On the construal on which I focus here, collective action occurs if and only if, as it would be put in the vernacular, two or more people are *doing something together*.

Cases of collective action in this sense include going for a walk together, investigating a crime together, running a country together. In this context the qualifier 'together' is used to mark the fact that a collective action is at issue rather than the fact that the parties are geographically adjacent to one another – which they may not be. This qualifier may be implied rather than explicitly stated when collective action is referred to in everyday life. Thus in referring to their collective action someone may well say, of herself and some other persons, 'We are running the country' rather than 'We are running the country together.' 'Together' is likely to be added when it seems necessary to avoid ambiguity. Thus, when reporting on what he and another person are doing, someone may think to add 'together' after 'We are playing tennis,' in order to make it clear that he is not referring to two separate tennis games.

Apart from its intrinsic interest, the topic of collective action is relevant to several other topics, including the nature of social groups. Thus it is often suggested in sociological discussions that those who do something together thereby constitute a social group, in one central sense of the term, though there may be as few as two people involved, and for a relatively short time. A clear understanding of acting together, then, may well throw light on the structure of social groups in general.

In spite of the importance of understanding collective action, philosophers of action have until relatively recently focused their attention on the actions of individual human beings. They have explored a number of related concepts, in particular that of intention, in relation, again, to particular individuals. There has been an increasing focus on the nature of collective action, however, within the past twenty years or so.

The key question in the philosophy of collective action is simply: what does it amount to? In other terms: under what conditions are two or more people doing something together?

The present discussion will start with some informal observations on how those who engage in collective action conceive of it. It then reviews three approaches to the topic and assesses them in light of these observations. Sometimes the phrases 'joint action' or 'joint activity' will be used to refer to the phenomenon at issue. The former phrases have the advantage of being at least somewhat less ambiguous than 'collective action.'

Observations on Collective Action

Take going for a walk together – or, for short, walking together – as an example. In practice a variety of conventions may exist relating to the way in which people are to go for a walk together, or the way in which people falling into specific categories are to do so. There may be a convention in certain circles, for instance, that, when they are out for a walk together, a man is to walk ahead of any woman who walks with him. Suppose, then, that two people, Hank and Jane, understand that they are going for a walk together, in a cultural context in which it is expected that, while people are out on a walk together, they are to walk alongside each other wherever possible. Informal observations on people walking together or otherwise acting together suggest the following.

If Jane starts drawing ahead of Hank, he will take himself to have the standing or entitlement to call her back, or to rebuke her for drawing ahead, although he may not do either of these things. Should he call out, in a mildly rebuking fashion, 'Hey, Jane, slow down!' – she will understand that he has the standing to voice such a demand, tinged with rebuke. She will not feel the same about a stranger, or even a friend who is passing by. She might put the point this way: 'I don't owe it to either of them to keep pace with Hank,' and she might explain this by saying, simply, 'I'm walking with him, not with them.'

In addition to considering that they owe each other actions that are appropriate to their walking together, such as keeping pace with one another, those who are out on a walk together will consider that they owe it to one another to discourage behavior of their own or of the other participants that is not appropriate to their walking together, and to correct such behavior if it occurs. Such corrective action need not involve demands or rebukes, though it may. It may also take various gentler forms, including messages of encouragement and help of various kinds.

In short, as they see it, those who are walking together have a special standing to demand of one another appropriate actions; and the same goes for other types of joint action. They also have a special standing to rebuke one another for inappropriate action. In both cases, this special standing may be explained by reference to owing: those who do something together owe each other actions appropriate to the action in question. They also owe each other correction of inappropriate actions.

Another observation on acting together, as seen by the participants, can be introduced in terms of the previous example. Suppose Jane responds to Hank's call by saying: 'We're not walking together anymore – I've decided to go on without you!' Hank could quite properly respond: 'But you can't just decide that we are no longer walking together!' Of course Jane has the physical capacity to break away from her walk with

Hank, but apparently she is not in a position to terminate their walk simply by deciding that it is over.

The foregoing discussion refers to the way people conceive of their acting together. One way to envisage the task of an account of acting together is as an account of the everyday, non-technical concept at issue. Some theorists (in particular Margaret Gilbert) explicitly undertake this task. Some (for instance Michael Bratman) explicitly identify their primary aim differently. Others are not explicit either way. The present discussion will characterize three distinctive approaches to collective action that have emerged in the literature and discuss them by reference to their relationship to the everyday concept of acting together as so far characterized.

Approaches to Collective Action

Theorists writing on collective action have tended to focus on the inner or mental states of the individual human participants, asking in effect: what aspect of the inner life of the parties distinguishes two or more people who act together from others, behaving in similar ways, who are not acting together? Though this may not be true if we take into account their whole trajectory, including the preliminaries from which their collective action starts, two people who are out on a walk together, for example, may indeed be behaviorally indistinguishable, at a single point in time, from two people who are simply walking alongside each other.

Three main approaches to collective action have been taken in the literature. One appeals to intentions, in each participant, which are expressible by statements of the form 'I personally intend ...' Such intentions will here be labeled 'personal intentions.' A prominent proponent of this approach is Michael Bratman.

Another approach appeals to intentions of each participant expressible by statements of the form 'we intend to' or 'we intend that.' Such intentions will here be labeled 'we-intentions.' This approach has been associated with the work of Wilfrid Sellars and, more recently, John Searle.

A third approach is that of Margaret Gilbert, who proposes that neither personal intentions nor 'we-intentions' of the individual participants lie at the heart of collective action. Rather, she appeals to a technical notion of joint commitment (on which more is said below). Gilbert's joint commitment approach has a broadly speaking contractual element that is absent from the others.

The Personal Intentions Approach

According to the personal intentions approach, the inner aspect of a collective action is a set of personal intentions of the participants. The content of such intentions may be characterized in different ways.

With respect to walking together, Michael Bratman would invoke a personal intention, present in each of the parties, *that we walk together*. He also invokes personal intentions, present in each participant, that we walk together in accordance with, and because of, the intentions just mentioned. In his earlier discussions this comes close to the complete account, which is complemented by the parties' common knowledge of the existence of the said intentions. For present purposes we can think of 'common knowledge' informally, as a matter of the intentions in question being out in the open as far as the various parties are concerned. In his more recent work Bratman has added a number of further conditions on what he refers to as a 'shared' intention. The points to be made below apply to the more complicated versions of his position, as they apply more generally to accounts that put personal intentions at the heart of collective action.

Suppose we consider that all there is to our walking together is each of us acting in accordance with personal intentions of the type in question in the truncated version of Bratman's account just given, intentions of which there is common knowledge between us. Do we have a case of walking together according to the everyday conception of this as it was characterized earlier?

There are two main issues. First, when the personal intentions of the sort now in question are present, do the parties owe each other actions appropriate to their walking together? The term 'owe' is ambiguous, so in asking this question it is important to emphasize that the kind of owing at issue here is enough to give one who is owed an action by another the standing to demand that action, and to rebuke the other person for not performing the action. It is by no means clear that the parties in the situation now envisaged owe each other actions appropriate to their walking together, in this sense of 'owe.'

Bratman has argued that in many such situations a moral principle of fidelity along the lines of that proposed by Thomas Scanlon may apply to the parties, so that in the case under consideration each may be morally required to act appropriately to their walking together, depending on the circumstances. As Gilbert has argued, however, even when Scanlon's principle applies to someone, it is by no means clear that the person in question owes anyone the action she is morally required to perform – in the sense of 'owe' in play here.

What of the observation made earlier concerning the inability of one party to a collective action to terminate that action simply by deciding that it is over? In the case of the interlocking personal intentions invoked by Bratman, it seems that this observation does not apply. Given that personal intentions lie at the core of a collective action, and given that such intentions can be unilaterally revoked by the person whose intentions they are, a given party is in a position, in effect, to terminate the collective action at will, by destroying one of its crucial elements.

The 'We-Intentions' Approach

John Searle and, earlier, Wilfrid Sellars proposed that, in addition to the personal intentions of individuals expressible by sentences of the form 'I personally intend to do such-and-such' and so on, there are intentions of individuals that are not expressible in this way. Rather they are expressible in sentences of the form 'We intend to do such-and-such,' and so on. According to the we-intentions approach to collective action, the 'inner' element at the core of a collective action is a corresponding set of 'we-intentions,' one for each participant. Thus, in order for two or people to go for a walk together, each must 'we-intend' their walking together.

This suggestion needs further development. As it stands, it amounts to little more than the negative point to the effect that the inner life of a collective action is not, or is not simply, a matter of personal intentions in favor of the collective action in question. This may be true and important, but much remains to be explained. For instance, we need to know whether there are conditions under which a given we-intention is appropriate, and, if so, whether these conditions have to do with anyone other than the possessor of the we-intention.

The normative implications of a given person's we-intending also need further discussion. Suppose that Anne, Bob, and Carrie all 'we-intend' to go for a walk with the others, and, at this point in time, each is acting appropriately in that each is making an effort to keep pace with the others. Suppose Anne suddenly slows her pace. Does Bob owe it to her and Carrie to do what he can to bring it about that her pace equals his and Carrie's? Is he in a position to demand that she move faster? If so, what precisely puts him in this position?

Finally, it is not clear, from what we-intentions theorists have said, whether or not one is in a position to revoke one's own we-intention without the concurrence of the other parties – as one is in a position to revoke a personal intention of one's own. If one is in this position, then each party is once again able, by a simple act of will, unilaterally to destroy one of the crucial elements of the collective action. This runs counter to the understandings of those who participate in collective actions without special background understandings.

The Joint Commitment Approach

Margaret Gilbert has argued that, in order to understand the everyday conception of acting together, one needs to invoke the concept of a joint commitment. This concept may be introduced by reference to the concept of a personal decision, roughly as follows. If Peter has decided to go to Paris tomorrow, he is committed to going to Paris tomorrow, in the sense that, all else being equal, if he does not go to Paris tomorrow he will not have acted appropriately. Thus, by making a given decision, one imposes a kind of normative constraint upon oneself. This is true of personal intentions also, although decisions and intentions differ in various ways. For instance, whereas an intention can simply disappear, a decision needs to be intentionally revoked, or it stands. Gilbert sums up the situation by saying that decisions and intentions give their possessors sufficient reason to act in accordance with them.

She proposes that people can be subject to both personal commitments – by personally deciding and intending – and to joint commitments. One is not subject to a joint commitment as a matter of one's having made a personal decision or formed a personal intention that corresponds in some way to the personal decision or intention of one or more other people. There would then be an aggregate of personal commitments, in which each person committed him or herself, albeit as a result of the fulfillment of some condition involving the other person. Rather, two or more people jointly commit each other. They do so by mutually expressing to one another their readiness jointly to commit them all in a particular way, where these expressions are common knowledge.

These mutual expressions may involve a variety of processes. One of them is the process of making an agreement. In other words, the making of an agreement is the making of a particular kind of joint commitment. There are other, more subtle ways of making such commitments as well.

Collective actions often, but not always, begin with an agreement. Thus Hank and Jane may have agreed to go for a walk together. Or they may not have done anything that amounted to agreement-making. Perhaps Hank said 'I'm going for an hour's walk,' Jane replied 'Oh, why don't you wait for me,' he waited, and then they set off.

In this case, according to Gilbert, the crucial joint commitment will be something like this: Hank and Jane are jointly committed to emulate as far as possible a single being which intends that they go for a walk together, where 'their going for a walk together' is understood in behavioral terms. Each is now committed through the joint commitment to do his – her part – in this emulation. A joint commitment as Gilbert construes it cannot be unilaterally be rescinded by any one party without some special background understanding. That which the parties create together they must revoke together.

How does Gilbert's account of the inner core of joint action cohere with the observations on collective action made earlier? It can be argued that it coheres very well.

As to the observation about the parties owing each other conformity, one can argue that the parties to any joint commitment owe each other conformity to the commitment in the pertinent sense of 'owe.' As suggested earlier, that sense is closely linked with the standing to demand conformity. Those who are owed conformity in the pertinent sense have such standing, and vice versa.

It is hard to doubt that, if I am committed through a process of joint commitment, then the other parties to the commitment have the standing to demand of me my conformity to that commitment. If that is right, we can infer that the parties to a joint commitment owe each other conformity to it.

Given a joint commitment account of joint action, then, it seems possible to allow that, even when morality requires one not to continue with a given joint action and this is understood by the parties, they will take it that they owe each other such continuance in the absence of their concurrence on the ending of the action. This does not mean that they will understand that they are bound to 'give what they owe' in spite of morality's dictates. Rather, they will understand that the other has the usual standing to demand compliance, whether or not, all things considered, he or she is justified in making such a demand.

With respect to the observation about the need for concurrence on bringing a collective action to a close, this is taken care of by the point that a joint commitment cannot be rescinded unilaterally without a special background understanding.

Concluding Remarks

The foregoing discussion suggests that an account of acting together in terms of personal intentions or we-intentions of the participants will not be able satisfactorily to take account of the informal observations on joint action made at the outset of this discussion. A joint commitment account, whatever its precise details, is more promising.

The philosophical debate on collective action continues, and many philosophers other than those named in the course of the foregoing discussion have contributed and continue to contribute to the discussion. These philosophers include Raimo Tuomela and Kaarlo Miller, Christopher Kutz, Christopher MacMahon, Abraham Roth, and David Velleman. The philosophical literature on collective action has provoked considerable interest in fields with a more empirical focus such as communication sciences, economics, social and developmental psychology, and primatology.

See also: PLURALISM ABOUT ACTION (12); INTENTION (14); DELIBERATION AND DECISION (32); ACTION IN HISTORY AND SOCIAL SCIENCE (50); THE PREDICTION OF ACTION (51); WEBER (67).

Further reading

Bratman, M. (1999). *Faces of Intention*. Cambridge: Cambridge University Press.

Bratman, M. (2009). Modest sociality and the distinctiveness of intention. *Philosophical Studies*, 144, 149–165.

Gilbert, M. (1989). *On Social Facts*. Princeton: Princeton University Press.

Gilbert, M. (2004). Scanlon on promissory obligation: The problem of promisees' rights. *Journal of Philosophy*, 101, 83–109.

Gilbert, M. (2009). Shared intention and personal intentions. *Philosophical Studies*, 144, 167–187.

Kutz, C. (2000). Acting together. *Philosophy and Phenomenological Research*, 61, 1–31.

MacMahon, C. (2005). Shared agency and rational cooperation. *Nous*, 39, 284–308.

Roth, A. S. (2004). Shared agency and contralateral commitments. *The Philosophical Review*, 113, 359–410.

Scanlon, T. (1998). *What We Owe to Each Other*. Cambridge, MA: Harvard University Press.

Searle, J. (1990). Collective intentions and actions. In P. R. Cohen, J. Morgan, and M. E. Pollack (eds), *Intentions in Communication*, Cambridge, MA: MIT Press, 401–415.

Sellars, W. (1963). Imperatives, intentions, and the logic of 'ought.' In G. Nakhnikian and H.-N. Castañeda (eds), *Morality and the Language of Conduct*. Detroit: Wayne State University Press, 159–218.

Tuomela, R., and Miller, K. (1988). We-intentions. *Philosophical Studies*, 53, 115–137.

Velleman, D. (1997). How to share an intention. *Philosophy and Phenomenological Research*, 57, 29–50.

10

Habitual Actions

BILL POLLARD

The Place of Habit in Human Life

Few would dispute that much of what we human beings do is habitual. Our daily lives are dominated by practiced routines of varying importance, which we achieve quite without thought, conscious decision, or awareness. From dressing in the morning to making breakfast, leaving for work, finding our way around our home town, greeting and interacting with others, cooking, washing, playing sport, dancing and making music, we find ourselves exercising countless habits. Habits transform performances which may once have required attention and concentration into actions which come so naturally and easily that we just find ourselves doing them, whilst we think about other things.

Habits help us on many levels. We acquire them effortlessly and utterly rely on them to do countless mundane tasks, as well as more complex ones. We encourage good habits in our children, as we know that this will help them throughout their lives. As adults, we harness the power of habits to give us new abilities, as when we learn a sport or an instrument, and also to take control of our weaknesses, as when we change our diet or exercise regime. The habits we have also reveal a good deal about who we are, and may represent our true selves better than the sometimes aspirational or delusional things we tell ourselves and each other.

But creatures of habit we may be; analytic philosophy has yet to appreciate that fact. I hope this chapter might help matters.

I begin by describing the place of habit in current philosophy of action. I then survey the tradition of habit-friendly philosophy. Next I make some suggestions about how an analysis of habit could proceed. Finally I describe some of the benefits of a philosophy of habit, and challenges that lie ahead.

Habits in Current Philosophy of Action

Habitual actions do not fit comfortably into contemporary philosophical conceptions of action, or not at least in analytic philosophy. Under the influence of Anscombe (1957) and Davidson (1980), debate has focused on the nature of intentional actions;

on issues such as the role of the reasons 'for which' we act; and on the nature of psychological antecedents of actions such as beliefs, desires, and intentions. But habitual actions are not obviously intentional, since, on the face of it, we do them without any intention (though they are not by that token unintentional). Neither do habitual actions seem to be done 'for reasons,' if reasons are to be understood as considerations which lie before the agent at the time of action. Habits, after all, spare us the need for any consideration. Similarly, if an account of action is cashed out in terms of psychological antecedents such as beliefs and desires, it will be tricky to include exercises of habits in the class of actions at all without stretching these concepts to the point of vacuity.

In this conceptual framework, if habitual actions are mentioned at all, they tend to be pushed to the margins of human action, where they can safely be relegated to being 'mere behaviors' rather than exercises of agency proper. We are thereby invited to think of them as little more than reflexes or nervous tics. Talk of 'habitual actions' is, strictly speaking, an oxymoron.

This skepticism is not purely driven by theory. After all, we tend to notice our habits when they are a hindrance. Smokers and nail-biters are fully aware of the grip their habits have on them. And anyone who has learned to do something badly, like a golf swing, will recognize the difficulty of losing a habit. What's perhaps most frustrating is that we pick them up with no effort at all. Habits, then, seem to work against our will, our rationality, our ability for self-control; indeed against agency itself. With our gaze fixed on bad habits, it is perhaps easy to see why habits per se are marginalized. But of course not all habits are bad.

There is another response within the current framework which is at first glance hospitable to habitual actions. This is to point out that, just because we don't *consciously* intend, or *consciously* deliberate about, an action before we do it, it does not follow that we don't intend, or don't have reasons, to do it: intentions and reasons can be entertained unconsciously. Philosophers who respond in this way will point out that, with habitual actions, there is often good reason to attribute such intentions and reasons (other than the mere fact of the action itself). These states can be modelled on the conscious states the agent had when she first acquired the habit. So, when I first put this kettle on in the morning, I did so with a conscious intention, and for a reason: it was a way of making a cup of tea, and I intended to do just that. Now that putting the kettle on in the mornings has become habitual, it is reasonable to say that I still have the same sort of intention and reason, and we needn't fuss about the fact that these states are now unconscious. So we can subsume habitual actions under the same theoretical structure as (supposedly) run-of-the-mill consciously deliberated actions.

But this is not a habit-friendly response either. This time the skepticism is not about the very possibility of habitual actions, but about their distinctiveness. Habitual actions are little more than actions which the agent happens to have done before, and it's not clear why that should matter at all.

This skepticism about habitual actions and their distinctiveness is, I believe, symptomatic of a philosophy of action which deserves to be termed 'intellectualist.' That is to say, it overestimates the role of the intellect by modelling all actions on the deliberated kind. But there is a long tradition of habit-friendly philosophy which might provide the ingredients for a corrective.

The Habit-Friendly Tradition

The tradition starts with Aristotle, who, in Book 2 of the *Nicomachean Ethics*, draws the analogy between learning crafts and learning to be a good person. In particular, he emphasizes the importance of the right kinds of practice (*ethos*) during upbringing, which will eventually develop the 'fixed and permanent disposition' (*hexis*) required for virtuous action (1105^b1).

David Hume is also noted for his appeal to habit, which plays a fundamental role in his account of human understanding. 'Custom or Habit' (terms that Hume uses interchangeably) is nothing short of 'the ultimate principle [...] of all our conclusions from experience' (1975: 43). Habit is a 'principle of human nature' upon which reason fundamentally depends. Habits are also central in Hume's moral philosophy: 'the *tendencies* of actions and characters, not their real accidental consequences, are alone regarded in our moral determinations' (ibid., p. 228n., my emphasis).

Habits also feature strongly in the early pragmatist philosophy of C. S. Peirce, William James and John Dewey. Peirce's analysis of thought identifies a number of 'habits of mind,' such as the inference from premises to conclusions, as well as the idea of belief itself, which is nothing more than 'some habit which will determine our actions' (Peirce 1877).

In his chapter devoted to habits in the *Principles of Psychology* (1890), James describes how acquiring a habit means that the actions become 'more accurate' and 'diminish fatigue,' as well as reducing 'conscious attention.' And for James, the importance of habit extends far beyond the individual. 'Habit,' he writes, 'is the enormous fly-wheel of society, its most precious conservative agent.' He also draws out some implications for education. He regarded children as 'mere walking bundles of habits' (1890: 127).

In *Human Nature and Conduct* (1922), Dewey develops James' suggestion about children into the striking claim that all habits 'constitute the self':

> In any intelligible sense of the word will, [habits] *are* will. They form our effective desires and they furnish us with our working capacities. They rule our thoughts, determining which shall appear and be strong and which shall pass from light into obscurity. (Dewey 1922: 25)

The conception of the self suggested here contrasts sharply with any other that identifies it with the intellect.

Despite the contribution of pragmatism, habits are scarce in the emerging analytic tradition of the twentieth century. One might think that Gilbert Ryle would seize on the notion as part of his anti-intellectualist manifesto. But in *The Concept of Mind* (1949) Ryle explicitly denies that mental terms can be understood as 'mere habits' (pp. 41–44), as he disparagingly calls them. Only what he calls 'intelligent capacities' can represent genuine mindedness, since (*inter alia*) their exercises are characterized by 'care, vilgilance and criticism.' But, as Nathan Brett (1981) argues, Ryle's distinction cannot be sustained, since exercises of habits can also have these features.

Though perhaps only on the fringes of analytic philosophy, Ludwig Wittgenstein's *Philosophical Investigations* (2001) contains some important support for the distinctiveness of habitual action. His investigation into linguistic meaning led him to diagnose various misconceptions of what it means to 'follow a rule.' What is at stake is the very idea of using a word or symbol correctly, as opposed to incorrectly. According to John McDowell's analysis (1998: 242), our sense of what is right cannot be determined by something else (such as a reason for doing it this way), since our enquiry requires us to ask: what makes *that* determination 'right'? But neither do we want to reduce the phenomenon to mere mechanical operations, which would not be subject to judgments of correctness at all.

The solution Wittgenstein proposes is that to follow a rule is a 'custom' (2001, § 199), though 'habit' would also be a permissible translation. Wittgenstein's central point is that what underlies our judgments of correctness is essentially unguided, yet established, ways of acting. Exercises of habits are such actions. If this is right, it would be particularly unfortunate for a philosophy of action to have no access to, or interest in, such actions.

In contrast to habit's rather modest influence on the analytic tradition, the notion plays an important role for a number of continental philosophers. Reflecting on his own early work, Gilles Deleuze writes of Hume that '[t]here is no more striking an answer to the problem of the Self' than that 'we are habits, nothing but habits' (1991: x) – a view which he adopts in his own philosophy. In *Phenomenology of Perception*, Maurice Merleau-Ponty uses the notion of habit as the central concept for undermining traditional dualisms such as those between active and passive, mind and body, subject and world. He emphasizes the sense in which habits both represent a form of intelligence and are essentially embodied; a 'knowledge in the hands' (2002: 144). Like Dewey and Deleuze, he emphasizes the identity between one's habits and one's self (see Carlisle 2006). It may be that all of these writers were influenced by the earlier work of Félix Ravaisson (2008), whose 1838 essay *Of Habit* was itself inspired by Aristotle.

Analyzing Habit

What, then, is a habit? Here I give some suggestions concerning the features any account of habit might profitably capture.

First, any account will have to acknowledge that a habit is acquired through the repetition of a certain kind of action in certain characteristic circumstances, and perhaps also with the involvement of various kinds of equipment, as in learning an instrument or sport. It is a conceptual truth that, if you have a habit of doing something, you have done the thing repeatedly before. This separates habits from the sorts of dispositions philosophers routinely discuss, such as fragility, which need not have been manifested.

Second, an account will have to capture the change of state in the organism. The agent becomes 'habituated' to the pattern of behavior that she has performed before. Of course, there are no guarantees that any particular set of repetitions will establish habituation for a given agent. Acquiring some habits will take more practice than others. And some people will pick up a given habit through fewer repetitions than others. Some people may never acquire a habit, no matter how many times they repeat the same action.

How, then, should we characterize the change? It appears to have both active and passive aspects (see Butler 1843: 72–73; Ravaisson 2008: 37):

1 The intellect is required less and less for the successful performance of the repeated actions and, once habituation is complete, will not be required at all. No deliberation, decision, choice or monitoring need take place. We develop a 'disposition' or 'tendency' to do the same sort of thing again. The mere encounter with the sorts of circumstances in which (and presence of the sorts of objects with which) the habit was learned is sufficient to initiate and sustain the exercise of the habit. Our actions become spontaneous reactions to the way the world is.
2 The awareness the agent may have had of sensations which accompanied the actions at the acquisition stage fade, so the agent's awareness of performing the action diminishes. Once habituation is complete, the awareness of the sensations may be absent altogether. This 'dulling' effect of repetition is the familiar process of becoming 'accustomed,' or 'used' to things we regularly encounter. We stop noticing the things we are most familiar with.

What is striking about the above two features of habituation is the inseparability of active from passive aspects. If one attempts to isolate the active aspect, the passivity of a habit becomes evident. The habituated agent is passive both in the sense that the habit is only exercised if the world is a certain way; and also in the sense that the way she responds is determined by actions over which she no longer has any control, namely actions in the past. (These senses are in addition to the sense in which an agent is passive in all actions, in addition to any resistance that the world, or the agent's body, offers in performing it).

Conversely, the dulling effect is also inseparable from the agent's active involvement with the objects in question. First, it is only by repeated engagement with these objects that the dulling of the senses takes place. And it is only when we actively engage in the habitual way with the object that the dulling is evident. We could engage with the same object in a novel way, and there would be no dulling.

The following additional features of habituation have been noted, which may be thought to be more or less important:

3 During habituation the actions become more fluent or 'natural' for the agent (James 1890: 112). As the body becomes familiar with the changes associated with the action, accuracy and dexterity improve. This change in the *way* the actions are performed does not seem adequately captured by saying merely that the intellect is not required. Rather we should say that the intellect is necessarily absent. This is illustrated when one starts to think about the movements involved in walking as one walks. Walking becomes difficult, hesitant and stilted.
4 Whilst habituation involves a dulling of our awareness of some things, it may also *enhance* our awareness of other things. Following habituation, one can make more sensitive discriminations among the circumstances and objects that characteristically go with the habit in question. We achieve an enhanced awareness of what is unusual, or perhaps unique, about the present situation. Most obviously, one is immediately sensitive to factors which make the usual exercise of the habit difficult

or impossible. Less obviously, we become more sensitive to subtle differences in what we are engaging with and adjust to these differences, as the guitarist adjusts his hands to the shape of a new guitar.

5 It has also been suggested (Carlisle 2006: 27) that, once a habit has been acquired, the agent becomes attached to the people, places, and objects which give her the opportunity to exercise her habits. We miss them when they are gone. The exercise of habits therefore becomes a source of comfort and brings with it a sense of belonging and a feeling of being 'at home.' Accordingly, we may seek opportunities to be in these places and among these things and people: one's usual 'habitat.' In this way the acquisition of a habit can be said to change profoundly the agent's motivations.

Third, any account of habit will have to do justice to the fact that the deliberative will has at least some degree of control over it. The agent can, for instance, choose whether to exercise the initial actions which may become a habit; whether to cultivate a habit deliberately, by repeating certain action; whether to inhibit or modify particular exercises of habits (a capacity I have called 'intervention control,' Pollard 2003); and whether to adopt strategies to break habits.

Fourth, in order to do justice to the sense in which exercises of habits are actions, any account will need to spell out the relationship between habit and agent. Does the agent, for instance, have a role only indirectly, by instigating the initial actions, and thereafter by failing to inhibit them once the habit is acquired? Or is there a more direct relation, in the sense suggested by Dewey and Merleau-Ponty, according to whom the agent is constituted (either partly or wholly) by her habits? In the former case, one may make do with a conception of agency which is based on the intellect, but the challenge would be to show how habits amount to more than trained reflexes. In the latter case, a more radical conception of agency is required, according to which the agent is at least partly constituted by her habits, and is thus extended in time and situated in a specific environment in just the way each of her habits are. In becoming habituated, she makes the actions her own; in an important sense, she can do them *authentically*.

Philosophy of Habit: Benefits and Challenges

There are many potential benefits of a philosophy of action that is habit-friendly. It allows us to understand better the interdependence between activity and passivity. It promises to relieve us of traditional dualisms. It invites us to reconsider the very notion of agency. Also – a topic hardly touched upon in this chapter – an understanding of human action as habitual may have important implications for moral and political philosophy.

Notable for contemporary debate is the role habit can play in the project of 'naturalizing' human action and the mind in general. In Pollard (2005) I explore how a proper understanding of habit can strengthen John McDowell's (1996) naturalistic project. According McDowell, our acquired second nature consists in 'habits of thought and action' (p. 84). Obviously, considerable work needs to be done to give some content to the notion of a 'habit of thought.' This opens the intriguing possibility that not just action, but thought itself can be thought of as habitual.

There are other challenges. First, what is the role of habit in the explanation of action? Explanations through habit such as 'He did it because it was his habit' or 'through force of habit' are not, on the face of it, stating the reason 'for which' the agent does something. Indeed one might explain an action in this way precisely to contrast it with an action that was done for one of the agent's reasons. Habit explanations do, however, seem to state what philosophers call 'reasons why' (Dancy 2000: 5–6). The question would then be how habit explanations explain actions. I have argued that such explanations are not causal, teleological, or psychological, but rather *constitutive* (Pollard 2006). When we explain an action in terms of a habit, we are fitting that action into a broader pattern of actions, of which the action in question is a constitutive part. This is not to say that teleological or causal explanations cannot also be given of the same habitual action. If this is right, it illustrates, again, the distinctiveness of habitual actions.

A related challenge is to show how habitual actions can be said to be 'rational.' As stated above, habitual actions are not rational in the sense that they are done 'for' something or 'in the light of reasons,' at least not if that means the considerations before the agent at the time of action. It is of the essence of habitual action that there is no consideration. Rather, habitual actions are performed, as we might say, 'in the *dark* of reasons' (Pollard 2008: 124). But this is not to say that they are incorrect, or indeed completely independent of the intellect. The habitual action may be an exercise of a good habit in an appropriate context. And it may be that, for the well brought-up and suitably self-critical agent, whose habits represent what she would choose to do anyway, many of her habitual actions can be said to be rational. The rationality here is not to be understood as the content of (possibly unconscious) deliberation, but as what the agent would have chosen had she deliberated, and this is shown in the agent's capacity to give reasons for her action, were she required to (Pollard 2003: 424). Clearly not all habitual actions would qualify as rational in this sense.

There seems to be little doubt that at least some of our agency is habitual. Perhaps indeed that is our better perfected or more authentic part. But it can't be denied either that some of our agency also proceeds from operations of the intellect; from deliberation, creativity, imagination, and free choice. Perhaps the greatest challenge for a philosophy of habit, then, is to spell out how these intellectual operations can themselves be seen as habitual. If that could be done, we would be able to call ourselves, in the fullest sense, creatures of habit.

See also: INTENTION (14); TELEOLOGICAL EXPLANATION (16); REASONS AND CAUSES (17); ARISTOTLE (54); HUME (63); RYLE (69); ANSCOMBE (74).

References

Aristotle (2004). *The Nicomachean Ethics*, translated by J. A. K. Thompson. London: Penguin.
Anscombe, G. E. M. (1957). *Intention*. Oxford: Basil Blackwell.
Brett, N. (1981). Human habits. *Canadian Journal of Philosophy*, 11, 357–376.

Butler, J. (1843). *The Analogy of Religion, Natural and Revealed, to the Constitution and Course of Nature* [1736]. New York: Dayton and Newman.

Carlisle, C. (2006). Creatures of habit: The problem and the practice of liberation. *Continental Philosophy Review*, 38, 19–39.

Dancy, J. (2000). *Practical Reality*. Oxford: Oxford University Press.

Davidson, D. (1980). Actions, reasons, and causes [1963]. In D. Davidson, *Essays on Actions and Events*. Oxford: Oxford University Press, 3–39.

Deleuze, G. (1991). *Empiricism and Subjectivity*, translated by C. V. Boundas. New York and Chichester: Columbia University Press.

Dewey, J. (1922). *Human Nature and Conduct*. New York: Henry Holt and Co.

Hume, D. (1975). *Enquiries Concerning Human Understanding and Concerning the Principles of Morals* [1777]. Oxford and New York: Oxford University Press.

James, W. (1890). *The Principles of Psychology*, Vol 1. New York: Henry Holt and Co.

Merleau-Ponty, M. (2002). *Phenomenology of Perception* [1945]. London and New York: Routledge.

McDowell, J. (1996). *Mind and World*. Harvard: Harvard University Press.

McDowell, J. (1998). *Wittgenstein on Following a Rule*. In J. McDowell, *Mind, Value, and Reality*. Cambridge, MA and London: Harvard University Press, 221–262.

Peirce, C. S. (1877). The fixation of belief. *Popular Science Monthly*, 12, 1–15.

Pollard, B. (2003). Can virtuous actions be both habitual and rational? *Ethical Theory and Moral Practice*, 6, 411–425.

Pollard, B. (2005). Naturalizing the space of reasons. *International Journal of Philosophical Studies*, 13, 69–82.

Pollard, B. (2006). Explaining actions with habits. *American Philosophical Quarterly*, 43, 57–68.

Pollard, B. (2008). *Habits in Action*. Saarbrücken: Verlag Dr Müller.

Ravaisson, F. (2008). *Of Habit* [1838], translated by C. Carlisle and M. Sinclair. London and New York: Continuum.

Ryle, G. (1949). *The Concept of Mind*. Harmondsworth: Penguin.

Wittgenstein, L. (2001). *Philosophical Investigations* [1953], translated by G. E. M. Anscombe. Oxford and Malden: Blackwell.

11

Cambridge Actions

DAVID-HILLEL RUBEN

Token action *a* = token action *b* iff. ... Well, iff what? An agent, *X*, bends his finger, pulls the trigger, shoots the gun, kills the Queen, and thereby reduces the world's population by one. *X* did each action on the list by doing its predecessor (if it has one). How many things did the person do?

The alternative theories that attempt to answer this question are well known. The most austere theory says that *X* did only one thing, and that what the list above provides are five different descriptions of one token action. Actions are, on austere theory, a moving of the body, variously described.

The most prolific theory says that, in the list above, *X* performed five different actions. Each action description on the list is a description of an action different from the action any other description on the list describes. A prolific theorist finds the plurality in the action, not in the description.

Both the austere and prolific theories are thought to have numerous counterintuitive consequences, but let's focus only on those having to do with the times (and, to less extent, the locations) of action that arise on the prolific theory. I shoot the Queen in London at *t*. Imagine that the Queen dies in Balmoral six months after I shoot her, at *t* + six months; poor dear, she lingers that length of time in her country estate before expiring.

The time argument against the prolific theory is this: if my killing of the Queen ≠ my bending of my finger, then the finger bending occurs at *t*, but the killing presumably occurs only when she died, namely at *t* + 6 months. What proponents of the time argument against the prolific theory almost invariably say is that, if prolific theory were true, the agent's action may commence or continue even after the agent dies. Suppose that I bend my finger at *t*, the Queen dies at *t* + six months, and I die at *t* + three months (no doubt from finger strain induced by all that finger bending). I will have killed her *after* I have died.

What is the location argument against the prolific theorist? Presumably, if my killing ≠ my finger bending, and *if* my killing of her is to have any location at all, then my killing should be placed wherever the Queen died rather than where I bent my finger, namely in Balmoral. But I may have never been north of the border, and how, it might be asked, could I have acted at a location where I may never have been? On prolific theory, I could have killed the Queen in some *p* and at some *t* in and at which I no longer exist or have never been. How serious an objection is this to prolific theory?

Peter Geach has introduced into the literature a distinction between real change and Cambridge change (1981, 318–323; 1969, 66–67, 70–73, 98–99). A real change is a change as ordinarily and intuitively understood. The change in a schoolchild if he comes to admire someone he did not admire before, the change in a woman when she gives birth to a sixth child, the change in an object when its color changes, are all real changes.

Real changes pair in some way with Cambridge changes: the change in Socrates every time a fresh schoolchild comes to admire him, the change in the number six each time it becomes or ceases to be the number of someone's children,[1] the change in Adam and Eve each time they acquire a new descendant. Socrates' death and the birth of my eldest daughter are real changes; Xantippe's widowing, the change in the number six, and Adam and Eve's descendant gain are only Cambridge events. What makes them 'Cambridge'? In some sense yet to be adumbrated, they are not 'real' changes at all. They merely shadow real changes.

Cambridge event pairs break down into at least two different types. (The reader interested in my somewhat fuller account of Cambridge change should see Ruben 1988.) The first type includes cases like admiring and being admired by, becoming taller than and becoming shorter than, and eulogizing and being eulogized by. In the case in which Chirac eulogizes Napoleon and Napoleon is eulogized by Chirac, there is but a single token event or change. Let's say that the schoolchild's coming to admire Socrates and Socrates' coming to be admired by the schoolchild, for instance, or Chirac's eulogizing Napoleon and Napoleon being eulogized by Chirac, provide an 'active–passive' pair of event descriptions, both of which refer to a single token event, where the descriptions are related by a simple grammatical transformation between the active and the passive voice. Also included in this first type are cases in which the event descriptions are related by a straightforward semantic relation, like that between 'x becoming taller than y' and 'y becoming shorter than x.'

In this sense, 'Cambridge' or 'real' do not denote two kinds of events or states, but rather refer to two different senses in which the multiple subjects of a single relational event may change. Is the event itself Cambridge or real? This is an ill-formed question as it stands. Concerning a single event with two (or more) subjects of change, one subject may change really and the other may change only in a Cambridge fashion. Strictly speaking, the event itself is neither real nor Cambridge.

Still, we can apply the Cambridge–real distinction even to these changes, in a somewhat derivative way. We tend to think of a change as categorized by what happens to the positionally first grammatical subject of the change. So we can say, if we wish, that Socrates' coming to be admired by a fresh schoolchild is a Cambridge change, but we only mean thereby that the change in Socrates is a Cambridge one. On the other hand, if we describe the *same* token change as the fresh schoolchild coming to admire Socrates, we could call it a real change, meaning thereby that the change in the schoolchild is real. I will use the terms 'Cambridge' and 'real' in this derivative sense, as well in the non-derivative sense which I explain below; but it is crucial to remember what these terms mean in the case of active–passive pairs.

What about the other type of example? In the cases above, there is but one token event under discussion, described in two different ways, actively and a passively. But other real–Cambridge event pairs, unlike the cases of eulogizing and admiring, do not follow this active–passive model and seem, indeed in my view are, pairs of different events: Socrates' death and Xantippe's becoming a widow; the birth of my daughter in 1972 and Adam and Eve's acquisition of an *n*-th remote descendant. In these cases, I think, we have two non-identical changes, although they are not distinct either. There is some sort of close conceptual relation between the death of a person and the widowing of his spouse, even if that relation is not one of identity.

Assuming that, in these cases, the partner changes are *not* numerically identical, the real–Cambridge distinction applies to the two changes or events themselves, and not just to the change or event which is numerically the same, as it differentially involves the two subjects. Socrates' death and the birth of my eldest daughter are real changes; Xantippe's widowing and Adam and Eve's descendant gain are different from (not identical to) the former, but they are only Cambridge events. In these cases, although the Cambridge change is always relational, the real change need not be. Socrates' death is not a relational change. Assuming that relations are not essential to events, the very same death could have occurred in a universe in which nothing else changed, indeed his death could occur in a universe which only contained Socrates. The widowing of Xantippe is relational. In any universe in which her widowing occurs, someone else must die.

No event that happens only to Socrates (namely his death) could be identical to an event that happens both to Xantippe and to Socrates (namely, her becoming his widow), and no event that happens to my daughter and her mother (Anna's birth) could be identical to an event that befalls both Anna and the pair Adam and Eve (their gaining her as their latest remote descendant), no matter how intimately or even logically related the latter event might be to the former. Finally, there are important asymmetries: Xantippe became a widow through Socrates' death, and not conversely; Adam and Eve gained a new remote descendant through my daughter's birth, and not conversely.

Geach, as far as I am aware, never offered an account of this difference between real and Cambridge changes. I think that the basic idea is that, in terms of their dependence on one another, there is somehow an asymmetry between what changes really and what changes in a Cambridge fashion. In some sense, the latter depends on the former in a way in which the former does not depend on the latter.

Adam and Eve Cambridge changed in 1972 by obtaining another remote descendant – and, if anywhere, in Glasgow, where and when my eldest daughter was born. This is so despite the fact that Adam and Eve died almost 4,840 or so years ago, somewhere far to the east of Glasgow. Xantippe became a widow in an Athenian prison, which is where and when Socrates died, in spite of her never having been to prison or even having visited one herself. The correct placing and dating of the Cambridge event is taken from the placing and dating of the partner real event, or the partner real changer.

Adam and Eve procreated, which involved them undergoing some real changes, about 5,770 years ago, just outside the Garden of Eden (they were quick off the mark), and that act of procreating is on a causal line that leads all the way to my eldest daughter's birth in 1972. The change, the new remote descendant gaining they undergo now, is a Cambridge event, dated and placed where they no longer exist, but when and where my eldest daughter was born.

So too for Socrates and his good lady. He drank some hemlock at *t* in *p*, one room in an Athenian prison, and that, for the purpose of this example, was the initiating event. At *t′*, he died in *p′*, a different room of that prison, as a causal consequence of that drinking. Place *p′* and time *t′* are where, if anywhere, and when, Xantippe became a widow. The dating and locating (if such there be) of Cambridge changes are tied to the date and location of the partner real change – the death of Socrates, or the birth of my daughter – not to any temporal or spatial features of the Cambridge changer.

Further, the Cambridge event is certainly not dated and placed by the grounding or initiating event. That is, no one would date or place Adam and Eve's remote descendant gain by the dating and placing of their 'grounding' act of procreation, so long ago, rather than by my eldest daughter's birth. So too, no one would, or should, date or place Xantippe's widowing by using the date and place of Socrates' drinking hemlock earlier in that other room, in *p* at *t*, rather than by locating his death at *t′* in room *p′*.

Let's return the discussion specifically to actions. The same account as I gave above for events holds for actions, I think. Indeed, it would be surprising if there could be Cambridge changes or Cambridge events, but no Cambridge actions. If we distinguish between 'real' and 'Cambridge' specifically for acts, then it must be true that agents can act – that is, Cambridge act – after they cease to exist and at locations they have never occupied.

Reconsider in this light my action of killing of the Queen. There is my earlier bending of my finger (compare the initiating or grounding events: Adam and Eve's procreating; Socrates' drinking hemlock). There is also a subsequent pair of 'partner' changes: the Queen's death and my killing of the Queen.

The Queen's death, a real event, is a causal consequence of my finger bending (compare the birth of my daughter and the death of Socrates, as causal consequences of Adam and Eve's act of procreation and of Socrates' drinking hemlock, respectively). And there is the Cambridge change, an action in this case, namely my killing of the Queen (compare Adam and Eve's gaining another remote descendant and Xantippe's becoming a widow). In the cases above, the partners were non-actional events (Socrates' death and Xantippe's widowing; my eldest daughter's birth and Adam and Eve's gain); of these new partners, only one is a non-actional event, whereas the other is an action.

So there are three 'elements' to consider in this last case, as well as in the earlier ones:

1 the initiating or grounding act: my finger bending, which is a real act of mine, dated (let's say) at *t* and placed in *p*;
2 the action: my killing of the Queen, which is relational – it relates me to the Queen. The act presupposes a change in me and a change in the Queen (the Queen's being killed by me). Of course this is a single change, but it occurs both in me and in her. My killing of her = her being killed by me, but I refer to my killing of her as a Cambridge act, in the derivative sense of that term; finally,
3 there is the Queen's death at *t′* in *p′*.

What really happens at t'? It is the Queen who really changes at t' (by dying). But when do I kill her? I kill her at t', when she dies, not at t, when I bend my finger. I merely Cambridge change when I kill her. If I am dead when the Queen dies, it is clear that the change, my killing of the Queen, can be only Cambridge. But, even if I am alive, my body may by then have stopped moving in any way relevant to her death (at least my finger bending will be six months in the past).

My killing of the Queen, (2) above, takes its temporal and spatial locations from the Queen's death, (3), just as Adam and Eve's gaining another remote descendant took its date from its 'partner' real event, my eldest daughter's birth, and not from their own much earlier act of procreation; and similarly for the Socrates–Xantippe case. So, as in the case of Adam and Eve, my killing of the Queen is to be dated when its partner real change occurs, that is, at t', when the Queen dies, and (if it has a location at all) at the place where its partner real change occurs, at Balmoral. My killing of the Queen acquires the place and date of my finger bending, (1), no more than Xantippe's widowing, or Adam and Eve's gaining an *n*-th remote descendant, get placed and dated by Socrates' drinking hemlock, or by Adam and Eve's act of procreation. These Cambridge actions, like Cambridge changes generally, do not take the spatial and temporal locations of their initiating events. On the contrary, they are placed in space and in time (if they are temporally placed at all) through the spatial and temporal positions of their real partners.

On the view that recognizes Cambridge actions, my killing of the Queen ≠ my bending of my finger, since my bending of my finger, the initiating event, occurs six months earlier, in London. My killing of the Queen is a Cambridge action, placed and dated by her death. Although my action, my killing of the Queen, is not identical to my bending of my finger, yet it is only a Cambridge action, because it attributes only a Cambridge change to me.

In the case of non-actional events, we have no difficulty in saying that the change in one of the relata is merely a Cambridge change for that relatum. So the remarks I made about Adam and Eve gaining a new remote descendant seem right. Why might we be more reluctant to say, in the case of actions such as my killing of the Queen, that the Cambridge change, the killing, is in the actor, whereas the real change, the dying, is in the patient, the Queen?

Perhaps this is because we tend, albeit wrongly, to associate the idea of effort with our idea of action. How can Cambridge action be any sort of action, since, as Bennett pointed out, the agent expends no effort additional to the effort expended in the bona fide act – say, in his pulling of the trigger? (Bennett 1973: 315–323). To that extent, the observation is simply correct: there is action without additional effort: 'the rest is up to nature.' When I Cambridge act, what my action is no longer depends on my effort, but on whether the Queen dies, for example. I act, yet without exercising any more effort beyond what I did when I bent my finger (see chapter 2).

What about my shooting of the gun? Since all the arguments about the dating and locating of the Queen's death apply *mutatis mutandis* to the gun's going off, the real change is in the gun, the Cambridge change in me. So my shooting of the gun occurs at the time that the gun undergoes a change, and, since this time is not identical to the time at which my finger bent, the bending of my finger ≠ my shooting of the gun. My shooting of the gun, like my killing of the Queen, is one of my Cambridge actions. The dating of my shooting the gun is taken from where and when the gun goes off. Most, but perhaps not all, of my non-basic physical actions are Cambridge actions.

Suppose a time switch that creates a longer delay than normal between an agent's switch-flipping and the light's going on. X flipped the switch at *t*. The light went on at *t′*, some time later. When did X turn on the light? Not, I think, at *t*, for the reasons already given: a person can't have turned on the light before the light went on. He turned on the light when the light went on. It may indeed, at first, sound unnatural ('incorrect') to say that he flipped the switch and *then* (later) turned on the light, but so too does saying that he turned on the light before the light went on.

The longer the time delay, the less unnatural it sounds in any case. He flips the switch at *t*, and the valley floods hours later. He did not flood the valley at *t*, when he flipped the switch. Of course, he did something at *t* that lead to the flooding. And he certainly flooded the valley by flipping the switch, but he flooded it after *t*, after he flipped the switch.

When it does sound unnatural to say that a person A-ed and *then* B-ed, I think one can explain the unnaturalness of the expression – while accepting its literal truth – in terms of remarks I made above: 'I act yet without exercising any more effort beyond what I did when I bent my finger.' There are of course genuine cases of actions related in a series in which extra effort is required: a person walks to Balmoral, shoots the Queen, climbs into his waiting get-away car, and then drives away. In this case there are, on everyone's view, four actions: the walking, the shooting, the climbing, and the driving. The four actions might be part of an agent's overall action plan. Each one is later in time than its predecessor(s) and requires additional effort on the agent's part. In cases like this, 'later in time' and 'more effort required' go together.

In the different case of the flipping of the switch and turning on of the light, it is literally true that the second action is dated later than the first. But the later-in-time-thus-more-effort nexus is broken. In cases like the flipping and the turning on, saying 'later' may sound wrong, since so saying often carries the pragmatic or informal implication that more effort is required by the agent to turn on the lights, in addition to what he expended in flipping the switch; and this, of course, is not so in the case we are considering. This informal or conversational (as it is sometimes called) implication is no part of the semantics of 'he A-ed, and then he B-ed,' but saying 'he flipped the switch and then he turned on the lights' can lead to a conflation of that case with the walking–shooting–climbing–driving case.

As long as there is a finite time interval (or locational difference), however small, between the bending of my finger and the event associated with any action I do through the bending of my finger (like the shooting of the gun or the killing of the Queen), the same argument will apply. What about my reducing the world's population by one? As far as I can see, I reduced the world's population by one exactly when I killed the Queen and at the same place, if anywhere. If events e_1 and e_2, or actions a_1 and a_2, occur at different times or different places or occur to (or are done by) different subjects, then they cannot be numerically identical. But the Cambridge theory can remain neutral about the so-called Goldman–Kim view that, if e_1 and e_2 exemplify different properties, then $e_1 \neq e_2$ (see for example Goldman 1970, ch. 1).

My own intuitions tell me that my reduction of the world's population by one = my killing of the Queen, but nothing in the Cambridge theory, concentrating as it does on times, places, and subjects, would force it to take a stand on this one way or another.

So the Cambridge account is neutral on the question of the identity of actions performed at the same time and in the same place by the same agent, like my bending of my finger and my giving a signal by so doing, or my saying 'I promise' and my promising by so doing, or my bending of my finger (when it is as a matter of fact the left index finger that I bend) and my bending of my left index finger. Where there is a series of action descriptions which run from the very general to the very specific, the descriptions in the series may refer to one and the same action, as far as the Cambridge theory goes. So a Cambridge theory may be a prolific theory, but it need not be a most prolific theory.

What of (what seems to be) my basic action, my bending of my finger? Could this action involve a real change to only one relatum and a mere Cambridge change to another, as in the case of my killing of the Queen? I do not think that cases of basic action could be construed in this way. The change in my (attached) finger is real. What other change could there be, Cambridge or otherwise, in me, as opposed to a change in my attached finger? Presumably the bending of my finger just is the relevant change in me. I am not distinct from my attached finger; the change in my finger just is a change in me. There is no real change and Cambridge change, or even two real changes. There is only one change in this case, a real one: my bending of my finger.

Like austere theory, the Cambridge change theory has the resources to limit real (in other words, non-Cambridge) physical actions to the movements of one's body. Like prolific theory, it holds that actions like an agent's shooting of the Queen are non-identical to basic actions like his bending of his finger. However, such non-basic physical actions as the theory licenses are not real actions, only Cambridge ones, because the actors or agents in such cases only Cambridge change. The challenge launched by the austere theorist to the prolific theorist was for the latter to account for the fact that, on prolific theory, I may be credited with acting at a place where I am not, and even after I die (or at least I stop moving my body in any relevant way). The prolific theorist's reply is that these are my Cambridge actions, since they presuppose only Cambridge changes in the actor.

See also: ACTION THEORY AND ONTOLOGY (1); BASIC ACTIONS AND INDIVIDUATION (2); BODILY MOVEMENTS (4); REFRAINING, OMITTING, AND NEGATIVE ACTS (7); COLLECTIVE ACTION (9).

Note

1 For Cambridge changes in numbers, see Dummett 1973, ch. 14, 'Abstract objects.'

References

Bennett, J. (1973). Shooting, killing, and dying. *Canadian Journal of Philosophy*, 2, 315–323.
Dummet, M. (1973). *Frege: Philosophy of Language*. London: Duckworth.

Geach, P. (1969). *God and the Soul*. London: Routledge and Kegan Paul.

Geach, P. (1981). *Logic Matters*. Oxford: Basil Blackwell.

Goldman, A. (1970). *A Theory of Human Action*. Princeton: Princeton University Press.

Ruben, D.-H. (1988). A puzzle about posthumous predication. *Philosophical Review*, 97, 211–236.

12

Pluralism about Action

ELIJAH MILLGRAM

Action theory has traditionally addressed itself in the first place to the question of what, metaphysically, an action is. Millgram (2005b) surveys some representative answers from recent moral philosophy, and I will take up the content of that question in due course. But we can already identify one assumption visibly made throughout the enterprise: that there is *one* kind of thing that action is. The standard philosophical payoffs of an account of action require the correctness of that assumption. Constitutivist arguments move from the premises that anything you do will inevitably be an action, and that an action is such-and-such, to the conclusion that whatever you do will be such-and-such. And it is arguments of this form that have motivated much of the work in the field. (See Enoch 2006 and Ferrero 2009 for some back and forth on the merits of constitutivist arguments.)

Actions are what agents do, and products of human activity often do not end up being one kind of thing: for instance, there is no one basic structure that chairs share, because people make chairs with very different structures (Fiell and Fiell 1997). Games are what people play, but the apparent logical tightness of that connection does not lend itself to constitutivist argumentation: as Wittgenstein (1998, §§ 66–70) famously pointed out, there are no features that all games share, and so, even if people necessarily play only games, because there are no substantive and true claims to the effect that games are such-and-such, you cannot argue successfully that, if one is a player, one inevitably engages in activities that are such-and-such. Likewise, if 'action' (or 'agent,' the other side of the conceptual coin) is a family resemblance concept, or even if there are several discrete metaphysical types of action, constitutivist arguments will fail – in which case much recent action theory will not deliver its intended payoffs. I will now review an emerging body of work which, in different ways, argues for pluralism about action.

Recent Work on Pluralism

In the so-called Canberra Plan, the object of metaphysics is to elicit the implicit folk theory of one or another domain of interest (Jackson 1998). One way (not the only way) of positioning the emerging sub-field of experimental philosophy treats it as generating empirical inputs to reconstructions of folk theory. For instance, Knobe (2003) suggests, on the basis of pencil-and-paper surveys, that the ascription of intentional action is sensitive to the valences of the outcomes: when you are uninterested in the foreseen consequences and the outcome is bad, it was something you did, whereas, if the outcome was fine, it was just something that happened. (See also Vogler 2008 for a point of entry into a much older tradition that attempts to make sense of this and related phenomena.) On the Canberra Plan approach to action theory, this sort of valence sensitivity is thus a feature of folk action theory. Now, Nichols and Ulatowski (2007) argue that, when you look at the patterns of minority responses in the surveys, the apparently startling asymmetry in the folk concept of intentional action turns out to be a misreading of interpretive diversity within a population; there are two diverging understandings of intentional action (one tying the ascription of action to motives, the other tying it to foreknowledge of outcomes). If this is correct, and if it is representative of future results, then '*the* folk theory of action' is a failed definite description: there is no *one* folk theory of action, in roughly the way there is no *one* folk tale of Little Red Riding Hood.

Not all of the metaphysics of action is an attempt to reconstruct folk theory. Of the models of action in play in the philosophical literature, Lelanuja (in progress) argues that many of them fit different sorts of action with varying degrees of success. She suggests that it is natural to tie much of the effect to the metaphorical size of the actions in question; a metaphysical account of action should not assume scale invariance. For instance, Vogler (2002) advances a view on which actions exhibit stepwise progress towards a termination point or 'end.' That model is a good fit for an action such as baking a cake: the completed cake is the finish line, and, when the cake comes out of the oven, the action is complete. However, when some (not all) actions become sufficiently 'large,' the would-be finish line itself has breadth. Suppose (the example is due to Sarah Buss) you are considering a move to London. When is the move over? When you get off the plane? When you sign the lease on your new apartment? When you have settled into the neighborhood (and when is *that*)? When you have found a permanent job? There is no unique and non-arbitrary answer, and so there is no crisp termination point that can serve as a criterion for the selection of previous phases of the action. In fact, the problem is deeper yet: because moving to a new city often requires you to leave much of the shape of your life up in the air, you don't know up front whether you *will*, in the course of moving to London, rent an apartment, or purchase a house, or move into university housing; whether you will get a permanent job or a series of freelance assignments, or perhaps gradually become one of the not-quite-employed … and so it is not just that choosing a crisp finish line out of the fixed menu of them would be arbitrary. You can't know *which* of the possible crisp finish lines is likely to be relevant until you are well along, and so you cannot realistically use any of them as a selection tool when you are choosing 'means' to your 'end.' (For a survey of literature on the problem of incompletely specified ends, see Millgram 2008.)

Here is a second example of the point Lelanuja is pressing. Recent Kantian accounts take the blueprint of an action to be a 'maxim'; a maxim designates generally framed trigger conditions and an objective to be attained by executing the action, along with a core characterization of the action itself (Nell 1975; see also Millgram 2005a: 90–91 for a summary). This control structure is held to be a precondition for attributing the action to the agent, and attributability further depends on the action's ties to organizational features of the agent that have the role within the agent of the constitution of a political state (Korsgaard 1999).

However, when the actions once again get 'large' enough, deviations from the pattern become apparent. We have recently seen a spate of non-state political actors making what seems to be the strategic choice (or meta-choice) not to conform to the Korsgaardian model of agency. Not only do these non-state actors resist constituting themselves into organized agents with a Korsgaardian constitution, they also generate actions which are not performed on the basis of well-defined and repeatable trigger conditions and which are not matched with well-defined and achievable objectives. The choice of this sort of quasi-agency has various rationales: well-organized agents can be effectively pressured, whereas these half-coalesced agents cannot be; the complications involved in attributing actions to the agents provide plausible deniability; the lack of well-defined trigger conditions make such an agent's actions harder to predict and preempt. These large-scale agents – or quasi-agents – are a bad fit for the Kantian model of actors and actions: so bad that a typical response to the picture I have been sketching is to deny that these activities count as actions at all. (And, generally, a response with which pluralism about action has to cope is the insistence that putative actions which do not fit one or another favored model are merely borderline or failed actions.) Briefly, Lelanuja's view suggests that the different theories of action in play are best construed not as competing accounts of the entire field of human action, but as suited to one or another range of it.

Bowman (in progress) relatedly argues that we embark on a great many long-term plans that – if we think about it for a moment – we fully expect to abandon long before completion; it is not just 5-year olds whom we do not seriously expect to grow up to be firemen. (*Pace* Harman 1976 and a large follow-on literature, we seem to intend to do a great many things that we believe we will not do.) Because we expect ourselves to drop such plans before we complete them, their point must not be attaining the official end of the course of action, but rather orientation in the here and now. For example, faculty know very well that the content of a dissertation often changes quite dramatically over the course of its execution, and a thoughtful student will understand this also; nevertheless, it is normal to insist on a fairly elaborately worked-out thesis prospectus. Or, again, we all know that what a faculty member has accomplished at the end of a fellowship year is likely to be quite different from what the applicant said he or she was going to do beforehand; that's what happens when you're doing real research. Still, it is good practice to require fellowship applicants to write an essay explaining what they are going to do with the time and money. Laying out such a plan for one's large-scale action frames the near-in actions that are the first stages of it, and so helps one select among them.

The Bowman-Lelanuja Thesis is an intriguing consequence of these two lines of argument: that the realism which it is reasonable to require of a plan of action is sensitive to scale. If you are actually going to bake the cake, it matters that the recipe is kitchen-tested and effective. But if you can already be pretty sure that your late-on career and retirement plans are going to be junked before you get to them, and if their real cognitive function is to serve as something like a self-image – a cognitive device which can be used to filter short-term options when they present themselves to you and to modulate their execution – then those plans need not be all that realistic in the first place. The thesis reinforces Bowman's suggestion that long-term and close-in courses of action are likely to be very different *kinds* of thing: the similar-seeming patterns that structure them are subject to functionally very different constraints, and thus the apparent similarity turns out to be mostly an illusion.

In short, we are seeing the beginnings of a wave of work in action theory pressing on the shared assumption we identified at the outset: action, it is being argued, comes in more than one metaphysical kind. Can we explain why that would be?

Action and Process Control

Action theory may be about what actions are, metaphysically, but what does that mean? The central competing accounts of action amount to different models of process control. Recall that Vogler's account treats actions as structured by a series of checkpoints on the way to a final stopping point: for Vogler, actions come in phases. On the closely related account in Thompson (2008, Part II), actions (always!) contain other, 'smaller' actions as their parts: an action consists of modules which are themselves actions. (For some discussion of the downward regress apparently implicit in Thompson's view, see Millgram 2009 § 9.4.) On another, still closely related account, the 'motivating reasons' that explain an action's actually being performed are anchored by the goal of the action, that is, by a desire, understood as a representation with a characteristic 'direction of fit' (Smith 1987). (This means: a representation such that, when there is a mismatch between the representation and the way the world is, what gets changed is the world, rather than the representation; the notion originates in Anscombe 1985, § 32.) On this account, actions are controlled by backward chaining from a specified target state. Finally for now, recall the Kantian notion that one acts on the basis of a maxim. Pairing generally specified trigger conditions with a core description of an action type makes actions out to be rule-driven activity. Since maxims also specify objectives, the Kantian picture of process control is one of both rule- and goal-governed activity.

Smith (1996: 72) describes recursion theory as a 'theory of the effective,' and suggests that it is our 'best candidate yet for a scientific theory of causation.' This seems to me to miss the mark, but not by too much: the computer programs that represent recursive functions in actual applications schematize the control structures of *actions* (rather than causation in general); it is not just accidental homonymy that functional units of code get called 'procedures.' So I want to introduce what I think will be a helpful analogy: between distinctive programming styles (along with the programming languages meant to enforce them), and the models of process control that distinguish competing accounts of action.

Return for a moment to Thompson's nesting model of action, on which actions are composed of further actions, which are in turn composed of still further actions ... That model is a useful way of thinking about action when the actions in question are neatly modularized, in something like the way subroutines are, say, in a highly structured language like Pascal. In a Pascal-like language, executing a subroutine is typically a matter of invoking further, separately defined subroutines; analogously, in Thompson's model, performing an action is matter of performing subsidiary actions.

The analogy is a useful reality check on such models. For instance, Thompson considers actions that can be decomposed into subsidiary actions in arbitrarily many ways. (His argument requires that all actions can be so decomposed.) Some actions evidently can be: when you roll a rock from point A to point B (his example), you can treat that as two actions, that of rolling the rock to a point C, in between A and B, and then rolling the rock from C to B; since it does not matter where C is, in an action like this one, any subsequence of the activity can be a subsidiary action. However, now that we have the programming analogy on board, it is obvious that this sort of arbitrary decomposition will be characteristic of outliers – that is, of actions that are not well modelled by the theory. The nested control structure is a good fit for actions that are assembled in roughly the way Pascal programs are. Most decomposable actions decompose cleanly because modularization is enforced in the design of the action, and they decompose, semi-uniquely, into the modules out of which they were assembled. When shampooing turns out to break down into lathering, rinsing, and repeating, that is because you are following the step-by-step instructions on the bottle.

If the programming analogy is a reason to think twice about whether a particular model of action is suitable for one application or another, it should also make us think twice as to whether we can treat any such model as a theory of (*all*) action. Sticking with the example, recall that the modularized programming typical of function-based languages was the product of something of a revolution in the field. (A program written in such a language is normally a function invoked on an argument; it is itself typically composed of further functions, invoked on further arguments.) Back in the 1950s and 1960s, programs were impossible-to-unravel tangles of GOTOs, appropriately called 'spaghetti code,' written in languages like Fortran or Cobol or in machine-specific assembly languages, none of which enforce clearly modularized coding. With the analogy before us, it is apparent that actions can also have that sort of flow of control as well. Not coincidentally, it's hard to gesture at clean examples, but the way I write my own papers often has this mode of organization (or lack thereof). Working on a sentence, I realize that the word I've chosen is too close to a word I've used earlier in the draft. Dropping what I'm doing, I go back to clean up the previous sentence. In the course of doing that, I realize that I have to make a choice about content; there's a distinction to draw, and I need to decide which side of it I'm going to come down on. This takes me to yet another paragraph in the paper ... and so the paper gets written (in a way that is very different from writing to outline, which really does typically conform to the stepwise and the modularized control models).

The point for now is that, just as structured programming was an achievement, so analogously structured action is evidently also an achievement. Because it is an achievement, it is not what actions turn out to be, willy-nilly. To the extent that the metaphysics of action has to do with the control structures that organize activity, the analogy makes it clear that our real question cannot be: What *are* actions (as a matter of metaphysical necessity)? And so we have identified a second assumption of most previous work in action theory: that the question of what actions are asks about what they *already* are, as a matter of standing fact.

It would be crazy for computer scientists to argue about what style of programming is metaphysically necessary (as though *it* were a matter of standing and immutable fact); I suggest that it is likewise an unpromising avenue of approach to their subject when philosophers argue over what control structures are metaphysically essential to actions (as though *that* were a matter of standing and immutable fact). The structure and composition of actions is evidently an engineering problem, one which can take various and novel solutions: the real question is not what actions *are*, but what sorts of control structures for action we can design and implement, with an eye to whatever benefits are to be had from them.

Is it clear, as I suggested a paragraph back, that there is no room for the traditional question of what an action is? Perhaps there are two levels at which treatments of action could be developed, and even if one of these turns out to be an engineering exercise, the other might still amount to traditional metaphysics. After all (the objection continues), if we did not have a metaphysical criterion for what actions are, how could we speculate about the different forms that their flow of control can take? And haven't we implicitly supplied a metaphysical analysis of action in the course of the discussion – namely that action is activity exhibiting this sort of process control? Argumentation at the presumed lower level might contest assumptions in the constitutivist argument we used to frame the debate: should we really conclude, from the fact that people perform actions, that actions are a product of human activity (in particular, that they are performances)? (Talbott Brewer and Carla Bagnoli have both pressed this objection in unpublished work.) Should constitutivists insist that actions *have* such-and-such features, or rather that the features in question are constitutive aims, which a defective action might not fully manage (as in Velleman 2000)?

Here the programming analogy continues to be a helpful guide. It used to be thought that, beneath the differing styles of programming, there was room for a theory of what computation really is, the most popular answer being given by the Turing-Church Thesis, on which computation is what Turing machines do. In retrospect (that is, now that there are live alternatives), Turing machines are themselves just another model of process control; it really *was* engineering all the way down, and we shouldn't expect action theory to turn out otherwise. The observation suggests two follow-up points. First, what the history of broadening out the available models of computation shows us is that 'process control' looks to be as much a family resemblance concept as 'action.' If that is right, the proposal that an action is activity plus process control is no more an essentialist analysis of action than 'games are what people play' is an essentialist analysis of games. Second, the questions we raised, as samples of debates that would be *prima facie* properly conducted as more traditional metaphysics, now seem much more like engineering problems. We could choose to generate actions as though they were exercises in performance art – or not. We could design actions with one constitutive aim (say, that of self-understanding, as in Velleman 2000), or with another – or actions controlled by no such objective at all.

If all this is right, we have on hand a very plausible candidate explanation for pluralism about action. Even if we have, by accident or tradition, always manufactured actions in one way, once we put our minds to it, we will certainly end up inventing many different sorts of action, actions that will be produced in many different ways. If action theory is really an engineering science (one that is closely related to industrial process control and to robotics), then pluralism is inevitable.

Acknowledgments

I am grateful to Chrisoula Andreou, Sarah Buss, Mariam Thalos, and Constantine Sandis for comments on an earlier draft.

See also: ACTION THEORY AND ONTOLOGY (1); BASIC ACTIONS AND INDIVIDUATION (2); TRYING TO ACT (3); BODILY MOVEMENTS (4); SPEECH ACTS (8); COLLECTIVE ACTION (9); HABITUAL ACTIONS (10); CAMBRIDGE ACTIONS (11); INTENTIONAL ACTION IN FOLK PSYCHOLOGY (45); INDIAN PHILOSOPHERS (52); WITTGENSTEIN (68); ANSCOMBE (74).

References

Anscombe, G. E. M. (1985). *Intention*, 2nd edn. Ithaca: Cornell University Press.
Bowman, M. (in progress). Are our goals really what we're after? PhD thesis, University of Utah.
Enoch, D. (2006). Agency, schmagency: Why normativity won't come from what is constitutive of action. *Philosophical Review*, 115 (2), 169–198.
Ferrero, L. (2009). Constitutivism and the inescapability of agency. *Oxford Studies in Metaethics*, 4, 303–333.
Fiell, C., and Fiell, P. (1997). *1000 Chairs*. Cologne: Benedikt Taschen Verlag.
Harman, G. (1976). Practical reasoning. *Review of Metaphysics*, 29 (3), 432–463.
Jackson, F. (1998). *From Metaphysics to Ethics*. Oxford: Oxford University Press.
Knobe, J. (2003). Intentional action and side effects in ordinary language. *Analysis*, 63, 190–194.
Korsgaard, C. (1999). Self-constitution in the ethics of Plato and Kant. *Journal of Ethics*, 3, 1–29.
Lelanuja, M. (in progress). The assumption of scale invariance. PhD thesis, University of Utah.
Millgram, E. (2005a). *Ethics Done Right: Practical Reasoning as a Foundation for Moral Theory*. Cambridge: Cambridge University Press.
Millgram, E. (2005b). Practical reason and the structure of action. In E. N. Zalta (ed.), *The Stanford Encyclopedia of Philosophy*. http://plato.stanford.edu/entries/practical-reason-action/.
Millgram, E. (2008). Specificationism. In J. Adler and L. Rips, (eds), *Reasoning*. Cambridge: Cambridge University Press, 731–747.
Millgram, E. (2009). *Hard Truths*. Oxford: Wiley-Blackwell.
Nell, O. (1975). *Acting on Principle*. New York: Columbia University Press.
Nichols, S., and Ulatowski, J. (2007). Intuitions and individual differences: The Knobe effect revisited. *Mind and Language*, 22 (4), 346–365.
Smith, B. C. (1996). *On the Origin of Objects*. Cambridge, MA: MIT Press.
Smith, M. (1987). The Humean theory of motivation. *Mind*, 96 (381), 36–61.
Thompson, M. (2008). *Life and Action*. Cambridge, MA: Harvard University Press.
Velleman, J. D. (2000). *The Possibility of Practical Reason*. Oxford: Oxford University Press.
Vogler, C. (2002). *Reasonably Vicious*. Cambridge, MA: Harvard University Press.
Vogler, C. (2008). For want of a nail. *Christian Bioethics*, 14 (2), 187–205.
Wittgenstein, L. (1998). *Philosophical Investigations*, 2nd edn, translated by G. E. M. Anscombe. Oxford: Blackwell.

Part II

Agency and Causation

13

Volition and the Will

LAURA W. EKSTROM

When we act intentionally, we initiate changes in ourselves and in the world more broadly. How do we do so? How is it that we make things be a certain way? To understand action, we have to understand what 'we' stands for in these questions. In other words, we have to understand our selves. A basic aim of action theory is to understand what is doing the work of ensuring that the self is behind the event that is thought to be an intentional act. When one's self is 'behind' the event, then the event is not one behind which there is a different self (as when one's child is the victim of a crime), and it is not an event behind which there is no human self (such as one's friend's dying of a sudden stroke). It is, rather, something one has intentionally done. This role – ensuring that the self produces the event said to be an intentional action – unifies varying uses of the terms 'volition' and 'will' by action theorists.

Will as Faculty, Capacity, or Power

In speaking of 'the will,' many philosophers mean roughly the capacity for choice, or the faculty in virtue of which we have the power to choose and to act. We commonly think that persons have this capacity and that things like tables do not – and that it is unclear which, if any, living beings other than us have it, too.

Possession of this capacity may be thought to ground, in part, certain moral obligations, and the lack of it may explain, in part, why some actions are morally permissible. One is not morally required to consult the table, for instance, before moving it about in the room. This moral claim may be thought to be grounded, at least in part, by the fact that the table has no will. On the present understanding of the term 'will,' this means that the table has neither the capacity to choose where it goes nor the capacity to move itself. It is, rather, at the mercy of the whims and wishes of those of us in possession of the capacity for choice. On the other hand, one is not morally permitted to move one's friend about in the room without his permission – in fact one is morally obligated not to do so – since to move him of one's own accord would be to treat him as an object rather than as a being in possession of a will. In saying so, we treat the term 'will' as a power, capacity or faculty – in this case, one's friend has the power to choose for himself where he goes.

Other cases are more difficult: do infants for instance, or the severely mentally disabled, have a will? In the sense of will as faculty for choice, or as capacity to choose, one might reasonably think so. However, infants and some people who are severely mentally disabled lack the ability to exercise the faculty for choice and action, which leads some theorists to prefer an understanding of will as power or ability over an understanding of it in terms of bare capacity.

On the sense of will as power or ability, exercises of will are choices, or mental acts, which some call volitions or willings. The label 'theory of volitions' has been given to the view that whatever one does is the causal product of a unique mental act, called 'willing' (O'Shaughnessy 1956: 443). Some theorists defend a view on which volitions are uncaused simple mental acts at the core of every complex bodily free action (Ginet 1990; for further discussion, see chapter 27 here). Others take volitions to be not mental acts but states of mind – in particular, attitudinal precursors to action that serve the function of ensuring that the self is behind the relevant event.

For those who posit the existence of volitions, 'the will' may be understood as that which produces volitions, on either of these construals: volitions as mental acts, or volitions as psychological states preceding action. If volitions are mental acts, then the will, construed as the maker of volitions, is whatever faculty enables us to perform mental acts. Roughly the will, on this construal, is the ability for choice or for willings. If volitions are rather mental states, then to say that the will is that which produces volitions is to say that the will is the faculty or power which is the source of certain of our motivations.

Since one's will is, on the faculty or power construal of 'will,' one's own power to choose (or power to perform mental acts of volition or willing), an act's source in the will may be thought to be what makes the act one's own, an event behind which there lies one's self.

Will as an Attitude or Collection of Attitudes

Alternatively, one might understand the will not as a faculty or ability, but rather as being itself some attitude, drive, or motivation. (For a discussion of will as a drive toward, or hunger for, the good, see chapter 56.) We could say, for instance, that a person's will *is* her volition or her structure of volitions, or that her will is a complex of mental states of some sort other than volitions.

This second sense of 'will' is recognizable in our everyday talk of one's will as, roughly, what one has resolved to do. On a natural construal of the term 'what' in 'what one has resolved to do,' the 'what' is the course of action upon which one has deliberately decided. It is inaccurate, however, to equate one's will with an action one performs, or with an action one will perform or intends to perform. We may sensibly say that one 'performed an action *willingly*' or that one 'acted *by will*,' but in saying so we describe a feature or property of the action in question. (We may sensibly speak of an act called willing, but one's will is not one's act.)

When we say, then, that one's will is 'what one has resolved to do,' what we ought to mean is that one's will is one's mental resolution; or, if not a resolution precisely – to leave open at present what a resolution might be – then rather some sort of mental state, one we may describe roughly (to begin with) as an attitude of favoring, or perhaps of committing to, some course of action or some state of affairs. By saying that the child has 'developed a will' in this second sense of will, we mean roughly that she has begun to exhibit attitudes of her own. No longer is she fully compliant with her parents' wishes, but instead she has ideas, preferences, judgments, or desires about where to go and what to do: this rather than that, here rather than there.

On the second account of 'one's will,' then, will is an attitude or state of mind, or a collection of these. Call this the attitudinal sense of will. In inquiring of someone, 'What is your will concerning your possessions, once you are deceased?' – we mean something in the neighborhood of these questions: what is your considered (or settled or stable) intention concerning the distribution of your worldly goods? What do you want done? What are your wishes, your plans? Each of these queries is expressed in rough terms, which stand in need of fuller examination.

There is a variety of ways in which philosophers have worked to fill in the notion of will as an attitude or state of mind, or as a complex or collection of these. Some philosophers, in the tradition of Hobbes, conceive of a person's will as her strongest desire, or as the appetite that leads to bodily motion in the direction of the desired object (Hobbes 1969). An instance of this type is Harry Frankfurt's account in his 'Freedom of the will and the concept of a person,' which defines *the will* as the first-level desire that is effective in leading one to act, when or if one acts (Frankfurt 1971).

One might find this account too simple, on the grounds that one's motivating desire and one's will can come apart. Other philosophers favor a view on which the true will of a person is taken to be not what she most wants – what she wants with felt gusto or strength – but rather what she authentically or truly wants.

To see why this more complex notion of will has attracted significant attention in recent work in action theory, consider cases of angst experienced while navigating an internal struggle. In a famous passage of the *Confessions*, Augustine describes such an experience, which in his case involved a conflict between temptations of the flesh and his higher spiritual ambitions. Augustine writes: 'My inner self was a house divided against itself.' In the 'agony of indecision,' he says, 'I tore my hair and hammered my forehead with my fists.' He concludes that 'there are two wills in us, because neither by itself is the whole will' (Augustine 1961: 170–172).

Augustine's report illustrates a certain predicament of the human will. Sometimes we feel volitionally stuck: our way forward is unclear, not because we lack information about what options are available, but rather because we lack information about ourselves. We are simply not sure where we stand. We do not know what our will is, because our will, in some sense, is divided. It is not clear, however, how a will can be divided, or how there could be 'two wills in us.' (More on this below.)

Will and Free Will Theory

On the broad sense of will identified first – according to which beings with a will are those with the ability to choose and to act – there are, arguably, no special issues concerning freedom of the will, distinct from the question of what it is to act freely. Some philosophers, in fact, have supposed that the will, in its sense as a faculty, is by definition free (Descartes 1996). Most philosophers, however, maintain that one can act by will (and also perform mental acts of willing) without thereby acting freely.

Recognition of the sense of the term 'will' as a faculty or ability helps to explain the way in which many contemporary analytic free will theorists construe their project: namely, as an attempt to explicate what it is to act freely (see for instance Ekstrom 2000: 71; Mele 2006: 17; Pereboom 2007: 200; van Inwagen 1983). For such theorists, freedom of will is not of separate interest from freedom of action, and rightly so, since the notion of will, as a faculty or ability, does not introduce any additional advantageous concepts into the analysis of free action. It simply stands as a prerequisite for being an agent who can act freely. To act freely requires that one can act. To choose freely requires that one can choose. The real work in free will theory, on the first understanding of will, is to explain what makes exercises of will – the power of choice and action (or the faculty in virtue of which we have the power) – free. In other words, the work is to explain what makes choices and actions free. If choices are actions, then the work is, simply, to explain what makes actions free.

One might object by asserting that appeal must be made to efforts of will, understood in the first sense, in order to understand action or free action. However, appealing to efforts to exercise the capacity for choice – or, similarly, to exertions of effort or to *endeavorings* to exercise this capacity – seems unhelpful to those who would separate the issue of freedom of will from that of freedom of action. This is so because efforts, exertions, and endeavorings, if they were to exist, would need to be actions themselves, or parts of actions, or sub-actions or behaviors of some sort (for further discussion, see chapter 3). If they were actions, as they seem to be, then, still, at issue would be the freedom of action, not the freedom of will. If they are alleged to be 'basic' actions, then, at issue are still these two concerns: we need an account of that in virtue of which they count as actions, and we need to know what makes them free or unfree. If efforts to exercise the capacity for choice are not actions, but rather sub-actions or behaviors of some sort, then we need an account of how they ground or generate actions, and we still need an account of the freedom of actions. The nature and freedom of action is what is at issue on the first sense of will, not freedom of the will.

Some philosophers who urge contemporary agency theorists to focus attention on the notion of freedom of will in addition to the notion of freedom of action, equivocate in their use of the term 'will.' This equivocation may obscure the matter of whether or not there is a separate issue concerning the freedom of the will. For instance, the 'will-forming' language used by Robert Kane in his work on free action suggests that his usage of the term 'will' is not univocal (Kane 1996, 2002, 2007). On Kane's view of self-forming willings, also called self-forming actions or SFAs, willings are taken to be actions. The efforts of will, which are central to accounting for directly free actions on Kane's account, are exertions of 'will,' understood as the power to act. Yet when Kane emphasizes that the will of a person should be formed by her, if she is to be its ultimate source and so if she is to be able to be ultimately responsible for her acts, Kane treats the will not as a faculty or power, but as itself a complex of attitudes. In Kane's example, the businesswoman's free decision to help a stranger in need in an alley, rather than to continue on her way to a meeting, shapes her will in the sense that it influences what kind of person she is and will be in the future. The decision shapes her will – not understood as the faculty for choice, but rather understood as her character traits and motives, what Kane has called her 'self-network.'

The standing of work on will in free will theory is clearly quite different when it comes to the attitudinal sense of 'will.' Here there is room for different particular *theories* of the will. The contenders are many, and work on the matter is nuanced and rich (see Arpaly 2003; Bratman 1996, 2000, 2003; Dworkin 1988; Ekstrom 2005a, 2005b; Frankfurt 1971, 1988; Mele 1995; Moran 2002; Scanlon 2002; Velleman 2000; Watson 1975, 1987; Wolf 2002). Not all of these writers cast their work explicity in terms of giving a theory of the will, though some concerns in their work may be fruitfully understood in those terms. Michael Bratman, for instance, suggests that his planning theory of intention, developed in part in the context of discussions concerning the phenomena of agent alienation from, and identification with, desire, offers 'a modest theory of the will' (Bratman 2007: 48, n. 10). The will, for Bratman, is a complex structure of attitudes, including intentions, plans, and policies (ibid., p. 67). Though not as simple as the Hobbesian or Frankfurtian account of will as effective desire, Bratman's account does contrast with a Kantian notion of the will, according to which, as Christine Korsgaard describes it, it is the claim to universality that gives one a will, that makes one's will distinguishable from the operation of impulses and desires in one (Korsgaard 1996: 232; for discussion of the Kantian notion of will, see chapter 64 here).

On the attitudinal sense of will, then, there are unsettled and interesting issues concerning both the nature and freedom of the will. These issues are clearly the ones of concern in Augustine's puzzlement over the 'two wills in us.'

Volitional Disunity and Wholeheartedness

What is the best theory of will in the attitudinal sense, and how does it point toward a way out of the volitional predicament Augustine describes?

One simple view of our psychology understands disunity in the volitional structure of the self as a matter of conflict between desires to act in various ways, and it offers, as a way out of the conflict, a sheer exertion of will (that is, an exercise of the power for choice) in one direction or another. However, we ought to avoid two tempting but untenable ideas. First, we may be tempted to imagine that there is a little agent in the head (or an 'eye' in the I) choosing one desire over another. Second, we should avoid the view that desire conflict resolution is to be accomplished arbitrarily by sheer fiat, in a way that gives us no confidence that *our* volitional discord has been resolved, or, to put it another way, that we have settled on what it is we really want (Bratman 2003).

Hierarchical accounts (on which see Dworkin 1988; Frankfurt 1971; Lehrer 1997; Neely 1974; Stump 1988; Thalberg 1989) offer a more complex and potentially more satisfying picture. They allow us to move from understanding disunity in the will as a matter of conflict between first-level desires (desires concerning action) to a conception appealing to a lack of mesh between second-level desires (desires concerning desires) and first-level ones. They thus suggest the following solution to the problem of volitional discord. When torn among competing desires to do this and that, one might reflectively form higher-order volitions concerning the lower-level attitudes. Some of these higher-order volitions will endorse certain first-level desires as legitimate candidates for satisfaction. Others will reject different first-level desires, giving them outlaw status. The idea, then, is that higher-order volitions allow us to settle on our true will, by 'putting our weight behind' certain attitudes and not others. Because the attitudes that we reject are no longer internal, they cannot fuel internal volitional conflicts.

The adequacy of the hierarchical approach depends on the strength of the claim of higher-order volitions to constitute the agent's authentic perspective and so to be the source of her free action. Many have argued that this claim is suspect. Difficulties include a charge of arbitrariness in the account of authenticity and the problem of a threatened regress of desires of higher and higher orders. Frankfurt's response to these central concerns about the hierarchical approach has been, broadly speaking, to deny that identifying with an attitude requires the formulation of a higher-order attitude of endorsement of that attitude. He has proposed that the series could be cut off non-arbitrarily by a person's satisfaction, construed as a state of the entire psychic system, 'a state constituted just by the absence of any tendency or inclination to alter its condition' (Frankfurt 1999: 104). In more recent work, Frankfurt sets out an account of identification as acceptance, rather than as the type of positive endorsement that generates a regress (Frankfurt 2002: 160–161).

Some theorists are dissatisfied with Frankfurt's proposed way out of the relevant problems. The pertinent objection is that certain explanations for the required 'satisfaction' or 'acceptance' – namely exhaustion, external manipulation, depression, boredom, and frustration, all allowed by Frankfurt – seem not to be the sorts of states or processes which authenticate satisfactorily an agent's desires. Why should we think that a certain act – letting my toddler take a bath without my supervision, for instance – is what I 'really want,' if I am only satisfied with the desire to do so because I am too exhausted or too distracted to think any harder about the matter? Even worse, why think so if my satisfaction traces to the hypnotic influence of someone who wishes my child harm?

An alternative way of illuminating volitional disunity and volitional accord is by developing a structural coherence account of the true self that is not reliant on the notion of higher-order desires. On one view of this sort, a self-determined act is understood as one non-deviantly caused by a desire of a particular sort: one that (1) has withstood critical evaluation with respect to the agent's conception of the good; (2) has been formed and is maintained without the coercive influence of another agent which the agent herself has not autonomously arranged; and (3) coheres with the agent's convictions and other reflectively evaluated desires (Ekstrom 1993, 2005a, 2005b).

The importance of the first condition on the motivationally effective desire lies in the fact that our ability to subject our attitudes to critical evaluation with respect to our conception of the good enables us to ensure that our desires do not automatically move us to act, making us the passive vehicles through which the strongest impulses hold sway. Our critical engagement with reasons, our evaluation of desires and courses of action with respect to worth, and our endorsement of some of them – these activities constitute the participation of the self. The structural coherence condition is motivated by this observation: the cohering elements of one's collection of convictions and reflectively evaluated desires are not directly opposed to each other, but instead have some mutual support, so that they are defensible in the face of challenges. They are not oddball attitudes that the agent cannot defend or explain. Rather they fit with, in fact they constitute, her 'party line.' In acting on a cohering preference, one acts without significant mental reservation, and one is wholeheartedly behind what one does, in a structural sense.

Thus, rather than characterizing the true will of a person in terms of desires about desires, and of desires about desires about desires – generating a regress of desires of higher and higher orders, which is said to be terminated, in a foundationalist way, by 'keystone preferences' (Lehrer 1997; Ekstrom 1999) or by higher-order desires to which one has decisively committed – we can take a cue from coherentists concerning epistemic justification and see our truly, volitionally internal attitudes as attitudes that form an interwoven network of support: a raft or an interconnected web, rather than a pyramid or an anchored chain.

A coherence theory of the authentic will and of self-directed action, then, can provide guidance for coping with the problem of volitional paralysis described by Augustine. From it we can derive suggestions for dealing with a common and distressing predicament involving human will.

See also: TRYING TO ACT (3); INTENTION (14); REASONS AND CAUSES (17); MENTAL ACTS (27); PRACTICAL REASONING (31); MOTIVATIONAL STRENGTH (33); RESPONSIBILITY AND AUTONOMY (39); AUGUSTINE AND AQUINAS (56); DUNS SCOTUS (57); HOBBES (58); NIETZSCHE (65); RYLE (69).

References

Arpaly, N. (2003). *Unprincipled Virtue: An Inquiry into Moral Agency*. New York: Oxford University Press.

Augustine (1961). *Confessions*. New York: Penguin.

Bratman, M. (1996). Identification, decision, and treating as a reason. *Philosophical Topics*, 24, 1–18.

Bratman, M. (2000). Valuing and the will. *Philosophical Perspectives*, 14, 249–265.

Bratman, M. (2003). A desire of one's own. *Journal of Philosophy*, 100, 221–242.

Bratman, M. (2007). *Structures of Agency*. Oxford: Oxford University Press.

Buss, S., and Overton, L. (eds) (2002). *Contours of Agency: Essays on Themes from Harry Frankfurt*. Cambridge, MA: MIT Press.

Descartes, R. (1996). *Meditations on First Philosophy* [1641], edited and translated by J. Cottingham. Cambridge: Cambridge University Press.

Dworkin, G. (1988). *The Theory and Practice of Autonomy*. Cambridge: Cambridge University Press.

Ekstrom, L. (1993). A coherence theory of autonomy. *Philosophy and Phenomenological Research*, 53, 599–616.

Ekstrom, L. (1999). Keystone preferences and autonomy. *Philosophy and Phenomenological Research*, 59, 1057–1063.

Ekstrom, L. (2000). *Free Will: A Philosophical Study*. Boulder, CO: Westview Press.

Ekstrom, L. (2005a). Alienation, autonomy, and the self. *Midwest Studies in Philosophy*, 29, 45–67.
Ekstrom, L. (2005b). Autonomy and personal integration. In J. S. Taylor (ed.), 143–161.
Frankfurt, H. (1971). Freedom of the will and the concept of a person. *Journal of Philosophy*, 68, 5–20.
Frankfurt, H. (1988). *The Importance of What We Care About*. Cambridge: Cambridge University Press.
Frankfurt, H. (1999). The faintest passion. In H. Frankfurt, *Necessity, Volition, and Love*. Cambridge: Cambridge University Press, 95–107.
Frankfurt, H. (2002). Reply to Gary Watson. In Buss and Overton (eds), 160–161.
Ginet, C. (1990). *On Action*. Cambridge: Cambridge University Press.
Hobbes, T. (1969). Of liberty and necessity [1654]. In *British Moralists, 1650–1800*, edited by D. D. Raphael, Vol. 1. Oxford: Oxford University Press, 61–70.
Kane, R. (1996). *The Significance of Free Will*. New York: Oxford University Press.
Kane, R. (ed.) (2002). *The Oxford Handbook of Free Will*. Oxford: Oxford University Press.
Kane, R. (2007). Libertarianism. In J. M. Fischer, R. Kane, D. Pereboom, and M. Vargas, *Four Views on Free Will*. Malden, MA: Blackwell, 5–43.
Korsgaard, C. (1996). *The Sources of Normativity*. Cambridge: Cambridge University Press.
Lehrer, K. (1997). *Self-Trust*. New York: Oxford University Press.
Mele, A. (1995). *Autonomous Agents*. New York: Oxford University Press.
Mele, A. (2006). *Free Will and Luck*. New York: Oxford University Press.
Moran, R. (2002). Frankfurt on identification: Ambiguities of activity in mental life. In Buss and Overton (eds), 188–217.
Neely, W. (1974). Freedom and desire. *Philosophical Review*, 83, 32–54.
O'Shaughnessy, B. (1956). The limits of the will. *Philosophical Review*, 65, 443–490.
Pereboom, D. (2007). Response to Kane, Fischer, and Vargas. In J. M. Fischer, R. Kane, D. Pereboom, and M. Vargas, *Four Views on Free Will*. Malden, MA: Blackwell, 191–203.
Scanlon, T. M. (2002). Reasons and passions. In Buss and Overton (eds), 165–183.
Stump, E. (1988). Sanctification, hardening of the heart, and Frankfurt's concept of Free will. *Journal of Philosophy*, 85, 395–412.
Taylor, J. S. (ed.) (2005). *Personal Autonomy*. Cambridge: Cambridge University Press.
Thalberg, I. (1989). Hierarchical analyses of unfree action. In J. Christman (ed.), *The Inner Citadel*. Oxford: Oxford University Press, 123–136.
Van Inwagen, P. (1983). *An Essay on Free Will*. Oxford: Oxford University Press.
Velleman, J. D. (2000). *The Possibility of Practical Reason*. New York: Oxford University Press.
Watson, G. (1975). Free agency. *Journal of Philosophy*, 72, 205–220.
Watson, G. (1987). Free action and free will. *Mind*, 96, 145–172.
Wolf, S. (2002). The true, the good, and the lovable: Frankfurt's avoidance of objectivity. In Buss and Overton (eds), 227–244.

Further reading

Arpaly, N., and Schroeder, T. (1999). Praise, blame and the whole self. *Philosophical Studies*, 93, 161–188.
Bourke, V. (1964). *Will in Western Thought*. New York: Sheed and Ward.
Fischer, J. M. (1994). *The Metaphysics of Free Will*. Oxford: Blackwell.
O'Shaughnessy, B. (1980). *The Will*, Vols 1 and 2. Cambridge: Cambridge University Press.
Pereboom, Derk. (2001). *Living Without Free Will*. Cambridge: Cambridge University Press.

Piper, A. (1985). Two conceptions of the self. *Philosophical Studies*, 48, 173–197.
Shatz, D. (1986). Free will and the structure of motivation. *Midwest Studies in Philosophy*, 10, 451–482.
Stump, E. (1997). Aquinas's account of freedom: Intellect and will. *Monist*, 80, 576–597.
Velleman, J. D. (2006). Identification and identity. In *Velleman, Self to Self*. Cambridge: Cambridge University Press, 330–360.
Wallace, R. J. (2006). *Normativity and the Will*. New York: Oxford University Press.
Wolf, S. (1990). *Freedom within Reason*. Oxford: Oxford University Press.

(1) The will is not a collection of attitudes, because these are transient and therefore mental objects that may come and go without affecting the existence of the subject as such (though they may affect his existence as an actor as such). The will is the actor's bare subjectivity, that which is essential for making a subject, that which is sufficient and necessary for making him a him. One may object that certain physical bodies (i.e. the brain) and certain mental objects (i.e. mental categories, knowledge objects) are required to produce this will, or at least are necessary for its existence, that the will "dies" without them. This may be true, but the requirement that the will have "tether" to the world does not mean that the will is the world or that these objects the will is tethered to need be of it essentially. On the contrary, the will is the capacity or power to choose, that makes the subject a subject as such.

(2) The will is not "what one has resolved to do" but who is doing the resolving. (pg. 100)

(3)

14

Intention*

ALFRED R. MELE

Philosophical work on intention is motivated by three general concerns. First, philosophers of action want to understand what it is for an event to be an intentional action and how intentional actions are produced by their agents. They have good reason to think hard about what intentions are and how they may be involved in the production of intentional actions, because, even if it is unclear exactly how intentional actions and intentions are related to each other, it is clear that they are intimately related. Second, moral philosophers and others in the business of developing theories of the evaluation of actions and their agents need an account of intentional action, and such an account is likely to involve intention in an important way. Moral evaluations of actions have intentional actions as their primary subject matter, even if people sometimes are proper targets of moral blame for some unintentional actions (e.g. a drunk driver's accidentally injuring or killing people). Third, some philosophers have the goal of crafting analyses of philosophically interesting concepts as they are reflected in ordinary language.

Intentions and Related States of Mind

It is generally agreed that intentions are closely linked to desires – especially *action-desires*, desires to do things – and beliefs. An intention to do something *A* has a motivational dimension, as does a desire to *A*. Having an intention also is widely regarded as requiring the satisfaction of a belief condition of some sort. Few philosophers of action would maintain that people who believe that their chance of winning today's lottery is about one in a million intend to win the lottery, no matter how strongly they desire to win. A relatively popular claim is that having an intention to *A* requires believing that one (probably) will *A*. The proposal is designed to capture, among other things, the confidence in one's success that intending allegedly involves. A less demanding claim is that having an intention to *A* requires that one lack the belief that one (prob-

* A. Mele, Intention. From D. M. Borchert (ed.), *Encyclopedia of Philosophy*, 10 vols, 2nd edn, Macmillan: Gale Press, 2006. Reproduced here by permission.

ably) will not *A*. (The agent might have no belief on the matter.) Other alternatives include the requirement that the agent believe to some non-zero degree (even a degree associated with a subjective probability well below 0.5) that he will *A* and the requirement that the agent believe that there is a chance that he can *A*.

Philosophers are divided on how tight the connection is between intentions, on the one hand, and desires and beliefs, on the other. In particular, they disagree about whether intentions are reducible to combinations of action-desires and beliefs. The central point of contention is whether the settledness that intention encompasses can be captured in terms of beliefs and desires. One who desires to *A* – even someone who desires this more strongly than he or she desires not to *A* and who believes on inductive grounds that he or she probably will *A* – may still be deliberating about whether to *A*, in which case the person is not settled on *A*-ing. Ed wants more strongly to respond in kind to a recent insult than to refrain from doing so, but, owing to moral qualms, he is deliberating about whether to do so. He is unsettled about whether to retaliate, despite the relative strength of his desires and despite his inference from his past behavior in similar situations that he is more likely to retaliate than not to do so (Mele 1992). In acquiring an intention to retaliate – or an intention to refrain from retaliating – Ed becomes settled (but not necessarily irrevocably) on a course of action.

Two ways of coming to intend to *A* should be distinguished. Many philosophers claim or argue that to decide to *A* is to perform a mental action of a certain kind – an action of forming an intention to *A*. According to one version of this view, deciding to *A* is a momentary mental action of intention formation, and it resolves uncertainty about what to do (Mele 2003). The assertion that deciding to *A* is momentary is meant to distinguish it from, for example, a combination of deliberating and deciding. Students who are speaking loosely may say, 'I was up all night deciding to major in English,' when what they mean is that they were deliberating or fretting all night about what major to declare and eventually decided to major in English. Not all intentions are actively formed. For example,

> When I intentionally unlocked my office door this morning, I intended to unlock it. But since I am in the habit of unlocking my door in the morning and conditions [...] were normal, nothing called for a *decision* to unlock it. (Mele 1992: 231)

If I had heard a fight in my office, I might have paused to consider whether to unlock the door or walk away, and I might have decided to unlock it. But given the routine nature of my conduct, there is no need to posit an act of intention formation in this case. My intention to unlock the door may have been acquired without having been actively formed.

Some intentions are for the non-immediate future and others are not. Ann might decide on Tuesday to attend a meeting on Friday, and she might decide now to phone her mother now. The intention formed in the former decision is aimed at action three days in the future. The intention Ann forms when she decides to phone her mother now is about what to do now. Intentions of these kinds are, respectively, distal and proximal intentions. Proximal intentions also include intentions to continue doing something that one is doing and intentions to start *A*-ing (e.g. start running a mile) straightaway. Temporally mixed intentions have both proximal and distal aspects.

Consider an intention to watch the movie *Dangerous Intentions* in one sitting, beginning now. Executing it requires doing something now and continued activity for some time.

Intention's Functions and Constitution

What work do intentions do? And how are they likely to be constituted given that they do this work? Functions plausibly attributed to intentions include initiating and motivationally sustaining intentional actions, guiding intentional action, helping to coordinate agents' behavior over time and their interaction with other agents, and prompting and appropriately terminating practical reasoning (see Brand 1984, Bratman 1987, McCann 1998, Mele 1992, and Searle 1983).

Intentions, like many psychological states, have both a representational and an attitudinal dimension. The representational content of an intention may be understood as a *plan*. The intending attitude toward plans may be termed an executive attitude. Plans, on one conception, are purely representational and have no motivational power of their own. People have many different attitudes toward plans, in this sense. They may believe that a plan is too complicated, admire it, hope that it is never executed, and so on. To understand the executive dimension of intention – something at work in the initiation of action – recall that intending to *A*, unlike desiring to *A*, is partially constituted by being settled on *A*-ing. To have the intending attitude toward a plan is to be settled (but not necessarily irrevocably) on executing it. In virtue of this motivational feature of intentions, acquisitions of proximal intentions are well suited to the task of initiating actions and the persistence of intentions that initiate actions is well suited to sustain them. (In the case of an intention for a not-doing – for example, an intention not to vote in tomorrow's election – the agent may instead be settled on not violating the simple plan embedded in it, the plan not to vote.)

Why do acquisitions of proximal intentions initiate and sustain the actions that they do? Why, for example, does acquiring a proximal intention to order a hamburger and fries initiate and sustain one's ordering a hamburger and fries rather than one's ordering a salad or one's singing a song? Attention to the representational side of intentions provides an answer. An intention to *A* incorporates a plan for *A*-ing, and which intentional action(s) an intention generates is a partial function of the intention-embedded plan. In the limiting case, the plan in an intention has a single node. It is, for example, a prospective representation of one's pushing a window closed. Often, intention-embedded plans are more complex. The proximal intention to check his bank account on-line that Bob is executing incorporates a plan that includes clicking on his bank's link, then typing his ID and password in a certain pair of boxes, and so on. Agents who successfully execute an intention are guided by the intention-embedded plan. The guidance depends on agents monitoring progress toward their goals. The information (or misinformation) that Bob has entered his ID, for example, helps to produce his continued execution of his plan.

Although the content of an intention is a plan, such expressions as 'Bob's intention to check his bank account now' and 'Ann intends to shoot pool tonight' are common. It should not be inferred from such expressions that the agent's intention-embedded plan is structurally very simple. Often, ordinary expressions of an agent's motivational attitudes do not identify the full content of the attitude and are not meant to. Bob says, without intending to mislead, 'Ann wants to shoot pool tonight,' even though he knows that what she wants is to play eight-ball with him at Pockets tonight for a dollar a game until the place closes, as they normally do.

Intention's coordinative capacities lie both in its executive aspect, which includes settledness, and in its plan-component. Comprehensive plans for extended activity can be constructed out of plans embedded in less inclusive intentions, and developments in plans will be influenced and constrained by what one is already settled on doing. (This is not to deny the possibility of revising earlier intentions.) Moreover, knowledge of what others are settled on doing assists one in forming intentions and plans for cooperative ventures. To the extent to which coordination depends on practical reasoning, intention promotes coordination by providing motivation for required reasoning – motivation deriving from the settledness intention encompasses. Michael Bratman argues that the coordinating roles of distal intentions rest on several features of these intentions: they have the capacity to control behavior, they 'resist (to some extent) revision and reconsideration,' and they involve dispositions to reason with a view to intention-satisfaction and 'to constrain one's intentions in the direction of consistency' (1987:108–109). All of these features are tied to the settledness intentions encompass.

Intention is an appropriate terminator of practical reasoning precisely because in forming or acquiring an intention one becomes settled on a course of action. Practical reasoning is aimed at action; and, if all goes well, one does what one has become settled on doing on the basis of one's practical reasoning. Intention's capacity to prompt such reasoning, as just noted, also derives from the settledness it involves.

Intentions and Reasons

Are people's reasons for intending to *A* limited to their reasons for *A*-ing? Gregory Kavka's (1983) 'toxin puzzle' suggests that they are not. In this puzzle, a trustworthy billionaire offers you a million dollars for intending tonight to drink a certain toxin tomorrow afternoon. You are convinced that he can tell what you intend independently of what you do. Although drinking the toxin would make you ill for a day, you do not need to drink it to get the money. Constraints on prize-winning intentions include prohibitions against creating special incentives for yourself to drink the toxin, various tricks, and forgetting relevant details of the offer. For example, you will not receive the money if you hire a hitman to kill you should you not drink the toxin or persuade a hypnotist to implant the intention in you. If, by midnight tonight, without violating any rules, you intend to drink the toxin tomorrow afternoon, you will find a million dollars in your bank account when you awake tomorrow morning. Because you are well aware of this point and would love to be a millionaire, you seemingly have a great reason to form the intention. Now, you probably would drink the toxin for a million dollars. But can you, without violating the rules of the offer, intend tonight to drink it tomorrow? Apparently, you have no reason to drink the toxin and an excellent reason not to drink it. Seemingly, you will infer from this that you will not drink the toxin. Indeed, it seems that you will be very confident that you will not drink it, and your confidence in that seems inconsistent with your having an intention to drink it.

Kavka draws the moral that intentions are 'dispositions to act that are based on *reasons to act* – features of the act itself or its (possible) consequences that are valued by the agent' (1983: 35). However, because not all the work in Kavka's puzzle is done by truths about intention, reasons, and the like, his perfectly general claim about intentions cannot be established by reflection on the puzzle. Were it not for the rule against forgetting, for example, you could become a millionaire. If, tonight, you can so arrange things that at midnight you will be confident that the toxin will be in your favorite afternoon drink tomorrow and confident, as well, that by tomorrow you will have forgotten about the toxin, then at midnight you can intend to drink the toxin tomorrow. The content of your intention may be described roughly as follows: 'Tomorrow afternoon, I drink the toxin unintentionally while sipping my customary afternoon tea.' Even though you will have a reason tomorrow to drink tea, you will have no reason at all to drink the toxin; and that is clear to you at midnight. This scenario falsifies the idea that all possible intentions to *A* are based on reasons to *A*. A more cautious diagnosis of your apparent inability to intend to drink the toxin given the constraints Kavka imposes is that having an intention to *A* is inconsistent with being convinced that one will not *A*.

The preceding scenario leaves open a more modest version of Kavka's moral. Perhaps all possible intentions to *A* such that in executing them one would *intentionally A* are based on reasons to *A*. Although one cannot find in reasons for *A*-ing a necessary basis for all possible intentions to *A*, one might find in them a necessary basis for all intentions of the sort just identified – *orthodox intentions*. The relatively cautious diagnosis previously mentioned provides a hint about how to test this hypothesis. Might there be agents who know that they have no reason to drink the toxin, have not forgotten anything relevant, and nevertheless believe that they will drink it?

Consider the following story. An evil genius tricks Ted into drinking nonlethal liquid toxins whenever such toxins happen to be nearby, and Ted is well aware of this. Ted also has – as he knows – a condition called intention perseverance: once he forms an intention, he will not abandon it unless he has a good reason to abandon it. Finally, Ted is indifferent between drinking toxins unintentionally and drinking them intentionally: only the subsequent illness bothers him.

Seemingly, Ted can get the big prize in Kavka's scenario. Although normal folks are confident that they will not drink the toxin, Ted is confident that he will drink it. He also has an excellent reason to decide to drink it: in so deciding he would form an intention that will make him a millionaire. And he can count on the intention formed in his decision to persist and to result in intentional toxin drinking, given that he lacks a good reason to abandon the intention after he forms it. Ted's intention to drink the toxin is such that, in executing it, he intentionally drinks the toxin. So he undermines even the more modest version of Kavka's moral. His intention to drink the toxin is based on his reasons for forming that intention, and it is not based at all on reasons for drinking the toxin. This leads back, then, to the relatively cautious diagnosis of one's apparent inability to intend to drink the toxin. The diagnosis is about a completely general connection between intention and belief, not a completely general connection between intention and reasons: having an intention to *A* is inconsistent with being convinced that one will not *A*.

Sometimes people consider reasons for and against taking a prospective course of action. Gilbert Harman (1986) and Michael Bratman (1987) argue that the concept of intentional action is sensitive to reasons agents have for not doing what they do in a way in which the concept of intention is not. The upshot is that agents sometimes intentionally do things that they lack an intention to do. For example, Bill knows that his vacuuming his carpets today will cause Beth to sneeze, and he counts that as a reason not to vacuum them today. Even so, because he believes that it is important to vacuum today, he does so, and he notices Beth sneezing as he works. Harman and Bratman would say that even though making Beth sneeze is no part of what Bill intends, he intentionally makes her sneeze. This judgment may be in line with ordinary usage of the terms at issue, and it may be a judgment that a majority of nonspecialists would make. However, granting the existence of intentionally produced side effects that the agent does not intend to produce would complicate the task of philosophers of action who say that they are in the business of explaining how intentional actions are produced by their agents. They would need a theory that explains intentional actions of two very different kinds: actions the agent is trying to perform and actions the agent is not trying to perform. Such philosophers may do well to seek – and to set up as the target of their explanatory efforts – a more circumscribed notion of intentional action that is no more sensitive to reasons against doing what one does than Harman and Bratman say the concept of intention is.

See also: ACTION THEORY AND ONTOLOGY (1); TRYING TO ACT (3); THE CAUSAL THEORY OF ACTION (5); COLLECTIVE ACTION (9); VOLITION AND THE WILL (13); PRACTICAL REASONING (31); AKRASIA AND IRRATIONALITY (35); INTENTIONAL ACTION IN FOLK PSYCHOLOGY (45); DAVIDSON (73); ANSCOMBE (74).

References

Brand, M. (1984). *Intending and Acting*. Cambridge, MA: MIT Press.
Bratman, M. (1987). *Intention, Plans, and Practical Reason*. Cambridge, MA: Harvard University Press.
Harman, G. (1986). *Change in View*. Cambridge, MA: MIT Press.
Kavka, G. (1983). The Toxin Puzzle. *Analysis*, 43, 33–36.
McCann, H. (1998). *The Works of Agency*. Ithaca, NY: Cornell University Press.
Mele, A. R. (1992). *Springs of Action*. New York: Oxford University Press.
Mele, A. R. (2003). *Motivation and Agency*. New York: Oxford University Press.
Searle, J. (1983). *Intentionality*. Cambridge: Cambridge University Press.

Further reading

Anscombe, G. E. M. (1957). *Intention*, 2nd edn. Ithaca, NY: Cornell University Press.
Audi, R. (1993). *Action, Intention, and Reason*. Ithaca, NY: Cornell University Press.
Bratman, M. (1999). *Faces of Intention*. Cambridge: Cambridge University Press.
Davidson, D. (1980). *Essays on Actions and Events*. Oxford: Clarendon Press.

15

Desire and Pleasure

TIMOTHY SCHROEDER

There are theories of desire that make clear desire's connection to action but leave obscure its connection to pleasure. There are also theories of desire that make clear desire's connection to pleasure but leave obscure its connection to action. There are theories that attempt to make clear both aspects of desire, and there are theories that fail to make clear either aspect. In short, there are more than enough theories of desire for almost any purpose, short of making one confident that one of them is correct.

If there is an overabundance of theories of desire, this is, at least partly, because the experience of desiring something is different on different occasions.

If I am parched after two hours of working in the hot summer sun and I desire water, my experiences tend to be of a familiar sort. I feel unpleasantly dry in my mouth and my hands feel unpleasantly swollen. The thought of getting water occurs to me spontaneously, and the idea is delightful. Thinking of water, I feel inclined to go and get some; my muscles tense up in a way preparatory to walking to the nearest source of water, and I feel myself poised to act. As I walk to where I can drink, I will be anticipating the drink. And then, once I drink water, I will experience pleasure. This pleasure will be intense at the first sip but will soon diminish to the point at which there is no more to be had, and if I go on drinking it will become unpleasant. Somewhere around this point I will stop drinking and declare that I have slaked my thirst.

Compare all this to experiences of desiring had on other occasions. I desire to be clothed when I am outdoors. This desire is not one that I develop under the summer sun and then satisfy with a sigh of contentment. It does not preoccupy me throughout the time when I have it, and it does not cause me to feel poised to take action. I do, of course, act to satisfy the desire, but I never have what one would call an impulse to do so. Such pleasure as I get from being clothed when I am outdoors tends to be modest, but tends also not to diminish: I will never feel that I have had enough of being clothed outdoors, and that more would now be unpleasant. I do not feel that my desire to be clothed is slaked; it is satisfied only in the technical sense that I have what I want. In rough outline, there are similarities to the experience of a desire to drink: I am motivated to act in a certain way, and I am disposed to feel distress if my desire is frustrated. In the details, however, there seem to be many dissimilarities.

Some theorists of desire appear to have in mind the experiences that come with desiring to drink water, and other theorists appear to have in mind less stirring experiences. Taking thirst as a paradigm of desire suggests (without forcing the conclusion) that desires are strong feelings, or dispositions to strong feelings; it also suggests that desires are (normally) for pleasure, or for relieving displeasure, and that, as it becomes true that there is no more pleasure to be gained (or displeasure to be evaded) through a given course of action, one ceases to desire it. Taking the desire to be clothed when one is outdoors as a paradigm of desire suggests (without forcing the conclusion) that desires are enduring states which guide action more than feelings. It also suggests that desires are often for things other than pleasure, things which one might continue to desire whether or not one feels pleasure as one gains one's end.

As it happens, theories of desire centered on desire's control of action dominate philosophical thought at present; pleasure-based theories of desire tend to be neglected as a result, although they retain a number of defenders. And there remain more theoretical options than this dichotomy suggests, as efforts are made to integrate all the familiar features of desire.

Action-Based Theories of Desire

The leading theory of desire may be called 'the action-based theory of desire.' A sophisticated version of the theory (for instance in Smith 1987) holds that to desire that *p* is to be disposed, all else being equal, to take any action one believes will make it the case (or contribute to making it the case) that *p*. A thirsty woman who desires a drink of water is disposed to take the actions she believes will get her a drink of water, and a man who desires to be clothed when being outdoors is disposed to take the actions he believes will make it the case that he is clothed when he is outdoors.

Action-based theories of desire leave open the relation between desire and pleasure. The anticipated or actual satisfaction of a desire could cause pleasure, but it could fail to do so, and this is a matter of theoretical indifference, so far as action-based theories are concerned. Similarly, action-based theories of desire permit pleasure to be an object of desire, but do not require that it be one, and permit other objects of desire as well.

Because of their indifference to feelings and emphasis on action, action-based theories of desire seem to do a good job of theorizing the desire to be clothed when one is outdoors. I am indeed disposed to take the actions that, I think, will keep me clothed outdoors, and my desire to be clothed does not, in my experience, seem to involve much more than this. Action-based theories of desire can seem less compelling when it comes to other desires, though. My desire to drink after a hot afternoon of work does dispose me to act, but this seems a small part of having this desire: the feelings I have are much more prominent. Still, it is possible to hold that my strong feelings are mere causes, or effects, of my desire, and that the desire itself is simply the disposition to action.

Pleasure-Based Theories of Desire

An important alternative to the action-based theory of desire is what may be called 'the pleasure-based theory of desire.' A sophisticated version of the theory (for which see Strawson 1994) holds that to desire that *p* is to be disposed to pleasure if it seems that *p* or to displeasure if it seems that not-*p*.

The pleasure-based theory of desire pushes to the foreground the strong feelings characteristic of thirst. According to the theory, the unpleasantness of being parched and the disposition toward having pleasure at drinking are the things which make it true that I have a desire to drink: it is my dispositions to these salient feelings that make up my desire. The feelings might also dispose me to action, but that is not what matters.

Notice that the theory does not identify desires with strong feelings, but with dispositions to strong feelings. This is probably a strength of the theory: if desires are identical to strong feelings, then desires cannot explain why we are disposed to strong feelings. But desires seem to do just this: that I desire my father to be healthy explains why I feel displeasure upon finding out that he has cataracts and pleasure upon finding out that his cataracts have been treated successfully. Similarly, my desires seem to explain why I tend to have my attention captured by newspaper stories about cataract treatments, even when I am not having any strong feelings at all. If desires were strong feelings, they could not play any role in causally explaining these facts about me. On the contrary, if desires were (the bases of) dispositions to strong feelings, they could well play these roles.

One worry about a pleasure-based theory of desire might be that it requires that, when we act on our desires, we act (ultimately) to attain pleasure. There are defenders of pleasure-based theories who have supported this conclusion (Morillo 1990), but the conclusion is not inescapable. Pleasure might make it true that a desire exists without being the ultimate content of the desire in question: in Strawson's version of the theory, for instance, the fact that I get displeasure from hearing about my father's cataracts makes it true that I desire him not to have them, but my desire is for him not to have cataracts – it is not a desire to escape my own displeasure (Strawson 1994).

Another worry about any theory of desire based purely on pleasure is that such a theory requires no connection at all between desire and action. As it stands, my motivation to be clothed when I go outdoors is only tenuously linked to pleasure. Suppose I were emotionally indifferent (perhaps inured to public humiliations) but still motivated to dress in the morning. It might then seem that I still desire to be clothed when I go outdoors; but this would fail to satisfy the requirements of a pleasure-based theory.

Combined Action-Based and Pleasure-Based Theories

Some theorists (Davis 1986; Schueler 1995) have argued that there is an ambiguity in the term 'desire' that resolves some of the tensions between action-based and pleasure-based theories. These theorists hold that there are desires in a generic sense of 'desire,' and desires in a proper or strictly-so-called sense of 'desire.' Any motivational state – any state satisfying the conditions of a reasonable action-based theory of desire – is a desire in the generic sense, according to these theorists. But only a desire that both disposes an agent to motivation and disposes an agent to strong feelings (especially of pleasure) can be called a desire in the strict sense.

Following these theorists, a reasonable theory of strict desire would hold that to desire that *p* is to be in a state which (1) disposes the agent to take any action which appears likely to make it the case that *p*; and (2) disposes the agent to feel pleasure if it seems that *p*, and displeasure if it seems that not-*p*. My desire to drink would then be a desire in the strict sense, because it exemplifies both of these features. But my desire to be clothed when I am outdoors might not be a desire in the strict sense. Within this theoretical framework it might well be a desire only in the generic sense, since I do not normally get any particular delight from being clothed.

The motivational states of maximum concern to theorists who have advocated action-based and pleasure-based theories of (true) desire have generally been motivations to do what is moral. Though I am disposed to pay my taxes, this disposition is not accompanied by a disposition to be delighted as I pay my taxes. I act 'dutifully,' as one says. It is held that I desire in the generic sense to pay my taxes, but in the strict sense I do not desire to pay my taxes. Likewise, I desire in the generic sense, but not in the strict sense, to return contempt with respect, to possess only what I have earned the right to possess, and so on. These motivational states have been of particular concern because it has seemed phenomenologically obvious to many that being moved to do what is right is not similar to being moved to drink water on a hot day and that this phenomenological difference marks an important difference in the underlying psychological states.

One problem for the proponents of this distinction between strict desires and generic desires is that they have focused on pleasure while neglecting displeasure. It is true that I do not get pleasure from paying my taxes. Yet, were I to cheat on my taxes, I would tend to feel displeasure (in the form of guilt). Were I to take what is not mine, or to return contempt with contempt, I would also feel bad. According to the pleasure-based theory of desire, this suffices for it to be the case that I desire not to do such things. Why, then, would it not suffice to make my desire to pay my taxes and so on a desire in the strict sense?

Holistic Theories of Desire

Holistic theories of desire hold that to desire that *p* is to have enough of some large body of features associated with desiring that *p*. An interpretationistic form of a holistic theory might hold that to desire that *p* is to display behavior which is best interpreted (through various holistic principles) as the behavior of an agent who desires that *p* (see Davidson 1980). A functional form of a holistic theory, on the other hand, might hold that to desire that *p* is to contain a state that plays at least half of the functional roles that common sense associates with desiring that *p* (see Lewis 1972). So long as the holistic theory considers both action and pleasure to be among the important features associated with desire, holistic theories make quite clear the relation between the two features and desire itself.

The primary virtue of any holistic theory of desire is that such a theory never disagrees with commonsensical intuition about whether a given state of mind is a desire, because there is nothing to having or being a desire – according to holistic theories – beyond having or being the sort of thing that satisfies most or all of our commonsensical ideas about what it is to be a desire.

This same virtue is also the source of a criticism of holistic theories: they render too many explanations trivial (Schroeder 2004). If the fact that a state causes pleasure is part of what makes it true that the state in question is a desire, then an attempt to explain where the pleasure came from by saying that it was caused by the desire seems trivial. If the fact that a state moves a person to action is part of what makes it true that the state is a desire, then an attempt to explain where the action came from by appeal to desire would also seem trivial; and so on, for the various features associated with desires.

Natural Kind Theories

If holistic theories threaten to give desires a trivial role in explanations, then another theoretical option is to treat desires as natural kinds: namely as the natural kinds that are causally responsible for action, pleasure and displeasure, and other effects associated with having a desire. If desires were such a natural kind, there would be no question of their explanatory relevance.

This strategy has been pursued by a pair of philosophers who have reached similar conclusions about the natural kind in question, but different conclusions about how to interpret it. Morillo (1990) and Schroeder (2004) use neuroscientific evidence to argue that there is a unique, discrete structure in the brain which is responsible for the various effects associated with desires – most centrally, for the causation of action and pleasure. Both philosophers argue that this unique structure in the brain is the brain's so-called reward system, a group of cells that release a chemical, dopamine, which has a well-confirmed and central role in action production (loss of dopamine causes Parkinson disease and ultimately paralysis) and in pleasure stimulation (most pleasant drugs, from nicotine to cocaine, stimulate or mimic the release of dopamine). According to Morillo, the release of dopamine from the reward system is identical to pleasure; this is why she holds a pleasure-based theory of desire. According to Schroeder, the release of dopamine is an unconscious learning signal, and pleasure is merely one of its effects.

Schroeder's work – a descendant of the view of desire first developed in Dretske 1988 – faces a challenge that Morillo's does not. According to Schroeder, desire is a natural kind – a generator of a certain sort of unconscious learning – that is not constituted by anything familiar about desire. This is standard in thinking about natural kinds: an H_2O molecule has no important property commonly associated with water, but its interaction with other H_2O molecules causally explains those commonly associated features. Still, it ends up being true that a very small quantity of water can lack the properties commonly associated with water. Likewise, on Schroeder's account, it turns out that a desire can exist that does not cause action, or pleasure, or any other phenomenon commonly associated with desires. This will seem a grave worry to those who doubt that mental kinds are likely to be natural kinds.

The Nature of Pleasure

There are other theories of desire not yet discussed (theories that link it to appearances of the good, or to apparent reasons to act, are the most important among those not yet mentioned), but these other theories leave obscure the connections of desire to both action and pleasure, and so will be set aside here.

Instead, this discussion will conclude with a survey of theories of pleasure and displeasure that say something substantial about the link between pleasure and desire.

Pleasure and displeasure have received behavioristic treatments (see for instance Ryle 1971) and treatments as propositional attitudes (Feldman 2004). But it is most common to think of pleasure and displeasure as feelings (Morillo 1990; Prinz 2004; Schroeder 2004). The pressing question at this point is the relation between the feelings of pleasure and displeasure on the one hand and desire satisfaction on the other.

One view (clearly set out in Pollock 2006) holds that dispositions to pleasure and displeasure are psychologically basic, and that desires are (always, often, or ideally) for those states of affairs which, as a basic psychological fact, tend to generate pleasure. On this view, I do not feel displeasure over immoral acts because I desire to be morally decent. The view holds rather that it is a basic fact about my psychology that immoral acts are a source of displeasure to me, and as a consequence I desire (more precisely, I am motivated to bring it about) that I am morally decent.

An opposed view holds that pleasure and displeasure are (always, often, or ideally) caused by desire satisfaction and frustration. In one formulation, the degree of pleasure (or displeasure) is held to represent net positive (or negative) change in desire satisfaction relative to unconscious, 'gut-level' expectations (Schroeder 2004; compare Davis 1981). On this view, the displeasure of immoral acts stems from the more basic psychological fact that I desire to act morally, along with the fact that I (unconsciously, at a 'gut' level) expect myself ordinarily to do what is moral.

One piece of evidence in favor of the representational view of pleasure is the way people use feelings of pleasure and displeasure as fallible epistemic guides to their desires. If pleasure is taken to be an indicator that I really did want whatever I just got, and disappointment an indicator that I really did not want it after all, then this suggests that pleasure and displeasure should be treated as caused by desire satisfaction (Schroeder 2004).

If pleasure and displeasure represent change in desire satisfaction relative to some baseline, this might go some way toward explaining the way I feel about satisfying my desire to be clothed. I get no particular pleasure from satisfying my desire, but I am also jaded with respect to it: I expect to be clothed whenever I want to be. If I were forced to go out without clothing for a time, not only would I experience displeasure, but when I was finally able to return to being clothed I would take pleasure in it. This suggests that I am indeed disposed to be pleased at wearing clothes given the appropriate baseline conditions, only these conditions are rarely met. Application of this thinking to moral desires (generic or strict) has not yet featured in the literature of moral psychology, but it might provide some insights into the way people feel about doing what is right. Perhaps most people who desire to do what is right are jaded with respect to doing what is right: they viscerally expect that they will do what is right, and so they derive no pleasure when their desires are satisfied in the expected manner. Because they viscerally expect to do what is right, they should (on this theory) be particularly prone to displeasure at the idea or actualization of doing what is wrong. This reasoning opens up the possibility of other people, who also desire to do what is right but who are (for whatever reason) of much less reliable virtue, hence who do not viscerally expect themselves to do what is right and whose feelings are correspondingly different. These people would be expected to derive more pleasure from doing what is right – even when doing so is otherwise unremarkable – than those who are accustomed to right action as their default mode of action, and to derive less displeasure from the idea or actualization of doing what is wrong. Whether or not this is a plausible thought remains to be investigated.

See also: MOTIVATING REASONS (19); HUMEANISM ABOUT MOTIVATION (20); WHAT A DIFFERENCE EMOTIONS MAKE (25); MOTIVATIONAL INTERNALISM AND EXTERNALISM (37).

References

Davidson, D. (1980). *Essays on Actions and Events*. Oxford: Clarendon Press.

Davis, W. (1981). A theory of happiness. *American Philosophical Quarterly*, 18, 111–120.

Davis, W. (1986). The two senses of desire. In J. Marks (ed.), *The Ways of Desire: New Essays in Philosophical Psychology on the Concept of Wanting*. Chicago: Precedent, 63–82.

Dretske, F. (1988). *Explaining Behavior: Reasons in a World of Causes*. Cambridge, MA: MIT Press.

Feldman, F. (2004). *Pleasure and the Good Life: Concerning the Nature, Varieties, and Plausibility of Hedonism*. New York: Oxford University Press.

Lewis, D. (1972). Psychophysical and theoretical identifications. *Australasian Journal of Philosophy*, 50, 249–258.

Morillo, C. (1990). The reward event and motivation. *Journal of Philosophy*, 87, 169–186.

Pollock, J. (2006). *Thinking about Acting: Logical Foundations for Rational Decision Making*. New York: Oxford University Press.

Prinz, J. (2004). *Gut Reactions: A Perceptual Theory of Emotion*. New York: Oxford University Press.

Ryle, G. (1971). Pleasure [1954]. In G. Ryle, *Collected Papers*, Vol. 2: *Collected Essays 1929–1968*. London: Hutchinson, 325–336. [Original publication in *Proceedings of the Aristotelian Society*, Supplementary Volume 27.]

Schroeder, T. (2004). *Three Faces of Desire*. New York: Oxford University Press.

Schueler, G. F. (1995). *Desire: Its Role in Practical Reason and the Explanation of Action*. Cambridge, MA: MIT Press.

Smith, M. (1987). The Humean theory of motivation. *Mind*, 96, 36–61.

Strawson, G. (1994). *Mental Reality*. Cambridge, MA: MIT Press.

16

Teleological Explanation

SCOTT SEHON

A teleological explanation of human behavior explains the behavior by citing a state of affairs or a goal towards which it was directed. Canonical teleological explanations of action comprise mentioning an agent, the agent's behavior, a teleological connective, and the state of affairs towards which the behavior was directed. Take the statement:

Jane went to the kitchen in order to get coffee.

In this example, the connective is the phrase 'in order to,' but explanations can be explicitly teleological with other connectives as well. For example,

Jane went to the kitchen for the purpose of getting coffee.
Jane went to the kitchen to get coffee.
Jane went to the kitchen with the aim of getting coffee.

These teleological explanations of behavior are paradigm cases of explaining an agent's action in terms of her *reasons*, and thus they count as reason explanations of behavior.

Like the examples above, many reason explanations of human behavior are couched in explicitly teleological form. Others are not:

[i] Jane went to the kitchen because she wanted coffee.
[ii] Hayden shucked corn because his father told him to.
[iii] Josephine went upstairs because her shoes were there.

According to some authors, such explanations should nonetheless be construed teleologically. That is to say, the explanations can be read as claiming,

[i a] Jane went to the kitchen in order to satisfy her desire coffee.
[ii a] Hayden shucked corn in order to fulfill his father's request that he do so.
[iii a] Josephine went upstairs in order to get her shoes.

Most philosophers would agree that many commonsense explanations of human action are already in teleological form and that others, like [i]–[iii] above, can be plausibly construed teleologically, as in [i a]–[iii a]. After all, acting for reasons or purposes is part of what makes us agents, and teleological explanations capture that directly.

The true controversy concerns whether action explanation is *irreducibly* teleological. Many philosophers of mind would claim that talk of *goal-direction* and *purpose* is a useful heuristic, but it is ultimately to be cashed out in other terms. In the first section I briefly discuss some of these attempts to reduce teleology to other forms of explanation and I mention some of the problems some of these approaches face. In the next section I turn to positive accounts of teleology, according to which teleological explanations are not reducible to other forms of explanation. In the final section I consider objections to the view that action explanation is irreducibly teleological.

Reductionist Accounts of Teleology

Prior to Darwin, purpose seemed to pervade the physical world even beyond the goal-directed behavior of human beings and beyond designed artefacts like hammers. Clearly, it seemed, bird wings were designed for flight, eyes were designed for sight, and so on. When asking about the purpose of a hammer, we naturally assumed that some agent *designed* the hammer for some end. Similarly with bird wings and the like: it was a natural thought, even if not inevitable, that there must be a designer. Whatever the merits of these pre-Darwinian thoughts as an argument for the existence of God, certainly the scene changed considerably after Darwin. As Darwinian biology shows, wings that fly and eyes that see can arise through random variation and natural selection in the process of reproduction. We can thus explain the prevalence of biological adaptations, and there is no need for a designer with conscious (or unconscious) purposes.

With reason explanation, the item to be explained is individual behavior rather than a thing like a wing or an eye. But there is nonetheless a similarity. Consider for example an artefact like a hammer or a stapler. Just as these artefacts are designed for a particular purpose, one might think of particular bits of human or animal behavior as designed by the agent for its goal. Just as some agent first fashioned a hammer for striking nails, Jane designed her walking for the end of getting coffee. But here too, at least in the case of certain animal behaviors, Darwinian explanation can eliminate the need for genuine talk of design. Why do cats arch their backs in the presence of a perceived threat? There is a selectional explanation. When cats arch their backs, they appear larger and more threatening, and this sometimes scares away potential predators. So cats with that behavioral disposition survived longer and had a higher differential reproductive rate, and thus the disposition came to dominate the population. Why did Fluffy, in particular, arch her back when Rover approached? Well, evolution explains her having the general disposition to do that in circumstances of the appropriate type – and Rover's approach is a circumstance of the appropriate type. Of course many details would need to be worked out. But the basic idea is broadly reductionist; for the goal-directed behavior exhibited by Fluffy can be cashed out in evolutionary terms, and Fluffy's role as the conscious agent or designer of the behavior drops out. The realm of *sui generis* teleological explanation seems to be much narrower than might have been originally thought. Where we once had apparently irreducibly teleological explanations for birds' wings and all sorts of animal behavior, the realm of *sui generis* teleological explanation now shrinks to the more idiosyncratic and intelligent behavior of human beings, and perhaps of other higher-level rational animals.

But now the question becomes: can this evolutionary approach be applied even to human behavior? Human beings are certainly part of the evolutionary story, and we explain the fact that our eyes are good for seeing in the same evolutionary way in which we explain that bird wings are good for flying. And we can likewise give selectional explanations for many of our general behavioral tendencies – from our disposition toward sweet foods to more complex dispositions, like our practice of burying or burning human corpses. One might think that we will be able to follow the evolutionary line of thought even for ordinary actions, like Jane's going to the kitchen for coffee. If so, this would take the apparently *sui generis* teleology concerning the behavior of animate agents and would reduce it to purely naturalistic explanation in terms of variation and natural selection.

There are obstacles to such a reductionist approach. When we explained the arching of Fluffy's back, the evolutionary explanation cited a disposition that led, in Fluffy's ancestors, to higher differential reproduction. A great many human actions seem, at best, neutral toward differential reproduction: writing philosophy papers, arranging to meet a friend, shoveling snow from the driveway, and so on. And some of our actions, even seemingly rational actions, appear to be quite inimical to differential reproduction: pledging celibacy and using birth control are obvious examples. So, if the goal-directedness of human behaviors is to be cashed out in the language of natural selection, there will be many challenges, and it is, to say the least, controversial whether those challenges can be met. For attempts that are oriented, at least roughly, in this direction, see Wright (1976), Millikan (1984), and, more recently, Okrent (2007).

Other authors attempt to reduce teleology not by tying it directly to evolution, but by giving a more straightforward causal reduction. This tradition begins with Donald Davidson's classic 1963 article 'Actions, reasons, and causes,' in which he maintains that standard reason explanations are to be construed as a form of causal explanation in which appropriate mental states of the agent are cited as the effective cause of the behavior. So, for example, an explanation like

> Jane went to the kitchen in order to get coffee

would be construed as saying something like this:

> Jane's desire for coffee, and her belief that coffee could be obtained in the kitchen, caused her going to the kitchen.

Alternatively, one might want to assert that intentions constitute the causally effective mental state. See for example Mele (1992) for a detailed working out of a broadly Davidsonian approach. For an approach that is still causal, but is within the agent causation rather than event causation tradition, see O'Connor (2000).

On the causalist approach, the apparently distinctive teleological element in reason explanations drops out. Reason explanations, even when in superficially teleological form, are ultimately a species of causal explanation. To say that an agent does something for the sake of some goal just is to say that an appropriate mental state caused the behavior. But this can't be quite right as it stands. Consider an example from Davidson:

> A climber might want to rid himself of the weight and danger of holding another man on a rope, and he might know that by loosening his hold on the rope he could rid himself of the weight and danger. This belief and want might so unnerve him as to cause him to loosen his hold, and yet it might be the case that he never chose to loosen his hold, nor did he do it intentionally. (Davidson 1980a: 79)

Here it seems that the agent's desire to let go of the rope caused him to do just that. But we don't want to say that the agent let go of the rope intentionally; we don't want to say that this was goal-directed behavior. Hence something more needs to be added to the causalist analysis. The causalist might reply that, in the case of the mountain climber, the causal chain was deviant in some way, and that genuinely goal-directed behavior requires that the mental state cause the behavior in the right way.

But now the challenge for the causalist is to spell out 'in the right way' in purely causal terms. This is the problem of deviant causal chains. It has been pressed upon the causalist most forcefully by Wilson (1989; for representative replies, see Mele 2000, Peacocke 1979, and Bishop 1989; for counters, see Sehon 2005). Beyond the problem of deviant causal chains, other arguments have been raised against the causalist reduction of teleology (see for example Okrent 2007, Sehon 2005, and Schueler 2003).

Non-Reductionist Accounts

Among recent authors, Wilson (1989), Schueler (2003), and Sehon (2005) are most explicit in taking action explanation to be irreducibly teleological. (There are other authors, for instance Anscombe 1957, Stoutland 1976, Dancy 2000, Tanney 2009, who suggest that action explanation is not causal, without quite saying that action explanation is irreducibly teleological.) On each of the teleological accounts, reason explanations, even when not in explicitly teleological form, work by citing a goal state as the crucial explanatory factor. In saying that Jane went to the kitchen to get coffee, we are saying that Jane's physical behavior was directed, by Jane, at the objective or goal of getting coffee. Two aspects of this form of explanation are of special note: the fact that the behavior is directed, and the mention of the agent herself as the director of the behavior. On the view that takes reason explanations to be irreducibly teleological, neither of these elements is eliminable. This is, of course, in marked contrast to the causalist view, where the goal-direction itself is cashed out in terms of a specific type of causal chain, and the causal factors are mental states.

On the teleological view, the fact that an agent is directing her behavior to some state of affairs is not grounded in, or reducible to, some further facts. Goal-direction on the part of agents is an ineliminable part of the universe. (Well, you could kill all the agents and thereby eliminate the phenomenon; but, insofar as the phenomenon exists, it is not reducible to other features.) But to say that goal-direction is ineliminable and in that sense *sui generis* is not to say that the concept is completely isolated from other concepts. Bedau (1992) noted that teleological explanations involve normative notions, and proponents of irreducible teleology explicitly tie teleology to the concepts of rationality and value.

Schueler (2003) claims that, when we teleologically explain an agent's action by citing some goal, we assert that the agent assigned that purpose to the behavior as part of a plan. Schueler's account is modeled on the practical syllogism: when we attribute a goal to an agent, we are imputing to the agent a plan that could be the conclusion of a piece of practical reasoning. More strongly yet, we are thereby attributing to the agent the normative judgment that her reason for acting represents that which she had 'the strongest reason to do,' that which has 'the most to be said for it' (ibid., p. 136). Thus teleological explanation is normative, in that each teleological explanation attributes to the agent a fairly strong normative judgment.

In Sehon (2005), I offer a picture that is similar to Schueler's in some ways but is less modeled on conscious practical reasoning or on the relatively rare acts of deliberately assigning a purpose to some behavior. According to my account, since facts about teleology do not reduce to some other set of causal facts, one cannot give definitive truth conditions for teleological explanations in non-teleological terms. However, there is still much that one can say about how we in fact make teleological explanations. Loosely following Davidson's views of interpretation (but not his endorsement of the causal theory of action), I argue that we arrive at teleological explanations as part of an overall attempt to construct a theory of the agent, and a constitutive part of reason explanation is to produce a theory according to which the agent is as rational as possible. Rationality can be judged in different ways, but two axes are particularly relevant to judging a candidate teleological explanation: the degree to which the explanation makes the behavior appropriate for achieving a goal, and the degree to which the goal in question is of value. We aim to maximize both of these in forming our theory of persons.

In simple and straightforward cases, application of this view is almost entirely automatic. Recall Josephine who went upstairs, and suppose that the circumstances were these: another 10-year-old friend has shown up at the door and asks if Josephine wants to come outside to play; Josephine starts to run excitedly outside, but her father says, 'Wait! you need your shoes! they're upstairs.' And off she goes up the stairs. Here it is quite obvious that going upstairs would be appropriate to achieving the goal of getting her shoes, and we can easily understand the value that this would have for Josephine. We might also believe various counterfactual conditionals that point in the same direction: if Josephine had believed that her shoes were in the kitchen, she would have gone there instead of going upstairs; had she believed that she already had shoes on, as perhaps she did prior to her father's admonition, she would have simply gone outside; and so on. The general point is that our theory of Josephine is constructed so as to make the most rational sense we can extract out of her behavior in the actual and in nearby counterfactual circumstances.

Naturally, these rationalizing principles do not constrain our theorizing about the behavior of inanimate things like rocks or planets. Or, to put it the other way around, on any theory according to which a rock was an agent, the rock would either come out as quite irrational, or would have too impoverished a set of goals to count as a genuine agent. If we attribute to the rock one and only one desire, the desire to follow the laws of physics, then of course the rock comes out as always acting in ways appropriate to its one goal. But it is not clear why this one goal would be of value to a rock or anything else. On the view in question, being an agent requires a complex set of goals – a life. We cannot successfully attribute anything of the sort to the rock. So we conclude that the rock is not an agent at all, and no teleological explanation of its behavior will be true.

Prospects and Consequences

Davidson (1963) famously raised a challenge for any non-causal account of action explanation. He pointed out that an agent's action might be justified by two distinct reasons, but that the agent in fact acted on only one of the reasons. For example, Jane walks downtown and thereby accomplishes two things of value: she gets out of the office for some fresh air, and she meets a friend, as planned; but in fact she may have acted only for the latter reason. Davidson says that the causalist can easily make sense of this scenario: Jane's real reason for action is determined by whichever desire or intention caused her behavior. But the teleological account might seem to have more of a problem. How can the teleologist claim that Jane really acted simply in order to meet her friend, given that the goal of fresh air would also make good rational sense of her behavior?

The teleologist's answer lies in the fact alluded to above: in seeking rationalizing explanations of the agent's behavior, we aim to make sense of the person both in the actual and in nearby counterfactual circumstances. If an agent's behavior is truly directed at a goal, then we expect that, in nearby counterfactual circumstances, the agent would have done what it took to accomplish that goal. So, in the case of Jane, if she really walked downtown in order to meet her friend rather than to get some fresh air, we would expect that, had she believed she could meet the friend by staying in her office, that is what she would have done. In other words, different teleological explanations of the same behavior support different counterfactuals, and this will be enough to answer Davidson's challenge.

Even if the teleological account can meet Davidson's challenge, there is perhaps a more serious worry waiting in the wings, namely that the teleological account seems to run afoul of Occam's razor. There are many differences of opinion about the details, but it is fairly clear that our theorizing about the world is constrained by some version of the following principle:

(S) Given two theories, it is unreasonable to believe one that leaves significantly more unexplained mysteries.

If teleological explanation is irreducible, then the teleologist has no account of why teleological explanations work, or why, more specifically, the behavior of certain systems is such that the rationalizing mode of teleological explanation works consistently over time. A reductionist, by contrast, simply reduces teleological explanations to some form of causal or selectional explanation, and thus has no further mysteries with teleologically explicable behavior. Thus it would seem that the reductionist theory leaves fewer unexplained mysteries, and should therefore be seen as preferable to the teleological account.

In answer to this objection, let's first compare another case. The standard model in physics postulates the following:

(SP) Four fundamental and independent forces: strong force, weak force, electromagnetic force, and gravity.

Suppose that Joe, a sophomore in Philosophy of Science, tells us that he thinks this is wrong and that there is just one force. He is, namely, an advocate of Joe's physics:

(JP) Just one force which suffices to explain the nature of the four 'subforces' as well as the relationships between them.

Should we just accept that (JP) is a simpler theory than (SP) and reject the standard model? Of course not. Joe has not actually provided a physical theory that works. All we know is that, *if* Joe can come up with such a theory, then we would have a simplicity argument strongly in its favor.

Now compare two theories, the teleological account (T) and the reductionist account (Rd):

(T) Principles of physical science plus independent rationality principles underlying teleological explanation.

(Rd) Just the principles of physical science, which suffice to explain why the principles underlying teleological explanation hold.

Should we immediately conclude that (Rd) is simpler, and that we should reject (T)? No. All we know is that, *if* philosophers can come up with such a reductionist account, then there is a simplicity argument in its favor. And this is indeed a motivation for seeking such an account. However, non-reductionists have argued against the likelihood of finding any such reductive account of teleology. And at least some of us would agree with George Wilson's words: 'the evidence points to more than infelicity or incompleteness in the various causalist proposals – it points, that is, to a global breakdown in the whole project of reduction' (1989: 258). If there is no successful recipe for reduction, then there is no simplicity argument against non-reductionist views. It would be desirable to have a reduction of teleology in the same sense in which it would be desirable to have a physical theory that unifies the four forces. But, if the world does not cooperate and no unifying theory accounts for the facts as we know them, then it is a mistake to affirm reductionism, and we must live with the teleological explanation of human action as an ineliminable feature of the world.

See also: THE CAUSAL THEORY OF ACTION (5); VOLITION AND THE WILL (13); INTENTION (14); REASONS AND CAUSES (17); DEVIANT CAUSAL CHAINS (21); MENTAL CAUSATION AND EPIPHENOMENALISM (23); DAVIDSON (73).

References

Anscombe, G. E. M. (1957). *Intention*. Ithaca, NY: Cornell University Press.

Bedau, M. (1992). Goal-directed systems and the good. *The Monist*, 75, 34–49.

Bishop, J. (1989). *Natural Agency: An Essay on the Causal Theory of Action*. Cambridge: Cambridge University Press.

Dancy, J. (2000). *Practical Reality*. Oxford: Oxford University Press.

Davidson, D. (1963). Actions, reasons and causes. *Journal of Philosophy*, 60, 685–699.

Davidson, D. (1980a). Freedom to act [1973]. In D. Davidson (1980b), 63–81.

Davidson, D. (1980b). *Essays on Actions and Events*. Oxford: Clarendon Press.

Mele, A. (1992). *Springs of Action: Understanding Intentional Behavior*. New York: Oxford University Press.

Mele, A. (2000). Goal-directed action: Teleological explanations, causal theories, and deviance. *Philosophical Perspectives*, 14, 279–300.

Millikan, R. G. (1984). *Language, Thought, and Other Biological Categories: New Foundations for Realism*. Cambridge, MA: MIT Press.

O'Connor, T. (2000). *Persons and Causes: The Metaphysics of Free Will*. New York: Oxford University Press.

Okrent, M. (2007). *Rational Animals: The Teleological Roots of Intentionality*. Athens, OH: Ohio University Press.

Peacocke, C. (1979). *Holistic Explanation: Action, Space, Interpretation*. New York: Oxford University Press.

Schueler, G. F. (2003). *Reasons and Purposes: Human Rationality and the Teleological Explanation of Action*. Oxford: Clarendon Press.

Sehon, S. (2005). *Teleological Realism: Mind, Agency, and Explanation*. Cambridge, MA: MIT Press.

Stoutland, F. (1976). The causation of behavior. In J. Hintikaa (ed.), *Essays on Wittgenstein in Honor of G. H. von Wright*. Amsterdam: North Hollandsche, 286–325.

Tanney, J. (2009). Reasons as non-causal, context-placing explanations. In C. Sandis (ed.), *New Essays on the Explanation of Action*. New York: Palgrave Macmillan.

Wilson, G. (1989). *The Intentionality of Human Action*. Stanford, CA: Stanford University Press.

Wright, L. (1976). *Teleological Explanations: An Etiological Analysis of Goals and Functions*. Berkeley: University of California Press.

17

Reasons and Causes

TIMOTHY O'CONNOR

Each of the two main terms in this entry's title has multiple senses. In the context of human action, 'reasons' can refer to *normative reasons*, or the conditions (generally external to the agent's psychological states) that rationally or morally justify a particular course of action for an agent in a given circumstance, whether or not the course of action is taken or the agent even acknowledges the existence of the reason. 'Reasons' can also refer to *motivational reasons*, the agent's own reasons for doing what he does, wise or foolish as it may be. In this latter sense, 'an agent's having reason *R* for doing *A*' is a psychological state or set of states (such as beliefs, desires, and intentions) that motivates the agent toward, and potentially explains, certain courses of action. It is this latter sense of 'reason' that is in view here (for further discussion of this distinction, see chapters 19 and 5). 'Causes' is employed in multiple senses as well in the context of the explanation of actions, and these will be adumbrated over the course of this essay.

Reasons as Not (Efficiently) Causal, Underwriting Irreducibly Teleological Explanations

Beginning in the 1950s, in the shadow of Wittgenstein, several philosophers argued that the reasons which explain an action cannot be among the factors which causally produce it. According to one such argument, the explanatory connection forged in citing reasons for actions is (allegedly) conceptual and hence logically necessary rather than empirical and contingent, as all efficient causal connections (allegedly) are (Melden 1961). According to another argument, which runs in a rather different direction, a causal explanation must cite a completely general 'covering law' encompassing types under which the cited cause and effect fall; but it is evident on the face of it that no plausible covering laws exist in the case of reasons and actions (Hart and Honoré 1959). These arguments are of less interest here than the non-causal account of the explanation of action to which they led many thinkers. On this view, explanations of action are teleological: they explain by citing an agent's goal or purpose in performing the action. Further, teleological explanations are basic; they are not reducible to, or a shorthand for, another form of explanation such as the causal one. In particular, the adequacy of a teleological explanation does not rest on an implicit assumption that the agent's desire to attain the goal and her belief that an action of a certain type would contribute to attaining that goal were among the set of factors which causally produced the action. Teleological explanations are different in kind from, but no less legitimate than, the mechanistic causal explanations characteristic of science. Proponents of irreducible teleological explanation (for example von Wright 1971 and Sehon 2005) will often allow that human actions are identical to, or are wholly realized by, sub-personal physical phenomena, and that these underlying phenomena admit of wholly causal explanations. But this does not show that teleological explanations are fundamental, let alone dispensable, since only they are capable of accounting for what occurs as an *action* – as opposed to mere movement. Other non-causalists are motivated in part by the desire to account for autonomous or morally responsible agency and make stronger claims concerning the independence of teleological explanation. They will say either that the goal-directed formation of an intention or volition which is the originating core of an action cannot be identical to, or realized by, an event which admits of an efficient causal explanation (McCann 1998) or that it is at best contingent that this is so (Ginet 1990, 2002).

In a widely influential essay, Davidson (1963) challenged this whole tradition by arguing that true explanations of actions must cite events which are in fact causes. His central argument rests on the observation that 'a person can have a reason for an action, and perform the action, and yet this reason not be the reason why he did it' (p. 9). The non-causalist, he argued, has no resources for making the required discrimination between those goals of which the agent is aware but which merely accompany the action and those which actually move the agent to act. Your rich uncle lies dying, in great and continuous pain. You want to see his suffering cease; you also want to receive your inheritance. You pull the plug on his life-preserving respirator. Why? We seem to be able to distinguish three basic scenarios – you were motivated by compassion, you were motivated by greed, you were motivated by both – where the non-causalist can discern only one. The causal theorist, by contrast, bid us to look to the actual causes in each case, an intuitively satisfying basis for determining the true reason(s) for the action.

The most important replies by non-causalists to Davidson's challenge point to the agent's intention in acting as grounding the required discrimination (Wilson 1989, Ginet 1990, McCann 1998, Sehon 2005). This action-guiding intention is conceived in somewhat different ways by these authors, but all posit that actions involve, or are accompanied by, an intention which refers to the purpose the agent is acting for. In the case of Davidson's rich uncle, the three scenarios are distinguished by there being in each case a distinct content to the intention that accompanies the agent's action. Critics of this content-of-intention strategy argue (1) that the teleological theories invoking intentions in acting cannot ground explanations of why an action occurred in the absence of a causal account of the formation and sustenance of the intention in acting and of its connection to the action itself; and (2) that it is implausible, on empirical grounds, that all actions feature intentions with the requisite content (see especially Mele 1992 and 2003; also Clarke 2000/2008 and O'Connor 1993; for a reply, see Ginet 2002 and Sehon 2005).

Reasons as Efficient Causes

A great many theorists over the last forty years have followed Davidson's lead in defending some version of the idea that typical explanations through reasons are implicitly causal, or – to focus directly on the claim about how things are with respect to actions rather than on the claim about how people typically take them to be – that *true* explanations of actions in terms of reasons implicitly or explicitly identify the state/event of the agent's having reason *R* for doing action *A* as being among the salient factors which causally produced his *A*-ing. Such a reason might consist of an appropriately paired belief and desire, as Davidson originally suggested (for example your desire for beer and your beliefs that beer is in the fridge, that, if you start walking to the fridge, you will arrive there, and so on caused you to walk to the fridge). Or the reason might involve a richer set of states, for instance nested intentions that constitute wide-ranging and longer-term plans of action (Bratman 1987).

Soon after Davidson's essay, a number of authors, including Davidson himself (Chisholm 1966, Taylor 1966, Davidson 1980), noticed a serious obstacle to attempts to provide a plausible causal theory. It is easy to conjure up scenarios where one's reasons cause one to perform an action suited to the reasons, despite one's not having acted intentionally. Here is Davidson's example:

> A climber might want to rid himself of the weight and danger of holding another man on a rope, and he might know that by loosening his hold on the rope he could rid himself of the weight and danger. This belief and want might so unnerve him as to cause him to loosen his hold, and yet it might be the case that he never *chose* to loosen his hold, nor did he do it intentionally. (1980: 79)

Here the climber has a reason for loosening his hold on the rope and this reason causes him to do so, but in such a way that it is evident that he did not intentionally act as he did. The *way* the reason caused the action was of the wrong sort for the action to have been intentional. The challenge for the causal theorist, then, is to say in general terms what the *right* way consists in. What kinds of causal process between motivating reasons and behavior must occur for the action to be intentional, according to the causal theorist?

This is the much discussed problem of 'wayward or deviant causal chains,' which is treated thoroughly on its own in this volume (chapter 21). Some have taken the problem to bring a decisive refutation of the causal theory, which led them to propose that causation *by the agent* should be taken as an ontological (Taylor 1966) or as a (merely) conceptual (Bishop 1983) primitive in the theory of action. Others have seen in the problem the futility of analyzing intentional action in fundamentally causal terms of any kind, and proposed a return to teleology (Wilson 1989, Sehon 2005). Sophisticated attempts to overcome the problem by advancing complicated conditions for the kind of reason-action causation involved in intentional action may be found in Bishop (1989) and Mele (1992). These are exercises in conceptual analysis; see chapter 5 for the suggestion that an account of the required causal process should come instead from a mature psychology and neuroscience, and chapter 21 for an argument that the problem is not distinctive to the causal theory of *action*, as we might imagine; we could see this by inserting irregular links within *any* kind of regular causal process, by raising difficulties for any attempt to give a precise and fully accurate causal analysis of an original type of process. We would not abandon an otherwise promising causal theory of these processes in the face of the challenge, so why should we do so in the case of a causal theory of action?

Reasons, Causes, and Physicalism

We noted above that one objection to the thesis that reasons are efficient causes of actions was rooted in the twin claims that a genuine causal explanation must cite a general 'covering law' encompassing types under which the cited cause and effect fall and that there are no covering laws available for reason and action types (given the endlessly open-ended range of circumstances needed to ensure the outcome, and even given the reason). Davidson conceded these premises but argued that individual (token) mental events could be causes by being identical to physical events which are linked to them by causal laws. Token mental events can be classified in various ways by distinct kinds of predicates (for instance physical–chemical, neurophysiological, and psychological). Davidson supposed that every token mental event is identical to a token physical event, although there is no systematic way to correlate mental and physical event types, since token mental events of the same mental type can be identical to token physical events that do not fall under any unified physical type. Although there are no general causal laws that link event types under mental terms, for every instance of mental causation (for example, Fred's desire for beer and Fred's belief that beer is available in the fridge causing Fred to get up from his chair and walk to the fridge), there is (we may suppose) a causal law that links the token events under some physical description. In short, you can have mental causation without mental causal laws by embracing mental–physical token identity without type identity.

Davidson's picture seems to face a serious problem. It allows that mental events can be causes, but it doesn't appear to allow that there are distinctively mental causal processes: it is never *qua* mental that a mental event causes an effect, but always *qua* physical. This would seem to imply a kind of epiphenomenalism, in that mental event types as such lack causal efficacy (McLaughlin 1989). The threat of epiphenomenalism is not confined to Davidson's distinctive philosophy of mind, however. Many contemporary philosophers of mind accept the claims of mental–physical token identity and type non-identity, while they depart from Davidson by seeking to make room for distinctively mental-level causation. (This departure is facilitated by a rejection of the 'covering law' model of causal explanation, a model that is now widely seen as implausible.) On their views, mental properties are in every case 'realized by' physical properties, though the same kind of mental property can be realized by a wide variety of physical properties, given appropriately different circumstances. (My dog and I might both believe that there is food in her bowl without its being the case that the physical realizations of these beliefs share any interesting neurophysiological description.) Most such philosophers hold, further, that the realm of purely physical causation is 'complete' or 'closed': in tracing the thread of causes running through my brain at a fundamental, physical level, one will not reach any mental event that makes an independent contribution. It is only at a level of organization which is subject to mental and actional description that mental causes make their mark. Mental processes are coarse-grained patterns running through a small, hierarchically organized portion of the physical world. These patterns neither are just a special case of physical patterns (they are in this sense irreducible) nor give rise to explanations that compete with the more fundamental physical explanations on which they supervene. The resulting picture of the physical world is one of multiple levels of causal processes (including physical, chemical, biological, psychological) that are independent of, and irreducible to, each other, each giving rise to true, mutually non-redundant causal explanations of distinctive kinds of phenomena.

It seems to some, however, that this resolution is an attempt to have one's cake and eat it, too. Consider again Fred, whose desire for beer and beliefs concerning its ready availability supposedly cause his decision to move towards it. On the view under consideration, each of the relevant beliefs and desires is realized by causal-explanatorily prior physical events, where realization is a kind of one-way ontological dependency, such that the occurrences of the more fundamental physical events suffice in the circumstances for the mental events to occur. If this is so, then it might seem that, after all, the purely physical events cause, and thereby explain, Fred's decision to move and subsequent action. By hypothesis, there is a complete, purely physical causal path at the lower level and, for each mental event at the higher level, there is a subvening physical event, which is ontologically prior and suffices for it. It appears that there is, after all, a competition between candidate physical and mental causes of Fred's decision. Assuming that the decision is not overdetermined – that is, caused both by Fred's relevant beliefs and desires *and* by purely physical causes – one set of causes must not be genuine. The ontological priority of the physical suggests that it is the claim about the causal efficacy of the mental that must go (Kim 1998).

The foregoing 'causal exclusion' argument challenges the reconcilability of non-reductive physicalism not just with a causal theory of action, but with the causal efficacy of mental states in general. There has been an enormous amount of discussion of this issue in the past few decades, and some of it turns on basic metaphysical issues concerning properties, events, and causation and on how views on these matters impact on the way in which mental events might be said to depend upon physical events. We cannot survey that discussion here. Interested readers are directed to Robb and Heil (2003/2008) and Bennett (2007), which include discussion of various attempts to demonstrate the unsoundness of the exclusion argument, and to O'Connor and Churchill (forthcoming), who argue that the argument goes through only under a certain view of causation. Here I wish to note two accounts of the causal role of mental states, including reasons for actions, which, if successful, would defang the exclusion argument's conclusion. On both accounts, mental states can be causally relevant to decisions and to subsequent bodily movements even if they are not straightforwardly efficient causes of them.

Causally Relevant, though Not Causes

Jackson and Pettit (1988 and 1990) distinguish 'process' and 'program' explanations. A process explanation specifies the causally efficacious properties that directly contribute to the effect's production. Even for high-level effects such as an agent's choices, these causally efficacious properties will be low-level ones, ultimately of fundamental physics. So mental events are not, strictly speaking, causes of any effects. They are, however, *causally relevant*, insofar as they figure essentially in informative program explanations; and these provide a kind of information not given by the corresponding process explanation:

> The realization of the property ensures – it would have been enough to have made it suitably probable – that a crucial productive property is realized and, in the circumstances, that the event, under a certain description, occurs. The property-instance does not figure in the productive process leading to the event but it more or less ensures that a property-instance which is required for that process does figure. A useful metaphor for describing the role of the property is to say that its realization programs for the appearance of the productive property and, under a certain description, for the event produced. The analogy is with a computer program which ensures that certain things will happen – things satisfying certain descriptions – though all the work of producing those things goes on at a lower, mechanical level. (1990: 114)

I shall not consider here whether this retreat from causation to causal relevance allows the theorist to retain everything that is essential to a straighforwardly causal theory of action. I merely note that one's views concerning the nature of causation may affect whether, on the picture Jackson and Pettit provide, reasons are *causally* – as opposed to *explanatorily* – relevant in a weaker sense.

Structuring Causes

Motivated by a different set of concerns than to respond to the causal exclusion argument, Dretske (1988, 1989) nonetheless presents a picture of mental causation that could be marshaled in response to it. (For fuller discussion, see chapter 18 here.) Drestske suggests that, for many kinds of naturally and artificially organized processes, we need to distinguish two kinds of causes. There is the triggering cause of the outcome and the structuring cause of the entire causal process. We may explain the distinction via an example. When you press the button outside my door, the doorbell rings. Your pressing the button triggered the ringing of the bell. That the type of event which is the triggering cause reliably has the bell-ringing effect has a distinct explanation, however – one which lies in the factor which created a causal pathway between the button and the bell. The electrician's establishing a circuit that can be opened by the pressing of the bell is a structuring cause of the effect, for each occasion when the button is pressed.

Likewise, in the case of animal and human action, each instance of, say, movement away from a predator has an electrochemical triggering cause within the agent's brain. The intentional properties of that event – it's being a desire to avoid harm and a belief that moving in a certain direction will potentially enable that desire to be realized – do not directly trigger the effect, only certain electrochemical properties do. The movement, then, has purely physical causes. However, we should also step back from the particulars of the triggering cause and its effect in this instance, and take note of the fact that a certain kind of electrochemical event in the brain reliably issues in certain kinds of movement (relative to a set of external circumstances). As in the bell-ringing case, although here for purely natural reasons, a kind of process is being exhibited that has a distinctive cause, a structuring cause. The reason why there is a reliable causal pathway of this sort is that the relevant events in the brain have not just electrochemical properties, but also meaning. Dretske's suggestion is that the process of learning operates on the agent's particular kind of cognitive system, recruiting its natural causal and informational regularities, so that certain kinds of representational states come to function as beliefs and desires. As a result, the physical causal sequence of brain state and movement is also a *behavior*, something that the agent is purposively doing. Beliefs and desires cause movements through their physical properties. The *causing* of movements that constitutes behavior is, however, explained by facts about *what* is believed and desired; and the latter facts are themselves, in part, historical – a function of a process of learning. In behavior based on learning, beliefs and desires play the causal roles they do precisely because of their acquired intentional content. In this way they are causally relevant to – structuring causes of – the behavior of which they are a part (Dretske 1990: 831). For a critical discussion of Dretske's conception of the causal role of reasons in action, see Stampe (1990) and Kim (1991).

Reasons, Causes, and Free Will

A different set of concerns comes to the fore when philosophers consider the nature – not of action *simpliciter*, which encompasses the range of animal and human action from the most instinctual or automated to that which is carefully and reflectively deliberated upon through complex considerations – but of actions that are done freely or autonomously, such that the agent is properly subject to moral praise and blame for the action. It is a debated empirical question whether human actions ever are undertaken freely, as we commonly assume in everyday life. (For a discussion of the present status of this question, see O'Connor forthcoming and Mele 2009.) Quite apart from giving a verdict on that matter, however, philosophers can and do ask what it would take to be free agents – to possess 'free will.'

Some philosophers ('compatibilists') endorse a view of freedom of action on which to act freely is, roughly, for one's act to be caused in a suitable way by one's own reasons – whichever reasons are motivationally the strongest at the time one acts – and for this to occur in such a way that one is not subject to any form or external manipulation or internal compulsion. Certain philosophers will adorn this basic account with certain additional requirements, which are not of concern here. All that we need to note is that, on this broad family of views, no special issues about the causal role of reasons arise.

Other philosophers, however, deem this sort of view to be fundamentally inadequate. On their view, free actions are (or would be) actions in which the agent selects from among alternative possibilities in such a way that it is not predetermined by factors influencing the action, including the agent's own reasons, which possibility the agent shall choose. Freedom of action, then, requires the action not to be causally determined by the action's past. This raises two questions: how is this indeterministic variety of control conceived, and how is its exercise influenced by the agent's reasons?

There are three broad types of indeterminist views of free action. Non-causalist views (Ginet 1990, McCann 1998) take control to be an intrinsic property of choices or volitions and espouse a purely teleological view of how choices are guided by reasons. Causal indeterminist views (Kane 1996) understand an agent's control much like the compatibilists discussed above. It is a function of the fact that the causes issuing in the action include the agent's own reasons for acting. What is different is simply the requirement that the causation between reasons and the action be indeterministic: the reasons cause the action in fact, but it might have been the case that they did not: there was a non-zero probability in the total set of circumstances that a different action might have been caused (by different or perhaps the same set of reasons, as the case may be). Twentieth-century physics has taught philosophers to be comfortable with the idea of indeterministic (or 'probabilistic') causation, though how exactly one is to think of this idea is much debated, and the differences will matter for accounts of the way in which reasons cause free choices indeterministically.

Finally, there is the agent causationist view of freedom. Agent causationists think that free control over one's own actions requires not merely that one's actions be undetermined by one's reasons and other influencing factors, but also that one have a capacity directly to determine which of the several alternatives with a non-zero probability actually occurs. On such a view, this sort of control is an ontologically basic causal capacity of free agents.

Assuming that they reject the adequacy of purely teleological views of the way reasons explain actions, agent-causal views seem to face a dilemma when it comes to the influence of reasons. If they say that reasons influence free actions by causing the agent to cause her decision, then it seems that the view is not a real advance on the causal indeterminist view. In the end, what action the agent selects is settled by the indeterministic activity of the agent's reasons. Why, then, incur the theoretical cost of positing the ontological primitive of agent causation? However, if agent-causal views deny that reasons cause agent-causal events, then it seems that they have no account of how reasons guide free actions. Agent causation would then be a causally unconstrained but 'blind' capacity, one whose exercise would seemingly be random, and not obviously the capacity of a free and responsible agent.

In response to this dilemma, two strategies have been proposed. Clarke (2003) suggests an 'integrated account,' on which an action is caused *both* by the agent and by the agent's reasons so to act. But the cooperative activity of the agent and of her reasons is not fortuitous. Instead, we may suppose that a law of nature governs the fact that the agent's causal capacity is exercised when and only when the appropriate reasons act, and vice versa. (For criticism of this proposal, see O'Connor and Churchill 2006).

O'Connor (2000, 2008) suggests, alternatively, that reasons might causally 'structure' the agent-causal capacity, in the sense of inducing or altering, in the agent, an objective propensity or likelihood (greater than zero but less than one, which designates certainty of outcome) to cause an appropriately matching decision to act. On this approach, nothing produces the agent's causing her decision, and hence nothing calls into question the ultimacy of the agent's control capacity. The causal activity of the agent's reasons is exhausted by their alteration of the likelihoods of various outcomes. But the capacity is inherently subject to the continuous influence of factors, chief among them being the agent's own reasons. (For critical discussion of this proposal, see Clarke 2003, Hiddleston 2005, and, in reply, O'Connor 2008.)

See also: THE CAUSAL THEORY OF ACTION (5); TELEOLOGICAL EXPLANATION (16); TRIGGERING AND STRUCTURING CAUSES (18); MOTIVATING REASONS (19); HUMEANISM ABOUT MOTIVATION (20); DEVIANT CAUSAL CHAINS (21); MENTAL CAUSATION AND EPIPHENOMENALISM (23); AGENT CAUSATION (28); VON WRIGHT (72); DAVIDSON (73).

References

Bennett, K. (2007). Mental Causation. *Philosophy Compass*. http://www.blackwell-compass.com/subject/philosophy/article_view?article_id=phco_articles_bpl063.

Bishop, J. (1983). Agent-causation. *Mind*, 92, 61–79.

Bishop, J. (1989). *Natural Agency*. Cambridge: Cambridge University Press.

Bratman, M. (1987). *Intention, Plans, and Practical Reason*. Cambridge, MA: Harvard University Press.

Chisholm, R. (1966). Freedom and action. In K. Lehrer (ed.), *Freedom and Determinism*. New York: Random House, 28–44.

Clarke, R. (2000/2008). Incompatibilist (nondeterministic) theories of free will. *Stanford Encyclopedia of Philosophy*. http://plato.stanford.edu/entries/incompatibilism-theories/.

Clarke, R. (2003). *Libertarian Accounts of Free Will*. New York: Oxford University Press.

Davidson, D. (1963). Actions, reasons, and causes. *Journal of Philosophy*, 60, 685–700.

Davidson, D. (1980). Freedom to act. In D. Davidson, *Essays on Actions and Events*. Oxford: Oxford University Press, 63–81.

Dretske, F. (1988). *Explaining Behavior: Reasons in a World of Causes*. Cambridge, MA: MIT Press.

Dretske, F. (1989). Reasons and causes. In J. Tomberlin (ed.), *Philosophical Perspectives 3: Philosophy of Mind and Action Theory*. Atascadero, CA: Ridgeview Publishing Co., 1–15.

Dretske, F. (1990). Replies to reviewers. *Philosophy and Phenomenological Research*, 50 (4), 819–839.

Ginet, C. (1990). *On Action*. Cambridge: Cambridge University Press.

Ginet, C. (2002). Reasons explanations of action: Causalist versus noncausalist accounts. In Robert Kane (ed.), *The Oxford Handbook of Free Will*. New York: Oxford University Press, 386–405.

Hart, H. L. A., and Honoré, A. M. (1959). *Causation in the Law*. Oxford: Oxford University Press.

Hiddleston, E. (2005). Critical notice: Timothy O'Connor, *Persons and Causes*. *Nous*, 39 (3), 541–556.

Jackson, F., and Pettit, P. (1988). Functionalism and broad content. *Mind*, 97, 381–400.

Jackson, F., and Pettit, P. (1990). Program explanation: A general perspective. *Analysis*, 50 (2), 107–117.

Kane, R. (1996). *The Significance of Free Will*. New York: Oxford University Press.

Kim, J. (1991). Dretske on how reasons cause behavior. In B. McLaughlin (ed.), *Dretske and His Critics*. Cambridge, MA: Blackwell.

Kim, J. (1998). *Mind in a Physical World: An Essay on the Mind–Body Problem and Mental Causation*. Cambridge, MA: MIT Press/Bradford Books.

McCann, H. J. (1998). *The Works of Agency: On Human Action, Will, and Freedom*. Ithaca: Cornell University Press.

McLaughlin, B. (1989). Type epiphenomenalism, type dualism, and the causal priority of the physical. In J. Tomberlin (ed.), *Philosophical Perspectives 3: Philosophy of Mind and Action Theory*. Atascadero, CA: Ridgeview Publishing Co., 109–135.

Melden, A. I. (1961). *Free Action*. London: Routledge and Kegan Paul.

Mele, A. R. (1992). *Springs of Action*. New York: Oxford University Press.

Mele, A. R. (2003). *Motivation and Agency*. New York: Oxford University Press.

Mele, A. R. (2009). *Effective Intentions*. New York: Oxford University Press.

O'Connor, T. (1993). Indeterminism and free agency: Three recent views. *Philosophy and Phenomenological Research*, 53, 499–526.

O'Connor, T. (2000). *Persons and Causes: The Metaphysics of Free Will*. New York: Oxford University Press.

O'Connor, T. (2008). Agent-causal power. In Toby Handfield (ed.), *Dispositions and Causes*. Oxford: Clarendon Press, 189–214.

O'Connor, T. (forthcoming). Conscious willing and the emerging sciences of brain and behavior. In Nancey Murphy, George F. R. Ellis, and Timothy O'Connor (eds), *Downward Causation and the Neurobiology of Free Will*. New York: Springer Publications, 173–186.

O'Connor, T., and Churchill, J. (2006). Reasons explanation and agent control: In search of an integrated account. *Philosophical Topics*, 32, 241–254.

O'Connor, T., and Churchill, J. (forthcoming). Nonreductive physicalism or emergent dualism? The argument from mental causation. In George Bealer and Robert Koons (eds), *The Waning of Materialism: New Essays*. Oxford: Oxford University Press, 261–280.

Robb, D., and Heil, J. (2003/2008). Mental causation. *Stanford Encyclopedia of Philosophy*. http://plato.stanford.edu/entries/mental-causation/.

Sehon, S. (2005). *Teleological Explanations*. Cambridge, MA: MIT Press/Bradford Books.

Stampe, D. W. (1990). Discussion notes on Fred Dretske's *Explaining Behavior: Reasons in a World of Causes*. *Philosophy and Phenomenological Research*, 50 (4), 787–793.

Taylor, R. (1966). *Action and Purpose*. Englewood Cliffs: Prentice Hall.

von Wright, G. H. (1971). *Explanation and Understanding*. London: Routledge and Kegan Paul.

Wilson, G. (1989). *The Intentionality of Human Action*. Stanford, CA: Stanford University Press.

Further reading

Setiya, K. (2003). Explaining action. *The Philosophical Review*, 112, 339–393.

18

Triggering and Structuring Causes

FRED DRETSKE

Causal explanations are context-sensitive. What we pick out as the cause of *E* in causal explanations of *E* depends on our interests, our purposes, and our prior knowledge. Almost any event *E* depends on a great variety of other events in such a way as to make any one of them eligible, given the right context, as the cause in causal explanations of *E*. My purpose here is not to dispute this doctrine, but instead, by assuming its correctness, to describe two kinds of causal explanation – a triggering and a structuring explanation – and to exhibit the usefulness of this distinction for understanding causal explanations of human behavior.

An operator moves the cursor on a screen by pressing a key on the keyboard. Pressure on the key is the triggering cause of the cursor's movement. By this I mean that movement would not have occurred (in these circumstances) if the key had not been pressed. Pressure on the key *made* the cursor move. In these circumstances, pressure on the key (this type of event) is regularly followed by cursor movement (this type of event). It is this sort of arrangement – the sort which is characteristic of a triggering cause – that allows us to say that the operator moved the cursor by pressing the key, and to explain cursor movement by citing the fact that the key was pressed.

On the other hand, we sometimes speak of the events that produced hardware and software conditions (electrical and mechanical conditions in the computer) as the cause of cursor movement. This is especially evident when cursor movement (in response to key presses) is unexpected or unusual in some way. Imagine a puzzled operator watching the cursor move as he pokes the key, asking, 'Why is the cursor moving?' Since pressure on the key is making the cursor move – that, in fact, is what the operator finds puzzling – clearly a different explanation is being sought. He wants to know what brought about, or caused, the machine to occupy a state, to be in a condition, in which pressure on this key has this effect. He knows, or he can easily be assumed to know after a few presses on the key, that *C* (pressing this key) is causing *E* (the movement of the cursor). What he wants to know is why it is so. Who or what made *E* depend on *C* in this way? He is looking for an explanation of why one thing (in this case pressure on the key) is causing *E* (in this case movement of the cursor). He is looking for a structuring cause.

A terrorist plants a bomb in the general's car. The bomb sits there for days, until the general gets into his car and turns the key to start the engine. The bomb is detonated and the general is killed. Who killed him? The terrorist, of course. How? By planting a bomb in his car. Although the general's own action (turning the key in the ignition) was the triggering cause, the terrorist's action was the structuring cause, and it will be his action, something the terrorist did a week ago, that will certainly be singled out, both in legal and in moral inquiries, as the cause of the general's death. Some causes of death are triggering causes, others are structuring causes. I put the poison in your coffee, yes, but you drank the poisoned coffee. I am the structuring, you the triggering, cause of death.

Triggering causes give rise to regularities. Push the key (in these circumstances) again and again, and the cursor will move – again and again. Turn on the ignition (once again, in these circumstances – that is, when there is a bomb wired to the ignition) and you will get the same result: an explosion. In this case, of course, the explosion destroys the conditions (a bomb wired to the ignition) in which the one event is regularly followed by an event of the second type. So consider a similar case in which the condition persists. I wire a switch to a light so that one can – again and again – turn on the light by throwing the switch. The structuring cause of the light's going on Tuesday is the same as that of its going on Wednesday: my wiring the switch to the light on Monday. The triggering causes may be different each time the light goes on, but the structuring cause remains the same.

Structuring causes, therefore, do not give rise to the sort of regularities associated with triggering causes. The effect may or may not occur. Structuring causes need a suitable trigger. The terrorist caused the general's death, yes, but in the circumstances that obtained at the time when he planted the bomb, the result – an explosion – would never occur. If no one ever turns on the ignition, no explosion takes place. Structuring causes need a suitable trigger to produce their effect.

When *C* is the triggering cause of *E*, one can think of the structuring cause of *E* as a (triggering) cause of those standing conditions (call them *B*) in which *C* causes *E*. The terrorist's activities a week ago, *A*, produced (or are the triggering cause of) those conditions of the automobile, *B* (bomb wired to the ignition), in which turning the key in the ignition (*C*) causes an explosion (*E*). So the triggering cause of *B* is a structuring cause of *E*.

Though triggering and structuring causes of a particular event are always distinct, they may sometimes appear to collapse into a single event. A dim-witted terrorist forgets he planted a bomb. Or he forgets which car it was he planted a bomb in. Needing a car, he steals the wired car and blows himself up. Is the terrorist both the triggering and the structuring cause of his own death? He created the conditions that enabled him to blow himself up, yes, but that only means that one and the same person was involved in both causes. It doesn't show that the causes were the same. What he did to trigger this outcome is different from what he did to structure it. It was his turning on the ignition that triggered the explosion. It was his wiring the bomb to the ignition – quite a different action – that structured it.

This point will be important in thinking about the explanation of behavior, because different states of a single internal object can function as triggering and structuring causes of behavior. In the case of human behavior, for instance, it might turn out that the brain's possession of certain electrical–chemical properties is the triggering cause of some bodily movement, while its possession of an altogether different property –

possibly a relational or semantic property – is the structuring cause of the same movement.

This, then, is the distinction. Why is it useful? How does it help us to understand explanations of animal and human behavior? Let us begin with the behavior of inanimate devices – simple instruments. We will come to the behavior of persons and animals – the main target – in a moment.

A careless electrician wires the room thermostat to the garage door opener instead of the furnace. Whenever it gets cold in the house, then, the thermostat opens the garage door instead of turning on the furnace. Someone observing this effect over time wants to know why the thermostat behaves in this unusual way. Why does it open the garage door instead of turning the furnace on when it gets cold? Thermostats do not usually behave like this. The explanation? An electrician mis-wired the device. He created conditions in which an event occurring in the thermostat, an event that normally (when things are wired properly) turns on the furnace, is now activating the garage door opener. Notice: this explanation of the thermostat's behavior (its opening the garage door) appeals to a structuring, not to the triggering, cause of the event (movement of the garage door) that results from the thermostat's behavior. If we follow standard practice and distinguish behavior (say, moving one's arm) from the events or conditions that necessarily result from the behavior (the movement of one's arm), then it would seem that this explanation of behavior (why the thermostat is opening the garage door) adverts to a structuring, not triggering, cause of the movements (garage door movements) that result from such behavior. If you are looking for the cause of the garage door's movements, look in the thermostat. Therein lies the triggering cause (the closure of an electrical circuit by the movement of a temperature sensitive piece of metal) of the garage door's movement. If, on the other hand, you want an explanation of the thermostat's behavior, why it opened the garage door, you have to look elsewhere – at who or what brought about this causal arrangement, at who or what made events in the thermostat cause the door to open. You have to find the structuring cause of the garage door movement.

If *C* is the (type of) event inside that thermostat that triggers the garage door opening *E*, then the thermostat's behavior is not *E*, but *C* causing *E*, and the explanation of this behavior is not the explanation of *E*, but of *C*'s causing *E*. Knowing what it is in the thermostat that causes (triggers) the garage door to open is not (yet) to know why the thermostat behaves the way it does, why it opens the garage door. By looking in the thermostat and at the associated wiring, you may come to know *how* the device opens the garage door, but not *why* it does. The explanation for that lies in the structuring cause – in this case, the shoddy work of the electrician. He is the one who made the thermostat behave in this strange way.

It should be noticed that the facts mentioned in a structuring explanation of a device's behavior do not supervene on the current physical state of that device. Two thermostats that are physically identical and therefore behave in exactly the same way (opening a garage door when it gets cold in the house) might nonetheless have their behavior explained in quite different ways. The first one behaves that way because it was mis-wired by the electrician. The second one behaves that way because lightning struck the house and produced a short-circuit. The device whose behavior is being explained is a material system, yes, and its behavior is a thoroughly material process

– yes, again – but to understand why, in causal terms, it behaves the way it does one must, sometimes at least, go outside the system, to understand how things got arranged that way.

Turning, then, from mechanical devices to living systems, consider an explanation of plant behavior (I'll come to animals in a minute). The explanatory pattern is the same. Some plants change color as their flowering season progresses. Why do they do this? In the case of the Scarlet Gilia – one of the plants that behave this way – the explanation lies in the adaptive value of this behavior: it attracts pollinators. Early in the flowering season, hummingbirds are the chief pollinators, and hummingbirds are more attracted to red blossoms. Later in the season the hummingbirds migrate and hawkmoths, who prefer whiter blossoms, become the principal pollinator. The Scarlet Gilia changes color, then, 'in order to' exploit this seasonal alteration in its circumstances. It yields more fruit by changing color, and this is why it does it.

Here, again, we have a structuring explanation of behavior, an explanation which adverts to the historical circumstances which caused the plant to be so constituted that the internal chemical changes brought about (triggered) by the weather give rise to (trigger) changes in color. Someone might know all there is to know about the internal chemical changes – what brings them about and what they bring about – and still not understand why the plant behaves this way. This is because an explanation for the plant's behavior is, typically at least, a structuring explanation – why things are now arranged the way they are in the plant.

Once again, the explanation of behavior does not supervene upon the system whose behavior is being explained. A physically similar plant will behave the same way – it will change color at a certain time each summer – but it might behave this way for quite different reasons. The second plant has a different history. It changes color in order to repel rapacious beetles, which dislike white blossoms. This is the reason why, the explanation for the fact that this plant changes color; but you could never discover this reason by examining the plant itself. This plant is similar to another plant that behaves the same way for quite different reasons. You need to know something about the history of the plant if you want to know why it behaves that way.

Consider, finally, animals: You observe animal *S* retreating at the approach of *O*. *S* appears to be avoiding *O*. Why? Why is S behaving this way?

There are at least two possible answers – one corresponding to the triggering cause of *S*'s movements, the other corresponding to the structuring cause.

A Triggering Causal Explanation

S is running because it saw (sensed, perceived) *O* approaching. This is a triggering causal explanation because one is merely citing a link in a causal chain that results in *S*'s movements. The approach of *O* caused in *S* an event (a perceptual experience of *O*), which then produced (caused) those bodily movements, *M*, which we describe as a retreat from (an avoidance of) *O*.

Although this gives us a triggering cause of *M*, we may still have a problem about understanding why *S* ran. Perhaps we don't know that *O*-s are predators. Or it may be that, although *we* know that *O* is dangerous (to *S*-s), we don't know whether *S* knows it. *S* saw a predator approaching, yes, and its approach triggered flight; but why did it trigger flight? Did *S* recognize the predator as a predator? Did *S* think that what it had seen was a predator? Was there something about the way *O* approached *S* that triggered an instinctive reaction in *S*? Is *S* afraid of *O*-s and, if so, is its avoidance a learned or an instinctive response to *O*-s? These are obviously questions about the way *S* represents *O*, questions not about what S sees, but about what *S* knows (believes, thinks) about what it sees. They are questions the answers to which will tell us why *S* ran from the *O* it saw. After all, as we all know, two animals may both avoid *O* (the approach of *O* is a triggering cause of flight in both); but, like the plants described above, they avoid *O* for quite different reasons. One avoids *O* because it represents *O* as dangerous, a threat; the other, because it represents *O* as a friend to whom (as it turns out) *S* owes a lot of money. So *O*'s approach can be recognized as the triggering cause of *S*'s avoidance behavior without our knowing *why S* avoids *O*. To explain *S*'s behavior, we need an explanation that gives us more than a triggering cause of movement. We need to know the structuring cause of those movements. What is it that made, or is currently making, *S*'s perception of *O* into a triggering cause of flight?

A Structuring Causal Explanation

In supplying an animal's reasons for running from the (external) triggering cause of flight, we are providing a structuring cause of *S*'s movements. Just as our keyboard operator knew it was pressure on the key that controlled cursor movement but still wanted to know *why* it did, an observer of animal *S* may know (after watching *S* long enough) what triggers *S*'s movements (the sight of an *O*). What he doesn't know, and what he seeks an explanation for, is why the sight of *O* (some internal event that registers *O*'s presence) causes these movements. He is looking for a structuring cause of the *S*'s movements. What caused the sight of *O* to cause these movements rather than some other movements, or no movements at all? That is the same kind of question that the botanists were asking about the plant, or homeowners about their eccentric thermostat.

Sometimes the answer to this kind of question, a question about the structuring cause of movement, is a fact about the internal (triggering) cause of movement. In other words, sometimes, a fact about *C* (the internal cause of movements *M*) is what explains why *C* causes *M*. Suppose, for example, that originally, when *S* was just a little boy, the sight of *O* did not cause *S* to run. The sight of *O* did not trigger avoidance movements. So *S* got bitten. It hurt. *S* escaped this original encounter. Another *O* approached and *S* carelessly allowed it to get too close again. He got bitten again. These painful experiences taught *S* to avoid *O*-looking things. *S* now runs when he sees an *O* (and anything that looks like an *O*). The sight of an *O* (this internal event) has now become a triggering cause of *S*'s avoidance movements. Why? What explains the promotion of this internal event – the sight of an *O* – into a cause of avoidance movements?

Quite clearly, what helps to explain the current causal arrangements is the fact that this internal event – the sight of an *O* – signals, it is a sign of, it indicates, the presence of an *O*. It is a certain extrinsic, relational fact about this internal event that explains why it has acquired its current role in the production of flight, concealment, and avoidance. It was recruited as a cause of these movements because it enables *S* to avoid closer, potentially painful, contact with *O*-s. This internal event has a host of electrical–chemical properties (I assume it is some event or condition in *S*'s nervous system), and these electrical–chemical properties will certainly be involved in neurophysiological explanations of just how (and why) *S*'s body moves the way it does (how, for example, leg muscles are made to contract). If you want to know, however, *why* an internal event with these neurobiological properties causes this kind of movement (it didn't before the first biting), the answer lies in the extrinsic, relational facts about it – facts about what it signifies about external affairs. It signals the presence of an *O*. It means that an *O* is approaching.

This, then, is the beginning of a psychological explanation of *S*'s behavior. *S* runs away from *O* because, whether correctly or not, it represents what it sees as an *O*, one of those creatures that S (given its painful earlier experiences) wants to avoid. It is the beginning of a psychological explanation because it is here that we see the extrinsic, relational facts about *S*'s internal states (what they signify or mean about external affairs) figuring in the explanation of *S*'s current behavior. Biologists may be primarily interested in triggering causes of behavior, but psychologists, who are interested in the reasons we have for behaving in certain ways, are interested in structuring causes.

See also: ACTION THEORY AND ONTOLOGY (1); BASIC ACTIONS AND INDIVIDUATION (2); BODILY MOVEMENTS (4); REASONS AND CAUSES (17); MENTAL CAUSATION AND EPIPHENOMENALISM (23); RATIONAL AGENCY IN EVOLUTIONARY PERSPECTIVE (47).

Further reading

Bratman, M. (1990). Dretske's desires. *Philosophy and Phenomenological Research*, 50 (4), 795–800.

Dretske, F. (1988). *Explaining Behavior: Reasons in a World of Causes*. Cambridge, MA: MIT Press.

Dretske, F. (1990a). Précis. *Philosophy and Phenomenological Research*, 50 (4), 783–786.

Dretske, F. (1990b). Reply to Reviewers. *Philosophy and Phenomenological Research*, 50 (4), 819–839.

Dretske, F. (1998). Minds, machines, and money: What really explains behavior. In J. Bransen and S. Cuypers (eds), *Human Action, Deliberation and Causation*, Philosophical Studies Series 77. Dordrecht: Kluwer Academic Publishers, 157–173.

Stampe, D. W. (1990). Discussion notes on Fred Dretske's *Explaining Behavior: Reasons in a World of Causes*. *Philosophy and Phenomenological Research*, 50 (4), 787–793.

Tuomela, R. (1990). Are reasons-explanations explanations by means of structuring causes? *Philosophy and Phenomenological Research*, 50 (4), 813–818.

19

Motivating Reasons

STEPHEN EVERSON

According to what is still often described as the standard account of agency, not only is every action explicable as resulting from a belief and desire of the agent, but the beliefs and desires that explain actions do so because they stand as reasons for the actions they explain. Indeed, it can readily seem that the second claim follows straightforwardly from the first: in explaining an action, we come to know why the agent acted as he did; and to know why someone does something is to know the reason for his doing it. So, if it is true that Brutus assassinated Caesar because he wanted to protect the Roman Republic, his reason for assassinating Caesar was his desire to protect the Roman Republic (together with his belief that in killing Caesar he was protecting the Republic). Although it will be convenient to continue to label this as the 'standard account,' one should note that this label has become increasingly misleading: such has been the fragmentation of views about the conditions for agency, the nature of reasons for action, and their role in the explanation of actions that it would now be fairly arbitrary to single out any account as being standard or orthodox. Criticism of the standard account has in fact come from various directions. Some have complained, for instance, that it imposes too rationalist a structure on agency, implausibly requiring that agents always believe that there is value in what they do. Others, in contrast, have argued that it rests on an impoverished understanding both of practical rationality and of the notion of a reason for action.

To get some sense of the pressures on the standard account, and of why these might push one to distinguish between reasons of different kinds, it will be helpful to consider in a little detail what has been its most influential modern version – that provided by Donald Davidson in his paper 'Actions, reasons, and causes,' first published in 1963. According to Davidson, every action can be explained by what he called a 'primary reason,' consisting of a suitably paired belief and desire (or 'pro attitude'):

> *R* is a primary reason why an agent performed the action *A* under the description *d*, only if *R* consists of a pro attitude of the agent towards actions with a certain property, and a belief of the agent that *A*, under the description *d*, has that property. (1980: 5)[1]

This may sound rather technical, but it merely allows Davidson to give a properly general formulation to what is, at root, a simple idea. In order to explain an action, one needs to determine what the agent is intending to do by performing it, and 'to know a primary reason why someone acted as he did is to know an intention with which the action was done' (1980: 7). So, whenever someone does something intentionally, he must have a favorable attitude toward performing actions of that type and believe that the action he performs is of that type.

To explain an action is to rationalize it: by specifying the primary reason for an action, it 'is revealed as coherent with certain traits, long- or short-termed, characteristic or not, of the agent, and the agent is shown in his role of Rational Animal' (1980: 8). Moreover, the ability of a suitable belief–desire pair to explain an action rests, Davidson thinks, on their actually having caused it. This is because an agent may have a belief and a desire which are suitable to make his action rational, but yet it may not be true that he acts because of these. An agent may have more than one desire whose satisfaction would be achieved or furthered by his acting in some particular way. Having inappropriately claimed something on expenses, for instance, someone might both want to do the right thing and to get off the hook: it does not follow from this, however, that when he does repay the money he does so for both reasons. Although each desire is a reason for him to repay the money, it will not be (part of) *the* reason why he does this unless it has caused him to do so. Davidson thus provides a nicely unified account of the explanation of actions. Actions, like events generally, are susceptible to causal explanation; but, unlike the explanations of non-mental events, those we give for actions need to make manifest the practical rationality of their agents. In citing an agent's primary reason to explain what he does, one manages to fulfill both these requirements at the same time.

It is one thing, however, to claim that every action can be explained as resulting from a suitable belief and desire, and quite another to maintain that every such successful explanation is sufficient to show the agent in the role of rational animal. It is easy to be misled here by the fact that, in practice, when we cite an agent's desire to explain his action, this will place the action in a pattern of means–end reasoning. If I explain someone's moving a piece of wood by citing as his primary reason the desire to place an opponent in check together with his belief that his moving that piece of wood is placing his opponent in check, I will certainly have shown him to have acted rationally. It is, however, no requirement on primary reason explanations that they should do this: not everything one does intentionally is done for the sake of achieving something else, nor need it be done because it is thought to have any value in itself.

This last point is worth emphasizing, since critics of the standard account have sometimes thought that it commits its adherents to the claim that, whenever someone acts, he must believe that there is something, however minor, of value in what he does. Rosalind Hursthouse, for instance, has argued that what she calls 'arational actions' – actions that, whilst done intentionally, are done '(just) because [the agent] wants to' do them, such as 'leaping up reaching for leaves on trees' or 'pounding the table' – falsify the standard account because they allow no role for belief in their explanation (Hursthouse 1991: 59). To illustrate her point, she gives the example of Jane, who, 'in a wave of hatred for Joan, tears at Joan's photo with her nails':

> I can agree that Jane does this because, hating Joan, she wants to scratch her face, and gouge out her eyes; I can agree that she would not have torn at the photo if she had not

> believed that it was a photo of Joan; and if someone wants to say, 'So those are the reasons for the action,' I do not want to quarrel, for these 'reasons' do *not* form the appropriate desire–belief pair assumed by the standard account. On the standard account, if the explanatory desire in this case is the desire to scratch Joan's face, then the appropriate belief has to be something absurd, such as the belief that the photo of Joan *is* Joan, or that scratching the photo will be causally efficacious in defacing its original. (Ibid., pp. 59–60)

Hursthouse's paper usefully brings into focus a kind of action that has been too often neglected within the philosophical discussion of agency – but she is wrong to think that they cannot be accommodated by the standard account. For Davidson will have no problem in determining the primary reason for Jane's action: she tears at the photo because she wants to tear at the photo and believes that in performing this action she is tearing at the photo. That, of course, would not be a very interesting explanation to give – but this is not to the point here.

Davidson himself is properly insistent that 'pro attitudes must not be taken for convictions, however temporary, that every action of a certain kind ought to be performed, is worth performing, or is, all things considered, desirable.' An agent, that is, can intentionally do something – so that his action is duly susceptible to a primary-reason explanation – and yet see no value in what he does. To use Davidson's own vivid example: 'a man may all his life have a yen, say, to drink a can of paint, without ever, even at the moment he yields, believing it would be worth doing' (1980: 4). The agent in the example drinks the can of paint because he has a pro-attitude toward actions of paint-drinking and believes that his action is such an action. Whilst this allows Davidson's account to cover actions which are arational in that the agent believes neither that they are worth doing in themselves nor that they contribute to achieving something else which is worth achieving, it reveals how weak is the claim of primary-reason explanation to show an agent in his role of rational animal. Rational agency must involve more than merely satisfying a whim that not even the agent thinks is worth satisfying.

In fact, Davidson himself provides the materials for a more robust understanding both of reasons for action and of rationalization. For he acknowledges that in practice we often explain people's actions by citing facts not about their beliefs and pro-attitudes, but directly about the actions themselves and their consequences, intended or actual:

> Straight description of an intended result often explains an action better than stating that the result was intended or desired. 'It will soothe your nerves' explains why I pour you a shot as efficiently as 'I want to do something to soothe your nerves,' since the first in the context of explanation implies the second; but the first does better because, if it is true, the facts will justify my course of action. Because justifying and explaining an action so often go hand in hand, we frequently indicate the primary reason for an action by making a claim which, if true, would also verify, vindicate, or support the relevant belief or attitude of the agent. (1980: 8)

Davidson accepts here that, to justify an action, we (generally) need to look outside the agent's own beliefs and desires. He accepts, too, that in practice we can provide a justification for an action when we seek to explain it. What he denies is that a fact which justifies an action is thereby such as to explain it. His idea is rather that, when some fact justifies an action, this entails the truth of an underlying primary reason explanation:

> your stepping on my toes neither explains nor justifies my stepping on your toes unless I believe you stepped on my toes, but the belief alone, true or false, explains my action. (Ibid., p. 8)

Even if for the moment we accept this division between justification and explanation, Davidson's acknowledgment that to justify an action we generally have to look beyond the agent's own propositional attitudes highlights that his sliding between talking of primary reasons as reasons *why* someone acts and talking of them as reasons *for* someone to act is problematic.[2] If Davidson stepped sharply on Quine's toes because he falsely believed that Quine had stepped on his, that belief would form part of the reason why he acted as he did; but, contrary to what he believed, he did not in fact have a reason for doing what he did. Again, whilst we can find, with Davidson, that his paint-drinker acted intentionally, since his action can be explained by specifying a primary reason, our earlier worry that this is insufficient to make the paint-drinking rational can now be underpinned by our finding that he did not have a reason for drinking the paint. In this case, it is not that he wrongly thought that he had a reason, but that he didn't even think he had a reason for doing what he had a yen to do. To think that one has a reason for doing something is precisely to think that it would be worth doing.

Davidson, then, acknowledges that our everyday explanations of people's actions appeal both to facts about their states of mind and to entirely non-psychological facts. I may explain Ian's running down Victoria Street by saying that he thinks his bus is about to leave or by saying that he is in danger of missing his bus. Davidson tries to impose order on this by distinguishing explanation from justification and by allowing non-psychological facts a role only in the latter. The difficulty for him is that rationalization cannot be separated from justification in this way. To justify an action is to show what made it worth doing – what reason the agent had for performing it. As we have seen, bare primary-reason explanation is not sufficient to rationalize what it explains, and to think that justifications are not themselves explanatory will not be to honor Davidson's own insight that to show an agent in his role of rational animal is to rationalize, and hence to explain, his action.

The tension here can be eased by distinguishing between two kinds of reasons and two kinds of explanation. In making the first distinction we can, with a little caution, follow Michael Smith:

> [We] ordinarily distinguish two senses in which we have a reason for action. The first is the sense in which we are happy to acknowledge that to do something intentionally is to do that thing for a reason. Here our talk of reasons is talk about the psychological states that motivate what we do, the complex of psychological states that teleologically, and perhaps causally explain our actions [...] Let's call these our 'motivating' reasons.
>
> In the second sense, however, we have a reason to do all and only those things for which we can construct a certain kind of *justification*. Justifications may, of course, be of quite different kinds [...] Let's call these our 'normative' reasons. (Smith 1992: 329)

Having now distinguished between reasons *for* and reasons *why*, we should resist Smith's claim that he is finding two senses in which we can be said to have a reason *for* action. Nevertheless, his distinction here between motivating and normative reasons provides the resources for a more flexible, and hence more satisfactory, account of the explanation of action than Davidson's monolithic account can provide.[3]

To cite the normative reason for which an agent acts is to rationalize it, since it precisely succeeds in showing that, in acting as he does, the agent is responsive to a reason for acting. We can also say that, in providing a psychological explanation for an action – an explanation that specifies relevant beliefs and desires of the agent – we specify the motivating reasons why the agent acted. Crucially, the sense in which normative reasons are reasons is different from that in which motivating reasons are. The latter count as reasons merely because they can be cited in the explanation of actions. The fact that the reason why someone drank paint was his desire to do so does not entail that the desire was a reason *for* him to drink paint, any more than the fact that the reason why the engine exploded was that the valve was blocked entails that the blockage of the valves was a reason *for* the engine to explode. In contrast, normative reasons will also count as explanatory reasons, but they do so because they are reasons for the actions they can be cited to explain.[4]

A challenge to the propriety of distinguishing between normative and motivating reasons in this way can be found in Jonathan Dancy's book *Pratical Reality* (2000). Like Davidson, Dancy adheres to a monistic rather than a pluralist account of the explanation of action; but, whereas Davidson is led to treat beliefs and desires as reasons for action because they feature in the explanation of action, Dancy moves to deny them an explanatory role on the grounds that they are not reasons for actions. I shall not try to deal here with the difficulties occasioned by this view, though they are extreme, but it will be helpful briefly to consider the force of his challenge.

Dancy's main argument against an account that takes motivating and normative reasons to be reasons of different kinds is that it will not be able to satisfy what, he argues, are two conditions on any satisfactory account of reasons: the 'explanatory constraint' and the 'normative constraint.' The first stipulates that the account should show 'that and how any normative reason is capable of contributing to the explanation of an action that is done for that reason' (2000: 101); the second

> requires that a motivating reason, that in the light of which one acts, must be the sort of thing that is capable of being among the reasons in favour of so acting; it must, in this sense, be possible to act for a good reason. (Ibid., p. 103)

In fact the first constraint is readily met: it would only cause difficulty if one followed Davidson in thinking that normative reasons have a direct role in the justification of actions but only an indirect role in their explanation. The natural consequence of distinguishing motivating from normative reasons is to allow each its proper explanatory role. Once one sees that they are not in competition for the same explanatory space, Dancy's explanatory constraint poses no problem: normative reasons contribute to the explanation of actions precisely because they, unlike motivating reasons, are capable of rationalizing them. The explanatory role of normative reasons is in no way compromised by the fact that the rationalization of an action entails an underlying explanation specifying the agent's motivating psychological states.

It is Dancy's second constraint that is the more difficult for the pluralist to meet: indeed it is formulated precisely to make this impossible. For it is not just that Dancy specifies two different relations – being a normative reason for an action and being a motivating reason for an action – and leaves it open that something might stand in both relations to a particular action (as, on Davidson's account, the same thing may be both the cause of and the reason for an action). Rather, since the items that may stand as normative reasons for actions are different in kind from those that may stand as motivating reasons, this rules out 'the possibility that motivating and normative reasons should be capable of being identical' – and unless one leaves that possibility open, Dancy argues, one will be unable to make sense of a claim such as 'It must be possible for the reasons in the light of which one acts to be *among* the reasons in favour of doing what one does' (ibid., p. 106).

Here there is an echo of the consideration which motivated Davidson's claim that the primary reason for an action should be its cause: namely that an agent may have several reasons for acting in some way but not act on all of them. Certainly, this is as much a feature of normative reasons as it is of an agent's beliefs and desires. Just as someone may want to do the right thing by paying back some money and yet not pay back the money because of that desire, so it can be an open question whether he paid back the money because that was the right thing to do or because it was his only way to avoid prosecution. So Dancy is certainly right that one needs to be able to distinguish, among the normative reasons one has for doing something, between those that actually motivate one, as one might say, and those that do not. It is also perfectly reasonable to describe the first as 'motivating reasons.' If one uses the phrase in this way, Dancy's normative constraint is unobjectionable – but this is not how the explanatory pluralist uses it. The point of distinguishing between normative and motivating reasons as the pluralist does is to deny that only the latter can be cited to explain actions: by insisting on his normative constraint, Dancy simply misses that point.[5]

Any account of how actions are to be explained must honor the fact that human agents are rational, but fallibly and inconsistently so. So, whilst agents are distinctive in being able to recognize and be motivated by reasons for action, people can, and often do, perform actions that do not manifest such rational responsiveness. One can falsely believe that there is reason for doing what one does – either because one falsely believes that something obtains which would be a reason if it did obtain, or because one wrongly takes something to be a reason when it is not[6] – just as one can do something which one knows one should not, since the reasons against are stronger than the reasons for performing it. Again, one can do things without thinking that one has any reason to do them at all. An account of explanation that builds on a distinction between motivating reasons and normative reasons to secure two distinct, but not unrelated, types of action explanation has the ability to respect both the rationality of human agency and its fallibility. In contrast, an account that tries to fit all action into a single explanatory pattern will either fail to do justice to those instances of agency in which someone's action conforms to (at least some of) the reasons there are for him to act or will be embarrassed by those actions that manifest no sensitivity to rational norms.

This is why it is not merely a terminological matter whether one follows Davidson in excluding justifying facts (that is, normative reasons) from the explanation of actions, allowing a role only for facts about the agent's states of mind. To provide an explanation of something is thereby to make it intelligible; and to claim that actions admit of only one kind of explanation is to allow for only one kind of intelligibility. Following this line, either one will need to think that the action of someone who, for instance, saves for his pension is no more – or differently – intelligible than that of another, who blows his spare money on buying paint to drink (each is explained merely as a case of someone's doing what he happens to want to); or one will be unable to find the latter's action to be a case of intelligible agency at all. Both these positions have been held, of course, but neither squares with the ordinary phenomena of agency. That people should drink paint or collect bottle-tops is puzzling in a way in which actions conforming to normative reasons are not – but the puzzlement is not such that we cannot find these to be cases of agency. That an action is susceptible to a primary-reason explanation is just what secures its status as an action. When we cannot also explain it as a response to normative reasons, this will push us back to look for further, causal, explanations of why the agent should want to do what cannot be rationalized. This is an inescapable feature of the way we understand ourselves and others – but it is complementary to, and not in competition with, our ability to understand those actions that are motivated by the recognition of the reasons we have to act.

See also: THE CAUSAL THEORY OF ACTION (5); TELEOLOGICAL EXPLANATION (16); REASONS AND CAUSES (17); PRACTICAL REASONING (31); AKRASIA AND IRRATIONALITY (35); MOTIVATIONAL INTERNALISM AND EXTERNALISM (37); DAVIDSON (73).

Notes

1 The point of using the technical term 'pro-attitude' rather than the ordinary 'desire' is that the latter can be used in such a way as to make sense of someone's intentionally doing something he does not want or desire to do – doing it out of duty, say, or because of prudential considerations. Someone who acts out of duty is motivated to act the way he does, and such a motivation will count as a pro-attitude.

2 Although his definition of a primary reason specifies it as the reason *why* an agent performs an action, elsewhere he also says that one can attribute a suitably paired belief and pro-attitude whenever someone acts *for* a reason: on his account, to give the reason why someone does something is to give the reason for which he does it.

3 Others have used different terminology to effect this distinction: thus Joseph Raz, for instance, contrasts reasons – i.e. normative reasons ('facts in virtue of which [...] actions are good in some respect and to some degree') – with 'explanatory reasons,' which are the agents' beliefs 'that there is reason for their action, or a specific belief of theirs in something which they take to be a reason' (Raz 1999: 23 n. 5). He restricts the range of explanatory reasons in this way because, unlike Davidson, he does maintain that intentional agency requires the agent to believe that he has a (normative) reason for action. (For a challenge to this 'classical' conception of agency, see Everson 2004.)

4 For a more sustained discussion of this, see Everson 2009: 25–28.

5 We can note, too, that, by denying any explanatory role to an agent's beliefs and desires, Dancy is forced to conclude that it will simply be a brute fact that an agent acted on one normative reason rather than another. The pluralist, in contrast, can explain this by appealing to the truth of one primary-reason explanation rather than another. It will be true that Tom paid back the money because that was the honest thing to do and not because it was the only way to avoid prosecution, since his desire to do the honest thing was part of the cause of his action (whilst his desire to escape prosecution was not).

6 The 'something' here is deliberately vague: there is a dispute as to what kind of items can stand as normative reasons for action. Dancy, for instance, maintains that only spatiotemporally located items such as states of affairs can do this (2000: 115). For a defense of the view that reasons must be propositional, see Everson (2009).

References

Dancy, J. (2000). *Practical Reality*. Oxford: Oxford University Press.

Davidson, D. (1980). Actions, reasons, and causes. In D. Davidson, *Essays on Actions and Events*. Oxford: Oxford University Press, 3–19.

Everson, S. (2004). In defence of ungrounded desires: Against Raz's classical account of agency. *European Journal of Philosophy*, 12, 282–303.

Everson, S. (2009). What are reasons for action? In C. Sandis (ed.), *New Essays on the Explanation of Action*. New York: Basingstoke, 22–47.

Hursthouse, R. (1991). Arational actions. *Journal of Philosophy*, 88 (2), 57–68.

Raz, J. (1999). Agency, reason, and the good. In J. Raz, *Engaging Reason*. Oxford: Oxford University Press, 22–45.

Smith, M. (1992). Valuing: Desiring or believing? In D. Charles and K. Lennon (eds), *Reduction, Explanation, and Realism*. Oxford: Oxford University Press, 323–360.

20

Humeanism about Motivation

MICHAEL SMITH

The Humean theory of motivation (hereafter HTM), named after the Scottish philosopher David Hume (Hume 1975), is a theory about the nature of the psychological states that constitute *motivations*. According to HTM, the psychological states that constitute motivations are pairs of *intrinsic desires* and *means–end beliefs*. Intrinsic desires are desires that agents have for things for their own sake; means–end beliefs are beliefs agents have about which of the options available to them (the means) will lead to the outcomes that they intrinsically desire (the ends). According to HTM, an agent who is motivated to act in some way thus has an intrinsic desire for the world to be a certain way and a belief that her acting in the relevant way, a way which represents an option available to her, will result in the world's being the way she intrinsically desires it to be.

Motivations, so understood, play an important explanatory role, according to HTM, as they figure in *constitutive explanations* of actions: that is, explanations whose availability is what makes it the case that certain bodily movements are actions (Davidson 1980). A bodily movement is an action, according to HTM, in virtue of being explicable in the right kind of way by the motivations of the person who performs them: that is, by an intrinsic desire and a means–end belief. Consider a simple example. Imagine that Bloggs moves his finger against a switch, thereby turning on a light. According to HTM, what makes Bloggs' moving his finger an action is the fact that his moving his finger is explicable in the right kind of way by some intrinsic desire that he has – perhaps he intrinsically desires that the room be illuminated – and a belief he has to the effect that his moving his finger in the way he moved it will bring it about that the room is indeed illuminated. Since Bloggs may move his finger in that way without its being so explicable – he may do so as a result of a nervous twitch, say – it is a contingent matter whether any particular bodily movement is an action. But it is a conceptual truth that, whenever a bodily movement is so explicable, it is an action – or so the HTM tells us.

Note that, although desire and belief pairs figure in constitutive explanations of actions, HTM is consistent with there being other, non-constitutive explanations of actions. For example, if Bloggs' belief that he can illuminate the room by moving his finger against the switch is itself explicable in terms of the fact that he can illuminate the room by moving his finger against the switch, then we could cite this fact in explaining Bloggs' moving his finger. Moreover, this explanation would be preferable in many contexts, conveying as it does more information. Importantly, however, the availability of such an explanation isn't required for Bloggs' moving his finger to be an action. Whether or not we can explain Bloggs' finger movement in terms of what actually happens, so long as his *belief* that certain things will happen, together with a relevant desire, explains his moving his finger in the right kind of way, his moving his finger is an action (Smith 1998).

HTM thus assumes, plausibly enough, that whenever an agent performs an action we can associate his action with some bodily movement or other which is among the agent's options, where any bodily orientation, including standing still, is to count as a bodily movement for the purposes of the theory. In Arthur Danto's terms, HTM thus presupposes that the agent's moving his body in the relevant way is a *basic action* (Danto 1963): something he knows how to do, where his knowledge of how to do this thing isn't explained by his knowledge of how to do something else. Raising an arm, wiggling a finger, moving one leg in front of another, and standing still – these are all examples of bodily movements that meet this condition for most people. Whether some putative action is indeed an action is thus a two-step process. We begin by seeing whether the putative action is associated with some bodily movement, and then we see whether that bodily movement is explicable in the right kind of way by some intrinsic desire and means–end belief the agent has. If so, then the agent acts; if not, he doesn't.

More controversially, HTM also assumes that, whenever an agent performs some action, there is some intrinsic desire in the offing that explains what she does. This is a more controversial assumption, because we readily describe agents as doing things that they don't really want to do. Think of someone who does her duty reluctantly, for example. Taking such descriptions at face value would, however, commit us to supposing, implausibly according to HTM, that an agent's believing that an act is her duty may suffice *all by itself* to explain her doing her duty. This supposition is implausible because it would make it impossible to understand why, when an agent does her duty, her doing what she does is explicable in *teleological* terms: that is, in terms of some goal that she has. This is the crucial feature of motivations, according to HTM: motivations are what make it possible to explain actions in teleological terms. The appeal of HTM is that it makes it transparent why this is so.

What it is for an agent to have something like a goal is, after all, for him to have, within himself, a representation of how the world is to be. An agent who has doing his duty as a goal has, within himself, a representation of the world as being such that his own duty is to be done. But having a representation of how the world is to be just is what it is for an agent to desire something. Indeed the difference between desires and beliefs is couched in precisely these terms: desires are *representations of how the world is to be*, whereas beliefs are *representations of how the world is* (Smith 1987). Insofar as an agent does his duty, it therefore follows that he does something teleologically explicable; and it follows from this that his doing what he does is explicable in terms of his having doing his duty as a goal; and it follows from this that he has, within himself, a representation of the world's being such that his duty is to be done; and it follows from this that he desires to do his duty. Strictly speaking, then, the idea that agents can do their duty without really wanting to is a contradiction in terms.

The same point emerges if we begin by focusing on what it is for an agent to believe that doing such-and-such is his duty. Such an agent has, within himself, a representation of how the world is with regard to his duty: the world is such that it is his duty to do such-and-such. But whether or not he has a motivation to do his duty depends on whether he has doing his duty as a goal: that is, whether he has, within himself, a representation of the world as being such that his duty is to be done. Since the fact that an agent has the first kind of representation within himself seems to leave it open whether or not he has the second kind, it follows that his having the belief that it is his duty to do such-and-such is insufficient for his having a motivation to do his duty.

Hume put this point by saying that belief and desire are *distinct existences*. His idea was that, no matter what intrinsic desires and beliefs we consider, we can always imagine an agent who has some belief but lacks some desire, and vice versa. An agent's possession of a psychological state of the one kind doesn't entail his possession of a psychological state of the other kind. The reason why an agent's merely believing that it is his duty to act in a certain way is insufficient for motivation, according to HTM, is thus that an agent who has such a belief may or may not desire to do his duty.

This presents us with a puzzle. What is going on when we say that agents may *reluctantly* do their duty, or that they may do their duty *without really wanting to*? There are various possibilities. We might be trying to convey the fact that the agent who does his duty gets no pleasure from doing so: that the desire he acts on isn't one of those whose satisfaction brings with it any *feelings* of satisfaction. On this construal, the things that agents 'really' want to do are a sub-class of the things they want to do: that sub-class where getting what one wants brings with it feelings of satisfaction. Or perhaps we are trying to convey the fact that the agent has a strong inclination not to do his duty, and that his doing it therefore requires a special exercise of self-control. On this construal, the things that agents 'really' want to do are, once again, a sub-class of the things they want to do: that sub-class of the things they want to do which they can get themselves to do without having to exercise self-control. When we understand the idea of what an agent 'really' wants to do in one of these ways, the puzzle disappears.

Those who oppose HTM do so for a wide variety of reasons. Some object that motivations are not psychological states at all, but are rather *facts* or *considerations* (Dancy 2000). Consider again the example of Bloggs, and let us imagine asking him what his motivation was for flicking the switch. His answer, fully spelled out, might be something like: 'My motivation was that the room would thereby be illuminated.' This suggests that his motivation is a fact, or anyway a putative fact, not a psychological state – or so the objection goes.

But this objection isn't very deep. No one thinks that facts that bear no relation at all to the psychology of an agent are able to explain that agent's actions. So, even though the objector says that motivations are facts or considerations, their own choice of which facts or considerations constitute these motivations is mediated by their knowledge of the psychology of the agent. There is therefore an easy translation from HTM's preferred account of motivations as psychological states into the terms preferred by those who deny that this is so. The facts or considerations that are candidates for explaining an agent's actions, according to those who offer the objection, are simply those that the agent believes to link the means to the desired end. There is therefore no deep disagreement here, just a superficial disagreement about whether to use the word 'motivation' to refer to the psychological states that explain an action or to the contents of those psychological states.

A deeper objection to HTM is that Hume was wrong to suppose that desire and belief are distinct existences. Though some desires and beliefs are distinct existences, the objection goes, there are other beliefs, whose very possession entails the possession of certain desires. Someone who is virtuous, for example, has certain characteristic desires, and these desires make her see things differently from the way in which those who lack her desires see things. Her desires make salient certain features of her situation rather than others. Imagine a social situation in which someone is shy and sensitive. His vulnerabilities will make certain features of the evolving social situation command the attention of the virtuous person. The virtuous person will therefore see this situation quite differently from the way in which someone who isn't virtuous will see it. On the plausible assumption that the way in which a virtuous person sees things affects the way he believes things to be, it follows that he will have beliefs which those who lack his special concerns simply don't have (McDowell 1979).

The trouble with this objection, however, is its empirical grounding. The premise of the argument is that, as it happens, having certain desires is the only way in which certain features of an evolving social situation will become salient. Differences in belief will therefore be explicable, *as a matter of fact*, by differences in desire. But Hume's claim that belief and desire are distinct existences is a conceptual claim, not an empirical claim. The question is not whether, as a matter of fact, there are beliefs that you will possess only if you have certain desires, but whether it is *logically impossible* to have those beliefs without having the relevant desires. So: is it logically impossible for the very same features to be salient to a virtuous person and to a non-virtuous person – and hence for the non-virtuous person to have exactly the same beliefs about his situation as the virtuous person – without the explanation of why those features are salient to the non-virtuous person being the same as the explanation of why those features are salient to the virtuous person? This option does indeed seem to be at least *logically* possible. But if it is logically possible, then Hume's claim that desires and belief are distinct existences remains intact. The second objection therefore collapses.

A final objection targets HTM's characterization of desire. The objection is that to desire something isn't just to have a representation of the world as being such that things are to be the way you desire them to be, but that it is in addition to have a representation of its *being good* that they are that way, or at least of its *seeming to be good* that they are that way. Desire itself is thus supposed to include a belief-like element. Note that the objection is not that HTM denies, implausibly, that an agent *rationally should* desire something only if he believes that it is good, or that it seems good. Though Hume denied that this is so, HTM, at least as I have characterized it, takes no stand on whether this is so. The objection is rather that HTM denies, implausibly, that an agent *can* desire something only if he believes that it is good, or that it seems good (Scanlon 1998).

The objection is really two objections rolled into one: an initial objection, which is itself just another variation on the objection that belief and desire are not distinct existences – to which there is an obvious reply; and a second version of that same objection – to which the reply is less obvious. The initial objection is that it is logically impossible for an agent to desire something without believing that it is good, to which the obvious reply is that it clearly is logically possible. Indeed, it also seems to be an empirical possibility, since all sorts of human pathologies seem to consist in agents' desiring things that they do not believe to be good, and indeed in their desiring things that they believe to be bad (Stocker 1979). To give just one example, psychopaths seem to be unintelligible unless we suppose that they believe that what they want to do is bad. What's so puzzling about them is precisely that they are so idiosyncratically indifferent, notwithstanding their relatively conventional evaluative beliefs (Kennett 2006).

The second version of the objection takes to heart the response to the initial version and reformulates the objection. Perhaps it isn't logically impossible for someone to desire something without believing it to be good, but it is logically impossible for someone to desire something without its at least seeming good to that person. To desire something you know to be bad is to be in the grip of an *evaluative illusion*. Just as we can know full well that the two lines in the Müller-Lyer illusion are the same length, though it seems to us that they are of different lengths, so an agent may know full well that something isn't good, but, if he desires it, it will seem good to him. The psychopath, for example, may know that what he desires to do is bad, but it must at least seem good to him.

The problem with this second version of the final objection is that it is left unclear what it is for something to seem good to someone; for, once this idea is made clear, it emerges that it is no more plausible to suppose that an agent can desire something only if it seems good to him than it was to suppose that he can desire something only if he believes it to be good. Consider what seems the most plausible account of what it is for something to seem good to you, namely, for the *thought* that it is good, a thought that you may know full well to be false, to occur to you persistently. The objection is then in trouble, as something can obviously seem good to someone in this sense without his desiring it, and hence without his being motivated; and someone may desire something, and hence be motivated, without its seeming good to him in this sense.

An agent may well, after all, have a representation within himself of the world's being such that it is to be a certain way without having the persistent thought that its being that way is good, and he may have the persistent thought that its being that way is good without having, within himself, a representation of the world's being such that it is to be that way. These psychological states are distinct existences in the sense that it is logically possible to imagine someone having the one but not the other, and vice versa. Yet all that is strictly necessary in order for an agent to have a goal, and hence to be motivated, is for him to have, within himself, a representation of the world's being such that it is to be a certain way. His having the persistent thought that its being that way is good thus seems to be neither necessary nor sufficient for his having a goal. It is thus neither necessary nor sufficient for motivation. The final objection therefore collapses as well.

See also: BASIC ACTIONS AND INDIVIDUATION (2); BODILY MOVEMENTS (4), THE CAUSAL THEORY OF ACTION (5); DESIRE AND PLEASURE (15); TELEOLOGICAL EXPLANATION (16); MOTIVATING REASONS (19); HUME (63).

References

Dancy, J. (2000). *Practical Reality*. Oxford: Oxford University Press.

Danto, A. C. (1963). What we can do. *Journal of Philosophy*, 60, 434–445.

Davidson, D. (1980). Actions, reasons, and causes [1963]. In D. Davidson, *Essays on Actions and Events*. Oxford: Oxford University Press, 3–19.

Hume, D. (1975). *Enquiries concerning Human Understanding and concerning the Principles of Morals*. Oxford: Clarendon Press.

Kennett, J. (2006). Do psychopaths really threaten moral rationalism? *Philosopical Explorations*, 9, 69–82.

McDowell, J. (1979). Virtue and reason. *Monist*, 62, 331–350.

Scanlon, T. (1998). *What We Owe to Each Other*. Cambridge, MA: Harvard University Press.

Smith, M. (1987). The Humean theory of motivation. *Mind*, 96, 36–61.

Smith, M. (1998). The possibility of philosophy of action. In J. Bransen and S. Cuypers (eds), *Human Action, Deliberation and Causation*. Dordrecht: Kluwer Academic Publishers, 17–41.

Stocker, M. (1979). Desiring the bad: An essay in moral psychology. *Journal of Philosophy*, 76, 738–753.

Further reading

Lewis, D. (1988). Desire as belief. *Mind*, 97, 323–332.

Mele, A. R. (1995). Motivation: Essentially motivation-constituting attitudes. *Philosophical Review*, 104, 387–423.

Sinhababu, N. (forthcoming). The Humean theory of motivation reformulated and defended. *Philosophical Review*.

21

Deviant Causal Chains

ROWLAND STOUT

Suppose I intend to cough loudly in a concert to upset my enemy, the conductor, but that this very intention makes me nervous and that nervousness makes me cough. I have intended to cough, and that intention has caused me to cough; but I have not coughed intentionally. Here we have an example of a deviant causal chain, a type of example that is supposed to raise difficulties for causal theories of intentional action.

Causal theories of intentional action take it to be both necessary and sufficient, for someone to act intentionally, that the person in question is in some mental state which represents the intended target of her action, and that her being in that state causes her to achieve this target. An example of such a theory might be this:

A subject intentionally ϕ-s if and only if his intending to ϕ causes his ϕ-ing.

For example, I intentionally cough if and only if my intending to cough causes me to cough. The deviant causal chain example at the start is a straightforward counterexample to this. Whether or not the causal condition is necessary, it is certainly not sufficient for intentional action. Roderick Chisholm (1966) provided one of the first deviant causal chain examples with the case of the man whose intention to kill his uncle made him so agitated that he drove too fast and accidentally killed a pedestrian who happened to be his uncle. And Donald Davidson presented a classic example of this sort in his paper 'Freedom to act,' first published in 1973:

> A climber might want to rid himself of the weight and danger of holding another man on a rope, and he might know that by loosening his hold on the rope he could rid himself of the weight and danger. This belief and want might so unnerve him as to cause him to loosen his hold, and yet it might be the case that he never *chose* to loosen his hold, nor did he do it intentionally. (Davidson 1980: 79)

A natural response to this sort of deviant causal chain example is to say that the thing done in these cases is not the same as the thing intended. The agent in these cases might well say, 'I did not intend *that*.' So if we require that ϕ in the formula above is specified with sufficient precision, we might see that the agent's intending to ϕ causes them to ϕ', where ϕ and ϕ' are slightly different. Then the right-hand side of the formula above would not be satisfied either, and the counterexample would fail.

One way to make the specification of ϕ more precise is to ensure that it refers to the *particular* thing done rather than to the type of thing done. The nervous climber did not intend that particular loosening of the grip, but another one of the same sort. The nervous cough I actually produced was not the particular cough I intended to produce. But this strategy, although it defeats the deviant causal chain counterexamples, does not help the causal theory of intentional action. Intending a particular action – that very action – is not a state that could possibly count as a cause of that particular action. It is only in retrospect – when the action has come into being – that one can identify that particular action as what was intended. At the time of any causally prior state of intention, there is nothing that can be picked out as a *particular* action in the content of that intention. So to say that a particular action of ϕ-ing was intended by me is not to describe my mental state in advance of that action. Psychological realism about intentions should not be extended to such talk.

Another way is to require that the specification of ϕ-ing should describe an *intentional* action. The climber did not intend to let go of the rope accidentally; he intended to let go of the rope intentionally. But if we try to factor this into the causal theory we get a circular and self-referential account, which is no good as an explanatory theory: the only explanation it can provide for the fact that Davidson's climber's letting go of the rope is not done intentionally appeals to the fact that it is not an intentional action.

There are two more differences worth noting between what the climber does and what he intended to do. One is that he intended to let go of the rope at a slightly later time from when he actually lets go of the rope. The other is that he intended to let go of the rope in a certain way, or following a certain plan, which is different from the one that actually occurred. His plan was simply to let go of the rope; it was not to utilize his nervousness to make himself let go of the rope. Let me consider these in turn.

One does not usually intend to do something at an absolutely precise moment. Even if one is intending to do something right now, that intention is usually satisfied if one does it within a split second or two. So we can easily imagine that the climber intends to let go of the rope right now, and does indeed let go of the rope right now as a result of this intention; yet his letting go of the rope is the result of a deviant causal chain. Suppose the climber suffers from such nerves that, whenever he forms a life-endangering intention like the one in question, he gets so nervous that he cannot go through with it. He might start to loosen his grip on the rope and terrify himself so much by the thought of what he is doing that he cannot go on. He might continue to intend to let go right now, but keep deferring the implementation of this intention until, say, ten seconds later he gives up and decides not to let go. And, just to be clear about it, let us suppose that this inability to follow through with such intentions is a preexisting condition – a verifiable neurosis. Finally, suppose that on this occasion his nerves were so bad that, as a result of his nervousness, he did accidentally release his grip and let go of the rope within the ten seconds. He let go of the rope while having the intention to let go of the rope right now and as a result of having that intention, but he did not do it intentionally. He might not even realize that he did not let go intentionally. But we, who know about his neurosis, know that he could not have done it intentionally.

So deviant causal chains can be constructed that match the intended time of action and the actual time of action. But what about the means or plan of action? In the case just considered the climber's action does not match his intention in terms of its means. He lets go of the rope as a result of nervousness, but he intends to let go of the rope without any such causal mediation. The problem with this line of thought is that the plan that figures in someone's intention is always to a certain extent vague. It could not include all the causally necessary elements, nor exclude as causally unnecessary everything else. A climber who acts intentionally in letting go of a rope does not have in mind the precise causal pathway that leads to his letting go of the rope. He does not need to know anything about muscles and nerve signals in order to act intentionally. He might not even have the concept of nervousness, and hence he might not have the conceptual resources to exclude that particular way of letting go of a rope. Whatever way of acting figures in the agent's intentions – whatever causal intermediaries are intended to be present and to be absent – it will be easy to construct an example where there is a deviant causal chain that includes and excludes these causal intermediaries in the intended way and where the action is clearly unintentional.

Many philosophers take the intractability of the problem of deviant causal chains to show that a causal approach to intentional action is mistaken. But if that were right, it would also show that a causal approach to absolutely anything is mistaken. For the very same intractable problem of deviant causal chains afflicts the attempt to construct a causal theory for any notion. For example the causal theory of perception is vulnerable to the same sort of counterexample. In order for you to be said to perceive an object, it is not sufficient that the object simply causes you to have an experience as of that object. If the causal chain between the object's presence and the experience as of that object is deviant – for example the light from the object somehow triggers a convincing hallucination of the object – then the object is not being perceived.

And there are indefinitely many causal notions whose analyses would face the same challenge. For example it would not work to say that the heat of the oven cooks the chicken if and only if the heat of the oven causes the chicken to be in a cooked state. The heat of the oven might trigger some microwave activity elsewhere which causes the chicken to be in that state; in this case the heat would not have cooked the chicken. Likewise, it would not work to say that the mass of an object attracts another massive object if and only if the object's having that mass causes the other object to be under a force towards it, or to accelerate towards it. We can easily construct examples where this causal condition is met in some deviant way; and it is wrong to describe the first object as attracting the second.

What all this seems to show is that causal theories should not employ a *generic* notion of causation to relate cause and effect, but should instead employ the idea of the effect being caused *in a certain way* by the cause. These 'ways' will differ from one kind of causal process to the next. Only if one mass' accelerating towards another is caused by way of the process of gravitational attraction between those masses can we say that it is being attracted by that mass. Only if an observer's experience as of an object being present is caused by the presence of that object by way of a perceptual process can we say that the observer is perceiving the object. And, in the same way, only if an agent's ϕ-ing is caused by her intention to ϕ by way of a process that is characteristic of her intentionally ϕ-ing can we say that she is intentionally ϕ-ing.

So a causal theory of action cannot rely only on there being an intention to do something (specified in a certain way), that thing being done according to the specification in question and there being a causal relation between them. The causal theory must also say something about *how* the thing done is caused by the intention to do it. It must be done in the right sort of way, even when this right sort of way is not captured in the content of the intention. This means that the original formula for the causal theory of intentional action must be changed to something like this:

> *S* intentionally ϕ-s if and only if *S*'s intending to ϕ causes *S*'s ϕ-ing in a way that is characteristic of *S*'s intentionally ϕ-ing.

This general strategy for constructing causal theories faces two new challenges: explaining what is meant by a 'way' of being caused – this is to explain the notion of a causal process; and explaining what way, or process, is characteristic of perceiving things, cooking things, attracting things, doing things intentionally, and so on. The first challenge is a general one for the philosophy of causation, while the second one is specific to each area of philosophy which deals with each causal notion.

There are two contrasting approaches to explaining the notion of a causal process: a Humean approach and an Aristotelian approach. The Humean approach takes causation to be a generic relation between real things, but not itself a real thing. The Aristotelian approach takes causation itself to be a real thing with an identity independent of the cause and effect. For Hume, a causal process can only be a chain of causal relations. According to this approach, specifying the way *A* causes *B* is to specify the intervening stages in the causal chain between *A* and *B*; that is, *A* causes *B* via *C*, *D*, *E*, and *F*. It is always a matter of relatively little philosophical imagination to conjure up a new deviant causal chain counterexample in response to any such specification; just have the normal link between *C* and *D* exchanged for a deviant one, in which some bizarre mechanism is triggered by *C* and results in *D*.

The Aristotelian approach takes a causal process to be the actualization of a potentiality of a certain sort – or, as we might say instead, the realization of a disposition or the operation of a mechanism. According to this approach, specifying the way *A* causes *B* is to specify what sort of mechanism it is whose operation *B* belongs to and that takes *A* as an input, or is set off by *A*, or is somehow embodied in *A*. If an effect belongs to the operation of the right sort of mechanism, then it is caused in the right sort of way. In this approach, a causal process is not understood as a causal chain, so deviant causal chains are irrelevant.

On the Aristotelian approach, what characterizes the way one mass is caused to accelerate towards another when it is gravitationally attracted by it is not a special kind of cause or sequence of causal chain links between the presence of the other mass and the acceleration. What characterizes the way the mass is caused to accelerate is the nature of the mechanism to whose operation its acceleration belongs. It is a fact that the mechanism is one which has those characteristic results when its operational conditions are satisfied and nothing interferes. In a deviant causal chain example, where the presence of the other mass triggers some other force, which makes the first mass accelerate, this acceleration belongs to the operation of a different mechanism, and so it is caused in a different way.

While this approach offers a way in which a causal theory can avoid deviant causal chain examples, it involves a huge wrench from the standard modern way of thinking about causation in philosophy. It requires one to be realist about causal mechanisms and their operations. It requires one to accept the existence of things which, by their very nature, have implications (albeit implications that are conditional on nothing interfering) for what happens in the future. Although philosophers of science like Peter Machamer are beginning to take mechanisms more seriously (see Machamer et al. 2000), many philosophers would consider this move back from Hume to Aristotle to be a move in quite the wrong direction.

But it is a move that is implicitly made in many of the most promising recent attempts to defeat deviant causal chain counterexamples to the causal theory of intentional action by using the notion of guidance or control. Harry Frankfurt (1978: 158) argued as follows:

> [T]he state of affairs while the movements [of a person's body] are occurring is far more pertinent [than the causes from which they originated]. What is not merely pertinent but decisive, indeed, is to consider whether or not the movements as they occur are under the person's guidance. It is this that determines whether he is performing an action. Moreover, the question of whether or not movements occur under a person's guidance is not a matter of their antecedents. Events are caused to occur by preceding states of affairs, but an event cannot be guided through the course of its occurrence at a temporal distance.

For Frankfurt, what distinguishes guided action is the causal mechanism, not the causal antecedents. And the characteristic quality of the sort of mechanism whose operation constitutes intentional action is its guidedness or goal-directedness. The idea is that, when such a mechanism is operating and not being interfered with, it results in those bits of behavior that belong to the agent's repertoire of possible behavior and that should happen if the agent's goal is to be achieved. This idea is spelled out by John Fischer and Mark Ravizza, who are some of Frankfurt's recent champions, as the idea of a 'reasons-responsive mechanism' (Fischer and Ravizza 1998: 54).

The climber's letting go of the rope in Davidson's example does not belong to the operation of such a mechanism; it belongs to the operation of a mechanism that characteristically results in uncontrolled bodily movements as a response to extreme nervousness.

Clearly the philosophy of action still has plenty of work to do to characterize precisely what goal-directedness, guidedness, control, sensitivity or reasons-responsiveness amount to in the description of how a mechanism works. But it would be a real advance if it could pass the problem of deviant causal chains to the philosophy of causation, so as to concentrate on this task, which belongs more properly to its domain.

However, this Aristotelian approach to controlled causal processes seems to exclude a whole class of cases which we tend to describe as intentional actions. Sometimes we are not in control of an action all the way up to the achievement of the goal, but rather we set off a process which, we think, will result in that achievement, and then we let nature take its course. Because this sort of case is puzzling, it often dominates discussion in the philosophy of action, to the exclusion of the more ordinary sort of action, which is controlled all the way. Someone might intentionally hit a pool ball into the centre pocket, or someone might intentionally assassinate the President by detonating a bomb. Their goal in these cases is achieved after the process involving their intentional agency is completed. Before the goal has been achieved but after the control has been relinquished it sounds wrong to describe them as intentionally potting the pool ball into the centre pocket or intentionally assassinating the President. (Consider the possibility of their falling down dead during this interval.) But after the goal has been achieved it sounds right to say that they have intentionally potted the ball into the centre pocket or assassinated the President.

Since a causal theory in terms of controlled or guided processes does not explain why these secondary effects are correctly described as intentionally achieved, one might be tempted to try for a Humean causal chain account for the uncontrolled part of the process. But then, of course, deviant causal chains come back into the story. In the literature, this is described as secondary or consequential deviance or waywardness. Suppose that the pool player's intentionally hitting the pool ball in the direction of the centre pocket means that the ball passes over a trigger which sets up a huge magnetic field drawing all the pool balls into the centre pocket. Our intuitions may be a bit unclear about what to say here, but it does not sound quite right to say that the pool player intentionally hit the ball into the centre pocket. Or suppose that the terrorist's bomb is a damp squib, which after being detonated only has the result of jogging the hand of some other bomber and thereby of detonating her bomb, which does result in the death of the President. Again, it may not be quite clear what to say, but I would not be inclined to say that the first person intentionally assassinated the President.

An alternative response to examples of secondary deviance is to give up on a causal theory for the uncontrolled part of the process while holding onto an Aristotelian causal process theory for the controlled part. One advantage of this strategy is that it allows for intentional omissions. For it seems that we can be said to have intentionally allowed things to happen just as much as we can be said to have intentionally made things happen. The goal keeper might intentionally allow the ball to pass between his legs, without being involved at all in the causal process that results in the ball passing between his legs. What seems relevant here is some notion of responsibility, which ties in with whether the agent knew or should have known what would happen given his action or lack of action. The inept bomber did not know that her detonating her bomb would kill the President (although he may have had a justified true belief that it would); and perhaps this means that he was not morally responsible for the President's death, despite intending it and in this case causing it.

See also: ACTION THEORY AND ONTOLOGY (1); BASIC ACTIONS AND INDIVIDUATION (2); TRYING TO ACT (3); BODILY MOVEMENTS (4); THE CAUSAL THEORY OF ACTION (5); INTENTION (15); TELEOLOGICAL EXPLANATION (16); REASONS AND CAUSES (17); TRIGGERING AND STRUCTURING CAUSES (18); HUMEANISM ABOUT MOTIVATION (20); AGENT CAUSATION (28); ARISTOTLE (54); DAVIDSON (73).

References

Chisholm, R. (1966). Freedom and Action. In K. Lehrer (ed.), *Freedom and Determinism*. New York: Random House, 28–44.

Davidson, D. (1980). *Essays on Actions and Events*. Oxford: Oxford University Press.

Fischer, J., and Ravizza, M. (1998). *Responsibility and Control*. Cambridge: Cambridge University Press.

Frankfurt, H. (1978). The problem of action. *Amercian Philosophical Quarterly*, 15, 157–162.

Machamer, P, Darden, L., and Craver, C. (2000). Thinking about mechanisms. *Philosophy of Science*, 67, 1–25.

Further reading

Stout, R. (2006), *Action*. Teddington: Acumen.

22

Action Explanation and the Unconscious

EDWARD HARCOURT

Any question about action explanations that appeal to the unconscious raises the prior question of what is meant by unconsciousness and by unconscious mentality. Though a full treatment of these questions lies beyond the scope of the present chapter, some comment on them is needed in order to avoid taking for granted conventional philosophical uses of 'unconscious' as introducing a well-demarcated topic or set of topics. As regards action explanations that appeal to the unconscious themselves (henceforth, for brevity, 'unconscious action explanations'), the questions addressed here are mainly two. First, to what extent are unconscious action explanations of a distinctive kind or kinds; in particular, how, if at all, do they differ from the kinds of action explanations supplied by conscious factors, and from the kinds of explanation, conscious or unconscious, of doings of ours which are not actions? Secondly, how closely is the phenomenon of irrationality in action connected with the availability of an unconscious explanation?

Many things people do are explained by things about themselves that they don't know – that is, by things about themselves of which they are, in a non-technical sense, unconscious. A man knocks over a glass thanks to a Parkinsonian twitch, without knowing he has the disease; a woman vomits because she is pregnant, though she doesn't know it yet. But these doings of ours do not qualify as actions. Irritably criticizing a friend, however, *is* an action, and might be explained by the fact that my blood sugar is low, which I don't know. But when philosophers speak of 'unconscious explanations of action,' this is often not the kind of case they have in mind. For some, this is because the explanation is not 'Freudian,' in other words because (whatever else there is to say about Freudian explanations) it does not refer to the kinds of unconscious mental processes distinctively discussed by Freud. But even among some philosophers who are skeptical about the validity of explanations of *that* kind, there's an unwillingness to treat the explanation in the blood sugar case as an example of an unconscious explanation of action, thanks to an assumption that the term 'unconscious' is properly applied only to *mental* states. Since Descartes defined the mental as the conscious (in a certain, specialized sense of that term) and his definition has been highly influential, it is of some polemical interest to assert that there are phenomena (and thus potential explanations of action) which are both unconscious and mental. But now compare 'He irritably criticized his friend because his blood sugar was low' and 'He irritably criticized his friend because he was hungry.' Hunger is a state one can easily be unaware of (for example, because one is so busy being irritated by one's friend) and, at least to the philosopher's ear, it is mental. But is there any reason of principle for distinguishing between the explanations involved in the two cases as being of different kinds? Arguably not. Moreover, the kind of explanation of action offered in both these cases seems to be the same as the following unconscious mental explanation of a non-action: 'She was tearful because she was suffering from depression.' I'm assuming here a case where, although the subject may consciously feel miserable, (a) she does not know she is depressed because she has not been diagnosed yet; but (b) when she gets her diagnosis, the state ascribed in it is a mental state. Indeed the kind of explanation in this third example seems to be the same as in the following unconscious *non*-mental explanation of a non-action: 'She was tearful because she was pregnant (without knowing it).' From cases of these kinds it may appear that the class of unconscious mental explanations of actions is carved arbitrarily from a much larger class: the class of explanations of things we do which cite facts about ourselves of which we are unaware. The class is even larger if we do not restrict it to facts about ourselves; compare 'She was irritable because of the Mistral,' whose blowing up she hadn't noticed because she was so absorbed by the object of her irritation. Since it is very hard to give a tidy non-stipulative definition of the mental, there is all the more reason to expect not to find well-motivated distinctions within the class of facts about ourselves of which we are unaware when it comes to explaining behavior.

What the above cases have in common, however, is that the explanations all explain without providing a reason: this is why it is so easy to be indifferent as to whether the behavior explained is a non-action (doings of ours for which there never are reasons) or an action, and as to whether the *explanans* is mental or not (because, though some mental *explanantia* are rationalizing, the ones in these examples are not). But there does seem to be a sub-class of explanations of actions which readily leap to mind when 'unconscious explanations of action' are mentioned, and which are of special interest. A neat way to introduce it is as the sub-class of cases where the *explanans* is a state of a kind which makes it apt to provide a rationalizing explanation (regardless of whether or not it does so in the particular case), and which is unconscious. Since propositional attitudes are widely thought to be the only states of this sort, we have a rationale for singling out explanations which invoke unconscious propositional attitudes for special attention. It should be noted, however, that this neat way of introducing the interesting sub-class depends on another issue, which lies beyond the scope of this chapter – namely the issue of the kinds of thing which can constitute a reason for action. According to an alternative view on this issue, any old facts can be reasons ('Why did you do that?' 'Because of the weather'; 'Because of the look on your face'). So there is no kind of *explanans* which is rationalizing or non-rationalizing per se. Moreover, the role unconsciousness plays in action explanation cannot reliably be put down to the unconsciousness of an explaining mental state (since there need not be one), and will have to rest instead on something like the agent's (conditional) inability to give the explanation.

However, factoring this controversy into what follows would make for excessive complication, so I am going to set the more liberal view of reasons on one side. And in any case, whether or not mental states which are apt to rationalize actions are the only things which are apt to rationalize them, advocates of the more liberal view of reasons need not deny that there can be unconscious desires, beliefs, and so on. So it is worth asking what further features, if any, such states have in common. There is at least one further feature which they don't share with non-mental causes, either of actions or of non-actions, or even with every mental cause of either – as the depression example above might be taken to show. For, although depression is a mental state, ascriptions of it do not display first/third person asymmetry, either in the strong sense that we are authoritative about whether we have it (we aren't), or in the weak sense that evidenceless self-ascriptions of it have a special status in confirming others' ascriptions of the state to one: I may just come to accept that I am depressed by accepting the expert diagnoses of those who have evidence that I am. In the case of propositional attitudes, by contrast, my evidenceless self-ascriptions do have a special status in confirming the ascription of the state to me (though of course I can be insincere, self-deceived, and so on). By the same token, it is doubtful whether I could count as *consciously* intending something if my only reasons for thinking that I intended it were indirect (for example the fact that others, who behaved the same way as me, had all accepted that they had the intention in question). It may thus be said that there are (at least) two senses in which a state of mine may be unconscious: one where evidenceless self-ascription has a special status in relation to the ascribability of the state to me; the other where it does not. Where a state is unconscious and evidenceless self-ascription has a special status in relation to the ascribability of the state to me, let us call the unconscious state 'avowable'; and let us call it 'non-avowable' where evidenceless self-ascription does not have this special status. The apparent fact that only mental states are avowable in the sense explained further fuels the common assumption, noted earlier, that 'unconscious' means 'unconscious *and* mental.'

Before leaving the subject of how unconsciousness is to be defined, it's appropriate to mention one more distinction commonly applied to unconscious mental states, sometimes termed the distinction between the 'procedural' and the 'dynamic' unconscious. According to this distinction, states that are procedurally unconscious are unconscious (roughly) because they don't need to be conscious. Such is for example my belief that there is a hole in the road, which explains my swerving to avoid it, though when I am asked about it I say, 'What hole?' Dynamically unconscious states are unconscious (roughly) because they need not to be conscious – for example any state that is unconscious as a result of repression. But things are more complicated than this distinction allows. Consider a case of what we might call simple lack of self-knowledge, as when I am upset about something but haven't realized it yet. At a given time I am not disposed to *assert* that I am upset (despite behaving as if I were), so my state is, at that time, unconscious. But when it is put to me that I am upset, I agree readily and find it helpful to be able to put my state into words; this means that, before that moment, the state was not repressed. So was it procedurally rather than dynamically unconscious? In the example, being upset is an avowable state in the sense previously explained: my ready agreement has a special status in confirming the suggestion that I am indeed upset. But this is not the case with my belief about the hole in the road: my sole reason for accepting that I had the belief may be that there was a hole, I was in a position to form the belief that there was, and I swerved. ('I suppose I must have believed there was one.') One response to these various observations would be to deny that the state I was in was an unconscious mental state at all. To see why the response seems too radical, contrast yet another case. There is evidence that male preference for female faces tracks female pupil size, though subjects report no awareness of differences in pupil size (Rey 1998: 523). Here again, then, subjects would accept that they were aware of differences in pupil size solely on the basis of indirect evidence, if at all. The pressure to deny that this awareness is an unconscious mental state is strong: the supposedly unconscious state does not do the explanatory work in the way it would if it were conscious: since pupil size does not *rationalize* preference, conscious awareness of it would presumably either leave preference unaffected or indeed confuse it. In the light of this example, consider again the 'hole' case. Here the state I was in *does* explain my swerving in the way a conscious belief would have done ('Oh look, there's a hole') – that is, through the rational relation it bears to the way things were, my wants and so on. This is why to deny that it is a mental state is going too far. But there is still the interesting fact that, like pupil-size awareness, the state is non-avowable. So in place of the two-way procedural unconscious/dynamic unconscious distinction we appear to need a three-way distinction, namely between those unconscious mental states that are not avowable but not repressed either; those that are avowable but not repressed; and those that are avowable and repressed.

With these clarifications out of the way, I want to focus on the interesting sub-class I picked out before, namely unconscious explanations of action that appeal to mental states that are both avowable and apt to rationalize the actions they explain.

One question immediately arising in this connection is whether such states do in fact rationalize the actions they explain when the states are unconscious. According to one line of thought, propositional attitudes provide the same kind of explanation when they are unconscious as when they are conscious. In some cases, at least, this seems right. Suppose that love rivalry with another suitor rationalizes my monopolizing a woman's attention (I love her, I don't want her to fall for him, so I form the intention of keeping them apart). My behavior would, it seems, be equally rational relative to my own state of mind if I did not know I was in love and offered instead a self-deceiving explanation for my monopolizing behavior (for example that, if I didn't set out the argument of my very long book all in one go, she wouldn't be able to form a proper opinion of it). This is not to say that this is a good wooing tactic; but it is what I would have done, rightly or wrongly, even if I had not been self-deceived. Indeed there are cases where my desires are more likely to be fulfilled if motive and intention remain unconscious than if they are conscious. Suppose I am in love with someone and want to become close to that person, but I am so painfully shy that, were I to become conscious of what I wanted, I would be inhibited and would fail. By self-deceivingly describing my conversations with the object of my desire as 'routine discussions with a colleague' or as 'just passing the time of day,' I may become close to the person in question before I realize what is happening, and so succeed. Or, to take a case reported by Freud, a Jewish convert to Christianity went on a family holiday to friends who did not know his background. When his hostess began to make anti-Semitic remarks he felt that he ought to declare it, but at the same time he was afraid of making a scene, so he said nothing – or perhaps 'said nothing.' For, although he meant to say 'run along to the garden, you boys [*Ihr Jungen*]' to his sons, what came out was 'run along to the garden, you Jews [*Ihr Juden*]' (Freud 2002: 87–88). On one reading of the episode, the slip was motivated by an unconscious desire on the speaker's part to communicate his Jewish origins. What is more, this was a desire he would have acted on, had he not akratically yielded to his fear of making a scene. Both examples remind us that our rationality may be compromised in more than one way at a time – shyness and self-deception; weak will and (I guess) a further specialized form of incontinence with respect to utterance – and that one defect can correct another.

From this it does not follow, however, that explanations of action which appeal to unconscious propositional attitudes are *always* rationalizing explanations. In a recent Preface to his *The Unconscious*, Alasdair MacIntyre emphasizes the distinction between acting for reasons and 'acting *as if* unconsciously guided by reasons.' In the latter case, 'the motives that control [one's] behaviour preclude one from acting as a practical reasoner does,' since it's constitutive of the notion of a reason that one should be capable of asking whether the reason one acts for is a *good* reason for one's action. But where our motivations 'give expression to infantile wishes and early traumas' we are unable to do this (MacIntyre 2004: 25–26). Insofar as this is so, the exercise of our rational powers is inhibited or subverted; so there are cases where, though the *explanantia* are of a kind that makes them apt to provide reasons, the explanation itself displays a defect in our rationality. Interestingly, however, this defect is not, on MacIntyre's account, due to the unconsciousness of the desires or emotions per se: the latter explain action in the way 'an attack of panic terror' does – panic terror, too, being a state in which we are not capable of evaluating our reasons for acting, but one where the explaining state is fully conscious. Here we may compare Davidson on akrasia: 'the standard case of akrasia is the one where the agent knows what he is doing, and why, and knows that it is not for the best, and knows why' (Davidson 1982: 304). On this type of account, then, the connection between the impaired rationality of the action and the unconsciousness of the states appealed to in explaining it is very loose. Apparently actions can be fully rational but unconsciously explained; and they can be irrational, and the reasons for this can be the same whether the explaining states are unconsciously explained or not.

Another type of explanation which cites unconscious states which, in turn, are apt to rationalize but don't do it in the particular case is exemplified by some other Freudian cases of 'symptomatic error':

> Frau F. said, of her first lesson in a language course [...]: 'It's really interesting, the tutor is a nice young Englishman. In the very first lesson he indicated to me *durch die Bluse* [through my blouse]' – and corrects herself: '*durch die Blume* [lit. through the flower, but colloquially with veiled hints] – that he would rather give me private tuition.' (Freud 2002: 78)

Though desires are states apt to provide rationalizing explanations, there is no unconscious communicative intention on Frau F.'s part in this case: her attraction to the tutor simply betrays itself involuntarily in her utterance, much as emotions betray themselves in gestures and facial expressions. Here as with the essentially non-rationalizing causes of action cited earlier, we find a pattern of unconscious explanation of action that is common to the explanation of non-actions, and indeed to the explanation of non-actions by *conscious* states (I can express amusement by smiling involuntarily, but I know perfectly well that I am smiling because I am amused).

Equally indebted to psychoanalysis, however, is a different model of the unconscious explanation of action (Gardner 1993), which insists on its difference from rationalizing explanation; discerns patterns of explanation common to actions (for example obsessional behavior) and non-actions (for example dreams); draws on the notion of expression and of expressive behavior; but tries to make the connection between the irrationality of the *explananda* and the unconsciousness of the *explanantia* much tighter than it is in any of the models reviewed so far. Does this model compete with the others for logical space? No: although Gardner claims that, if the correct explanation of the action is 'unconscious rationality' (as in the case of the monopolizing suitor), we have the operations not of the unconscious but of the 'preconscious,' the disagreement here is surely over the choice of our terminology rather than over the viability of the other models of explanation.

As an example of this most exigent model of unconscious explanation, consider the case given by Freud, of a girl's obsessive bedtime ritual which involved arranging her bedding in a particular way (Freud 1952: 224–227). Notice first of all that the behavior consists of a series of intentional actions such as arranging the bolster so that it does not touch the end of the bedstead. It is also irrational (reminding one of the man in Anscombe's *Intention* who fills a saucer with mud 'for no reason'), since the agent's reasons for acting this way give out immediately, and yet the action – unlike whistling or running one's fingers through one's hair – does not remotely begin to make sense *without* a further reason. It is natural, then, to look for further, unconscious reasons, of the kinds canvassed before: beliefs, desires, and so on – reasons which, although unconscious, either fully rationalize the action or at least display it as a case of action performed *as if* for reasons, even if this remains in fact a case of impaired rationality because of the agent's incapacity to evaluate them. Indeed reasons of this kind are ready to hand. The girl's ritual (which included preventing her parents from going to bed till it was over) might be seen as manifesting her unconscious intention to prevent her parents from having sexual intercourse; thereby it would avert an outcome which she unconsciously very much does not want – namely a sibling, who would be her rival. Gardner concedes that rationalizing factors (including perhaps pleasure in the ritual) may help to perpetuate the obsessional behavior and make it hard to shift. However, the primary function of the behavior, dependent as the latter may be on the content of unconscious states and hence not merely mechanical, is not to rationalize but depends on: (1) unconscious phantasy; (2) expression; and (3) symbolism. The girl is motivated by a wish-fulfilling phantasy of undoing her mother's pregnancy, which expresses itself in intentional action in the way anger may express itself in smashing a glass, only it does so symbolically, through the details of the ritual (fluffing the eiderdown in such a way that it makes a hump, then smoothing it again, thereby symbolically undoing pregnancy). The ritual is thus irrational not only because of the inadequacy of the reasons the girl herself is able to offer, but also because the mental states that explain it are themselves irrational (though representational, they are 'not subject to the requirements of rationality that govern belief, desire and preference,' Gardner 1993: 116). It is not that the girl unconsciously wants her mother to cease to be pregnant and believes, unconsciously and falsely, that wishing for this state of affairs will bring it about (which would make her wish instrumentally rational in relation to her false belief); rather the phantasy itself functions, by its very nature, as if wishing something makes it so. But states of this kind are also, as a rule, minimally accessible to consciousness (Gardner 1993: 89). Hence the special irrationality of the action and the unconscious character of its explanation don't go together just by accident.

This psychoanalytic account of irrational action and its unconscious explanation draws attention to a feature of explanation by intentional states overlooked by the previous accounts of rationalizing explanation, namely that, even when explaining actions by appeal to *conscious* emotions 'makes sense' of them (as in the case of smashing the glass in anger), it need not do so by representing the action as practically rational relative to the agent's desires, beliefs, and so on: the action may simply express the subject's state. However, there is room for controversy about the view of unconscious mental states in play on this account, both with respect to the states' content and with respect to their alleged inaccessibility to consciousness. On a psychoanalytical model of mental structure emphasized by Bion, Winnicott and others, ego-formation or self-formation is favored by the availability of a mirroring or containing other, who articulates the growing child's thoughts and experiences in such a way that the child can grasp them and make them its own; from this pattern of nurture the child gradually acquires the capacity to 'contain' its own thoughts and experiences (Shuttleworth 2002: 36). Perhaps because they are traumatic, or because of the absence of a containing other, or both, these contents may, however, make themselves felt in other ways – for example through symptom-formation, 'concrete thinking' (Dubinsky 1997: 8), or 'acting out.' When this happens, irrationality results, since the agent's incapacity to articulate the contents to himself debars them from interacting in the right way with the rest of his beliefs, desires and so on. But there is nothing about the nature of the states themselves that precludes them from interacting with the subject's other mental states in the right way. Insofar as it aims to help the subject 'contain' these contents – or, in Jonathan Lear's words, converts 'physical throwings-up into verbal throwings-up [of meanings]' (Lear 1999; cf. Lear 1990: 7) – psychoanalysis sees itself as restoring or enhancing the subject's rational powers.

See also: VOLITION AND THE WILL (13); TELEOLOGICAL EXPLANATION (16); REASONS AND CAUSES (17); MOTIVATING REASONS (19); THE EXPLANATORY ROLE OF CONSCIOUSNESS (24); AGENTS' KNOWLEDGE (30); AKRASIA AND IRRATIONALITY (35); RESPONSIBILITY AND AUTONOMY (39); INTENTIONAL ACTION IN FOLK PSYCHOLOGY (45); NIETZSCHE (65).

References

Davidson, D. (1982). Paradoxes of irrationality. In R. Wollheim and J. Hopkins (eds), *Philosophical Essays on Freud*. Cambridge: Cambridge University Press, 289–305.

Dubinsky, A. (1997). Theoretical overview. In M. Rustin, M. Rhode, A. Dubinsky and H. Dubinsky (eds), *Psychotic States in Children*. London: Duckworth, 5–26.

Freud, S. (1952). *Introductory Lectures on Psycho-Analysis*, translated by J. Riviere. London: George Allen and Unwin.

Freud, S. (2002). *The Psychopathology of Everyday Life*, translated by Anthea Bell. London: Penguin.

Gardner, S. (1993). *Irrationality and the Philosophy of Psychoanalysis*. Cambridge: Cambridge University Press.

Lear, J. (1990). *Love and Its Place in Nature*. London: Faber.

Lear, J. (1999). Love and its place in nature. www.psychoanalysis.org.uk/lear.htm.

MacIntyre, A. C. (2004). *The Unconscious*, rev. edn. London: Routledge.

Rey, G. (1998). Unconscious mental states. In E. J. Craig (ed.), *The Routledge Encyclopedia of Philosophy*, Vol. 9. London: Routledge.

Shuttleworth, K. (2002). Psychoanalytic theory and infant development. In L. Miller, M. Rustin, M. Rustin [*sic*] and J. Shuttleworth (eds), *Closely Observed Infants*. London: Duckworth.

23

Mental Causation and Epiphenomenalism

JOHN HEIL

Epiphenomenalism is most often cast as a thesis in the philosophy of mind according to which:

1 mental events (or properties) are distinct from physical events (or properties);
2 mental events (or properties) depend on physical events (or properties);
3 mental events (or properties) lack causal efficacy.

Mental events (or properties) resemble the smoke given off by a steam locomotive. Smoke is a byproduct of the process of combustion, not a contributing factor in the locomotive's operation. The analogy is in one way misleading. Smoke is a byproduct, but smoke can have numerous effects of its own. Epiphenomenalists deny any sort of efficacy to the mental.

If you think of causal sequences as chains, then you might think of an epiphenomenal byproduct on the model of a branching chain (Figure 23.1):

Here *C* is depicted as a byproduct of *B* that has no further effects. Imagine that *A*, *B*, *D*, *E*, and *F* are goings on in your brain, and that *C* is a sensory occurrence – a painful sensation, for instance. *C* is produced by neurological goings-on, themselves effects of goings-on in your body that have resulted from your barking your shin. What matters to your body – and to your subsequent behavior – is the physical sequence, not the feeling that accompanies it. It might *seem* to you that you groan and rub your shin because you are in a painful state, but this is an illusion. The illusion is understandable because the same physical occurrence that gives rise to your feeling, in this case *B*, also gives rise to your responses. Unpleasant feelings of this kind are typically followed by such responses, so it is natural to regard the feeling as producing the response.

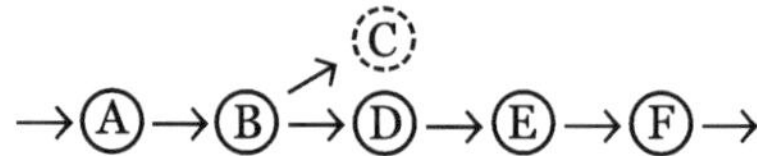

Figure 23.1 Epiphenomenalism

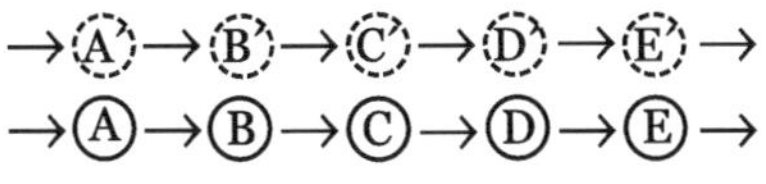

→(A')→(B')→(C')→(D')→(E')→

→Ⓐ→Ⓑ→Ⓒ→Ⓓ→Ⓔ→

Figure 23.2 Parallelism

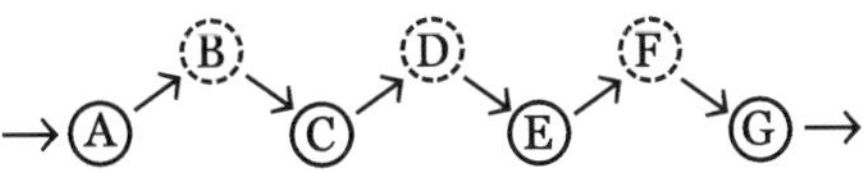

Figure 23.3 Interactionism

Epiphenomenalism is to be distinguished from *parallelism*, the doctrine that the mental and the physical constitute autonomous, causally self-contained, non-interacting realms of being. Parallelists allow that mental goings-on can have causal efficacy in the production of other mental goings-on, but no physical efficacy (compare Figures 23.1 and 23.2). Similarly, physical events can have only physical effects. In contrast, a central tenet of epiphenomenalism is that epiphenomena are physical side effects, dependent (causally or in some other way) on physical occurrences.

Both epiphenomenalism and parallelism differ from interactionism, according to which the mental and the physical differ dramatically but interact causally (Figure 23.3).

Why should anyone be attracted to epiphenomenalism? One reason is that we are increasingly coming to see the physical world as a closed system of purely physical causes and effects. Every physical occurrence apparently has a wholly physical explanation. To the extent that mental states, events, and properties stand outside the physical system, they seem powerless to affect physical goings-on. Indeed, the possibility that non-physical items might make a physical difference apparently violates conservation laws lying near the heart of physics.

A second reason why you might be attracted to epiphenomenalism is the intimate connection between physical goings-on, in particular goings-on in the brain, and conscious experiences. On the one hand, conscious experiences appear to be distinct from, but somehow dependent on, neurological occurrences: mental phenomena 'arise from' purely physical goings-on. On the other hand, neurological occurrences seem wholly explicable by reference to other neurological – or at any rate physical – occurrences. Epiphenomenalism provides a straightforward explanation of these appearances.

Epiphenomenalism, which has a long history (Caston 1997; Robinson 2007), has recently returned to prominence, largely as a result of philosophers' attraction to the three pillars of epiphenomenalism: the irreducibility of the mental to the physical; the dependence of the mental on the physical; and the causally closed nature of the physical world. One popular view, 'non-reductive physicalism,' makes mental properties dependent on physical properties (mental properties 'supervene on' or are 'realized by' physical properties), while cleaving to a fundamental distinction between the mental and the physical. Such a position might be thought to have epiphenomenalist consequences. If your being in pain 'supervenes on' or is 'realized by,' but is nevertheless distinct from, goings-on in your brain, how could the feeling of pain, as distinct from the brain states that 'ground' or 'realize' that feeling, have physical effects?

Most non-reductive physicalists see epiphenomenalism as a threat, to be answered by accounts of the mental–physical relation that allocate efficacy to the mental without violating the causal autonomy of the physical realm. Some (for instance Chalmers 1996) are more sanguine about possible epiphenomenalist implications of their position, arguing that the reality of the mental, as well as its distinctness from the physical, are undeniable. If this implies epiphenomenalism, so be it.

Indeed, epiphenomenalism might be thought to be innocuous. Conscious creatures undergo all sorts of conscious – 'phenomenal' – experiences. These accompany complex physical goings-on. If the conscious, experiential, phenomenal nature of experiences plays no role in the production of behavior – or, for that matter, in the production of subsequent conscious experiences – why should we care? Conscious experiences reliably co-vary with physical episodes that have all the right causal consequences. We can save the appearances without supposing that the physical realm is affected by anything non-physical.

Opponents regard this picture as specious. States of mind are important, they argue, not merely because they have a distinctive qualitative nature, but because we take them to play a vital role in what we think and do. You form the belief that you are in pain in part *because* of the painfulness of your experience. An epiphenomenalist must deny this seemingly obvious connection. Many philosophers regard reasons as 'rationalizing' actions only insofar as they cause bodily motions that constitute those actions (Davidson 1963). If reasons – agents' beliefs and desires, for instance – are inefficacious, no action could be reasonable. Norman Malcolm (1968; see also Lowe 2008) goes further, noting that mental categories are causally imbued. An intention to flip the switch, for instance, is a state that produces switch-flipping behavior unless something intervenes to prevent it. A state that had or could have no such effect would not be an intention. Malcolm parlays this line of thought into an argument that epiphenomenalism is, in a certain sense, self-defeating: if you reasonably believe epiphenomenalism is true, it must be false!

One way around these worries would be to distinguish states of mind such as beliefs, desires, and intentions from qualitatively distinctive states of consciousness. The former might be thought to lack the kind of 'phenomenal character' essential to the latter, hence to be more susceptible to a purely physical accounting. David Chalmers (1996) deploys this strategy in distinguishing between 'phenomenal' and 'psychological' conceptions of mind. 'Psychological' goings-on – beliefs, desires, intentions – appear to be physically explicable. 'Phenomenal' states, in contrast – the *qualia* – 'arise from' physical states and evidently stand outside the physical realm as it is currently conceived. We must, Chalmers thinks, either find a way to let in consciousness – 'phenomenal' properties, qualia – at the fundamental physical level (panpsychism), or accept consciousness as epiphenomenal.

Epiphenomenalists of whatever stripe must deny a plausible metaphysical principle (the 'Eleatic Principle,' or 'Alexander's Dictum') to the effect that to be real is to possess causal potency. Not only do epiphenomena have no effects; they *could* have no effects. Epiphenomena would be what J. J. C. Smart calls 'nomological danglers' (Smart 1959).

Laws governing the generation of epiphenomena would be 'dead end' laws, wholly unlike any other laws of nature.

The causal inertness of epiphenomena might be thought to imply that epiphenomenal states of mind are unknowable. To see the difficulty, start with the idea that we certainly seem to be aware of our own conscious states, our own thoughts and feelings. Knowledge of an entity apparently requires, however, that the knower be connected causally with the entity. We can know about our surroundings or about spatially or temporally distal goings-on because such things belong to a causal network within which we ourselves are embedded. Your beliefs about your own states of mind, let alone the states of mind of others, could not be caused by those states of mind, however, if states of mind were causally impotent.

Even if knowledge of an entity requires the knower to be causally connected to it, however, it need not require a direct causal connection. We are only indirectly connected with spatially or temporally remote events. An epiphenomenalist can allow – indeed will insist – that we are indirectly connected to epiphenomenal states of mind. A neurological event that gives rise to a painful sensation might also be responsible for the production of your belief that you are undergoing a painful sensation. Perhaps this is sufficient for your belief to constitute knowledge of your sensation.

Traditional formulations of epiphenomenalism of the sort depicted in Figure 23.1 presume that epiphenomena are *events*: particular, datable effects of causal sequences which themselves could have no effects. This is what Brian McLaughlin (1989) calls 'token epiphenomenalism.' Non-reductive physicalism, however, is most often taken to imply 'type epiphenomenalism,' a view according to which mental types or properties are 'causally irrelevant' to the production of physical goings-on. Given the dependence of the mental on the physical, mental types would seem thereby causally irrelevant to the production of mental goings-on as well.

An appreciation of McLaughlin's distinction requires a conception of *causal relevance*. Suppose, as many philosophers do, that causal relata – causes and effects – are events. What an event causes depends on its properties. A ball's being spherical is responsible for its making a circular, concave impression in the carpet. Were the ball differently shaped, were it a cube, for instance, its resting on the carpet would have a different kind of effect. Even if properties are not themselves causes, then, the properties of a cause evidently make a difference to the properties of its effect.

Now suppose an occurrence in your brain 'realizes' your sensation of pain, and suppose this occurrence has a certain physical effect: it causes you to groan. Did the occurrence have this effect in virtue of its physical properties or in virtue of its mental properties? Closure considerations suggest that mental properties are epiphenomenal: this is property (or type) epiphenomenalism. Jaegwon Kim (2005) argues that, if a physical effect can be explained wholly by reference to physical features of the cause, mental features are 'excluded' as causal contributors. The options, he thinks, are: (a) reduction of mental properties to physical properties; (b) violation of closure; or (c) epiphenomenalism. A fourth option (d), 'causal over-determination,' apparently implies that events with mental causes are systematically 'over-determined': they have sufficient physical causes *and* they have sufficient mental causes. (See Bennett 2003 and Gibbons 2006 for a rebuttal.)

Assessing the consequences of property epiphenomenalism requires a look behind the scenes at the metaphysics of events. An object – say, this ball of wax – might be taken to be a substance that posesses various properties: it is spherical in a lumpy sort of way, white, rigid. Over time, an object might gain or lose various properties. If you place the wax in an oven, its shape changes; it becomes transparant; it is no longer rigid. One way to think about events is to regard them as occurring when substances gain or lose properties. The wax's becoming warm, then, or its becoming transparent, might be thought of as events. Although these events occur simultaneously, they are, as events, distinct, just as the wax's being spherical and its being white are distinct *states* of the ball.

Events, then, could the thought to be the objects' coming to be in particular states, where a state is an object's possession of a property. (Some philosophers will differ on the nature of events, but the aim here is to spell out the ontology that underlies current worries about the epiphenomenalist implications of non-reductive physicalism.) This way of understanding events is associated with Kim (1973), but it is reflected in a widely accepted conception of states of affairs as the objects' possession of properties at particular times (see for example Armstrong 1997). Because the difference between events and states of affairs is not ontologically deep, it is common to think of events as having the following form: an object *a*'s possessing a property *P* at a given time *t*. (To streamline the discussion, I omit explicit reference to times in what follows.) It is natural to think of events as *changes* of state, but you might regard an object's *remaining* in a particular state as a kind of event. The strength of a bridge requires that the bridge's parts interact in the right way and that they persist in so interacting.

According to non-reductive physicalists, an object's possession of a mental property depends on the object's possession of some physical property. This is often put in terms of realization. Your undergoing a painful sensation depends on your brain's being in a particular state. The sensation is realized somehow in your brain. But what is realization? On most views, realization is a relation among properties or 'property instances.' In your case, an instance of a certain mental property *M* is realized by an instance of a certain physical property *P*.

Is a property instance a state? Is it that your being in *M* is realized by your being in *P*? For the purposes of the present discussion, the answer to this question is not important. What is important is that, for a non-reductive physicalist, the properties *M* and *P* are distinct. This is the heart of the non-reductivist position: mental properties are not reducible to, not identifiable with, physical properties.

Non-reductivists often describe their position as one that accepts the 'token identity' of mental and physical events but denies 'type identity': mental events could be identical with physical events, although mental properties are distinct from physical properties. Such a position is usually attributed to Donald Davidson (1970). Davidson holds that every mental event is a physical event, although there is no principled way of correlating mental and physical types: particular mental events of the same kind could turn out to be identical with physical events of very different kinds. A view of this sort meshes nicely with the idea that mental properties are multiply realizable – a non-reductionist staple.

But how are we to understand the token identity thesis? Consider a particular mental event *m*. This event is identical with a physical event *p*: $m = p$. The event is mental by virtue of its incorporating a mental property *M*, and physical by virtue of including some physical property *P*; but $M \neq P$. The good news is that we can allow for the causal efficacy of mental events: if *p* has assorted physical effects, then *m*, by virtue of being identical with *p*, has those very same effects. The bad news is that we seem to have a new problem: the *qua* problem. Granted that *m* (= *p*) has various physical effects, are these effects due to *m*'s being *M* or to its being *P* – in other words, does the event cause what it does *qua* mental or *qua* physical?

We are imagining token identity, type diversity. The worry is that such a view yields McLaughlin's property or type epiphenomenalism: whenever a mental event causes a particular effect, it does so not by virtue of including some mental property, but by virtue of incorporating a particular physical property. To think otherwise, to think that non-physical, mental properties could affect physical causal relations, is to risk violating closure. And, given the dependence of the mental on the physical, a mental property could make a mental difference only by making some physical difference. Epiphenomenalism!

Non-reductive physicalists have offered a number of arguments aimed at defusing this epiphenomenalist worry (see, among others, Pereboom 2002; Bennett 2003; Gibbons 2006; Shoemaker 2007). This is not the place to examine the success of such arguments. Let us instead look more closely at the idea that particular mental events might be identical with particular physical events in spite of the fact that mental and physical types are distinct. This is the possibility that yields a distinction between traditional token epiphenomenalism and an epiphenomenalism of properties or types thought to plague non-reductive physicalism.

When philosophers discuss mental and physical events and speak of token identity, what are the tokens said to be identical? You might think that the tokens are particular – token – events. But this seems wrong. It is certainly wrong if events consist in the possession of properties by objects, as described above. An event *m* and an event *p* are identical just in case their constituents are identical. Suppose *m* consists in *a*'s having *M*, and *p* consists in *a*'s having *P*. Unless *M* and *P* are the same property, *m* and *p* must be distinct. There is no question here of *the same* event exhibiting different properties. True, we have token identity of a sort: the object, *a*, in each event is the same object. But *a* is merely a *constituent* of distinct events.

Given, then, the conception of events with which we began, there is no way for the notorious '*qua*-problem' to get off the ground. This is not because there is no problem. We can still doubt that mental events have causal efficacy. But this is just the prospect of traditional 'token epiphenomenalism' all over again.

You might try revising the account of events. Perhaps there *is* a single event that possesses both a mental property and a physical property. But what story about events allows for this possibility? Sometimes Davidson is described as embracing a 'coarse-grained' conception of events (as distinct from our 'fine-grained conception'). When a mental event occurs, there is a single event, which is both mental and physical.

This account might sound appealing to some, but it leaves the ontology of events entirely open. How is the ontology to be spelled out? One bad idea would be to accept the initial characterization of events and to tack on the idea that events, so characterized, *have* mental and physical properties (see Macdonald and Macdonald 2006). The problem is that events so characterized appear to belong in the wrong metaphysical category. You can think of a substance or an object possessing (or 'instantiating') properties, but an event is not a substance or an object: it is a substance's having a property. Can a substance's having a property *itself* have a property?

There are undoubtedly truths about events: that they occur at a particular time and place, that they occur slowly or rapidly. But are the truth-makers for these truths properties *of* the events? That an event occurs at *t* is made true by the fact that *t* is a constituent of the event. That it occurs slowly is made true by the event's occuring over an extended temporal duration. Philosophers are too ready to assume that every truly applicable predicate must correspond to a property.

This brings us back to Davidson. It is natural to describe Davidson as advocating token identity, type diversity. Every mental event is a physical event, although the mental is not reducible to the physical. The mistake is to imagine that Davidson holds that events are mental by virtue of possessing a mental property, physical by virtue of possessing a physical property. For Davidson, the mental–physical distinction is a distinction of conception, not a distinction in being or reality. An event is mental if it could be picked out using a mental description, and physical if it could be singled out by deploying a physical vocabulary. Davidson thinks that any event which can be identified mentally also has some physical designation or other. This is ontological reduction without conceptual reduction; token identity without type identity – with one important proviso: the types in question are not properties or constituents of events, but predicates or classificatory vehicles.

Epiphenomenalists assume that mental states, events, and properties are nonphysical – an assumption many philosophers have challenged. Perhaps, as Davidson thinks, mental and physical concepts merely reflect different ways of classifying worldly goings-on – a kind of 'neutral monism.' Or perhaps the mental is just a sub-category of the physical: mental states, events, and properties make up a special class of physical states, events, and properties. A more radical thesis, *eliminativism*, holds that the mental category is empty: there are no distinctively mental states, events, or properties.

One question is: What is required for 'realism' about the mental? Is Davidson's view, for instance, a kind of anti-realism, a kind of eliminativism? Does accepting the reality of the mental mean accepting the thesis that mental states, events, and properties are distinct from physical states, events, and properties? If it does, and if you think of the mental as in some fashion dependent on physical goings-on while you regard the physical realm as causally autonomous, it is hard to see how epiphenomenalism could be avoided. If you regard epiphenomenalism as unacceptable, then you will want to consider dropping one of the three theses spelled out at the outset of this chapter.

See also: ACTION THEORY AND ONTOLOGY (1); REASONS AND CAUSES (17); THE EXPLANATORY ROLE OF CONSCIOUSNESS (24); MENTAL ACTS (27); AGENT CAUSATION (28); DAVIDSON (73).

References

Armstrong, D. M. (1997). *A World of States of Affairs*. Cambridge: Cambridge University Press.

Bennett, K. (2003). Why the exclusion problem seems intractable, and how, just maybe, to tract it. *Noûs*, 37, 471–497.

Caston, V. (1997). Epiphenomenalism, ancient and modern. *Philosophical Review*, 106, 309–363.

Chalmers, D. (1996). *The Conscious Mind: In Search of a Fundamental Theory*. New York: Oxford University Press.

Davidson, D. (1963). Actions, reasons, and causes. *Journal of Philosophy*, 60, 685–700.

Davidson, D. (1970). Mental events. In L. Foster and J. Swanson (eds.), *Experience and Theory* (Amherst: University of Massachusetts Press): 79–101. Reprinted in *Essays on Actions and Events* (Oxford: Clarendon Press, 1980): 207–225.

Gibbons, J. (2006). Mental causation without downward causation. *Philosophical Review*, 115, 79–103.

Kim, J. (1973). Causation, nomic subsumption, and the concept of event. *Journal of Philosophy*, 70, 217–236.

Kim, J. (2005) *Physicalism, or Something Near Enough*. Princeton: Princeton University Press.

Lowe, E. J. (2008) *Personal Agency: The Metaphysics of Mind and Action*. Oxford: Oxford University Press.

Macdonald, C., and Macdonald, G. (2006). The metaphysics of mental causation. *Journal of Philosophy*, 103, 539–576.

McLaughlin, B. P. (1989). Type epiphenomenalism, type dualism, and the causal priority of the physical. *Philosophical Perspectives*, 3, 109–135.

Malcolm, N. (1968). The conceivability of mechanism. *Philosophical Review*, 77, 45–72.

Pereboom, D. (2002). Robust nonreductive materialism. *Journal of Philosophy*, 99, 499–531.

Robinson, W. (2007). Epiphenomenalism. In E. N. Zalta (ed.), *Stanford Encyclopedia of Philosophy*. http://plato.stanford.edu/entries/epiphenomenalism/.

Shoemaker, S. (2007) *Physical Realization*. Oxford: Oxford University Press.

Smart, J. J. C. (1959). Sensations and brain processes. *Philosophical Review*, 68, 141–156.

24

The Explanatory Role of Consciousness

NAOMI EILAN

The Problem

The problem we are interested in when we ask about the role of consciousness in explaining action is vividly illustrated by 'anarchic hand' syndrome. Patients suffering from this syndrome sometimes find one of their hands performing complex, apparently goal-directed movements they are unable to suppress (except by using their 'good' hand). Sometimes the anarchic hand interferes with intentional actions performed by the other hand – for instance it may unbutton a shirt the patient is trying to button up. Sometimes it performs movements apparently unrelated to any of the agent's intentions, such as (in one notorious example) a movement resulting in picking up some leftovers from somebody else's plate in a restaurant. In most of these cases patients go on to claim that it feels as if the actions performed by the anarchic hand are not theirs, and that the hand is doing something they did not intend or want, and cannot control (Della Salla 1994, 2000).

Now, although the activities of the anarchic hand are, in some sense, skillfully controlled – they are not pure reflexes – intuitively we do not have in play in these cases the kind of control we take ourselves to have *qua* rational agents, in virtue of which we speak of freedom of the will; and the question is precisely about the relation between consciousness and that kind of control. Similarly, although some kind of awareness of the action being performed is involved on the subject's part, there is a sense in which this awareness is of the kind one might have as an observer of someone else's actions, rather than the first-person or inside awareness we normally have of our actions. And the question is specifically about the explanatory role, if any, of that kind of first-person awareness in generating the kind of control of our actions we think we have as free agents.

A first response to such cases is to treat them as confirming the thought that in normal situations there is a kind of awareness of one's intentions and of what one is doing which causally controls one's actions, and that in the case of the anarchic hand there is no such awareness and therefore not the right kind of control. In fact, however, the bare description of the syndrome leaves open the following three options:

1 The absence of the right kind of control in anarchic hand syndrome is indeed to be explained by the absence of such awareness.
2 The absence of the right kind of control in such cases is to be explained wholly by the absence of the right kind of sub-personal causal mechanism – where this mechanism (in normal life, but not here) also generates, as a by-product, the right kind of consciousness.
3 The absence of control and the absence of consciousness in anarchic hand syndrome are each to be explained by the absence of two independent sub-personal mechanisms, which in normal circumstances are both operative.

In both (2) and (3), consciousness has no role in explaining the distinctive kind of control we think we have of our actions. It is epiphenomenal.

During the past three decades there has been much work in psychology which has often been treated as lending support either to (2) or to (3). For example, in the mid-1980s Benjamin Libet conducted a series of experiments which, he argued, showed that we are aware of beginning to act only after the brain area responsible for initiating action has already been activated. On his view, which was shared by others, the conclusion we should draw is that our brain 'decides' on courses of action independently of our consciousness; consciousness is epiphenomenal (Libet 1985). Similarly, David Milner and Melvyn Goodale have suggested that the conclusion to be drawn from their experimental and theoretical work on normal and pathological subjects is that the causal mechanisms underpinning environmentally directed action-control are independent of those underpinning visual experiences of the objects on which we act and, hence, that experience has no contribution to make to action control (Milner and Goodale 1995).

The significance of these theses depends in part on the account one gives of the kind of consciousness distinctive of intentional action. On any account of such consciousness, we need to explain both ownership – the sense in which one feels the actions to be one's own – and awareness of what one is doing. And we need also to account for the relation between these phenomena. A central question here is whether there is a characterization of what it is to be aware of what one is doing when one is in control which simultaneously yields an account of the sense of ownership. A further issue turns on whether one thinks that there is a distinctive *experiential* phenomenology to these various aspects of conscious action, and, if there is, how it is to be accounted for.

Now, the first thing to note about the epiphenomenalist challenges is that they have a variety of targets. Libet for example is interested in consciousness of action initiation, whereas Goodale and Milner are interested in the visual consciousness of the object toward which we direct our actions. Other psychologists have been concerned specifically with proprioceptive experiences (the direction in which one feels one's arm to be moving, for example). The significance of this or that epiphenomenalist challenge to the general question of the explanatory role of consciousness depends in part on whether (and for what reasons) you think that the kind of consciousness targeted in the experiments on which the challenge is based is, in fact, the kind of consciousness you hold to be distinctive of the actions we control.

A second ingredient relevant to the assessment of these theses is this. Many accounts of the distinctive phenomenology of acting are driven by epistemological concerns, in particular by the question of how we know what we are doing. The scene for these debates was set by Elizabeth Anscombe, who held (a) that we acquire knowledge of what we are doing by way of rationally controlling our actions rather than on the basis of (experiential) observation or introspection; and (b) that what it is for an action to be rationally controlled is for it to be the (practical) outcome of a piece of practical reasoning. Experience plays a role neither in causing action nor in yielding knowledge of what we are doing (Anscombe 1957). Obviously, if this is your view, demonstrations of the causal irrelevance of experience are grist to your mill. Much of the most interesting work on the phenomenology of action in recent years has been driven by Anscombe's claims – including attempts to prove her wrong – and by the general question of the extent to which epistemological concerns should (if at all) constrain accounts of phenomenology (see for instance Dokic 2003; Peacocke 2003; Proust 2003; Roessler and Eilan 2003).

The significance of empirical research for the question of the explanatory role of consciousness is also modulated by which account you adopt of the information-processing mechanisms involved in controlling action. The failures of control displayed in the anarchic hand syndrome serve as one kind of input to such theorizing; but so too do different kinds of pathological failures – for instance 'utilization behaviors' (see Humphreys and Riddoch 2003; Norman and Shallice 1986) and everyday failures, which are often referred to as 'capture errors' (Reason 1984; Monsell 1996). Theories about the relation between consciousness and control can vary according to which failure is treated as a springboard for an account of the normal case. Two relevant debates that emerge when such differences are taken into account are as follows. Many information-processing theories of action control adopt some version of a two-level theory, in which higher-level intentions prime 'automatic' lower-level information-processing mechanisms that respond to stimuli. However, on some (but not all) views, 'automatic' means 'non-conscious.' Thus finding (perhaps to the surprise of common sense) that various aspects of control are delegated to automatic sub-systems will have a different significance for the causal role of consciousness, depending on which account of automaticity you adopt. Secondly, there is the major theoretical question of whether the operation of the higher-level information-processing system can simply be equated with the operation of conscious intentions. If you hold that it can, then showing that this system has a causal role will also vindicate a causal role for consciousness. But you might hold that such a reduction of personal to information-processing level is impossible – in which case questions about the causal role of consciousness remain wide open. (On these issues, see Eilan and Roessler 2003: 3–15; Perner 2003; Humphreys and Riddoch 2003.)

So, when we ask about the role of consciousness in controlling action, there are questions about:

1 how to characterize the distinctive first-person awareness that accompanies the actions we control;
2 whether epistemology constrains accounts of phenomenology, and, if it does, how;

3 which information processing theory of causal control is right;
4 how the latter relates to personal level explanations of intentional action.

These represent but a handful of illustrations from the minefield of issues we encounter here. Our understanding of these issues is, in many respects, in its infancy. One thing which is certain, though, is that recent work in psychology, in which control and awareness come apart in various ways, provides materials aplenty, both for formulating commonsense intuitions about the nature of the connection between intentional control and awareness and for putting them to the test. In what follows I make do with some illustrations of the issues that open up when such work is used as a springboard for asking about the role of consciousness in explaining action.

Perceptual Consciousness and Action: Experimental Dissociations and Commonsense Connections

Proprioceptive experience and action control

In a series of experiments conducted by Tony Marcel, the arm and hand of various subjects were occluded by a surface that had a number of lights placed on it. The subjects in question were asked to move their hand to a particular position, identified by reference to one of the lights on the surface. Crucially, the subjects' proprioceptive experience of the position of their arm was demonstrably illusory (this emerged from an experimental technique called 'vibro-tactile stimulation,' which involves vibrating a muscle tendon): subjects experienced their hand as being to the left of the light when it was actually to its right. Despite this abnormal set-up, subjects had no difficulty complying with the instruction – they moved their hand to the correct position. However, many were mistaken about the direction in which they moved – they claimed, say, to have moved their hand to the right when in fact they moved it to the left (Marcel 2003; for an extensive discussion of the philosophical significance of these findings, see Peacocke 2003). Important experimental work by Marc Jeannerod also points to the irrelevance of proprioceptive experiences in determining subjects' beliefs about the way they act, and therefore, on the face of it, to the rational intentions on which they act and which control their actions (see for instance Fourneret and Jeannerod 1997; Jeannerod 2003).

Most people would find these results, at least initially, surprising. And there is little doubt that the surprise is relative to some set of expectations about the contribution made by proprioceptive experience to the content of the intentions which control action. One such expectation is this: we think that moving the hand to the left, in Marcel's experiment for example, is something which subjects do intentionally. Yet they are either unaware of the direction of their movement or have an erroneous experience of it. One way of articulating our surprise is to say that, when we act intentionally, we are aware of our 'basic actions,' – the things we do directly rather than by doing something else. In Marcel's experiments we would want to say that subjects moved their hand to the position of the light *by* moving it to the left. This description of their action seems to be basic. Yet, while they certainly intentionally moved their hand to the light (and were aware of doing so), they were unaware of moving it to the left. Hence they were unaware of their 'basic' action.

Marcel himself argues that that getting right the description under which agents are aware of their intentional bodily movements requires taking into account the object of their perceptual attention. He suggests that, in his experiments, subjects are aware that they are moving their hand to the position of 'this' (perceptually presented) light; they are not aware of moving 'this' (perceptually presented) hand – in intentional acting, the agent's body normally occupies the background of attention. Correlatively, the direction of the movement was not part of the content of their conscious intention; and the control exercised by consciousness here derives solely from the visually presented light, rather than from proprioceptively informed experience of the hand's location. Marcel also suggests that this is true in many normal cases of action, and he draws on Wolfgang Prinz's common coding thesis. A key claim of the thesis is that it is the representation of the spatial location of the distal stimulus (the seen object) that primes, or pre-activates, the representation of the target location of the response, and that this representation controls movement directly, independently of any proprioceptive awareness of movement (see Prinz 2003).

One thing the experiments certainly put pressure on is the idea that, in all cases of intentional action, it is proprioceptive awareness of movements that provides us with the basic description under which our action is intentional. This result still leaves open the question of whether in all cases of action we are proprioceptively aware of some bodily movements, and, when we are, what the role of such awareness might be. A pathological case that makes this issue vivid is that of 'deafferented' subjects: subjects who, in the absence of proprioceptive awareness of the limbs they move, succeed in learning to act in response to conscious visual stimulation (Cole and Paillard 1995). On the face of it, there is something quite radically different here from the way we normally control action, but the question of how exactly we should explain this difference is still wide open (for a discussion, see Brewer 1995).

Visual experience and action control

In the work described above, it is left open that visual experience of the target of action does play a role in controlling action. However, pioneering work by Bruce Bridgeman and his colleagues puts pressure on that too (Bridgeman et al. 1975, 1981). Their experiments show that, when subjects are instructed to point to an object they see and visual illusions of movement are induced, the same subjects nonetheless point to the right location. Conversely, if changes of location are introduced during saccades so that subjects have no visual awareness of them, the same subjects will take them into account when they act. Visual awareness does not seem to control the spatial parameters of the action.

These and many other experiments suggest that, in normal conditions as well as in in illusory and pathological ones (for instance in blindsight), visual experience does not set the spatial parameters of our intentional action. There is accumulating evidence that the spatial parameters of your movement (how far and in what direction you reach) are determined on the basis of non-conscious representations of the relevant properties; and that the execution of the movement is controlled by various comparator mechanisms which operate non-consciously, checking for mismatches such as between the goal and the perceived effect of a motor command, rapidly correcting any deviations. (For a review, see Jeannerod 2003; Milner and Goodale 1995.)

In normal cases, object-directed actions are controlled by experientially based demonstrative intentions (say, to move one's arm towards 'this' object). A traditional and plausible thought is that such demonstrative intentions are necessary for acting on an object because awareness of the object sets the parameters of the action. But such work seems to undermine precisely this account of why demonstratives are important.

One way of saving the importance of consciousness here, proposed by John Campbell, is to give an alternative account of the role played by conscious experience. Roughly, the importance of consciousness, he suggests, is not that it tells you *how* to act, but rather that it tells you *which object* you are acting on; and this in turn:

1 identifies the object for non-conscious control of action; and
2 provides you with the materials for understanding why what you are doing is the right thing to do.

With respect to (1), Campbell suggests that conscious attention to an object does have a limited causal role. It is required to identify the target for the non-conscious determination of the spatial parameters of object-directed actions. More specifically, it is what enables the visually driven semantic system to 'communicate' with the pragmatic system, because both systems use location to identify objects. With respect to (2), Campbell suggests that, in the absence of consciousness, the subject lacks understanding of why what she is doing, say, in configuring her hands in a particular way is the right thing to do. This is because, in the absence of consciousness, all she perceives are affordances, whereas consciousness provides for awareness of the categorical grounds of these affordances. Awareness of the latter provides for an understanding of why what one is doing is right, and such understanding, in turn, is required for intentional action or action performed for a reason (see Campbell 2003).

Note that Campbell's solution comes with a price, as it rests on endorsing Milner and Goodale's suggestion that visual information used in the recognition of objects (the semantic system), processed in the ventral stream, is what yields conscious experience; whereas visual information used for the control of action (the pragmatic system), processed in the dorsal stream, operates wholly outside conscious awareness. To adopt such a proposal is to reject both long-standing and recently advocated claims (to be found both in philosophical and in psychological literature) that assert the existence of an empirical and a constitutive connection between one's consciousness of a perceived object and the actions one is disposed to direct at it. Two critical questions here are:

1 Can we make sense of a consciousness of dispositional properties (affordances) only? For this is what an independent pragmatic system is conceived of as delivering.
2 Do we need to appeal to the relation between perception and action to explain the nature of the subjects' point of view in perceptual consciousness of the environment?

(For a discussion of such issues, see e.g. Eilan and Roessler 2003: 31–34.)

Awareness of Intentions and Action Initiation

Perhaps the strongest challenge to the causal role of consciousness comes from Libet's classical studies, in which subjects were instructed to make a hand movement at a 'freely chosen' time. They were then asked to report, by reference to a clock, (a) when they moved, and these were labeled M (movement) reports; or (b) when 'they first felt the urge to move,' and these were labeled W (conscious will) reports. Libet found that M reports preceded the onset of muscle activity (on average by 86 ms); and that neural preparation for the movement (the so-called 'readiness potential') preceded the W reports or the reported time of 'conscious willing.' It was the latter finding in particular that led Libet to claim that consciousness is epiphenomenal in a way that shows that freedom of action is an illusion (Libet 1985).

In a series of experiments, Haggard and his collaborators extended Libet's work by investigating whether awareness, both of movement and of intention ('conscious will'), is associated with specific stages in pre-motor processing. They found (a) that awareness of movement is associated with processes which prepare the issuing of motor commands – and this, Haggard argues, lends support to the view that awareness of bodily action is 'pre-motor'; and (b) that awareness of intention is associated with the 'lateralized readiness potential,' a stage of action preparation known to be devoted to the selection of the specific movement to be made – and this, he argues, shows that what subjects are aware of is an intention for a specific kind of movement (for example to press a button with the left rather than with the right hand; Haggard 2003).

One response to Haggard is to see his results as dovetailing two claims made in the philosophical literature. The first is the suggestion that the distinctive first-person phenomenology linked with acting derives, a least in part, from the phenomenology of pre-motor trying to act or from an awareness of such tryings. The second is the suggestion that our knowledge of what we are doing is based (wholly or partially) on such tryings. (For different versions of the latter view, see O'Shaughnessy 2003 and Peacocke 2003.) If this is the line we take, then it is, at least partly, to the causal role of such awarenesses that we should look when we ask about the explanatory role of consciousness. And a natural gloss on both Libet's and Haggard's findings is that, although we do have such awareness, it is a mere epiphenomenal offshoot of the various stages of pre-motor processing unfolding in our brains. It has no causal role in controlling action.

One immediate question concerns the relation between prior and immediate intentions in the process of securing the kind of consciousness which is necessary for rational control. For example, a natural suggestion in response to Libet's findings is to say that, in this particular set-up, the causally relevant contribution of the subjects' conscious intentions lies in their prior decision to move their hand 'sometime,' whereas the task of deciding exactly when to move is delegated to some sub-personal mechanisms (which may then initiate pre-motor processing before the subject becomes aware of the present-tense intention to move). Under the particular circumstances of the experiment, delegating control to sub-personal mechanisms may be a way of choosing when to act. (This 'consciousness saving' move is analogous, structurally, to the move Campbell makes in response to the challenge that visual consciousness is epiphenomenal.) Of course, even if this move is right in these circumstances, it still leaves open many questions. These include the question of how, in general, we should explain the relation between prior and immediate intentions in yielding the kind of consciousness we think is necessary for rational control; and also the question of the sense in which we should account for the role of consciousness in controlling action in cases where there is no prior intention.

References

Anscombe, G. E. M. (1957). *Intention*. Oxford: Blackwell.

Bermudez, J., Marcel, A., and Eilan, N. (eds) (1995). *The Body and The Self*. Cambridge, MA: MIT Press.

Bridgeman, B., Hendry D., and Stark, L. (1975). Failure to detect displacement of the visual world during saccadic eye movements, *Vision Research*, 15, 719–722.

Bridgeman, B., Kirsch, M., and Sperling, A. (1981). Segregation of cognitive and motor aspects of visual function using induced motion. *Perception and Psychophysics*, 29, 336–342.

Brewer, B. (1995). Bodily awareness and the self. In Bermudez, Marcel, and Eilan (eds), 291–310.

Campbell, J. (2003). The role of demonstratives in action-explanation. In Roessler and Eilan (eds), 150–164.

Cole, J., and Paillard, J. (1995). Living without touch and peripheral information about body position and movement: Studies with deafferented subjects. In Bermudez, Marcel, and Eilan (eds), 245–266.

Della Salla, S. (1994). The anarchic hand: A fronto-mesial sign. In F. Boller and J. Graffman (eds), *Handbook of Neuropsychology*, Vol. 9. Amsterdam: Elsevier, 233–255.

Della Salla, S. (2000). Clinical aspects of anarchic hand: Disowned actions. Paper presented at the Sixteenth European Workshop on Cognitive Neuropsychology, Bressanone, Italy.

Dokic, J. (2003). The sense of ownership: An analogy between sensation and action. In Roessler and Eilan (eds), 321–344.

Eilan, N., and Roessler, J. (2003). Agency and self awareness: Mechanisms and epistemology. In Roessler and Eilan (eds), 1–48.

Fourneret, P., and Jeanneord, M. (1998) Limited conscious monitoring of motor performance in normal subjects. *Neuropsychologica*, 36. 1133–1140.

Haggard, P. (2003). Conscious awareness of intention and action. In Roessler and Eilan (eds), 111–128.

Humphreys, G., and Riddoch, J. (2003). Fractionating the intentional control of agency: A neuropsychological analysis. In Roessler and Eilan (eds), 201–208.

Jeanneord, M. (2003). Consciousness of action and self-consciousness: A cognitive neuroscience approach. In Roessler and Eilan (eds), 128–150.

Jeannerod, M. (1997). *The Cognitive Neuroscience of Action*. Oxford: Blackwell.

Libet, B. (1985). Unconscious cerebral initiative and the role of conscious will in voluntary action. *Behavioural and Brain Sciences*, 8, 529–566.

Marcel, A. (2003). The sense of agency: Awareness and ownership of action. In Roessler and Eilan (eds), 48–94.

Milner, A. D., and Goodale, M. A. (1995). *The Visual Brain in Action*. Oxford: Oxford University Press.

Monsell, S. (1996). Control of mental processes. In V. Bruce (ed.), *Unsolved Mysteries of the Mind*. Hove: Erlbaum, 93–148.

Norman, D., and Shallice, T. (1986). Attention to action. In R. Davidson, G. Schwartz, and D. Shapiro (eds), *Consciousness and Self-Regulation*. New York: Plenum, 1–18.

O'Shaughnessy, B. (2003). The epistemology of physical action. In Roessler and Eilan (eds), 345–357.

Peacocke, C. (2003). Action: Awareness, ownership and knowledge. In Roessler and Eilan (eds), 94–110.

Perner, J. (2003). Dual control and the causal theory of action: The case of non-intentional actions. In Roessler and Eilan (eds), 218–243.

Prinz, W. (2003). Experimental approaches to action. In Roessler and Eilan (eds), 165–187.

Proust, J. (2003). Perceiving intentions. In Roessler and Eilan (eds), 296–320.

Reason, J. (1984). Lapses of attention in everyday life. In R. Parasuraman and D. R. Davies D. (eds), *Varieties of Attention*, Orlando, FL: Academic Press, 515–549.

Roessler, J., and Eilan, N. (eds) (2003). *Agency and Self-Awareness*. Oxford: Oxford University Press.

25

What a Difference Emotions Make

SABINE A. DÖRING

Ever since Aristotle, philosophers have held that explanations of intentional actions must always make essential reference to some desire the agent has. The desire is claimed to provide the end, purpose, or goal seen as constitutive of intentional action. Intentional action is then explained by the agent's desire for something, in combination with his belief that the action in question is a suitable means for attaining that thing. The agent wants to listen to the news, for example, and he believes that turning on the radio will result in his listening to the news; and he consequently turns on the radio. By providing a goal for action, his desire is supposed to motivate the agent to act so that this goal is achieved. In combination with the belief, the desire is also supposed to equip the agent with a reason for action: from his perspective, it speaks in favor of the action that it is expected to bring about a desired thing. In this sense, the explanation is a rational explanation of his action (see Davidson 1980).

Let us call this model of the explanation of intentional action the 'belief–desire model' (BD for short). I shall explain emotional actions against the backdrop of BD because BD is the standard model, and not only in philosophy. As desires and beliefs are the only mental states involved in BD, it seems that emotions, if they have to play a role in the explanation of intentional action, must be desires or beliefs. This is, however, denied by contemporary emotion theorists, who are all agreed that emotions cannot be reduced to desires, nor to beliefs, nor simply to combinations of both, plus perhaps certain Jamesian bodily sensations (on which see James 1884). What consequences do the insights of contemporary emotion theory have for BD?

The most influential way of cashing out BD is the Humean theory of motivation (HTM for short), whose origin's lie with David Hume's notorious claim that 'reason alone can never be a motive to any action of the will' (Hume 1978, Book 2, Part 3, § 3, p. 413). In addition to BD, HTM states that beliefs and desires constitute two distinct classes of mental states, which mutually exclude each other (Smith 1994: 111–129). It follows that the mental state which provides the goal for, and thereby motivates, an intentional action, if it is a desire, cannot assume the form of a belief (reason state). This possibility is not excluded by BD: 'desire' here is a technical term, also called 'pro-attitude,' and is understood simply as *any* mental state that could possibly be held to move anyone (Davidson 1980: 3–4). The 'pro-attitude' sense of 'desire' is entailed by the very definition of intentional action: it follows from the fact that an agent does something intentionally that he wants to do whatever it is that he thinks the action will achieve (Nagel 1970: 29). But, as G. F. Schueler has pointed out (1995: 29–38), it does not follow that what moves the agent is a *proper* desire, as opposed to a belief. In this second sense of 'desire' it is perfectly possible to say that someone acts, even though he has no desire at all to do so. Someone may, for example, listen to the news even though she would much rather listen to music; and yet she does listen to the news because, say, she regards it as her citizen duty to keep herself informed about politics and world issues. To establish his core doctrine, the Humean must supplement BD with an extra argument, which restricts the class of pro-attitudes to proper desires and makes a clear-cut distinction between desires and beliefs.

Traditionally this distinction is made in terms of the notion of direction of fit. As opposed to 'cognitive' beliefs, which are held to aim at truth – that is, at fitting with the world – it is claimed of 'conative' desires that they aim at bringing about goals – that is, conversely, at changing the world in such a way that it fits the desire. In whichever way the content of these unsatisfactorily metaphorical formulations is spelled out, it is a disputed question whether there are, or can be, states that have *both* directions of fit. This anti-HTM (yet not necessarily anti-BD) claim is held not only by ethicists who analyze moral judgments as inherently motivational states (McDowell 1978). It is also found in contemporary emotion theory (see Goldie 2000; Helm 2001; Döring 2003; Roberts 2003). The emotion theorist does not say, however, that an emotion combines cognitive belief and conative desire into one unitary 'besire.' Instead, she distinguishes both the representational characteristics of emotion from belief and the motivational characteristics of emotion from desire.

It is common ground to contemporary theorizing that emotions represent the world, but that they do so in a different way than beliefs. Consider even a simple emotion like fear. In experiencing fear, say, at a snake that you suddenly encounter on a woodland path, it seems to you that the snake is in fact dangerous: your occurrent emotional state puts forward your fear's content as correct. One main contrast with belief consists in the fact that an emotion may persist despite the subject's better judgment and knowledge: you need not be able to rid yourself of your fear even when a closer look has convinced you that the putative snake is in fact a harmless blindworm. As this is similar to perceptual illusions like the famous Müller-Lyer illusion, many have drawn an analogy between emotion and perception rather than between emotion and belief (see de Sousa 1987; Roberts 1988; 2003; Tappolet 2000; Döring 2003; 2007; 2009a; Prinz 2004; Zagzebski 2004). Even those who claim that emotions are value judgments do not identify them with ordinary judgments, but conceptualize emotions as judgments of a special and irreducible kind (compare Nussbaum 2001 and Solomon 2004).

As regards the motivational characteristics of emotion, theorists are less unanimous. Some would even deny that it is constitutive of emotion to motivate action, although they might agree that emotions typically involve tendencies to act in certain ways (so already Alston 1967). The main dispute is about *how* the emotions motivate and explain actions. While some emotion theorists remain committed, if not to HTM, then at least to BD (for instance Goldie 2000), others abandon the notion of direction of fit, and even BD (see Helm 2001; Döring 2003).

By clear contrast with desires, emotions have motivational force independently of whether they provide goals for action. There are many cases in which emotions – or rather the evaluative representations they contain (for instance as dangerous) – do not provide goals for action. This is so not only when there is nothing the agent *can* do to make the world fit his emotion – as when he sentimentally longs for his former lover, who will not come back, or grieves for a beloved one's death, which he cannot undo. There are also cases in which the agent does not *want* to change the world because of his emotions. Sometimes emotions do not, so to speak, call for any change in the world but appreciate it as it is. Thus an agent may swell with pride at the look of her beautiful horse, or she may be full of joy about her unexpected success in an exam. In both cases the world appears perfect to the agent, not in need of any change at all – and yet her emotion is not deprived of its motivational force: the lucky horse-owner may be moved to pet her horse's neck, while the successful examinee may jump for joy or hug the next best person.

As this already indicates, emotions motivate different kinds of behavior, including not only intentional actions aiming at some end, but also expressions of emotions. Expressions of emotions, in their turn, can be non-intentional, as in the case, say, of facial expressions (Darwin 1998; Ekman 1972); or they can be intentional actions, as in the examples just mentioned (and compare Hursthouse 1991). The explanation of expressive action is a touchstone for BD, not just for HTM. For it is characteristic of this kind of action that it is intentional, and yet it is not performed by the agent as a means to some further end. Here we may consider even so sophisticated an emotional expression as, in a wave of hatred, scratching out the eyes in a photograph of the hated person – to borrow Rosalind Hursthouse's example in which a woman named Jane does exactly this to the photograph of another woman named Joan. If Jane did what she did because she actually wanted to harm Joan and believed that she can achieve this by scratching out the eyes in a photograph of Joan, Jane's action would not qualify as a genuine expression of an emotion.

To withstand the challenge to BD, Michael Smith (1998) has suggested attributing to Jane a desire to scratch out the eyes in Joan's photograph, combined with a belief that she can achieve this just by doing it: BD (in the form of HTM) is maintained by an explanation of expressive action that *identifies* means and end. But this explanation is distinctly unsatisfying; in particular, it fails to mention the expressed emotion. To remedy this defect, Smith adds the emotional factor to his BD explanation: Jane's hatred is introduced as the cause of her otherwise unintelligible desire, yet without this having any impact on the rational explanation of her action.

Does this suffice to make us understand Jane's action as an expression of her hatred? Hardly. As Peter Goldie (2000, ch. 5) has noted, it is by no means clear *why* the emotion of hatred might cause an agent to desire such a bizarre thing as scratching out the eyes in a photo of the person one hates. According to Goldie, what has to be added to the BD explanation of Jane's behavior in order to render it intelligible as an expression of her emotion is a further desire, namely Jane's desire to scratch out the real Joan's eyes. This desire is claimed to be Jane's true desire, and is ascribed to the 'animal blood' which has its residue in us, civilized adults. Goldie thus explains Jane's action as a sublimation of her brutish desire to scratch out Joan's eyes: because Jane respects the constraints of modern civilization and is well aware of the fact that scratching out someone's eyes does not quite fit these constraints, she 'symbolically satisfies' her desire by scratching out the eyes in a photograph of Joan.

Elsewhere (Döring 2003) I have discussed this extended version of BD at some length. Here let me just point out two objections against it, to make clear why expressive action presents a severe challenge to BD. First, expressive action need not involve symbolic satisfaction of brutish desires. To recall the example of the successful examinee: if this person jumps for joy after having learned that she unexpectedly passed the exam, it would hardly make sense to insist that she thereby sublimates some brutish desire of hers. Secondly, it may be doubted, even in Jane's example, that her true desire is to scratch out Joan's eyes and not just the eyes in a photo of Joan. In any case, Jane's action is not the symbolic satisfaction of a brutish desire. Scratching out someone's eyes is certainly no option in our culture; but, if it were, it would not be an expression of 'animal blood.' As far as I can tell, animals do not specifically scratch out each others' eyes. Furthermore, it is only women who are thought to express their hatred for another woman, typically a rival, by scratching out the eyes – men, by contrast, are associated with actions such as breaking every bone in their rival's body. Together, these facts constitute strong evidence that Jane's action is in any case culturally mediated by a certain construction of femininity.

It thus seems that all available attempts to put forward a BD account of expressive action fail. Expressive action cannot be explained in terms of goal-directedness. Quite to the contrary, expressive actions are often performed *because* the agent lacks a goal for action, and yet his emotions move him to do something. The emotions' motivational force is then canalized into certain culturally established forms of behavior. This must not be misunderstood as a 'hydraulic' BD explanation, stating that expressive actions are performed as means to the end of relieving the agent from emotional pressure. Not only would such an explanation miss the distinctive characteristic of expressive action. It would also fail to account for the determinate ways in which emotions are expressed: Why is it that scratching out the eyes in a photograph of someone qualifies as an expression of hatred, but not of love? Why do we, conversely, accept kissing the photo of a person as an expression of love, but not of hatred?

Answering such questions requires reference to the specific kind of evaluations which emotions contain. We must here distinguish between mere evaluations and the 'felt' or 'affective evaluations' which are characteristic of emotion (cf. Goldie 2000; Helm 2001; Döring 2003). Goldie (2000: 61) illustrates this difference through what happens when you suddenly realize that the door to the cage of a fierce gorilla in front of you has been left open. Until this moment, you may have thought of the gorilla as dangerous, yet normally without *feeling* fear. The gorilla's dangerousness did not affect you, so to speak, for you did not see the animal as presenting a danger *to you*. The very moment when this changes, your feelingless evaluation turns into a felt evaluation, thereby revealing your concern to escape unharmed. This concern manifests itself in the emotional evaluation and makes it an affective evaluation, as is indicated by the fact that you are now poised for action out of your emotion (with the only exception that you are paralyzed with fear). Somewhat surprisingly, Goldie seems to be saying here that the emotions' motivational force is due to their being concern-based felt evaluations, while elsewhere – as is exemplary in his account of expressive action – he ascribes this motivational force to emotional desires. Others hold that emotions motivate precisely because we feel in them the worth or import which the evaluated thing has for ourselves (cf. Helm 2001; Döring 2003).

Thus it seems that emotions gain their motivational force from the feeling or affect which accompanies them. But, as Goldie and also Bennett Helm have conclusively argued, affect cannot be separated from evaluation (contrast Roberts 2003). This explains why emotions are expressed in determinate ways: the expression must fit the emotional evaluation. When Jane feels hatred toward Joan, Jane's emotion represents Joan as an awful person (who has stolen her job or husband, say). An appropriate expression of her hatred must be of such a kind that it expresses *this* evaluative content. In that sense, expressive actions, traditionally dismissed as arational, may well be assessed for rationality, though not in terms of instrumental, means–end rationality, but on the criterion of the action's appropriateness as an expression of a particular emotional evaluation (we find the most sophisticated expressions of this kind in art).

The emotions' concern-based evaluative content also explains why sometimes they do provide goals for action. One and the same emotion may even explain both a rational action (in the sense introduced at the beginning of this chapter) and an expressive action: while your fear of the gorilla may rationally explain your running away as a means to the end of avoiding danger, it may at the same time expressively explain your clinging tightly to your bag. Certainly this cannot mean that the motivational force of emotion is due to its goal-directedness in some cases, but not in others. But doesn't this open up the possibility of adhering to BD? Could we not decouple the intentional action associated with emotion from mere emotional behavior, by restricting the former to goal-directed and, *in that sense*, rational behavior?

A more convincing strategy is to look for an alternative account of intentionality, which allows for different sub-varieties of intentional action (for example Brian O'Shaughnessy 1980 holds that what makes something an action is the fact that it is caused in a suitable way by one of the agent's 'tryings'). This strategy becomes all the more attractive when we consider that goal-directedness as such is neither necessary nor sufficient to make actions rational. Not only do expressive actions constitute a class of non-goal-directed and yet – in a different sense – rational actions. The merely functional goal-directed desires, which are central to HTM in its most elaborated form (see Smith 1994), also fail to qualify as reasons (in the above sense). So, to use Warren Quinn's example (1993: 236), I could find myself with an urge to turn on every radio, without seeing anything good about doing so. To feel this urge and to act out on it, I need not attach any value either to turning on radios or to the outcome of this move, be it music, news, or the avoidance of silence. I could simply be disposed to turn on any radio that I see to be off.

From examples such as this one, some have drawn the moral that the Humean view of desire is misconceived (Anscombe 1957; Scanlon 1998; Johnston 2001). This critique is echoed in contemporary emotion theory (Helm 2009). Its essence is that, in cases like those described by Quinn, the agent has no desire. Desires, it is claimed, include an evaluation of the desired goal as desirable or good. Desire is thus understood as an evaluative notion, so as to guarantee both that desires give their agent reasons for acting from his personal perspective and that desires render actions intelligible from an impersonal perspective.

Helm expands on this critique by shifting the focus from single actions to agency, where agency is the constitutive characteristic of an agent which guides his actions rationally, so that these actions may be understood as belonging to one personality who continues over time and is the subject of a life. Helm rejects HTM for the reason that it fails to account for agency. Insofar as a chess-playing computer displays a goal-directedness that is rationally mediated by its informational states, HTM may well describe the computer's behavior as intentional, and hence classify the computer as an agent. To anyone not in the grip of a theory, this sounds like a mistake, claims Helm (2009: 247). As he emphasizes, agents do not simply have goals that they mechanically pursue; they rather find certain goals worth pursuing and pursue them because of their worth. On Helm's view, this is precisely what makes Quinn's example so powerful against HTM: turning on every radio remains unwarranted, unless there is some special story making intelligible why the agent cares about doing so.

Does this suffice to establish that desires must be evaluative states, and specifically emotions, as Helm suggests? I don't think so, and that is not Quinn's point either (see also Velleman 1992). Quinn carefully distinguishes between the explanation of an action and its 'rationalization' – as he puts it, following Davidson. From his example, Quinn concludes neither that the person in question lacks a desire nor that desires under the functional interpretation may not have some significant role to play in the explanation of action. And is it not 'over-intellectualizing' to hold that humans – and, according to Helm, even higher animals like cats and dogs – desire only goals that they regard as good? What about the urges, cravings, or yens that sometimes overcome us – such as, say, the sudden urge to jump down when you look from a great height. This urge seems to be quite common in humans, and it certainly does not imply that the subject sees anything good about jumping or its probable outcome.

We thus arrive at Schueler's (1995) thesis that proper desires are, precisely, urges and cravings. This is not to deny that, in the default mode, agents do act because they value either the action itself or its expected outcome. Nor is this to dispute that such evaluation is indispensable to the rationalization of action. But the required evaluation is not due to Hum(e)an desire. Helm's shift of focus from action to agency does elucidate that, in agents, goal-directedness is typically, though not necessarily, backed up by suitable evaluation, where this evaluation, typically, does not come isolated but as part of a whole network of (ideally coherent) evaluations. This network comprises evaluative judgments and, essentially, the felt evaluations involved in emotions. Examples like Quinn's show that the apparent plausibility of rationalizing intentional action by its goal-directedness depends on the fact that the evaluation of the desired goal as good is *tacitly added* to the explanation. We tacitly assume that agents who turn on radios see something good about listening to them. Quinn's example is both powerful and disturbing because it deprives us of the possibility of making this essential tacit assumption.

Let me conclude by at least sketching the specific way in which emotions evaluate. Crucial is, again, the shift of focus from action to agency. I pointed out above that emotions differ from judgments in that, like perceptions, they need not be revised in the light of better judgment and knowledge. This characteristic becomes particularly important in view of the fact that emotions contain evaluative representations capable of being *correct*. On this basis many have argued that, when it comes to conflict with judgment, it need not be the emotion that gets things wrong; it may equally be the judgment. This is illustrated by the famous example of Huckleberry Finn who, after having helped his friend Jim to run away from slavery, decides to turn him in but, when he is given the opportunity, finds himself doing just the contrary: because he feels sympathy for Jim, Huck lies in order to protect his friend from the slave hunters. Assuming that Huck's emotion motivates the right action, some have even claimed that we have here a case of 'inverse akrasia' (see Arpaly 2000; Tappolet 2003; Jones 2003). Elsewhere (Döring 2009b) I have rejected this claim, although I agree with its proponents that it is Huck's emotion that fits his situation, either because it is more coherent than Huck's judgment is with Huck's evaluations as a whole or because it corresponds to the facts. In any case, his emotion's persistence may lead Huck to question his judgment and to reconsider the moral principles he had hitherto accepted, which may in turn lead him to formulate new, better, more comprehensive moral principles. Such a 'productive' role can be played by any emotion. Accordingly, we better dismiss the traditional view that rational agents must discard their emotions, which would be both hopeless and counterproductive. What agents ought to do instead, and they can do it, is to cultivate their emotions over time for the sake of the ongoing improvement of their practical reasons.

See also: DESIRE AND PLEASURE (15); REASONS AND CAUSES (17); MOTIVATING REASONS (19); HUMEANISM ABOUT MOTIVATION (20); PRACTICAL REASONING (31); MOTIVATIONAL INTERNALISM AND EXTERNALISM (37); VIRTUOUS ACTION (40); ARISTOTLE (54); DAVIDSON (73).

References

Alston, W. (1967). Emotion and feeling. In P. Edwards (ed.), *Encyclopedia of Philosophy*, Vol. 2. New York: Macmillan, 479–486.

Anscombe, E. (1957). *Intention*. Oxford: Blackwell.

Arpaly, N. (2000). On acting rationally against one's best judgment. *Ethics*, 110, 488–513.

Davidson, D. (1980). Actions, reasons and causes [1963]. In D. Davidson, *Essays on Actions and Events*. Oxford: Clarendon Press, 3–19.

Darwin, Ch. (1998). *The Expression of Emotions in Man and Animals* [1889], with an Introduction, Commentary and Afterword by P. Ekman. New York: Oxford University Press.

De Sousa, R. (1987). *The Rationality of Emotion*. Cambridge, MA: MIT Press.

Döring, S. (2003). Explaining action by emotion. *Philosophical Quarterly*, 211, 214–230.

Döring, S. (2007). Seeing what to do: Affective perception and rational motivation. *Dialectica*, 61, 363–394.

Döring, S. (2009a). Why be emotional? In P. Goldie (ed.), *Oxford Handbook of the Philosophy of Emotion*. Oxford: Oxford University Press, Ch. 12.

Döring, S. (2009b). The logic of emotional experience: Noninferentiality and the problem of conflict without contradiction. In Reisenzein and Döring (eds), 237–243.

Ekman, P. (1972). Universals and cultural differences in facial expression. In J. Cole (ed.), *Nebraska Symposium on Motivation*. Lincoln, NE: University of Nebraska Press, 207–283.

Goldie, P. (2000). *The Emotions. A Philosophical Exploration*. Oxford: Oxford University Press.

Helm, B. (2001). *Emotional Reason. Deliberation, Motivation, and the Nature of Value*. Cambridge: Cambridge University Press.

Helm, B. (2009). Emotions as evaluative feelings. In Reisenzein and Döring (eds), 245–252.

Hume, D. (1978). *A Treatise of Human Nature* [1739/40], edited by L. A. Selby-Bigge and P. H. Nidditch. Oxford: Clarendon Press.

Hursthouse, R. (1991). Arational actions. *Journal of Philosophy*, 88, 57–68.

James, W. (1884). What is an emotion? *Mind*, 9, 188–205.

Johnston, M. (2001). The authority of affect. *Philosophy and Phenomenological Research*, 63, 181–214.

Jones, K. (2003). Emotion, weakness of will, and the normative conception of agency. In A. Hatzimoysis (ed.), *Philosophy and the Emotions*. Cambridge: Cambridge University Press, 181–200.

McDowell, J. (1978). Are moral requirements hypothetical imperatives? *Aristotelian Society Supplementary Volume*, 52, 13–29.

Nagel, T. (1970). *The Possibility of Altruism*. Oxford: Clarendon Press.

Nussbaum, M. (2001). *Upheavals of Thought. The Intelligence of Emotions*. Cambridge: Cambridge University Press.

O'Shaughnessy, B. (1980). *The Will: A Dual Aspect Theory*, Cambridge: University Press.

Prinz, J. (2004). *Gut Reactions: A Perceptual Theory of Emotion*. New York: Oxford University Press.

Quinn, W. (1993). Putting rationality in its place. In W. Quinn, *Morality and Action*. Cambridge: Cambridge University Press, 228–255.

Reisenzein, R., and Döring, S. A. (eds) (2009). *Perspectives on Emotional Experience (= Emotion Review. Journal of the International Society for Research on Emotion*, 1 (3), special issue). Newbury Park, CA: Sage.

Roberts, R. C. (1988). What an emotion is: A sketch. *Philosophical Review*, 97, 183–209.

Roberts, R. C. (2003). *Emotions: An Essay in Aid of Moral Psychology*. Cambridge: Cambridge University Press.

Scanlon, T. M. (1998). *What We Owe to Each Other*. Cambridge, MA: Harvard University Press.

Schueler, G. F. (1995), *Desire. Its Role in Practical Reason and the Explanation of Action*. Cambridge, MA: MIT Press.

Smith, M. (1994). *The Moral Problem*. Oxford: Blackwell.

Smith, M. (1998), The possibility of action. In J. Bransen (ed.), *Human Action, Deliberation and Causation*. Dordrecht: Kluwer, 17–41.

Solomon, R. (2004). Emotions, thoughts and feelings. In R. Solomon (ed.), *Thinking about Feeling*. Oxford: Oxford University Press, 76–78.

Tappolet, C. (2000). *Emotions et valeurs*. Paris: Presses Universitaires de France.

Tappolet, C. (2003). Emotions and the intelligibility of akratic action. In S. Stroud and C. Tappolet (eds), *Weakness of Will and Practical Irrationality*. Oxford: Clarendon Press, 97–120.

Velleman, D. (1992). The guise of the good. *Nous*, 26, 3–26.

Zagzebski, L. (2004). *Divine Motivation Theory*. Cambridge: Cambridge University Press.

Further reading

Arpaly, N. (2003). *Unprincipled Virtue. An Inquiry into Moral Agency*. Oxford: Blackwell.

De Sousa, R. (2003). Paradoxical emotions: On *sui generis* emotional irrationality. In C. Tappolet and S. Stroud (eds), *Weakness of Will and Practical Irrationality*. Oxford: Oxford University Press, 274–297.

Deonna, J., Clavien, C., and Wallimann, I. (eds) (2007). *Affective Intentionality and Practical Rationality (= Dialectica*, 61 (3), special issue).

Elster, J. (1999). *Alchemies of the Mind: Rationality and the Emotions*. Cambridge: Cambridge University Press.

Fehr, E., and Gächter, S. (2002). Altruistic punishment in humans. *Nature*, 415, 137–140.

Frank, R. H. (1988). *Passions within Reason: The Strategic Role of the Emotions*. New York/London: W. W. Norton and Company.

Frijda, N. (1986). *The Emotions*. Cambridge: Cambridge University Press.

Gigerenzer, G. (2000). *Adaptive Thinking: Rationality in the Real World*. New York: Oxford University Press.

Gigerenzer, G., and Selten, R. (eds) (2002). *Bounded Rationality: The Adaptive Toolbox*. Cambridge, MA/London: MIT Press.

Goldie, P. (ed.) (2009). *The Oxford Handbook of the Philosophy of Emotion*. Oxford: Oxford University Press.

Greenspan, P. (1988). *Emotions and Reasons: An Inquiry into Emotional Justification*. New York: Routledge.

Kenny, A. (1963). *Action, Emotion and Will*. London: Routledge and Kegan Paul.

Lambie, J. A. (2009). Emotion experience, rational action, and self-knowledge. In Reisenzein and Döring (eds), 270–278.

LeDoux, J. (1998). *The Emotional Brain: The Mysterious Underpinnings of Emotional Life*. New York: Simon and Schuster.

McIntyre, A. (1990). Is akratic action always irrational? In O. Flanagan and A. Rorty (eds), *Identity, Character, and Morality. Essays in Moral Psychology*. Cambridge, MA: MIT Press, 379–400.

Oakley, J. (1992). *Morality and the Emotions*. London: Routledge.

Reisenzein, R. (2009). Emotional experience in the computational belief-desire theory of emotion. In Reisenzein and Döring (eds), 212–220.

Reisenzein, R., and Döring, S. A. (2009). Ten perspectives on emotional experience. In Reisenzein and Döring (eds), 195–203.

Reisenzein, R., and Döring, S. A. (eds) (2009). *Perspectives on Emotional Experience (= Emotion Review. Journal of the International Society for Research on Emotion*, 1 (3), special issue). Newbury Park, CA: Sage.

Roeser, S. (2009). *Moral Emotions about Risky Technologies*. Heidelberg: Springer.

Sartre, J.-P. (1939). *Esquisse d'une théorie des émotions*. Paris: Hermann.

Scherer, K., Schorr, A., and Johnstone, T. (eds) (2001). *Appraisal Processes in Emotion: Theory, Methods, Research*. Oxford: Oxford University Press.

Slovic, P. (2004). Risk as analysis and risk as feelings: Some thoughts about affect, reason, risk, and rationality. *Risk Analysis*, 24 (2), 1–12.

Solomon, R. (1973). Emotion and choice. *Review of Metaphysics*, 17, 20–41.

Solomon, R. (1993). *The Passions: Emotions and the Meaning of Life*. Indianapolis: Hackett.

Stocker, M., with Hegeman, E. (1996). *Valuing Emotions*. Cambridge: Cambridge University Press.

Taylor, G. (1985). *Pride, Shame and Guilt: Emotions of Self-Assessment*. Oxford: Clarendon Press.

Thalberg, I. (1980). *Perception, Emotion and Action*. Oxford: Blackwell.

26

Agency, Patiency, and Personhood

SORAN READER

Introduction

When we ask 'What is a person?,' abject features of human life like suffering, vulnerability, constraint, dependency, though metaphysically and ethically important, are frequently neglected. Like Charles Taylor, who wrote a whole book 'tracing [...] our modern notion of what it is to be a human agent, a person, or a self' (1989: 3), we are culturally biassed towards thinking of persons as agents. We thus presume that people are, people count, only when they are agents, so that if persons are passive, incapable, constrained or dependent, society's duty is to help them back to agency and personhood.

Contemporary philosophers for whom social justice is central are tempted to bracket out 'metaphysical' inquiry from their agential conception. For John Rawls, for example, the conception of a person as citizen, while it may 'presuppose [...] metaphysical theses about the nature of persons,' does not 'distinguish between the distinctive metaphysical views – Cartesian, Leibnizian, Kantian; realist, idealist or materialist' (Rawls 1985: 240). However, these 'distinctive metaphysical views' all share the mistaken metaphysical presumption that persons are agents, which metaphysical analysis is needed to unsettle.

We already possess all the philosophical resources we need for such an analysis. For Aristotle (significantly not on Rawls' list), the human being is by nature 'an animal [...] capable of acquiring reason and knowledge' (*Topics* 112^{a}20), and also 'a political animal' (*Politics* 1253^{a}3). For him, all 'agents' have beings they act on as their correlates; and all beings acted on are 'patients,' not only those in the negative situation of being operated on in hospital, for the removal of some undesired occurrent state of need. I use the word 'patiency' (or 'passivity') in this chapter to refer to the silenced and 'othered' aspects of personhood, which are passive, but nonetheless as inalienable and central to personhood as 'agency' is commonly assumed to be. I shall consider four issues related to this 'other side' of agency: action and passivity; capability and need; freedom and constraint; independence and dependency.

Action and Passivity

Central to the agential conception of persons is the idea that persons *act* not merely in the broad sense in which animals and machines act, but in some special way best characterized as 'intentional action' (Velleman 2000), or *self*-movement (Dretske 1988: 1; Karlsson 2002). The philosopher of action Richard Taylor became disillusioned with the widely held assumption that 'persons are unique, in that they sometimes act' while 'other things are merely passive.' He rejected three possible accounts of the assumption. The assumption that action differs metaphysically from causation – what a person *does* differs from what a clock *does* – he rejected on the grounds that animals act, and that we perfectly comprehend talk about the 'actions' of inanimate artefacts. The assumption that actions are a special *kind* of causation, found only in agents – *self*-caused rather than caused by other things – he rejected on the grounds that a 'metaphysical self' acting in this mysterious way is an *ad hoc* postulate lacking explanatory basis and internal sense. The idea that actions are caused 'in the normal way' but by special objects – a pro-attitude towards the action and a belief that the latter is of the right kind (Davidson 1973) he rejected because it merely reprises the dilemma: either my willing is a special cause acting on my belief/pro-attitude pair, so that we have the *ad hoc* postulate again; or the pair itself causes my action, and then the action is not distinct from causation after all. Human action, Taylor concludes, is not distinctive of persons through any intrinsic metaphysical features, but is distinguished through the ordinary practices by which we decide what is or is not an action or an agent when we encounter one (Taylor 1982: 223–232).

What concerns us here, however, is the 'other side' of action: the passivity which action presupposes, the sufferings which doings involve. When agents act, necessarily they, as agents, suffer: in hitting you I suffer your resistance, in lifting a cup I suffer its weight. I do not suffer my action under its unifying description: I do not *hit* or *lift* myself, but, unless I suffer that resistance or weight, I have not hit or lifted anything. Again, when an action is done, necessarily some patient suffers it: when I hit you, you suffer, and, unless you suffer a hit, I have not hit you. Every action as such has, at the receiving end, a *patient* acted upon when the agent acts.

These twin features of patiency – the fact that we suffer both as agents and as patients – are inalienable, pervasive, and important in human social life. But this suggests that persons must be patients inasmuch as they are agents. It suggests that patiency, far from being a privation of personhood, must metaphysically and conceptually define us as much as agency does. C. B. Martin argues for an even stronger view, dispensing altogether with 'unhelpful distinctions such as power to give vs. power to receive, agent vs. patient, active vs. passive, causal conditions vs. standing conditions' (Martin 1997). But, although agency cannot be metaphysically 'prior to' patiency, I think the distinction helps to illuminate issues of harm, benefit, and responsibility.

How, then, can we avoid agential bias in our definition of persons? Aristotle distinguishes man from other animals as the animal 'able to *receive* knowledge' (*Topics* 112^{b}20). 'Knowledge' is a very broad concept, covering experience of action and of suffering; and to *receive* knowledge is of course to be passive to it, acted upon by it. The agent/patient distinction, therefore, is not the same as the subject/object distinction.

To be a patient is not to cease from being a human subject – a knower, a thinker, a moral being. A patient is not reduced to the status of an object: I am a patient all the time, and that is not, as such, a reduced or unpleasant condition. I am a patient not just when I am treated in hospital, but when I use the world's resistances to speak, and when I take my turn to be quiet and listen; not just when I 'lie back and think of England' but also when I experience my own lovemaking; not just when I am caught in a downpour, but also when I dive into a lake, or surf to shore on a wave. I am fully alive, fully human while I am a patient, and I may indeed be more myself: Hannah Arendt has expressed the evocative idea of conscience as the subjective presence of self to self, away from the distractions of action (Arendt 1971: 185–193).

We might note that personhood as passive is accepted in epistemology, where our concept of 'world' is of something given to, or inflicted upon, us – something to be noticed, recognized, acknowledged, accepted. Since Kant (1929, A51/B75), and arguably long before him (see Aristotle, *De anima* 430^{a}10–432^{a}14), the necessity of an agential contribution to experience and knowledge has been recognized. Boiling water unknowingly manifests the fact that it is hot; but, to be knowers, we must make sense of this given: we must use 'understanding' – which for Kant is the active complement of our 'sensibility.' 'Intuitions [experience of hot water] without concepts are blind,' as Kant said – and more recently McDowell (1996); but, equally, 'concepts [the idea of heat] without intuitions are empty.' Perhaps passion without action is also blind, and action without passion empty? Perhaps there is no action without suffering, and no personhood without patiency? The epistemological illustration itself may help to explain why this inalienability of passivity has been so overlooked. That, as knowers, persons might truly be passive, subject to that given Other, the world, may so have horrified a thinker like Kant, that he protested a role for spontaneity to avoid acknowledging subjectedness. No surprise, then, that in other areas of philosophical analysis of personhood the correlation of activity with passivity should be left out altogether.

There is an aspect of the non-agential human being which has particular moral and political importance, and to which philosophers have generally been sensitive. Human action that aims to harm is violence, and persons suffering such harm are victims. If philosophical efforts in ethics and politics are agentially focussed on the violence *done* by the perpetrator, or on what bystanders should *do* to punish or prevent it, the victim will typically be objectified, and our concern will be what can be *done* to restore that being to full personhood or *agency* (Reader 2006a: 205–210). This implicit denial of full personhood to victims compounds the harm they suffer: our communities shun them, pressing them to hide what they suffer and to 'recover' their humanity by 'getting past' their victimhood, to become 'survivor' agents.

Such denial of victimhood impacts asymmetrically on the two sexes. Women are more often and more completely victims, their vulnerability to violence from stronger males, coercion and economic dependency structuring what it is for them to be persons (MacKinnon 2006). Women themselves are socialized so as to be more accepting of male violence than men are of female violence, more disposed to respond to it with care and compassion than with judgment and counter-attack. They are thus more likely to see themselves as victims. Some feminists – Naomi Wolf, for example – attack 'victim-feminism' and advocate instead a 'power-feminism,' thus endorsing an agential conception of victimhood as a falling short of full humanity (Wolf 1994). When Carole Vance writes, 'If women [...] allow themselves to be viewed [as victims] [...] by others, they become enfeebled and miserable' (Vance 1992: 7), she expresses a common view, which almost blames victims for their victimhood. A balanced conception of the person would see the personal perspective of victims recognizing and living with themselves as victims as a necessary condition for living human life sanely, for understanding human persons fully, and for achieving more just social arrangements. Susan Brison's remarkable book *Aftermath* tackles this issue (Brison 2002).

We can learn something important about persons from well-known but philosophically disrespected female responses to violence. 'Fight or flight' does not exhaust the possible responses. In actual living, women more often endure the violence, protecting themselves and the everyday life of those near them as best they can, and trying to stop the perpetrator in non-violent ways. They endure not because they are masochists or fail to achieve full rational personhood, but because a powerful enough perpetrator often cannot be escaped from or beaten in a fight. Though endurance is not action, is not chosen or independent, and shows incapability, it may be the only way to be a person in adversity. It is passive, but also difficult and courageous, fully present and alive.

Through enduring we see, learn, and witness deep truths about violence and its perpetrators. In *Life and Words*, Veena Das records some profound metaphors which women-victims of violence used for endurance: 'drinking all pain' and 'digesting the poison' (Das 2007: 54–8 and 101). 'Drinking pain' suggests taking in the factual knowledge of violence revealed through the victim's unique epistemic perspective, respecting its demand to be uttered, articulated, and presented as truth's challenge to (male) power and violence. But 'digesting poison' suggests metabolizing, neutralizing, containing or living with the violence, so that human life can continue. Many victims believe that, far from demanding to be spoken, the knowledge that informs endurance demands silence, so that ordinary life can continue, or begin again, amid the rubble which violence has created.

Capability/Incapability and Need

Equally central to the agential conception of a person is a focus on capability: the *ability*, power, or potential of the self to act. For Locke, a person is a being who '*can* consider itself as itself' (Locke 1846: 217); for Rawls, it is 'someone who *can* take part in social life,' possessing 'two moral *powers*': 'a *capacity* for a sense of justice and a *capacity* for a conception of the good' (Rawls 1985: 233); for Amartya Sen and Martha Nussbaum, persons in political society are characterized by 'capabilities' rather than by actual 'functionings.' Nussbaum, drawing on Aristotle (*De Anima* 417^{b}30), conceives humans as having 'B [for basic] capabilities' to become some specific thing in virtue of the natural kind of being they are: capabilities which ground claims to political distribution that will facilitate the 'I [internal]' and 'E [external]' capabilities needed to become that thing – for example the acquisition of skills and the removal of constraints (Nussbaum 1988: 145–184 and 160–168). Sen, as an economist steering a middle course between the paternalistic objective good approaches and subjective wellbeing or preference-based accounts of political claims, emphasizes capability not just as potential but as freedom – potential which can be actualized or left un-actualized through agent choice.

But capabilities and powers also have a silent 'other side': the liability to suffer. Being truly able to do one thing (write a philosophy paper) implies being unable to do another (clean my house); and being able to write a philosophy paper implies having been unable to do so, and being vulnerable to losing the ability. Even Rawls' 'moral power' to act from 'a conception of the good' implies the vulnerability to act badly from a skewed conception of the good. As Eva Kittay points out, her profoundly disabled daughter was a good person, while extremely capable Nazi doctors did vast harm (Kittay 2005: 123).

Need, too, is a silenced 'other side' of capability (Reader 2006b). Amartya Sen writes:

> The perspective of positive freedom links naturally with capabilities (what can the person *do?*) rather than with the fulfillment of their needs (what can be *done for* the person?). The perspective of fulfilling needs has some obvious advantages in dealing with dependents (e.g. children), but for responsible adults the format of capabilities may be much more suitable. (Sen 1984: 514)

But having needs is not, in itself, a passive state. Persons have needs in order to act, in order to be capable, in order to make rational free choices, and in order to have such independencies as they can. A need is made passive, first, when it is *occurrent* – what is needed is currently lacked. My dispositional need for air makes me vulnerable only when I am, first, deprived of air and, second, made passive to that privation. For the need must also be one that *I cannot meet for myself*. If I am deprived of air but can break a window through to an air supply, I am as active as I will ever be. Every person, *qua* patient and *qua* agent, has needs; but only some are occurrent and unmeetable by the needy person. It is the agential conception of persons that leads Sen and Nussbaum to conceal our vulnerability to helplessness and dependence behind brave talk of capability.

Choice, Rationality, Freedom/Constraint

On the agential conception, a person is not just a being who *does* and *can*, but a being who *chooses* what to do, chooses which abilities to develop and exercise and when. And choice is not the random selection of options, but implies deliberating over them and selecting one to act on for *reasons*. Whoever is able to do this is, as Kant put it, *free*: free under moral laws, 'subject to no other laws than those which he (either alone or jointly with others) gives to himself' (Kant 1889: 24).

Margaret Walker discusses three dramatic ways in which this identification of personhood with free rational choosing has been elaborated (Walker 1998: 131–152). According to Rawls, a person is a being with a 'rational plan of life' (Rawls 1971: 407–416); but Walker points out that ordinary people in most circumstances cannot and do not live according to life plans. According to Bernard Williams, a person is a being stably disposed to practical deliberation by character, structured by 'constitutive projects' which answer 'the question of why we go on at all' (Williams 1981: 10); but

Walker empirically questions the 'claim that having character at all requires having literally life-driving, make-or-break commitments.' According to Charles Taylor, 'selfhood itself' is equated 'with having and sustaining a whole-life narrative' (Taylor 1989) – a view which Walker criticizes as 'presenting this richly specific ideal [of autonomous man-and-career self] as a [...] necessary idea of what persons, selves, or human agents "are." ' But here a stronger criticism is surely warranted: the 'richly specific' ideal of an independent career-self is mistaken, even pernicious.

Freedom's 'other side' is constraint: freedom to talk is constrained by the grammar of language; my choice of my child's school, by the schools on offer, my understanding of her, my ability to pay, and my past history. Rationality, too, if understood on the intellectualist paradigm of deliberation, has an 'other side.' To deliberate is to leave out things that might matter, to fail to apprehend completely, and to be subject to contingencies outside the deliberative scope. Deliberative rationality is a non-apt ideal for defining ordinary people as such (Das 2007).

Choice's 'other side' is necessity. In most of life we do not choose – when we need to eat, when our sick parents need us. When we become pregnant and have no access to abortion, we do not 'choose' the path our life then takes. Talking of choice in respect of some aspects of life makes little sense. I do not choose to be a woman or a member of a certain race; I do not even choose to be an agent, to be capable, to be a rational chooser, or to be independent. Nevertheless, what I go through and how I respond to these aspects is no less personal, expressive, or determinative of me, than what I do out of free rational choice. Margaret Walker's thoughtful study of such aspects of life reveals that there is plenty of moral and political importance to the way people act when they are deprived of choice and guided less by rationality than by thoroughly contingent relationships and practices of concern and response. But Walker herself does not entirely escape the agential conception. She may still be committed to the idea that 'free agency' is part of the essence of selfhood or personhood (Walker 1998: 196).

Independence and Dependency

The agential conception implicitly commits us further to the idea that persons are *independent*. In acting, nothing but their own decision causes their action, and their choosing is not constrained by others, not in need of others, nor inhibited or distracted by others. This idea of independence is so demanding that Spinoza concluded there could only be one independent being: the world (passively – *natura naturata*) or God (actively – *natura naturans*). Independence itself, which is at the core of the agential conception, if it is to make sense, must always be partial, woven from multiple dependencies which are total, or abject, in the sense that the agent is as truly helpless in relation to them, like any newborn baby. We depend, in the here and now alone, on health, space, surfaces on which to act, light, air, food, and drink. Beyond the here, we depend on the earth turning and on the sun shining, and on an absence of asteroids, violence, eruptions, or tsunamis. Beyond the now, we depend on a history of maternal gestation and care, family and social support, education, economic and political resources. It is astounding that the idea of the 'independent agent' ever got off the ground, let alone came to identify what persons are.

The significance of dependency for personhood has been explored by Eva Kittay. She points out that every capable person is 'some mother's child' (Kittay 1999: 25), depending on the care work of another for becoming what he is. So, into any defensible social contract, the double requirement must be built that (1) dependants must be cared for and that (2) 'secondary dependants' – those who must care for dependants – should be enabled to do their work of care. This double requirement Kittay calls 'the principle of *doulia*,' using the ancient Greek word for slavery (Kittay 1999: 107).

Martha Nussbaum thinks that Kittay makes dependency too central, obscuring the social needs for 'liberty and opportunity, the chance to form a plan of life, the chance to learn and imagine on one's own' (Nussbaum 2000: 64). For Nussbaum, dependency is a privation of citizenship, of personhood under its political aspect. But Kittay reminds us that less capable persons are less capable of doing inhuman harm (Kittay 2005: 123). To regard capability as per se desirable, Nussbaum insists, 'a full human life' must 'involve a kind of freedom and individuality' Nussbaum 2000: 65). I, on the other hand, think that Kittay's arguments do not go deep enough. Persons are necessarily dependent. The 'independent' person is inalienably dependent, even in their independence.

Nussbaum does criticize the damaging effects of a Kantian split between rational personhood and animality, urging us to prefer the Aristotelian conception, which makes animality fundamental, rationality and sociability specifying only the kind of animal we are (Nussbaum 2000: 53–4 and 62–63). But Nussbaum thinks of us as rational and social animals who are sometimes dependent and sometimes depended on, not as inalienably patient, incapable, needy, dependent in their very personhood.

We conclude then that there is as much of the self, or of the person, in the passive aspects of personal being as in the active ones. Full persons – all of us – are passive, needy, constrained, and dependent as well as active, capable, free, and independent. The complex philosophical task that now faces us is that of exploring what persons suffer as well as what they do; what they cannot do as much as what they can; the respects in which they are constrained, subject to necessities, respondent to contingencies, dependent on others. To progress with this, we need to attend to facts that do not demand our attention: the truths of the passive, weak, needy, helpless, confused, entangled and overwhelmed. We need to overcome our philosophical fear of passivity and give ethical recognition to each other as abject victims.[1]

See also: AGENT CAUSATION (28); BODILY AWARENESS AND BODILY ACTION (29); AGENTS' KNOWLEDGE (30); DELIBERATION AND DECISION (32); RATIONALITY (36); FREE WILL AND DETERMINISM (38); RESPONSIBILITY AND AUTONOMY (39); INDIAN PHILOSOPHERS (52); ARISTOTLE (54); DESCARTES (59); KANT (64); HEGEL (66); DAVIDSON (73); RICŒUR (75).

Note

1 This chapter is a slimmed-down version of 'The other side of agency' (*Philosophy*, 82 (4), 2007 (October), 579–604). Thanks to Catriona Mackenzie, Susan Brison, John O'Neill, Christopher Rowe, Eva Kittay, Marilyn Friedman, Bill Pollard, Margaret Walker, Lorraine

Code and Jonathan Lowe for help with that work. Especial thanks to Timothy McDermott for the same editorial help he has given to Thomas Aquinas: halving my chapter whilst retaining and even improving all I needed to say.

References

Arendt, H. (1971). *The Life of the Mind.* New York: Harcourt Brace.

Aristotle (1908). *Works of Aristotle*, edited by W. D. Ross. Oxford: Clarendon Press.

Brison, S. (2002). *Aftermath.* Princeton: Princeton University Press.

Das, V. (2007). *Life and Words; Violence and the Descent into the Ordinary.* Berkeley: University of California Press.

Davidson, D. (1973). Actions, reasons and causes. *Journal of Philosophy*, 60, 685–700.

Dretske, F. (1988). *Explaining Behavior: Reasons in a World of Causes.* Cambridge, MA: MIT Press.

Kant, I. (1889). *Critique of Practical Reason and Other Works on the Theory of Ethics* [1788]. translated by T. Kingsmill-Abbott. London: Longman.

Kant, I. (1929). *Critique of Pure Reason* [1781/1787], translated by N. K. Smith. London: Macmillan.

Karlsson, M. (2002). Agency and patiency: Back to nature? *Philosophical Explorations*, 5, 59–81.

Kittay, E. (1999). *Love's Labor.* New York: Routledge.

Kittay, E (2005). At the margins of moral personhood. *Ethics*, 116, 100–131.

Locke, J. (1846). *Essay concerning Human Understanding.* London: Thomas Tegg.

MacKinnon, C. (2006). *Are Women Human?* Cambridge, MA: Harvard University Press.

Martin, C. B. (1997). On the Need for Properties. *Synthese*, 112, 204.

McDowell, J. (1996). *Mind and World.* Cambridge, MA: Harvard University Press.

Nussbaum, M. (1988). Nature, function and capability: Aristotle on political distribution. *Oxford Studies in Ancient Philosophy* (Supplementary Volume), 145–184.

Nussbaum, M. (2000). The future of feminist liberalism. *Proceedings and Addresses of the American Philosophical Association*, 74, 47–79.

Rawls, J. (1971). *A Theory of Justice.* Cambridge, MA: Harvard University Press.

Rawls, J. (1985). Justice as fairness: Political not metaphysical. *Philosophy and Public Affairs*, 14, 223–251.

Reader, S. (2006a). After 9/11: Making pacifism plausible. In B. Bleisch and J.-D. Strub (eds), *Pazifismus.* Bern: Haupt.

Reader, S. (2006b). Does a basic needs approach need capabilities? *Journal of Political Philosophy*, 14, 337–350.

Sen, A. (1984). *Resources, Values and Development.* Oxford: Blackwell.

Taylor, C. (1989). *Sources of the Self.* Cambridge, MA: Harvard University Press.

Taylor, R. (1982). Agent and patient: Is there a distinction? *Erkenntnis*, 18, 223–232.

Vance, C. (1992). Pleasure and danger: Towards a politics of sexuality. In *Pleasure and Danger.* London: Pandora.

Velleman, D. (2000). What happens when someone acts? In D. Vellman, *The Possibility of Practical Reason.* Oxford: Clarendon Press, 123–143.

Walker, M. U. (1998). *Moral Understandings.* New York: Routledge.

Williams, B. (1981). Persons, character and morality. In B. Williams, *Moral Luck.* Cambridge: Cambridge University Press.

Wolf, N. (1994), *Fire with Fire.* New York: Fawcett.

Further reading

McDowell, J. (1979). Virtue and reason. *Monist*, 62, 331–350.
Reader, S. (ed.) (2005). *The Philosophy of Need*. Cambridge: Cambridge University Press.
Reader, S. (ed.) (2007). *Needs and Moral Necessity*. London: Routledge.
Reader, S. (2008). The Other Side of Agency. *Philosophy*, 82, 579–604.
Scanlon, T. (1998). *What We Owe to Each Other*. Cambridge, MA: Harvard University Press.
Warren, M.-A. (2000). *Moral Status*. Oxford: Oxford University Press.

27

Mental Acts

JOËLLE PROUST

There are two different ways of applying the phrase 'mental act,' which can be distinguished as the *actualization* sense and the *agentive* sense. In the sense of being an actualization, *act* is contrasted with *potentiality*. In Aristotle's use of the term, potentiality refers to 'a principle of change, movement, or rest,' in oneself or in other entities (*Metaphysics*, Θ, 1049^{b}7). An act, in contrast, refers to the actual expression of this potentiality. For example a seeing is an act, while the disposition to see is the potentiality associated with it (*Metaphysics*, Θ, 1049^{b}21). Mental acts, in this sense, are synonymous with 'mental events,' in other words with 'what happens in a person's mind' (Geach 1957: 1). In the agentive sense, in contrast, a mental act is the process of intentionally activating a mental disposition in order to acquire a desired mental property. Discussion of the scope of mental acts is complicated by the fact that the distinction between active and passive events is even less clear in the case of the mind than it is in the case of the body. A mental event of a given type (such as imaginings or rememberings) may qualify as a mental action on one occasion and not on another. A thinker can think about John, memorize a telephone number, mentally solve a math problem; but to what extent are these mental 'doings' under her control? Are these merely mental operations that are passively (that is, associatively) triggered in the agent by the context? If not, in what does the agentive involvement of the mind consist?

Mental Agency as Sensitivity to Reasons

A common answer is that agency consists in the capacity to respond rationally to practical reasons and to allow one's behavior to be guided and justified by them. Practical reasons are typically construed as inferences based on various beliefs and desires, which the agent normally offers when asked about her reasons for acting. An agent desires to visualize Mary's dress at the gala dinner, believes that she has the ability to do so, and, as a result, forms the intention to conjure up Mary's image at the gala dinner. The agentive aspect of mental actions, as of bodily ones, thus depends on the association between motivation and knowledge on the one hand, and changing conditions on the other: a behavior, or a mental process, is agentive when it is sensitive to reasons, that is, able to adjust flexibly its means and goals to varying constraints or opportunities.

Having instrumental reasons to perform a mental action, however, should not lead one to ignore a disanalogy with bodily action. In bodily actions, the overarching norms that govern the inferences involved are the *utility* of a given outcome and the comparative *effectiveness* of the alternative means–ends relations available. The fact that an agent acts on the basis of false beliefs, or on the basis of a false inference, does not constitutively impair the ability of this agent to act. Mental actions, on the other hand, also respond to constitutive norms: epistemic norms apply to the objective relations between informational states (and their propositional contents) and determine the success conditions for these actions. Directed rememberings, plannings or reasonings, for example, would not exist if there was no systematic, objective connection between various informational or cognitive facts. A usual satisfaction condition for an act of remembering is the truth or correctness of the memory retrieved, assuming that the information originally committed to the memory was correct; and the satisfaction condition for an act of planning or for an attempt to reason is its coherence and relevance, assuming that the problem or situation has been correctly represented – and so on.

Granting that epistemic norms are constitutive for mental actions, even moderate biases in recognizing epistemic norms result in systematic failures at the associated mental tasks.

This normative structure, however, seems to impose constraints on agents capable of mental action. An agent sensitive to epistemic reasons, that is, to evidential rationality, should be able to grasp that an epistemic norm differs from a mere instrumental norm of appraisal because it is *less concerned with effects than with how cognitive causes lead to these effects* (Sosa 2007). In other words, a mental agent must be able not only to evaluate the outcomes of her mental actions, but also to recognize consciously that her ability to grasp epistemic norms is crucially involved in these actions; mental agency, on this reading, involves an ability to take responsibility for one's mental performances (in contrast with the case of bodily agency, where an agent can deny responsibility for failing to execute what she wants to). For example, an agent who has evaluated her memory as non-reliable cannot be confident that the proper name she now seems to have recovered is correct. The claim that epistemic norm awareness is central to mental actions does not necessarily entail that bodily actions never involve an epistemic type of normative awareness. Rational decision needs to be sensitive to the truth of the beliefs on which one's decision is based. The point is that a mistaken belief, in this case, will not affect the agentive status of the subsequent action.

To summarize: the specific way in which rational evaluation operates in mental action seems to play a defining role in mental agency. Mental agency is a domain structured by constitutive epistemic norms, where agents form a decision to act which is based on their sensitivity to these norms, in addition to a sensitivity to instrumental reasons, which inspire the specific goals they pursue.

Two objections, however, can be made to this view. First, how could the conclusion of a practical syllogism move an agent to act and guide her action to the goal? As many causal theorists have claimed in the case of bodily action, the proximate cause of an action needs to be distinguished from the set of inferences preceding it (Brand 1984;

Mele 1992). On this alternative view, agency is essentially tied to the fact that the action is initiated and executed in a specific way, rather than being tied to its inferential, rational background. Consider the case of impulsive or emotional actions (Hursthouse 1991): an agent may voluntarily perform actions that go against her rational preferences. This is also true in the realm of mental agency: a subject can search her memory even when she knows that she should not trust it; or allow herself to imagine and plan for a (virtual) 'second life' while knowing that this activity violates her epistemic, moral, or instrumental norms. The sensitivity to reasons account seems to be ill-equipped to deal with these cases of common irrational or akratic mental actions, where agents act against their best judgment.

The second objection has to do with the fact that a practical inference approach to mental action requires agents to have a conceptual grasp of their goals and means and, in particular, of the fact that they entertain beliefs, desires, and intentions, or that certain cognitive causes lead to certain effects. This condition seems to be arbitrarily restrictive: agents may certainly select ways of acting that worked in the past, as in the circular reactions described by developmental psychologists, without having to represent them conceptually. Certainly a child can search her memory for a name before she finds herself able to make explicit her practical reasons for doing so, by relying on a conceptual knowledge of the mental. Moreover, recent work in comparative psychology suggests that non-human primates are also able to search their memory selectively. They can correctly predict whether they can remember, after a delay, the color or shape of an earlier stimulus in order to decide what to do (Hampton 2001). Granting, however, that no evidence for mind-reading abilities has been found in macaques, they must do so without representing the task through mental concepts such as belief, desire, memory, and so on.

In sum: granting that at least some mental actions are in the repertoire of non-humans and of human children, a practical inference (or sensitivity to reasons) approach does not seem to furnish a necessary condition for mental agency. Moreover, this approach does not account for executive force, and therefore does not provide a sufficient condition either.

Mental Agency as Voluntary Control

An alternative view to the practical inference approach, then, is to emphasize that mental agency, just like bodily agency, involves a trying or a willing (Locke 2006; O'Shaughnessy 2000; Ginet 1990; Proust 2001; Peacocke 2008a). In bodily and mental cases, trying may only involve a change in posture or in mental set; or it may aim to attain a distal goal. A mental trying may thus constitute the action (as when one tries to concentrate), or be, in addition, aiming at some distal effect (as in trying to remember a name). In this latter case, the outcome is *mediated, that is, brought about* by enabling cognitive operations on which the agent has no personal control.

The 'trying' or 'executive' view has several attractive features. First, it provides a unified causal account for mental and bodily agency (and bodily agency always has a mental component): trying to produce a bodily or a mental change, represented as the goal of an action, is what constitutes – or, in mediated cases, contributes to causing

– the desired change to occur. Second, it applies to impulsive actions – that is, to actions that cannot result from prior rational deliberation – and to 'negative actions' – that is, to actions that involve inhibiting a disposition to act (such as wanting to avoid thinking about John). Third, it is compatible with non-conceptual forms of action representation; for you can try to attain a goal that is non-conceptually represented. Finally, the willing or trying can account for the distinctive experience of agency that one has when one tries to remember, or tries to imagine, in contrast with passive cases (Peacocke 2008a, Proust 2009).

The nature of trying

This view, however, has raised various doubts and objections. It has been blamed for failing to assign a real explanatory role to willing and to make its nature clear (Brand 1984). Research in the neurosciences of action provides nevertheless a response to this worry, by showing that 'trying to *A*' has a cognitive role and a physiological realization. When *A* is bodily, the activation of a pre-motor area in the contralateral brain hemisphere suggests that 'trying' corresponds to preparing the action by setting in motion a program of sequential movements selected in the repertoire. A copy of the command, or 'efference copy,' subserves the feeling of agency in voluntary action: the ability to predict subsequent perceptual and motor effects seems to explain contrasts in the phenomenology of voluntary action, as opposed to that of passive movement (Haggard 2003). In the case of mental actions, one can suppose that some equivalent of the 'efference copy' allows subjects to have a sense of mental effort, permitting them to distinguish the case of a spontaneous recall from that of a directed one (Proust 2006; Peacocke 2008b).

Is trying an independent mental action? The infinite regress objection

Another traditional puzzle concerns the metaphysical status of 'trying' or 'willing': is it itself an independent mental action? For some of the proponents of the 'trying' view (Locke 2006; Peacocke 2008a) the answer has to be positive; the main interest of introducing the notion of a mental action is, for them, to lay bare the spring of agency rather than define it. Mental agency explains bodily agency; nothing can explain in turn the more primitive mental action of trying or willing to *A*: 'one can merely observe' that it consists in initiating within oneself a movement or a directed thinking episode. This version of the 'trying view,' however, seems to be open to a regress argument, which Ryle expressed in this way:

> So what of volitions themselves? Are they voluntary or involuntary acts of mind? Clearly either answer leads to absurdities. If I cannot help willing to pull the trigger, it would be absurd to describe my pulling as 'voluntary.' But if my volition to pull the trigger is voluntary, in the sense assumed by the theory, then it must issue from a prior volition and that from another *ad infinitum*. (Ryle 1949: 67)

Regress can only be involved, however, if an action needs to be *caused* (rather than *constituted*) by a prior trying. This is Locke's argument:

> A man is not at liberty to will, or not to will, because he cannot forbear willing: Liberty consisting in a power to act, or to forbear acting, and in that only. (2006, II, § 24, p. 246)

The structure of the will thus precludes the possibility of willing to will, or trying to try:

> The will is conversant about nothing, but our own Actions; terminates there, and reaches no farther; and Volition is nothing but that particular determination of the mind, whereby, barely by a thought, the mind endeavours to give rise, continuation, or stop to any action, which it takes to be in its power. (Ibid., II, § 30, 250)

What is, then, the cause of a willing? A motivation or a desire to act are obvious candidates.

Illusory trying

Another conceptual difficulty concerns how we are to pry apart failed trying from illusory trying. According to the 'trying' view, trying to do *A* and failing is still to act. An agent may fail, on a given occasion, to reach her proximal goal (to move, to concentrate), or her distal goal (to illuminate the room, to capture the argument) in spite of her efforts. This gives rise to a puzzle: if someone mistakenly takes herself to be trying to do something which, in fact, is impossible for her to do, such as speeding up her heartbeat, and either fails to produce the expected change or obtains it through deviant causes, shall we say that she has nevertheless acted? How can we account for the agent's sense of trying while we preserve the truth of the matter? McCann (1974), observing that the heartbeat rate can be sped up through the excitement produced by the false expectation, proposes strengthening the condition for trying through a voluntary control condition (VCC):

> *VCC* *Trying to A necessarily involves an actual capacity of exerting voluntary control over a bodily or mental change.*

Having voluntary control means that the agent knows how, and is normally able, to produce a desired effect; in other words, the type of procedural or instrumental activity that she is trying to set in motion must belong in her repertoire. Even though interfering conditions may block the desired outcome, the agent has tried to act if and only if she started to exert voluntary control in an area in which she is able to act. An important consequence of McCann's suggestion is that the agent has no authority with respect to the actual content of what she tries to do. All she knows is that she seems to be trying to perform action *A*.

Are there mediated mental actions?

It is compatible with VCC that bodily or mental properties which seem *prima facie* uncontrollable, such as sneezing, feeling angry, or remembering the party, can be indirectly controlled by an agent, if she has found a way to cause herself to sneeze, feel angry about *S*, or remember the party. She can then bring it about that she feels angry about *S*, or that she remembers the party. Are these *bona fide* cases of mental action?

The mediated kind does not seem to belong to mental action, according to Mele (2009), because 'the things that agents can, strictly speaking, try to do, *include no nonactions*' (INN).

All the mental events listed above, however, seem to violate this INN condition by including non-actions. Take Mele's task of finding seven kinds of animal whose name starts with 'g' (Mele 2009). There are several things that the agent actively tries to do: exclude names not beginning with 'g,' make a mental note of each word beginning with 'g' that has already come to mind, keep her attention focused, and so on. Her retrieval of 'goat,' however, does not qualify as a mental action, because 'goat' came to her mind involuntarily, in other words it was a non-action. Bringing it about that one thinks of seven animal names is intentional and can be tried, while forming the conscious thought of seven individual animal names is not (Mele 2009).

Is mediated epistemic agency conceptually incoherent?

Another serious conceptual problem is raised when a thinker's mediated goals are epistemic attitudes with pre-specified contents (Williams 1973; Dorsch 2009; Mele 2009). Let us suppose that a thinker wants to believe that her partner is faithful and is ready to resist potentially conflicting evidence, if required. Granting that mental actions respond to epistemic norms, a mental action which would include, as a sub-goal, fiddling with the epistemic norms associated with its type would no longer qualify as a mental action *of that type*. This is particularly clear with believing and judging: if one manages to bring oneself to will *P* to be true (ignoring potential conflicting evidence), then one no longer *believes* or *judges* that *P*, for believing or judging entails that one uses all the unbiased evidence available in forming one's belief or judgment (Williams 1973). The self-manipulative case in which a subject wants to believe that *P* should rather be analyzed as a distinctive propositional attitude: an accepting which, in contrast to believing and judging, qualifies as a mental action (Cohen 1992; Engel 1998).

In sum: the difficulties of the executive view are not insuperable. They point to the importance of making the notion of control more precise and of allowing cross-fertilization of the executive and rationalizing views. A third type of account of mental agency tries to instantiate such a junction.

Mental Agency, 'Evaluative Control,' and Metacognition

A third group of theories accepts the executive, 'trying' aspect of mental actions, but emphasizes the constitutive role of self-evaluation in mental agency. Proposals in this group agree that a sense of mental agency needs to incorporate the constitutive–normative commitments and decisions taken by an agent. They diverge, however, on whether self-evaluation constitutes an alternative case of agentive control, irreducible to object-oriented actions, or is rather an ingredient of every mental action.

Evaluative control

A basic assumption of this view is that some attitudes, like beliefs and intentions, constitute answers to questions or to sets of self-addressed questions (Hieronymi 2009).

While theories of mental agency focus on 'managerial control' (acting on attitudes for a purpose, just as we act on objects and situations), 'evaluative control' is an alternative form of agency, associated with *commitment* – seen as a product of attitude evaluation. For example, if one forms a belief that *P* after raising the associated question of whether *P*, one is committed to a positive answer to the question of whether *P*. In this analysis, epistemic control does not mean that one aims at entertaining selected belief contents; it means, rather, that one is ready to form and revise one's judgments in the light of one's answer to one's self-directed questions. Evaluative and managerial control, on this view, normally work in tandem, although evaluative control is seen as the basis of mental agency.

Mental action monitoring

A worry with the 'evaluative control' view is that epistemic or conative evaluative control generally fails to be voluntary. The term 'control,' as it is usually understood (Nelson and Narens 1994), does not apply to the evaluation of one's epistemic or conative attitudes; a more adequate term would rather be 'monitoring.' The alternative, 'metacognitive' view takes self-evaluation to be a necessary ingredient of any mental action and to be involved in two different steps. First, a mental action cannot be rationally tried without an agent having first appreciated its feasibility: 'Self-probing' is an operation allowing a thinker to estimate whether this token of mental action can be executed, given the mental resources available to her at that moment ('Am I able to remember this word?' is a question that must be answered before searching one's memory). Second, 'post-evaluating' allows an agent to assess retrospectively whether her mental action has been successfully completed ('Is this word the one I was looking for?'). Neither question need be articulated conceptually; the reflexive structure of command and monitoring, and the intervention of epistemic feelings, allow an agent to conduct mental actions on the basis of non-conceptual contents (Proust 2009).

In contrast to the evaluative control view, it is not claimed that the evaluative interventions of an agent can be made independently of a mental action. But, in contrast to the 'simple' executive view, the metacognitive view allows mediated mental actions to be included within the scope of mental agency. Mental agency surfaces in the ability to appraise the fluency and availability of the very cognitive processes on which 'bringing it about that *P*' depends.[1]

See also: TRYING TO ACT (3); VOLITION AND THE WILL (13); AGENTS' KNOWLEDGE (30); PRACTICAL REASONING (31); AKRASIA AND IRRATIONALITY (35); RESPONSIBILITY AND AUTONOMY (39); ARISTOTLE (54); RYLE (69).

Note

1 I am grateful to Dick Carter for his linguistic help and his philosophical comments on a prior version of this chapter.

References

Aristotle (1933–1935). *Metaphysics*, translated by H. Tredennick, 2 vols. Cambridge, MA: Harvard University Press (Loeb Classical Library).

Brand, M. (1984). *Intending and Acting*. Cambridge, MA: MIT Press.

Cohen, J. (1992). *An Essay on Belief and Acceptance*. Oxford: Oxford University Press.

Dorsch, F. (2009). Judging and the scope of mental agency. In O'Brien and Soteriou (eds), 38–71.

Engel, P. (1998). Believing, holding true, and accepting, *Philosophical Explorations*, 1 (2), 140–151.

Geach, P. (1957). *Mental Acts: Their Content and Their Objects*. London: Routledge and Kegan Paul.

Ginet, C. (1990). *On Action*. Cambridge: Cambridge University Press.

Haggard, P. (2003). Conscious awareness of intention and of action. In J. Roessler and N. Eilan (eds) *Agency and Self-Awareness: Issues in Philosophy and Psychology*. Oxford: Oxford University Press, 111–127.

Hampton, R. R. (2001). Rhesus monkeys know when they remember. *Proceedings of the National Academy of Sciences USA*, 98, 5359–5362.

Hieronymi, P. (2009). Two kinds of agency. In O'Brien and Soteriou (eds), 138–162.

Hursthouse, R. (1991). Arational actions. *Journal of Philosophy*, 88 (2), 57–68.

Locke, J. (2006). *An Essay concerning Human Understanding* [1689], 2 vols London: Elibron Classics.

McCann, H. (1974). Volition and basic action. *Philosophical Review*, 83, 451–473.

Mele, A. R. (1992). *Springs of Action. Understanding Intentional Behavior*. Oxford: Oxford University Press.

Mele, A. R. (2009). Mental action: A case study. In O'Brien and Soteriou (eds), 17–37.

Nelson, T. O., and Narens, L. (1994). Why investigate metacognition? In J. Metcalfe and A. P. Shimamura, *Knowing about Knowing*. Cambridge, MA: MIT Press, 1–25.

O'Brien, L., and Soteriou, M. (eds) (2009). *Mental Action*. Oxford: Oxford University Press.

O'Shaughnessy, B. (2000). *Consciousness and the World*. Oxford: Oxford University Press.

Peacocke, C. (2008a). *Truly Understood*. Oxford: Oxford University Press.

Peacocke, C. (2008b). Mental action and self-awareness. In O'Brien and Soteriou (eds), 192–214.

Proust, J. (2001). A plea for mental acts. *Synthese*, 129, 105–128.

Proust, J. (2006). Agency in schizophrenics from a control theory viewpoint. In W. Prinz and N. Sebanz (eds), *Disorders of volition*. Cambridge, MA: MIT Press, 87–118.

Proust, J. (2009). Is there a sense of agency for thought? In O'Brien and Soteriou (eds), 253–279.

Ryle, G. (1949). *The Concept of Mind*. London: Hutchinson.

Sosa, E. (2007). *A virtue epistemology: Apt Belief and Reflective Knowledge*, Oxford: Oxford University Press.

Williams, B. (1973). *Problems of the Self*. Cambridge: Cambridge University Press.

Further reading

Anscombe, G. E. M. (1959). *Intention*. Oxford: Blackwell.

Buckareff, A. A. (2005). How (not) to think about mental action. *Philosophical Explorations: An International Journal for the Philosophy of Mind and Action*, 8 (1), 83–89.

Burge, T. (1998). Reason and the first person. In C. Wright, B.C. Smithy, and C. Macdonald (eds), *Knowing our own Minds*. Oxford: Oxford University Press, 243–270.

Davidson, D. (1980). *Essays on Actions and Events*. Oxford: Clarendon Press.

Goldman, A. (1970). *A Theory of Human Action*. New York: Prentice Hall.

Hornsby, J. (1980). *Actions*. London: Routledge and Kegan Paul.

Mele, A. R. (ed.) (1994). *The Philosophy of Action*. Oxford: Oxford University Press.

O'Brien, L. (2007). *Self-Knowing Agents*. Oxford: Oxford University Press.

O'Shaughnessy, B. (1973) Trying (as the mental 'pineal glan'). *Journal of Philosophy*, 70, 365–386. [Reprinted in A. R. Mele (ed.) (1994), *The Philosophy of Action*, Oxford: Oxford University Press, 53–74.]

O'Shaughnessy, B. (1980). *The Will. A Dual Aspect Theory*. Cambridge: Cambridge University Press.

Proust, J. (2008). Epistemic agency and metacognition: An externalist view. *Proceedings of the Aristotelian Society*, 108 (3), 241–268.

Strawson, G. (2003). Mental ballistics or the involuntariness of spontaneity. *The Proceedings of the Aristotelian Society*, 77, 227–256.

28

Agent Causation

RANDOLPH CLARKE

Introduction

When we act intentionally, we cause things to happen. If you raise your arm, you cause your arm to go up; if you do this during an auction, you might thereby cause the auctioneer to recognize you as entering a bid. We agents, then, are capable of causing things, and in acting intentionally we exercise these causal capacities. So much is common sense and commonly acknowledged by philosophers of action. In this respect, we all believe in agent causation.

But we can distinguish (at least) three different views of agent causation. As many theorists see it, what happens when someone performs an intentional action such as bidding at an auction is that certain mental states or events involving that agent – for example his wanting to acquire a certain photograph and his believing that, in order to acquire it, he must raise his arm to enter a bid – cause (in some specifiable way) certain motions of his body – his arm's going up – and these bodily motions cause some further things, such as the auctioneer's response. And some writers hold that intentional action can be analyzed entirely in terms of such causal transactions among states or events. (For brevity, causation of this sort will henceforth be called causation by events, or event causation.) As this view has it, a philosophical theory of action need make no appeal to agent causation as something either conceptually or ontologically basic.

A second view holds that, although each instance of agent causation is ontologically realized in causation by events, no reductive conceptual analysis of it is possible. Analysis is said to be precluded because the distinctive way in which, for example, one's having a certain desire and belief must cause one's arm to go up if the episode is to count as one's intentionally raising one's arm cannot be characterized without appeal to agent causation (see further below). This position, then, takes agent causation to be conceptually basic but not ontologically fundamental.

On a third view, causation by an agent is said to be not only conceptually irreducible but also ontologically on a par with – or more fundamental than – event causation. (Alternatively, sometimes agent causation is held to be the only kind of causation there is.) Agent causation of this sort is sometimes claimed to be necessary for intentional agency. Other theorists take agent causation (understood in this way) not to be required for action but to be necessary for free will; we might be genuine agents without it, but we could not, then, be free agents. All theorists of this third sort take agent causation, in contrast with causation by an event, to be causation by an enduring substance – by the agent who performs the action in question. Some (for instance Taylor 1966: 135–138) take human agents to be physical beings, human animals; others (for instance Berkeley 1998) take agents to be immaterial spirits.

The view that the causation by agents which characterizes intentional agency can be reductively analyzed in terms of causation by events is dealt with in chapter 5. The present chapter concerns views of agent causation either as conceptually irreducible or as ontologically fundamental.

Why Agent Causation?

Why accept any such view? One argument favoring agent causation as ontologically basic observes that, when someone acts, he does not passively undergo change; rather he makes something happen, initiates something, brings something about. However, it is said, when prior events alone cause us to move in one way or another, we are passive with respect to the resulting motions. We are, on such occasions, moved rather than self-moving. We are truly active only when we are ourselves the ultimate causes of what we do. Our causing our actions, then, must be something that is ontologically fundamental (Taylor 1966, chs 8–9).

These claims express an intuition which is open to question. Suppose that your assessment of your situation was what caused your intending to enter a bid by raising your arm, and your intending to do so initiated and guided (in response to information feedback) the rising of your arm. Could this not be an instance of genuine agency, of your intentionally raising your arm? Perhaps a judicious answer can be given only in light of a detailed causal theory of action.

An argument for taking agent causation to be conceptually irreducible concerns the problem of causal deviance. It is often observed that an individual might do something as a causal result of mental events of just the sorts to which the causal theory appeals, and yet that person might not act intentionally, because of the way in which those events cause what is done. For example, a climber might want to rid himself of the burden of supporting his partner; it might occur to him that, by releasing a rope, he can free himself; his grip might then loosen and the rope might slip; and yet he might not have performed an action of letting go of the rope. For the realization of what he was contemplating might have so unnerved him that he lost his grip on the rope rather than intentionally releasing it (Davidson 1980b: 79). Intentional action, apparently, requires that the causation of one's behavior must not be deviant or wayward in this fashion. The causal theory, then, faces the task of spelling out the special, non-deviant way in which mental events must cause behavior if what one does is to be an instance of intentional action (for discussion of this problem, see chapter 21). Some proponents of agent causation maintain that the problem cannot be solved, at least not without appeal to a conceptually basic notion of agent causation (Bishop 1983; but see Bishop 1989 for a proposed solution).

Both considerations mentioned up to this point leave unchallenged the philosophically popular view that at least many of the causes of things are events. But this view is sometimes countered with the claim that only substances can be causes, or that event causation is reducible to causation by substances. Some philosophers have held that only a being with understanding and will – only an intentional agent – can be a cause (Berkeley 1998, §§ 25–27), or a cause in the 'proper and strict sense' (Reid 1852: 67). This view is far from our ordinary understanding (and scientists' understanding) of the causal roles of hurricanes, pollination, nuclear fission, and the like.

Other writers hold that inanimate substances – a magnet, some salt – as well as animate ones – plants and animals – can be causes, but that nothing other than a substance can be a cause (Swinburne 1997), or that all causation is fundamentally substance causation (Lowe 2008, ch. 6). In fact we commonly talk both of objects causing things and of events causing things. We might say, for example, that the rock broke the window (caused it to break), or that the rock's striking the window broke it. When it comes to a philosophical account of the matter, we might consider competing reductions. The second claim might be offered as a partial analysis of the first, in line with a view of event causation as the more basic. Alternatively, favoring substance causation, it might be said that the second claim is to be analyzed as: the rock, by striking the window, broke it. Which reductive claim, if either, is correct?

One argument against the former focuses first on what is known as basic intentional action. A basic action is, roughly, an action which one performs without (on that occasion) performing any other action as a means to performing it (see chapter 2). Your entering a bid in the auction would not be a basic action, for you enter the bid by raising your arm. It might be thought that your causing the auctioneer's recognition of your bid can be analyzed in terms of event causation: the raising of your arm causes the recognition of the bid. But your raising your arm – or your trying or choosing to do so – is a basic action; and, it is claimed, in this case your causing something (perhaps the motion of your arm) cannot similarly be given an event-causal analysis (Lowe 2008: 126–132; Swinburne 1997: 87–89). One might then recommend a view on which substance causation is basic in all cases, on the grounds that a uniform account is to be preferred (Swinburne 2006: 185).

An account of basic intentional action in terms of event causation is, of course, what proponents of the causal theory of action attempt to work out. The argument here can be assessed only by considering their proposals.

A second consideration said to favor taking substance causation as more fundamental is the fact that persisting objects – magnets, vases, grains of salt – are the things to which we commonly attribute causal powers and liabilities, such as being magnetic, fragile, or soluble. It is, then, such objects or substances that we see as exerting and manifesting causal powers and liabilities. And what exerts or manifests a causal power or liability would seem to be a cause (Lowe 2008: 138).

However, causal powers and liabilities are grounded in the properties that things possess. And our discourse is consistent with its being the case that when, for example, water dissolves salt, the causes are states or events: the water's having a power to dissolve salt, and the salt's being disposed to dissolve in water. Some further comparison of events and substances is required if we are to decide which, if either, of event causation or substance causation to take as ontologically more basic.

Many appeals to agent causation as something ontologically fundamental are made with the aim of providing an account of free will. It might be allowed that intentional actions can be caused only by prior events; but, it is said, such actions could not be free. Most agent causalists of this sort hold that, if every event – including all of our doings – were causally determined by events, then we would never act freely. (But see Markosian 1999 for a view that invokes agent causation but takes free will to be compatible with causal determinism.) At the same time, they maintain, behavior that was not caused by anything at all would not be under our control at all. And they deny that we could act freely if our behavior were caused but not determined by prior events, and by nothing else. (Events are non-deterministic causes if they cause a certain effect and yet they might have occurred in exactly the same circumstances without bringing about that effect.) There might, then, be genuine alternatives open to us, but it would not be up to us which open alternatives we actually pursue. In order for this to be under our control, it is said, we must ourselves cause what we do, and our causing what we do must not be causally determined by any other thing. In this way we are genuine sources, uncaused causes, of our behavior (Clarke 2003, chs 8–10; O'Connor 2000; Pereboom 2001, ch. 2).

Views of free will which require indeterminism are often said to confront a problem of luck, and it is sometimes argued that the appeal to agent causation provides no help in dealing with this problem. For example, suppose that on some occasion a certain individual, *S*, decides at time *t* to raise his arm, and that in so deciding what *S* directly causes is the event *e*, which occurs at *t*. Suppose that, as the indeterminist agent causalist would have it, prior events do not causally determine *S*'s decision, that it was causally open for him to decide at *t* not to raise his arm, in which case *S* would have caused, not *e*, but some other event at *t*. There is, then, a possible world with the same laws of nature as the actual world, and with the same history prior to *t*, in which *S* causes, not *e*, but some other event at *t*. Given the exact similarity between the actual world and this other possible world up until *t*, there is no difference between the two worlds that can account for the difference between *S*'s causing *e* at *t* and his causing a different event at *t*; nothing accounts for this difference. Since nothing accounts for this difference between the two worlds, the difference is just a matter of luck. And, since this difference is just a matter of luck, it does not seem to be up to *S* whether he decides to raise his arm on this occasion (Mele 2006, ch. 3; see also van Inwagen 2000: 10–18).

If in fact *S*'s causing *e* constitutes his exercising free will, then the difference between *S*'s causing *e* and his causing something else instead is not *just* a matter of luck; it is a matter of how he exercises free will. But what can be said to support the claim that an agent's causing something is his exercising free will? A basic conception of free will has it that, when one acts freely, a plurality of alternatives is open to one, and one determines oneself which alternative one pursues. When one does this, one is a source or origin of one's behavior. One might defend the claim in question by observing that an agent-causal theory of free will nicely fills out this basic conception (Clarke 2004). Whether this is so would seem to depend on just what agent causation is supposed to be – a topic to which we will turn in the final section.

What Is Agent-Caused, and What Else (if Anything) Causes It?

Some theorists who appeal to agent causation in accounts of intentional action or free will take it that actions – whether mental actions such as deciding to enter a bid or overt bodily actions such as raising one's arm – are the things which are agent-caused when one acts, or when one acts freely (see for instance Clarke 2003, ch. 8; Pereboom 2001, ch. 2; Taylor 1966). Others hold that agents directly cause only certain cerebral events (Chisholm 1966) or mental actions of certain sorts – volitions (Reid 1969) or choices (Donagan 1987) – which might then cause further things, such as the rising of one's arm. On a quite different view, actions are not events that are agent-caused; they are rather agent causings (Alvarez and Hyman 1998; Bishop 1983; O'Connor 2000: 72, n. 11). For example, my action of raising my arm is said to be my causing my arm to rise, or my causing my coming to intend to raise my arm, plus a sequence of events issuing from that intention acquisition, culminating in the rising of my arm.

Between the view that actions are agent-caused events and the view that actions are agent causings, is there any decisive reason to favor one over the other? The latter is sometimes favored (for instance by Bishop 1983: 71–72) on the grounds that a view of the former type aims to explain agency by invoking an obscure notion of a causing which is not a doing (a charge raised by Davidson 1980a: 52). However, the problem of explicating agent causation (discussed in the next section) falls equally on views of both types. It is also said that the former view has no principled way of distinguishing between those agent causings which are actions (some evidently are, for instance your causing the auctioneer to recognize your bid) and those which are said not to be (Alvarez and Hyman 1998: 222–223). Here it might be responded that agent causings are actions when and only when the agent causes something by performing an action. This principle would serve to distinguish between your causing the auctioneer's response and your causing the raising of your arm.

It is common for agent causalists to require, at least for free action, that the agent be the sole cause of what is directly agent-caused (Chisholm 1966; Pereboom 2001, ch. 2; O'Connor 2000; Taylor 1966). Such a view, however, raises questions about how actions (or free actions) can be things done for reasons, and thus explicable by citing the reasons for which they are done. A popular causal model has it that acting for reasons requires that certain of one's reason-states (such as desires and beliefs) cause one's behavior. A view that takes the agent to be the sole cause of what is done must develop some other account of acting for reasons and of reasons explanation (on this point, see chapter 17).

A causal model of acting for reasons can be accommodated by a view that takes agent causation to combine with event causation of what is directly agent-caused. It might be held that the causal theory has the right view of intentional action, but that agent causation is needed for free will. On such a view, when one acts freely, one's action is co-caused by oneself and (non-deterministically) by events such as one's having certain desires and beliefs. Provided that prior events do not causally determine what one does, one will face genuinely open alternatives. And the two types of causation are required to be integrated in such a way that one will pursue a given alternative only if one agent-causes one's doing so. With these requirements satisfied, it is said to be up to oneself what one does (Clarke 2003, ch. 8). However, whether agent causation can be combined with event causation in this fashion is a matter of some dispute (O'Connor 2000: 76–79; O'Connor and Churchill 2004).

Some theorists who take actions to be agent causings (Alvarez and Hyman 1998; Bishop 1983) similarly allow that the events which agents cause directly are also caused by prior events (such as neural events). Indeed, one such theorist (Bishop 1983) allows, even for free action, that prior events causally determine the events which agents cause when they act.

What is Agent Causation?

Contemporary theories of causation offer conflicting views on what sort of thing causes are, the favored candidates including events, states, states of affairs, facts, properties, universals, and tropes. While it is a good bet that most such views are mistaken, in none of the cases just mentioned is the claim commonly dismissed as incomprehensible. Yet critics often purport to find the thesis that agents are causes unintelligible, when it is denied that agent causation is conceptually or ontologically reducible to event causation. The appeal to agent causation in accounts of acting freely is sometimes said merely to give a name to a mystery (Nagel 1986: 115).

We observed above that several philosophers in the early modern period held that only thinking substances can be genuine causes. Among the late scholastics (for example Suarez 1994), the standard view was that all efficient causes, whether involving animate or inanimate beings, are substances. As already noted, some theorists have recently advanced a similar view. However, most writers who appeal to agent causation nowadays accept that there also exists event causation that is not reducible to causation by substances. Given such a view, how might one explicate agent causation?

Some agent causalists leave the notion unanalyzed, though they might exhibit its interconnections with other important concepts that we employ in our understanding of intentional agency – such as those of intending to act, of carrying out an intention, or of a repertoire of basic actions (Bishop 1983: 74–76). Others seek to characterize agent causation by way of comparison and contrast with event causation.

One move along these lines is to take causal powers, constituting the properties things have, as metaphysical bedrock. Causation, whether by an event or by a substance, is held to be the manifestation of such a power. In a case of event causation, it is said, an object's causal power is exerted by nature; given that the object has certain properties and is in certain circumstances, it is necessary that its having those properties cause a certain effect, or that there be a certain determinate probability that this event-causal transaction take place. In contrast, in a case of agent causation, it is held, the agent has both a power to cause a certain effect and a power not to cause it. If she does cause it, her causal power is freely exercised, or exercised at will. Further, agent causation is said to be essentially purposive; its exercise is an agent's causing his coming to have a certain intention for certain reasons (O'Connor 2000: 71–72 and 121; see also Donagan 1987: 168).

Another approach takes agent causation to be a species of substance causation, one distinguished by its role in intentional action. Regarding substance causation in general, this view stresses the similarity with causation by events, taking the relation between cause and effect to be the same in the two cases, the only difference being the ontological category of the cause. For its account of causation, such a view might appeal to causal powers as ontologically basic; or it might take the causal relation to be an irreducible theoretical entity, definable by postulates that specify the role it occupies in the domain of properties and events. On the latter alternative, for a substance to cause something is for that substance to stand to the effect in the relation specifiable in this manner – the same relation in which one event stands to another when the first event causes the second (Clarke 2003: 186–191).

Even if such a claim is intelligible, is it genuinely possible for a substance to be a cause? Perhaps the best known argument for impossibility concerns the timing of causal effects. When something is caused, it is caused to occur at a certain time. There must, then, be something about the (direct) cause of that effect that 'enters into the moment' from which the effect issues. A cause, then, must be something to which the notion of date, or time, applies; and such a notion has application only to events (Broad 1952: 215).

Agent causalists typically hold that, when a substance causes something directly, it does so at least partly in virtue of possessing at that time certain properties, which ground its power to cause that thing. The cause might then be said to 'enter into the moment' by virtue of possessing those properties at that time. To take this line, however, is tantamount to accepting that the cause is, after all, an event – the thing's having those properties then. (Clarke 2003, ch. 10 examines additional arguments for impossibility.)

Though agent causation is widely regarded as either incomprehensible or impossible, surprisingly little effort has been expended by critics either to understand what it is supposed to be or to explain why it could not exist. If there were thoroughly satisfactory accounts of agency and free will that made no appeal to agent causation, there might be no need to give it careful consideration. But, in the case of free will at least, this does not appear to be so.

See also: BASIC ACTIONS AND INDIVIDUATION (2); THE CAUSAL THEORY OF ACTION (5); REASONS AND CAUSES (17); DEVIANT CAUSAL CHAINS (21); FREE WILL AND DETERMINISM (38); BERKELEY (61); REID (62); CHISHOLM (71); DAVIDSON (73).

References

Alvarez, M., and Hyman, J. (1998). Agents and their actions. *Philosophy*, 73, 219–245.

Berkeley, G. (1998). *A Treatise Concerning the Principles of Human Knowledge* [1710], edited by J. Dancy. Oxford: Oxford University Press.

Bishop, J. (1983). Agent-causation. *Mind*, 92, 61–79.

Bishop, J. (1989). *Natural Agency: An Essay on the Causal Theory of Action*. Cambridge: Cambridge University Press.

Broad, C. D. (1952). Determinism, indeterminism, and libertarianism. In C. D. Broad, *Ethics and the History of Philosophy: Selected Essays*. New York: Humanities Press 195–217.

Chisholm, R. M. (1966). Freedom and action. In K. Lehrer (ed.), *Freedom and Determinism*. New York: Random House, 11–44.

Clarke, R. (2003). *Libertarian Accounts of Free Will*. New York: Oxford University Press.

Clarke, R. (2004). Reflections on an argument from luck. *Philosophical Topics*, 32, 47–64.

Donagan, A. (1987). *Choice: The Essential Element in Human Action*. London: Routledge and Kegan Paul.

Davidson, D. (1980a). Agency. In D. Davidson, *Essays on Actions and Events*. Oxford: Clarendon Press, 43–61.

Davidson, D. (1980b). Freedom to act. In D. Davidson, *Essays on Actions and Events*. Oxford: Clarendon Press, 63–81.

Lowe, E. J. (2008). *Personal Agency: The Metaphysics of Mind and Action*. Oxford: Oxford University Press.

Markosian, N. (1999). A compatibilist version of the theory of agent causation. *Pacific Philosophical Quarterly*, 80, 257–277.

Nagel, T. (1986). *The View from Nowhere*. New York: Oxford University Press.

Mele, A. R. (2006). *Free Will and Luck*. New York: Oxford University Press.

O'Connor, T. (2000). *Persons and Causes: The Metaphysics of Free Will*. New York: Oxford University Press.

O'Connor, T., and Churchill, J. R. (2004). Reasons explanation and agent control: In search of an integrated account. *Philosophical Topics*, 32, 241–253.

Pereboom, D. (2001). *Living Without Free Will*. Cambridge: Cambridge University Press.

Reid, T. (1852). *The Works of Thomas Reid, D.D.*, 3rd edn, edited by Sir William Hamilton. Edinburgh: MacLachlan and Stewart.

Reid, T. (1969). *Essays on the Active Powers of the Human Mind* [1788]. Cambridge, MA: MIT Press.

Suarez, F. (1994). *On Efficient Causality: Metaphysical Disputations 17, 18, and 19* [1597], translated by A. J. Freddoso, New Haven, CT: Yale University Press.

Swinburne, R. (1997). The irreducibility of causation. *Dialectica*, 51, 79–92.

Swinburne, R. (2006). Relations between universals, or divine laws? *Australasian Journal of Philosophy*, 84, 179–189.

Taylor, R. (1966). *Action and Purpose*. Englewood Cliffs, NJ: Prentice Hall.

Van Inwagen, P. (2000). Free will remains a mystery. *Philosophical Perspectives*, 14, 1–19.

Further reading

An important historical work on agent causation is Thomas Reid's *Essays on the Active Powers of the Human Mind* (MIT Press, 1969). Two recent studies of Reid's theory are William Rowe's *Thomas Reid on Freedom and Morality* (Cornell University Press, 1991) and Gideon Yaffe's *Manifest Activity* (Clarendon Press, 2004).

Perhaps the most important twentieth-century proponents of agent causation are Roderick Chisholm and Richard Taylor. Chisholm's most accessible presentation of his view is his 'Human freedom and the self,' in Keith Lehrer (ed.), *Freedom and Determinism* (Random House, 1966). Taylor's view is presented in his *Action and Purpose* (Prentice Hall, 1966).

Recent work concerning agent-causal theories of free will includes Randolph Clarke's *Libertarian Accounts of Free Will* (Oxford University Press, 2003); Timothy O'Connor's *Persons and Causes* (Oxford University Press, 2000); and Derk Pereboom's *Living Without Free Will* (Cambridge University Press, 2001).

John Bishop's 'Agent-causation' (*Mind* 92, 1983, pp. 61–79) argues that a theory of intentional action must appeal to agent causation as conceptually basic. E. J. Lowe's *Personal Agency* (Oxford University Press, 2008) advances a theory of action and free will that takes agent causation as ontologically basic.

The most detailed recent proposals concerning what agent causation might be are found in the books by Clarke, Lowe, and O'Connor. Clarke's book offers an examination of arguments concerning whether agent causation is possible.

29

Bodily Awareness and Bodily Action

HONG YU WONG

The body is at the centre of physical action. Even when one's action ranges beyond the boundaries of one's body, as it often does, one is (typically) acting with one's body in some way. The normal situation of an agent is thus one where she is striving with her body in some way in order to achieve her aims in the circumstances she is faced with. Are there conditions on striving with one's body? Intuitively, to act with a body part, one needs to know the state and position of that body part in order to have some sense of how one can strive with it to achieve one's aims in a particular scenario. This sense of how one might strive with a body part may be inarticulate; it may consist in no more than the agent being able to demonstrate what she will do, which she might express with 'I'll do something like *this*.' But what puts the agent in a position to know the state and position of the body parts she is acting with, so that she may even begin to have some inarticulate sense of what she can do? Is it sight, touch, or any of the familiar sense modalities? We are not always sensing the body parts we are acting with through the familiar perceptual modalities, since our attention is drawn outwards to the external objects we act on; yet we are able to strive with our body on demand. How is this possible?

What is less noticed is another set of sense experiences that are ubiquitous and yet unattended to. These experiences tend to lurk in the background, in the shadow of our experiences of the world outside. On occasion, they cry out for attention, as when one experiences an acute pain, an intense pleasure, or an urgent itch. But their typical manifestation is inconspicuous. I am referring to our experiences of our bodies and of their various parts 'from the inside,' experiences which we may unify under the label of *bodily awareness*. Bodily awareness really consists of a ragtag group of ways of sensing one's body: familiar instances include experience of the location, movement, and temperature of parts of one's body, awareness of whether one is fatigued or hungry, whether some part of one's body is hurt, and whether one is upside down. Once we bring out the presence of this 'modality,' its importance is obvious. We have noted that the normal situation of an agent involves her striving with her body in some way to accomplish her ends. The thought, then, is that bodily awareness is *always there* to provide these parameters about the state and position of body parts, presenting them to the agent so that she can control her actions. Thus bodily awareness can come to seem central to the possibility of bodily action.

Despite the intuitive force of these initial thoughts, the alleged centrality of bodily awareness in bodily action is hard to articulate and, as a consequence, it is hard to evaluate. My approach in this chapter will be to sketch the orthodox account of the relation between bodily awareness and bodily action and to attempt to convey a sense of the depth and difficulty of the topic by way of exploring various problems with it.

The forms of bodily awareness are various. In connection with bodily action, that is, with acting *with* one's body, the modes of bodily awareness that are most important are those that relate to sensing spatial and kinematic properties of one's body – proprioception and kinaesthesia – and, to a lesser extent, properties like fatigue and effort.

The most natural claim concerning the relation between bodily awareness and bodily action is that bodily action is possible because of bodily awareness. This corresponds to the natural direction of explanation for how we think experience rationalizes and guides behavior (though there may be critical differences between bodily awareness and exteroceptive modalities). This line of thought is developed in the work of Brian O'Shaughnessy (1980, 1995, 2001, and 2008). O'Shaughnessy's work is immensely rich and complex; it is the most detailed exploration of our topic in the philosophical canon. Our discussion will not be able to do justice to the richness of his discussion, but let us focus on the core of his central claim that bodily awareness is necessary for bodily action. This claim may be developed in many different ways. Three important ways are:

1 bodily awareness is a condition on bodily action in some general sense;
2 bodily awareness is required for the control of bodily action; and
3 bodily awareness is necessary for knowing what one is doing when one acts with one's body.

Observe that, even if the latter two claims were false, the former might still be true. The most straightforward of the three theses is the second one, and it has some claim to capturing the intuitive force of the thought behind the necessity of bodily awareness for bodily action. We might make the claim more precise by stating it as follows: acting directly with a body part requires feeling that body part 'from the inside' at the time of acting. Call this *Necessity*. By 'acting directly,' I mean to pick up on an intuitive notion of 'basic action' (roughly corresponding to teleological basicness): that which I perform not by performing any distinct action. So I act directly with my left hand when I just raise it, as opposed to raising it with my right hand. We can discern three strands of argument for Necessity in O'Shaughnessy's work. The first is that acting with a body part is inconceivable without feeling that body part 'from the inside.' The second is that bodily awareness provides the necessary information, including feedback, for the control of the body part one acts directly with. The third is that bodily awareness provides a 'target-object' for the bodily will to engage with.

Support for the feedback strand comes from considering how we might correct mistakes in the direction, trajectory, and speed of movement without feedback from bodily awareness. Acting requires one to know the state of one's limbs, and bodily awareness puts us in a position to know the state of one's limbs. Furthermore, actions – unlike reflexes – are robust, in that agents can act to achieve the desired goal state in a very large number of ways. (For example, if you are reaching for the salt and there are bottles blocking a direct approach to it, you can reach around them.) Changes in one's environment and changes in one's bodily state thus require that one gets feedback which allows for fine-tuning, so that the agent can be sensitive to conditions affecting the performance of his task.

The image of bodily awareness providing a 'target-object' for the bodily will to engage with is both suggestive and obscure. The easiest way to explicate the idea is to rely on the inconceivability argument, but this does not fully reflect its plausibility. Valberg captures O'Shaughnessy's 'target-object' idea in the following passage (2007: 272):

> [W]e are not talking here about numbness – the sort of thing you get, say, with local anaesthesia. [...] We are talking about the more extreme possibility of a total loss, a sheer absence, of feeling. If this happened to your arm, could you move it (in the normal way)? It is not that if you tried to move it you would fail. You could not even *try* to move it. Without feeling, there is, so to speak, nothing at which the will might aim. Feeling is what makes the body 'visible' to the will. And if something is not visible, you cannot aim at it.

Various ideas are at work in this evocative passage. The basic premise is that striving with a body part requires that one is able to 'latch onto' that body part in some way. It is then claimed that bodily awareness provides the necessary means of engagement, so that body parts are *presented* to the agent; in feeling her body 'from the inside,' the agent is presented with her body as a 'target-object' for her will. But if striving requires the provision of a 'target-object' and only bodily awareness can furnish it, then it is the case that, if a body part is not presented to the agent, then, *a fortiori*, it is not presented to the agent as a body part that he might act directly with at all. A fuller analysis of this line of thought must await another occasion; for now we will simply record a number of observations.

One question that arises is the sense in which bodily awareness is distinctive in presenting the agent with her own body. So far we have not indicated any sense in which bodily awareness is a special source of information about one's body, except that it is constant. We have relied on the thought that we can strive with our bodies on demand and that this requires the agent to know the spatial dispositions of her body – but only bodily awareness appears to be always on hand to provide these parameters for motor control. This, in itself, does not show that there is anything distinctive about the *content* of bodily awareness. If the constancy claim is correct, then it may provide some support for the claim that bodily awareness is required for feedback in motor control. But the 'target-object' idea goes beyond this. Valberg remarks that one could not even *try* to move a limb which is entirely unfelt. This is a very strong claim: it excludes the possibility that other sense modalities might provide the bodily will with its 'target-object' and it rules out the possibility of trying to act on the basis of one's memory of one's limb and of how to move it. This brings out the distinctive character of bodily awareness: it is that which presents certain body parts as parts that one can strive with. Why think that bodily awareness is special in this way?

Descartes remarked in his *Sixth Meditation* that we are not in our bodies as pilots are in their ships: one experiences one's body and its various parts 'from the inside,' and not just as one material object among others. Bodily awareness presents only one object – one can only be aware of one's own body 'from the inside' – in contrast with the multiplicity of objects that visual awareness can present. One's body is not the only material body one can be visually aware of. When one experiences one's body in sight, one's body is given as one among many other possible objects of perception. In contrast, for each and every mode of bodily awareness, one can only be aware of one's body: when one feels a limb moving, one feels that it is one's own limb which is moving, and not anyone else's; when one feels a pair of hands stretched out, one feels that it is one's own hands which are stretched out and not another's. This provides for a sense of ownership of one's body, as one is not presented with one's body among other bodies which one also feels, but is only aware of one's body in this way – yet one's body is also experienced as an element of the objective order, which also contains other bodies and objects (Martin 1995). If we couple this with the observation that one is able to act with one's body in ways in which one is incapable of acting with other bodies or objects, we can begin to see how bodily awareness can underwrite the agent's sense that her body is the distinctive respondent to her will.

In sum: the case for Necessity comes from seeing how bodily awareness seems to provide an indispensable source of information for the control of action and how it presents the body as a 'target-object' for the will. Though distinct, the feedback and the 'target-object' strands are not unrelated. One is not simply put in some brute relation of acquaintance with one's body, but awareness provides the spatial parameters for control of one's action. The picture embodied in Necessity accords with our ordinary experience of agency: it is hard to conceive how even sundry everyday activities would be possible in the absence of bodily awareness; just imagine running after a bus under conditions of complete anaesthesia.

It does seem compelling that, in agency as we know it, bodily awareness has an intimate connection with bodily action. Despite its intuitive plausibility, there are immediate challenges to Necessity. There are 'deafferented' agents, who retain a capacity to act with parts of their body that they no longer have sensation in. (This is not to say that bodily action is possible in the *complete* absence of bodily awareness – a definitive answer to that question would require further empirical investigation than has previously been carried out.) There is the much discussed case of IW, who is able to dress himself, walk, write, and even drive, despite being deafferented from the neck down (Cole and Paillard 1995). Thus bodily action *is* possible even if one's bodily awareness is drastically reduced. Since IW can act directly with limbs in which he has no sense of position, movement, or touch, bodily awareness is not required in order to provide a 'target-object' for his bodily will, and he can control his limbs without feedback from bodily awareness. The case also refutes the inconceivability claims.

There is no doubt that what it is like for IW to act is radically different from the phenomenology of agency of normal human beings. But that is not our question. Unless one shows that IW cannot be understood as capable of bodily agency at all with those parts of his body he doesn't have sensation in, this constitutes a counterexample to Necessity. There are no grounds for denying that IW is capable of bodily action because he lacks proprioception and kinaesthesia in those parts; IW clearly is able to do various things with parts of his body. IW was only able to perform many mundane tasks, such as walking and even sitting, by painstakingly relearning them; for now he has to be able to perform them without the benefit of bodily awareness. He compensates for this by paying close visual attention to the state of his body and he needs to anticipate his next moves constantly, so as to deal with the environmental obstacles that turn up.

One response to this case is to say that Necessity concerns the *normal* or non-pathological cases of physical agency (where by 'normal' we mean the conceptually paradigmatic cases, as opposed to whatever is statistically predominant); and we have not shown that Necessity fails there. However, such a move already represents a significant retreat from the initial position offered; it is now unclear what the modal force of the alleged necessity comes to. O'Shaughnessy is willing to concede that, even in the repertoire of normal agents, there may be extreme cases which require an alternative treatment; but, he stresses, 'the normal acts of reaching are scarcely on a par with sudden high-speed duckings from what shows as a mere blur in one's visual field!' (1995: 201). Unfortunately, O'Shaughnessy's contention is false. There is overwhelming empirical evidence that, even if we restrict ourselves to central cases of ordinary bodily action, (1) in most instances, these are accomplished automatically and without constant bodily awareness, and (2) even when movement involves bodily awareness, the online control involved in fine-tuning actions is mostly non-conscious. This, unsurprisingly, is due to the workings of various sub-personal mechanisms, which monitor the state of our body and underwrite our ability to act.

The first claim can be established by comparing the various execution times of actions with the time required for sensory feedback to arrive from the periphery. Lashley (1951) observed that the frequency at which finger alternations take place while a subject is playing a fast musical passage can reach up to sixteen strokes per second. The speed of finger movements during these passages precludes the possibility of any sensory feedback influencing the command system. (Other examples of fast actions are speed typing and various movements in sporting activities.) This example also bears on our second claim, concerning the role of sensory feedback for online fine-tuning of many ordinary bodily actions, which are often very quick and accurate: sensory feedback is delayed. Proprioceptive information is delayed because of the time it takes for neural signals to propagate from the limbs to the brain. Therefore, if motor control relied on sensory feedback for online control of fast actions, the reafferent information would be inevitably out of date and would lead to instability (Miall et al. 1993; Haggard 2001).

Fast actions also generate problems for the 'target-object' line of thought, since events of awareness of body parts have to precede, or at least be simultaneous with, acting with them, otherwise there will be no 'target-object' for the will. However, the neural circuits responsible for conscious awareness of motor performance appear to be far slower than the circuits involved in the online fine-tuning of actions (Castiello et al. 1991, Jeannerod 2006, ch. 3). If so, then, for ordinary actions which are fast, conscious bodily awareness cannot be temporally prior in a way that the priority is what the will exploits to know what to latch on to and how to control it. Since these fast actions form a large and important part of an agent's repertoire, Necessity cannot hold even for the normal acts of normal agents.

Recent empirical evidence for dissociations between perception and action present further problems. Marcel's (2003) experiments exploiting vibro-tactile illusions are a case in point. Subjects experience illusions of arm position and movement when a muscle tendon at the joint of the arm is vibrated and the resulting reflex movement inhibited. The illusion is particularly pronounced when subjects cannot see their arm. The task is to move one's concealed arm to the position of a target light. When subjects are under the vibro-tactile illusion, their judgments tend to reflect the illusion, both before and after the experiment; yet their performance is unaffected. They are consistently successful, even in situations where they have to move their arm in a direction opposite to what would be expected on the basis of their illusory experience. There is room to quibble about the exact ramifications of results like these, but Marcel's results suggest that the parameters for the initial position of the arm and motor specification for movement cannot be derived in this case from bodily awareness. Insofar as the movement requires feedback, this cannot be provided by parameters from bodily awareness either, since these would specify the opposite direction of movement.

The upshot of these points is that feeling a body part 'from the inside' at the time of acting cannot be necessary for striving with it. This leads us to a wrinkle in the debate with O'Shaughnessy, which concerns his two notions of body image. Theorists of the body image have typically distinguished between (at least) two senses of body image (where the relevant kind of body image is that which is exploited in direct action control): a long-term and a short-term (or here-and-now) body image (see O'Shaughnessy 1980: 241–248; Lackner 1988).

The *long-term body image* is, roughly, a settled picture of one's own physical dimensions, which may change (slowly) depending on the development of the body (grafts, amputations, growth). This describes the *structure* of one's body – how it is shaped, sized, and hinged – and thus what possibilities of movement are open to one. It tells us what basic actions the body can afford. However, the long-term body image only tells us what range of actions are possible for one, given the structure of one's body. It tells us nothing about the current state of one's body, including its current position and spatial dispositions. One's long-term body image remains the same whether one is upside down or downside up, whether one is cooking or skiing. What we need, then, is a body image which gives us a sense of the range of actions which are *currently* possible for one. And this requires an image that describes one's current posture and dispositions of body parts. This is what O'Shaughnessy calls the 'short-term body image.' It is

> given by the description or drawing or model one would assemble in order to say how the body seems to one at a certain instant. For example: torso straight, right cylindrical arm stretched out from body, crooked at right angles, etc. (O'Shaughnessy 1980: 241)

The debate regarding Necessity is concerned only with the short-term body image as these images are the occurrent, but usually recessive experiences of the body that are claimed to be essential to bodily action. However, why not retreat to the claim that all we need is the long-term body image, which contains information about possible sites of sensation, bodily structure and bodily dispositions, but is not a form of occurrent experience of one's body? Conceding this much is already to concede that Necessity is false as it stands. This indicates that the connection between bodily awareness and agency is more complicated than the model embodied in Necessity suggests, and may involve different factors contributing in complex ways. But this is not to say that there is no intimate connection between bodily awareness and bodily action, for bodily awareness may have a role at a remove from online control.

At the beginning, we noted that the claim that bodily awareness is necessary for bodily action may be developed in other ways: it might still be that bodily awareness is a condition on bodily action in some general sense, or that bodily awareness is necessary for knowing what one is doing. There is no space to consider these other claims here; but we will conclude by briefly remarking on them, in reverse order. The points we have marshalled against Necessity suggest that certain versions of the knowledge claim are problematic as well: in the case of fast actions, it appears that one knows what one is doing before proprioception and kinaesthesia return a verdict. It may be, however, that even though awareness of position and movement 'from the inside' is not required for knowing that one is striving, the capacity for knowing what one is doing requires, in the case of normal agents, that one is able to feel one's body 'from the inside.' (And even if the mooted suggestion is feasible, the question may arise as to whether perception of one's body through these channels is a constitutive or simply an enabling condition on knowledge of action.) Similar strategies may be pursued with respect to a general claim, which is not necessarily connected to knowledge of action. One proposal would be to chart out a connection between bodily awareness and action through the long-term body image. If, in acting intentionally with one's body, one acts with some sense of how one can strive with it to achieve one's aims in a particular scenario, then the long-term body image would seem to be required for action, since it is what underwrites one's sense of what actions are possible for one. The question would then be whether bodily awareness has an essential role in the construction of the long-term body image for normal agents. There are also other ways a connection between bodily awareness and agency might be pursued. One obvious option is the opposite direction of explanation: bodily action might be thought to be a condition on bodily awareness (Brewer 1995 and Hurley 1998). Whatever the attractions of this view, it faces a serious difficulty with paralyzed subjects. Paralysis removes the possibility of striving with certain body parts, but leaves intact the ability to feel these parts 'from the inside.' If the response is that the condition can be satisfied by the possession of behavioral dispositions even when these are *merely* dispositional (Evans 1982: 161), then the question is what notion of disposition is in play and whether this strategy remains explanatory, especially since the neural structures underlying motor control may be damaged.

Though there are at present no definitive accounts of the relation between bodily awareness and agency, there remains a powerful sense in which bodily awareness appears to be implicated in bodily actions as we know them. Another way to put this is that our conception of ourselves as agents is already as *embodied* agents; our relation to our bodies, both in action and in perception, is not as a pilot to his ship. So we are obliged to understand the intimate connection between bodily awareness and agency. Part of the excitement of our topic is that we have more questions to ask than answers to give.

See also: BODILY MOVEMENTS (4); THE EXPLANATORY ROLE OF CONSCIOUSNESS (24); AGENTS' KNOWLEDGE (30); DESCARTES (59).

References

Bermúdez, J., Marcel, A., and Eilan, N. (eds) (1995). *The Body and The Self*. Cambridge, MA: MIT Press.

Brewer, B. (1995). Bodily awareness and the self. In Bermúdez, Marcel, and Eilan (eds), 291–309.

Castiello, U., Paulignan, Y., and Jeannerod, M. (1991). Temporal dissociation of motor responses and subjective awareness: A study in normal subjects. *Brain*, 114, 2639–2655.

Cole, J., and Paillard, J. (1995). Living without touch and peripheral information about body position and movement: Studies with deafferented subjects. In Bermúdez, Marcel, and Eilan (eds), 245–266.

Evans, G. (1982). *Varieties of Reference*. Oxford: Clarendon Press.

Haggard, P. (2001). The psychology of action. *British Journal of Psychology*, 92, 113–128.

Hurley, S. (1998). *Consciousness in Action*. Cambridge, MA: Harvard University Press.

Jeannerod, M. (2006). *Motor Cognition: What Actions Tell the Self*. Oxford: Oxford University Press.

Lackner, J. R. (1988). Some proprioceptive influences on the perceptual representation of body shape and orientation. *Brain*, 111, 281–297.

Lashley, K. S. (1951). The problem of serial order in behavior. In L. A. Jeffress (ed.), *Central Mechanisms and Behavior*. New York: Wiley, 112–136.

Marcel, A. (2003). The sense of agency: Awareness and ownership of action. In J. Roessler and N. Eilan (eds), *Agency and Self-Awareness*. Oxford: Oxford University Press, 48–93.

Martin, M. G. F. (1995). Bodily awareness: A sense of ownership. In Bermúdez, Marcel, and Eilan (eds), 267–285.

Miall, R. C., Weir, D. J., Wolpert, D. M., and Stein, J. F. (1993). Is the cerebellum a Smith predictor? *Journal of Motor Behaviour*, 25, 203–216.

O'Shaughnessy, B. (1980). *The Will: A Dual Aspect Theory*, 2 vols. Cambridge: Cambridge University Press.

O'Shaughnessy, B. (1995). Proprioception and the body image. In Bermúdez, Marcel, and Eilan (eds), 175–203.

O'Shaughnessy, B. (2001). *Consciousness and the World*. Oxford: Oxford University Press.

O'Shaughnessy, B. (2008). *The Will: A Dual Aspect Theory*, 2 vols, 2nd edn. Cambridge: Cambridge University Press.

Valberg, J. J. (2007). *Dream, Death, and the Self*. Princeton and Oxford: Princeton University Press.

Further reading

Bermúdez, J. (1998). *The Paradox of Self-Consciousness*. Cambridge, MA: MIT Press, Ch. 6.

Bermúdez, J. (2006). The phenomenology of bodily awareness. In A. Thomasson and D. W. Smith (eds), *Phenomenology and Philosophy of Mind*. Oxford: Oxford University Press, 295–317.

Brewer, B. (1993). The integration of spatial vision and action. In Eilan, McCarthy, and Brewer (eds), 294–316.

Campbell, J. (1993). The role of physical objects in spatial thinking. In Eilan, McCarthy, and Brewer (eds), 65–95.

Eilan, N., McCarthy, R., and Brewer, B. (eds) (1993). *Spatial Representation*. Oxford: Oxford University Press.

Knoblich, G., Thornton, I., Grosjean, M., and Shiffrar, M. (2005). *Human Body Perception from the Inside Out*. New York and Oxford: Oxford University Press.

Martin, M. G. F. (1993). Sense modalities and spatial properties. In Eilan, McCarthy, and Brewer (eds), 206–218.

Merleau-Ponty, M. (1958). *Phenomenology of Perception*, translated by Colin Smith. London and New York: Routledge.

O'Brien, L. (2007). *Self-Knowing Agents*. Oxford: Oxford University Press.

Roessler, J., and Eilan, N. (eds) (2003). *Agency and Self-Awareness*. Oxford: Oxford University Press.

30

Agents' Knowledge

JOHANNES ROESSLER

According to both common sense and philosophical tradition, agents enjoy a distinctive kind of knowledge of their own intentional actions. A helpful way to bring out the intuitive force of the idea and to introduce some of the philosophical questions raised by it is to look at pathologies of action awareness. Consider the following report by a patient in the pre-onset phase of schizophrenia:

> One might think that my person is no longer there. I walk like a machine; it seems to me that it is not me who is walking, talking, or writing with this pencil. When I am walking, I look at my legs which are moving forward; I fear to fall by not moving them correctly. (Quoted in Parnas and Sass 2001: 106)

We can distinguish three themes here. First, the patient's 'sense of agency' is impaired: he experiences his actions as not (fully) his own. As Parnas and Sass comment, 'he has a feeling of *observing* his actions as a witness without being actively involved' (ibid., my emphasis). Second, there is an impairment of intentional control, or at least the patient has lost confidence in his ability to control his movements appropriately. Third, the patient suffers from what might be called a sense of disintegration or depersonalization ('One might think that my person is no longer there').

The first theme is the one that is most immediately related to the topic of agents' knowledge. Obvious questions here include: how does the patient's experience of his actions differ from non-pathological awareness of agency? What is the source, and the scope, of the distinctive kind of knowledge agents ordinarily have of what they are doing? How, if at all, can we make sense of the idea of an *impairment* of the way we are ordinarily aware of our actions? But the other two themes – intentional control and self-awareness – also correspond to traditional philosophical concerns around the topic of agents' knowledge. A number of philosophers, including for example Kant and Anscombe, have put forward versions of the strong thesis that agents' awareness of their actions is in some sense constitutive of rational or intentional agency. And some philosophers (again, including Kant and Anscombe) have appealed to agents' knowledge in their account of the nature of first-person thought.

The following brief review will be limited in a number of ways. I will focus on contemporary work – more precisely, work coming downstream from Anscombe's path-breaking *Intention* (1957). I will not be able to take up any of the important philosophical issues arising from recent experimental and theoretical work in psychology in this area (though I will come back to the interpretation of pathologies). I'll follow current practice and concentrate on first-person knowledge of *what* one is doing, at the expense of first-person understanding of *why* one is doing it. (See Velleman 1989 for a welcome exception to that practice.) And I will have nothing to say on the relation between agents' knowledge and first-person thought.

My review will be organized around two basic distinctions. The first distinction concerns the explanatory role of experience. Consider two cases. In the first case you intentionally raise your arm. In the second case, someone else grabs your arm and raises it. On what I will call an 'empiricist' view of agents' knowledge, we can identify a type of experience which is distinctive of the first case and which provides the source (or part of the source) of your knowledge that you are raising your arm. There is a good deal of room for internal disagreement among empiricists, both on the nature of the relevant experience and on the way it grounds agents' knowledge. What empiricists of various stripes have in common is the idea that agents' knowledge has what might be called an experiential source. My first distinction, then, is between empiricism and anti-empiricism, the position of whose who deny that agents' knowledge has an experiential source.

My second distinction concerns the issue of epistemic justification. Some philosophers think that an account of agent's knowledge has to take the form of an account of the source of an agent's epistemic justification in holding certain non-inferential beliefs about her actions. Others reject this view. The issue leads to an interesting division amongst anti-empiricists. According to what I will call a 'rationalist' approach, while agents' knowledge lacks an experiential source of knowledge, there is nevertheless a substantive, informative account to be given of how agents' beliefs as to what they are doing are epistemically justified – an account that helps to make it intelligible how such beliefs qualify as knowledge. According to what I will call a *minimalist* approach, no such account can be given; nor is one needed.

I will set out these options in slightly greater detail, and then look at what I take to be the three critical issues between them: (1) the relation between agents' knowledge and intentional action; (2) the phenomenology of action; and (3) the relation between agents' knowledge and practical rationality.

The empiricist approach was strongly discouraged by Anscombe, who ridiculed it as the fantasy of a 'very queer and special sort of seeing eye in the middle of acting' (1957: 57). More recently, though, empiricism has had a growing number of defenders. Ginet (1990) invokes what he calls 'the actish phenomenal quality' to explain agents' distinctive access to their voluntary actions. O'Brien (2003) argues that actions occupying attention are conscious events which provide the agent with reasons for beliefs as to what they are doing. Peacocke (2003) argues for the existence of a 'belief-independent' conscious state of 'action awareness,' a state agents are normally entitled to 'take at face value.' According to O'Shaughnessy (2003), action involves a conscious psychological event of trying, given immediately in experience. What these proposals have in common is that they seek to make agents' knowledge intelligible in a certain way. They offer a certain kind of answer to questions such as: 'How do I know I am currently writing?' Empiricists claim that the key to answering the question lies in the relation between my judgment 'I am writing' (or, according to some empiricists, my judgment 'I am trying to write') and the distinctive kind of experience which provides its epistemic basis. If this sort of explanation can be sustained, this would have a number of important ramifications. It would have an immediate bearing on the scope of agents' knowledge. The difference between those descriptions of one's actions under which one is aware of them 'from within' and those under which one is not would turn on the question of what sorts of judgments are licensed by the critical sort of experience. The explanation would also encourage a particular account of the traditional, and intuitive, contrast between the perspectives we occupy *qua* agents and *qua* spectators. Empiricists understand the contrast as one between two experiential sources of knowledge: a first-personal source, available only to the agent engaged in an action, and a third-personal source, available to external observers.

Those who reject the empiricist framework tend to give a central role to the notion of intention in their account of agents' knowledge. They tend to endorse what I'll call Anscombe's thesis:

(AT) We express agents' knowledge by expressing intentions.

Intentions are based on practical reasons rather than on theoretical evidence or experience. Correlatively, what we aim to get right in expressing our current intentions is the goal of some current or future action of ours, and how we aim to achieve that goal. This is why AT, despite being silent on how we should understand the source of agent's knowledge, is incompatible with the empiricist approach: on the latter, expressing agents' knowledge should be a matter of articulating the content of a certain experience, not the goal of an action or the means to achieve it.

How is it possible to express *knowledge* of one's current or future actions by expressing intentions? There are two sorts of assumptions that can make this possibility look deeply mysterious. The first assumption is simply that intention and knowledge are different sorts of psychological states. If they are different states, how can you express the one by expressing the other? The second assumption is that it must be possible to give an account of the epistemic justification of the beliefs constituting agents' knowledge. Given that intentions are held for practical, not for epistemic, reasons, it is not clear how beliefs expressed by expressing intentions are supposed to meet the requirement of epistemic justification.

Some of Anscombe's remarks seem to commit her to the rejection of both assumptions. She characterizes agent's knowledge as knowledge 'in intention' (1957: 57), and she speaks of 'practical knowledge' (p. 82), where a defining feature of the latter is this: if a claim to such knowledge turns out to be mistaken, even though the agent didn't change her mind as regards the intention expressed, the mistake (in Theophrastus' words) 'is one of performance, not of judgment' (p. 5). Connectedly, Anscombe maintains that, if 'I'm replenishing the house water-supply' is a claim to practical knowledge, the way to contradict my claim would not be to say 'You aren't, since there is a hole in the pipe,' but '"Oh, no, you aren't," said by someone who thereupon sets out, e.g. to make a hole in the pipe with a pick-axe' (p. 55). Thus on Anscombe's account, while the concept of practical knowledge is not the same as that of intention, the two concepts pick out the same psychological state: a successfully executed intention constitutes practical knowledge. At least this is a natural and common reading of the Theophrastus point. The incorrectness of what you say when you express an unrealized intention is no objection to your claim, any more than failure to carry out a command is an objection to the command. This account of 'practical knowledge' implies a version of what I called earlier 'minimalism': it is plausible that, as regards 'practical knowledge' in Anscombe's sense, the issue of how beliefs acquire epistemic justification simply does not arise, 'practical knowledge' being a matter of intention, not of belief. In other words, Anscombe's rejection of the first assumption (that intention and agents' knowledge are distinct psychological states) goes hand in hand with her rejection of the second assumption (that an account of agents' knowledge has to be an account of the epistemic justification of certain beliefs).

The classical objection to Anscombe's account of practical knowledge is due to David Pears:

> Why must we assume that, in the circumstances described, the speaker has made only one mistake, a mistake in his performance? It is surely obvious that he has made two mistakes, one in his performance (which failed to fit his intention), and one in his earlier utterance (which failed to fit his performance). (1975: 51)

One problem with Anscombe's 'one mistake' assumption is that it receives no defense. Another problem is that it may be incoherent. For it's hard to see why, on her account, it should not be possible (indeed natural), in expressing an intention, to aim to express *both* an intention *and* practical knowledge. But, relative to the aim to express practical knowledge, incorrectness would turn out to be an objection to the utterance after all. For these and other reasons, Anscombe's account of practical knowledge has been somewhat less influential than AT itself.

Suppose we try to develop AT under the 'two mistakes' view. How should we conceive of the relation between intentions and the beliefs constituting agents' knowledge? We can distinguish three positions here. One is that expressing an intention serves as an *epistemic basis* for knowledge of one's current and future actions. The idea may not have to be that I *infer* what I'm doing from expressed intentions (which would hardly be consistent with AT). Rather, as Kevin Falvey (2000) has argued, perhaps I 'employ' an expression of intention as a description of what I am doing. The second position is to embrace a reductive account of intention in terms of beliefs about future action: expressions of intention *just are* expressions of belief (Velleman 1989). According to the third position, an intention to do something (normally) *commits* us to the factual belief that we will do the thing (Wilson 2000; Moran 2001). Now the first two positions, as developed by Falvey and Velleman respectively, are explicitly rationalist: they are designed to explain the epistemic entitlement in virtue of which certain beliefs constitute knowledge. The third theory is less clear on this issue. It insists, in what is sometimes described as a broadly Kantian spirit, on the distinctively practical source of agents' knowledge. A good illustration is the following passage from Moran:

> It is as an expression of the authority of reason that [the agent] can and must answer the question of his belief or action by reflection on the reasons in favour of this belief or action. To do otherwise would be for him to take the course of his belief or action to be up to

> something other than his sense of the best reasons, and if he thinks *that*, there's no point in his deliberating about what to do. (2001: 127)

Whether this should be taken to provide materials for satisfying, or grounds for rejecting, the demand for an account of epistemic justification is not obvious. Moran apparently seeks to construct a rationalist account. For one of his main concerns is with our 'right' to take the answer to a 'deliberative question' to settle the factual question of our actions or beliefs (2003: 405). The interesting question is whether the sort of explanation one might offer here – for example, Moran's neo-Kantian proposal that we deliberate under the idea of deliberation being efficacious – provides materials for an informative and completely general account of the *epistemic* justification of agents' beliefs as to what they are doing.

At this point, I want to bring in the three issues mentioned earlier:

1 the relation between agents' knowledge and intentional action;
2 the phenomenology of action; and
3 the relation between agents' knowledge and practical rationality.

I will not explore the three issues individually. Rather I want to articulate two lines of argument that illustrate some of the complex interconnections between them.

First, consider what might be called the realist argument for empiricism, connecting (1) and (2). Suppose that our view on (1) is a robust form of realism: intentional actions are events which exist, and are constituted, independently of the agent's awareness of them. An obvious question, then, is how facts concerning such independently constituted events get round to the agent. A plausible answer is that the agent draws on a distinctive source of knowledge; a natural way of developing this answer is in terms of a distinctive experience of agency; and an obvious commitment of this way of developing the answer is a certain, completely general, claim about (2), to the effect that agency involves a distinctive type of experience.

Here is a counterargument, connecting (3) and (2). Suppose we label Confidence the disposition to believe that one is (or will be) doing the things one intends to do. The passage from Moran quoted earlier offers one way of thinking about Confidence. Moran claims that Confidence is a necessary, and completely general, condition of engaging in practical deliberation. One might object that it is possible, and can be perfectly sensible, to reach an intention of doing something while one is suspending judgment on whether one will actually do it. (See Bratman 1987 for a defense of what he calls 'intention–belief incompleteness.') Even so, one might agree that violations of Confidence have to be exceptional – that intending to ϕ involves a (defeasible) commitment to the belief that one is (or will be) ϕ-ing. Spelling out the source and scope of the commitment is a delicate matter, but the basic idea is simple: it is surely a datum that, if you definitely believe you won't ϕ or won't be able to ϕ, it would be irrational for you to intend to ϕ. If intending to ϕ (perhaps defeasibly) commits one to the belief that one is (or will be) ϕ-ing, the datum would be readily intelligible. Now on this view there is an interesting sense in which the question of what I am/will be doing is not, for me, a theoretical issue. The question will often be settled for me in virtue of my intentions, held for practical reasons. Moreover, we should not, on this view, think of AT merely as a description of ordinary practice, but as something of a requirement. Insofar as I have an intention to ϕ, it's a requirement of practical rationality that I answer the question of whether I am (or will be) ϕ-ing by expressing my intention. These points encourage two kinds of objection to the empiricist project. A weaker objection might be that there is no *need* for an experiential source of knowledge of one's own intentional actions, given that such knowledge is available in virtue of one's intentions. A stronger objection might be that there can be no *room* for an experiential source: relying on such a source would involve a form of irrationality. It would involve treating the question of what one is doing as a wholly theoretical matter, contrary to the requirements of practical rationality. Of course neither argument would directly cast doubt on the existence of a 'distinctive experience of agency' of the kind, or kinds, appealed to by empiricists. Nevertheless, by subverting the empiricist project, the two arguments would question the assumption that it *has to be* possible to identify a single distinctive type of experience, as opposed to, say, a range of different sorts of experience that may be involved in acting intentionally (for instance various sorts of perceptual experience, sometimes effort, attention or inattention, and so on). Moreover, reversing the empiricist direction of explanation, anti-empiricists might argue that the phenomenological difference between active and passive movements partly consists in the fact that, in the active case, one's experience is informed by agents' knowledge.

A detailed analysis and assessment of the dialectical situation here is beyond the scope of the present review. But I want to highlight the importance of the issue of realism and its connection with the nature of action explanation. At the heart of Anscombe's account of intentional action lies the dual commitment that (a) actions are intentional in virtue of being intelligible in terms of the agent's reasons, and (b) the agent's possession of non-observational knowledge is an essential prerequisite of her action's being intelligible in this way. Contrary to the robust form of realism underpinning the realist argument for empiricism, on this view intentional actions are not constituted independently of agents' knowledge: the latter has to be appealed to in an account of *what it is* to act intentionally. Anscombe's view is, of course, consistent with a more modest form of realism. On her view, agents can certainly be mistaken about their actions and, anyhow, there is no prospect of reducing intentional action to agents' awareness. Still, on this sort of view, intentional actions and agents' knowledge are, as it were, made for each other. Correlatively, a certain general skepticism about the justification of agents' beliefs would arguably be incoherent. This has an important bearing on how to think about the sort of explanation we should expect from a philosophical account of agents' knowledge. Thus one suggestion might be that both empiricism and rationalism rest on the mistaken assumption that a general skepticism concerning the justification of agents' beliefs is coherent and needs to be addressed, and refuted, by an empiricist or rationalist epistemology. One the other hand, of course, many would argue that (b) should be rejected – specifically, that it has been superseded by the causal theory of action. For the latter is often taken to provide an account of what it is to act intentionally that makes no reference to agents' knowledge at all. Thus, explicitly or (more often) implicitly, theories of agents' knowledge reflect the theorist's views on the nature of action explanation.

I want to conclude by looking at the way the debate between empiricists and advocates of AT affects the interpretation of pathological cases such as the disorder of self-awareness mentioned at the beginning. On an empiricist account, the following is conceivable. An agent may fail to be informed of her intentional actions in the normal way due to a loss or impairment of the experience of agency. Some empiricists speculate that the latter may be caused by a breakdown of the sub-personal monitoring mechanisms underpinning the ordinary experience of agency (see for example Campbell 1999). Put schematically, the picture is this:

> Defective sub-personal monitoring → loss of the experience of agency → lack of first-person knowledge of agency → 'it seems to me that it is not me who is walking, talking, or writing.'

This kind of account encourages us to think of the impairment of agents' knowledge as a matter of defective *access* to one's intentional actions. Such an approach has two notable implications. One is that the impairment of agents' knowledge does not conceptually entail an impairment of intentional action (though of course it may *give rise* to many sorts of problems, including problems of action control). Another implication is that it should be possible to make *rational* sense of the patient's 'impression' of not being the agent of his actions. Indeed, the account provides materials for a rational explanation of a patient's later *belief*, or delusion (during the psychotic phase of schizophrenia), that it is not he who is walking or talking or writing.

On both of these points, advocates of AT will disagree. On their view, the disorder of self-awareness of which the patient complains has to be understood as a disorder of intention and practical rationality. Specifically, they may suggest that understanding the impression of not being the agent of one's actions requires understanding an impairment of Confidence: of our ordinary disposition to believe that we are, or will be, doing what we intend to do. Commonsense psychology is arguably not unfamiliar with the phenomenon. There seems to be an intelligible connection between, for example, severe depression and a lack of conviction about one's efficacy (see Marcel 2003). The question is whether that sort of explanation can be adapted and extended to the case of disorders of self-awareness in schizophrenia. (See some of the papers in Hoerl 2001 for discussion.) What is clear is that, on this approach, the impairment of self-awareness is not so much a matter of impaired epistemic access to one's intentional actions as a matter of impaired intentional agency.

See also: VOLITION AND THE WILL (13); INTENTION (14); THE EXPLANATORY ROLE OF CONSCIOUSNESS (24); BODILY AWARENESS AND BODILY ACTION (29); KANT (64); ANSCOMBE (74).

References

Anscombe, G. E. M. (1957). *Intention*. Oxford: Blackwell.

Bratman, M. (1987). *Intention, Plans, and Practical Reason*. Cambridge, MA: Harvard University Press.

Campbell, J. (1999). Schizophrenia, the space of reasons, and thinking as a motor process. *Monist*, 82, 609–625.

Falvey, K. (2000). Knowledge in intention. *Philosophical Studies*, 99, 21–44.

Ginet, C. (1990). *On Action*. Cambridge: Cambridge University Press.

Hoerl, C. (guest editor) (2001). *On Understanding and Explaining Schizophrenia* (= *Philosophy, Psychiatry, and Psychology*, 8 (2/3), special issue).

Marcel, A. (2003). The sense of agency: Awareness and ownership of action. In Roessler and Eilan (eds), 48–93.

Moran, R. (2001). *Authority and Estrangement*. Princeton: Princeton University Press.

Moran, R. (2003). Reponses to O'Brien and Shoemaker. *European Journal of Philosophy*, 11, 402–419.

O'Brien, L. (2003). On knowing one's own actions. In Roessler and Eilan (eds), 358–382.

O'Shaughnessy, B. (2003). The epistemology of physical action. In Roessler and Eilan (eds), 345–357.

Parnas, J. and Sass, L. (2001). Self, solipsism and schizophrenic delusion. In Hoerl (guest ed.), 101–120.

Peacocke, C. (2003). Action: Awareness, Ownership, and Knowledge. In Roessler and Eilan (eds), 94–110.

Pears, D. (1975). Wanting and intending. In D. Perars, *Questions in the Philosophy of Mind*. London: Duckworth.

Roessler, J., and Eilan, N. (eds) (2003). *Agency and Self-Awareness*. Oxford: Oxford University Press.

Velleman, D. (1989). *Practical Reflection*. Princeton: Princeton University Press.

Wilson, G. J. (2000). Proximal practical foresight. *Philosophical Studies*, 99, 3–19.

31

Practical Reasoning

BART STREUMER

To be able to say what practical reasoning is, we first need to say what reasoning is and what the conclusion of a process of reasoning is. I shall do this in the first two sections. We can then make a distinction between practical and theoretical reasoning. There are three main ways to do this, which I shall survey in the next two sections. I shall end by suggesting that there are different kinds of practical reasoning.

Reasoning

As Harman (1986) has emphasized, reasoning should be distinguished from logic. Whereas logic is the study of relations of entailment between propositions, reasoning is the process of modifying one's mental states in a rational way, either by forming additional mental states or by giving up existing ones. But this does not mean that there is no relation between reasoning and logic. For the fact that one or more propositions that we believe entail a further proposition can make it rational to reason in a certain way.

Consider a simple example. Suppose that I have the following two beliefs:

(BELIEF:) It is going to rain.
(BELIEF:) If it is going to rain, the streets will get wet.

The propositions that are the contents of these two beliefs together entail the proposition that the streets will get wet. This fact is a reason not to retain beliefs in the former two propositions while forming a belief in the negation of the latter proposition (Streumer 2007a).[1] Now suppose that I am planning to go outside, and that I need to decide which shoes to wear. In that case, I also have a reason to form a belief about whether or not the streets will get wet. And these two reasons together make it rational for me to engage in the following process of reasoning:

(BELIEF:) It is going to rain.
(BELIEF:) If it is going to rain, the streets will get wet.
So, (BELIEF:) The streets will get wet.

Of course, actual processes of reasoning are normally much more complex. Moreover, though this example may suggest that reasoning is a fully conscious processes, actual processes of reasoning are often partly or wholly unconscious. But I think this example nevertheless gives us a broadly accurate picture of the nature of reasoning, and in what follows I shall assume this picture to be correct.[2]

The Conclusion of Reasoning

What is the conclusion of a process of reasoning? Logicians sometimes talk about the conclusion of an argument, but what they mean by this is a proposition that is entailed by the propositions that are the premises of this argument (Sainsbury 2001). The conclusion of a process of reasoning cannot be a conclusion in this sense, since it is not a proposition but a mental state.

It may instead be thought that the conclusion of a process of reasoning is the mental state that results from this process. But this cannot be right either. Suppose that I go through the process of reasoning that I have just described, and that my going through this process results in my being anxious about going outside. My being anxious is clearly not the conclusion of this process, since it is not a response to the reasons to which this process of reasoning was a response (that is, the reason given by the fact that the contents of the first two beliefs entail the content of the third belief and the reason given by the fact that I need to decide which shoes to wear). So perhaps we should say instead that a mental state is the conclusion of a process of reasoning if and only if it results from this process of reasoning and it is formed in response to the reasons to which this process is a response.

The First View: The Conclusion of Practical Reasoning Is an Action

There are three main views about the distinction between practical and theoretical reasoning. According to the first view, whereas the conclusion of theoretical reasoning is a belief, the conclusion of practical reasoning is an action. Following Anscombe (1957, § 33), this view is almost universally attributed to Aristotle, though some deny that he held this view (Charles 1984).[3] Contemporary philosophers who hold this view include Dancy (2004) and Tenenbaum (2007).

Consider another example. Suppose that I have the following two mental states:

(DESIRE:) To avoid getting wet.
(BELIEF:) I will only avoid getting wet if I take an umbrella.

The first of these mental states is a desire and the second is a belief about a necessary means to achieve the thing desired. According to this view, taking these two mental states as premises, I can go through a process of reasoning that has the following conclusion:

So, (ACTION:) Taking an umbrella.

Philosophers who hold this view should adopt a wider definition of reasoning and of the conclusion of a process of reasoning: they should say that reasoning is the process of modifying or acting on one's mental states in a rational way, and that a mental state or an action is the conclusion of a process of reasoning if and only if it results from this process of reasoning and it is formed or performed in response to the reasons to which this process is a response.

The example I gave in the first section suggested that we engage in processes of reasoning partly in response to reasons that are given by facts about relations of entailment between propositions. That seems to be a problem for this view, since actions do not seem to have propositions as their contents. Philosophers who hold this view can deal with this problem in two different ways. First, they can say that the content of an action is identical to the content of the intention with which it is done, and that the contents both of this intention and of the desires and beliefs that are the premises of a process of practical reasoning are propositions.[4] But then they seem forced to say that the relations of entailment between these propositions are different from the relations of entailment between propositions that are the contents of beliefs. For consider the following process of reasoning:

(DESIRE:) To avoid getting wet.
(BELIEF): I will avoid getting wet if I take an umbrella.
So, (ACTION:) Taking an umbrella.

The second premise of this process says that taking an umbrella is a sufficient means to avoid getting wet, not that it is a necessary means. Therefore, if the propositions that are the contents of the premises of this process were the contents of beliefs, they would not entail the proposition that is the content of the conclusion. But this nevertheless seems to be a rational process of practical reasoning. Philosophers who deal with the problem in this way therefore seem forced to say that the logic that applies to practical reasoning is different from the logic that applies to theoretical reasoning: according to the logic that applies to practical reasoning, they seem forced to say, the fallacy of affirming the consequent (that is, the fallacy of inferring *p* from *if p then q* and *q*) is not a fallacy, but a valid inference (Kenny 1966).[5]

A second way to deal with the problem that actions do not seem to have propositions as their contents is to deny that practical reasoning is a response to reasons given by facts about relations of entailment between propositions, and to say instead that it is a response to reasons of a different kind (Dancy 2004). Philosophers who deal with the problem in this way usually deny that the premises of a process of practical reasoning are a desire and a belief about a necessary or sufficient means to achieve the thing desired, and claim instead that the premises are beliefs that make it rational to perform an action. For example, suppose that I have the following two mental states:

(BELIEF:) Getting wet will be unpleasant.
(BELIEF:) I will only avoid getting wet if I take an umbrella.

According to these philosophers, the content of the first belief corresponds to a fact that is a reason for action: that is, it corresponds to the fact that getting wet will be unpleasant, which is a reason for taking an umbrella. The content of the second belief corresponds to a fact that is what Dancy (2004) calls an enabling condition: a fact that is not itself a reason for action, but that must obtain for the fact that getting wet will be unpleasant to be a reason for taking an umbrella. If that is so, these two beliefs together make it rational to reason to the following conclusion:

So, (ACTION:) Taking an umbrella.

The view that practical reasoning is not a response to reasons that are given by facts about relations of entailment between propositions is sometimes expressed by saying that practical reasoning is not a form of inference or that practical reasoning is non-inferential (for discussion, see Streumer 2007b).[6] This need not apply exclusively to practical reasoning: if practical reasoning is non-inferential, some theoretical reasoning is likely to be non-inferential as well.

The Second View: The Conclusion of Practical Reasoning Is an Intention

The second view about the difference between practical and theoretical reasoning is that, whereas the conclusion of theoretical reasoning is a belief, the conclusion of practical reasoning is a desire or an intention. According to Charles (1984), Aristotle's real view was that the conclusion of practical reasoning is a desire to perform an action. But most contemporary philosophers who hold a view of this kind, such as Broome (1999, 2002, 2009), think that the conclusion of practical reasoning is an intention.[7]

This view is generally defended by raising objections to the view that the conclusion of practical reasoning is an action. For example, Broome writes:

> Forming an intention [by reasoning] is making a decision. Making a decision is as close to acting as reasoning can possibly get you. Reasoning could not actually get you to act, because acting requires more than reasoning ability. (1999: 407)

And Raz writes that the view that the conclusion of practical reasoning is an intention

> allows for failure to act in the way entailed by the premises which is not a failure of reasoning but is due to inability, forgetfulness, weakness of will, etc. [...] [This] view is better able to represent the difference between non-action owing to failure of reasoning and non-action owing to other factors. (1978: 5–6)

Perhaps the best way to formulate this objection is this. Suppose that a process of practical reasoning goes as well as it possibly can, except that it does not lead to the performance of an action. We would not normally describe this as a fault *in* one's reasoning. Instead, we would describe it as a failure to act *on* one's reasoning. This suggests that the conclusion of practical reasoning is not an action, but is instead the mental state that comes as close as possible to the performance of an action, which is an intention.[8]

In response to this objection, philosophers who think that the conclusion of practical reasoning is an action can admit that their view conflicts somewhat with our normal use of the term 'reasoning,' but they can say that, all things considered, this does not mean that the conclusion of practical reasoning is not an action. For they can remind us that something is the conclusion of a process of reasoning if it results from this process of reasoning and if it occurs in response to the reasons to which this process of reasoning is a response. And, since it must surely be possible for practical reasoning to be a response to reasons for action, they can say, it must be possible for the conclusion of practical reasoning to be an action rather than merely an intention. This reply is strongest if it is combined with the view that practical reasoning is non-inferential, since, on this view, practical reasoning is not even partly a response to reasons that are given by facts about relations of entailment between propositions; it is instead wholly a response to reasons for action.

A second objection to the view that practical reasoning results in an action is that practical reasoning can result in an action that is not performed immediately, but is performed much later instead. For example, I can now reason about whether I shall travel to New York next year, and such a process of reasoning seems practical even if it will only lead to my travelling to New York a year from now. But it seems implausible to say that this process of reasoning keeps going for whole year until the time at which I finally travel to New York: after all, for most of this time, I am not actively considering either the premises of this process or the action that it will lead to. Moreover, if part of the criterion for whether a process of reasoning is practical is whether it results in an action, we will not know for a whole year whether this process of reasoning is really practical or whether it merely seems practical because it will not actually result in my travelling to New York. But we surely do not have to wait for a whole year to find out whether this process of reasoning is practical. In such cases, therefore, it seems more appropriate to say that the conclusion of practical reasoning is an intention.

Unlike the previous objection, however, this objection cannot show that the conclusion of practical reasoning is never an action. It can only show that the conclusion of practical reasoning is sometimes an intention, which leaves it open that, in other cases, the conclusion of practical reasoning is an action.

The Third View: The Conclusion of Practical Reasoning is a Normative Belief

The third view about the distinction between practical and theoretical reasoning is that, whereas the conclusion of practical reasoning is a belief about reasons for action or about what we ought to do, the conclusion of theoretical reasoning is a belief of a different kind. This view is defended less often, but it is favorably discussed by Raz (1978) and endorsed by Audi (1989).

One reason for holding this view is that we may think that, if someone engages in reasoning about what someone else ought to do, such a process of reasoning is practical, even though its conclusion will not normally be an intention but a belief about what the other person ought to do (Raz 1978). Of course, defenders of the other two views may not be impressed by this: they may deny that reasoning that does not affect one's own intentions or actions is practical, and they may defend this denial by saying that practical reasoning must be first-personal in some way. Another reason for holding this view is similar to the second objection that I discussed in the previous section: we may think that a process of practical reasoning can result in an intention that is not formed immediately but that is instead formed much later, and we may think that the conclusion of such a process of reasoning is a belief about reasons for action or about what I ought to do.

As before, however, these objections cannot show that the conclusion of practical reasoning is never an intention or an action. They can only show that the conclusion of practical reasoning is sometimes a belief about reasons for action or about what we ought to do, which leaves it open that, in other cases, the conclusion of practical reasoning is an intention or an action.

There is also a further objection to all three views about the distinction between practical and theoretical reasoning that I have discussed. In the first section I suggested that processes of reasoning can result not only in forming additional mental states, but also in giving up existing mental states. Processes of reasoning that result in giving up mental states do not result in an action or an intention, and it is unclear what we should take their conclusions to be instead (Harman 1999). But it does seem that such processes of reasoning can be practical, as long as they result in the non-performance of an action that I might otherwise have performed, in giving up an intention, or in giving up a belief about reasons for action or about what we ought to do.

Different Kinds of Practical Reasoning

The most plausible conclusion to draw from this, I think, is that there are different kinds of practical reasoning: reasoning that concludes with a belief about reasons for action or about what we ought to do, reasoning that concludes with an intention, and reasoning that concludes with an action. These processes of reasoning often succeed each other and, if they do so immediately, they can be said to form one continuous process of practical reasoning. But these processes may not always succeed each other immediately, and practical reasoning can also result in the non-performance of an action, in giving up an intention, or in giving up a belief about reasons for action or about what we ought to do.[9]

See also: MOTIVATING REASONS (19); DELIBERATION AND DECISION (32); MOTIVATIONAL STRENGTH (33); AKRASIA AND IRRATIONALITY (35); RATIONALITY (36); DAVIDSON (73); ANSCOMBE (74).

Notes

1 I here use the term 'reason' to mean normative reason, and I take normative reasons to be facts that count in favor of, or count against, actions or mental states.

2 For a different picture of reasoning, see Broome (1999, 2002, 2009, this volume). Broome takes reasoning to be a means to bring ourselves to satisfy requirements of rationality, and he takes it to be an open question whether rationality gives us reasons.

3 For Aristotle's brief remarks on this subject, see *The Movement of Animals*, 701^a6–24, and the *Nicomachean Ethics*, 1141^b21–22, 1147^a24–b5.

4 They can say that these contents are propositions because they can be reformulated from, for example, 'To avoid getting wet' to 'That I avoid getting wet' and from 'Taking an umbrella' to 'That I take an umbrella.' For doubts about this, see Dancy 2009.

5 Alternatively, however, they can also say that the same fact about a relation of entailment between propositions can give us different kinds of reasons, and that practical and theoretical reasoning are responses to these different kinds of reasons. For example, they can say that the fact that *p* and *if p then q* entails *q* is a reason against both believing *p*, believing *if p then q* and believing *not-q*, and that this very same fact is also a reason against both desiring *q*, believing *if p then q*, and failing to do *p*. And they can say that, whereas theoretical reasoning is a response to a reason of the first kind, practical reasoning is a response to a reason of the second kind. Anscombe (1995) makes a suggestion along these lines, though she does not formulate it in terms of reasons.

6 Philosophers who hold this view usually also deny that practical reasoning is a response to reasons that are given by facts about relations of probabilification between propositions.

7 Harman (1999) similarly claims that practical reasoning 'is concerned with' intention.

8 This formulation of the objection was suggested to me by Joseph Raz.

9 I am grateful to Jonathan Dancy, Andrea Lechler, and Constantine Sandis for helpful comments.

References

Anscombe, G. E. M. (1957). *Intention*. Cambridge, MA: Harvard University Press.

Anscombe, G. E. M. (1995). Practical inference.' In Rosalind Hursthouse, Gavin Lawrence and Warren Quinn (eds.), *Virtues and Reasons*. Oxford: Clarendon Press, 1–34.

Aristotle (1984a). *Nicomachean Ethics*. In Aristotle, *The Complete Works of Aristotle*, edited by J. Barnes, Vol. 2. Princeton: Princeton University Press.

Aristotle (1984b). *The Movement of Animals*. In Aristotle, *The Complete Works of Aristotle*, edited by J. Barnes, Vol. 1. Princeton: Princeton University Press.

Audi, R. (1989). *Practical Reasoning*. London: Routledge.

Broome, J. (1999). Normative requirements. *Ratio* 12: 398–419.

Broome, J. (2002). Practical reasoning. In J. Bermúdez and A. Millar (eds), *Reason in Nature: New Essays in the Theory of Rationality*. Oxford: Oxford University Press, 85–112.

Broome, J. (2009). The unity of reasoning? In S. Robertson (ed.), *Spheres of Reason: New Essays in the Philosophy of Normativity*. Oxford: Oxford University Press, 62–92.

Charles, D. (1984). *Aristotle's Philosophy of Action*. London: Duckworth.

Dancy, J. (2004). *Ethics without Principles*. Oxford: Clarendon Press.

Dancy, J. (2009). Action, content and inference. In H.-J. Glock and J. Hyman (eds), *Wittgenstein and Analytic Philosophy: Essays for P. M. S. Hacker*. Oxford: Oxford University Press, 278–298.

Harman, G. (1986). *Change in View*. Cambridge, MA: MIT Press.

Harman, G. (1999). *Reasoning, Meaning, and Mind*. Oxford: Clarendon Press.

Kenny, A. (1966). Practical inference. *Analysis*, 26: 65–75.

Raz, J. (1978). Introduction. In J. Raz (ed.), *Practical Reasoning*. Oxford: Oxford University Press, 1–17.

Sainsbury, M. (2001). *Logical Forms*, 2nd edn. Oxford: Blackwell.
Streumer, B. (2007a). Reasons and entailment. *Erkenntnis* 66: 353–374.
Streumer, B. (2007b). Inferential and non-inferential reasoning. *Philosophy and Phenomenological Research*, 74: 1–29.
Tenenbaum, S. (2007). The conclusion of practical reason. In S. Tenenbaum (ed.), *New Trends in Philosophy: Moral Psychology*. Amsterdam: Rodopi, 323–343.

Further reading

Bratman, M. (1987). *Intention, Plans, and Practical Reason*. Cambridge, MA: Harvard University Press.
Millgram, E. (ed.) (2001). *Varieties of Practical Reasoning*. Cambridge, MA: MIT Press.
Raz, J. (ed.) (1978). *Practical Reasoning*. Oxford: Oxford University Press.
Raz, J. (1999). *Practical Reason and Norms*, 2nd edn. Oxford: Oxford University Press.

32

Deliberation and Decision

PHILIP PETTIT

The Decision-Theoretic Picture

Does every action originate in a decision to perform that action? It cannot do so if decision is itself an intentional action: if it is a mental act, as some have taken it to be, in which an agent resolves uncertainty about what to do in a given context. For if action were always supposed to originate in decision, and decision were itself an action, then we would face a regress. The regress would be similar to that which Donald Davidson (1980) invoked in criticism of the idea that every intentional action must originate in an act of will, repeating – without apparently being aware of it – a point that Thomas Hobbes (1994: 125) had made in 1640: 'a man can no more say he will will, than he will will will, and so make an infinite repetition of the word will.'

But decisions do seem to count as actions. Thus, if you claim to have decided something, we naturally assume that you were led to do so on the basis of your desires and beliefs, and we treat the decision in just the way we would treat an action. Then, while we certainly think that some actions begin in distinct decisions, we cannot think that all do so. It seems that we are committed to thinking that there are two types of action: those which originate in decisions and those which do not.

This dichotomy need not cause problems by suggesting a bifurcation in the nature of action. For there is one obvious basis on which actions do fall into two categories of the kind envisaged. Some actions are planned in advance and some are not, and we may equate those that originate in decision with those that are planned in advance, those that do not originate in decision with those that are not diachronically planned. The claim, perfectly plausible in itself, is that some actions originate in prior decisions, others do not.

But does not the tie between decision and action seem to be closer than that? After all, we ask about the decision you made in taking such and such an action even in cases where there is no question of your having had a prior plan. How to build this assumption into the emerging picture?

The way to build it in, I think, is to say that there are prior decisions and there are simultaneous decisions, and to hold that, while only some actions originate in prior acts of decision-making, still all actions are, simultaneously or synchronically, acts of decision-making; all actions involve, incorporate, or display simultaneous decisions.

The simultaneous act of decision-making, on this account, is not something distinct from the action, something in which the action might originate; it is that very action, taken under a certain description.

To adopt this picture is to equate deciding with forming an intention, as it is sometimes said. The decision is distinct from the action decided upon when the intention is formed in advance of the behavior that enacts it – when it involves making a plan for that future behavior (Bratman 1987) – and it is not distinct when there is no such temporal lag: when acting thus and so is just acting with this or that intention, not enacting an intention previously formed. Deciding, on this way of thinking, is forming an intention in respect of a certain set of options – if you like, choosing between those options – and it is distinct from enacting the chosen option only in the case where the intention is formed, or the choice made, in respect of options that are not yet available to the agent.

This nexus of claims makes sense of assumptions that are presupposed in decision theory, and I describe it as the decision-theoretic picture (Jeffrey 1983; Joyce 1999). Decision theory is supposed to explicate something that deserves to be described as decision, and yet is meant to apply to every case of intentional action, at least among suitably rational agents. Rational agents will have well-defined probability and utility functions – regimented versions, by most accounts, of systems of belief and desire – and they will act in such a way as to maximize expected utility: they will act so as to maximize the satisfaction of their desires according to their beliefs. Any action of that kind will count as a decision in the sense of the theory. And it will count as a decision, whether it is an action that relates to what is to be done at a future time or an action that relates to what is to be done now: whether or not it is a decision that is distinct from the action decided upon.

To sum up the discussion so far, there are three claims built into the decision-theoretic picture, all of them being well grounded in our common assumptions and ways of speaking:

- First, every decision is an action.
- Second, on pain of regress, while some actions originate in decisions – that is, prior acts of decision-making – not every action does so.
- Third, there is nonetheless no action without decision: actions that do not originate in prior decisions are, simultaneously, decision-making acts.

The Decision-plus-Deliberation Picture

But at this point the notion of deliberation has to be put in the picture. Whenever you make a decision, we are liable to ask about what weighed with you in deciding as you did: what tilted the balance, to use a standard metaphor, in favor of the line you took. We generally think that it makes sense to ask that sort of question, treating you as an authority in seeking the 'weighing reasons' that led you one way or another (Broome 2004; but see Dancy 2004). The assumption amounts to an assumption that, wherever there is a decision, there is deliberation: the agent considers and compares the features of the options available and is led on that basis, as by reasons, to a choice.

The word 'deliberation' derives etymologically from the Latin word *libra* for a weighing scale and it seems appropriate to link it with this sort of process rather than to use it with less demanding connotations, as is sometimes done (Skyrms 1990). I shall assume in what follows that deliberation is a process in which an agent explicitly or implicitly considers the features of the options available in a certain choice and, all going well, is led to the decision which those features recommend as being the best.

Does decision theory in itself make room for deliberation? Decision theory starts from the degrees of utility that an agent attaches to certain states of affairs – that is, roughly, from the intensities with which the agent ranks those states of affairs against one another – and from the probabilities with which the agent links each of an available set of options to those states of affairs, no matter how the probabilities are understood. Then it identifies that option (or sub-set of options) in the relevant set which the agent is rationally required to select, and hence will select, under the assumption of rationality. But does decision theory have to make suppositions about the features of those options that weigh with the agent in anything that might deserve to be called deliberation?

This question may be introduced by analogy with a question raised in the theory of inference – in particular, inference of the sort a robot might display. Suppose that there is a system of artificial intelligence built so as to satisfy, for example, *modus ponens*. Whenever the system counts as endorsing sentences or propositions of the form '*p*' and 'if *p*, then *q*' – whenever it counts as representing its environment in corresponding ways – then, so long as the conditions satisfy normal specifications, it transitions to endorsing the proposition or sentence '*q*' – that is, to forming a *q*-representation of how things are (Cummins 1983). Should we say that such a system draws inferences in accordance with the *modus ponens*?

In one sense, yes; in another, no. Clearly the system forms new representations on a pattern which conforms to that rule. But, equally clearly, it does not relate to that rule in the way you or I might. It need not have any awareness of that rule as such: not in the way logicians are aware of it. And, more important still, it need not have any awareness of what the rule requires in particular circumstances; it need not form the belief that '*q*' on the basis of forming the belief that the truth of '*q*' follows from the truth of '*p*,' taken together with 'if *p*, then *q*.' It need not have the wherewithal to form the belief that '*p*' on the basis of forming the belief which most of us would express in the words: 'so *q*' or 'so therefore, *q*.' There is nothing about how it performs that would force us to ascribe to it the ability to think in 'so–therefore' terms.

Let us say that a system that draws *modus ponens* inferences without being able to think in 'so–therefore' terms conforms to the rule but does not apply it. The question that confronts us about deliberation and decision theory can be phrased in parallel terms. Does the decision-theoretic agent who conforms to the theory's principles of rational decision-making have to apply such principles, thinking in 'so–therefore' terms? In particular, does the agent have to register properties of the rival options in any choice and let a consideration of those features indicate how it is rational to choose? Or might such an agent merely conform to the principles of rational decision-making, as the robot conforms to the *modus ponens*?

Once this matter is raised, it is pretty obvious that, for all that decision theory says and the decision-theoretic picture supposes, the rational agent is not required to register those features of rival options which might make salient the rationality of choosing this option rather than that; there need be nothing that would correspond to thinking in 'so–therefore' terms. The decision-theoretic picture merely supposes that, when the agent has beliefs and desires which make a certain choice rational, then, other things being equal, the agent will make that choice. It says nothing about how the agent is led to the choice. In particular, it does not suppose that there has to be any process of registering and weighing the features of the rival options or any process which might deserve to be described as 'deliberation.'

This is to say that decision theory as such does not rule in deliberation, making it an obligatory feature of rational choice. But does it actively rule it out?

A theory of rational inference would ideally tell us what it was right to infer on the basis of any given set of beliefs, going beyond what strict logic would deliver (Harman 1986). But it might do this without offering any view on the process whereby the rational agent is moved to draw rational inferences, and without any commitment to there being a process in which the agent is moved by registering what deserves to be described as 'reasons' – a process, for example, in which the agent is moved by the recognition that the truth of '*p*' and of 'if *p*, then *q*' ensures the truth of '*q*' and provides reasons for believing that '*q*.' The theory of rational inference would not rule in a process of reasoning of this kind. But neither, of course, would it rule out the relevance of such a process. It would just be silent on the matter.

By analogy with a theory of rational inference, a theory of rational decision will tell us what it was right for an agent to do or decide on the basis of a given set of beliefs and desires. But it can do this without any view on the sort of process whereby the rational agent is moved to make rational decisions, and without any commitment to there being a process in which the agent is moved by registering the properties of rival options and is led by them, as by reasons, to make the rational choice. Decision theory will not rule in a process of deliberation, as the theory of rational inference will not rule in a process of reasoning. But neither will it rule out the presence of such a process. It will posit nothing one way or the other.

On this account, the three claims encoded in the earlier picture stand, but they can be supplemented by a fourth claim, as in the following schema, which spells out the elements in the decision-plus-deliberation picture:

- Every decision is an action – that is, an act of decision-making.
- Some actions originate in prior decisions, but not all of them do.
- All actions, however, involve simultaneous acts of decision-making.
- There is no decision, prior or simultaneous, without deliberation.

As already mentioned, we expect people to be able to provide an account of the reasons that weighed with them in any choice, or at least in any choice in the general run. We expect them to be able to speak about their reasons with a certain authority, whatever its source, and not just to speculate about them as they might speculate about hidden influences. Insofar as we expect this, we appear to endorse the decision-plus-deliberation picture. But is that picture really gripping? Are we really as reflective and intellectual as it makes us seem?

It is certainly unlikely that non-human animals live up to the picture. According to this description, the options over which agents deliberate are *abstracta*, not *concreta*: they are ways-things-might-be – ways the agent knows how to make things be – not actual events. Human beings can identify such entities on the basis of how they answer to abstract linguistic specifications: my helping the beggar is that way-things-may-be, under certain contextual constraints, which makes true the sentence 'I help the beggar.' But it is unclear how creatures without language could ever entertain options as objects of thought and ever deliberate about the features of such options (Pettit 2007).

This restriction does not apply to human beings. But isn't it still implausible to hold that, in the general run of choices, humans invariably deliberate about the options they face: they are invariably in deliberative control?

There are two ways in which deliberation might control a decision and provide support for something like the decision-plus-deliberation picture. It might actively control the decision, as when I go painstakingly through the pros and cons of a particular choice and make up my mind on the basis of this reflection. Or it might control the decision just in a virtual manner. Suppose I go through a certain train of action more or less unthinkingly, as when I drive home or go to the shop to pick up something to eat. There may be no active deliberation whatsoever involved; I may go through the required motions on automatic pilot. But deliberation will still be in virtual control if the following is true: should things go wrong, as in my taking a wrong turn or beginning to pick up hardware rather than food, then the red lights will go on – I will become aware that something is amiss; deliberation will be activated; and deliberation will put me back on the right track (Pettit 1995).

The decision-plus-deliberation picture is committed, not to the view that deliberation is actively present in all our decisions, but only to the view that deliberation generally has at least this sort of virtual or standby control over what we decide and do. And that observation may help to make the picture more persuasive. The presence of even virtual deliberative control would explain why it generally makes sense to ask a human agent for the reasons which carried weight in a decision. The reasons which carried weight may not have been actively considered. They may be the reasons which would have been invoked, had an otherwise unthinking pattern of action gone amiss. After all, it is true of such reasons that the agent's pattern of behavior was required to satisfy them, however unthinking the agent may have been, on pain of putting on the red lights. They exercised control over the behavior, albeit only virtual control, and in that sense they carried weight.

A Common Mistake

Those who master decision theory may be tempted to think that the properties registered in deliberation are properties that decision theory enables us to identify with precision. Thus they may be tempted to think that the property in virtue of which a given option or a probabilistically associated outcome is found attractive by a rational agent is the property of having such-and-such a utility score: being preferred with such-and-such intensity to alternatives. This line of thought would support the idea that a good way to make people more rational would be to have them use decision theory as a deliberative calculus. They would compute the utility and probability scores of different outcomes, do the usual expectational computations, and in that way identify the option it is rational for them to choose.

This is a mistaken and seriously confused way of thinking (Pettit 2002). In the first place the recommended methodology is not really feasible, since there is no way in which we can tell the degrees with which we desire different scenarios, or even the degrees of probability we associate with them. These may show up in our preferences, in particular our preferences over certain gambles (Ramsey 1990), but they are not available to us at will, as in a process of introspection (Harman 1986).

In the second place, and perhaps even more strikingly, the recommended methodology would force us to revise an established and intuitively attractive way of thinking (Pettit and Smith 1990; Pettit 2006). When I decide to help a beggar on the street, I may do so out of a desire to be rid of a sense of guilt. But in less pathological cases I will do so out of a desire to help a person in obvious need. On the recommended way of thinking, the property of the philanthropic option which should register with me is that it has a high utility count: it promises to satisfy my philanthropic desire. But, were I to go over to that way of thinking, then there would be a serious shift from the way in which I think in the normal, non-pathological case of philanthropy. In the normal case, I think in such a way that, on my view, helping the beggar is the thing to be done in any scenario where he or she remains in need, other things being equal. But were I to go over to the recommended methodology, I would think in such a way that, on my view, helping the beggar is the thing to be done only in scenarios where I continue to have the philanthropic desire.

There are some desires with which it makes sense to endorse the options they motivate only so long as the desires remain in place. I will make plans to have a smoke after a meeting, or to have a snack later, only on the assumption that I continue to have a yen for a smoke or a snack. But with most desires this is not the case (Parfit 1984). I can sensibly make plans to fulfill such a desire even when it is possible, as I recognize, that I will have ceased to have the desire at the time I am required to act. In such a case, the property of the option which prompts me to desire that very option is not its promising to satisfy my desire – to relieve me of it, as I might be relieved of an itch – but rather an independent property: say, its being just, or generous, or spontaneous, or likely to improve the existing state of things in some way.

Were I to adopt the recommended methodology, the effect would be that I would treat all desires in the manner in which it is appropriate to treat only a yen such as for a smoke or a snack. I would help the beggar, not on the grounds of his or her need, but rather on the grounds that doing so provides me with the best available opportunity for desire-satisfaction. Decision theory may be consistent with deliberation, as on the decision-plus-deliberation picture, but it is not a good guide as to the form which deliberation ought to take.

See also: COLLECTIVE ACTION (9); MOTIVATING REASONS (19); HUMEANISM ABOUT MOTIVATION (20); PRACTICAL REASONING (31); AKRASIA AND IRRATIONALITY (35); RATIONALITY (36); MOTIVATIONAL INTERNALISM AND EXTERNALISM (37).

References

Bratman, M. (1987). *Intention, Plans, and Practical Reason*. Cambridge, MA: Harvard University Press.

Broome, J. (2004). Reasons. In J. Wallace, M. Smith, S. Scheffler, and P. Pettit (eds), *Reason and Value: Themes from the Moral Philosophy of Joseph Raz*. Oxford: Oxford University Press, 28–55.

Cummins, R. (1983). *The Nature of Psychological Explanation*. Cambridge, MA: MIT Press.

Dancy, J. (2004). *Ethics Without Principles*. Oxford: Oxford University Press.

Davidson, D. (1980). *Essays on Actions and Events*. Oxford: Oxford University Press.

Harman, G. (1986). *Change in View*. Cambridge, MA: MIT Press.

Hobbes, T. (1994). *Human Nature and De Corpore Politico: The Elements of Law, Natural and Politic*. Oxford: Oxford University Press.

Jeffrey, R. C. (1983). *The Logic of Decision*, 2nd edn. Chicago: University of Chicago Press.

Joyce, J. M. (1999). *The Foundations of Causal Decision Theory*. Cambridge: Cambridge University Press.

Parfit, D. (1984). *Reasons and Persons*. Oxford: Oxford University Press.

Pettit, P. (2002). Decision theory and folk psychology [1991]. In P. Pettit (2002), *Rules, Reasons, and Norms*, Oxford: Oxford University Press, 192–222.

Pettit, P. (1995). The virtual reality of *Homo economicus*. *Monist* 78: 308–329. [Expanded version in U. Maki (ed.), *The World of Economics*, Cambridge: Cambridge University Press, 2000; reprinted in P. Pettit (2002) *Rules, Reasons, and Norms*, Oxford: Oxford University Press.]

Pettit, P. (2006). Preference, deliberation and satisfaction. In S. Olsaretti (ed.), *Preferences and Well-Being*. Cambridge: Cambridge University Press, 131–153.

Pettit, P. (2007). Rationality, reasoning and group agency. *Dialectica* 61: 495–519.

Pettit, P., and Smith, M. (1990). Backgrounding desire. *Philosophical Review* 99: 565–592. [Reprinted in F. Jackson, P. Pettit, and M. Smith (2004), *Mind, Morality and Explanation*, Oxford: Oxford University Press.]

Ramsey, F. P. (1990). *Philosophical Papers*. Cambridge: Cambridge University Press.

Skyrms, B. (1990). *The Dynamics of Rational Deliberation*. Cambridge, MA: Harvard University Press.

33

Motivational Strength

ALFRED R. MELE

In an article expressing skepticism about the idea that desires vary in motivational strength, Irving Thalberg asks what 'theorists mean when they rate the strength of our [...] desires, aversions [...] and so forth' (1985: 88), and he contends that, 'as soon as we endeavor to clarify what philosophers of action and drive theorists in psychology mean by motivational strength, we run across one obscurity after another' (ibid., p. 103). This chapter's aim is to clarify the notion of motivational strength in the course of reviewing literature on the topic.

Background

Ann's desire to sell her car and Bob's desire to wash his car are *action-desires* – that is, desires to *act* in certain ways. What does the motivational strength of action-desires, in particular, amount to? If desires to *A*, by their very nature, are inclinations to *A*, the motivational strength of a desire to *A* may be the strength of this inclination. What does that amount to? Three answers which have been discussed by skeptics about the idea that desires differ in motivational strength should be rejected. None of these answers has been advanced by any recent friend of this idea – 'the motivational strength idea,' or MSI, for short.

First, the strength of an action-desire is not the desire's 'felt violence or intensity' (Charlton 1988: 127; see Thalberg 1985: 89–90). Friends of MSI claim that a desire with great affective intensity may be motivationally weaker than a competing desire with little or no affective intensity. Ann, a morally upright therapist who experiences, to her own consternation, an intense desire to have sexual relations with a seductive patient, may, in a desire that has little affective intensity, have a stronger inclination to exercise self-control.

Second, having a stronger desire to *A* than to *B* is not to be identified with believing that it would be better to *A* than to *B* (Charlton 1988: 127–128). Agents with this belief may be more strongly motivated to *B* than to *A*, as in ordinary cases of weakness of will. So, at least, some friends of MSI argue (Mele 1987).

Third, by the motivationally stronger desire, friends of MSI do not mean 'the desire which actually prevails, the desire on which the agent acts' (Charlton 1988: 127; see

Thalberg 1985: 89 and 99). Bob's desire to write a book before he dies may be stronger than his desire to visit China before he dies, even if an accident takes his life before he has time to do either. Friends of MSI tend to be realists both about attitudes in general (desires, beliefs, intentions, and the like) and about the motivational strength of such attitudes as action-desires. On a realist view of these things, even if no one – including Bob himself – has behavioral evidence that one of the desires is stronger than the other, there is a fact of the matter about which desire is stronger.

Realism about states that encompass motivation is evident in a definition of 'motivation' offered by psychologist John Atkinson:

> [T]he term *motivation* is used to designate the activated state of the person which occurs when the cues of a situation arouse the expectancy that performance of an act will lead to an incentive for which he has a motive. (1982: 25)

By 'motive,' Atkinson means

> the disposition within the person to strive to approach a certain class of positive incentives (goals) or to avoid a certain class of negative incentives (threats). The definition of a particular class of incentives constitutes the general aim of a particular motive. (Ibid., p. 25)

Motivation, as Atkinson understands it, may perhaps be identified with action-desire or a species thereof.

In the same article, Atkinson writes:

> If a certain kind of activity has been intrinsically satisfying or rewarded [...] there will be an *instigating force (F)* for that activity. This will cause a more or less rapid increase in the strength of an inclination to engage in that activity, an *action tendency (T)*, depending on the magnitude of the force. If a certain kind of activity has been frustrated or punished in the past, there will be an *inhibitory force (I)* and a [...] growth in the strength of a disinclination to act or *negaction tendency (N)*. This is a tendency *not* to do it. The duration of exposure to these forces [...] will determine how strong the action or negaction tendency becomes. The latter, the tendency not to do something, will produce *resistance* to the activity. It opposes, blocks, dampens, the action tendency. That is, it subtracts from the action tendency to determine the *resultant action tendency*. [...] The resultant action tendency competes with resultant action tendencies for other incompatible activities. The strongest of them is expressed in behavior. (1982: 34)

Although this passage has a deterministic ring, a notion of motivational strength need not presuppose determinism (neither global determinism nor local determinism about the workings of the human brain). This is a source of comfort to any libertarians inclined to believe that some desires have more motivational strength than others (Clarke 1994). ('Libertarianism' is the conjunction of incompatibilism and the assertion that there are free actions, including decisions. 'Incompatibilism' is the thesis that determinism is incompatible with there being free actions.) Even if Ann's desire to strike an offensive person is stronger than her desire to walk away instead, it may be open to her to do the latter. Whether this is open depends on what else is true of her. Perhaps an agent can resist a stronger action-desire and act on a weaker one, and perhaps the connection between action-desires and actions is indeterministic in such a way that there is only a probability (less than 1) that one will act on the stronger of two action-desires if one acts on either.

MSI and Vacuity

If Atkinson's position is meant to apply to action-desires, he conceives of such desires as causal forces. Depending on their preferred metaphysics of mind, some friends of MSI may think of the causal force of a desire as the force of the physical condition that realizes the desire, whereas others may view the force as a more intimate feature of the desire. In this chapter, neutrality on this issue is appropriate.

A common criticism of principles which link the motivational strength of action-desires to intentional action – and an indirect criticism of MSI itself – is that such principles are 'vacuous' because there is no way to gauge the relative strengths of our desires to *A* and of our desires to *B* aside from seeing whether we do *A* or *B* (Charlton 1988: 127; Gosling 1990: 175; Thalberg 1985: 96–99). This objection merits attention. Suppose it is claimed that my arms are stronger than my daughter's arms and that her car is faster than mine. We can stage contests to test these claims – relevant weight-lifting contests and drag races. But the claims can be tested in other ways too: for example, we can measure the size of relevant muscles and examine mechanical features of the motionless cars. Because action-desires are internal states, and because their strength is not to be identified with their affective qualities, it may seem that there is, in principle, no possible way to gauge relative strength aside from seeing what the agent does. But is this true?

If one were concerned to measure the strength of an action-desire in some other way, how might one proceed? One who holds a certain view about physical correlates of states of mind might monitor neural activity in the brain. (Obviously, judgments about what mental phenomena are indicated by neural activity of various kinds require a background that includes assumptions about the meanings of mental predicates and past observation of extracranial occurrences statistically correlated with various types of neural activity.) Assuming that action-desires are realized in the brain, this procedure need not be misguided *in principle*, even if current technology is not up to the task. Hypothetical readings might indicate the relative strength of contemporaneous action-desires. And what would they be indicating by indicating this? In a properly functioning agent, they would indicate the relative causal capacity of each desire (or its physical realizer) to issue in a corresponding attempt, given the way the agent is constituted. (In hypothetical agents who, owing to manipulation, cannot try to act as they desire to act, matters are more complicated.)

It should also be observed that, even if seeing whether agents do *A* or *B* is *in fact* our only way of gauging the relative motivational strengths of their competing desires to *A* and to *B*, this does not entail that 'motivational strength' is an empty notion. Imagine a planet on which there are poisonous plants but no understanding of chemistry. Some people there claim that eating a gram of a plant of kind *x* causes a higher fever than eating a gram of a plant of kind *y* because *x*-s contain a more potent or stronger poison than *y*-s. Their only way of gauging the relative strength of poisons requires seeing how ill poison-eaters become. But their claim is not vacuous. As it happens, they are embroiled in a bitter dispute with others, who contend that there are no poisonous plants and that the fevers are caused directly by God, who has issued rules against eating certain plants: God takes different degrees of offense at the eating of different kinds of plant and directly causes proportional illness as punishment. When chemists finally emerge in that world, they provide considerable support for the claim of the former group of inhabitants.

It might be claimed that, because there are in fact no appropriate physiological tests of motivational strength, it is likely that principles linking motivational strength to intentional action are held on conceptual grounds, and that conceptual principles of this kind are useless for explanatory purposes. This claim merits consideration too.

It is, I think, a conceptual truth that acting intentionally at a given time requires having some relevant purpose or objective at that time. Suppose it were shown, on conceptual grounds, that desiring or some motivational attitude like desiring is an essential ingredient in having a purpose or objective of the relevant sort. (Bricks and bikes have purposes of another sort.) Then motivational attitudes would have a firm place in any conceptual scheme that includes intentional actions (Mele 1992: 17–25, 39–42). Suppose it were also shown, again on conceptual grounds, that proper *explanations* of intentional actions must appeal to, or presuppose, *causal* roles for motivational attitudes or for the physical states which realize them, if they are so realized (see Mele 2003, ch. 2). For example, it might be shown that we can make sense of an agent's acting *for* a particular reason or purpose only on the assumption that motivational attitudes associated with the agent's having that particular reason or purpose – or the physical realizers of those attitudes, if the attitudes are so realized – make a causal contribution to the pertinent intentional action. Then motivational strength would apparently gain a foothold too.

It is often observed by opponents of MSI that the claim that agents were most strongly motivated to *A* does not *explain* why they *A*-ed (Thalberg 1985: 97). I agree. And some friends of MSI might say that we do not regard the claim as explaining why agents *A*-ed precisely because we *take it for granted* that agents do, or at least try to do, what they are most strongly motivated to do at a given time. Now, imagine that, in light of Bob's reasons and other features of the case, we learn *why*, at a given time, he was more strongly motivated (that is, he wanted more) to *A* than to do anything else at that time. For example, we learn why Bob, who bought a certain car at *t*, wanted more to do that at *t* than to do anything else at *t*. Would we be satisfied that we understood why he bought that car? Perhaps – at least normally. And, as I observe elsewhere,

> when such information does satisfy us, there is a background presumption at work, namely, that the agent *A*-ed *because* (in some sense) that is what he wanted most to do at the time. If his wanting most to *A* were *irrelevant* to his *A*-ing, the explanation that we have of his wanting most to *A* would also be irrelevant to his *A*-ing, or, at best, tangentially relevant. (Mele 1992: 83)

If this is right, principles linking motivational strength to intentional action may have an explanatory significance for intentional action. They may articulate background presumptions about intentional action in the context of which people offer explanations of particular intentional actions in terms of such attitudes as desires, beliefs, and intentions. One who presupposes the existence of a tight connection between motivational strength and intentional action would take information about why agents were most strongly motivated to do what they did to improve one's understanding of why they did it.

Action-Desires and Ordinary Dispositions

Action-desires may be instructively compared with familiar dispositions – for example fragility and elasticity. David Lewis writes: 'I take for granted that a disposition requires a certain causal basis: one has the disposition [if and only if] one has a property that occupies a certain causal role' (1986: 223–224). (This is not to say that dispositions of the same type must have bases of the same type. To use an example Lewis offers, the basis of Ann's immunity to a certain virus might be her having certain antibodies, whereas the basis of someone else's immunity to the virus might be 'his possession of dormant anti-body makers' (ibid., p. 224).) Consider a fragile vase. If its fragility is manifested in a shattering, the basis of its fragility (for example, its crystalline structure) is a *cause* of this manifestation (ibid., p. 224). And, even if the vase's fragility is never manifested, the basis of its fragility is still present and capable of playing the pertinent causal role under suitable conditions.

In human beings and other animals with action-desires, such desires presumably are realized physically. But then, just as the fact that one vase is more fragile than another is grounded in differences in the respective physical bases of the fragility of the two vases (for example, in their different crystalline structures), the fact – if it is a fact – that one member of a pair of contemporaneous action-desires of mine is stronger than another is grounded, presumably, in differences in the respective physical bases of the strength of the two desires. If there are action-desires, perhaps a future science will uncover the physical bases of their strength, and the physical grounds of relative desire-strengths. It may reasonably be suggested that we can conceive of the relative strength of a human agent's action-desires at a given time as analogous, in the respect mentioned, to the relative fragility of the vases stored in my son's kitchen and to the relative elasticity of the various rubber bands in my desk-drawer: there is a physical basis in each case, and comparative truths about the fragility, the elasticity, and the motivational strength of the relevant items are grounded in differences in the physical bases.

To say that vase x is fragile is to say something more like (ii) than like (i):

(i) If x were struck a hard blow, it would shatter.
(ii) x is so constituted that (i).

And to say that vase x is more fragile than vase y is to say something more like (iv) than like (iii):

(iii) There is some range of forces such that, if x and y were struck with the same force within that range of forces, in the same way, and under the same conditions, x would shatter and y would not.
(iv) x and y are so constituted that (iii).

Similarly, to say that my desire to *A* is stronger than my contemporaneous desire to *B* is to say something more like (vi) than like (v):

(v) If I were to act either from my desire to *A* or from my desire to *B*, I would act from my desire to *A*.
(vi) The two desires at issue are so constituted or so realized that (v).

(I am not suggesting that the even-numbered statements are proper analyses of the relevant notions, but only that they are significantly closer to the mark than their odd-numbered counterparts.)

So what might some theorists have in mind when they claim, for example, that, at *t*, my *proximal* desire to *A* – that is, my desire to *A* straightaway – is stronger than any proximal desire I have to do anything else? Perhaps this:

S The physical realizers of the pertinent action-desires have physical properties suitable for playing 'a certain causal role' in me – a role that amounts to contributing to the production of an attempt that is appropriate to the action-desire they realize – and the pertinent realizers differ internally in such a way that, other things being equal, if, at *t*, I were to proceed to make an attempt appropriate to any of my pertinent proximal action-desires owing to relevant properties of the desire's realizer, I would proceed to make one appropriate to my desire to *A* (or it is *more probable* that I would make one appropriate to my desire to *A* than that I would make any other attempt. (See Mele, 2003: 173 for a more detailed version of *S*.)

Suggestion *S* includes the following theses: agents like us have action-desires; these desires are realized in physical states; the realizing states have physical properties suitable for playing an action-causing role; in agents like us, an action-desire's strength is grounded in physical features of the physical state that realizes the desire; differences in the strengths of a human agent's contemporaneous action-desires are grounded in physical differences in the realizing states. And the suggestion links the concepts of desire-strength and intentional action. The relative *strength* of contemporaneous proximal action-desires of mine is conceived here partly in terms of what I (probably) would *attempt to do* at the time if I were to make an attempt appropriate to any such desires of mine owing to relevant properties of the bases of these desires.

To be sure, the suggestion raises a number of difficult issues, not the least of which is the mind–body problem. But Thalberg (1985) and others challenge people to say what they mean by the claim that an agent's desires have different motivational strengths, and the suggestion offers a coherent interpretation of the assertion as it applies to proximal action-desires.

This section has offered opponents of MSI something that they can try to falsify. Complaints about the obscurity of MSI can be replaced by arguments for the falsity of this application of MSI. The interpretation offered here of the idea that proximal action-desires vary in motivational strength undermines the charge that motivational strength is an empty notion and the objection that the notion is irremediably obscure.

MSI and Agency

Does suggestion *S* diminish our agency by leaving no room for intentions or practical reasoning in the production of intentional actions? No. I myself favor the view that attempting to *A* requires a relevant intention and that action-desires (or their physical realizers) contribute variously to corresponding intentional actions by contributing to the formation or acquisition of corresponding intentions or by providing enabling conditions for the effectiveness of intentions (Mele 1992). This idea is consistent with suggestion *S*. The 'causal role' mentioned there – 'a role that amounts to contributing to the production of an attempt that is appropriate to the action-desire' – may include the two roles just identified. Furthermore, the formation or acquisition of an intention may influence the strength of the relevant desires (Mele 1992: 190).

Suggestion *S* also is compatible with the idea that our practical reasoning often plays an important role in generating action-desires and influences their strength. Action-desires for means presumably often issue partly from practical means–end reasoning, and the strengths of our action-desires for means are influenced by our assessments of the chance that we will achieve the end if we attempt the means. Furthermore, suggestion *S* is compatible with its being the case that the strength of our intrinsic desires (desires for ends) is subject to the influence of critical reflection (Mele 1995: 118–121). For the most part, desires – including intrinsic desires – do not come equipped with immutable strengths (Mele 1992, ch. 4).

The suggestion is compatible with a libertarian view of agency as well. Many libertarians endorse the idea that free actions are caused, and those who do are not all agent causationists (see Kane, 1996). But even an agent causationist may hold that free actions are produced by mental states or events in conjunction with irreducible agent causation (see Clarke, 2003). The worry is about deterministic causation, and suggestion *S* makes no commitment to the thesis that intentional actions are deterministically caused.

In this chapter, the idea that some of our desires are motivationally stronger than others (MSI) has been given a relatively precise content in one major application – its application to proximal action-desires. A thorough defense of MSI would feature a detailed argument for the thesis that proper explanations of intentional actions are *causal* explanations, and that motivation-encompassing attitudes have a significant place in such explanations. Support for MSI would also be found in a persuasive defense of a familiar causal view of the *nature* of action: the view that actions are events with a psycho-causal history of a certain kind. I defend causalism in both connections in Mele 1992 and 2003.

See also: THE CAUSAL THEORY OF ACTION (5); INTENTION (14); TELEOLOGICAL EXPLANATION (16); REASONS AND CAUSES (17); MOTIVATING REASONS (19); PRACTICAL REASONING (31); AKRASIA AND IRRATIONALITY (35); CHISHOLM (71).

References

Atkinson, J. (1982). Old and new conceptions of how expected consequences influence actions. in N. Feather (ed.), *Expectations and Actions*. Hillsdale: Lawrence Erlbaum, 17–52.

Charlton, W. (1988). *Weakness of Will*. Oxford: Basil Blackwell.

Clarke, R. (1994). Doing what one wants less: A reappraisal of the law of desire. *Pacific Philosophical Quarterly*, 75, 1–10.

Clarke, R. (2003). *Libertarian Accounts of Free Will*. Oxford: Oxford University Press.

Gosling, J. (1990). *Weakness of the Will*. London: Routledge.

Kane, R. (1996). *The Significance of Free Will*. New York: Oxford University Press.

Lewis, D. (1986). *Philosophical Papers*, Vol. 2. New York: Oxford University Press.

Mele, A. (1987). *Irrationality: An Essay on Akrasia, Self-Deception, and Self-Control*. New York: Oxford University Press.

Mele, A. (1992). *Springs of Action: Understanding Intentional Behavior*. New York: Oxford University Press.

Mele, A. (1995). *Autonomous Agents: From Self-Control to Autonomy*. Oxford: Oxford University Press.

Mele, A. (2003). *Motivation and Agency*. Oxford: Oxford University Press.

Thalberg, I. (1985). Questions about motivational strength. In E. LePore and B. McLaughlin (eds), *Actions and Events*. Oxford: Basil Blackwell, 88–103.

Further reading

Brand, M. (1984). *Intending and Acting*. Cambridge, MA: MIT Press.

Goldman, A. (1970). *A Theory of Human Action*. Englewood Cliffs: Prentice-Hall.

Velleman, J. D. (2000). *The Possibility of Practical Reason*. Oxford: Oxford University Press.

34

Addiction and Compulsion

NEIL LEVY

Addiction, at least in its clinically significant form, is characterized by a loss of control over reward-seeking behavior (West 2006). Addicts typically wish to modify their behavior; they would like to abstain completely from the drug or activity to which they are addicted, or at least to moderate their intake. They are usually keenly aware of the costs they pay to be able to continue to indulge their habit: financial costs and personal costs. Typically, they value the goods they risk – jobs and family, not to mention liberty and life – more than they value the drug. Yet they continue to consume it. Why? One common answer, given both by laypeople and by scientists, is that addicts are *compelled*. In this chapter I will argue that, on the common understanding of compulsion, this is false: insofar as the folk-psychological notion of compulsion requires that the agent be moved by a desire that is unusually strong, addicts are not compelled to take their drug. Nevertheless, there are grounds for revising the notion of compulsion so as to permit the loss of control experienced by addicts to be regarded as compulsive.

On the folk-psychological understanding of compulsion, an agent is compelled to perform an action by an irresistible desire, and desires are irresistible on account of their enormous strength. Addicts are compelled to consume their drugs because their desire for the drug is so great that only very extraordinary countervailing incentives could persuade – or cause – them to abstain. This conception of addiction is common, both among laypeople and among scientists. The view was eloquently expressed by William James more than a century ago:

> The craving for a drink in real dipsomaniacs, or for opium or chloral in those subjugated, is of a strength of which normal persons can form no conception. 'Were a keg of rum in one corner of a room and were a cannon constantly discharging balls between me and it, I could not refrain from passing before that cannon in order to get the rum'; 'If a bottle of brandy stood at one hand and the pit of hell yawned at the other, and I were convinced that I should be pushed in as sure as I took one glass, I could not refrain': such statements abound in dipsomaniacs' mouths. (James 1890: 543)

More recent expressions of the addiction-as-compulsion view are not hard to find. For Louis Charland, for instance, 'the brain of a heroin addict has almost literally been hijacked by the drug' (Charland 2002: 43). For Carl Elliott, the addict 'is no longer in full control of herself. She must go where her addiction leads her, because the addiction holds the leash' (Elliott 2002: 48). For Alan Leshner, the initially voluntary behavior of drug-taking gradually transforms into 'involuntary drug taking, ultimately to the point that the behavior is driven by a compulsive craving for the drug' (Leshner 1999: 1316).

A first reason to reject the view that addicts are compelled, when compulsion is understood folk-psychologically, is that, far from being in the grip of an especially powerful desire, addicts may not desire their drugs *at all*. Drugs may be 'wanted' – that is, they may have high incentive salience – without being 'liked' at all (Robinson and Berridge 2003). Balfour (2004) has identified the neural basis for this dissociation between the causal strength of a desire and the liking of its object as a consequence of the effects of dopamine on different regions of the *nucleus accumbens*. One region is involved in the subjective feelings of reward associated with a drug, while the other confers incentive salience on the stimulus, independently of its being pleasurable.

A second reason to reject the idea that addicts are (folk-psychologically) compelled to take their drugs is that it is apparently false that the incentive salience of drugs is extraordinarily strong in addicts, at least when measured by the sensitivity of drug-taking behavior to counterincentives. Price increases affect the amount of drugs consumed by addicts (Elster 1999; Neale 2002). Alcoholics are sensitive to the cost of alcohol even after a priming drink (Fingarette 1988: 36–42). Moreover, many addicts give up their drug, often without outside help. When given a powerful reason to abstain permanently, many addicts succeed in overcoming their addiction. New mothers, for instance, are often able to give up their addiction in order to care better for their child (Carlson 2006).

Despite these facts, addicts clearly have a self-control problem. One piece of evidence for this claim is self-report: addicts say, repeatedly and apparently sincerely, that they desire to give up their addiction more than they desire to indulge. Of course, we might suspect them of self-deception: it might serve many addicts' interests to claim that they lack control, inasmuch as the claim seems to relieve them of responsibility for their actions (Levy 2003). A second piece of evidence is arguably more compelling: it consists in the lengths addicts will go to in an attempt to be free of their addiction, and the costs they pay as a consequence of failing (West 2006). These costs are much higher than we should expect, were their failures due to ordinary weakness of the will; the loss of self-control is therefore correspondingly greater.

If we cannot understand the loss of self-control that occurs in addiction by utilizing the folk-psychological conception of compulsion, how should we understand it? Some philosophers have suggested that duress is a better model for addiction than compulsion (Watson 1999). There is no doubt that addicts often experience withdrawal symptoms and cravings which are powerfully aversive. These states constitute a strong impetus in favor of consumption. But not all the drugs of addiction produce withdrawal symptoms beyond perhaps a depressed feeling and mood. Nicotine, one of the most powerfully addictive of all drugs, is not associated with intense withdrawal or cravings (West 2006). Moreover, addiction is a relapsing disease: even after the withdrawal stage has been successfully negotiated and the intense cravings of the acute addiction phase have been seen off, the addict remains vulnerable to lapses. The duress model lacks resources to explain this fact.

A satisfactory theory of addiction must be capable of explaining the loss of control characteristic of addicts without postulating desires or incapacities that are greater than those to which addicts are actually subject. I suggest that recent research on the mechanisms of self-control promises to illuminate the self-control deficit to which addicts are subject. This body of research, on the so-called 'ego-depletion' hypothesis, aims to understand ordinary failures of self-control, but it seems equally applicable to the failures of self-control seen in addiction.

According to the ego-depletion hypothesis, self-control (so-called ego strength) is a deplatable resource. The classic ego-depletion experiment compares the performance of two groups of subjects on a common task, which requires self-control (Baumeister et al. 1998; Baumeister 2002). Subjects are randomly assigned to the ego-depletion group or to the control group. Each group is then given a task to perform. The ego-depletion group is given a task requiring self-control – say, watching a brief funny film without smiling – while the control group is given a task which is thought to be equally fatiguing, but which doesn't require much self-control (say, performing a series of 3-digit multiplications using pen and paper). Then both groups are given the common self-control task; typical tasks include the cold-pressor task (keeping one's hand immersed in icy water as long as possible), or attempting insoluble anagrams. The experimenters simply measure how long subjects persist at the task. The frequently confirmed finding is that subjects in the ego-depletion group persist a significantly shorter time at the task than subjects who have not been called upon to engage in a prior self-control task.

There is good evidence that ego-depletion involves a reduction of self-control resources. Part of the evidence comes from studies of the effects of ego-depletion on chronic dieters. Chronic dieters who were also ego-depleted consumed more cookies or ice-cream, in what were ostensibly taste-perception studies, than either ego-depleted non-dieters or non ego-depleted dieters (Vohs and Heatherton 2000; Kahan et al. 2003). Ego-depletion does not therefore increase basic appetites. Instead, it affects our ability to avoid acting in ways that conflict with our prior commitments. Ego-depletion apparently depletes a resource required for self-control. Lacking sufficient resources to maintain self-control, the subject gives in to prepotent desires.

The ego-depletion hypothesis can explain many of the features of addiction. In particular, it explains the fact that addiction is a relapsing disease. Holding out against an urge – whether a 'want' or a 'liking' – cannot be maintained indefinitely; self-control reserves must be replenished if resistance is to be successful. This helps to explain the cue and context sensitivity of addiction. Addicts are known to have relatively little trouble giving up their drugs if the cues which trigger cravings are absent; hence the fact that few of the many American GIs who returned from Vietnam addicted to heroin remained addicted after discharge (Loewenstein 2000). The ego-depletion hypothesis helps us to understand this phenomenon: though the GIs were almost certainly subject to cravings for heroin, some of them of great strength, they were able to resist them because these cravings were intermittent. When an addict attempts to give up his drug in the environment in which he became addicted, however, he experiences urges to consumption which are much more frequent and longer lasting, since (through operant and classical conditioning) he has come to associate the features of that environment with the drug. Ego-depletion also helps to explain the observed association between lapse–relapse and stress (West 2006), since stress is independently ego-depleting.

Recent research strongly suggests that ego-depletion leads to an alteration in the agent's 'all-things-considered' judgment as to how it is best to act. That is, ego-depleted subjects temporarily judge that abiding by their resolutions is less choiceworthy than some tempting alternative. There are two pieces of evidence supporting this conclusion. First, there is the fact that ego-depletion affects not only immediate choice, but also choice for future occasions: ego-depleted subjects do not just (say) choose to eat more cookies *now*, they also select less healthy menus for future occasions (Wang et al. under submission). This is not the pattern one would expect if the agent retained the judgment that abiding by their diet is better than consuming cookies. Second, there is evidence from studies which examined directly the effects of ego-depletion on judgments. Wheeler and colleagues (2007) gave ego-depleted subjects as well as controls counterattitudinal arguments. They found that, although ego-depletion had no effect on the persuasiveness of strong counterattitudinal arguments, ego-depleted subjects were significantly more convinced by weak arguments than were the controls. If their self-reports are reliable, this was not the result of any less attentiveness on the part of these subjects, or any less effort. Instead, ego-depletion seems to degrade the quality of argument assessment. There is independent evidence that taking claims to be true is the cognitive default; in the absence of adequate resources to assess a claim fully, we will tend to accept it (Gilbert 1991). Ego-depletion seems to lead to a reduction in the resources needed to generate contradictory arguments and to apply them to the message content. The default tendency to accept claims as true therefore predominantes.

Zaragoza (2006) argues that there is a categorical difference between compulsion, which for him is characteristic of addiction, and weakness of the will. He recognizes that the loss of control in compulsion is caused (*inter alia*) by the over-exertion of inhibitory resources, although for him the proximate cause of giving in is duress, not judgment-shift; but he believes that compulsion is the result of 'an abnormality [...] located in the systems that initiate the causal sequence leading to action,' whereas weakness of the will is a product of abnormality in the agent's 'resistive capacities' (Zaragoza 2006: 265). In fact, both in weakness of the will and in compulsion – *if* there is a defensible distinction to be drawn between the two – the failure of resistance is contextual. There need be no abnormality in the agent's capacities, understood (as Zaragoza clearly does) as a weakness in the agent existing independently of the context, for weakness of the will to occur. We will all give in to temptations if our self-control resources have been taxed sufficiently. Moreover, there need be no abnormality in the systems that lead to action: an addict might simply be someone for whom a certain rewarding behavior has high incentive salience and who is exposed to continual or frequently repeated cues triggering an urge for that behavior. When an agent gives in to the urges caused by drug addiction or by ordinary temptations, the causal route to action is normal in almost every respect. The agent judges that she ought to give in, and acts accordingly.

The very same mechanism is likely to be at work in ordinary weakness of the will, which is generally regarded as free, and in the consumption of drugs by addicts. Should we therefore conclude that drug-consumption behavior by addicts is *not* compulsive? Though it certainly isn't compulsive when judged against the standard of the folk-psychological notion, there may nevertheless be grounds for revising that notion in such a manner as to accommodate addictive behavior.

As we saw, compulsion is normally thought of as produced by irresistible desires, where an irresistible desire is abnormally strong. But whether a desire can be resisted depends not only upon its strength, but also upon the strength of the agent who attempts resistance. Hence irresistibility should be relativized to agents and times: a desire is not irresistible in itself, but irresistible to a given agent at a given time. Mele (1990) argues that a desire is resistible to an agent if there is a strategy, epistemically and motivationally open to that agent and within that agent's skills and capacities, for intentionally resisting or circumventing the desire in question (where 'circumventing' a desire means to implement a course of action incompatible with the action which would satisfy that desire, though without directly resisting it). To discover whether the temptations to which ego-depleted individuals give in count as resistible, we need to ask whether continued resistance is available to them.

It might be thought that empirical evidence supports the view that continued resistance is motivationally open to the agent. When subjects are reminded of their values, or offered cash incentives, they are able to hold out for longer periods against the urge to succumb (Baumeister et al. 2008). Philosophers commonly test whether an agent could have done otherwise than she actually did by asking how she would have acted given the appropriate incentives or reasons; by this test, the agent would have been able to do otherwise, and the urge was therefore resistible. But while the suggested test tells us something about the agent that is relevant to whether she could have done otherwise – it tells us what capacities and skills she possesses – it does not tell us whether, *in the circumstances that actually prevailed*, exercising those capacities and skills was motivationally open to her. Offering her incentives or reasons for acting otherwise is *altering* her motivational set, not revealing its pre-existing state.

As Mele argues, there is good reason to construe the basis of the ability to do otherwise broadly, by including in it motivational and epistemic elements – else we get the absurdity that, say, agoraphobics are not compelled to remain indoors, since, given the appropriate incentives, they would leave. Of course, the incentives to refrain which are given to participants in ego-depletion experiments are relatively trivial – not the risks to life and limb that might motivate the agoraphobic to leave his house; but the principle is the same. Given a large change in the motivational set, an agent otherwise compelled to perform an act at t will hold out until $t + 10$; given a small change, the agent might hold out only until $t + 1$. But in both cases it is the change in the motivational set that enables further resistance.

It might be held that agents ought to give *themselves* the relevant inducements. Presumably (to focus on a particular case), when it is true that an agent would hold out longer were she reminded of her values, this is because there is some kind of conflict, or at least tension, between her values and the contemplated action; in cases like this, she ought to remind herself of her values. However, though there is something compelling about the thought that agents ought to remind themselves of their values and thereby bring themselves to act consistently with them, putting this advice into practice has epistemic preconditions. After experiencing judgment shift, agents do not remind themselves of their values or take other steps to test whether their (new) 'all-things-considered' judgment coheres with their values – and this is precisely *because* they have experienced judgment shift and are satisfied with their decision. But prior to experiencing judgment shift agents do not take steps to shore up their self-control resources (like reminding themselves of their values) and thereby forestall the judgment shift, because they are typically unaware of the need to engage in this kind of activity. Instead, they believe that resistance is best achieved by an effort of will, a belief which is fostered by a focus on the importance of willpower in achieving our ends. Both before and after judgment shift, there are things we could do which would increase the likelihood that we make (by our own lights) better decisions; but most of us are unaware either that there are steps we should take or what those steps are. Thus addicts will regularly fail to possess the epistemic resources for continuing to resist their urges.

At, or near, the time of consumption, addicts will typically lack the motivational resources to resist the temptation to consume; prior to this moment, they may lack the epistemic resources to ensure that, at the appropriate time, they will possess (or not need) the motivational resources. To that extent, there are grounds for holding that they are compelled to take the drug, though the motivational salience of the temptation may not be unusually strong. A caveat: the line of argument here is far more persuasive in showing that addicts are compelled to consume their drug, when it is available, than it is in showing that they compelled to engage in the activities of procuring the drug (though it is worth noting that there is good evidence that steps regularly taken as part of the process of drug-taking can themselves acquire incentive salience for addicts: West 2006). Nevertheless, I suggest that viewing drug consumption through the lens of ego-depletion, while bearing Mele's analysis of irresistible desires in mind, gives us good reason to regard at least some drug-taking behavior as genuinely compelled. The ego-depletion hypothesis also suggests, incidentally, that we ought to respond to drug abuse not so much by exhorting addicts to 'just say no,' but by giving them the skills – and that means, crucially, the knowledge – to ensure that their cravings do not endure so long, or recur so often, as to overwhelm their self-control resources. Not only can they remind themselves of their values; they can also structure their environments so as to avoid the cues that trigger cravings. They will frequently need help in so doing, especially since they will often lack the financial resources to move from their neighborhoods. Here, too, there is an important role for social support in helping addicts to refrain.

See also: HABITUAL ACTIONS (10); VOLITION AND THE WILL (13); MOTIVATIONAL STRENGTH (33); AKRASIA AND IRRATIONALITY (35); RESPONSIBILITY AND AUTONOMY (39); ACTION AND CRIMINAL RESPONSIBILITY (42).

References

Balfour, D. J. (2004). The neurobiology of tobacco dependence: A preclinical perspective on the role of the dopamine projections to the nucleus accumbens. *Nicotine and Tobacco Research*, 6, 899–912.

Baumeister, R. F., Bratslavsky, E., Muraven, M., and Tice, D. M. (1998). Ego-depletion: Is the active self a limited resource? *Journal of Personality and Social Psychology*, 74, 1252–1265.

Baumeister, R. F. (2002). Ego depletion and self-control failure: An energy model of the self's executive function. *Self and Identity*, 1, 129–136.

Baumeister, R. F., Sparks, E. A., Stillman, T. F., and Vohs, K. D. (2008). Free will in consumer behavior: Self-control, ego depletion, and choice. *Journal of Consumer Psychology*, 18, 4–13.

Carlson, B. E. (2006). Best practices in the treatment of substance-abusing women in the child welfare system. *Journal of Social Work Practice in the Addictions*, 6, 91–115.

Charland, L. C. (2002). Cynthia's dilemma: Consenting to heroin prescription. *American Journal of Bioethics*, 2, 43.

Elliott, C. (2002). Who holds the leash? *American Journal of Bioethics*, 2, 43.

Elster, J. (1999). *Strong Feelings: Emotion, Addiction and Human Behavior*. Cambridge, MA: The MIT Press.

Fingarette, H. (1988). *Heavy Drinking: The Myth of Alcoholism as a Disease*. Berkeley: University of California Press.

Gilbert, D. (1991). How mental systems believe. *American Psychologist*, 46, 107–119.

James, W. (1890). *Principles of Psychology*. New York: Henry Holt and Company.

Kahan D., Polivy, J., and Herman, C. P. (2003). Conformity and dietary disinhibition: A test of the ego strength model of self-regulation. *International Journal of Eating Disorders*, 33, 165–171.

Leshner, A. (1999). Science-based views of drug addiction and its treatment. *Journal of the American Medical Association*, 282, 1314–1316.

Levy, N. (2003). Self-deception and responsibility for addiction. *Journal of Applied Philosophy*, 20, 133–142.

Loewenstein, G. (2000). Willpower: A decision theorist's perspective. *Law and Philosophy*, 19, 51–76.

Mele, A. (1990). Irresistible desires. *Nous*, 24, 455–472.

Neale, J. (2002). *Drug Users in Society*. New York: Palgrave.

Robinson, T. E., and Berridge, K. C. (2003). Addiction. *Annual Review of Psychology*, 54, 25–53.

Vohs, K. D., and Heatherton, T. F. (2000). Self-regulatory failure: a resource-depletion approach. *Psychological Science*, 11, 249–254.

Wang, J., Novemsky, N., Dhar, R. and Baumeister, R.F. (under submission). Effects of depletion in sequential choices. *Marketing Science*.

Watson, G. (1999). Excusing addiction. *Law and Philosophy*, 18, 589–619.

West, R. (2006). *Theory of Addiction*. Oxford: Blackwell Publishing.

Wheeler, S. C., Briñol, P. and Hermann, A. D. (2007). Resistance to persuasion as self-regulation: Ego depletion and its effects on attitude change processes. *Journal of Experimental Social Psychology*, 43, 150–156.

Zaragoza, K. (2006). What happens when someone acts compulsively? *Philosophical Studies*, 131, 251–268.

Further reading

Ainslie, G. (2001). *Breakdown of Will*. Cambridge: Cambridge University Press.

Elster, J. (1999) (ed.). *Addiction: Entries and Exits*. New York: Russell Sage Foundation.

Schoeman, F. (1991). Alcohol addiction and responsibility attributions. In M I. Bockover (ed.), *Rules, Rituals, and Responsibility: Essay Dedicated to Herbert Fingarette*. La Salle, IL: Open Court, pp. 11–36.

Vihvelin, K. (1994). Are drug addicts unfree? In S. Luper-Foy and C. Brown (eds), *Drugs, Morality, and the Law*. New York: Garland, pp. 51–78.

Wallace, R. J. (1991). Addiction as defect of the will: Some philosophical reflections. *Law and Philosophy*, 18, 621–654.

Yaffe, G. (2002). Recent work on addiction and responsible agency. *Philosophy and Public Affairs*, 30, 178–221.

35

Akrasia and Irrationality

SERGIO TENENBAUM

Akrasia and accidie are traditionally recognized as two of the clearest cases of practical irrationality. An 'akratic action,' to a first approximation, is an intentional action that the agent recognizes to be in conflict with what she judges to be the best course of action. So an agent who continues smoking even though she thinks it would be better if she were to quit smoking would be engaging in akratic actions. In a state of accidie, by contrast, the agent recognizes that there is something of value that he can and ought to bring about, and yet he does not engage in any action to bring it about, or in any other course of action that he judges he ought to undertake, or in any other course of action that he judges to be more or equally valuable. So, for instance, a depressed agent who knows that he can go to work and help support his family but stays in bed nonetheless is suffering from accidie. Akrasia, accidie, and other forms of practical irrationality are philosophically interesting in themselves, but they are also phenomena that are taken to make test cases for various philosophical theories in the realm of ethics and practical reason. For instance the acceptance of the 'guise of the good' thesis (the view that all intentional action aims at the good) is often taken to be incompatible with the possibility of akrasia or accidie (see Stocker 1979; for an argument that they are compatible, see Tenenbaum 2007). Ethical internalism, the view that moral judgments necessarily motivate, is often taken to be incompatible with the possibility of accidie (Smith 1994). More generally, some philosophers have argued that theories of rationality such as the view that rationality only commands that one takes the means to one's given ends leave no room for the possibility of practical irrationality (Korsgaard 1997, Pears 1982).

These kinds of claims are often put forward on the assumption that it is a matter of empirical fact that phenomena such as akrasia and accidie exist; but the grounds for this assumption are not clear (Korsgaard is a notable exception, since she thinks that the possibility of irrationality is constitutive of the norms of rationality). An action can count as a case of akrasia or accidie, if the action (or inaction) the agent chooses conflicts with some kind of evaluative judgment the agent makes. However, it is not immediately obvious why we must attribute the relevant evaluative judgment to the agent in question. Philosophers often rely on the supposition that agents in these situations would sincerely assent to certain propositions. But agents might be self-deceived, confused, or simply they may change their minds. Given the yeomen's work that the possibility of such irrational behavior is supposed to perform, one would expect that philosophers would have done a better job of showing that 'akrasia' and 'accidie' denote real phenomena.

References to weakness of will are common in ordinary parlance, but doubtless the words 'akrasia' and 'accidie' are terms of art (at least in English). Since philosophers have traditionally assumed that the ordinary notion of weakness of will and the philosophical conception of akrasia coincide, they could at least draw some comfort from the fact that it is a well-entrenched part of our ordinary understanding of agents that they can be irrational exactly by exhibiting weakness of will. However, it has been recently suggested that what is ordinarily described as weakness of will is not the same phenomenon as the one covered by the philosophers' notion of akrasia. In what follows I'll try first to argue that, insofar as the ordinary notion of weakness of will denotes some kind of irrationality in the agent, the traditional view which identifies weakness of will with akrasia is the correct one. Then I'll try to suggest more general and more promising ways of establishing the reality of such phenomena. I'll focus on akrasia, but much of what I'll say, especially in the second part of the argument, should apply to accidie too.

Davidson's classic paper on weakness of will (Davidson 1980) defines this phenomenon as a failure to act in accordance with what one acknowledges (or at least thinks) to be the correct evaluative judgment. In other words, a weak-willed agent is one who judges that *A* is better than *B*, all things considered, but (freely) chooses *B* over *A*. Versions of this view seem to have been endorsed by historical figures, from Aristotle to Kant (Aristotle 1985; Kant 1998). On Davidson's explication of akrasia, the agent's privileged evaluative judgment is identified with what he calls an 'all-things-considered judgment.' The 'all-things-considered' judgment is best understood when contrasted with *prima facie* evaluative judgments such as 'insofar as *A*, but not *B*, will cause me to feel pleasure, *A* is better than *B*.' *Prima facie* evaluative judgments would be conditional judgments of the following form:

[i] Insofar as *A* is more pleasant than *B*, *A* is better than *B*.

All-things-considered judgments are also conditional judgments of the same form, but they are is conditioned on all the relevant considerations as follows:

[ii] Insofar as all the relevant considerations are considered, *A* is better than *B*.

According to Davidson, the principle of continence is a rational requirement; the principle of continence states that one should always act according to one's all-things-considered judgment. (Davidson 1980b: 41). The weak-willed agent is irrational exactly by violating the principle of continence. Davidson also asserts that, by acting against her all-things-considered judgment – by choosing *B* over *A* while judging that *A* is better than *B*, all things considered – the weak-willed agent accepts an *unconditional*, or 'all-out' judgment of the form:

[iii] *B* is better than *A*.

According to Davidson, the rational conflict between [ii] and [iii] is what makes actions that violate the principle of continence irrational. Many philosophers reject Davidson's view that the weak-willed agent accepts [iii]. In fact, some philosophers think that some forms of akrasia involve the agent's acting against her 'all-out' judgment (see for instance Pears 1982 and Bratman 1979). However, until recently there was wide agreement that weakness of will involved acting against one's all-things-considered judgment, or at least against something that was classified as one's 'best' evaluative judgment. However, there is no longer consensus among philosophers even on this point. Holton (1999 and 2004) and MacIntyre (1990) have both defended the claim that akrasia, or weakness of will, consists in certain types of failures to act on a future-directed intention. I am weak-willed if I form at t_0 an intention to *A* at t_1, and yet I do not *A* at t_1. Of course, this claim needs to be qualified; I might have, for instance, overwhelming reasons to change my mind between t_0 and t_1, in which case my failure to act as I intended would not count as an instance of weakness of will. More particularly, Holton claims that instances of weakness of will are instances of reconsidering intentions which are 'contrary inclination defeating'; intentions that are formed at least partly as 'an attempt to overcome contrary desires that one believes one will have when the time comes to act' (Holton 1999: 250).

It is worth noting that these authors will often admit that there is a distinctive failure of rationality, which involves acting against one's best judgment (and they even concede the label 'akrasia' to this form of irrationality). Although Holton, for instance, insists that his view captures the 'ordinary' use of 'weakness of will' by non-philosophers, there are reasons to doubt that his claim is true; Holton reports only anecdotal evidence in support of this claim, and more systematic attempts to test his hypothesis about ordinary usage do not confirm his claim (see Mele, fothcoming). Holton's view on weakness of will has the advantage of singling out a phenomenon whose existence there is very little reason to doubt; it would be hard to deny that we often fail to act in accordance with our future-directed intentions. On the other hand, the more particular definition of weakness of will as a phenomenon encompassing those cases in which the failure concerns the inclination to defeat a contrary inclination does postulate psychological phenomena that might not be as ubiquitous as Holton supposes (I'll come back to this point in a moment).

More importantly, it is far from clear that weakness of will defined in this way is a form of irrationality; it is far from clear that reconsidering one's intention is ever irrational per se (see Broome 2001 and Tenenbaum, unpublished manuscript). Let us look more precisely at what Holton considers to count as cases of weakness of will. According to Holton, sometimes we form intentions to overcome the inclination to act in a certain way. So I might form an intention not to eat dessert, and I might do it with the purpose of resisting my momentary preferences for certain sweets when they are served right in front of me. According to Holton, if I now revise this intention as a result of my inclination to eat a certain dessert, I exhibit weakness of will; weakness of will is a tendency to revise intentions formed with the purpose of defeating some contrary inclination.

However, am I necessarily irrational in eating the dessert, and, if so, am I irrational precisely because I have revised my intention? Let us look at two cases in which this kind of intention revision does not seem to be irrational. Suppose that we have the same basic case – namely an agent who forms an intention not to eat dessert in order to defeat an inclination for sweets. But let us assume now that this is an agent whose modest appetites and particular physiology are such that his health or figure would not be negatively affected even if he were to eat all the desserts he would ever feel like eating. However, the agent suffers from anorexic tendencies and consequently forms now the intention not to eat any more desserts. Suppose that the agent is served with dessert and, rather than simply turning it down, he reconsiders his intention and comes to the conclusion that he should enjoy himself more, and not be such a 'slave of the scale.' If the agent decides to eat the dessert on these grounds, there seems to be no reason to impute him with any kind of irrationality or weakness of will. Why should an agent who revises his intention correctly be deemed irrational or weak-willed on the basis of an ill-considered intention he had made in the past? (Arpaly 2003, p. 18 uses a similar example to make a different point.) This is not to deny that, *in some cases*, a decision of this sort might express some kind of irrationality. Suppose the agent had come to the conclusion that he does not deliberate well in situations in which he is faced with certain temptations; he concludes, for instance, that he is likely to engage in rationalizations and overlook important features of his choice situation in these circumstances. Given these tendencies, he judges that he ought not to rely on his 'momentary' deliberation, but rather stick to his prior intentions. If he now considers revising his intention while retaining (or unwarrantedly revising) the judgment that, all things considered, he should not be engaging in (or at least acting in accordance with) such a deliberation, he does exhibit weakness of will; but this is a case that falls straight within the purview of the traditional conception of weakness of will. In this case, even though he is not acting against his better judgment that he should eat the dessert, he is acting against his better judgment that he should not be acting in accordance with his momentary deliberation (or that he should not revise his judgment in the face of temptation). But the failure of the will is still a case in which the agent does not follow his better judgment.

Finally, the very idea that we form contrary inclination-defeating intentions in such a widespread manner would need defense. It is true that many cases of weakness of will are cases in which we act against a general intention, which is supposed to apply to various situations in which we face temptation. But are such intentions 'expressly made in order to get over one's later reluctance to act' (Holton 1999: 249)? Let us take a case that seems to fit in well with the idea that some of my intentions are formed, at least in part, in order to defeat contrary inclinations. So perhaps when I form an intention never to drink again in light of my past difficulties with alcohol, one might claim that I am forming the intention precisely to combat the temptation that a cocktail holds for me. If I now find myself in a party and I decide that it would be fine, just this once, to have a beer, I might indeed be manifesting weakness of will. However, if we look more closely at this case, it is not clear that the intention would have been formed as 'an attempt to overcome contrary desires.' Suppose I formed this intention as follows: I used to think that I could drink socially. But now I notice that this is impossible for me; when I start drinking socially, I quickly slip into my old drinking habits.

Consequently, I judge that I should never drink; I judge that it is best that I simply refrain from drinking on all occasions (see Rachlin 2000). Suppose I now form the intention simply on the basis of this judgment, but with no further aim to overcome contrary desire (of course, I realize that I'll have contrary desires, but certainly not all intentions formed in the awareness that one will also have desires to act differently are formed as an attempt to overcome contrary desires). It seems that, if I fail to act on this intention, I suffer from the exact same kind of irrationality as if I had formed the intention in an attempt to overcome a contrary inclination.

And I see no reason to think a priori that most cases of my forming such general intentions are cases in which contrary inclination-defeating intentions are also at work. In fact, even if I don't form the relevant intention but only make the judgment that the best thing to do is never to drink alcohol, I would still be suffering from the same kind of irrationality; and this is exactly what the traditional conception of weakness of will predicts. In sum, even though Holton is right to think that many cases of weakness of will are failures to act on general intentions, and that many such general intentions are formed when the agent recognizes that it is not best to deliberate on the merits of the particular case rather than on the merits of the general policy, he is wrong to think that this presents a challenge to the traditional conception of weakness of will.

Although Davidson took it for granted that a rational agent should always follow his all-things-considered judgment, some philosophers have disputed this claim (see for instance Arpaly 2000). Huck Finn seems to have acted better by not following his all-things-considered judgment. Huck Finn seems to have thought that, all things considered, he should turn in Jim, the runaway slave, to his owner, since Jim was, on Huck Finn's view, the slave owner's rightful property. However, Huck Finn akratically lets his fondness for Jim prevail and presumably acts better by letting Jim run away. But exactly such cases show the difficulty in establishing that we have a genuine case of akrasia at hand. After all, one could argue that, despite Huck Finn's pronouncements and musings, which indicate that he acted against what he *thought* (perhaps confusedly) to be something like an all-things-considered judgment (after all, it's unlikely that Huck Finn put the matter to himself in terms of 'all-things-considered' judgments), Huck Finn never judges that it is better to turn Jim in, all things considered. Of course, since Huck Finn is a fictional character, it is tempting to think or simply stipulate that he does make the all-things-considered judgment. But it is not clear that this is a coherent stipulation. Why should we not say that, given that Huck Finn chose the right action in response to the right reasons, we have no reasonable grounds to assert that Huck Finn still judged that, all things considered, he should turn Jim in? We can think that we have various pieces of evidence about Huck Finn which might be relevant: Huck Finn's musings about what he ought to do, his various emotions before and after the action, and his actual behavior. It is not clear which piece of evidence should be conclusive here.

But this leads to a more general concern about whether we have any grounds to ascribe to an agent an all-things-considered judgment. Why should we ever think that an agent's assent to an all-things-considered judgment would be better evidence than her actual behavior of what she has, or take herself to have, most reason to do? Isn't it just as good an explanation of an apparently akratic action that the agent changes her mind at the time of the action and then regrets later having changed her mind in this manner? (For a position roughly along these lines, see Scott-Kakures 1997.) This might be further confirmed by the psychologist George Ainslie's work on weakness of will (see Ainslie 2001). According to Ainslie, behavior under the heading of weakness of will typically involves hyperbolic discounting; we do not simply discount linearily future rewards, but the rate of discounting changes dramatically as we approach a certain reward. So, even though Tuesday I might prefer waking up sober on the following Monday after drinking on Sunday, I will discount the rewards of being sober more dramatically as Sunday evening approaches, until I finally experience a preference shift as I walk into the bar. We could then say that an agent in such a situation changes her evaluative judgments in lockstep with her preference shifts, and that the claim that she chose against her best judgment can be understood as expressing the evaluative judgments she made before and after the action, but not *at the time of the action* (for an attempt to use Ainslie's work in order to show that there is at least no intentional counterpreferential choice, see Heath 2008).

One might object that this line of reasoning establishes, at best, that we cannot *know* that an agent is akratic in a particular case, but gives us no reason to suspect that akrasia might not be a widespread phenomenon, whether or not we can ascertain its existence. However, it is not clear that all-things-considered judgments have any psychological reality which is independent of what one is warranted to ascribe to the agent in attempting to provide intentional explanations of that agent's behavior. Davidson himself argued that the ascription of mental states such as beliefs and desires depends on a constitutive use of the principle of charity: the agent's beliefs and desires are those that would make most sense of her behavior in the light of the assumption that the agent is a 'believer of truths and lover of the good' (Davidson 1980a: 222). But even if one does not accept Davidson's extreme contention, it seems plausible to think that the correct ascription of mental states to an agent is partly determined by the role played by such mental states in explaining the agent's actions and that, *ceteris paribus*, we should not attribute needless irrationality to the agent.

But this very thought gives us a way to confirm our confidence that cases of akrasia are not only possible but widespread. For on many occasions it is plausible to conclude that failing to ascribe akrasia would be a greater violation of the principle of charity than not ascribing it. Suppose I am a divorce lawyer to whom a famous client has told various risqué stories about herself and her husband. It is tempting to gossip about the case with my friends, but I know that I have overwhelming prudential and moral reasons not to break my client's confidentiality. I understand very well the force of these reasons; I know for instance that my career is at stake, and that it would not be fair on my client to spread around stories about intimate aspects of her life. Moreover, I have on many occasions resisted the temptation to gossip this way. Now I am at a party where people have been gossiping, and I finally succumb to the temptation to tell a salacious story my client related to me. After telling the story, I immediately regret what I did and judge that I have done something tremendously stupid. In this case, denying that I behaved akratically would have very implausible consequences about how I revise judgments. The judgment that I should not break my client's confidentiality was, *ex hypothesis*, formed on good grounds, and perhaps after a great deal of reflection; it was probably grounded on deep features about my character and on central aspects about some of the projects that are very important in my life. This judgment was also reaffirmed just after my indiscretion. So if indeed I changed my mind momentarily, this would mean that I have revised a well-grounded, previously stable judgment, on the basis of reasons which I am clearly capable of knowing to be bad reasons, when no new information was available, and then immediately reverted to my original judgment despite, again, having no new evidence. This would be highly irrational behavior; certainly no less irrational than simply acting against one's all-things-considered judgment. And, again, whatever one thinks about the principle of charity, it seems a much simpler explanation to say that the agent acted against her best judgment than to say that the agent underwent all these irrational revision processes.

Notice that the argument that the ascription of akrasia was warranted depends, at least in part, on the claim that the agent formed the evaluative judgment for good reasons and held it in a stable manner. Thus it seems that akrasia is, at the very least, more easily attributed in cases in which the agent acts contrary to her knowledge of the good, rather than when she acts against what she merely believes to be good. One of Davidson's many contributions to the literature on akrasia has been to claim that akrasia is best defined in terms of action contrary to an evaluative *belief*, rather than, as it had been traditionally defined, in terms of action contrary to a piece of practical knowledge. Davidson's position has been nearly unanimously accepted in the literature on akrasia (for a notable recent exception, see Engstrom 2009). However, reflection on the possibility of akrasia raises the suspicion that the traditional view of akrasia might be the correct one.

See also: PRACTICAL REASONING (31); DELIBERATION AND DECISION (32); MOTIVATIONAL STRENGTH (33); ADDICTION AND COMPULSION (34); RATIONALITY (36); ARISTOTLE (54); DAVIDSON (73).

References

Ainslie, G. (2001). *Breakdown of Will*. New York: Cambridge University Press.

Aristotle (1985). *Nicomachean Ethics*, translated by T. Irwin. Indianapolis: Hackett Publishing Co.

Arpaly, N. (2000). On acting rationally against one's best judgment. *Ethics*, 110, 488–513.

Arpaly, N. 2003. *Unprincipled Virtue: An Inquiry into Moral Agency*. New York: Oxford University Press.

Bratman, M. (1979). Practical reasoning and weakness of the will. *Nous*, 13, 153–171.

Broome, J. (2001). Are intentions reasons? And how should we cope with incommensurable values? In C. Morris and A. Ripstein (eds), *Practical Rationality and Preference: Essays for David Gauthier*. New York: Cambridge University Press, 98–120.

Davidson, D. (1980a). Actions, Reasons, and Causes. In D. Davidson (ed.), *Essays on Actions and Events*. Oxford: Clarendon Press, 3–20.

Davidson, D. (1980b). How is weakness of the will possible? In D. Davidson (ed.), *Essays on Actions and Events*. Oxford: Clarendon Press, 21–42.

Davidson, D (1980c). Mental Events, In D. Davidson (ed.), *Essays on Actions and Events*. Oxford: Clarendon Press, 207–224.

Engstrom, S. (2009). *The Form of Practical Knowledge*. Cambridge, MA: Harvard University Press.

Heath, J. (2008). *Following the Rules: Practical Reasoning and Deontic Constraints*. New York: Oxford University Press.
Holton, R. (1999). Intention and weakness of will. *Journal of Philosophy*, 96, 241–262.
Holton, R. (2004). Rational resolve. *Philosophical Review*, 5 (113), 507–535.
Kant, I. (1998). *Religion within the Boundaries of Mere Reason and Other Writings*, translated by A. W. Wood, G. Di Giovanni, and R. M. Adams. New York: Cambridge University Press.
Korsgaard, C. M. (1997). The normativity of instrumental reason. In G. Cullity and B. Gaut (eds), *Ethics and Practical Reason*. New York: Clarendon Press, 215–254.
MacIntyre, A. (1990). Is akratic action always irrational? In O. Flanagan and A. Rorty (eds), *Identity, Character, and Morality*. Cambridge, MA: MIT Press, 379–400.
Mele, A. (forthcoming). Weakness of will and akrasia. *Philosophical Studies*.
Pears, D. (1982). How easy is akrasia? *Philosophia*, 11, 33–50.
Rachlin, H. (2000). *The Science of Self-Control*. Cambridge, MA: Harvard University Press.
Scott-Kakures, D. (1997). Self-knowledge, akrasia, and self-criticism. *Philosophia*, 25, 267–295.
Smith, M. (1994). The moral problem. *Philosophical theory*. Oxford: Blackwell.
Stocker, M. (1979). Desiring the bad: An essay in moral psychology. *Journal of Philosophy*, 76, 738–753.
Tenenbaum, S. (unpublished manuscript). Intention and commitment.
Tenenbaum, S. (2007). *Appearances of the Good: An Essay on the Nature of Practical Reason*. New York and Cambridge: Cambridge University Press.

Part III

Action in Special Contexts

36

Rationality

JOHN BROOME

Rationality as a Property and Rationality as a Source of Requirements

The word 'rationality' often refers to a property – the property of being rational. This property may be possessed by people, and also by beliefs, acts, conversations, traffic schemes and other things. I shall concentrate on the rationality of people. The rationality of other things is derivative from the rationality of people.

One task for an account of rationality is to describe the contours of the property of rationality, when it is ascribed to people. That is to say, the account should tell us when we are rational and when we are not. An account of rationality also needs to describe what rationality requires of us. At first this may seem to be nothing different, because 'rationality requires' seems to be definable in terms of the property of rationality. But that turns out not to be so.

We do often speak of what a property requires of us. For instance, we say 'Beauty requires hard work.' This sentence specifies a necessary condition for possessing the property of beauty, or perhaps for possessing this property to a higher degree. It means that hard work is necessary for being beautiful, or more beautiful. The notion of a necessary condition is not entirely determinate, so there is room for different interpretations of the sentence 'Beauty requires hard work.' It may mean that, necessarily, if you do not work hard you are not beautiful. Or it may mean that, if you were not to work hard, you would not be beautiful. Or that, necessarily, if you do not work hard you will not be more beautiful. And so on.

We could understand 'rationality requires' on the same model. We could take 'Rationality requires you to *F*' to mean that your *F*-ing is a necessary condition for you to be rational, or to be more rational. For instance, because being alive is a necessary condition for being rational, we could intelligibly say that rationality requires you to be alive. But that would not be giving 'rationality requires' its most natural meaning; we most naturally make a distinction between what is necessary for being rational and what rationality itself requires of us. We would naturally say that, although being alive is necessary for being rational, rationality does not itself require you to be alive. What rationality itself requires is such things as intending means to ends that you intend, not having contradictory beliefs, and so on. So 'rationality requires' has another, more natural meaning.

We would more naturally understand 'rationality requires' on the model of 'convention requires' or 'the law requires.' This brings us to recognize that 'rationality' is not only the name of a property; it is also the name of an abstract entity in a category that I believe has no generic name. Others in the category are convention, the law, morality and prudence. Members of this class issue requirements; they are sources of requirements. The law requires you not to defraud people; convention requires you to use your right hand for shaking hands; morality requires you to keep your promises; rationality requires you to intend means to ends that you intend; and so on.

I call this second sense of 'rationality' the 'source sense,' and the first the 'property sense.' When we speak of requirements of rationality, we generally use 'rationality' in the source sense. In this sense, 'rationality' is synonymous with one of the senses of 'reason.' 'Rationality requires' generally means the same as 'reason requires.'

Rationality in the source sense requires you to intend means to an end you intend, not to have contradictory beliefs, to intend to do what you believe you ought to do, and so on. Many of rationality's requirements are hard to formulate precisely, and several are controversial; I shall give more careful attention to a few requirements later. The list of requirements may be very long. Nevertheless, it does not include every necessary condition for being rational. Being alive is not a requirement of rationality in the source sense, for instance.

Requirements of rationality in the source sense cannot be defined in terms of the property of rationality. However the property of rationality can be defined in terms of requirements of rationality in the source sense. I shall next explain how.

The first step is to define a person to be fully rational if and only if she satisfies all the requirements of rationality she is under.

Next we need to define the ordering relation 'more rational than.' Compare two states a person might be in, *A* and *B*, where she is under the same requirements of rationality in both. Suppose that in *A* she satisfies all the requirements she satisfies in *B*, and some others as well. Then she is more rational in *A* than in *B*. This gives a sufficient condition for being more rational, but not a necessary one. The person may also be more rational in *A* than in *B* if the requirements she satisfies in *A* are together more important than those she satisfies in *B*. To apply this criterion, we must have some scale for the importance of requirements; I assume we do intuitively. No doubt the scale is very indeterminate, which means the ordering of states by 'more rational than' will be very partial.

We may define a person as rational (rather than fully rational) if and only if her state is sufficiently high in this partial ordering, and irrational if and only if her state is sufficiently low in it. 'Sufficiently' will have to be left vague, and no doubt dependent on the context.

In this way, we can define all the features of the property of rationality. The definitions capture one feature that the property obviously possesses: that rationality is a matter of degree.

A complication is that, once we have the property of rationality, we can identify necessary conditions for you to possess this property, and we *could* say that rationality requires those conditions of you. If we did, we would be talking of the requirements of rationality in the property sense. This is a different from the source sense, and requirements in one sense are not necessarily requirements in the other, even though the property of rationality is defined on the basis of requirements in the source sense.

Requirements in the property sense are not necessarily requirements in the source sense; I have already given the example of being alive. Moreover, requirements in the source sense are also not necessarily requirements in the property sense. For the sake of an example, let us assume that rationality in the source sense requires a person to intend to do whatever she believes she ought to do; I shall later say this is indeed so. Suppose Huck Finn believes he ought to hand over Jim, an escaped slave, to the authorities. (I take this example from Arpaly 2003.) Then, if he does not intend to hand Jim over, he is violating a requirement of rationality. But suppose that Huck would nevertheless be more rational overall if he were not to intend to hand Jim over. Perhaps having that intention would entail conflicts among Huck's deeply held moral beliefs. Then, in one sense of 'necessary condition,' a necessary condition for Huck to be more rational is that he does not intend to hand Jim over. So we might say that rationality in the property sense requires Huck not to intend to hand Jim over. There might nevertheless be no such requirement in the source sense. Moreover, we should not forget that, if Huck believes he ought to hand Jim over but does not intend to, he is violating a requirement of rationality in the source sense.

Since requirements of rationality in the source sense cannot be defined in terms of the property of rationality, but the property of rationality can be defined in terms of requirements of rationality in the source sense, these requirements are the key to describing rationality. I shall concentrate on them.

The rationality of things other than people is derivative from the rationality of people. Start with mental attitudes such as beliefs and intentions. We say a mental attitude of a person is irrational if the person would be more rational without it, and it is rational if it is not irrational. Next acts. An act has a mental component: you cannot do a particular act unless you have a particular mental attitude. We say an act is irrational if its corresponding attitude is irrational, and it is otherwise rational. The rationality or irrationality of other things such as conversations and traffic schemes derives from the rationality or irrationality of people in more remote ways that depend on the particular case.

Rationality and Normativity

What is the relation between rationality and normativity? Since rationality in the source sense issues requirements – we might say 'rules' – it is automatically normative in one sense. 'Normative' in one sense just means 'to do with rules.'

But for any source of requirements, there is a question of whether you have any reason to satisfy its requirements. Have you any reason to satisfy the requirements of convention, for instance? This is the question of whether convention is normative in a different sense. In this sense 'normative' means 'to do with reasons.' This is the sense that is commonest in moral philosophy, and it is the one I shall adopt. There is a real question of whether rationality is normative in this sense. To put it another way: have you any reason to satisfy the requirements of rationality?

I think this is a substantive question, which I shall not try to answer here. Instead, I shall respond to the common view that it is not a substantive question at all. Many philosophers think it is a conceptual truth that rationality consists in responding correctly to reasons. If that were so, it would follow that if rationality requires something of you, you have a reason to achieve that thing. So these philosophers think it is a conceptual truth that you have a reason to satisfy the requirements of rationality. There is no substantive question whether rationality is normative.

An objection to this view is that often you have false beliefs about reasons. You may believe your reasons require you to do something, whereas actually they require you not to do it. Then you are irrational if you intend not to do it, even though intending not to do it is the correct response to your reasons. So rationality cannot consist in responding correctly to reasons. I think this is a sound objection, and it remains a substantive question whether you have any reason to satisfy the requirements of rationality.

In answer to this objection, some philosophers make a distinction between subjective rationality and objective rationality. When you have the false beliefs I described, they say that subjective rationality requires you to intend to do what you believe your reasons require you to do, but objective rationality requires you to intend to do what your actual reasons require you to do. Objective rationality consists in responding correctly to actual reasons.

This is a bad answer. It flies in the face of something that is indeed a conceptual truth: that the property of rationality, when ascribed to a person, is a mental property. If, in one possible situation, your mind has just the same properties (apart from rationality) as it has in another, then your degree of rationality is exactly the same in one as it is in the other. Consequently, requirements of rationality are requirements on your mind only. The idea of objective rationality violates this principle, unless all your actual reasons are themselves properties of your mind. I assume they are not.

Suppose the hotel is on fire and the only way to escape is to jump from the window. Your actual reasons require you to jump. But suppose you have no idea the hotel is on fire, and you believe your reasons require you not to jump. It is implausible to say that you are in some way rational if you intend to jump. This is because rationality is a mental property. Since objective rationality is not a mental property, it is not rationality at all.

I conclude it is not the case that rationality consists in responding correctly to reasons. I believe the idea that it does arises largely from a confusion over the meaning of 'reason.' Some philosophers seem unhesitatingly to associate rationality with reasons, but actually the connection between rationality and reasons is not very close. It is true that 'rational' in the source sense is synonymous with the mass noun 'reason' in one of its senses. But the count noun 'reason,' whose plural is 'reasons,' has a quite different meaning. It is a normative word, whereas the meaning of the mass noun is not normative.

To illustrate the point, think of David Hume's remark that 'Tis not contrary to reason to prefer the destruction of the whole world to the scratching of my finger' (Hume 1978, Book 2, Part 2, § 2). Hume means that this preference is not contrary to rationality: that he might have this preference without violating a requirement of rationality. He does not mean that the preference is not contrary to his reasons. I assume Hume recognized he had a strong reason not to have this preference, since it is contrary to morality and to prudence. His claim is that it is not contrary to rationality.

Requirements of Rationality

How may we identify what the requirements of rationality are? Are there any guiding principles to follow? I have already mentioned one: that the property of rationality, when ascribed to a person, is a mental property. A second is that rationality is associated with good order in the mind; to be rational is to have a mind that is internally coherent. Correspondingly, requirements of rationality require coherence within the mind.

These two principles give us some limited guidance in identifying requirements of rationality. I know no other broad principles. Some philosophers think that particular requirements follow from the nature of certain mental states. For instance, it is said to be a constitutive feature of the state of belief that it aims at the truth, and certain requirements of rationality on beliefs are supposed to follow from this feature. But I have not seen this idea worked out convincingly in detail. So beyond those two general principles, I am guided largely by an intuitive idea of what rationality requires.

Mental coherence includes simple consistency, so some requirements of rationality require consistency. For instance, rationality requires you not to believe a proposition and also believe its negation, and not to intend to do something and also intend not to do it.

But rationality probably does not require you to have no inconsistent beliefs at all. Unless you are very complacent, you no doubt believe that not all your beliefs are true. That is to say, you believe that not all the propositions you believe are true. On the other hand, of each proposition you believe, you believe it is true. So your beliefs are inconsistent. Does rationality require you not to be in this state? Probably not; that would be implausibly demanding.

The requirements of rationality go beyond narrow consistency to wider sorts of coherence. One example is the instrumental requirement of practical rationality: the requirement to intend a means to an end that you intend. Practical requirements turn out to be surprisingly complicated to formulate precisely. This is my formulation:

Instrumental requirement. Rationality requires of *N* that, if

[1] *N* intends at *t* that *e*, and
[2] *N* believes at *t* that, if *m* were not so, because of that *e* would not be so, and
[3] *N* believes at *t* that, if she herself were not then to intend *m*, because of that *m* would not be so, then
[4] *N* intends at *t* that *m*.

Condition [1] says that you (more formally '*N*') intend an end *e*. Condition [2] says that you believe *m* is a means to *e*, and moreover that it is a means 'implied' by *e*, as I put it. It is commonly recognized that rationality requires you to intend what you believe is a necessary means to an end that you intend. But we rarely encounter means that we believe are strictly necessary, so that requirement is rarely applicable. My requirement is often applicable because condition [2] is frequently satisfied. Condition [3] says that you believe the means is 'up to you,' to put it informally. Rationality does not require you to intend a means to your end if you believe the means will happen anyway, without your intending it.

The formula as a whole says that rationality requires of you that, if you satisfy these conditions, you satisfy condition [4], which is to intend the means *m*.

An equally important requirement of practical rationality is one that requires you to intend to do what you believe you ought to do. I formulate it (slightly simplifying) as:

Enkrasia. Rationality requires of *N* that, if

[1] *N* believes at *t* that she herself ought to *F*, and
[2] *N* believes at *t* that, if she herself were then to intend to *F*, because of that, she would *F*, and
[3] *N* believes at *t* that, if she herself were not then to intend to *F*, because of that, she would not *F*, then,
[4] then *N* intends at *t* to *F*.

Clauses [2] and [3] say that it is up to you whether or not you *F*.

This is a central requirement of practical rationality. It is important because it links the theoretical with the practical. We often spend time on theoretical deliberation, forming beliefs about what we ought to do; enkrasia makes the results of our deliberation practical, because it requires our intentions, which are practical attitudes, to follow the beliefs we form. Implicitly, enkrasia has appeared twice in my argument previously: once in talking about Huck Finn, and once in discussing 'objective rationality.' (There I used 'your reasons require you to' rather than 'you ought to,' but the meaning is the same.)

Though enkrasia is crucially important, it is also controversial whether it is genuinely a requirement of rationality. Enkrasia is the requirement not to be akratic. It has traditionally been regarded as a requirement of rationality, because akrasia has traditionally been regarded as irrational. Moreover, it requires a sort of coherence between your normative beliefs and your intentions, and coherence is a mark of rationality. However, enkrasia seems intuitively not to be of a piece with the requirement not to have contradictory beliefs, or even with the instrumental requirement of practical rationality. Perhaps this is because it may sometimes require a difficult act of will. I shall not pursue this controversy here.

Reasoning

What role does the activity of reasoning play in our rationality? We satisfy many requirements of rationality naturally, without our doing anything about it. Unconscious process within us bring us to satisfy them. For instance, suppose you believe it is raining, but then you look up from your work and see the rain has stopped. Now you believe it is not raining. As you acquire this new belief, unconscious process within you cause you to stop believing it is raining. Those processes ensure you satisfy the requirement not to have contradictory beliefs, in this instance.

For another example, suppose you look up from your work and notice the time. You come to believe you ought to go home soon. At the same time, unconscious processes bring you to intend to go home soon. They bring you to satisfy enkrasia in this instance.

But sometimes automatic processes let you down, and you find yourself violating a particular requirement of rationality. In this case, there is something you can do for yourself that can bring your to satisfy the requirement, and that is reasoning.

For instance, suppose you intend to visit Venice, and you believe you will not visit Venice unless you buy a ticket to get there, but you do not intend to buy a ticket. You violate the instrumental requirement. You may say to yourself:

I shall visit Venice.
Buying a ticket is a means implied by my visiting Venice.
Buying a ticket is up to me.
So I shall buy a ticket.

(No doubt you would use less stilted language.) The second and third of these sentences express beliefs of yours. The first and fourth express intentions. You have the beliefs and the intention to visit Venice when you start your reasoning, and you acquire the intention to buy a ticket in the course of the reasoning. So this reasoning brings you to satisfy the instrumental requirement of rationality.

So reasoning can contribute to your rationality by giving you a means of bringing yourself to satisfy particular requirements of rationality.

See also: PRACTICAL REASONING (31); DELIBERATION AND DECISION (32); AKRASIA AND IRRATIONALITY (35); RESPONSIBILITY AND AUTONOMY (39); ACTION IN HISTORY AND SOCIAL SCIENCE (50); THE PREDICTION OF ACTION (51); HUME (63).

References

Arpaly, N. (2003). *Unprincipled Virtue*. Oxford: Oxford University Press.

Hume, D. (1978). *A Treatise of Human Nature* [1739/40], edited by L. A. Selby-Bigge and P. H. Nidditch. Oxford: Oxford University Press.

Further reading

Audi, R. (2006). *Practical Reasoning and Ethical Decision*. London: Routledge.

Bratman, M. E. (1987). *Intention, Plans and Practical Reason*. Chicago: University of Chicago Press.

Broome, J. (forthcoming). *Rationality through Reasoning*. Wiley–Blackwell.

Castañeda, H.-N. (1990). Practical thinking, reasons for doing, and intentional action: The thinking of doing and the doing of thinking. *Philosophical Perspectives*, 4, 273–308.

Chisholm, R. (1974). Practical reasoning and the logic of requirement. In S. Körner (ed.), *Practical Reason*. Oxford: Blackwell, 2–13. [Reprinted in J. Raz (ed.) (1978), *Practical Reasoning*, Oxford: Oxford University Press, 118–27.]

Grice, P. (2001). *Aspects of Reason*. Oxford: Oxford University Press.

Hare, R. M. (1971). *Practical Inferences*. London: Macmillan.

Harman, G. (1986). *Change in View: Principles of Reasoning*. Cambridge, MA: MIT Press.

Kolodny, N. (2005). Why be rational? *Mind*, 114, pp. 509–563.

Mele, A. R., and Rawling, P. (eds) (2004). *The Oxford Handbook of Rationality*. Oxford: Oxford University Press.

Parfit, D. (2001). Rationality and reasons. In D. Egonsson, J. Josefsson, B. Petersson, and T. Rønnow-Rasmussen (eds), *Exploring Practical Philosophy: From Action to Values*. Aldershot: Ashgate, 19–39.

Price, A. (2008). *Contextuality in Practical Reason*. Oxford: Oxford University Press.

Scanlon, T. M. (2007). Structural irrationality. In G. Brennan, R. Goodin, F. Jackson, and M. Smith (eds), *Common Minds: Themes from the Philosophy of Philip Pettit*. Oxford: Oxford University Press, 84–103.

Searle, J. (2001). *Rationality in Action*. Cambridge, MA: MIT Press.

Wedgwood, R. (2003). Choosing rationally and choosing correctly. In S. Stroud and C. Tappolet (eds), *Weakness of Will and Practical Irrationality*. Oxford: Oxford University Press, 201–229.

37

Motivational Internalism and Externalism

G. F. SCHUELER

The internalist–externalist debate in moral philosophy is about the place of motivation in morality and in moral judgments (where 'motivation' can refer either to having a normative reason to do something or to being actually inclined to do it). The underlying issue is about the connection between motivation and judgment generally. Intuitively, moral requirements or prohibitions give those who are subjected to them reason to act in the way required or to refrain from acting in the way forbidden. Analogously, the *belief* that one is required to do something or prohibited from doing it should move one to act or to refrain from acting in the designated way. These are internalist intuitions.

Broadly speaking, internalists hold that moral judgments (or, alternatively, moral 'facts' such as obligations) always somehow involve the agent's having some motivation, either toward the thing positively evaluated or away from the thing negatively evaluated. Externalists deny these things. Part of the interest in these opposed positions is that, while the two are apparently incompatible, each seems to be supported by a very plausible metaethical intuition. On the one hand, moral judgments, especially those about one's own actions, seem paradigmatically practical. Someone who blithely and without hesitation did something she claimed to think to be morally wrong would be regarded as insincere in her claim, and as not really thinking it to be wrong at all. On the other hand, the most straightforward form of moral realism, the sort which holds that moral wrongness, say, is simply a property of some actions, seems to entail that one could realize that an action one was considering doing had that property and yet one could be unmoved by the fact, just as one could be unmoved by any other fact about it.

This debate over the role of motivation in moral judgments is strongly influenced by the wide acceptance of the Humean theory of motivation (see chapter 20). According to this view, there is a sharp difference between beliefs and desires (or between states with a 'mind-to-world direction of fit' and states with a 'world-to-mind direction of fit'). And, on the Humean theory, all motivation requires desire; beliefs alone cannot motivate. So, if one accepts this theory, one seems committed to one of two positions, each of which seems problematic. Holding the 'cognitivist' view that moral beliefs have truth values like any other beliefs seems to commit one to the externalist position that moral beliefs by themselves involve no motivation. This makes moral motivation dependent on an extra, apparently non-rational, desire to do what is right (or some similar desire).

Alternatively, if one wants to be an internalist about moral judgments, one seems committed to holding that what is *called* a 'moral belief' is really some form of desire or 'pro-attitude,' which makes one a 'non-cognitivist' about moral beliefs and seems to entail that such 'beliefs' cannot have truth values. So trying to combine these two initial intuitions – that moral beliefs both motivate and have truth values like any other beliefs – and to achieve a 'cognitivist internalism' seems to require rejecting the Humean theory of motivation.

There is yet another complicating factor. It might be thought that motivation takes place through reasons, or through the agent's conception of her reasons. And one could be an internalist or externalist about reasons, or reason judgments, as well as about moral facts or judgments. So there are two further issues. First, if one thinks that motivation takes place through reasons for acting (or through the agent's judgment about this), this requires understanding the question of whether moral judgments (or facts) motivate in terms of the question of whether such judgments or facts provide reasons to act. Second, since reasons, or reason judgments, also seem to move us, the same issue about the connection with an inclination to act arises for reason judgments (or facts) as for moral judgments (or facts).

To distinguish between whether we are speaking of judgments or the 'facts' these judgments are about, we can follow Darwall and distinguish 'judgment internalist' from 'existence internalist' views. Judgment internalists

> hold it to be a necessary condition of a genuine instance of a certain sort of *judgment* that the person making the judgment be disposed to act in a way appropriate to it.

Existence internalism, however,

> is the thesis that something is a ground of an act's actually having a certain property (being right, for example [...]) only if it is capable of motivating the agent.[1]

If we focus first on moral claims, the distinctions between moral judgments and moral facts and between reasons and motives mark out four possible versions of internalism.[2]

There is, first, the sort of existence internalism that claims a necessary connection between moral facts (such as obligations) and justifying reasons. That would seem to be true for instance if ethical egoism is the correct moral theory, since egoism says that what one morally should do is what will serve ones own interest and, presumably, one always has a good reason to do what is one's own interest.

Second, there would be the sort of existence internalism which held that the mere fact of the existence of a moral requirement is necessarily connected to the motivation of the agent under the requirement. This looks plausible if one holds that moral requirements are not independent of the attitudes of the agent, for example that it is a necessary condition of someone's being morally required to do something that she should have a certain attitude toward that thing. This later condition becomes plausible if, for example, one combines the view that moral facts entail justifying reasons (the first view just distinguished) with the idea that justifying reasons themselves entail some sort of internal motivating state in the agent (which is an existence internalist view about reasons, not about moral facts). Bernard Williams famously argues for this latter view.[3]

The other two sorts of 'ethical' internalism start with moral judgments, rather than moral requirements or other moral facts. So a third variety of internalism claims that there is a necessary connection between moral judgments and justifying reasons; more specifically, that having a good reason for doing or avoiding something is a necessary condition of judging some act to be morally required or prohibited. This form of internalism would be entailed if one held both that moral judgments involve, or contain, a motivation to follow them (the fourth variety of internalism, below) and that one's having some motive to act is a sufficient condition for having a reason to act.

The fourth variety of internalism holds that there is a necessary connection between moral or evaluative judgments and the motivation of the agent who makes the judgment. Emotivism, for instance, is this sort of judgment internalism (as are, I think, its contemporary, 'expressivist' descendants).[4] Emotivism claims that to make a moral judgment is just to express a certain attitude. And, since emotivists hold that attitudes are motivating states, on this view making a moral judgment involves, among other things, being inclined or motivated toward the thing evaluated if the judgment is positive, or against it if the judgment is negative.

If this kind of view were correct, it would solve (or 'dissolve') the apparent puzzle about the connection between moral facts and agent motivation in a very direct way. The apparent motivational 'pull' (or 'push') of things with evaluative properties would be an artefact of this feature of moral or evaluative judgments, rather than being a feature of the things themselves. According to this view, we only judge things to have such properties if we have some motivating attitude toward them.

As it stands, though, this taxonomy of internalisms is incomplete, since it leaves out internalism about either reasons or reason judgments. Bernard Williams' 'internal reasons' view is of the former sort. According to Williams, roughly, one only has a good reason to do something if that thing promotes the satisfaction of a preexisting desire (or some other 'subjective motivational' state).[5] This is a form of existence internalism about normative reasons rather than about any specifically moral fact such as a moral obligation. If one accepts the first variety of internalism presented above, the notion of an agent having a good reason to do something can provide a 'middle term' connecting claims about moral requirements and the actions that constitute following those requirements. Michael Smith, for instance, argues that a form of judgment internalism which claims a connection between moral judgments and motivation (the fourth variety presented above) is entailed by a form of existence internalism which connects moral facts with reasons (the first variety). This is because, he says,

> an agent who judges herself to have a reason to act in a certain way [...] is practically irrational if she is not motivated to act accordingly. For if she is not motivated accordingly then she fails to be rational by her own lights.

So Smith holds that the first variety entails the fourth variety because,

> according to the [first variety], the judgement that it is right to act in a certain way is simply equivalent to the judgement that there is a reason to act in that way.[6]

Williams' view also makes sense of (though it does not fit into) the second of the four categories just distinguished – the one which makes it a necessary condition of having a moral obligation that the agent have some motive to act on that obligation. Again, it does this if we accept the view delineated in the first category, that it is a necessary condition of having a moral obligation that one have some good reason to act on it. If this is true, then, if Williams is right and having some preexisting motive is a necessary condition of having such a reason, it follows that it is a necessary condition of having a moral obligation that one should have some preexisting motive, which would lead one to act on it.

But this fifth form of internalism, exemplified by Williams' internal reasons doctrine, though it connects reasons and motives, leads to a form of skepticism about morality. If one accepts it, then one is faced with an unhappy choice, which turns on one's view about the first kind of internalism. On the one hand, one can deny this kind of internalism – in other words deny that obligations and other such 'moral facts' entail reasons to act on them. This would mean, however, that, even though Gyges in Plato's famous story may have been under a genuine moral requirement not to do the immoral things his invisibility allowed him to do, he may still have had no actual reason to act on this requirement, if there was nothing which moved him to do so. Alternatively, if one wants to hold that moral requirements do entail reasons, then accepting Williams' internal reasons claim means that Gyges may have been under no actual moral requirement to forgo what he did, if he had no inclination to do so.

The plausibility of the forth sort of internalism – the judgment internalist idea that there is a necessary connection between an agent's judgment, say, that she has a moral obligation and that agent's being moved to act on the judgment in question – rests, at least partly, on the intuition mentioned above that someone who makes such a moral judgment but has no inclination to act on it would be revealed as insincere. A similar intuition holds for reason judgments and motivation. Someone who agrees that she has good reason to do something while remaining utterly unmoved to do it even when she thinks she has no reason not to looks insincere in her agreement. And, as Smith's argument suggests, it is plausible to think that the first intuition rests on the second, since the connection between moral facts and reasons (the first sort of internalism) is itself widely accepted. So it may help to evaluate at least some of the versions of *ethical* internalism to look more carefully at the *reasons* internalism, which connects reason judgments and motivation (which is the sixth variety to be distinguished). In the terminology adopted above, this is *judgment internalism about the agent's own normative or justifying reasons.*

The claim to examine is that:

JIR *It is a necessary condition of making a genuine judgment to the effect that one has a good reason to do something that one be, at least to some minimal degree, motivated or inclined to do it.*

The plausibility of this claim rests on the fact that it seems to provide something close to the minimum connection between the normative and the practical. Even if one doesn't think that obligations or reasons connect to motivation, or that ethical judgments automatically motivate, it seems hard to deny that judgments about *their own reasons* motivate those who make them, at least if these judgment-makers are rational. That seems to be what Smith has in mind when he writes, in the argument quoted above, that 'an agent who judges herself to have a reason to act in a certain way [...] is practically irrational if she is not motivated to act accordingly.' If JIR is not true, then it seems very difficult to explain what the connection is between the agent's own view of the reasons she has for doing something and her actually doing it. And it seems that there must be some connection. Otherwise judgments about one's reasons to act will make it no more likely that one will actually perform the action than will one's judgments about, say, whether the action will happen on an even-numbered day of the month.

What is it to make a judgment that one has good reason to do something? Expressivist and similar speech-act accounts of judgments, to be plausible at all, will have to make judgments into silent, inner speech, since not all judgments are in the form of actual utterances. But of course I can say things, even if only to myself, which I know to be false. And, similarly, most of the things I judge (believe) to be true I am not even thinking about at the moment, let alone talking about (even to myself). These are familiar points. But they apply to the judgments one makes about one's own reasons as much as to any other judgments. Sometimes, when I am trying to figure out what to do, I explicitly consider the various things that I take to count for or against the action I am considering. But such explicit deliberation is rare, and for the same reason explicit rehearsal of ones beliefs is rare. Life is just too short and our beliefs far too numerous. Besides, since deliberation is itself something one can have reasons for and against doing, engaging in it could itself be an object of deliberation. So, on pain of regress, it is not possible that all the things one does for reasons are things one deliberates about.

There are really two distinct questions: What is it to act for a reason? What is it to *judge* that one has a reason to do something? JIR is about the second question, but the first is the more general one. We can make a start at seeing what the connection between the two is if we make the simplifying assumption that, in some case, the agent does explicitly deliberate and then acts on the basis of her deliberation. Consider such a case.

A few moments ago I got up from my desk and walked to the kitchen to get some coffee. Suppose that, when I reach the point in the hallway where I need to turn left in order to get to the kitchen, I pause and consciously try to figure out what to do:

> 'Let's see,' I say to myself, 'I want to get some coffee and at this point in the hallway there are four possible ways to go.
>
> 1 I could continue down the hallway in the same direction I am now heading. That will take me into my wife's workroom.
> 2 I could turn left, which is the direction of the kitchen, where the coffee is.
> 3 I could turn around and go back to my desk. Or
> 4 I could just stand here in the hallway.
>
> Going to my wife's workroom is not a bad idea, since it is always nice to see what she is working on, but that might distract me from what I am doing and anyway I want to get some coffee at the moment and there is none in her workroom. There is nothing to be said for just standing in the hallway or turning back toward my desk in defeat. The coffee, which is what I am after, is in the kitchen to the left. So, I'll turn left.'

Notice that, though these judgments *set out* my reason for turning left, nowhere in this deliberation does the claim *that* I have reason to turn left appear. So did I, just as I turned, *judge* that I had good reason to turn left? I don't think it is obvious that the answer to this question is 'yes,' even though I clearly *had* a reason for turning at that point and I did indeed turn *for that reason.*

Someone might think that the above description just leaves out the relevant reasons claim. And, of course, I might have made that claim while deliberating. So the question is really whether without such a claim my deliberation would have been incomplete or defective. I think the answer is that it would not have been. What gives me reason to turn left is the fact that what I want, the coffee, is to the left. So how could there be anything wrong with the reasoning in which I take account of this fact and, as a result, decide to turn left?

Let's assume that, given that I want to get some coffee and the coffee is in the kitchen to my left, I have reason to turn left. That truth is not part of my reasoning, because it cannot be one of my reasons. What has to be part of my reasoning is what makes it true that I have reason to turn left, in other words the fact that what I want, the coffee, is to the left. Here is a different sort of example. Suppose I believe that *P* and that, if *P*, then *Q*. Assuming that these two beliefs are themselves well founded, I have good reason to believe that *Q*. Does this mean that, in order to be completely accurate, all reasoning via *modus ponens* should really be represented as follows?

[1] *P*.
[2] If *P*, then *Q*.
[3] Premises [1] and [2] provide good reason to believe that *Q*.
[4] So, *Q*.

No. As Lewis Carroll showed a long time ago, this immediately leads to a regress.[7] Exactly the same bad argument that seems to require the addition of [3] leads to the addition of another premise to the effect that [1]–[3] provide reason to believe that *Q*. And so on. The sentence labeled [3] here is not part of the reasoning at all. That does not mean that someone might not *utter* [3] in the course of her attempt to figure out whether *Q* is true. It means that the argument here is a perfectly good one (logically valid in fact) without the addition of [3].

Exactly parallel considerations apply to practical reasoning, and hence to whether we need to add the claim that I have reason to turn left in the description of my deliberation in the hallway. If the fact that I have a reason is itself a reason, on a par with the fact that the coffee I want is in the kitchen to the left, then my deliberation won't be correct until I include this further reason as one of my reasons. And then we get the same issue for that addition, and a similar regress.

The claim that some fact gives someone a reason to do something is a claim about the rational status of that action with respect to that fact. It is not, therefore, *part* of what makes it reasonable to perform the action in question. So the description of my deliberation given above is acceptable as it stands. Though I might have had the *thought* that I have good reason to turn left, that is not part of my deliberation. It is a comment *about* my reasons, not one of the reasons themselves.

JIR is the claim that a necessary condition of an agent's making a judgment that she has reason to do something is that she should be, at least to some minimal extent, motivated to act on that reason. This means that a good place to look for such judgments is where agents are motivated to act, and in particular where they do act for reasons. But when we examine the example of my turning left toward the coffee in my kitchen, it turns out that I need to make no actual reason judgment; in fact the thought that I must employ such a judgment generates a regress. Yet I still have a reason to act, and in this example I do indeed act for that reason.

This does not show that JIR is false, of course. I have been arguing that one can act for a reason without making the judgment that one has a reason, not that one can make such a judgment without being moved to act. But this argument does suggest that, even if this form of internalism is true, it doesn't really help us to make sense of what it is to act for reasons. It also raises the question of what the supposed 'motivation' claimed by this form of judgment internalism could possibly be. If the argument above is correct, then the motivation could not be the sort of motivational connection represented in practical deliberation, when someone considers what reasons she has and then acts on this deliberation. Judgments to the effect that I have a reason are not a part of practical deliberation at all. They are descriptions of the status of one's reasons. So, if such judgments somehow motivate actions, this must be some sort of extra- or non-rational form of motivation.

JIR is important because it links moral judgment and motivation, and it seems plausible because it appears to show that we can make sense of why people are moved to act on the reasons they judge they have – and that we can do so through the idea that having some inclination to act in the specified way is a condition for judging that one even has such a reason. But if JIR is to help us understand what it is to act for a reason, we must presuppose that, when someone acts for a reason, she judges that she has a reason to act in the way she does. As we have seen, this is not the case.

See also: SPEECH ACTS (8); MOTIVATING REASONS (19); HUMEANISM ABOUT MOTIVATION (20); WHAT A DIFFERENCE EMOTIONS MAKE (25); PRACTICAL REASONING (31); AKRASIA AND IRRATIONALITY (35); RATIONALITY (36); HUME (63).

Notes

1 Darwall 1983: 54.
2 This part of the taxonomy of varieties of internalism, which is to be explained below, follows Shafer-Landau 2003 (ch. 6).
3 See Williams 1979.
4 The classic expression of emotivism can be found in Stevenson 1963. For an example of contemporary expressivism, see virtually any of the essays in Blackburn 1993.
5 Williams 1979.
6 Smith 1994: 62.
7 Carroll 1995: 691–693.

References

Blackburn, S. (1993). *Essays in Quasi-Realism*. Oxford: Oxford University Press.
Carroll, L. (1995). What the tortoise said to Achilles [1895]. *Mind*, 104 (416), 691–693.

Darwall, S. (1983). *Impartial Reason*. New York: Cornell University Press.
Shafer-Landau, R. (2003). *Moral Realism*. Oxford: Oxford University Press.
Smith, M. (1994). *The Moral Problem*. Oxford: Blackwell.
Stevenson, C. (1963). *Facts and Values*. New Haven, CT: Yale University Press.
Williams, B. (1979). Internal and external reasons. In R. Harrison (ed.), *Rational Action*. Cambridge: Cambridge University Press, 17–28. [Reprinted in B. Williams (1981), *Moral Luck*, Cambridge: Cambridge University Press, 101–113.]

38

Free Will and Determinism

THOMAS PINK

Intentional human action is something we naturally take to be within our control; it is up to us how we act. This up-to-us-ness of our action is what philosophers call freedom or free will. But whether or not we really do enjoy free will is disputed. One central threat to free will is causal determinism. If all our actions were predetermined by causes outside our control, many would claim that those same actions could not still be within our control. So is determinism a real threat to free will; and what hangs on the issue? Why might it matter whether we possess free will?

Freedom as a Power

If the way we act is up to us, then we must have a capacity to determine our action for ourselves. But capacities to determine, or at least influence, what happens are powers. So our belief in the up-to-us-ness of our action is the belief in our possession of a power over how we act – a power which, ever since the Hellenistic period, philosophers, borrowing a term originally used in political theory, have termed *freedom*. What kind of power might freedom be?

One obvious case of power is displayed by causation. Causes have the capacity to determine or influence the occurrence of their effects, which is why we think of causes as exercising a power or force over what happens. Indeed, causation is such a central and familiar form of power that philosophers have tended to write as if all power were causal, and so as if freedom in particular must be a causal power. In which case to exercise control over one's actions would always be to produce effects (see Clarke 2003 and O'Connor 2000).

But we should not assume that all power is causal. For outcomes can be determined without being determined causally. Take a moral or a normative power, for example. As a promisee, I may well have the power to release you, as promisor, from your obligation under your promise to me. That is, I have the capacity to determine that you are no longer obliged to deliver on your promise. Now, when I exercise this moral power, my exercise of it may well consist in the utterance of certain words – such as 'I release you from your promise' – an utterance which determines that you are released. The relation between my declaration and your release is a relation of determiner to determined – but the determination is not causal. For the determining event and the event determined are not distinct in the way causes are distinct from the effects they determine. My declaration of your release is not distinct from the release it determines, but constitutes that very outcome (for an argument that freedom is not a causal power, see Pink 2004, ch. 8).

Freedom differs from ordinary cases of causal power in one very obvious respect. Causal power may perfectly well occur in one-way form. That is, a causal power may exist to determine only one outcome, not a range of alternatives. The brick's hitting the window may have the power to cause but one effect – that the window breaks. But, on our natural conception of it, freedom is quite different. Freedom seems by its very nature to be a two-way or multi-way power, which can be exercised in more than one way. The nature of freedom is to leave it up to us which actions we perform – whether we raise our hand or lower it. If it exists at all, the very power that could be exercised by us to determine one outcome could equally well be exercised by us to determine another. That indeed seems to be precisely how we identify the power of freedom: it is that power which leaves the way we act up to us, or within our control.

Some powers are powers primarily of states and events. Here, any ordinary talk of the power as attaching to substances is to be explained in terms of its attaching to events and states in the life of the substance. Causation is often thought of nowadays in just these terms. Granted, substances such as stones are ordinarily talked of as causing things; we naturally say that it was the stone that caused the window to break. But, according to many modern philosophers, this talk of stones as causes is supposed to be explained in terms of causal power attaching not immediately to stones themselves, but to occurrences or events involving them – such as to the event of the stone's hitting the window.

But perhaps some powers really do attach primarily to substances. And, whatever might or might not be true of causation, it does seem to be true of other powers that they are primarily possessed and exercised by substances. Take, again, my moral power as promisee to release you as promisor from your obligation to me. My exercise of this power may require an event to determine the release – such as the utterance of the words 'I release you.' But surely these words uttered by me can determine this outcome only because I, as a substance, possess a power to release you. It is to me as human substance that you owe the obligation; and it is I as a human substance who possess the right to release you, and so the moral capacity and power corresponding to it.

Freedom does seem, by its very nature, to be the power of a substance. For if we are free it is because we ourselves, and not just some event or state distinct from us, have the power to determine what we do. And because this power is one which we possess ourselves, if it is real, it can ground our moral responsibility for what we do. We are morally responsible for our actions insofar as we can be fairly held to blame for faults in what we do – because the faults in what we do are our own. And, if we are morally responsible, that must be because it is we who determine what we do, and not just events or states distinct from us. It is the agent, and not simply some state or event within him, that is responsible; because it is the agent, and not simply some such state or event, who is in control and who determines how he acts. Excuses which reduce moral responsibility can do so precisely by displacing responsibility from the agent himself to an event or state involving him. As we might say: the agent was not responsible for what he did; it was his overwhelming fear that made him do it.

Freedom and Determinism

Causal determinism is the claim that everything which happens, including our own actions, has already been causally determined to occur. Everything that happens results from earlier causes – causes which not only influence, but determine their effects by ensuring that these effects must occur, leaving no chance for things to happen otherwise. So, if causal determinism is true, then what will happen at any time in the future is already entirely fixed and determined by the past.

And there is a strong inclination to think that the truth of causal determinism would definitely remove our freedom. Suppose, for example, that, by the time of your birth, the world already contained causes – be they the environment into which you were born or the genes you were born with – which determined exactly what you were going to do throughout your life. Then, it is very tempting to think, at no stage could the way you act possibly remain up to you. If, from the very beginning, it has all along been determined exactly how you must act, how could you possibly be free to act otherwise?

'Incompatibilism' is the doctrine that freedom is incompatible with the causal predetermination of the way we act by factors outside our control. 'Libertarianism' about freedom of action combines incompatibilism with the further belief that we do actually possess control over the way we act. 'Compatibilism' asserts, by contrast, that freedom is perfectly compatible with the causal predermination of action by causal factors outside our control.

English-language philosophy has often treated the debate about the implications of determinism for our freedom as if it were a debate about the semantics of the expression '*X* could have done otherwise': does this expression have truth conditions logically consistent with causal determinism? And arguments such as the famous 'consequence argument' (see van Inwagen 1983 and Lewis 1986) have sought to determine the issue conceptually, by logical deduction from platitudes common to any competent user of the relevant English terms. But such conceptual arguments have not been found conclusive by the generality of philosophers, and this conceptual or semantic approach may be not be the right approach to the issue.

For the free will debate seems to be about power – about the relation of one power, a two-way power over our own actions, with another, the causal power attaching to other substances or occurrences outside our control. Now debates about the relations between various kinds of power – such as whether the existence or operation of one power precludes or defeats that of another – need not be conceptual or semantic. For example, if the two powers in question were causal, we might not be able to settle the matter by a priori reasoning at all. We might have to experiment or look. This raises the issue whether the power of freedom and its properties, including its relations to other powers such as ordinary causation, is represented to us in experience. For if it were so represented, the free will debate would have to refer to that representation as a possible source of our intuitions and to determine whether it was veridical or delusory. And theories of freedom have importantly differed on just this issue. Thus the medieval scholastic John Duns Scotus (see Wolter 1986) seems to have taught that our belief in, and view of, our own freedom is indeed based on an experiential representation of its existence as a distinctive two-way power. Whereas modern English-language philosophy has been deeply influenced by David Hume's doctrine that powers, and in particular causal powers, are not directly represented in experience. In which case it is tempting to suppose that the nature of freedom and its compatibility with determinism must be determinable conceptually rather than by reference to experience (for more on the phenomenology of free will, see Nahmias et al. 2004 and Pink 2009b).

Another possibility is that incompatibilist intuitions are based neither on the very concept of our power of freedom nor on any experiential representation of that power, but are instead ethically motivated. Belief in the moral responsibility and possible blameworthiness of agents comes first; and an ethical conception of what true moral responsibility would involve then generates an incompatibilist conception of freedom. On this view, we are incompatibilists about freedom because we think that our moral responsibility depends on its being we, and not causes distinct from us, that determine what we do; and we think of freedom as by its very nature taking just the form that our moral responsibility would require (for discussion, see Williams 1995).

On the other hand, it may be that the opposite is true. We hold agents responsible because we detect a power on their part to determine for themselves the way they act. It is then our independent understanding of the properties of this power that shapes our conception of moral responsibility and the conditions on which it depends. If we think that freedom is incompatible with causal determinism, that is because we have a conception of the relation between freedom and the power of prior causes that comes from outside of ethics. Perhaps it comes, as I suggested it might, from experiential representations of the powers concerned and of their relations. It is only because we believe, on such non-ethical grounds, that the power of freedom would be inconsistent with causal determinism that we then suppose that the moral responsibility which presupposes that power is also incompatible with determinism.

A central and still open question about freedom and causal determinism is whether the problem of their compatibility is primarily metaphysical, being immediately about the relations between various kinds of power; or whether it is a problem generated from within ethics by the central ethical notion of moral responsibility – in which case the key question is what it means to be truly morally responsible for what we do, so that the faults in what we do can be our own.

Freedom and Action

The power of freedom is exercised in and through our action. I can determine for myself whether the lights come on or not thanks to my having control over some action, such as operating the light switch, which would determine whether the lights come on; and I exercise that control in intentional agency – by intentionally operating the switch or by intentionally refraining from operating it. What is the relation between the power and the action? How have philosophical conceptions of the power been related to philosophical conceptions of action?

Some might say that it is in the very nature of intentional action to be determined by the agent. On this view, a philosophical theory of action will, precisely, specify intentional action as involving the exercise by the agent of a certain kind of power over what he does. Intentional action, after all, is what the agent *does*. An account of the nature of the power will give us an account of what action itself involves.

It is not entirely clear that this need be so, however. For not all action, even fully intentional action, need be determined by the agent. Can I not do something, and do it intentionally, but be compelled and determined to do it by some overwhelming fear or anger – so that it is the fear or anger that determines what I do, and what I do is no longer left up to me?

In any case, there seems to be a way of identifying intentional agency that does not, at least not obviously, involve appeal to the exercise of any power. For it has been natural to think of agency, ever since Aristotle, as involving the intentional adoption and employment of means to ends. An action is an event that is intentionally directed to the attainment of an end – an end the real or apparent desirability of which motivates the action's performance, and motivates the action as a means to its attainment. This model obviously still applies even when the action is performed for its own sake – even when the action's performance constitutes, just of itself, the attainment of the very end at which that performance is directed.

Goal-directedness, *A*-ing in order that *E*, does not obviously involve the exercise by the agent of any power over his action. For the exercise of power over his action by the agent involves, plainly, a relation of the agent, as determiner, to his action, as something determined. But goal-directedness seems to involve something very different – a relation between the action and an object of thought at which the action is directed, an object of thought which stands to the action as its goal. It is not clear why a theory of goal-directedness, of the relation of the action to its object, should deliver or be delivered by a theory of self-determination – which would be a theory of a very different relation: that of the agent to the action.

So what kind of relation is this one, between an action and its object? What is it for an event to be directed at an object as its motivating goal?

One venerable answer to this question once dominated action theory in the Middle Ages and early modern period – though it has been remarkably ignored by, and is absent from, English-language action theory in our day. On this *practical reason-based* view, the relation between an action and its object is a special case of a wider phenomenon – in which mental beings, or events and states within them, are directed at objects of thought (see Pink 2009a). Beliefs are directed at objects of thought, what is believed, as true. Desires are directed at objects of thought, what is desired, as good or desirable. Actions are directed at objects of thought, what is pursued or acted towards, as both good or desirable and attainable through the action – in other words, actions are directed at objects of thought as goals. And what determines the nature of the object-direction in each case is the way the rationality of the form of object-direction is determined. In the case of belief, the attitude is rational only if the object at which it is directed is sufficiently likely to be true. In the case of desire, the attitude is rational only if the object at which it is directed is sufficiently likely to be good or desirable. In the case of action, the direction towards the object is rational only if that object is both sufficiently likely to be good or desirable and sufficiently likely to be attained through the event directed at it. And that is a central and distinguishing feature of reason in practical or practice-governing – action-governing – form. An action is rationally performed only if the goal or end at which it is directed is sufficiently desirable; and only if the action's performance, the event directed at its attainment, is sufficiently likely to attain that end.

But then we are characterizing intentional action in terms of its involving one mode of rationally appraisable directing ourselves at an object of thought – a mode of direction that occurs not in cognitive, nor in simply desiderative form, but in a distinctively practical or goal-directed form, a form revealed by the application of a certain, specifically practical, kind of rationality. We have a conception of intentional agency that is indeed practical reason-based. And this does not obviously involve any conception of a power being exercised by the agent over his action. If such a power is involved, the nature of it must be determined from outside action theory.

But English-language philosophy has been dominated by a quite different conception of what action's goal-directedness involves, and one which does make appeal to power – a causal power attached not directly to agents, but to events or states in their life which are not the agents' own doing: they precede these agents' own actions, being causes of them.

On this view, goal-directedness involves what I shall term 'voluntariness' – an action's being caused by a pro-attitude or pro-attitudes to its performance. To cross the road voluntarily is to cross the road as an effect of a pro-attitude towards so crossing – for example a desire or an intention to cross, whether for its own sake or as a means to further ends to which the agent also holds pro-attitudes, such as reaching the shop on the other side. The goal or goals at which an action is directed come from the contents of all these motivating pro-attitudes.

This theory of action and its goal-directedness was pioneered by Thomas Hobbes (see Hobbes and Bramhall 1656), but has been most influentially defended in modern times by Donald Davidson (see Davidson 1980). And it characterizes action as an effect of prior motivating pro-attitudes – attitudes that, if the theory is not to prove viciously regressive, cannot arise as, or through, actions themselves. On this theory, the very occurrence of action involves the exercise of a power. The power in question is not, however, an inherently two-way power of the agents themselves, but rather a one-way causal power attaching to motivations or passions within the agent that are not themselves the agent's own doing.

Nevertheless, English-language compatibilism has characteristically identified freedom with this power. In the classical and simple formulation of the doctrine, the two-way power of freedom that leaves it up to us whether or not we cross the road is reduced to a combination of distinct one-way causal powers – a power of a will or motivation to cross the road to cause us successfully to cross, and a separate power of a will or motivation not to cross to cause us to refrain from crossing.

This reductive account of freedom is dubious, precisely because it seeks to explain a two-way power of agents themselves in terms of a merely one-way power of mere occurrences or states distinct from the agent and not of his own doing. Moreover, this reductive account leaves the freedom – conceived of as a two-way control over the actions we perform – immediately and obviously irrelevant to our moral responsibility for the way we act – which we do not ordinarily suppose freedom to be. For if freedom is indeed nothing but a combination of two distinct powers of voluntariness, then freedom will surely drop out as a distinct condition on moral responsibility. And this is because, on this classic reductive account of freedom, the only power of 'self-determination' ever exercised is voluntariness. Freedom as a power to do otherwise is left as a power that is never exercised at all.

On the classical English-language compatibilist reduction, whenever I do *A*, the power of self-determination exercised is the power of a will or motivation to do *A* to cause me to do *A*. Any power to act otherwise – to refrain – is quite distinct, and it is certainly not being exercised. It is quite inert. Its presence or absence would make no difference to the power I am actually exercising, since the two powers are distinct and independent of each other. In which case, the presence or absence of this unexercised power to act otherwise must be irrelevant to my moral responsibility for what I do. How can moral responsibility ever depend on a kind of power that is never actually exercised to determine what we do? But that, on this reductive account of freedom, is precisely what the freedom to do otherwise becomes.

Our moral responsibility for action depends on the fact that we ourselves determine the way we act. The question, then, is what kind of self-determining power we really exercise. For that will provide the true basis of our moral responsibility. Is it that we are exercising a power to act otherwise? Or is it that we are acting as we will, and because we so will? Which matters – control or voluntariness? The idea of freedom as two-way voluntariness is an attempt to combine both conceptions. But it is a deeply unstable compromise, and control is surely going to be the loser. And this is because, on this theory, the power to act otherwise is never actually being exercised to determine action – only a power to act as one wills. The power to act otherwise is present, but as a dummy that plays no active role at all. Why make moral responsibility depend on it, if it is irrelevant to any power that the agent actually exercises over the way he acts? (See Pink 2009a for further development of this argument.)

See also: VOLITION AND THE WILL (13); REASONS AND CAUSES (17); AGENT CAUSATION (28); ADDICTION AND COMPULSION (34); RESPONSIBILITY AND AUTONOMY (39); ACTION AND CRIMINAL RESPONSIBILITY (42); SCIENTIFIC CHALLENGES TO FREE WILL (44); DUNS SCOTUS (57); HOBBES (58); DAVIDSON (73).

References

Clarke, R. (2003). *Libertarian Accounts of Free Will*. Oxford: Oxford University Press.

Davidson, D. (1980). Actions, reasons and causes. In D. Davidson, *Essays on Actions and Events*. Oxford: Oxford University Press, 3–19.

Hobbes, T. and Bramhall, J. (1656). *The Questions Concerning Liberty, Necessity and Chance, Clearly Stated between Dr Bramhall Bishop of Derry, and Thomas Hobbes of Malmesbury*. London.

Lewis, D. (1986). Are we free to break the laws? In D. Lewis, *Philosophical Papers*, Vol. 2. Oxford: Oxford University Press, 291–298.

Nahmias, E., Morris, S., Nadelhofer, T., and Turner, J. (2004). The phenomenology of free will. *Journal of Consciouness Studies*, 11, 162–179.

O'Connor, T. (2000). *Persons and Causes*. Oxford: Oxford University Press.

Pink, T. (2004). *Free Will: A Very Short Introduction*. Oxford: Oxford University Press.

Pink, T. (2009a). Power and moral responsibility. *Philosophical Explorations*, 12, 127–149.

Pink, T. (2009b). Free will and consciousness. In Tim Bayne (ed.), *The Oxford Companion to Consciousness*. Oxford: Oxford University Press, pp. 296–300.

Van Inwagen, P. (1983). *An Essay on Free Will*. Oxford: Oxford University Press.
Williams, B. (1995). Nietzsche's minimalist moral psychology. In B. Williams, *Making Sense of Humanity*. Cambridge: Cambridge University Press, 65–76.
Wolter, A. (1986). *Duns Scotus on Will and Morality*. Washington, DC: Catholic University of America Press.

Further reading

Fischer, J. M. (1994). *The Metaphysics of Free Will*. Oxford: Blackwell.
Kane, R. (ed.) (2002). *The Oxford Handbook to Free Will*. Oxford: Oxford University Press.
Pereboom, D. (2006). *Living without Free Will*. Cambridge: Cambridge University Press.
Strawson, G. (1986). *Freedom and Belief*. Oxford: Oxford University Press.
Watson, G. (ed.) (2003). *Free Will*. Oxford: Oxford University Press (Oxford Readings in Philosophy).

39

Responsibility and Autonomy

JOHN MARTIN FISCHER

The Concept of Responsibility

We use the term 'responsibility' to pick out various different kinds of responsibility, including causal responsibility, role-responsibility, and moral responsibility. One is causally responsible for some upshot insofar as one is part of the causal chain leading to that upshot, quite apart from whether one is morally accountable for it (or morally accountable at all). So, for example, the lightning bolt might be causally responsible for the fire, the earthquake for the crack in the roof, and an individual who sneezed loudly might be causally responsible for waking up the baby. There might also be cases in which an agent is morally but not causally responsible for an upshot, but this is a bit more contentious. Imagine, for example, that one does not initiate or contribute 'positively' to a causal sequence issuing in a certain upshot, but that it is one's duty to prevent the upshot, and one intentionally fails to prevent it. This is arguably a case of moral responsibility for the upshot without causal responsibility, although it might be argued that one has caused the upshot through one's *omission* to act.

Role-responsibility is a matter of the duties associated with a specific role. So, for instance, the chair of the philosophy department is responsible for arranging for certain courses to be taught every year; the mayor is responsible for making sure that the city's officials are paid; and a parent is responsible for making sure that his or her child goes to school on time. Role-responsibility typically involves moral responsibility, because the relevant roles are usually assumed voluntarily. But the two kinds of responsibility can pull apart, especially if a certain role is 'thrust upon one.' Suppose, for instance, that one is forced by the dean to be department chair at gunpoint. (Whereas this is obviously fanciful, it is perhaps not wildly implausible!) In such a case, if the chair is really *compelled* to assume the role (and not simply cajoled or importuned), then she would presumably not be morally blameworthy for not fulfilling the chair's role-responsibilities (in case she does not fulfill them).

We might call an individual 'responsible,' or say that she is 'very responsible,' meaning that she fulfills her role-responsibilities well. At a wedding, I was once asked by a relative what I write about, and I answered that I was working on a book on moral responsibility. She replied, 'Good, we need more of that.' I interpreted her as saying that it would be desirable if people took their role-responsibilities more seriously. Perhaps there are role-responsibilities associated with being a human being; of course, these responsibilities are not undertaken voluntarily, but perhaps they are included in the relevant notion of responsibility, which we might dub 'substantive responsibility.'

Here I shall be concerned with a more 'abstract' notion of moral responsibility, which I shall simply call 'moral responsibility.' To be morally responsible in this more abstract sense need not entail that one is morally praiseworthy (or even blameworthy); it is a matter, very roughly speaking, of being *accessible to* or *an appropriate target for* certain distinctively normative responses.

We say that individuals or groups are morally responsible, and we also say that (for example) individuals are morally responsible *for particular items*: choices, actions, omissions, consequences, and even traits of character. Presumably an individual is a morally responsible agent insofar as he is morally responsible for at least some item. Further, it is often helpful to distinguish the *item* for which an agent is morally responsible, where this is a specification of what the agent is morally responsible for, from questions about the appropriate *degree* of praiseworthiness or blameworthiness of the agent, if indeed the agent is praiseworthy or blameworthy. It may be that an agent is not morally responsible for one item, but rather for another; and the specific nature of our response to the agent – including its 'degree' or 'intensity' – is a separate (although related) matter.

With respect to the abstract notion of moral responsibility, it is important to distinguish between 'being responsible' and 'holding responsible' (and the related notion of 'being held responsible'). The specific relationship between these notions is unclear. The standard view would be that being morally responsible is analytically prior, and thus it is appropriate to hold someone morally responsible only if he is indeed morally responsible (where the status of being morally responsible is independently established). Jay Wallace, however, has argued that the order of explanation is quite the opposite (Wallace 1994). He claims that one's being responsible is to be analyzed in terms of its being fair to hold one responsible. (For a critical discussion, see Smith 2007). Although I would agree with Wallace that there is a fundamental connection between 'being responsible' and 'holding responsible,' I do not think that Wallace has adequately captured this connection; after all, one could be an appropriate candidate for certain distinctively normative responses in the sense that it would not be a category mistake to target one with those responses, even though it might not be *fair* to target one in this way. Here I would contend that the agent is morally responsible (insofar as he is an appropriate target for the responses constitutive of holding responsible), even though it would not be fair to hold him responsible.

We have already seen that 'responsible' is multiply ambiguous. It should also become increasingly clear that even 'moral responsibility,' construed abstractly, is multiply ambiguous. Making the distinction between 'being responsible' and 'holding responsible' is just the beginning of uncovering the complexity; indeed, philosophers frequently 'talk past each other' precisely because they fail to recognize that they are operating with distinct notions of moral responsibility (Fischer and Tognazzini, forthcoming).

For an agent to be morally responsible for an item is, in my view, for that item to be attributable to the agent in a way that would make it in principle justifiable to react to the agent in certain distinctive ways (on the basis of the item in question). Being responsible, on this view, is a kind of 'attributability' (Watson 1996). More specifically, one might distinguish two sorts of attributability. For an agent to be responsible for an item might be for the item to be attributable to the agent in a way that would make the agent a sensible or appropriate target for what Watson calls 'aretaic appraisals'; these concern the agent's moral virtues and vices as manifested in thought and action (ibid.). On a slightly broader version of this first kind of attributability, for an agent to be responsible for an item would be for the item to be attributable to the agent in a way that would make the agent a sensible or appropriate target for distinctively moral judgments on the basis of the item (where these judgments could encompass more than virtues and vices).

We can distinguish the first sort of attributability from a second. For an agent to be responsible for an item, on the second view, would be for the item to be attributable to the agent in a way that would make the agent an appropriate or sensible target for what Peter Strawson called the 'reactive attitudes' (and related practices such as punishment; Strawson 1962). Strawson's reactive attitudes include gratitude, indignation, resentment, hatred, love, and forgiveness. That someone is an appropriate or sensible target for such an attitude implies that it would not be a category mistake to have such an attitude toward that individual; in contrast, it would seem to be a category mistake to be resentful of a goldfish, or to be grateful to a rodent. Importantly, when one is an appropriate or sensible target for such attitudes, it is in principle justifiable that one should be the target of the attitudes in question; but of course it does not follow that in any given context anyone is actually justified in targeting one with the attitudes. This point helps to explain the difference between 'being responsible' and 'holding responsible' (and the twin notion of 'being held responsible').

Being responsible, then, is a matter of attributability – either 'aretaic attributability' (or, more broadly, 'normative attributability') or 'reactive attributability.' *Holding* someone responsible, on the other hand, is a matter of actually targeting the individual with the relevant attitude or judgment. Again, the judgments and attitudes in question might be either 'aretaic,' 'normative in general,' or the 'reactive attitudes.' If one judges someone to be blameworthy, this could be considered a form of holding that individual responsible – quite apart from any outward expressions which flow from that inner judgment, any reactive attitudes or public expressions of such attitudes, or any sort of harsh treatment or condemnation. Similarly, having indignation or resentment toward someone is to hold that individual responsible, quite apart from any outward or public expression of these attitudes, or any further condemnation or harsh treatment. Of course, the outward or public expression of reactive attitudes would be an additional way of holding someone responsible; I simply wish to point out that these are not *essential* to holding responsible. Similarly, harsh treatment or condemnation would be forms of holding an individual responsible; but, again, they are not *essential* to holding responsible.

Moral responsibility, then, is a complex notion, involving various different aspects (or, in Watson's word, 'faces'). Here I have focused (in a sketchy way) on the concept of moral responsibility or, alternatively, on the 'essence' of moral responsibility (what it is to be morally responsible). This of course leaves open the conditions under which the concept applies (or the conditions in which moral responsibility is actually present). Perhaps the most salient and contentious issue here is whether moral responsibility is compatible with causal determinism (or universal causation of a deterministic sort). There are also questions about the relationship between moral responsibility and causal indeterminism, and between moral responsibility and various kinds of freedom or control.

Discussion of these issues is beyond the scope of the present chapter.

Responsibility and Autonomy

It is striking that there are 'parallel literatures' in contemporary philosophy about the similar – but different – notions of responsibility and autonomy. Indeed, similar analyses have been suggested, similar objections made, and so forth. Often there has been a perplexing lack of communication or contact between the two literatures; it is as if they were parallel philosophical universes. I seek to bring them together, at least in a preliminary way, here.

In my view, moral responsibility is a necessary but not sufficient condition for autonomy. (We have seen that responsibility is a complex notion; there is a similar complexity in the notion of autonomy.) In order to be an autonomous agent (or to act autonomously in a given context), one must be a morally responsible agent (or act in such a way as to be morally responsible). But some additional features must also be present; one can be morally responsible without being autonomous. Put metaphorically, the crucial additional ingredient is: 'listening to one's own voice' or 'being guided internally.' Of course, it is difficult to make these metaphors more precise, but the idea is that one can meet the conditions for moral responsibility without meeting the additional conditions for autonomy because one is not, in the relevant sense, being guided internally.

To exhibit the parallel nature of the contemporary discussions of moral responsibility and autonomy, and to bring out an important difference between the two notions, I shall begin by discussing the 'hierarchical analysis' of 'acting freely.' In the context of moral responsibility, this analysis has been developed by Harry Frankfurt (1971); in the context of autonomy, this sort of analysis has been developed by Gerald Dworkin (1970 and 1988).

Frankfurt distinguishes 'first-order preferences' – preferences for states of affairs or actions – from 'second-order preferences' – preferences about one's first-order preferences. He contends that we, unlike mere non-human animals, can step back from our first-order preferences and form preferences about them. A subset of our second-order preferences is the set of 'second-order volitions,' which, according to Frankfurt, are the second-order preferences that specify which of our first-order desires we wish to move us to action. Frankfurt gives us a 'mesh' theory of acting freely; that is, on his approach, an agent acts freely insofar as there is a mesh between his second-order volition and the first-order preference which actually does move him to action. On Frankfurt's 'hierarchical' approach, one fails to act freely insofar as the mesh does not exist, that is, insofar as there is not a harmonious match between one's second-order volition and the first-order preference that moves one to action. Although the details differ slightly, Gerald Dworkin gives a similar hierarchical account of 'acting freely' (in the context of his discussion of autonomy).

A crucial point for Frankfurt is that the second-order volition need *not* be based on any sort of rational reflection or normative considerations. On the view suggested by Frankfurt (1971), an agent 'identifies' with the selected first-order preference by forming a second-order volition (to act in accordance with it). That is, the view suggested by Frankfurt in his classic 1971 paper is that forming a second-order volition constitutes *identification*, and identification plus acting on the selected first-order preference (the first-order preference identified with) constitutes acting freely. On this view, it does not matter what the *basis* of the identification is, or whether it has any basis at all. It is also important to note that Frankfurt was seeking to characterize an element of an account of acting freely which would fit into a theory of moral responsibility. In his early work he seeks to give an account of 'acting freely,' which, he contends, is the freedom component of the conditions for moral responsibility. And his account of 'identification' is supposed to be the ingredient that, when added to action on the selected first-order desire, gives us the relevant notion of freedom – the notion that plays a role in the analysis of moral responsibility.

Now various problems have been raised for the analysis suggested by Frankfurt (1971). Perhaps the classic presentation of the main worries is Gary Watson's 1975 paper. Here Watson raises the 'regress' objection. The worry is that, if mere action in accordance with a first-order preference is not enough to confer the status of 'acting freely,' why exactly does it help to add a second level? That is, why exactly does it help that one has in place a mesh between a second-order volition and the preference on which one acts? Why does adding a second level help, when one can presumably ask the same questions about the provenance and basis of the preferences (volitions) at the second level as one can about those at the first? It is as if one were told that the earth is in place because it is standing on a giant tortoise, and, when one asked what keeps that tortoise in place, one were told that the first tortoise is standing on another giant tortoise. Perhaps it is not conceptually impossible for there to be tortoises all the way down; but is it really plausible that, whenever we act freely, we have an infinite number of levels of preferences, all in harmony?

Much of Frankfurt's subsequent work on these topics, especially the central notion of 'identification,' can be understood as attempts to answer Watson's regress objection (Frankfurt 1988). Dworkin also gives considerable attention to parallel worries in the context of his own development of the hierarchical approach to acting freely (Dworkin 1988). Whereas various theorists have insisted that we must add some ingredient which states that the *basis* of the second-order volition must include 'rational reflection' or some sort of normative notion, Frankfurt himself has resisted this move. He has consistently adhered to the contention that the 'identification' in question need not be based on rational reflection or have any particular substantive content.

I think this point is important, and I believe that it helps to clarify the difference between moral responsibility and autonomy. Recall that Frankfurt's initial suggestion of an account of identification in terms of a mesh between elements of the first and second levels in our motivational economy was made in the context of seeking an analysis of moral responsibility, *not* autonomy. I claim that Frankfurt's minimalist 'Humean' notion of identification fits better into an account of moral responsibility than into an account of the more substantive notion of autonomy. Further, I believe that there has been a subtle migration of the crucial notion of autonomy in Frankfurt's own thinking about these issues over the years – a migration that has lead to what might be called 'mission creep.' That is, Frankfurt initially discussed 'identification' in the context of seeking to specify the crucial additional element in an account of moral responsibility; in his later work, he speaks of 'identification' as helping to specify the 'true self' or 'real self.' Other theorists have also framed their discussions in terms of such notions and of the related idea of 'agential authority.' But it is unclear what exactly the relationship is between the notions of 'real self,' 'true self,' and agential authority on the one hand, and (mere) moral responsibility on the other.

To understand my view here, recall that various theorists have urged Frankfurt to *add* a value component to his hierarchical account of identification (and of acting freely). One such theorist is Eleonore Stump (1988). Others, including Gary Watson, have rejected the hierarchical approach entirely, but have nevertheless insisted on a 'normative' or 'value' component to their analysis of acting freely (Watson 1975 and 2004). Let us call any approach to giving an account of acting freely which contains a significant requirement that the agent should act in accordance with what he takes to be rationally or normatively defensible a 'value-added' approach. (I owe the term to Andrew Eshleman.) Clearly, there are hierarchical and non-hierarchical value-added models of acting freely.

The problem for *any* value-added approach to acting freely is weakness of the will. That is, it certainly seems that we can act freely but *against* what we take to be normatively defensible (in any of the senses given by the various value-added models). Given this, we cannot define acting freely in terms of acting in accordance with what one finds normatively defensible; similarly, we cannot define acting freely in terms of what we do or would reflectively endorse. Just as Frankfurt has spent much of his career seeking to respond adequately to the regress objection, Watson has given considerable attention to the problem of weakness of will. In my view, neither Watson nor any of the value-added theorists (sometimes called 'normative theorists') has addressed this problem successfully, insofar as the notion of acting freely is the notion relevant to *moral responsibility*. (Note that it does *not* seem straightforward that it is possible to act freely, in the sense required for moral responsibility, when one acts against a Frankfurtian second-order volition, where that is *not* necessarily based on rationality or normative defensibility. In my view, then, the problem of weakness of will does not threaten Frankfurt's 'minimalist' hierarchical approach to giving an account of the sort of freedom implicated in moral responsibility.)

But suppose that we make it explicit that the target of our analysis is the notion of acting freely in a sense which is relevant to autonomy. Now it is not so clear that the value-added model leads us astray. My claim is that we can act freely, in the sense relevant to moral responsibility, and nevertheless exhibit weakness of will; thus our acting freely in the sense relevant to moral responsibility must be consistent with acting against what we take to be normatively defensible, and the value-added approaches are problematic here. Insofar as the initial intention of Frankfurt was to give an account of acting freely that would play the required role in a theory of moral responsibility, he has been correct to resist the move to adding a 'rational' or 'normative' component to the basis of the second-order volition. But things are different if the target of our analysis is the notion of acting freely that is relevant to *autonomy*. It is not clear to me that one is acting *autonomously* if one is acting against what one takes to be normatively defensible. It is not implausible, then, that the value-added model (in contrast to Frankfurt's more minimalist approach) gives a promising account of acting freely, or at least a necessary element of such an account, insofar as this is the notion of freedom relevant to autonomy.

Think about it in terms of the admittedly metaphorical and vague terms, 'real self' or 'true self.' There is a notion of 'self-governance' that can be understood as governance by the real or true self. Further, if one identifies the real or true self with the value module, then it would turn out that self-governance (of the relevant sort) would be governance by the value module (that is, governance in accordance with what one takes to be normatively defensible). This sort of self-governance seems to me to be something more than mere moral responsibility; it appears to come close to the more substantive notion of autonomy.

If this is correct, then it suggests the following (no doubt oversimplified) diagnosis. Frankfurt originally suggested that the pertinent mesh (the harmony between the second-order volition and the first-order preference on which one acts) is a sufficient condition for identification, which is the crucial missing ingredient in the account of acting freely. But acting freely plays a role in an analysis of moral responsibility and also of the related but more demanding notion autonomy. The initial context in which Frankfurt's discussion took place was an attempt to give an analysis of moral responsibility. But there has been a 'slippage' or 'mission creep' over time, both in the work of Frankfurt and in that of others who have participated in these discussions, so that there has been a conflation of considerations relevant to moral responsibility and considerations relevant to autonomy. In particular, although the value-added approaches are inadequate as accounts of the freedom involved in moral responsibility, they are not thereby to be ruled out as accounts of the freedom involved in autonomy.

Autonomy, as is suggested by etymology, might be regarded as 'self-governance.' I have suggested above that the value-added model might be interpreted as giving an account of the relevant self-module, as it were, and thus of the notion of self-governance. I have further suggested that mere moral responsibility does not demand this sort of self-governance or inner guidance. This suggests that the value-added model of acting freedom gives a necessary condition for autonomy, but nor for moral responsibility. It is unclear, however, whether it also gives a *sufficient* condition for the kind of freedom involved in autonomy. This is because it might be that an individual's normative orientation is such that she takes it that it is normatively defensible for her to take her cues from others in certain ways. For example, a 'deferential housewife' might take it to be normatively defensible to be deferential to her husband in certain ways. If this is so, then it is not clear whether we should say that acting in accordance with such normative views renders the agent free in the sense implicated by autonomy. This is a complicated question, which I cannot take up here. The value-added model does seem to me to offer at least a necessary condition for the notion of freedom required for autonomy; after all, what would we make of an individual who acts against what she reflectively endorses, by failing to be deferential? That is, I do not think we would be confident in thinking that someone is acting autonomously in standing up for her own interests, when she does *not* think that this is normatively defensible. This problem illustrates a tension between a *structural* and a *content-based* account of autonomy.

See also: HABITUAL ACTIONS (10); VOLITION AND THE WILL (13); MENTAL ACTS (27); AGENT-CAUSATION (28); MOTIVATIONAL STRENGTH (33); ADDICTION AND COMPULSION (34); AKRASIA AND IRRATIONALITY (35); FREE WILL AND DETERMINISM (38); ACTION AND CRIMINAL RESPONSIBILITY (42); INTENTION IN LAW (43); SCIENTIFIC CHALLENGES TO FREE WILL (44).

References

Dworkin, G. (1970). Acting freely. *Nous*, 4, 367–383.

Dworkin, G. (1988). *The Theory and Practice of Autonomy*. Cambridge: Cambridge University Press.

Fischer, J. M., and Tognazzini, T. (forthcoming). The physiognomy of responsibility. *Philosophy and Phenomenological Research*.

Frankfurt, H. G. (1971). Freedom of the will and the concept of a person. *Journal of Philosophy*, 68, 5–20.

Frankfurt, H. G. (1988). *The Importance of What We Care About*. Cambridge: Cambridge University Press.

Smith, A. (2007). On being responsible and holding responsible. *Journal of Ethics*, 11, 465–484.

Strawson, P. F. (1962). Freedom and resentment. *Proceedings of the British Academy*, 48, 187–211.

Stump, E. (1988). Sanctification, hardening of the heart, and Frankfurt's concept of free will. *Journal of Philosophy*, 85, 395–420.

Wallace, R. J. (1994). *Responsibility and the Moral Sentiments*. Cambridge, MA: Harvard University Press.

Watson, G. (1975). Free agency. *Journal of Philosophy*, 72, 205–220.

Watson, G. (1996). Two faces of responsibility. *Philosophical Topics*, 24, 227–248.

Watson, G. (2004). *Agency and Answerability*. Oxford: Clarendon Press.

Further reading

Feinberg, J. (1987). *Harm to Others*. New York: Oxford University Press.

Feinberg, J. (1988). *Offense to Others*. New York: Oxford University Press.

Feinberg, J. (1989). *Harm to Self*. New York: Oxford University Press.

Feinberg, J. (1990). *Harmless Wrongdoing*. New York: Oxford University Press.

Fischer, J. M. (1994). *The Metaphysics of Free Will: An Essay on Control*. Oxford: Blackwell.

Fischer, J. M, (ed.) (2005). *Critical Concepts in Philosophy: Free Will*, Vols 1–4. London: Routledge.

Fischer, J. M. (2006). *My Way: Essays on Moral Responsibility*. New York: Oxford University Press.

Fischer, J. M., and Ravizza, M. (1998). *Responsibility and Control: A Theory of Moral Responsibility*. New York: Cambridge University Press.

Frankfurt, H. G. (1969). Alternate possibilities and moral responsibility. *Journal of Philosophy*, 66, 829–839.

Oshana, M. (2006). *Personal Autonomy in Society*. Aldershot: Ashgate.

Pereboom, D. (2001). *Living without Free Will*. Cambridge: Cambridge University Press.

Taylor, J. S. (ed.) (2005). *Personal Autonomy: New Essays in Personal Autonomy and Its Role in Contemporary Moral Philosophy*. Cambridge: Cambridge University Press.

40

Virtuous Action

ROSALIND HURSTHOUSE

In many contexts, the phrase 'virtuous action' is just virtue-ethics speak for 'right action.' In this use, it figures in debates within normative ethics about the relative merits of different virtue ethical accounts of right action and whether any of them is adequate. It is also used as a general phrase to apply to a smaller class than the phrase 'right action' – namely to actions which can be described using a virtue adjective: just actions, courageous actions, kind actions, honest actions. (When discretion is the better part of valor, the courageous (rather than foolhardy) agent may rightly run like mad, but his running isn't a courageous action.)

In either of these uses, 'virtuous action,' like 'right action,' allows for the possibility that an agent can do such an action without possessing virtue. Call this 'everyday virtuous action.' But, in the most interesting use of the term, a virtuous action has to come *from* virtue. Call this 'ideal virtuous action.' And, in the context of this volume, the concept of 'ideal virtuous action' is interesting not so much as the concept of morally ideal action (though it is that) but as the concept of ideal rational action (or 'acting for a reason' or 'from reason') *itself*, in some special sense – the upshot of an ideal practical rationality.

The concept is, of course, derived from Aristotle, though for some reason to do with Greek usage he rarely, if ever, uses the phrase whose literal translation would be 'virtuous/excellent action.' Instead he speaks of actions in accordance with virtue, or uses examples (just or temperate actions). All these phrases have the ambiguity of 'virtuous action' noted above, and Aristotle pinpoints the ambiguity in a famous passage of the *Nicomachean Ethics* (Aristotle 2000: 1105^{a}30–^{b}1).

Yes, we can perform everyday virtuous actions, actions that are in accordance with virtue in the sense of conforming to it; we can do what is just and temperate, and exactly what, in the circumstances, someone with the virtues of justice and temperance would do. Even quite small children can perform everyday virtuous actions. But we can do better than that, namely perform them *in the way* in which the just and temperate perform them, namely 'for their own sake,' *from* virtue. In the later passage, where he repeats the point, Aristotle is more explicit about the difference between ideal and everyday virtuous action (ibid., 1144^{a}14–20). Unlike the former, the latter might be done unwillingly, under compulsion (through fear of punishment perhaps) or 'for some other reason' – but not for its own sake.

That ideal virtuous actions are (for the most part) not done unwillingly flows immediately from the condition that they are done from virtue; and it is in this point that we find the most well-known difference between Aristotle and Kant in normative ethics. Virtues, in Aristotle, are settled dispositions to act *and* feel well (or excellently or virtuously). The distinction between the virtuous and the merely continent lies not in what they do, nor the reason(s) for which they do it – they both do the virtuous action for its own sake – but in how they feel about what they do. The merely continent execute the everyday virtuous actions because their reason 'urges them in the right direction,' but their emotions or desires 'conflict with or resist it' (ibid., 1102^{b}15ff.); so they do not take pleasure in what they do. The emotions of the virtuous agents, by contrast, are in harmony with their reason, so they do the everyday virtuous actions gladly or willingly, with no inner conflict, and thereby produce the morally ideal actions.

But what of the concept of the rationally ideal action? To grasp it, we need to begin with the special sense of 'action,' or 'acting for a reason,' which is at issue, for which I will use the capitalized terms 'Action,' 'Act,' and 'Acting' (in the phrase 'Acting for a reason'). Although my concern here is with Aristotle's account of Action, it is no accident that Korsgaard has written more influentially on this concept than any other modern philosopher; for, as will become clear, Action is as much a Kantian notion as an Aristotelian one.

Not every philosopher will agree that there is any sense to be made of the term Action (perhaps Hume would deny it), because the first thing we need to note about it is that children, at least young children, and the other animals don't Act. 'For we do not say that a child acts, or a brute either; only someone who is already doing things from reason,' as Aristotle asserts in the *Eudemian Ethics* (1982: 1224^{a}29). So Action isn't the same as intentional action, because children and some of the other animals certainly act intentionally and thereby, we might say, for a reason. One might want to insist that, although some of the other animals act 'for reasons' in a way – surely, the lioness chases off the marauding male *in order to* protect her cubs – there is another way in which they don't. Unlike us, they are not aware of their reasons *as* reasons. But in this respect they are also unlike children. Any child old enough to respond appropriately to Anscombe's question 'Why?' could be said to manifest awareness of his reasons as reasons in those responses and, further, in his responses to us when we give him reasons for doing one thing rather than another – as we can't do with the other animals. (I mean, by giving a child information such as 'You could make it stand up if you put it on the table instead of putting it on your knee' – not by coercion or by changing the circumstances.) So Action isn't the same as 'acting for a reason' in any ordinary sense of the phrase. It is acting *from* a sort of rational capacity that we think children and the other animals lack.

Philosophers may, naturally, be interested in giving an account of intentional action and/or of acting for a reason, but not in giving one of Action. But, given the premise that adult human beings can be rational agents in some sense in which children cannot, we would expect that their accounts, if adequate, should be able to generate a story about what changes as we move from acting as children to acting as rational adults do. (For example, does some set of things – say, beliefs, desires, intentions, plans – simply get bigger? Or get bigger by the addition of more complex things – say, desires about beliefs/desires – or more abstract or general ones? Or does something quite new happen?)

The terminus of those changes, whatever they may be, would be Action, the concept of the fullest expression or development of our rational agency or practical reason.

In Aristotle, Acting is acting from rational choice – *proairesis.* He introduces this idea in Book III of the *Nicomachean Ethics*, defining it simply as the outcome of deliberation, and deliberation is described as what we would now call instrumental reasoning (taking that to cover both means–end and part–whole reasoning): reasoning about what to do to achieve some end by working out ways and means to it. You consider means, and if the best, or only, means is not something you can bring about immediately, you consider by what further means it can be brought about, until you reach something you can do. Then you conclude that this is what you'll do – or you 'rationally choose' or 'decide' (another possible translation) – to do that.

But all that this gives us is 'acting for a reason' in the ordinary sense, which children and the clear-eyed akratic certainly do; and it remains a puzzle until Book VI why Aristotle denies that they act from rational choice (as he does in Book III). In Book VI, rational choice turns out to be (at least in the favored cases) the outcome, not of any deliberation, but only of ultimate end-directed deliberation, which is reasoning related to *the* 'architectonic' end of *eudaimonia* ('happiness' or the good life, or living well). And thereby Acting for a reason emerges as acting for – or at least in the light of – not just an end, but that ultimate, 'architectonic,' end.

Followers of Aristotle find it entirely plausible to make this the ideal of practical rationality (see Annas 1993: 27–46). Assuming that each of us wants our life to go well, is it not irrational – just folly – to make daily choices without having formed any conception of what we want our life to be like, given that so many choices, willy nilly, rule out future options? Practical reasoning is, after all, concerned with what to do quite generally, not just with some areas of action, and, as Aristotle implies, we shall be more likely to make the correct practical decisions if we have a target to aim at. But, even if the ideal is plausible, it does, surely, create the possibility that not only children and the other animals, but quite a few of 'us,' don't Act.

However, if this is a problem for Aristotelians, it is a problem that other philosophers aiming to give an account of Action share. This is hardly surprising, since 'Action' is the concept of an ideal, and when we are considering such ideals in philosophy we have to make some decision about how high we think it plausible to set the threshold, and tailor our account correspondingly. Do we think that most ordinary rational adults reach a threshold of this ideal of rational agency, or only a few of them?

If we are following Aristotle or Kant, which way we go (for the many or the few) is partly determined by what we want to say about the prevalence of virtue or a good will, since both philosophers give accounts according to which, when the virtuous agent (or an agent with a good will) acts, she Acts. But, whichever way we go, we must not over-intellectualize Acting for a reason in such a way as to guarantee that only people who have studied academic philosophy can do it. So we can't demand conscious reflective endorsement of such-and-such a conception of *eudaimonia*, nor an articulated *de dicto* recognition of the categorical imperative or anything similar (such as a consciously articulated theory of oneself, rather than an implicit one, as in Velleman 2007). The modern challenge is to find a way to describe those features of adults' capacities we take to be sufficient for attributing to them some form of whatever it is that figures in our account of Action, and this is currently still proving very difficult.

But now, assuming the virtuous Act, we may ask, can the wicked Act too? For most Kantians, the answer is 'No,' and there is an explanation of why not. Capital 'A' Acting is the outcome of a special sort of practical reasoning, which the wicked do not employ. But when Action is specified as the outcome of rational choice rather than reasoning in terms of the categorical imperative, things are more complicated. If the wicked can't Act, we need an answer as to why not; and if they can, what becomes of my initial claim that Aristotle's concept of ideal *virtuous* action is not only the concept of ideal rational action, but of ideal moral action as well?

In common with most moral philosophers, Aristotle does not say much about the wicked, and indeed seems to offer two competing pictures of them. We have, on the one hand, the view in Book IX of the *Nicomachian Ethics* of the wicked as psychological wrecks, torn, like the incontinent, by inner conflict. It is hard to conceive of the wicked, described as they are in this way, as Acting. How can they be acting from rational choice, unless we suppose that they take their ultimate end to be 'making myself miserable' or 'a ruined life'?

But, as we all know, one can't be confident that someone is not wicked on the grounds that they are not conflicted and miserable. And elsewhere (Book VII, chs 4 and 8) Aristotle presents a different view – one in which the intemperate (who do lots of wicked things in their pursuit of pleasure) are contrasted with the incontinent *and* the continent precisely insofar as they do not suffer from inner conflict. But, like the continent, they do act from rational choice, and hence Act.

Capital 'A' Acting for a reason is itself meeting some sort of norm of rational agency. So, if we can make out that, although the wicked do it, the virtuous do it better, then we can say that the practical rationality of the wicked falls short of the ideal – that their rational agency is indeed defective to some extent, and that the virtuous are ideally rational. But how can we say that?

According to Anscombe (1989), Aristotle offers a really neat account. She draws a tight analogy between the assessments of practical and theoretical reasoning. In the latter, as everyone learns in baby logic, we distinguish between sound and valid reasoning; the latter is good, but the former is better. The difference between them simply lies in their starting points or premises; sound reasoning proceeds from true premises; valid reasoning may not. Bearing the analogy firmly in mind makes it harder (though not impossible, of course) to accept the Humean idea that the exercise of practical reason can be critically assessed *only* in terms of the adequacy of the steps it takes to achieve the agent's ends. Although, when teaching philosophy, we always stress the importance of valid reasoning, and sometimes we recklessly say to our students 'I don't mind what conclusion you reach as long as you give a decent argument for it,' we take that back if they avail themselves of a premise which, in context or quite generally, is just plain false; sound reasoning is better. The same holds for practical reasoning. There is both sound and valid practical reasoning; the former is better; and the difference between the two lies in their starting points. Sound practical reasoning proceeds from a true/right/correct starting point or premise, namely that such-and-such an end is good to pursue; valid practical reasoning may not.

On the Aristotelian picture, the virtuous employ the best practical reasoning because theirs proceeds from a true premise; *as* virtuous, they have the correct conception of the ultimate end – the life of virtuous activity. But the wicked have a different, and hence false, premise: for example that the ultimate end is the life of pleasure – so, even if their reasoning is valid, it will still fail to be sound.

Aristotle's stress is all on the 'major' premise ('*The* ultimate end is ...') and on the impossibility of getting this right without the possession of virtue. But modern Aristotelians have laid as much stress on those among the 'particular' premises in practical reasoning which identify – correctly or incorrectly – the relevant features of the situation in which the agent is to act – and the impossibility, in many cases, of getting *these* right without the possession of virtue. And at this point the modern contrast between the fully virtuous and the merely continent comes to play a new role.

In its original role, as I noted above, this contrast figured in debates within normative ethics about what is formally required in order for one to be a morally excellent person. Can someone who always acts correctly but does not always feel correctly be as morally good a *person* (albeit, perhaps, not as good a human being, as people sometimes used to say) as someone who does both; or is she morally inferior? But, in its new role, we use the contrast to query whether that question is not based on a false assumption, namely that the merely continent agent *can* be supposed to reason soundly – and hence to reach correct practical conclusions and to act correctly – to the same extent as the virtuous agent does. ('To the same extent' rather than 'always,' because even the ideal virtuous agent is not infallible and may, incorrectly but quite innocently, identify the poisoned chalice as containing life-saving water.) Given the ways our emotions shape our perceptions, will the merely continent not be liable to misread (the term used in McDowell 1998) or misdescribe (the term used in Murdoch 1970) some situations and, as a result, to plug in false particular premises about them? 'This person (isn't in need of help but just) needs to pull herself together,' 'This person (isn't the victim of misfortunate but) has brought this trouble on himself' or, indeed, 'This human being (being of such and such a race, gender, age) is not an autonomous agent and, for her own good, needs me to make this decision for her.' If that is so, then the merely continent agent will sometimes fail to do what she should do, and culpably so, unlike the virtuous.

Finally, the way the emotions sometimes prompt us to immediate action brings us to a new version of the problem of over-intellectualizing Acting. Suppose we think of Acting for a reason or 'from reason' as acting from a clockable period of prior, conscious, ultimate end-directed practical thought. There is, as we noted above, a persisting difficulty in finding a way to describe that thought without making it too overtly philosophical. Now, the problem is whether to allow some actions which are clearly not preceded by such thought at all to be Actions, and, if so, how?

For the Aristotelian, the obvious cases are many of the 'everyday' virtuous actions of the virtuous (and, though they are not our concern, many of the 'everyday' vicious actions of the vicious.) A nice child might spring forward immediately, 'without thought,' to help someone who had fallen in front of them, but they, *ex hypothesi* do not Act when they do so. The mature virtuous agent might well do the same in the same circumstances. And there is nothing to be seen in the moment of acting which distinguishes what the virtuous agent does from what the child does, nor, necessarily, in what the agents can say afterwards in response to Anscombe's 'Why?' (A child raised in a pious household may well say sincerely that she did it because it was her duty, and an inarticulate virtuous agent, that he couldn't help it or 'just did it.')

But, in the life of the virtuous agent, such spontaneous action is just what is to be expected from him, since everyday uncomplicated virtuous actions are just what such agents do from habituated virtue. If in these circumstances the agent does *not* act immediately, spontaneously, 'without thinking,' his failure calls for explanation ('Did he not see?' 'Is he ill?' 'What was it about the situation that made him pause?'). And we have already assumed that, when the virtuous act, they Act. So when the virtuous agent springs forward, he Acts.

How can this be so? At this point we might insist that, though it may be unseen, there *is* something in the moment (roughly speaking) of acting which distinguishes what the virtuous agent does from what the nice child does. It is, obviously, what it was said to be before, namely that the virtuous agent's action, unlike the child's, comes from rational choice and thereby prior ultimate end-directed deliberation – it is just that, in these cases, the deliberation is split-second and unconscious. And then we try to give some further account of that.

Alternatively, we may stick with saying that, in these cases – of the child and of the virtuous agent – there is nothing in the moment of acting, or in its proximate antecedents, which distinguishes between the two. Instead we reconsider what we mean by Acting 'for a reason,' abandoning the idea that it has to involve prior reflection, conscious or unconscious, regarding the action done. We may take our lead from Anscombe on acting for a reason – that is, on intentional action quite generally – of which she says:

> We do not add anything attaching to the action at the time it is done by describing it as intentional. To call it intentional is to assign it to the class of intentional actions [...]. (1963: 28)

As a particular 'Eureka!' moment constitutes understanding in a subject with a certain past and a certain future, so a spontaneous virtuous action constitutes an Action, an operation of the ideal practical rationality of the agent, in the setting of a virtuous life. To call it 'Acting for a reason' is to assign it to the class of actions which manifest such a rationality, not to say that anything extra was going on in the agent at the time when it was done.

This would fit well with the one place in the *Nicomachean Ethics* where Aristotle mentions spontaneous virtuous actions, since there he apparently claims that the rational choice of such actions comes directly from the agent's character – his virtue – rather than from deliberation (Aristotle 2000: 1117^{a}17–22).

He thus leaves unquestioned his claim that deliberation takes time, but he suggests that the activity of the ideal practical reason of the virtuous agent is not limited to such time-occupying thought. Her practical reason is hardly having to work hard when she does what the nice child does; but it is still at work, informing what she does.

See also: INTENTION (14); TELEOLOGICAL EXPLANATION (16); PRACTICAL REASONING (31); DELIBERATION AND DECISION (32); ARISTOTLE (54); KANT (64); ANSCOMBE (74).

References

Annas, J. (1993). *The Morality of Happiness*. Oxford: Oxford University Press.

Anscombe, G. E. M (1963). *Intention*, 2nd edn. Oxford: Basil Blackwell.

Anscombe, G. E. M. (1989). von Wright on practical inference. In P. A. Schilpp (ed), *The Philosophy of Georg Henrik von Wright*. LaSalle, IL: Open Court, 377–404. [Reprinted as: Practical inference, in R. Hursthouse, G. Lawrence, and W. Quinn (eds) (1995), *Virtues and Reasons*. Oxford: Oxford University Press, 1–34.]

Aristotle (1982). *The Eudemian Ethics*, translated by M. Woods. Oxford: Clarendon Press.

Aristotle (2000). *The Nicomachean Ethics*, translated by R. Crisp. Cambridge: Cambridge University Press.

McDowell, J. (1998). *Mind, Value, and Reality*. Cambridge, MA: Harvard University Press.

Murdoch, I. (1970). *The Sovereignty of Good*. London: Routledge.

Velleman, D. J. (2007). *Practical Reflection*, new edn. Stanford, CA: University of Chicago Press (Center for the study of language and information, David Hume Series).

Further reading

Anscombe, G. E. M. (1965). Thought and action in Aristotle: What is 'practical truth'? In R. Bambrough (ed.), *New Essays on Plato and Aristotle*. London: Routledge and Kegan Paul, 143–158. [Reprinted in G. E. M. Anscombe (1981), *The Collected Papers of G. E. M. Anscombe*, Vol 1: *From Parmendes to Wittgenstein*, Minneapolis: University of Minnesota Press, 66–77.]

Audi, R. (1995). Acting from virtue. *Mind*, 104, 449–471.

Engstrom, S. and Whiting, J. (eds) (1996), *Aristotle, Kant, and the Stoics*. Cambridge: Cambridge University Press.

Korsgaard, C. (2005). Acting for a reason. *Danish Yearbook of Philosophy*, 40, 11–36.

Korsgaard, C. (2008). *The Constitution of Agency. Essays on Practical Reason and Moral Psychology*. Oxford: Oxford University Press.

McDowell, J. (2007). What myth? *Inquiry*, 50, 338–351.

41

The Doctrine of Double Effect

DAVID S. ODERBERG

Few moral theorists would disagree that the fundamental principle of morality – perhaps of practical rationality itself – is 'Do good and avoid evil.' Yet along with such an uncontroversial principle comes a major question: Can you fulfil both halves satisfactorily across your life as a moral agent? We all have opportunities to perform acts that do good with no accompanying evil, but these are not as common as we might think. We can avoid evil by doing nothing, but doing nothing implies doing no good either. Clearly the fundamental principle does not require that you go about your life doing good on any and every possible occasion any more than that you sit on your hands and abstain from action out of fear of doing evil. The principle tells us to avoid evil, not to refrain from ever causing it. And the simple fact is that the complexities of life make it inevitable that, much of the time when we go about doing good, we will also be doing evil. Further, they are such that sometimes we can avoid evil only at the cost of not performing a good act which reasonable people would regard as at least permissible, if not sometimes obligatory.

So how, as rational, morally responsible agents, are we to satisfy the fundamental principle in an adequate, harmonious fashion, given life's exigencies? This is where the so-called 'doctrine of double effect' comes into play. Some call it a doctrine, influenced by the fact that Catholic ethicists and moral theologians have, since the Middle Ages, codified and ratified it as something akin to a doctrine of Catholic moral philosophy. Others call it the 'principle of double effect,' though it breaks down into a set of principles unified by a common idea. Yet other writers see it simply as a kind of *reasoning* about certain types of hard case in ethics. Whatever the preferred nomenclature, the DDE, as I will call it here, is – for all its critics and the difficulties it faces – a keystone of sound moral thinking, without which the fundamental principle would remain nothing but a high ideal with little consistent applicability.

So consider a simple example. When I drive to work, I cause pollution from my car's exhaust. Getting to work, so that I can do my job, is good; causing pollution is evil. (Note that 'evil' here does not necessarily mean something monstrous or heinous; you can, if you prefer, use the word 'bad.' In this context, an evil is simply a bad state of affairs or a bad result or outcome of an act.) Now, I intend to drive to work: that is my objective in using the car (and this objective may be a means to a further objective, namely doing my job). I do not, however, *intend* to pollute the atmosphere, even though in fact I do so. I know that driving will cause pollution, but I think I have a *good reason* to drive my car. (Let's leave aside controversial environmental issues, though, if you wish, you can suppose that I live fifty miles away from work and using the car is my only available means of transportation.) And I think my good reason for taking the car to work *outweighs* the bad polluting effects of doing so.

The more you think about simple cases like this, the more you find them throughout the lives of agents. The doctor gives me antibiotics for an infection, knowing that they may cause a rash. In his judgment, the good effect (cure of the infection) outweighs the bad effect (risk, perhaps certainty, of a rash). He does not *intend* to give me a rash, any more than the dentist intends to cause you inevitable pain when he removes a tooth, though she knows that the pain is inevitable. You head off to an urgent appointment with your accountant, knowing that this will make you ten minutes late for lunch with a friend. You don't intend to be late and you don't want to be late; but you judge that this mild inconvenience to your friend is justified by the importance of the meeting. Maybe your judgment is wrong, but that's not the point. If it is correct, then, all things being equal, you are permitted to make the appointment and knowingly inconvenience your friend.

If morality is to comprise a coherent, rationally actionable system of behavior, there ought to be a way of codifying the ideas that justify, in some cases, actions with both good and evil effects. If so, then we really can have our cake and eat it: we can go about our lives doing good and avoiding evil, as long as the injunction to avoid evil does not mean that we may never permissibly be its cause. The idea that such a codification is possible goes back at least to St Thomas Aquinas (1225–1274), who famously introduced a sketch of DDE into his discussion of self-defense (Aquinas 1929: 208–210 = *Summa Theologica* II.II q.64 a.7). Asserting that it is sometimes permissible to kill in self-defense, he argues (I paraphrase) that an act may sometimes have a good and a bad effect, where the good effect is intended and the bad effect is merely foreseen ('beyond intention'). The death of the attacker is bad, but saving one's life is good. You may defend yourself even using lethal force, as long as you do not intend to kill, but you must use no more force than necessary: otherwise your act, for all its good objective of saving your life, will be 'out of proportion' to its end, and hence immoral.

The basic outlines of DDE are found in Aquinas' account of self-defense and in related discussions by him. (See Cavanaugh 2006, ch. 1, for details and for a general history of DDE; also Mangan 1949.) But it has taken generations of thinkers to refine and tease out the various principles that go to make it up. Aquinas' discussion, for instance, points to the need for proportionality both between ends and means and between the ends themselves. You may only use proportionate force to repel an attacker: if you can ward him off with a personal alarm but you choose instead to use your revolver, you act impermissibly. Also, if I kill someone who is trying to pick my pocket, the evil effect is clearly out of proportion to the good end.

The codification of DDE that has finally come down to us via many ethicists, mainly within Catholic moral theology, is as follows. There are four conditions to be satisfied before an act with both good and evil effects can be judged permissible overall:

1 The specific act intended by the agent must be at least permissible.
2 The good effect of this act must follow from it at least as immediately as its evil effect.

3 The evil effect must itself not be intended.
4 There must be a proportionate, or sufficiently serious, reason for causing the evil effect.

Some clarification is in order. As to (1), the act intended by the agent need not be good in the sense of obligatory or even admirable – just not itself evil. For example, if you defraud a bank you cannot appeal to DDE in justification on the grounds that the evil effect you foresee – say, that the bank has to close and people will lose their jobs – is outweighed by the good you intend – to distribute the money to the poor. With regard to (2), the point is that the evil effect must either be caused by the good effect or be caused directly by the act which also directly causes the good effect. In other words, the notion of immediacy here is causal, not temporal. What (2) rules out is using the evil outcome as a *means* to the good effect, since the ends do not justify the means. A classic case from just war theory illuminates this idea. The so-called 'tactical bomber,' who intentionally bombs a military target while foreseeing that he will kill innocent civilians, in no way uses the deaths as a means either to his immediate objective (destroying the target) or to his ultimate objective (winning the war); rather, the civilian deaths are a foreseen side effect. By contrast, the 'terror bomber' who intentionally bombs civilians in order to terrorize them into surrendering, uses their deaths as a means to his objective. Tactical bombing, say the defenders of DDE, can be justified; terror bombing cannot. Some object (Cavanaugh 2006: 29–30) that (2) as stated is incorrect, and that what is right about it is already captured by (3): the agent must never intend the evil effect – whether as end or means. For what if, in the tactical bomber case, the civilians are terrorized, albeit unintentionally, with this result: they flee the city, leaving the soldiers at the military installation without food, and thereby cause them to starve and the installation to cease functioning? The evil effect does in fact cause the good effect, but the tactical bomber did not *mean* for this to happen. The point to remember, however, is that DDE is not just a principle of retrospective justification, but mainly one of prior permissibility: it is designed as an action-guiding method for judging what to do. Certainly, the tactical bomber in the case I just outlined would be excused. But if he were to get into his plane *knowing* that by killing civilians he might well achieve his military aim, even though, if asked, he would claim only to intend to destroy the installation with his bombs, an observer would rightly hesitate. A plausible presumption in action theory is that he who wills the end also wills the means. If you know that an evil effect will cause a good effect, then it is open to others to question whether you really do not intend to use the former as a means to the latter. Even more is this so if you know that the evil effect is the *sole* means to the good effect. If the tactical bomber knows that he can bring the installation to a halt *only* by terrorizing the civilians, and he bombs, then his claim that he really only intended to achieve his aim by bombing will ring hollow. DDE, then, is as much about moral psychology as it is about after-the-fact justification.

The import of (3) should by now be evident. Even if the agent does not intend the evil effect as a means, she might still intend it as an end – in which case, according to DDE, she still may not act. A sadistic dentist who intends both to remove your diseased tooth and to cause you pain cannot absolve himself by claiming that the pain was not itself a means to his good end. If 'avoiding evil' means anything, it means, first and foremost, that one may never intend evil, whether as means or as end. One may, however, *permit* or *tolerate* it. Again, a subtle point needs to be clarified. By saying that evil may in some circumstances be permitted, I am not claiming that central to DDE is the doing/allowing distinction. The doctrine applies as much to the doing of evil as to the allowing of it. (For examples of the latter, which requires some ingenuity with thought experiments, see Cavanaugh 2006: 166–177.) The point, rather, is that an agent may, as it were, *permit himself* to do (or allow) evil if he meets the conditions of DDE. But condition (3) says that he must not intend it. More fully, he must, at most, only *foresee* that he will or may cause (or allow) the evil effect. Note at this point the distinction between acting *intentionally* and acting *with an intention*, the latter being sometimes called a 'further intention.' DDE presupposes, and applies to, acts done intentionally, whether the consequences are themselves intended (making the act an act with an intention) or only foreseen (in which case the act, to that extent, is not an act with an intention). In both cases, however, the act is still performed intentionally inasmuch as it is an intentional act.

Clause (4) is often mistakenly read as a consequentialist add-on. Peter Singer, for instance, thinks that DDE just is a form of disguised consequentialist judgment (Singer 1993: 210). Yet this is grossly to misread the fourth clause. The clause in no way requires one to compare good and bad states of affairs in order to judge the overall balance of good over evil. All it says is that there must be a proportionate *reason* for causing the evil effect. To be sure, when it comes to morality, sometimes only numbers count. If I have to rush my child to the hospital, and I foresee that if I take route *A* I will endanger more pedestrians than if I take route *B*, then, *all things being equal*, I must take route *B*. But all things are rarely equal. Route *A* might be much shorter, and if I do not take it my child might be far more likely to die on the way. If this consideration is a sufficient reason for taking the extra risk with pedestrians, I may go via route *A*. On a consequentialist calculation, however, the overall evil if I take route *B* is smaller than if I take route *A*, so I should go via route *B*. (Of course, consequentialists add refinements to their theories so as to rule out undesirable recommendations while maintaining faith in their calculus of the overall best state of affairs; but that would take us too far afield.) For the consequentialist, all that matters is the weighing of outcomes. For the defender of DDE, what matters is the relative importance of the reasons for taking a proposed course of action.

How, though, do we assess the proportionality of good and bad effects according to reasons? In simple cases, it is not so hard: to save my life I may endanger another's, since, all things being equal, I am permitted preferentially to save my life rather than another's. (Some would say that I am obliged to do so.) To be sure, there are martyrs, and of course a parent, for instance, may be bound to save her child rather than herself. But DDE is first and foremost a doctrine about what we *may* do, in other words it is a doctrine of permissibility. Once we get clear about what we may do, we are in a position to understand specific cases in which we are *advised* to do something else or we are *admired* or considered an exemplar of virtue if we take a more elevated course of action than simply doing what we are allowed. And we will be in a position to see how certain factors, such as special relationships and duties of office, might oblige us to do something other than what, in different circumstances, we would be allowed to do. For instance, in some cases a person is allowed to refuse highly risky medical treatment that might save their life. But if they are a parent with family obligations, or perhaps the president or prime minister of their country, they would generally be obliged to undertake the risky procedure for the good of others. Conversely, certain considerations might allow someone to do something they otherwise would be obliged *not* to do. So, for example, a police officer has greater justification for endangering the public in the pursuit of a criminal than an ordinary citizen has. A qualified doctor has a greater reason for causing you painful side effects in the administration of a treatment which, in his professional estimation, is warranted than has an unqualified person seeking to try out a remedy he saw mentioned on television.

Attending clause (4) are a number of sub-principles which aid in its interpretation. For instance, if the evil effect would probably occur whether or not the agent acted at all, the agent needs a lesser reason for acting than otherwise. Over-determination aside, the idea is that the less the risk of evil is down to you, the less you are required to take it into account in your decision-making. Conversely, if not acting would definitely prevent the evil, the agent needs a greater reason for going ahead than otherwise. 'Avoid evil' means that we should try to prevent it as far as we can; so, if our proposed action is the only way in which the evil will occur, we need a very good reason for forging ahead. Unpacking clause (4), then, requires attention to the whole body of reasons and justifications that permit or excuse certain kinds of action. No form of consequentialism can perform this task, but the rich history of casuistry in medieval and modern moral theology gives much guidance as to how an ethicist, whether religious believer or not, should apply DDE to the many hard cases for which it is designed. (For more on clause (4), see Oderberg 2000: 93–101.)

For all its reasonableness, in fact its necessity in handling hard cases, DDE has come under sustained attack for a long period of time. Perhaps the most serious criticism concerns the essential distinction between intention and foresight, which is built into the doctrine. Ontologically, DDE presupposes that such a distinction exists. Ethically, it asserts the relevance of the distinction to accounts of responsibility. On the first score, Blaise Pascal (1623–1662) famously attacked the Jesuit moral theologians, in his *Provincial Letters*, for their allegedly fine-grained approach to individuating intentions as a way of exculpating agents. One could, Pascal holds the Jesuits as claiming, 'divert one's intention' from the evil on which one was embarked, and 'direct' it to the good that one sought to achieve (Pascal 1850: 153). Imagine (not Pascal's example, but a similar one) a person who cut off another's head with a sword, and claimed in defense: 'I didn't intend to kill him, only to test my sword for sharpness.' No one would be convinced by such a feeble plea, indeed we would consider the killer either a liar or insane. It is highly doubtful whether any Jesuit taught that such implausible mental gymnastics could ever be used to escape responsibility for what one appears by all accounts to have really intended. Nevertheless, Pascal's satire has stuck, and DDE defenders have had to repel it ever since. Elizabeth Anscombe, for one, has pointed out that any such attempt to divert one's intention would itself have to be intentional, hence that such second-order intentions would still implicate the agent as fully responsible (Anscombe 1957).

Yet, even without resort to second-order intentions, one can argue that we should be metaphysical realists about intentions as subjective mental states, and that our judgments about the intentions of others are sometimes fallible. It might be very hard to know in a specific case what a person intended; nevertheless, we can usually question them, and interpret their behavior, in order to judge what they probably – or almost certainly – did intend. 'Diverting the intention' is nearly always belied by the behavioral and linguistic evidence: 'You say you didn't intend to kill, yet you left the victim to die.' Of course there might be a *prima facie* plausible alternative explanation for every piece of evidence pointing to intent, which is why our judgments are fallible. Still, there are more ways of being responsible than as an intentional agent (recklessness, gross negligence, and so on), so the friend of DDE would do better to find comfort in these extra categories than be obsessed over whether fine-grained individuation of intention can ever absolve an agent who does evil (see further Oderberg 2000: 101–126).

As to whether the foresight of inevitable consequences entails, or is identical to, intention, as critics have claimed, the friends of DDE must stand equally fast. If the agent knows that something bad will occur with certainty, he does not necessarily intend the result. Is the evil outcome something he has *chosen* as a means or as an end? Did it form part of his deliberative process and, if so, in what way? Was it part of a plan of action? Did the agent regret the evil effect? Did he try to minimize it or to avoid it altogether? The supporter of the doctrine has many questions that block any straight logical or conceptual connection between foresight and intent.

As to the ethical relevance of the intention/foresight distinction, the DDE supporter claims that this is crucial to our general theory of agency and responsibility. Intentional action is paradigmatic human action. We act for ends, and we choose the means to achieve them. As Cavanaugh (2006) points out, no one counts any old human behavior as voluntary, and hence as a matter of agency: think of involuntary bodily movements, reflex behavior, instinctive behavior. When it comes to agency, only the voluntary counts. Yet, if the critic is prepared to accept this cut-off point, it seems inconsistent that he is not also ready to acknowledge that, *within* the scope of agency, further distinctions can be made between what one does merely *knowingly* and what one does with *intent*. Such distinctions within the ambit of the voluntary have important applicability. We saw the distinction between terror bombing and tactical bombing in war. Similarly, is an ethical distinction to be made between a doctor who intentionally kills a suffering patient (euthanasia) and one who gives painkillers solely with the intent of relieving pain, but knowing that the patient will or may well die (terminal sedation)? Critics of DDE think that any ethical distinction between these cases is specious. Defenders see a world of difference, hinging on what the doctor intends to do. What is she trying to achieve? What is her objective? If it is pain relief, she acts as a doctor should. If it is the death of the patient, then, according to the vast majority of defenders of DDE, she is not acting as a doctor – that is, as a healer – but as a killer.

See also: REFRAINING, OMITTING, AND NEGATIVE ACTS (7); VOLITION AND THE WILL (13); INTENTION (14); INTENTION IN LAW (43); INDIAN PHILOSOPHERS (52); AUGUSTINE AND AQUINAS (56); ANSCOMBE (74).

References

Anscombe, G. E. M. (1957). *Intention*. Oxford: Blackwell.

Aquinas, T. (1929). *The 'Summa Theologica' of St. Thomas Aquinas*, Vol. 10, trans. by the Fathers of the English Dominican Province. London: Burns Oates and Washbourne.

Cavanaugh, T. A. (2006). *Double-Effect Reasoning: Doing Good and Avoiding Evil*. Oxford: Clarendon Press.

Mangan, J. (1949). An historical analysis of the principle of double effect. *Theological Studies*, 10, 41–61.

Oderberg, D. S. (2000). *Moral Theory: A Non-Consequentialist Approach*. Oxford: Blackwell.

Pascal, B. (1850). *The Provincial Letters of Blaise Pascal*, translated by T. M'Crie. New York: Robert Carter and Brothers.

Singer, P. (1993). *Practical Ethics*, 2nd edn. Cambridge: Cambridge University Press.

Further reading

Bennett, J. (1988). *The Act Itself*. Oxford: Clarendon Press.

Finnis, J. M. (1991). Intention and side-effects. In R. Frey and C. Morris (eds), *Liability and Responsibility*. Cambridge: Cambridge University Press), 32–64.

Nagel, T. (1980), The limits of objectivity. In S. McMurrin (ed.), *The Tanner Lectures on Human Values*, Vol. 1. Cambridge: Cambridge University Press, 75–139.

Oderberg, D. S. (2000). *Applied Ethics: A Non-Consequentialist Approach*. Oxford: Blackwell.

Quinn, W. S. (1989). Actions, intentions, and consequences: The doctrine of double effect. *Philosophy and Public Affairs*, 18, 334–351.

Woodward, P. A. (ed.) (2001). *The Doctrine of Double Effect*. Notre Dame: University of Notre Dame Press.

42

Action and Criminal Responsibility

R. A. DUFF

Actions and the Criminal Law

It is a familiar idea that a liberal criminal law properly focuses on actions (Moore 1993, ch. 2). Criminal law focuses on actions, as opposed to mere thoughts: I might think evil thoughts or plan criminal deeds, but these are private matters, not the law's business, until I begin to put them into effect by acting. Criminal law focuses on actions, as opposed to mere involuntary movements: the movements of my limbs as I suffer a fit might cause harm that would be criminal if it was caused voluntarily, but it would clearly be unjust to define such movements as criminal. Criminal law focuses on actions, as opposed to mere conditions: we might criminalize the use of certain drugs (though even that is controversial), but it would be unjust to criminalize the mere condition of being addicted to drugs. Criminal law normally focuses on actions, as opposed to mere omissions: although the law sometimes criminalizes omissions, notably when the agent had a special duty to act, we are not in general criminally responsible for harms that we do not prevent in the way that we are generally criminally responsible for harms that we avoidably cause. We are criminally responsible not for what we think, or fail to do, or for what merely happens to or through us, but for what we do – for our actions.

Such claims about criminal law's proper focus combine the descriptive or analytical with the normative (Husak 1998: 65–67). They purport to identify a central feature of existing systems of criminal law: the law generally criminalizes actions rather than mere thoughts, involuntary movements, conditions or omissions. However, they also purport to identify a normative principle by which criminal law should be structured: it *should not* criminalize mere thoughts, involuntary movements, conditions, or omissions. This normative dimension makes it possible to treat cases in which the law does (apparently) criminalize such things not as exceptions to a generalization whose truth they therefore threaten, but as mistakes – cases in which the law goes wrong. (The position is more complicated with omissions, since it is generally agreed that criminal responsibility for omissions is sometimes justified.)

This normative claim reflects a range of familiar liberal values, notably those concerning privacy (the law should leave us an extensive private realm, and coerce us only when we act in ways that have a deleterious impact on the public world) and individual choice (we should be criminally liable only for what we choose to do, or could choose to avoid doing).

Objects or Conditions of Criminal Responsibility?

The claim that criminal law is focused on actions might mean that actions are the proper objects, that is, are constitutive of, criminal responsibility: criminality consists in criminal action; it is for such actions that we are convicted and punished. It could be argued, however, that, while criminal responsibility does require action in that crimes should be so defined as to include an action, actions are not the objects, or essential constituents, of criminal responsibility (see Husak 1998: 65–73): that they are instead conditions of criminal responsibility, perhaps playing an evidential rather than a constitutive role.

Some argue, for instance, that criminal responsibility is grounded in character rather than in action: what makes me a proper object of the criminal law's attentions is not (primarily or merely) my actions, but the defective character traits that my actions reveal (Lacey 1988, ch. 3; Huigens 1995). Such theorists can still insist, however, that criminal responsibility requires action: for, they could argue, actions provide the only reliable evidence, obtainable by means that are not grossly intrusive or oppressive, of the character traits that are the proper objects of criminal responsibility. On such a view, action is still necessary for criminal responsibility: but it is necessary as a condition rather than as the proper object of criminal responsibility.

Whether actions are to be understood as objects, or conditions, of criminal responsibility, the claim that action is necessary for criminal responsibility invites the question: 'But what is action?'

Actions and (Voluntary) Acts

It might seem that this is one way in which philosophy can assist criminal law: since a central question in the philosophy of action is 'What is action?' an answer to that philosophical question should surely assist practitioners and theorists of criminal law, by showing what this necessary condition or object of criminal responsibility amounts to.

One familiar approach to the philosophical question 'What is action?' is a reductivist one, which seeks to analyze action into its most basic or simple elements – an approach that leads us to 'basic actions,' or to various versions of volitionism (see chapters 2 and 13). This approach appeals to many legal theorists, in virtue of a further feature of orthodox criminal law doctrine. Crimes, we are told, must consist in both an *actus reus*, or 'conduct element,' and a *mens rea*, or 'mental element'; they require a guilty act and a guilty mind. Now the 'act' that partly constitutes an *actus reus* must be understood in quite minimal terms: for, while it must be a voluntary act rather than a merely involuntary movement, it cannot be identified in terms of the agent's intentions, since intention belongs to *mens rea* rather than to the *actus reus*; and we must distinguish the 'act' from its circumstances and consequences (see Robinson and Grall 1983). Many legal writers therefore define the (voluntary) act that is required for an *actus reus* as a willed bodily movement (see for instance Williams 1983: 147–148; Ormerod 2008: 51–52; Dressler 2009: 87–91): a bodily movement, because that gives us the kind of minimal act, distinct from its circumstances and consequences, that this analysis of *actus reus* requires; a willed bodily movement, because the act must be voluntary. Moore (1993) offers a philosophically sophisticated development of this kind of account: an action consists in 'bodily-movement-caused-by-a-volition'; the act requirement is therefore the requirement that criminal responsibility should normally depend on an *actus reus* which includes a bodily-movement-caused-by-a-volition (only 'normally,' because the law does sometimes justifiably criminalize omissions).

There are three kinds of objection to this kind of account of the act requirement. First, it faces the objection that it depends on a philosophically untenable conception of action. The various objections brought against volitionist accounts of action and against accounts that rest on a conception of 'basic' actions as consisting in bodily movements are relevant here, but we need not discuss them now: for, even if they can be met, even if 'action theory' (Hornsby 1999) can provide a viable account of action along such lines, there are the two other major objections to this way of explaining either the act requirement in criminal law, or the idea of action as the proper focus of criminal responsibility.

The second objection is that the act requirement, understood in this way, does not specify a plausible condition or requirement of criminal responsibility. The objection is not just that no such requirement is actually respected by our existing criminal laws, which impose criminal responsibility in the absence of any such act: since any account of the proper role of action in criminal law is partly normative, theorists can reject such exceptions as mistakes. Rather, the objection is that it is not plausible to hold that criminal responsibility *should* depend on action understood in this way: there is no good normative reason why people should be held criminally responsible only for 'actions' that include, or consist in, voluntary bodily movements. Not only does the law often imposes liability for omissions; familiar offences, too, can be committed in ways that involve no (voluntary) bodily movements as easily as in ways that involve them: I can steal by keeping someone's property, or I can recklessly endanger others by doing nothing to stop the spread of a fire that starts in my house; in neither case is any bodily movement necessary (see Fletcher 1994; Duff 2007: 97–99).

The third objection could be seen as a development of the second: that such an account of action is not false so much as irrelevant as an account of a necessary condition of criminal responsibility. Action theory, as represented in accounts of action of this kind, focuses on our bodily agency, and thus on actions as events in the natural world. Criminal law, however, is concerned with our social rather than our merely physical being – with our roles in, and our impact on, our shared social world rather than with our physical impact on the material world. Whether or not acts, understood as bodily movements or movings, are necessary for criminal responsibility, they are not its focus: we do not capture what interests criminal law, or what constitutes the object of criminal responsibility, by investigating actions as thus understood. Nor, therefore, is action theory, understood in this way, 'suited to answering questions about the criminal law' (Hornsby 1999: 15).

Suppose that such objections are sound: what can we say, then, about the role of action in criminal law?

Abandoning the Act Requirement?

One response to the second objection noted above (that criminal responsibility cannot plausibly be taken to require an act understood as a willed movement) is to revise the account of acts or actions so that it becomes true that criminal responsibility should always require an act. The obvious danger here is that truth will be achieved at the cost of vacuity. Were we to say, for instance, that 'an act consists of events or states of affairs for which a person might be held responsible' (Gross 1979: 56), we would make it true that criminal responsibility is, properly, for an act, but we would render the act requirement substantively empty; it could then do no work in focusing or limiting the reach of the criminal law (see Husak 1998: 93).

Another response is to argue that we should simply abandon the act requirement, at least as specifying a necessary condition or an object of criminal responsibility, perhaps in favor of a control requirement to the effect that we can properly be held criminally responsible only for what lies within our control (see Husak 1998; Simester 1998). The traditional act requirement overlaps substantially with such a control requirement, if a 'voluntary' act is understood as a controlled bodily movement, and some kind of overt action might still often be necessary if guilt is to be securely proved: even if, for instance, we think it in principle appropriate to criminalize the firm intention to commit a crime, we might expect that some overt action to put that intention into effect will (usually) be needed if the intention's existence and firmness are to be proved beyond reasonable doubt. But we will not need now to engage in the futile search for a definition of action that will capture a necessary element of criminal responsibility; and we will realize that we can properly be held criminally responsible for bodily movements that do not amount to actions, or for conditions or states of affairs, or for omissions, so long as they lie within our control.

Consider just one example. There are many offences of possession: possessing certain categories of prohibited drug; or a firearm without a licence; or material that might be useful for terrorist purposes; or certain kinds of pornography; and so on (see Dubber 2001). Many such offences do mark objectionable over-extensions of the criminal law. But, first, what is objectionable is not that they impose criminal responsibility in the absence of bodily action. They are objectionable if they violate the control requirement, criminalizing 'possession' that is quite unavoidable. They are objectionable if they impose criminal responsibility for what is not morally wrong, or does not threaten harm to others, or is too remote from any wrong-doing. But the absence of (willed) bodily movement, or indeed of action at all, does not seem to be a legitimate ground for objection. Second, some offences of possession are legitimate – most obviously those involving dangerous items that have no legitimate use. But if we ask what makes their criminalization legitimate, or how such offences should be defined, bodily action will not figure either in the rationale or in the definition. Possession does often arise from an act, typically bodily, of acquisition; it also involves retention, which typically involves in turn a failure to undertake whatever acts (typically bodily) are required to end possession (though that is a matter of omission, not of action): the focus of the offence, however, is not on such acts or omissions, but on the way in which the item is available to (that is, under the control of) the possessor, or available to others, for wrongful or harmful use. Control is crucial; action is not.

There is much to be said for a control requirement, both as marking a clearly necessary condition for legitimate criminal responsibility, and as a possible replacement for an orthodox act requirement; but there also seems to be more to be said for some kind of act requirement than the proponents of the control requirement allow.

The control requirement specifies a condition, not an object, of responsibility: we are not responsible for our control over something; rather, we are responsible for something (an act, an outcome, a state of affairs) on condition that we have control over it. It might be said that this is the most we can hope for: while we can specify such general conditions on criminal responsibility as the control requirement, we cannot say anything comparably general about its objects; they are too diverse to admit of any unitary principle to the effect that criminal responsibility must be for *X*. But this does not do justice to the intuitive idea that actions are crucial to criminal responsibility: that there is something amiss with punishing a person for merely thinking or feeling something, and that criminal responsibility for omissions requires special justification – not because thoughts, feelings, or omissions are not controllable, but just because they are not actions. So it is worth asking whether, while accepting the objections noted above to the traditional act requirement, we can salvage or reconstruct something that will do justice to those intuitions.

An Action Presumption?

If we are to salvage anything, we must begin with a different account of action – one which avoids the charge of irrelevance as well as that of vacuity. To do so, we must look away from accounts of actions as events in the physical world, to an account of actions as engagements in a shared social world (see Melden 1961; Gustafson 1986; and also chapters 50 and 66). Action does typically involve the exercise of our capacities to move our bodies – which is the focus of accounts of action as bodily moving. But it also, and for present purposes more significantly, involves the exercise of our capacities to engage in practical reasoning and to actualize its results in ways that make a difference to the social world in which we live. It is action of this kind (and our failures to act in such ways) that properly interests criminal law for two reasons. First, only actions understood in this way can have the kinds of meaning that bring them within the purview of the criminal law: only such actions can, in particular, constitute wrongs, and criminal law is concerned with wrongs. Second, criminal law's interest in us as agents who can be held responsible is an interest in us as social beings who can recognize, and be guided by, reasons for action – as beings, therefore, who can engage in practical reasoning, formulate intentions, and actualize them in the world (see Duff 2007, ch. 5).

Since we are embodied beings, actions as understood in this way will of course typically involve bodily movings: we usually need to exercise our capacities for physical movement (together with other capacities) if we are to actualize the results of our practical reasoning in ways that impact on our shared world. But there is now no reason to pick such movings out as constituting the core or essence of action, or to focus our attention on them as the objects of criminal responsibility: they are simply aspects of most (but not all) of our actions.

Can we then replace the act requirement by an action requirement, and say that criminal responsibility requires, indeed is for, actions? There is a point to saying this; indeed there are two points. One is that criminal responsibility should (normally) require action that impinges on the world: that, for reasons to do with the familiar liberal values of privacy and freedom, thoughts, plans, and feelings which are not given concrete and world-affecting shape in action should not concern the criminal law (which is not to deny that our actions will often have the criminal meaning which they have only in virtue of the thoughts, intentions, and emotions they manifest). The other point is that criminal responsibility should not reach deeper than action: in particular, that we should be criminally responsible only for what we do in the world, not for the character traits which lie behind our actions (which is not to deny that our actions may have the criminal meaning they have only in virtue of the dispositions or character traits they manifest; see Duff 1993). In two ways, however, this principle does not do what the act requirement was supposed to do.

First, it does not pick out part of the *actus reus*, as the most basic constituent of criminal action, independently of any idea of *mens rea*: although action can of course be unintentional, and free from the other kinds of fault (knowledge, recklessness, negligence) standardly taken to constitute *mens rea*, we cannot understand what it is to act (in a way that could interest the criminal law) without reference to intention. But it is anyway arguable that the distinction between *actus reus* and *mens rea* should not be understood as distinguishing independently identifiable elements of a crime (see Robinson 1993; Duff 2007: 202–207).

Second and more importantly, it is not plausible to say that criminal responsibility *requires*, or is *always* for, action: there are simply too many cases in which criminal responsibility is imposed for what must be counted as omissions rather than actions, and in which it is not plausible to argue that this is unwarranted simply on the grounds that it imposes criminal responsibility for something other than an action. The most we can plausibly assert is an action presumption: that criminal responsibility should presumptively be for, and should therefore presumptively require, action. We will then need to ask about the conditions under which that presumption can be defeated, and whether they can all be shown to involve imposing criminal responsibility for omissions (possession offences will again be significant here). If that is the case, some might argue that we should replace such an action presumption by an 'act or omission' requirement: those who believe, however, that there is some morally significant distinction between acts and omissions (a topic which we cannot pursue here, but see Duff 2007: 107–115, and also chapter 7) will wish to reflect that distinction in an action presumption which needs to be defeated in those cases in which responsibility can be properly imposed for omissions.

See also: ACTION THEORY AND ONTOLOGY (1); BASIC ACTIONS AND INDIVIDUATION (2); BODILY MOVEMENTS (4); REFRAINING, OMITTING, AND NEGATIVE ACTS (7); VOLITION AND THE WILL (13); RESPONSIBILITY AND AUTONOMY (39); INTENTION IN LAW (43).

References

Dressler, J. (2009). *Understanding Criminal Law*, 5th edn. New York: LexisNexis.

Dubber, M. D. (2001). Policing possession: The war on crime and the end of criminal law. *Journal of Criminal Law and Criminology*, 91, 829–996.

Duff, R. A. (1993). Choice, character and criminal liability. *Law and Philosophy*, 12, 345–383.

Duff, R. A. (2007). *Answering for Crime: Responsibility and Liability in the Criminal Law*. Oxford: Hart Publishing.

Fletcher, G. (1994). On the moral irrelevance of bodily movements. *University of Pennsylvania Law Review*, 142, 1443–1453.

Gross, H. (1979). *A Theory of Criminal Justice*. New York: Oxford University Press.

Gustafson, D. (1986). *Intention and Agency*. Dordrecht: Reidel.

Hornsby, J. (1999). The poverty of action theory. *Philosophical Inquiry*, 21, 1–19.

Huigens, K. (1995). Virtue and inculpation. *Harvard Law Review*, 108, 1423–1480.

Husak, D. N. (1998). Does criminal liability require an act? In R. A. Duff (ed.), *Philosophy and the Criminal Law*. Cambridge: Cambridge University Press), 60–100.

Lacey, N. (1988). *State Punishment*. London: Routledge.

Melden, A. I. (1961). *Free Action*. London: Routledge.

Moore, M. S. (1993). *Act and Crime: The Philosophy of Action and Its Implications for the Criminal Law*. Oxford: Oxford University Press.

Ormerod, D. (2008). *Smith and Hogan Criminal Law*, 12th edn. Oxford: Oxford University Press.

Robinson, P. H. (1993). Should the criminal law abandon the *actus reus/mens rea* distinction? In S. Shute, J. Gardner, and J. Horder (eds), *Action and Value in Criminal Law*. Oxford: Oxford University Press, 187–211.

Robinson, P. H., and Grall, J. A. (1983). Element analysis in defining criminal liability: The model penal code and beyond. *Stanford Law Review*, 35, 681–762.

Simester, A. P. (1998). On the so-called requirement for voluntary action. *Buffalo Criminal Law Review*, 1, 403–430.

Williams, G. (1983). *Textbook of Criminal Law*, 2nd edn. London: Stevens.

43

Intention in Law

GIDEON YAFFE

The intentions of people who are entwined with the law are often of central importance for answering legal questions. A contract is not ordinarily legally enforceable unless each party intended to be bound by the agreement when it was made. An injured party is not ordinarily legally entitled to damages for battery unless the person who caused the injury intended the act resulting in it. A person cannot ordinarily legally inherit under a will unless the creator of that will intended that person to inherit. These are three of the many examples that one finds in private law, by which the state is overseeing and enforcing transactions between private parties. However, intention plays a more important role in criminal law, where the state specifies what people are to be legally punished for, determines whether they have committed acts for which they are to be punished, and administers sentences. In fact, the intentions of criminal defendants and, on occasion, of others involved in the crimes of which the former are accused are central to a very large number of criminal cases, and in several different ways.

Setting aside exceptions that need not concern us, criminal liability is imposed only after a finding to the effect that a defendant performed the *actus reus* ('guilty act') of a crime with *mens rea* ('a guilty mind'). To reach a guilty verdict, that is, the state must show that the defendant did something prohibited (with the results and in the circumstances in which it is prohibited), and did so while being in a certain mental state. Precisely what mental state the defendant needs to have been in for guilt to be established varies from crime to crime. However, there is a large class of crimes for which showing *mens rea* requires showing that the defendant had some intention when engaging in the *actus reus*.

The distinction between acts and mere happenings – between, for instance, nodding one's head and one's head nodding while one falls asleep in a chair – is reflected in the criminal law, but the criminal law does not make an explicit appeal (although perhaps it makes a tacit appeal) to intention in drawing this distinction. Under the relevant legal principle, known as 'the voluntary act requirement,' the *actus reus* of every crime includes a voluntary act. A defendant is never punished in the absence of a finding that he performed some prohibited voluntary action. A voluntary act is defined as a bodily movement guided by the mental state of 'volition.' Exactly what a volition is remains somewhat dark in criminal law. However, showing that a defendant engaged in a relevant voluntary act is thought to be part of what is involved in showing that he committed the *actus reus* of the crime with which he is charged. It is not taken in the law as part of what is involved in *mens rea*. But it is in showing *mens rea* that a defendant's intentions are thought to be relevant. Hence criminal law quietly takes the position that the intentions of relevance to criminal punishment are not those that distinguish acts from mere happenings (unless it turns out that volitions are a species of intention). Rather, the intentions of relevance to the law are those which guide our voluntary actions but do not account for the fact that they are voluntary actions. On this view, a person who hits another one in the face intending to shame the other person engages in the voluntary act of hitting another by virtue of his volition; his intention to shame is a distinct and separate mental state, which guides his performance of the act of hitting.

Although it is becoming of increasingly little legal relevance, crimes are still sometimes divided into the categories of 'general intent' and 'specific intent.' A general intent crime is a crime the commission of which requires some sort of objectionable mental state, but no particular intention is shared among all those who commit the crime. In fact, the phrase 'general intent crime' is misleading, since the *mens rea* requirements of many such crimes include no intention at all. A person who takes a nap while the fire from the pile of trash he is burning spreads and kills his neighbor might be guilty of a criminal homicide. Such a homicide is a general intent crime – the defendant might need to be shown to have been aware that there was a good chance that the fire would spread and hurt someone if not watched – but a defendant need not be shown to have had any intention whatsoever, much less an intention to kill his neighbor, in order to be proven to be guilty. In fact, the default rule is that recklessness in the absence of intent suffices for *mens rea* in general intent crimes. By contrast, a specific intent crime is a crime the commission of which requires some particular intention. Assault with intent to kill, as well as some other crimes such as burglary, the names of which do not mention intent, are specific intent crimes. All those who commit assault with intent to kill *intend to kill*; all those who commit burglary intend to commit some felony in the dwelling they illegally enter.

At times in the history of the criminal law, the question of whether a crime was properly classified as one of general intent or of specific intent has had legal consequences. For instance, it was at one time true under the British common law that a defendant could appeal in his defense to the fact that he had made an unreasonable mistake of fact – he had thought, for instance, that the white powder was sugar when it was actually arsenic, a mistake which a reasonable person would not have made – only if the crime with which he was charged was to be classified as a specific intent crime. The thought was that an unreasonable mistake might undermine the claim that the defendant had some particular intention, such as an intention to kill, but it could not undermine the claim that he was in one of the many possible objectionable mental states that might serve for *mens rea* in a general intent crime. However, primarily because there has been much confusion over which crimes are of general intent and which ones are of specific intent, and because the classification, per se, did not seem to matter if it was clear what mental states were involved and what mental states were not involved in the *mens rea* of the crime, the importance of the distinction has been eroding. Increasingly, judges reach decisions without appealing to the distinction, and legislators avoid drafting legislation that uses it.

It is not only in the phrase 'general intent' that criminal law uses the term 'intent' to refer to something which does not involve the mental state of intending at all. Three other potentially misleading legal usages of the term are worth mentioning, although this list is not exhaustive. First, a distinction is sometimes drawn in legal contexts between 'direct' and 'oblique' intention. A person's oblique intention is what he believes, with some high degree of confidence, will come to pass, should he do as he intends. His direct intention, by contrast, is what he intends to do. A defendant, for instance, who fires a gun at the chest of a police officer who is pursuing him might directly intend only to disable the police officer long enough to allow escape; but if he thinks it very likely that he will kill the police officer, should the bullet reach its mark, then he obliquely intends to kill the police officer.

Evincing awareness that oblique intention is not intention at all, judges sometimes use the term 'actual intent' to refer to direct intention and consider oblique intention to be an instance of 'constructive intention.' 'Constructive intention' is another usage of the term 'intention' in the law, made in order to refer to something which, properly speaking, is not an intention at all. A person's constructive intention is the intention that he is *taken, for legal purposes, to have*, despite a recognition that he actually lacks the mental state of intention attributed to him. We might think that firing a gun at the chest of a police officer intending to disable the officer but foreseeing his death is *just as bad* as intending the police officer's death. Such a thought motivates treating a person who acted that way *as though* he intended to kill. This thought is sometimes expressed by saying that such a person 'constructively intends' to kill, but does not actually so intend.

A third misleading usage of the term 'intent' in criminal law appears in the name of the doctrine of 'transferred intent,' which is of primary importance in homicide law. If a defendant intends to kill one person but misses and kills an innocent bystander, he is guilty of an intentional homicide under the doctrine of transferred intent. (He is similarly guilty, under the same doctrine, in mistaken identity cases in which a defendant kills one person believing it to be another.) This usage is sometimes rationalized on the grounds that the intention to kill the target 'transfers' to the bystander (or to the person mistaken for the target). The doctrine of transferred intent, then, seems to involve the assertion that the intention to kill the target somehow becomes an intention to kill the bystander, when a bystander is mistakenly killed. So understood, however, the doctrine involves asserting an absurdity. A mental state that precedes and guides an act cannot change in content given an unanticipated outcome of action. However, legal practitioners who employ the doctrine of transferred intent recognize that defendants in such cases do not actually intend to kill the people they kill – either before or after the death in question. In fact, such defendants may not even foresee the possibility, and may not even be negligent in their failure, when they act. Rather, the thought is that someone who kills one person while intending to kill another has acted just as badly as someone who succeeds in killing the person he intends; and thus the law is justified to treat him *as though* he did. There is only a metaphorical sense in which the intention to kill transfers to the bystander; in fact, applying the doctrine of transferred intent involves merely attributing to the defendant the constructive intent to kill the person who was actually killed.

Although the term is used in various misleading ways in criminal law, intention, properly so called – the mental state of intending – plays an important role there. Intent, in the proper sense, is ordinarily distinguished from 'motive.' This distinction is primarily drawn in order to convict defendants who intend something objectionable only as a means to some further end, which might itself be unobjectionable, or even laudable. In such cases, the further end is referred to as the defendant's 'motive' and deemed irrelevant as such to the question of his guilt. The person who commits euthanasia, for instance, would be said to intend to kill, but to be motivated to relieve suffering. But, since his motive is not relevant to the question of his criminal liability for murder while his intention is, he is guilty of an intentional homicide (assuming that he does not perform the act under a jurisdiction which has made euthanasia legal). The general rule that motive in this sense is irrelevant to criminal liability is, however, nothing more than a rule of thumb. A person, for instance, who intends to kill for its own sake – the killing is his end in acting, and therefore constitutes his motive for acting – will not be acquitted under this rule. We do not ignore such an intention in assessing guilt, despite the fact that it is an intention which favors an end. Further, there is a variety of circumstances in which a defendant intends something as a means, and such an intention is the needed *mens rea* of the crime, but the defendant is acquitted in virtue of his motive for acting or of the further end at which he aims. This is particularly common in the affirmative defenses. Someone who intends to commit a robbery but does so merely to comply with another's threat is, under certain circumstances, not guilty of robbery. Someone who intends to destroy another's property but does so in order to prevent a fire from burning much more property is, under certain circumstances, not guilty of destruction of property. His motive for acting – to prevent the destruction of much more property than he damages – allows him to escape criminal liability. The distinction between what a person intends and a person's motives serves only the legal purpose of establishing that it is possible to be guilty of a crime while aiming at an end which is not criminal. This is consistent with the legal practice of taking some motives to undermine guilt even in the presence of the intention involved generally in the completed crime. In other words, the importance of the distinction between motive and intent can be easily overestimated.

Criminal law has struggled, in several different domains, with the question of whether foresight should suffice for liability, or whether, instead, intent should be required and foresight be considered insufficient. For instance, should it be a greater crime to kill someone while intending to kill him than it is to kill him while only foreseeing his death? The law's answer, across jurisdictions, is that it should not. When it comes to homicide, foresight is as bad as intent. However, should it be a greater crime to intend to kill, to act on that intention, and to fail, than it is to expect that one's act will kill someone, and perform it nonetheless, yet without a death resulting? The law's answer, across the vast majority of jurisdictions, is that it should. Attempted murder requires an intention to kill; foresight will not do, even though foresight suffices for a completed murder of the worst sort. Or, to take another example, should performing an act that one foresees will help another to commit a crime suffice to make one an accomplice to the crime, or must one intend to help the other to commit the crime in order to be an accomplice? Although there is some variation across jurisdictions in answering this question, the standard approach is that intent to aid is required for accomplice liability; foresight is insufficient. On this view, the person who gives another directions to a drug dealer's home expecting thereby to help him to buy drugs, but not intending to help him buy drugs, is not an accomplice to a drug sale.

At various times in the history of criminal law, questions concerning criminal liability relative to the line between foresight and intent, let alone the law's answers to them, have been obscured by the law's usage of the term 'intent' to refer to things that were not properly designated by that term. Crimes of attempt – attempted murder, attempted robbery, for instance – were traditionally classified as specific intent crimes: a person can commit an attempt of a crime only if he 'intends' to commit the crime. But in saying that attempts are specific intent crimes, is the law referring to direct intention or to oblique intention? Is intent, properly so called, required, or does foresight suffice? Since the term 'intention' was used to refer to foresight ('oblique intention') the classification of attempt as a specific intent crime did not settle the question: in which sense of 'intent,' 'direct' or 'oblique,' was attempt a specific intent crime? In fact, it took many years of adjudication of attempt cases before the ambiguity was removed and the default rule that intent is required and foresight does not suffice for attempt was established.

A variety of additional difficult questions about intent in the law continues to be a subject of debate among theorists and legal practitioners. Since legal decisions cannot await the outcome of such debates, decisions are made in cases as though the answers to these questions were settled. And, given the rule of deference to prior judicial decisions – the principle of *stare decisis* ('to abide by what has been decided') – the answer to a difficult question that a court settles on in its decision will perpetuate in future decisions at least in that jurisdiction, even if there is uncertainty about its correctness even on the part of the judge who made it. One such question concerns conditional intent. It is common enough for our intentions to be conditional in content. A person, for instance, might not intend to sell drugs to another person; but that person may intend instead to sell them if the other person promises not to distribute the drugs to children. His intent to sell is conditional. When such a person is charged with possession of drugs with intent to distribute, is he guilty? Does his conditional intention suffice for the *mens rea* of the crime? Those who think that such a conditional intention does suffice must explain why some conditional intentions clearly do not. For instance, imagine someone who intends to take a bag from the baggage claim at the airport if that bag is his own. When he acts on this conditional intention and starts to take a bag that is not his, has he attempted theft? Such an attempt requires an intention to take something that is not one's own. Does such a person's conditional intention serve? Intuitively, it seems not. But what distinguishes these two hypothetical cases? It is fair to say that this issue is not definitively settled in the law, even though judges have employed various 'tests' in deciding whether defendants with conditional intentions are guilty or not of crimes which involve intent.

Another question about intent which remains a topic of debate among theorists and legal practitioners concerns the attitude towards so-called 'circumstantial elements' of crimes needed for guilt when intention is included in the *mens rea* of the crime. For instance, to attempt receipt of stolen property, a person must intend to receive stolen property. Say that a defendant intends to buy a stereo from a stranger off the back of a truck and does not know or care whether the stereo is stolen. Has such a person attempted receipt of stolen property? It would seem that, if the legal status of the property as stolen or unstolen were in the content of his intention, that would make a difference to what he would do in certain counterfactual circumstances. If the property's being stolen were in the content of his intention, then he would balk at the sale, were he to discover that the stereo is not stolen. And so it seems, given that he does not care whether the property is stolen, that the property's being stolen is not in the content of his intention. Does it follows that he is not guilty of attempted receipt of stolen property? Or does uncertainty about the property's legal status, even in the absence of intent, suffice for establishing guilt about the attempt to receive stolen property? In jurisdictions which have confronted this question, we ordinarily find acceptance of the view that such a defendant has the intention needed for attempt only if he believes that the goods are stolen. But there are other options. Perhaps awareness of a good chance that the goods are stolen, even in the absence of belief, suffices. Or perhaps not even belief suffices in the absence of some sort of pro-attitude towards the possibility. Perhaps, that is, the defendant must at least want, or hope, that the goods are stolen. Or perhaps true intent is required. Perhaps in order to be guilty the defendant must actually positively aim at receiving stolen goods and be ready to walk away from the transaction should he discover that the goods are not stolen. Which of these approaches is appropriate, and, more importantly, *why* one approach is superior to another, remain open questions, even in jurisdictions which have settled on a particular rule in such cases.

Guilt and innocence in criminal law, then, frequently turn on the answer to some question about intent. Sometimes this is a question about what kind of crime the defendant is charged with: for instance, is the crime one of general or of specific intent? Sometimes it is a question about what the law's actual standards are or should be: for instance, is intention required for guilt, or does foresight, or some other mental state entirely, suffice? And sometimes it is a question about whether the mental state that the defendant was actually in at the time of the crime meets the standard of guilt or falls short of it: for instance, is the intention to kill the target sufficient for guilt for intentional homicide of the bystander who was killed even though the defendant did not intend to kill that bystander? Some of these questions have settled answers in the law, some do not; some are answered uniformly across jurisdictions, some are not; some are answered on grounds of principle, some are not. But, unavoidably, intention and the questions that arise about it in adjudicating cases are and will remain fixtures of the criminal law.

See also: REFRAINING, OMITTING, AND NEGATIVE ACTS (7); VOLITION AND THE WILL (13); INTENTION (14); RESPONSIBILITY AND AUTONOMY (39); THE DOCTRINE OF DOUBLE EFFECT (41); ACTION AND CRIMINAL RESPONSIBILITY (42).

Further reading

NOTE These books are concerned with much more than intention. I single out pages that are concerned with the issues discussed in this chapter.

Duff, R. A. (1990) *Intention, Agency and Criminal Liability*. Oxford: Blackwell Press.

Fletcher, G. (2000) *Rethinking Criminal Law*, 2nd edn. Oxford: Oxford University Press (esp. 439–454).

Hart, H. L. A. (1968). Intention and punishment. In H. L. A. Hart, *Punishment and Responsibility*. Oxford: Oxford University Press, 113–135.

Husak, D. (1996). Transferred intent. In *Notre Dame Journal of Law, Ethics and Public Policy*, 10, 65–67.

Moore, M. (1997). *Placing Blame*. Oxford: Clarendon Press (esp. 449–470).

Yaffe, G. (2004). Conditional intent and *mens rea*. *Legal Theory*, 10, 273–310.

44

Scientific Challenges to Free Will

EDDY NAHMIAS

Scientists have recently claimed that their discoveries challenge free will. For instance, psychologist Jonathan Bargh concludes that 'The phenomenological feeling of free will is very real [...] but this strong feeling is an illusion' (2008: 148–149). Neuroscientist John-Dylan Haynes claims that his functional magnetic resonance imaging (fMRI) research shows that

> [t]here's not very much space for operation of free will. The outcome of a decision is shaped very strongly by brain activity much earlier than the point in time when you feel to be making a decision. (Youngsteadt 2008)

And neuroscientists Joshua Greene and Jonathan Cohen conclude: 'The net effect of this influx of scientific information will be a rejection of free will as it is ordinarily conceived with important ramifications for the law' (2004: 1776). Indeed, what scientists say about free will could have a significant impact not only on our legal practices, but on our conception of ourselves and of others as morally responsible agents. This impact is likely to be exacerbated by the way in which the research is presented by the science media. For instance, *ScienceNews* reports: ' "Free will" is not the defining feature of humanness, modern neuroscience implies, but is rather an illusion that endures only because biochemical complexity conceals the mechanisms of decision making' (12/6/08). And Jeffrey Rosen asks: 'And since all behavior is caused by our brains, wouldn't this mean all behavior could potentially be excused?' (*New York Times* 3/11/07).

It is therefore important to consider carefully what discoveries these scientists take to be challenging free will and whether these claims are justified. In the present essay I take on this task, first by distinguishing among various ways the research might pose challenges to free will, then by considering whether it actually does.

Philosophical debates about free will focus largely on one question: is free will compatible with *determinism*? So the most straightforward scientific challenge to free will would seem to be the discovery of determinism. Indeed, scientists often explicitly argue that:

[D1] Free will requires that determinism is false.
[D2] Science is showing that determinism is true.
[D3] So, science is showing that we do not have free will.

For instance Bargh writes: 'The psychological issue of whether free will exists thus boils down to whether *undetermined choices* of action exist' (2008: 130), and he and Ferguson take their research to 'present the case for the determinism of higher mental processes' (2000: 926). Lawrence Tancredi writes: 'Free will, long considered a hallmark of what makes us human, seems to be losing ground to claims of biological determinism' (2007: 305).

One problem with this argument is that the scientists simply *assume* that premise [D1] is true, ignoring the substantial philosophical literature supporting *compatibilism*, the view that free will does *not* require the falsity of determinism (see McKenna 2004). Perhaps these scientists take incompatibilism to be commonsensical, but this assumption is controversial and may be based on confusing determinism with different threats to free will (Nahmias et al. 2006, 2007b). More importantly, science is *not* showing determinism to be true. *Determinism*, as understood in the incompatibilists' arguments for [D1] (see for instance van Inwagen 1983), is the thesis that a complete description of a system at one time, conjoined with a complete description of the laws which govern that system, entails a complete description of that system at any future time. In a deterministic system, given identical circumstances, the same causal antecedent will always have the exact same effects. But the dominant interpretation in quantum physics suggests that determinism, so defined, is false. While some philosophers have looked to quantum indeterminism in the hope that it might allow for free will (Kane 1996), most conclude that such indeterminism would not provide us with any relevant type of control which we could not have without it. This should make us wonder why philosophers focus so much attention on determinism and whether they are neglecting scientific discoveries seemingly more relevant to human free will – namely discoveries about human psychology rather than discoveries in microphysics.

In fact the scientists who are claiming that free will is an illusion are not physicists. They are neuroscientists and psychologists. While, in practice, these scientists may aspire to offer deterministic explanations and laws for the systems they study, these sciences are not in a position to establish determinism. Most of their discoveries involve statistical correlations that are compatible with indeterminism. Moreover, it is implausible to think that indeterministic interactions at the microphysical level *never* have an effect on the way things happen at, say, the neurobiological level. And 'near-enough determinism' is simply not sufficient to make incompatibilist arguments go through (i.e., to justify premise D2).

It turns out that these skeptical scientists are not really working with a philosophical conception of determinism. Rather they tend to use 'determinism' to mean something else, namely *mechanism*. Mechanism is the view that mental phenomena can be fully explained in terms of their component neurobiological parts and in terms of the organization of, and interactions between, these parts (see Craver 2007). Consider how neuroscientist Benjamin Libet defines 'determinism' in terms of mechanism, explicitly setting aside quantum indeterminism:

> But we have not answered the question of whether our consciously willed acts are fully determined by natural laws that govern the activities of nerve cells in the brain, or whether conscious decisions can proceed to some degree independently of natural determinism [...] Quantum mechanics forces us to deal with probabilities rather than with certainties of events [...] [but] they might nevertheless be in accord with natural laws and therefore determined. (Libet 1999: 55)

Bargh and Ferguson make a similar move:

> We consider the discovery and delineation of the causal mechanisms that underlie these [conscious] processes and the quest for supplying mechanisms [...] as the critical and defining criteria of the deterministic stance. (Bargh and Ferguson 2000: 926)

This sort of mechanism could clearly be true even if determinism is false (for example if any of the component parts in a mechanistic system interact in *indeterministic* ways). Conversely, determinism could be true even in a non-mechanistic system (for example if both physical laws and psychological laws are deterministic, but psychological processes cannot be fully explained in terms of physical processes). Hence it is misleading to present determinism as a threat to free will by trading on threats posed by mechanism or vice versa.

We need a different argument to represent the challenge to free will that psychologists and neuroscientists have in mind:

[M1] Free will requires that mechanism is false.
[M2] Science is showing that mechanism is true.
[M3] So, science is showing that we do not have free will.

As with determinism, it is not clear that these sciences are *discovering* that mechanism is true [M2] rather than *assuming* it as a useful heuristic. One might, however, argue that these sciences provide inductive support for mechanism to the extent that they offer evidence that human decision-making and behavior can be explained and predicted in terms of underlying mechanisms. But in this case none of the *specific* results discussed as challenges to free will (for instance, those considered below) is particularly relevant to this argument.

Premise [M1] is more controversial. It may be motivated by the assumption that free will, by definition, involves non-natural powers. Consider the way neuroscientist Read Montague puts it:

> Free will is the idea that we make choices and have thoughts independent of anything remotely resembling a physical process. Free will is the close cousin to the idea of the soul – the concept that 'you,' your thoughts and feelings, derive from an entity that is separate and distinct from the physical mechanisms that make up your body [...] Consequently, the idea of free will is not even in principle within reach of scientific description. (Montague 2008: 584)

Psychologist Daniel Wegner assumes that we are dualists about free will: 'Seeing one's own causal influence as supernatural is part of being human' (2008: 228). And Greene and Cohen write: 'intuitive free will [...] requires the rejection of determinism and an implicit commitment to some kind of magical mental causation' (2004: 178). But it is entirely unclear whether most ordinary people assume that free will requires non-natural powers, and even less clear that they associate it *primarily* with such powers rather than with the sorts of powers compatibilists emphasize, such as self-control and rational deliberation. Philosophers certainly aim to analyze free will in ways that are consistent with our best scientific picture of decision-making; no serious contemporary accounts of free will appeal to substance dualism.

In order to examine whether specific scientific evidence about human decision-making challenges free will, we should begin with the assumption that a naturalistic account of free will is possible. On that assumption, some discoveries may help to *explain* free will rather than explaining it *away*. Nonetheless, recent evidence from psychology and neuroscience could challenge free will on the basis of an argument like this:

[E1] Free will requires that one's actions properly derive from one's conscious reasoning, decisions, and intentions.
[E2] Science is showing that our actions do *not* properly derive from our conscious reasoning, decisions, and intentions.
[E3] So, science is showing that we do not have free will.

Free will, as understood in [E1], is consistent with determinism. Whether it is consistent with mechanism or not is an issue which leads to metaphysical debates about mental causation and 'philosophical epiphenomenalism.' Some philosophers think that conscious mental states cannot play a causal role in action if they *supervene* on neural states – that is, if changes in mental states depend on changes in neural states (Kim 1998). But the scientific evidence is not relevant to these debates, since the debates *begin* with the assumption that our mental states supervene on our neural states. For the scientific evidence to be relevant to this argument, we need to consider whether it adds support to [E2] on the naturalistic assumption that all mental processes supervene on 'neural correlates.' This question then turns on whether there is evidence for a thesis which I call 'modular epiphenomenalism' (Nahmias 2002). This is the thesis that the neural correlates of our conscious experience of deciding or intending an action (the 'C module') are *not* causally responsible for producing that action; instead, distinct, non-conscious processes or modules (the 'NC modules') cause the action, while NC modules *also* cause the activity in the C modules (see Figure 44.1). Hence 'conscious will' is an illusion (Wegner 2002) in that the processes underlying our conscious choices and intentions do *not* in fact cause our actions – they are epiphenomenal.

Modular epiphenomenalism finally offers an empirical thesis that appears to challenge free will and can be informed by recent scientific evidence, rather than relying primarily on controversial philosophical claims. So now we are in a position to examine some of this research and then to consider whether it is properly interpreted as a challenge to free will.

Libet's much discussed work represented the first such challenge. Libet (1985) demonstrated that voluntary muscle movements (flexing one's wrist) are preceded by 'readiness potentials' (RPs), brain waves in the supplemental motor area (SMA) which occur about half a second (500 ms) before the movement. Libet also had subjects report

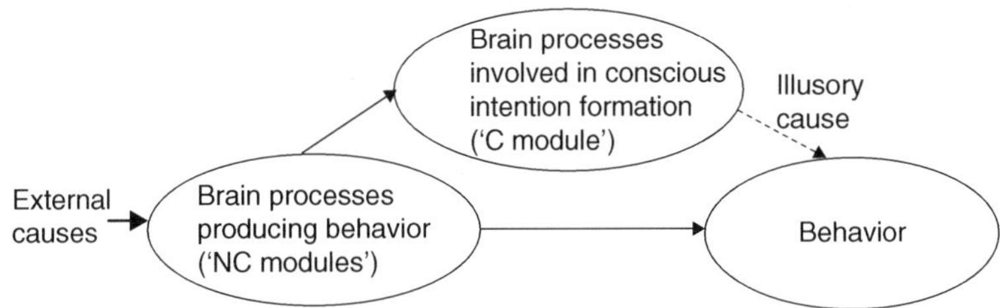

Figure 44.1 Modular epiphenomenalism (compare Wegner 2002: 68)

when they became aware of the 'intention, desire, or urge' to move, and this measure suggested that awareness occurred only 150 ms before the movement – 350 ms *after* the RP. Libet concluded that voluntary actions 'begin in the brain unconsciously, well before the person consciously knows he wants to act' (1999: 51). Libet interpreted this result as showing that our conscious intention to move is not the cause of our movement but, like the movement itself, an effect of earlier (non-conscious) brain activity. Libet seems to assume that conscious intentions are non-physical; but, if we reject this dualist assumption, his data look like evidence for modular epiphenomenalism: the RP in the SMA is a non-conscious process that causes the movement, while the neural correlates of the conscious experience of intending to move are shown to be epiphenomenal because they occur too late to initiate the movement. If this model of agency applied to all actions, it would appear to reduce the role of consciousness to one of merely *observing* unconsciously formed decisions instead of *making* them.

Libet's paradigm has recently been extended in an fMRI study. Soon et al. (2008) asked subjects to press a button either with their left or with their right index finger 'when they became aware of the urge to do so' and to pay attention to when 'their motor decision was consciously made.' Consistent with Libet's results, subjects generally reported that they were aware of their 'decision' less than half a second before pressing the button. But analyses of the fMRI data showed specific activity in the frontopolar cortex that predicted *which* button subjects would press *7–10 seconds* before the movement! And activity in SMA predicted *when* subjects would press the button about 5 seconds before the movement. It should be noted that, while statistically significant, these 'predictions' (actually post-hoc correlations) could be made with only 60 percent accuracy (that is, 10 percent above chance). The authors conclude that

> two specific regions in the frontal and parietal cortex of the human brain had considerable information that predicted the outcome of a motor decision the subject had not yet consciously made. (Soon et al. 2008: 545)

They take these findings to bolster Libet's case that the 'subjective experience of freedom is no more than an illusion and that our actions are initiated by unconscious mental processes long before we become aware of our intention to act' (ibid., p. 543). Assuming that further studies could drive the predictive accuracy much higher, modular epiphenomenalism and premise [E2] look plausible: non-conscious neural processes, *not* the neural correlates of conscious decisions, cause actions that we experience as freely chosen.

A third research paradigm suggesting modular epiphenomenalism appears in the work of psychologists such as Wegner and Bargh. As we have seen, these authors suggest that simply discovering that there are underlying brain processes for decisions and actions is a threat to free will. For instance, Wegner suggests that conscious will is an illusion because 'the real causal sequence underlying human behavior involves a massively complicated set of mechanisms' (2002: 27). But if we put aside such assumptions and focus on the actual *evidence* these psychologists discuss, we can consider whether this evidence lends support to modular epiphenomenalism. Though Wegner and Bargh discuss neuroscientific research such as Libet's, their focus is on psychological evidence – evidence, for instance, of people performing voluntary-looking actions without conscious awareness of performing those actions or without conscious decisions to perform those actions. This evidence is taken to suggest that, because non-conscious processes can produce actions normally accompanied by consciousness, consciousness is unnecessary and hence causally irrelevant. Bargh and Ferguson conclude:

> the same higher mental processes that have traditionally served as quintessential examples of choice and free will – such as goal pursuit, judgment, and interpersonal behavior – have been shown recently to occur in the absence of conscious choice or guidance. (2000: 926)

Wegner focuses on cases where people lack an experience of consciously willing a bodily movement that they in fact brought about (as in automatisms, or in hypnosis), and also on cases where people experience some sense of agency in relation to a bodily movement or an event which they do *not* in fact cause (see for example his I-Spy study, 2002: 74). Wegner takes these seemingly exceptional cases to represent the rule that our conscious intentions *never* cause our actions:

> Rather than conscious will being the rule and automatism the exception, the opposite may be true: Automatism is the rule, and the illusion of conscious will is the exception. (Ibid., p. 143)

And he suggests modular epiphenomenalism:

> The brain, in turn, shows evidence that the motor structures underlying action [NC modules] are distinct from the structures that allow the experience of will [C module]. The experience of will may be manufactured by the interconnected operation of multiple brain systems, and these do not seem to be the same as the systems that yield action. (Ibid., p. 49)

Wegner's explanation for our illusory experiences of conscious will is that we have relevant conscious thoughts just prior to the action, while being unaware of any competing causes of the action. But these thoughts are themselves caused by prior non-conscious brain activity, such that conscious intention 'might just be a loose end – one of those things, like the action, that is caused by prior brain and mental events' (ibid., p. 55; see Figure 44.1).

Now that we have seen the sort of evidence from neuroscience and psychology that has been taken to challenge free will, I will first argue that such evidence does not clearly demonstrate modular epiphenomenalism – that is, premise [E2] – and then argue that, even to the extent that it could, this would not pose much of a threat to free will, once we parse premise [E1] more carefully (for more detailed responses to Wegner and Libet, see Nahmias 2002 and Mele 2009).

Wegner and Bargh face a dilemma: they must either take the evidence they describe to suggest that the causal role of consciousness is limited in scope (and further work will delimit this scope), or use it as inductive evidence for the general rule that conscious processes are never causal. Bargh and Ferguson admit that the evidence they discuss shows only that conscious processes play a less significant role that we tend to assume: 'This research has found much of an individual's complex psychological and behavioral functioning to occur without conscious choice or guidance – that is, automatically' (2000: 941). Plugging this claim into the argument for epiphenomenalism would only generate the conclusion that we have *less* free will than we tend to think rather than none at all. Though I think the scope of this threat is more limited than the authors suppose (see below), not even Bargh's claim of 'mainly unconscious instead of conscious causation of action' (2008: 148) entails the skeptical conclusion that free will is an illusion.

Wegner tends to take the other horn of the dilemma and to draw more general conclusions about epiphenomenalism. However, to demonstrate that the neural correlates of conscious intentions are causally cut off from the neural processes which produce actions would require data from the neurosciences, and here Wegner has little to offer beyond Libet's work. The unusual cases from the psychological literature (voluntary-looking movements without the agent's experiencing control, and small increases in reported experiences of control over events which the agent did not actually cause) demonstrate only that the experience of will is not *always* veridical, not that it is *never* veridical. Without the neuro-anatomical data to demonstrate that the relevant brain processes are causally unconnected, the best interpretation for these 'illusions of will' should be guided by an analogy with visual illusions, which certainly do not demonstrate that our visual experiences are systematically mistaken. Indeed, as with visual illusions, explanations for illusions of will may be offered in terms of a generally *reliable* system, which sometimes produces inaccurate output because of some unusual feature of the situation (all the cases discussed by Wegner are unusual in important ways). The fact that we *sometimes* perform complex behaviors without conscious intentions (for example, under hypnosis or with subliminal priming) does not show that, on the many occasions when we do perform complex behaviors with conscious intentions, the conscious mental processes are causally irrelevant.

But doesn't the neuroscientific evidence presented by Libet and by Soon and colleagues give us reason to think that the neural correlates of conscious intentions and decisions are *not* causes of our actions? Not really. Their data are entirely consistent with other interpretations. For instance, RPs and the even earlier activity in the frontopolar cortex may correlate with non-conscious *urges* to move soon (or to push the left or right button), rather than with specific *intentions* or *decisions*. In the experiments, this non-conscious activity almost always leads to a consciously experienced intention and corresponding action, but in some cases the urge may be 'vetoed,' perhaps by the subjects' conscious intention not to act on that urge (Mele 2009). The data is simply not sufficient to show that the non-conscious neural activity *deterministically* causes a particular action (such that, given that activity, the action must happen). Libet did not even analyze data on brain activity in cases where subjects felt the urge to flex but did not flex. And recall that Soon's group could only show that the early brain activity predicted the choices at 10 percent above chance, which leaves open the possibility that, on some trials, later conscious thoughts, whose neural correlates could not be captured in the analyses, influenced which button was pressed and when. This interpretation, if true, allows that the neural correlates of conscious intentions can causally influence when, whether, and how a person acts, contra premise [E2].

Another possibility is that the early non-conscious brain activity just *is* part of the correlate of the conscious intention, or part of the necessary build-up to such intentions or decisions. After all, if we assume that conscious processes correlate with neural processes, we should expect that conscious experiences do not arise out of nowhere and in no time (Dennett 1991). Rather, they will be produced by earlier complexes of events, including external stimuli and neural activity, some of which may have been caused by even earlier *conscious* processes. For instance, in these experiments subjects consciously processed and accepted the experimenters' instructions, which in the trials conducted by Soon and his colleagues were 'to press either the left or right button with the index finger of the corresponding hand immediately when they became aware of the urge to do so' (2008: 15) and 'to avoid any form of preplanning for choice of movement or time of execution' (ibid., p. 17; Libet's instructions were similar). If the subjects followed these instructions, they probably formed a distal intention (or plan) to allow urges to press a button arise within them, and to pay attention to when the urge arises. In the circumstances, it is likely, on the one hand, that this (conscious) distal intention or plan causally influenced the spontaneous generation of non-conscious urges to act and, on the other hand, that subjects may not be reporting awareness of a consciously formed *intention* to act now, but rather awareness of an urge to act. (This interpretation becomes more plausible when we consider that subjects in these experiments must repeat tedious button-presses many dozens of times, so that the action may become more habitual and automatic.)

Of course, these alternative interpretations might be mistaken; evidence might surface to show that, whenever we consciously intend an action just before we act, our being conscious (and the underlying neural processes) simply occurs too late to influence the action causally (and the neural correlates of this proximal intention are not 'hooked up' to the action–production system). However, even *if* this turned out to be true – and again, the evidence has not yet shown it to be true – I do not think it would represent a significant threat to free will. Consider your own experiences of most voluntary actions. If they are like mine, they rarely involve specific conscious intentions to move in particular ways just prior to moving. Rather, they are preceded by more distal intentions and general plans to carry out various actions, which are followed by conscious monitoring of what we are doing to make sure that the actions correspond to these previously formed intentions and plans.

For instance, in these experiments, even *if* there are proximal conscious intentions to move and they occur too late to affect the action, it would not follow that *all* relevant conscious mental states were epiphenomenal, since the subjects' consciously agreeing to move when the urge strikes them surely plays a role in their later actions. Similarly, when we drive or play sports or prepare meals, we do not generally form conscious intentions to perform each of the component actions involved in these activities. When we lecture to students or converse with friends, we tend not to think about exactly what we are going to say right before we say it. Rather we may consciously consider what sorts of things we want to say, and then we 'let ourselves go,' though we consciously monitor what's happening and consider how to proceed, for instance, in response to what our students or friends say. Whereas I take these actions that accord with earlier conscious deliberations to be paradigmatic examples of freely willed actions, Bargh suggests just the opposite when he says:

> Our ability to take a vague thought and have it come out of our mouths in a complete coherent sentence, the production of which happens unconsciously, is ... *not something we need consciousness or free will for*. (2008: 145)

On many theories of free will, what is essential is not that conscious intentions formed *just prior* to action cause one's actions, but that conscious deliberations can have a proper downstream effect on the way one acts in the relevant situations, such that we act in accord with reasons that we have consciously considered and accepted at some point. There is simply no evidence (yet) to show that conscious deliberation, reasoning, and planning have no such effects on what we do, or that our conscious monitoring of our behavior is not critically involved in the way we carry out and adjust our actions. Indeed there is evidence to the contrary – situations which indicate the crucial roles that conscious intention formation, rational thinking, and 'willpower' play in some of our actions (Gollwitzer 1999; Baumeister 2008).

Of course, empirical evidence from neuroscience and psychology could show that *these* 'downstream' roles of conscious mental processes are less significant than we tend to think. Indeed some research on moral reasoning seems to suggest that, when people make moral judgments, they often act on immediate gut reactions and then their conscious deliberations merely come up with *post hoc* rationalizations of these reactions (Haidt 2001; Greene 2007). Furthermore, research in social psychology suggests that we are often influenced by situational factors of which we are unaware and whose influence we would not accept, were we aware of them. For instance, whether people help someone in need depends less on whether the person needs help or on whether one considers oneself a helpful person than on factors such as the number of bystanders, the ambient noise, or whether one is in a hurry (Ross and Nisbett 1991; Doris 2002). This view suggests one more scientific challenge to free will (Nahmias 2007a):

[R1] Free will requires that one's actions properly derive from decisions or intentions that one has at some point consciously considered, or at least that one *would* accept, as one's reasons for acting.

[R2] Science is showing that our actions do not properly derive from decisions or intentions that we have consciously considered or would accept as our reasons for acting. Rather, our actions are produced by other factors, and we *rationalize* them after the fact.

[R3] So, science is showing that we do not have free will.

I find [R1] plausible, and I think that most philosophical theories of free will accept something like it. Though the existing neuroscientific research does not say much about premise [R2], research in psychology offers evidence of numerous cases where we don't know why we do what we do and make up reasons for why we did what we did. This research has not, however, established that conscious reasoning is always *post hoc* and inefficacious, and I suspect it will not establish such a sweeping conclusion. On the other hand, it may show that we have *less* free will than we tend to think we have – that our capacities for conscious reasoning and control are less efficacious than we generally assume. Hence scientific research may challenge the *degree* to which we have free will – and perhaps, in turn, the degree to which we are morally responsible for our actions.

We now have a better sense of various ways to interpret recent scientific challenges to free will. If such challenges begin with the assumption that free will is incompatible with determinism or with mechanism, then they must rely on controversial philosophical arguments, and it is unclear how specific research in psychology and neuroscience will advance these arguments. Such research, however, could show that conscious processes (and their neural correlates) are *not* the proximal cause of action. Such 'modular epiphenomenalism,' however, has not yet been established by the relevant research in neuroscience and psychology, and the challenge it poses to free will might be minimal as long as conscious deliberation and planning have the proper 'downstream' influence on actions. Indeed, the scientific discoveries which seem to pose the most significant challenge to free will are those which suggest that our conscious deliberations and reasoning do *not* contribute to our later actions, but only to our *post hoc* rationalizations of such actions. As I am someone who thinks that free will, properly understood, is compatible with determinism, with mechanism, and even with modular epiphenomenalism, it is this evidence for systematic rationalization that I find most threatening. Luckily, I think that future research will show this challenge to be limited in scope. But I may just be rationalizing.

When science claims to have discovered that humans have no free will – and headlines read 'Case closed for free will?' (Youngsteadt 2008) – people will interpret such claims in terms of their own conceptions of free will. The danger is that most people do not take free will to involve (only) magical powers of non-physical souls but to involve more mundane psychological capacities – those that allow us to control our own behavior, change our habits, overcome addictions, exercise willpower, and consciously consider the sort of life we want to lead. If people regard free will as including these sorts of capacities, then telling them that they don't have free will could have detrimental effects on their self-conception, interpersonal relations, and moral behavior, as well as on our political debates and legal practices. It could make them more fatalistic, less likely to exert what powers of rational deliberation and willpower they do have, and less motivated to act morally (Baumeister et al. 2009). Hence it is crucial both that we understand people's conception of free will and that we examine critically what scientific discoveries actually tell us about free will.[1]

See also: VOLITION AND THE WILL (13); REASONS AND CAUSES (17); ACTION EXPLANATION AND THE UNCONSCIOUS (22); MENTAL CAUSATION AND EPIPHENOMENALISM (23); THE EXPLANATORY ROLE OF CONSCIOUSNESS (24); FREE WILL AND DETERMINISM (38); RESPONSIBILITY AND AUTONOMY (39); INTENTIONAL ACTION IN FOLK PSYCHOLOGY (45).

Note

1 I am grateful for helpful comments from Al Mele, Manuel Vargas, Andrea Scarantino, George Graham, and the audience at the 2009 meeting of the APA Central. This chapter was completed in part with support from a grant from the University of Chicago Arete Initiative and the John Templeton Foundation.

References

Baer, J., Kaufmann, J., and Baumeister, R. (eds) (2008). *Are We free? Psychology and Free Will.* New York: Oxford University Press.

Bargh, J. (2008). Free will is un-natural. In Baer, Kaufmann, and Baumeister (eds), 128–154.

Bargh, J. and Ferguson, M. (2000). Beyond behaviorism: On the automaticity of higher mental processes. *Psychological Bulletin*, 126, 925–945.

Baumeister, R. (2008). Free will, consciousness, and cultural animals. In Baer, Kaufmann, and Baumeister (eds), 65–85.

Baumeister, R., Masicampio, E., and DeWall, C. (2009). Prosocial benefits of feeling free: Disbelief in free will increases aggression and reduces helpfulness. *Personality and Social Psychology Bulletin*, 35, 260–268.

Craver, C. (2007). *Explaining the Brain: Mechanisms and the Mosaic Unity of Neuroscience*. New York: Oxford University Press.

Dennett, D. (1991). *Consciousness Explained*. New York: Back Bay Books.

Doris, J. (2002). *Lack of Character: Personality and Moral Behavior*. New York: Cambridge University Press.

Gollwitzer, P. M. (1999). Implementation intentions. *American Psychologist*, 54, 493–503.

Greene, J., and Cohen, J. (2004). For the law, neuroscience changes nothing and everything. *Philosophical Transactions of the Royal Society of London B*, 359, 1775–1778.

Greene, J. (2007). The secret joke of Kant's soul. In W. Sinnott-Armstrong (ed.), *Moral Psychology*, Vol. 3: *The Neuroscience of Morality: Emotion, Disease, and Development*. Cambridge, MA: MIT Press, 35–79.

Haidt, J. (2001). The emotional dog and its rational tail: A social intuitionist approach to moral judgment. *Psychological Review*, 108, 814–834.

Libet, B. (1985). Unconscious cerebral initiative and the role of conscious will in voluntary action. *Behavioral and Brain Sciences*, 8, 529–566.

Libet, B. (1999). Do we have free will? In B. Libet, A. Freeman, and K. Sutherland (eds), *The Volitional Brain*. Exeter: Imprint Academic, 47–57.

Kane, R. (1996). *The Significance of Free Will*. New York: Oxford University Press.

Kim, J. (1998). *Mind in a Physical World*. Cambridge, MA: MIT Press.

McKenna, M. (2004). Compatibilism. In E. Zalta (ed.), *The Stanford Encyclopedia of Philosophy* URL: http://plato.stanford.edu/entries/compatibilism.

Mele, A. (2009). *Effective Intentions: The Power of Conscious Will*. New York: Oxford University Press.

Montague, R. (2008). Free will. *Current Biology*, 18, R584–R585.

Nahmias, E. (2002). When consciousness matters: A critical review of Daniel Wegner's *The Illusion of Conscious Will*. *Philosophical Psychology*, 15, 527–541.

Nahmias, E. (2007a). Autonomous agency and social psychology. In M. Marraffa, M. Caro, and F. Ferretti (eds), *Cartographies of the Mind: Philosophy and Psychology in Intersection*. Dordrecht: Springer, 169–185.

Nahmias, E., Coates, J., and Kvaran, T. (2007b). Free will, moral responsibility, and mechanism: Experiments on folk intuitions. *Midwest Studies in Philosophy*, 31, 214–232.

Nahmias, E., Morris, S., Nadelhoffer, T., and Turner, J. (2006). Is incompatibilism intuitive? *Philosophy and Phenomenological Research*, 73, 28–53.

Ross, L. and Nisbett, R. (1991). *The Person and the Situation: Perspectives of Social Psychology*. New York: McGraw-Hill.

Soon, C., Brass, M., Heinze, H., and Haynes, J. (2008). Unconscious determinants of free decisions in the human brain. *Nature Neuroscience*, 11, 543–545.

Tancredi, L. (2007). The neuroscience of 'free will.' *Behavioral Sciences and the Law*, 25, 295–308.

Van Inwagen, P. (1983). *An Essay on Free Will*. Oxford: Oxford University Press.

Wegner, D. (2002). *The Illusion of Conscious Will*. Cambridge, MA: MIT Press.

Wegner, D. (2008). Self is magic. In Baer, Kaufmann, and Baumeister (eds), 226–247.

Youngsteadt, E. (2008). Case closed for free will? *Science NOW Daily News*, 4/14/2008.

45

Intentional Action in Folk Psychology

BERTRAM F. MALLE

What Intentional Action Is

There is consensus in psychology and cognitive science that the capacity to recognize a behavior as intentional is a central component of human social cognition; that this capacity has evolved for its adaptive value in social interaction; and that it develops rather rapidly in the early years of childhood (Malle et al. 2001; Zelazo et al. 1999). We also know that adults judge intentionality fast and with ease and that these judgments both regulate attention in social interaction and guide explanations and evaluations of behavior (Malle 2004). But exactly how do people conceptualize intentional action and how do they judge a given behavior as intentional?

People share a powerful folk concept of intentionality that is acquired by interacting with other people in human culture. At least some folk concepts are historically and cross-culturally stable, and the evidence suggests that intentionality is one of them (Malle 2008). Furthermore, the concept of intentionality is part of folk psychology – the larger conceptual and cognitive apparatus that allows people to make sense of human behavior in terms of mental states. In fact, intentionality may be the core concept of folk psychology, as it connects behavior directly with the mind, by classifying a behavior as intentional when it is characteristically caused by certain mental processes and states (such as belief, intention, and awareness).

Importantly, the folk concept of intentional action is not just a cultural hypothesis that could easily be defeated through philosophical analysis or scientific discoveries. If a scholar tried to convince people that the behaviors they previously judged to be intentional are in reality not intentional, these people would be puzzled rather than impressed; the scholar would appear to make a conceptual mistake, not an empirical claim. Likewise, if another scholar told people that intentions are not based on beliefs and desires but rather on the recursive firing of two particular brain structures, they may just shrug. An intention has to be *somehow* implemented in the brain (folk psychology is mute on the details here), but this does not mean that the agent did not integrate various beliefs and desires when forming the intention. The domain of human behavior is fundamentally framed by the concept of intentionality, and people may be incapable of thinking about behavior in any other way. Perhaps rightly so; for the adaptive advantage of sophisticated intentionality perceptions is at least partially grounded in their correspondence with the physical reality of human action – just as color and spatial concepts show a systematic correspondence with the physical reality of light and space.

There is of course plenty of room for error. In every given instance of a person judging a behavior as intentional, the behavior may or may not be truly intentional. However, if the person had enough information, he or she would recognize what the correct judgment is. The folk concept of intentionality allows cases of ambiguity or disagreement to be settled in accordance with relevant facts; it does not guarantee that social perceivers always have those facts.

So what are the facts that reveal a behavior to be intentional?

The Folk Concept of Intentionality

The philosophical and social–psychological literature had provided several theoretical analyses of intentionality. Malle and Knobe (1997) studied the folk concept of intentionality empirically. In a first study, participants read descriptions of twenty behaviors and rated them for their intentionality. About one half of the participants received no definition of intentionality before they made their ratings; the other half did ('It means that the person had a reason to do what she did and that she chose to do so'). Agreement on intentionality ratings across the twenty behaviors was high. On average, any two people's ratings correlated at $r = .64$, and any one person's ratings correlated at $r = .80$ with the remaining group. More importantly, whether or not participants received a definition of intentionality had no effect on agreement, so people appear to share a folk concept of intentionality that they spontaneously use to judge behaviors.

Given that there is a shared folk concept of intentionality, the next question was what specific components this folk concept has – what evidence an intentionality judgment requires. Malle and Knobe first asked people for explicit definitions of intentionality ('When you say that somebody performed an action intentionally, what does this mean?'). These definitions revealed four main components: For an agent to perform an action intentionally, the agent must have (a) a desire for an outcome; (b) beliefs about an action that leads to that outcome; (c) an intention to perform the action; and (d) awareness of fulfilling the intention while performing the action. Following previous theoretical postulates, Malle and Knobe also explored whether skill may be implicitly used in people's intentionality judgments, even if it was not explicitly mentioned. They presented participants with stories about behaviors and systematically varied the evidence, making certain components present or absent (particularly the agent's skill). They found that, for some difficult actions (such as in art or athletics), people look for evidence of the agent's skill at actually controlling the behavior. This skill component may have been omitted from explicit definitions of intentionality because people focused on social behaviors, for which skill can typically be assumed.

Malle and Knobe (1997) thus proposed a five-component model of the folk concept of intentionality, as displayed in Figure 45.1. According to this folk concept, the direct cause of an intentional action is the mental state of intention. For an intention to be ascribed, a desire (for an outcome) and a belief (about the action–outcome link) must be present. For an action to be seen as *performed* intentionally, however, skill and awareness have to be present as well. Thus people distinguish between intention as a

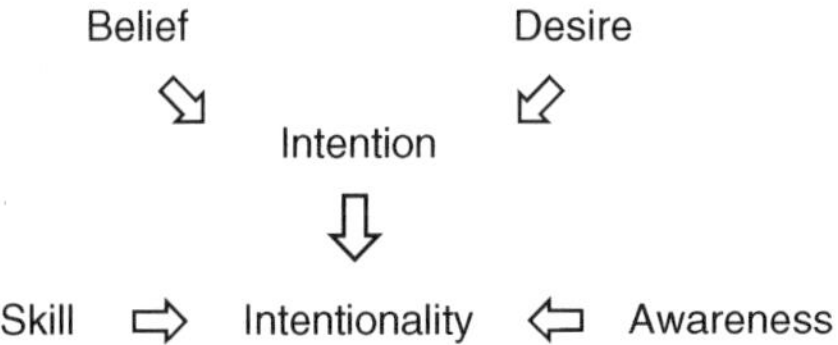

Figure 45.1 A model of the folk concept of intentionality. Adapted with permission from Malle and Knobe (1997)

mental state and intentionality as the quality of an action. This two-layer structure was supported by an additional experiment, in which belief and desire information was found to be necessary for intention ascriptions and, given an intention ascription, skill and awareness were found to be necessary for an intentionality ascription.

Development

Acquiring a five-component concept of intentionality is not an easy feat, and it is not done in one trial. Instead, humans build up this concept from simple beginnings over many years of conceptual and social development (Malle et al. 2001). During the first year of life, infants begin to identify intentional behavior by recognizing self-propelled movement, especially in recurring everyday actions such as grasping or putting. At the end of the first year, they parse streams of behavior into units that correspond to initiated or completed intentional actions, taking advantage of eye-gaze and verbal signals ('oops'), and become proficient at inferring goals from incomplete action attempts. The first truly mental concept appears to be that of desire, followed by belief, and finally by intention, which is not cleanly differentiated from desire before the age of five. Developmental change in the folk-psychological framework thus occurs primarily as a differentiation of the intentionality concept, from a simple behavioral understanding to a richly mentalistic understanding.

Animal work also hints at the evolutionary emergence of folk psychology. Many animals can recognize species-relevant actions, but it appears that primates distinguish more subtly between intentional and unintentional versions of the same movement. Apes are keenly sensitive to variations in behavior patterns that point to others' goals and upcoming actions. But, even though they identify intentional action, there is no clear-cut evidence that they have mentalistic concepts of desire, belief, and intention (Povinelli and Vonk 2006). This is consistent with the general assumption that chimpanzees are similar to 2-year olds, who are just at the transition from a sophisticated behavioral to a mentalistic understanding of action.

The Judgment Process

Modern human life presents a vast array of intentional actions. In most contexts, however, people do not check off each component of the intentionality concept; instead, they recognize intentional behavior in a configural manner. If it compellingly *looks* intentional, then it must be. This look may be driven by motion features, eye gaze, and similar surface cues that can be processed fast and efficiently. Even implemented in geometric figures, these cues can trigger people's impressions of intentional behavior (Heider and Simmel 1944). By contrast, in high-stakes situations (for instance in the courtroom) and when facing novel or ambiguous behaviors, people are likely to shift to a slower, more systematic gathering of information about the agent's mental states. In particular, deviations from the prototypical appearance of intentional behavior may raise doubts and encourage systematic analysis. If the agent did not have full control in performing the behavior, skill may be doubted; if the agent appeared somewhat absent-minded, awareness or even the presence of an intention may be doubted.

Whether fast or slow, assessments that a behavior is intentional are rarely sufficient for an adequate response to another person's behavior. The social perceiver must know what the agent's specific intentions, desires, and beliefs were. Intentionality judgments only guarantee *that* the agent had these mental states; their content requires additional processing.

The intention content gives the action its meaning by specifying what the agent is *trying* to do (for example she is either cracking her wrist or waving at you). This intention must be inferred both from features of the behavior itself and from the immediate context, from knowledge about the agent, and from cultural scripts. A given action may reflect a large number of candidate intentions, and an integrative inferential process constrains the candidates and helps the perceiver to converge on a single interpretation.

The desire content reveals the agent's primary *purpose* or *goal* (she is cracking her wrist to remove tension; or she is waving at you to reject your proposal). If the action is puzzling or deviates from a script, the perceiver may further wonder about beliefs (she must have thought that waving to reject my proposal would be more subtle than responding verbally) and even reconsider the agent's goals in light of them (she wanted to be subtle so as to not embarrass me). If, however, the action is scripted or familiar and the goal is quickly established, the perceiver may not further consider any beliefs, because they may be trivial (she thought that this action would help her fulfill her goal) or refer to unimportant details (it's the right hand that felt tense to her). So desires are inferred all the time, and quickly at that, whereas beliefs are not always inferred and, if they are, they take more time (Apperly et al. 2006; Barr and Keysar 2005).

One important source of information, both for the detection of intentionality and for the recognition of the agent's specific mental states, is the family of 'simulation' processes – motor mirroring, automatic empathy, projection, and perspective taking – by which other people's mental states are in some sense recreated in the perceiver (Goldman 2006).

Motor mirroring occurs when a perceiver observes another person perform a certain behavior and this observation triggers the perceiver's own performance of the behavior (Decety and Grèzes 2006). If the triggered behavior is intentional, then the perceiver will easily recognize the other person's behavior as intentional. In the case of automatic empathy, the perceiver cannot help but feel the same affective state as the other person and is likely to understand the person's ensuing actions. In projection, perceivers project their own mental states onto the other – that is, they assume that the other person knows, sees, or wants what they themselves know, see, or want. As a result, perceivers regard certain actions as intentional, or infer certain intentions, merely because they themselves would intend to so act. Perspective taking, finally, overcomes the limitations of these simpler mechanisms and occurs when perceivers try to infer intentions and other mental states that are true of the other person, not necessarily of themselves.

Intentionality and Moral Judgment

The folk concept of intentionality plays important roles in the assignment of responsibility and blame, in both moral and legal contexts (Malle and Nelson 2003).

First and most obviously, negative intentional actions are blamed more than (comparable) negative unintentional behaviors. Learning that some harmful behavior was performed intentionally causes outrage, whereas hearing that it was done accidentally mitigates (but does not necessarily remove) blame.

Second, for intentional actions, fine-grained levels of blame are assigned depending on the agent's reasons for acting – the particular beliefs and desires that led to the agent's forming of the intention. An agent who hurt someone intentionally may have had acceptable reasons (the dentist wanting to extract an unhealthy tooth) or unacceptable reasons (a schoolboy wanting to torture another) and will be blamed less or more, respectively.

Third, even for events that the agent did not bring about intentionally, responsibility and blame are assigned when the agent could have prevented the event and it was his or her obligation to do so. The notions of preventability and obligation both entail intentionality, because preventing is an intentional act, provided that the agent has the capacity and foreknowledge to do it, and assigning obligations to a person presupposes that the person can intentionally fulfill them. Without the folk concept of intentionality and its constituent mental concepts, moral judgment would either not exist at all or be entirely based on outcome. Supporting this contention, research into children's developing moral reasoning has discovered an important transition from judgments based solely on outcome severity to judgments that incorporate the agent's intentionality and mental states (Shultz and Wells 1985). This transition occurs in the pre-school period, just when children have learned to consider desires, beliefs, and abilities in the process of judging intentionality.

Recently the hypothesis has been proposed that even adult intentionality judgments may be biased by outcome severity – that negative behaviors are judged to be intentional even if not all the five components are present. Initial evidence has supported the hypothesis (Knobe 2003a, b), but more recent findings suggest otherwise (Guglielmo et al. 2009).

Explanations of Intentional Action

People's complex concept of intentional action is most clearly revealed when we examine how they explain such actions. Indeed, when explaining behavior, people

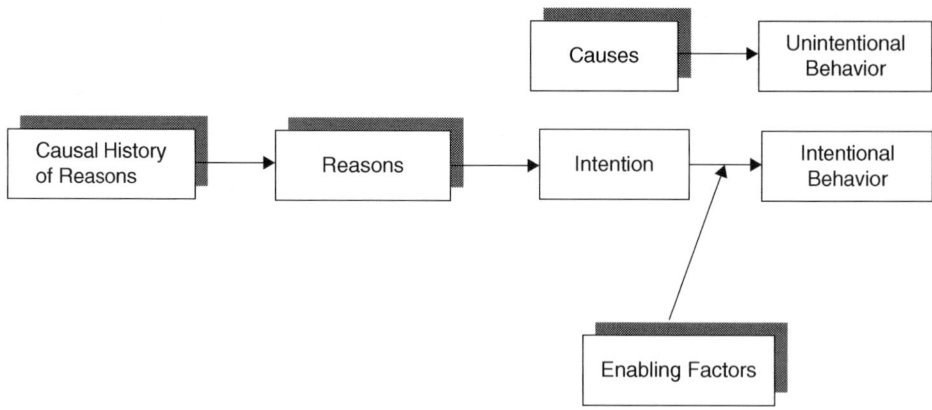

Figure 45.2 Four modes of explanation for unintentional and intentional behavior. Figure adapted from B. F. Malle (1999). How People Explain Behavior: A New Theoretical Framework. *Personality and Social Psychology Review*, 3, 23–48. © Lawrence Erlbaum Associates, Inc.

distinguish sharply between intentional and unintentional events (Malle 2004). They explain unintentional events such as accidental behaviors, experiences, and bodily states by referring to mechanical causal factors (for instance mental states, traits, others' behaviors, physical events) – and we may label these 'cause explanations' (see top of Figure 45.2). Traditional attribution models apply fairly well to these cause explanations, because people presuppose no other link between explanation and behavior apart from causality (in other words, no components of intentionality such as awareness or intention). Traditional attribution theory fails, however, in modeling the way people explain intentional behavior, which is a far more complex phenomenon. As a result of the complex definition of intentionality discussed earlier, explanations of intentional behavior break down into three modes (Figure 45.2): 'reason explanations,' 'causal history of reason explanations,' and 'enabling factor explanations.'

Reason Explanations

Reasons are the most frequently used mode of explanation, and they reflect the core of the intentionality concept – the reasoning process that leads to an intention. The concept of intentionality specifies two paradigmatic types of reasons that precede the formation of an intention: the agent's desire for an outcome and a belief that the intended action leads to that outcome. For example, a student explained why she chose psychology as her major by saying:

[DESIRE:] I want to go to graduate school in counseling psychology.
[BELIEF:] I think psychology is the right major for going into counseling psychology.

In many naturally occurring explanations, other reasons are mentioned either in addition to or instead of the paradigmatic reasons – for instance, desires to avoid alternative outcomes, beliefs about the context, beliefs about consequences, and expressions of valuing the action itself.

Reasons have two defining features: subjectivity and rationality (Malle 2004). Subjectivity refers to the fact that reason explanations are designed to capture the agent's own reasons for acting. That is, social perceivers try to reconstruct the agent's considerations that led to the intention to act, and thus they take the agent's subjective viewpoint when they explain the action. For example, the explanation 'She thought she was late for her class' offered to the question 'Why did she rush off?' illustrates the subjectivity assumption, because the explainer subtly distances himself from the agent's belief and implies that, in reality, she was probably not late. But it was that subjective belief (and not objective reality) that guided the agent's action and thus explains it.

Rationality, the second defining feature of reason explanations, refers to the fact that the contents of mental states that are cited as reasons have to hang together, so as to offer support for the 'reasonableness' of the intention and action they brought about. Philosophers often speak of a 'practical reasoning argument' that has reasons as its premises and the intention to act as its conclusion. The folk conception of rational support is probably not as strict; it demands that the intended action should be a reasonable thing to do in light of this agent's desires and beliefs. In the example above, the agent's action of rushing off was rationally supported by her belief that she was late for class (and it would not have been rationally supported if the agent had thought that there was plenty of time left, or if she had had no desire to be on time). To complete the practical argument in the first case – the rational one – we would need to add (at least) the student's desire to be on time and her belief that rushing off may help her to get to class on time. But one of the fascinating aspects of reason explanations is that the conceptual constraints folk psychology puts on reasons (and especially the assumptions of subjectivity and rationality) allow explainers to mention only a single reason and to trust the audience with filling in the remaining reasons and with comprehending why the agent decided to act.

Causal History of Reason Explanations

A less frequent but no less important mode of explanation refers to factors that lie in the causal history of reasons (CHR) and thus clarify what led to their formation in the first place. For example, the statement 'Anne invited Ben for dinner because she is friendly' attempts to explain Anne's action, but the content of the explanation ('she is friendly') refers to a factor in the causal history of her reasons, not to a reason itself. The explainer would not claim that Anne deliberated, 'I am friendly – hence I should invite Ben for dinner'; rather, the explainer cites Anne's friendly disposition as a relevant causal history or background to whatever specific reasons Anne had for inviting Ben. Causal history explanations can refer to a variety of factors, such as personality traits, past behavior, physiological states, culture, or context cues that triggered particular beliefs or desires.

Even though CHR explanations help to clarify intentional actions, they do not function in the same way as reasons do. Importantly, they are not subjected to the constraints of subjectivity and rationality. The agent need not have considered, or even been aware of, the causal history factors cited in the explanation; nor do CHR factors provide rational support for an explained action. In fact, the fundamental form of causality assumed for causal history explanations is identical to that of cause explanations: both describe a 'mechanical,' involuntary causal process. However, CHR explanations specifically capture the generation of reasons en route to intentional actions.

Enabling Factor Explanations

The third, and relatively rare, mode of explaining intentional action refers to factors that enabled the action to come about as it was intended. These enabling factor explanations refer to the agent's skill, effort, opportunities, or facilitating circumstances. Whereas reason explanations and CHR explanations focus on clarifying what motivated the agent's intention and action, enabling factor explanations take it as a given that the agent had an intention and attempt to clarify how it was possible for the intention to be successfully turned into action. For example, the explanation 'She hit her free throws because she had practiced all week' is not an account of why the agent *intended* to hit the free throws; rather, the agent's practicing is identified as the critical factor that allowed her to perform her intended action.

To summarize, the folk concept of intentionality gives rise to multiple modes of explanation, which people use in order to make sense of intentional behavior. They try to grasp the agent's reasons; they cite causal factors that lay in the history of those reasons; and, occasionally, they clarify what has allowed an agent to perform an intended action successfully.

Synopsis

Every day, people encounter and perform countless intentional actions, and they conceptualize them within the systematic conceptual framework of folk psychology. Specifically, the concept of intentional action consists of five components: desire, belief, intention, awareness, and skill. If any one of these components appears to be absent, people are reluctant to call a given behavior intentional. Developing from infancy into late childhood, judgments of intentionality are often fast and configural, triggered as they are by the characteristic appearance of intentional behavior. But sometimes people take each component into account and weigh the evidence for its presence. Whether fast or slow, judgments of intentionality play an essential role in moral judgments and in explanations of behavior. The concept of intentional action is not only a part of folk psychology; it may define its very core.

See also: ACTION THEORY AND ONTOLOGY (1); PLURALISM ABOUT ACTION (12); INTENTION (14); DESIRE AND PLEASURE (15); TELEOLOGICAL EXPLANATION (16); REASONS AND CAUSES (17); TRIGGERING AND STRUCTURING CAUSES (18); RATIONALITY (36).

References

Apperly, I. A., Riggs, K. J., Simpson, A., Chiavarino, C., and Samson, D. (2006). Is belief reasoning automatic? *Psychological Science*, 17, 841–844.

Barr, D. J., and Keysar, B. (2005). Mindreading in an exotic case: The normal adult human. In B. F. Malle and S. D. Hodges (eds), *Other Minds: How Humans Bridge the Divide between Self and Others*. New York: Guilford, 271–283.

Decety, J., and Grèzes, J. (2006). The power of simulation: Imagining one's own and other's [*sic*] behavior. *Brain Research*, 1079, 4–14.

Goldman, A. I. (2006). *Simulating Minds: The Philosophy, Psychology, and Neuroscience of Mindreading*. Oxford: Oxford University Press.

Guglielmo, S., Monroe, A. E., and Malle, B. F. (2009). At the heart of morality lies folk psychology. *Inquiry*, 52, 449–466.

Heider, F., and Simmel, M. (1944). An experimental study of apparent behavior. *American Journal of Psychology*, 57, 243–259.

Knobe, J. (2003a). Intentional action and side effects in ordinary language. *Analysis*, 63, 190–193.

Knobe, J. (2003b). Intentional Action in folk psychology: An experimental investigation. *Philosophical Psychology*, 16, 309–324.

Malle, B. F. (2004). *How the Mind Explains Behavior: Folk Explanations, Meaning, and Social Interaction*. Cambridge, MA: MIT Press.

Malle, B. F. (2008). The fundamental tools, and possibly universals, of social cognition. In R. Sorrentino and S. Yamaguchi (eds), *Handbook of Motivation and Cognition Across Cultures*. New York: Elsevier/Academic Press, 267–296.

Malle, B. F., and Knobe, J. (1997). The folk concept of intentionality. *Journal of Experimental Social Psychology*, 33, 101–121.

Malle, B. F., and Nelson, S. E. (2003). Judging *mens rea:* The tension between folk concepts and legal concepts of intentionality. *Behavioral Sciences and the Law*, 21, 563–580.

Malle, B. F., Moses, L. J., and Baldwin, D. A. (eds) (2001). *Intentions and Intentionality: Foundations of Social Cognition*. Cambridge, MA: MIT Press.

Povinelli, D., and Vonk, J. (2006). We don't need a microscope to explore the chimpanzee's mind. In S. Hurley and M. Nudds (eds), *Rational Animals?* New York: Oxford University Press, 385–412.

Shultz, T. R., and Wells, D. (1985). Judging the intentionality of action–outcomes. *Developmental Psychology*, 21, 83–89.

Zelazo, P. D., Astington, J. W., and Olson, D. R. (eds) (1999). *Developing Theories of Intention: Social Understanding and Self-Control*. Mahwah, NJ: Erlbaum.

Further reading

Gordon, R. M. (1992). The simulation theory: Objections and misconceptions. *Mind and Language*, 7, 11–34.

Heider, F. (1958). *The Psychology of Interpersonal Relations*. New York: Wiley.

Rizzolatti, G., Fadiga, L., Fogassi, L., and Gallese, V. (1996). Premotor cortex and the recognition of motor actions. *Cognitive Brain Research*, 3, 131–141.

Weiner, B. (1995). *Judgments of Responsibility: A Foundation for a Theory of Social Conduct*. New York: Guilford.

46

Attribution Theory

BERNARD WEINER

Introduction

The basic premise of an attributional approach to action is the commonsense notion that the perceived cause of an event determines subsequent behavior. For example, assume your car cannot start. To find a solution, you must determine the cause of the stoppage. If it is found that the car does not have gas, then the tank will be re-filled; if the battery is dead, then it will be replaced; and so on. It is so obvious that perceived causality influences subsequent behavior that attribution theory is often called 'naïve' – a psychology of common sense. Pejoratively, this status is sometimes labeled 'bubba' or 'grandmother' psychology: an approach that fails to advance psychology as a science because it does not exceed the knowledge of one's grandmother. Thus the task for attribution theorists has been to establish an empirical foundation and a conceptual system that includes predictions and understanding beyond the awareness of the general public.

Initially attribution theory was concerned with how one arrives at a causal understanding of human action; that is, it provided a system of epistemology. Guided by its accepted originator, Fritz Heider (1958), and by its foremost spokesperson, Harold Kelley (1967), the theory argued that co-variation provides the foundation for causal thinking. In addition, biases in causal understanding were revealed; these biases were more congenial to the study of psychology than to that of philosophy and included the observers' over-attribution of an event to personal dispositions; an underestimation of situational influences (labeled the fundamental attribution error); and the actors' tendency to attribute success more than failure to the self (a hedonic bias).

A concern with motivational processes and action (the results of attributional thinking) rather than with the antecedents of causal ascriptions came later in the history of attribution research. Empirical and conceptual advances have been made regarding the consequences of causal ascriptions, and they are the topic of this chapter.

Phenomenal Causality

The perceived causes of events are virtually infinite. For example, ability and effort are the main determinants in achieving success and failure, although a myriad of other causes, including the difficulty of the task, luck, strategy, and the contributions of others are also perceived as affecting achievement outcomes (see Weiner 1985). The perceived causes of success and failure also vary greatly between achievement contexts. If, for example, good crops are the achievement goal, then rainfall and other weather conditions are likely to be regarded as important causes. And if there was an unfulfilled achievement intention to increase exercise, then age and health are salient ascriptions for the outcome. Attribution theory embraces phenomenology and is concerned with perceived rather than 'real' causes, although reality of course influences causal beliefs. Furthermore, causal ascriptions are primarily sought after negative, unexpected, and important events. One does not ask: 'Why did the car start?' (unless this was unexpected), but rather: 'Why did the car not start?'

Causes do not merely apply to achievement outcomes; they are also desired in other motivational domains, giving rise to further causal possibilities. For example, the causes of social acceptance and rejection include physical characteristics, traits (such as 'boring,' 'dominating'), shared attitudes, religious beliefs, and so forth. These are unlikely to appear on lists of the ascriptions for success and failure in school settings. And the perceived causes of poverty include lack of education, laziness, few job opportunities, drug and alcohol use, and low wages. Such data are easily obtained by asking participants to list their perceived causes of various outcomes or states. In this way a large and useful, albeit somewhat 'bubba-like,' descriptive literature concerned with phenomenal causality was produced.

Causal properties or dimensions: From description to taxonomy

To convert perceived causality from qualitative to quantitative distinctions, researchers have identified the underlying properties or dimensions of causes. In so doing, they made it possible to compare and contrast causes, thereby advancing research and hypothesis testing and moving the study of attribution further away from 'bubba psychology.' It has been shown that the properties of causes rather than (in addition to) their particular specification are linked to motivational consequences.

Three fundamental characteristics of causes are known. The most central property, identified by Heider (1958) and by Julian Rotter (1966), was labeled 'causal locus' and pertains to the location of a cause either within (internal to) or outside (external to) an actor. For example, ability and effort as causes of success and failure lie within the actor, whereas teacher characteristics and chance are environmental causes of achievement outcomes. In a similar manner, social acceptance because of good looks or because of a pleasing personality are internal to the individual who seeks company, whereas acceptance because the other person wants to go to a party or is forced to comply by his or her parents indicates that the causes reside outside of the requestor and in the situation. Hence, rather than being qualitatively distinct, ability, effort, good looks, and a pleasing personality are alike in that they share a common property (namely, an internal causal locus) and they differ from genotypically similar causes such as teacher characteristics, chance, the other's desire to go to a party, and family pressure, which are external in terms of causal locus. Causes often are dichotomized, although ascriptions can be quantitatively compared as to their degree of internality or externality, which is a causal continuum.

A second causal property, orthogonal to locus, is 'stability.' Some causes, such as aptitude and physical appearance, tend to be regarded as enduring. On the other hand, ascriptions including luck and the weather are perceived as transient or unstable over time.

Finally, a third causal characteristic, which is not independent of the previous two, has been called 'causal controllability.' This property refers to the extent that the cause is subject to volitional change, or to the degree to which 'it could have been otherwise.' Effort, for example, is regarded as a controllable cause of achieving success and failure, whereas aptitude is considered uncontrollable by the actor.

In sum, causes can be placed within a three-dimensional taxonomy. Aptitude tends to be classified as internal, stable, and uncontrollable, whereas chance is considered external, unstable, and also uncontrollable. These dimensions provide the meaning or the connotation of a cause; for example, aptitude is a stable characteristic of a person that is not subjected to volitional alteration. Although there is substantial agreement on the taxonomic placement of aptitude and luck, for other causal perceptions there may be some dimensional disagreement. For example, while effort is considered to be internal and controllable, judged stability may vary depending on its construal as a trait ('She is an industrious person') or as a state ('He tried very hard that time').

From Classification to Dynamics

To understand the action consequences of causal beliefs, we must make a distinction between behaviors that center upon the self and are labeled intrapersonal motivation and behaviors that involve others and are labeled interpersonal motivation. Persistence at an achievement task is typically classified in the intrapersonal category, whereas help-giving and aggression involve actions in interpersonal contexts.

Intrapersonal motivation: Emotional and cognitive causal associations

The dimensional characteristics of causal ascriptions have unique dynamic qualities directed by a variety of linked emotions and other beliefs. The locus dimension of causality relates to the affective consequences of success and failure and self-perception. Experiences of pride and increments in self-esteem require internal attributions for success. For example, ascriptions of positive outcomes to ability or effort give rise to pride and augment views of the self. On the other hand, self-attribution for failure tends to lower self-worth. External beliefs in success and failure do not impact on pride or self-worth. One consequence of these relations is exhibited in the unexpected finding that individuals with a variety of stigmas rank as highly in self-esteem as non-stigmatized others. Their esteem is in part maintained because failure tends to be ascribed to the prejudice of others – an external attribution that protects self-worth.

The stability dimension of causality has affective consequences that are associated with the subjective expectancy of success. Ascriptions to stable causes intimate that the future will not differ from the past. For example, failure due to perceived lack of aptitude or to a superior opponent in an athletic contest promotes the thought that there will be future failures in those contexts. On the other hand, failure ascribed to temporary illness or bad luck, which are unstable causes, intimate that future success is possible. The former beliefs therefore give rise to feelings of hopelessness, whereas the latter ascriptions generate hope. In related research, for example, it has been documented that the likelihood of paroling a criminal from prison is reduced if the prior crime is ascribed to a stable personal characteristic ('He is a bad seed') as opposed to being ascribed, say, to poor economic conditions – an unstable cause. In the former case the perceived likelihood of future criminal activity remains high, whereas in the latter crime would not be expected if the economic situation of the person improved.

Many motivation theorists have proposed that a key determining fator of motivated behavior is the expectancy of future success: no matter how great the desire, if the expectancy of goal attainment is zero, then instrumental activity is unlikely to be undertaken. Thus causal stability and the linked emotions of hopelessness and hope are essential factors to take into account when examining the dynamics of action.

The controllability dimension of causality, in conjunction with causal locus, gives rise to feelings of guilt, regret, and shame (humiliation) in the event of failure. Given an internal, controllable cause of failure such as lack of effort, individuals experience guilt and regret when a goal has not been attained. On the other hand, failure due to an internal, uncontrollable cause such as lack of aptitude tends to elicit shame and other indicators of inadequacy. Note that ability attributions versus effort attributions produce greater emotional differentiation in situations of failure (shame and guilt) than in situations of success (pride) – which is consistent with the greater number of negative than positive emotions. In addition to these affects, beliefs of control are vaguely associated with attitudes of empowerment and with the courage to overcome obstacles. Thus controllability also relates, indirectly, to the other two properties of causes – locus and stability.

Intrapersonal motivation: From causal connections to action

From an attributional perspective, a motivated episode begins with an already completed event such as success or failure at an achievement activity. If that event was negative, unexpected, and/or important, a causal search is initiated. Guided in part by achievement history, the performance of others, and hedonic biasing, the search reaches a cause. This cause is characterized by three properties: locus, stability, and control. Locus relates to pride and self-esteem; stability, to hope/hopelessness and expectancy; and control, to guilt, regret, shame, and empowerment attitudes. For example, assume that a student failed an exam. He also failed in the past, whereas his peers are succeeding. On the basis of this information, the failure is ascribed by the student to lack of aptitude. Because this is an internal cause, self-esteem is lowered; inasmuch as aptitude is stable, the student experiences a low expectancy of future success and hopelessness; and, since aptitude is uncontrollable, he has experiences of shame and humiliation and the belief that obstacles cannot be overcome. Low self-esteem, hopelessness and low expectancy of success, and shame and low empowerment are motivational inhibitors. Hence it would be anticipated that this student will drop out of school or exhibit other indicators of reduced motivation. Depression ('learned helplessness') has been viewed as one consequence of this attributional pattern (see Abramson et al. 1978).

Now assume instead that this student ascribes the failure to going to parties rather than studying. Lack of effort is an internal, unstable, and controllable cause. Hence, although his self-esteem is weakened, expectancy of future success and hope are maintained, and there are experiences of guilt and regret along with thoughts that the cause is subject to volitional change. Because high expectancy, hope, guilt, regret, and positive control beliefs are motivational enhancers, this student is predicted to exhibit increased motivation and to work harder in the future.

A general theoretical structure embracing these two situations of motivational decrements and increments is depicted as follows:

> Outcome – Causal antecedents – Cause – Causal properties (locus, stability, control) – Affective and attitudinal effects – Motivational consequences

This sequence captures an attribution theory of intrapersonal action. The basic metaphor guiding this approach is that the person is a scientist seeking to understand and master the environment. This contrasts with other theories of action, which make use of a machine metaphor to describe energy-driven human behavior or of a selfish organism regulated by hedonistic desires.

Empirical evidence

Is this attribution sequence of action valid, and has it been supported by empirical evidence? The answer is: 'in part.' There is no doubt that individuals seek causal understanding, particularly after negative, unexpected, and/or important events; that causal decisions are guided by past personal history, social norms, and a variety of biases; that causes can be characterized by three basic properties (locus, stability, and control); that these properties relate to pride and self-esteem (locus), expectancy and hope or hopelessness (stability), and guilt and regret (control). However, the final links to action remain unclear. Competing motivation theorists have contended respectively that low expectancy (a difficult task), intermediate expectancy, or high expectancy (being close to the goal) maximize motivation. Similar disagreement has been voiced regarding the consequences of shame, guilt, and regret on action. Thus the last critical step in the sequence relating expectancy and affect to action remains somewhat uncertain, whereas the prior linkages to causes are well substantiated.

Interpersonal Motivation

A theory of social motivation from an attribution perspective shares much in common with the attribution theory of intrapersonal behavior. Again, it is assumed that an event has occurred (say, a person is in need of aid; someone has attacked another; a student is observed failing an exam). Furthermore, a cause is assigned and placed within the three-dimensional taxonomy. However, in this case the event and the cause pertain to someone else ('Why has she failed?') rather than to the self. In addition, following the causal determination, the sequence is assumed to vary somewhat and the dimensions take on partially different consequences from those specified in the intrapersonal theory.

Inferences of causal controllability and personal responsibility

Attribution theorists such as Heider (1958) presume that in interpersonal contexts beliefs about intent and responsibility play key roles in guiding social conduct. Inasmuch as perceptions of control ('Could it have been otherwise?') are essential determinants of beliefs about responsibility and ethical behavior, in an interpersonal context the control dimension of causality takes a more important role than the one assigned to it in the intrapersonal conception. In addition, attribution-related communications from an actor to others regarding causal locus and controllability also have important behavioral consequences. In social settings, the person is viewed not only as a scientist but also as a judge, determining if the other is good or bad, moral or immoral, and behavior is guided by beliefs about social justice and how best to maintain the social system (see Weiner 1995, 2006).

Consider, for example, the following situations. A pupil fails at school because of lack of effort. Effort is considered a controllable cause – it can be volitionally altered. Because the cause is controllable, in the absence of mitigating circumstances the student is regarded as responsible for the poor performance. Personal responsibility for a negative outcome generates anger – teachers as well as the parents are upset and mad. These negative affects give rise to various forms of punishment – taking away classroom privileges, withholding allowance, and so on.

On the other hand, assume the student failed because of low aptitude. Aptitude is regarded as genetically given and an uncontrollable cause. Hence, there is an absence of responsibility. Non-responsibility for a negative outcome tends to give rise to pity and sympathy. Imagine, for example, reactions in a classroom to the failure of a mentally handicapped child, or failure on the sports field of a physically handicapped person. Sympathy tends to generate pro-social behavior such as help-giving and the withholding of punishment.

These relations have been documented in many diverse contexts. For example, when mental illness such as schizophrenia or depression is perceived as controllable, family members react with anger, which increases relapse. Furthermore, behaviorally based stigmas such as addictions and obesity are associated with greater personal responsibility than are somatically based stigmas such as blindness or physical handicaps. The former stigmas are reacted to negatively and are less able to generate charity funding than the latter stigmas. In a similar manner, those in need of financial aid because of perceived controllable reasons such as laziness, lack of planning, or overspending are met with annoyance and receive reduced aid from others, by comparison with those who are in need because of uncontrollable causes such as illness or bad economic conditions. These perceptions need not be veridical, and there can be causal disagreement between individuals. Conservatives, for example, are more likely to hold others responsible for poverty than are liberals, who tend to emphasize environmental causality.

The motivation sequence from the attribution perspective in these social situations can be depicted as:

Outcome – Cause – Causal Controllability – Responsibility – Affect – Action

To illustrate this episode more specifically, in an achievement setting, the motivation sequence capturing reactions to failure due to lack of effort versus low aptitude is represented as:

Failure – Lack of Effort – Controllable – Person is responsible – Anger – Punish
Failure – Lack of Aptitude – Uncontrollable – Not responsible – Sympathy – Help

Impression management

The consequences of responsibility are well understood by the layperson, who uses a variety of impression management strategies to avoid negative sanctions from others. These include denial of the outcome, excuses attempting to alter causal perceptions from controllable to uncontrollable ('I could not help it – the bus was late'), justifications that mitigate the link between control and responsibility ('I was late because my mother needed aid'), and confessions that attempt to sever the connection between the act and the actor (who did something bad but is a good person).

The other causal dimensions and interpersonal motivation

To a lesser extent, the stability and locus dimensions of causality also play important roles in social motivation. Stability, as already discussed, is essential in consideration of expectancy calculations. Hence, for example, punishment decisions guided by utilitarian philosophy must take into account the stability of the cause of any prior negative action. A mentally handicapped killer may not be held morally responsible for an action, but nonetheless may be imprisoned because of being a threat to society (the cause of the action is stable, so the deed may happen again). And regarding the role of causal locus in social settings, internal causes, when communicated by the perpetrator of a deed, are valued by society because they suggest acceptance of the role of self in producing outcomes (although high ability ascriptions for success result in inferences of arrogance and social rejection).

Theoretical overlap

Although the intrapersonal and interpersonal theories of action have been presented separately, they overlap and are intertwined. For example, if sympathy is expressed by an observer, then the recipient of this affect is likely to attribute failure personally to an uncontrollable cause, which then gives rise to shame and beliefs of lack of control. On the other hand, expressions of anger, if acknowledged, elicit guilt because of the linkage with personal responsibility. Furthermore, at the heart of both theories is a sequence of thought (causal understanding) – feeling – action: in other words, causes produce feelings that direct action. That is the 'deep structure' representing motivation from an attribution perspective.

See also: THE CAUSAL THEORY OF ACTION (5); INTENTION (14); REASONS AND CAUSES (17); MOTIVATING REASONS (19); THE EXPLANATORY ROLE OF CONSCIOUSNESS (24); WHAT A

DIFFERENCE EMOTIONS MAKE (25); FREE WILL AND DETERMINISM (38); RESPONSIBILITY AND AUTONOMY (39); INTENTIONAL ACTION IN FOLK PSYCHOLOGY (45).

References

Abramson, L. Y., Seligman, M. E. P., and Teasdale, J. D. (1978). Learned helplessness in humans: Critique and reformulation. *Journal of Abnormal Psychology*, 87, 49–74.

Heider, F. (1958). *The Psychology of Interpersonal Relations*. New York: Wiley.

Kelley, H. H. (1967). Attribution theory in social psychology. In D. Levine (ed.), *Nebraska Symposium on Motivation*, Vol. 15. Lincoln: University of Nebraska Press, 192–238.

Rotter, J. B. (1966). Generalized expectancies for internal versus external control of reinforcement. *Psychological Monographs*, 80 (1, Whole No. 609), 1–28.

Weiner, B. (1985). An attribution theory of achievement motivation and emotion. *Psychological Review*, 92, 548–573.

Weiner, B. (1995). *Judgments of Responsibility: A Foundation for a Theory of Social Conduct*. New York: Guilford.

Weiner, B. (2006). *Social Motivation, Justice, and the Moral Emotions*. Mahway, NJ: Erlbaum.

47

Rational Agency in Evolutionary Perspective

KIM STERELNY AND BEN JEFFARES

Introduction

Humans are rational agents, or so much contemporary philosophy supposes. Theorists as different as Daniel Dennett, Donald Davidson, and Philip Pettit have argued that there is a constitutive connection between agency and rationality: we can interpret other humans as agents with beliefs and preferences only if we take them to be rational (Dennett 1987; Pettit 1993; Davidson 2001). On these views, intentional agents act with a consistent, well-defined set of preferences; on beliefs which are largely true (or at least justified by the evidence to which they have access); while reasoning and choosing appropriately, given those beliefs and preferences. The aim of the present chapter is to place both this informal conception of humans and its more technical developments into an evolutionary perspective. For this informal conception of humans as rational agents is given more rigorous shape by decision theory and game theory. Evolutionary theory, in turn, vindicates important aspects of this framework, while challenging some of the assumptions traditionally made about human rational agency. We begin with a brief account of the conceptual framework and its elaboration in the social sciences as economic rationality. We then discuss ways in which the model can be modified and enriched by using an evolutionary framework, before considering more skeptical evolutionary assessments of rational agency.

Rational Agents and the Conceptual Background

Decision theorists treat human acts as rational bets. To do so, they presuppose that agents have systematic beliefs about the likely effects of their acts: we can judge odds. And they presuppose that agent preferences satisfy a set of formal conditions. Roughly, they presuppose that our preferences are transitive; that they are well defined, in the sense that agents know which, if any, of two possible outcomes they prefer; and that preferences are tradable, so that if an agent preferences *X* to *Y*, the agent also knows what would have to be added to *Y* to make that total package as good as *X*. Given those assumptions, a utility function can be constructed for an agent which gives quantitative expression to the value that agent places on the possible outcomes of acts. Agents' choices can then be represented as maximizing their expected utility (Elster 2008). In many contexts of choice, the expected utility of one agent's act is not independent of the choices of other agents. My deciding to hunt may have a high expected payoff if others hunt with me; low, otherwise. Game theory is the extension of decision theory that allows us to identify optimal choices in such interactive contexts.

Decision theory is applied empirically in 'rational actor' models in the various social sciences; most famously, in economics. The formal machinery of decision theory makes no substantial assumptions about preferences: an agent who cares about nothing but the welfare of penguins can be a rational maximizer. That typically changes when this formal conception is mapped onto social phenomena in rational actor models of the social sciences. In part, this is designed to give such models empirical content. If preferences are constrained only by the formal requirements necessary for utility to be defined, and if we take preferences to be revealed by actions, almost any action is consistent with some rational actor model. Sometimes the fact that the theory imposes no intrinsic constraint on preference is no problem, when rational actor models are informative because they show that aggregate outcomes can emerge *despite* the preferences of all the agents concerned. So, for example, in a classic paper Thomas Schelling showed that segregated patterns of housing can emerge even when all agents prefer to live in racially mixed environments, if they also have a trumping preference not to be the only household of their own race in a local patch (Schelling 1971).

Schelling's model, though, is a how-possibly model of the origins of segregation. The formal skeleton of decision theory needs to be enriched if it is to make rational actor models in the social sciences empirically tractable and explanatorily salient. For example, many in the sociology and cultural anthropology traditions place great stress on enculturation; on the fact that agents in particular cultures internalize the norms, customs and mores of their particular community and, as a consequence, this cultural imprinting is reflected in the agents' beliefs, preferences and actions (Geertz 2001). But, while the importance of enculturation is undeniable, with good reason defenders of rational actor models rarely incorporate culturally specific norms directly into agent preference structure. To do so would be to rob this approach of its explanatory power. We cannot explain, say, the gerontocentric distribution of sexual access in many traditional aboriginal communities (see Keen 2006) by supposing younger male and female agents to have a normatively shaped preference for such partners. For the origin, spread, persistence, and influence of such norms is a crucial *explanatory target*, not an *explanatory resource* (Sperber 1996). Similarly, the East Asian preference for boy children even in an environment of female rarity, as it is revealed in patterns of infanticide, is what we need to explain. We would learn nothing from a model of individual choice which simply factored into agent utility functions a strong preference for boys over girls.

Homo economicus

Those who develop rational actor models of social phenomena must have independent evidence that agents have the informational resources and motivations which their models presuppose. Moreover, those informational resources and motivations must be somewhat public to other agents, for agents typically make choices, and must make choices, with real though imperfect knowledge of what other agents want and believe. Finally, and this is the point illustrated by gerontocracy and male bias, those resources and motivations must also be explanatorily prior to the social and cultural phenomena that the models explain. Because it fulfills these requirements, frequently the economists' version of rational agency is rightly used in the social sciences.

The economist's *Homo economicus* version of rational agency takes humans to be rational decision-makers who care only about their own individual welfare. While this assumption simplifies the variety and idiosyncrasy of human motivation, that is also an advantage of the economists' approach to rational agency. For it gives it real predictive and explanatory power. The economists' version of rational agency may presume that agents have more access to information about the consequences of their actions, and more facility in using this information, than they really do. But the assumption that agents have self-regarding economic preferences enables models to be general, strategic, empirically tractable, and explanatorily salient. Economic decision-making is strategic, as decisions interlock. So it is important that others can identify self-regarding economic preferences and make a reasonable estimate of other agents' best economic choices. The assumption is not arbitrary. Agents do not care *only* about their economic welfare. But we have good reason to believe that they *do care* about it, often giving it a high priority. Moreover, this preference is not culturally contingent: across all cultures, agents place significant weight on their own welfare. Consequently, *Homo economicus* models do not presuppose what they are meant to explain. Finally, models making this assumption are general: they predict that agents in objectively similar circumstances will make similar choices, since their best economic options will be similar.

The *Homo economicus* construct underlines the idealizations inherent in the rational actor models of the social sciences, and equally inherent in the decision-theoretic framework from which the construct is derived and in the underlying conception of humans as rational agents. No one doubts that rational agency models are idealizations, but the extent and location of these idealizations remain very controversial. The rest of this chapter considers the impact of an evolutionary perspective on these issues. Evolutionary considerations can be used to complement rational actor models, enriching them and explaining their scope and limits. But they can also be used to build alternatives to rational actor models. One key issue in model choice is to identify the space of alternatives. We can think of agents not as utility maximizers but as adaptation executors or fitness maximizers. These are genuine alternatives to rational actor models, for they offer general pictures of human decision-making that identify key explanatory resources for the human sciences. Moreover, these models do not presuppose the phenomena to be explained. In this short chapter we do not aim to adjudicate between evolutionary–revisionist accounts of rational agency and alternatives to those conceptions of human action. Rather, we aim to sketch the options within the evolutionary research program.

Beyond *Homo economicus*

> Scratch an altruist and watch a hypocrite bleed.
>
> Ghiselin 1974: 2

The economist's *Homo economicus* model is implicitly evolutionary: one reason why the assumption of self-interest is not arbitrary is that it roughly matches our experiences of one another. But the deeper reason is that we expect evolutionary mechanisms to produce agents who safeguard their own interests; only such agents become ancestors. Even so, no one doubts that this picture of motivation is simplified, though there is considerable debate about the extent of that simplification, as Michael Ghiselin's robust remark shows. Ken Binmore defends models of human social interaction essentially based on self-interest, for he takes the simplification just to strip away noise. Most agents most of the time act in largely self-interested ways (Binmore 2006).

In contrast, Robert Frank (1988) and, more recently, Ernst Fehr, Sam Bowles, Herbert Gintis and their collaborators have argued that the extent and nature of human cooperation cannot be explained on the assumption that agents are typically self-interested. Cooperation among self-interested agents would decay in large groups with imperfect knowledge of one another's acts, and we live cooperatively in such groups (Bowles and Gintis 2003; Fehr and Fischbacher 2003; Gintis 2006, 2007, 2008). Moreover, experimental evidence shows that agents do indeed have 'social preferences': they cooperate if they expect others to cooperate (even if cheating is possible and profitable), and they punish cheating, even when that is not profitable. The central idea is that (first) humans have evolved in a selective regime in which it is important to have a reputation as an honest cooperator, and (second) the only way of building a reputation as an honest cooperator is to be an honest cooperator. The best way of seeming good is to be good.

In Frank's model, further developed by Bowles and Gintis, moral and prosocial emotions play a crucial role in generating and signalling our social preferences. The result is a technically messy picture of agent utility functions, for objective costs and benefits are modulated by subjective costs and rewards. But there emerges an alternative to the *Homo economicus* model that shares many of its virtues. Agent utilities are common across agents and stable over time. They are partially known among agents, for, while emotional signals can be faked, they are quite reliable. There is independent evidence for such social preferences, and their presence is independent of, and explanatorily prior to, the social phenomena – the networks of human cooperation – that these models explain. The bottom line: rational actor models can be empirically tractable, general, and explanatorily powerful without presupposing that agents have self-interested motivations. But these alternative models must be embedded in a coherent and empirically supported account of the evolution of agents with social preferences: one cannot simply claim history as justification, one must show how an evolutionary history shapes such prosocial emotions and thence cooperative groups.

Informational Resources

One problem for rational actor models of human agency is that they can easily seem to presuppose that we are better informed, or smarter, than we really are. If agents maximize expected utility in interacting with their environment, they must be able to judge odds. If they are to judge odds well, they need good information about their environment. Yet information is an expensive resource; it is rarely freely available. This fact is explicitly acknowledged only in models of strategic interaction. One key difference between Binmore and Gintis is that they have different views on what we can legitimately assume agents to know about one another in their strategic interactions: Binmore thinks that information is available for free, being generated as a side effect of other activities. Gintis thinks that information is expensive, and so agents have limited information about one another (Binmore 2006; Gintis 2006; Ross 2006). But, outside of contexts of strategic interaction, access to relevant information is rarely explicitly considered. So, for example, in human behavioral ecology models rarely show that agents have access to the information they would need in order to make optimal trade-offs between gathering and hunting.

One advantage of evolutionary models of human action is that they have the potential to bring access to information more systematically into our conception of human agency. The evolution of learning is central to much work on human cognitive evolution, and many ideas have been explored. Some emphasize the cultural accumulation of information about key problem domains. In their different ways, Tomasello (1999), Robson and Kaplan (2003), Sterelny (2003 and 2006), and Richerson and Boyd (2005) all develop theories of the kinds of information humans build access to, and of the mechanisms which make that information available at and across generations. Dan Dennett and Andy Clark emphasize the importance of epistemic technology in acquiring and using information (Dennett 2000; Clark 2008). Clark, in particular, argues that artefacts have become so important to our cognitive capacities that we should think of some artefacts as integral parts of the human cognitive system. These theories of the evolution of human access to information were not developed to supplement rational actor models of human agency. But they can be adapted for that use: they are theories of the scope and limits of informed rational agency. So, for example, Sterelny (2007) argues that humans in traditional societies make poor choices about medical intervention, because the mechanisms of accumulation of reliable environmental information are ineffective in the medical domain. The environment of pathogen and parasite is highly labile, and disease and recovery is often multi-causal. Hence our techniques for tracking success and failure – for judging the odds – work poorly. Herbert Gintis also takes up ideas about the limits of rationality, distinguishing between routine and deliberative choice. Routine choices are those for which our evolved psychology, the mechanisms of cultural information accumulation, and individual experience prepare us. In such cases we have, and we know how to use, the relevant information: these are the circumstances in which we act rationally (Gintis 2008).

It is one thing to have information; another to use it well. One pervasive criticism of rational actor models is that they fit poorly with empirical data on human reasoning. There is a rich empirical literature on the frailties of human reasoning, showing the importance of framing effects, neglect of base rates and the like (see Kahneman et al. 1982; Gigerenzer et al. 1999; Gigerenzer and Selton 2001). To some extent, this criticism can be deflected by treating rational actor models as specifications of human behavioral dispositions rather than of conscious, reflective deliberation. If Gintis' distinction between routine and deliberative decision-making is cogent, then we are most reliable in our practiced, fluent decision-making. We are least likely to be making optimal choices when we are engaged in deliberative reflection about our best, all-things-considered choice of action. So the most plausible version of a rational agent model suggests that, in many central areas of human decision, our heuristics, rules of thumb, and other cognitive habits typically generate near-optimal action. The same cultural–evolutionary mechanisms that explain the scope and limits of our access to information explain the scope and limits of its judicious use. We are boundedly rational agents (Kahneman 2003). Our cognitive machinery does not harness smooth and accurate probability calculation to an accurate world model and to a well-specified preference structure. But in important, stable and well-practiced areas of human decision-making we use rules of thumb fine-tuned by collective and individual experience, perhaps supplemented by cognitive technology and (in some hyper-stable domains) domain-specific cognitive adaptations. These work well enough to generate approximately optimal decisions.

The notions of bounded rationality, cultural learning, and the interplay of individual strategies in groups sometimes enable us to make good sense of historical data. Archaeological research reveals some highly efficient and economically sophisticated tool-making behavior. For instance, some historical groups have manufactured two sorts of tools; high turnover 'disposable' tools manufactured from readily available resources, and expensive high-quality long-life tools manufactured from rare materials, used on foraging expeditions (Odell 1996; Hiscock 2006). Models of these archaeological findings integrate use wear information with cost benefit analysis of manufacture modes and information about the geological sources of raw materials. These highly sophisticated strategies required information which could not be gathered and assessed by any one individual. However, no individual needed to gather the relevant information herself. Cultural learning allows an agent to parasitize her fellow tool-makers for tips, tricks, and strategies. Information preservation via story-telling and accumulated cultural experience gives an agent access to information about historical successes and failures. Rather than learning a sophisticated strategy from scratch, actors can access robust templates of sophisticated tool-making generated by their culture, which they may then modify. A culture might be 'smart' due to generations of trial and error feedback, even while individuals are constrained by their poor access to crucial information. So the informational cheat of copying successful strategies from others can be a good heuristic, given the insurmountable informational load of finding out everything for yourself. Mimicking the behavior of apparently successful individuals also mimics rational behavior. But such a strategy can have unforeseen consequences, entrenching sub-optimal historical accidents. Agents may imitate the ostentatious prayers of a community leader whose actual success depends on a subtle feature of his fish-net manufacture. Publicly accessible but economically epiphenomenal social displays can be elaborated through imitation, while the real keys to improvement remain unseen and uncopied. Information is expensive to get and difficult to assess, so individuals do well who have learning strategies that maximize their plagiarism of cultural templates, regardless of the nature of those templates; regardless of the rationality of the behaviors they direct.

A Poisoned Chalice?

At this point, the reader will have begun to wonder whether evolutionary biology comes to enrich rational actor models or to bury them. Evolutionary biology genuinely enriches rational actor models of motivation by showing that an empirically tractable version of rational decision-making need not treat humans as pure egoists. But perhaps the section on 'Informational Resources' shows that we are not smart and knowledgeable enough to count as rational decision-makers. Rational actor models deliver, at best, an approximate description of the patterns of human choice, while telling us very little about the information-processing mechanisms that generate those choices. Rather than being rational agents, we just mimic rational agency moderately well, in a restricted but important set of circumstances. Evolutionary biology (on this skeptical reading) does not vindicate rational actor models of human agency; it undermines them, while explaining why they have real but limited predictive utility.

The existence of two alternative models adds bite to this skeptical challenge. One alternative, human behavioral ecology, uses very similar tools to those of rational choice theorists, and like them, takes humans typically to make optimal choices. But we do not maximize *utility*, we maximize *fitness*. More radically, nativist evolutionary psychologists have consistently argued that it is a mistake to think of human minds as unified optimality engines. There is no single, general purpose evaluation and decision mechanism driving most of an agent's actions; a mechanism whose overall performance we can evaluate and explain (Tooby and Cosmides 1992). While we have some capacities in the general domain, our minds are integrated ensembles of domain-specific specializations. Many of the distinctive features of human decision-making depend on these adaptations. When we act in environments relevantly similar to those in which these specializations evolved, trying to solve the problems for which they are designed, we usually make fitness-enhancing decisions. If we are confronted with a new environment, or new problems, all bets are off. We can be lucky; old tools can sometimes be used for new tasks. But there are no guarantees. On this view, it simply makes no sense to give an overall assessment of intelligence or rationality. We are not *approximately rational*. Rather, we are superbly adapted to some cognitive challenges, and piss-poor at others. This conception of human psychology offers alternative micro-foundations for the human sciences. For, according to this picture, human cognitive profiles are developmentally robust. While enculturation makes some difference to agents' minds, our performance specifications are cross-culturally stable, and so are the explanatory resources for the social sciences. The Wilson-Daley explanation of the correlation between stepfather presence and increased violence towards children illustrates the explanatory strategy of nativist evolutionary psychology (Daly and Wilson 1988). Violence towards children is not an unfortunate side effect of individual optimization. It is maladaptive behavior caused by a mismatch between historical and current environments.

Nativist evolutionary psychologists are skeptical about human behavioral ecology, and not just about rational agency. Human behavioral ecology, like decision theory, sees humans as optimality engines, and it uses similar analytic tools. But we maximize fitness, not utility (Smith et al. 2001). These models, too, should be seen as specifications of human behavioral dispositions rather than of cognitive processes. The models assume that our proximate motivators and decision heuristics track fitness, but the models' focus is on the relationship between choice and fitness, not on the cognition of choice. This focus on fitness brings the same theoretic benefits as the *Homo economicus* focus on resource acquisition. The quantity maximized is explanatorily important; it is objectively measurable; it can be estimated by other agents; and it predicts similar choices by agents in similar situations. Indeed, in many traditional societies fitness depends largely on resource acquisition, so human behavioral ecology models will be roughly equivalent to economic versions of rational actor models. However, to the extent that fitness is decoupled from resource acquisition, and to the extent that rational actor models take a less constrained view of utility, the models' empirical predictions go separate ways. In one set of cases, rational actor models seem to work better. It is very hard to give behavioral ecology models of the demographic transitions in the western world over the last century, as urbanization and increasing wealth co-vary with falling family sizes.

What Is to Be Done?

The issues are in part empirical. Nativist evolutionary psychology has yet to show the consistency of its basic ideas with the observed variety of human culture and with the versatility of individual minds. There has been very little systematic attempt to compare utility-based and fitness-based models of human agency. We do not yet know the extent to which human decision-making in the wild (rather than in experimental situations) departs from the optimum, especially when we take into account the role of environmental support and the costs of information.

However, the issues are not just empirical. For one thing, it is not clear that we should select a single model of agency. Many of those who analyze human action accept some version of a dual process picture of our cognitive architecture: a late-evolving, conscious, reflective, culturally influenced and slow system works in conjunction with a faster, more ancient, less conscious, less linguistically mediated system (Stanovich 2004). Perhaps the choice of model might depend on which sub-system has been triggered by which external stimuli. Knowing the context of a decision becomes even more important. This may be complicated if triggering is itself learnt in a cultural setting: the eliciting of moral judgments and of associated motivating emotions may well be such a culturally derived trigger; we may well learn to be indignant at certain behaviors of others. The result is that understanding agency might require knowledge of our evolutionary history (to understand the evolved mechanisms); knowledge of the cultural context (to understand learned behaviors); and knowledge of the personal circumstances (to understand the informational environment relevant to the individual decision-maker). Only then might we understand rationality. But this suggests that assumptions of pure rationality are problematic and overly abstracted from the underlying cognitive mechanisms of agents, from their evolutionary history, and from their environmental contexts.

Given this complexity, Dan Dennett may be right in suggesting that the question 'Is Abe rational?' is not like 'Is Abe a mammal?': Abe's taxonomic status is settled by the facts of history. Perhaps Abe's status as a rational being depends in part on objective facts about Abe, and in part on our predictive and explanatory interests and on our cognitive toolkit. Whether a pixel pattern is a picture of an elephant is, as Dennett points out, in part an objective feature of the pattern. Some pixel distributions cannot be elephant pictures. But many can be, and there is no objective threshold of resemblance which sorts the elephant pictures from other pixel distributions. Likewise, some agents are so cognitively limited that there is no reasonable way to see them as rational agents. But there is no magic threshold of cognitive competence which Abe must satisfy to count as rational (Dennett 1991). Perhaps multiple models of agency are needed not just to capture the way in which new capacities have been grafted on top of an older rootstock of skills, but also to reflect the variety of our intellectual projects and the conditional nature of rationality, agency, and action.

See also: DELIBERATION AND DECISION (32); AKRASIA AND IRRATIONALITY (35); RATIONALITY (36); INTENTIONAL ACTION IN FOLK PSYCHOLOGY (45); ANIMAL AGENCY (48); ACTION IN COGNITIVE ETHOLOGY (49); ACTION IN HISTORY AND SOCIAL SCIENCE (50).

References

Binmore, K. (2006). Why do people cooperate? *Politics, Philosophy, and Economics*, 5 (5), 81–96.

Bowles, S., and Gintis, H. (2003). Origins of human cooperation. In P. Hammerstein (ed.), *Genetic and Cultural Evolution of Cooperation*. Cambridge, MA: MIT Press, 429–443.

Clark, A. (2008). *Supersizing the Mind*. Oxford: Oxford University Press.

Daly, M., and Wilson, M. (1988). *Homicide*. New York: Aldine de Gruyter.

Davidson, D. (2001). *Inquiries into Truth and Interpretation: Philosophical Essays*. Oxford: Oxford University Press.

Dennett, D. C. (1987). *The Intentional Stance*. Cambridge, MA: MIT Press.

Dennett, D. C. (1991). Real patterns. *Journal of Philosophy*, 87, 27–51.

Dennett, D. C. (2000). Making tools for thinking. In D. Sperber (ed.), *Metarepresentation: A Multidisciplinary Perspective*. Oxford: Oxford University Press, 17–29.

Elster, J. (2008). *Exploring Social Behaviour: More Nuts and Bolts for the Social Sciences*. Cambridge: Cambridge University Press.

Fehr, E., and Fischbacher, U. (2003). The nature of human altruism. *Nature*, 425, 785–791.

Frank, R. (1988). *Passion within Reason: The Strategic Role of the Emotions*. New York: W. W. Norton.

Geertz, C. (2001). *Available Light: Anthropological Reflections on Philosophical Topics*. Princeton: Princeton University Press.

Ghiselin, M. T. (1974). *The Economy of Nature and the Evolution of Sex*. Berkeley: University of California Press.

Gigerenzer, G., and Selton, R. (2001). *Bounded Rationality: The Adaptive Toolbox*. Cambridge, MA: MIT Press.

Gigerenzer, G., Todd, P., and the ABC Research Group (eds) (1999). *Simple Heuristics That Make us Smart*. Oxford: Oxford University Press.

Gintis, H. (2006). Behavioral ethics meets natural justice. *Politics, Philosophy and Economics*, 5 (1), 5–32.

Gintis, H. (2007). A framework for the unification of the behavioral sciences. *Behavioral and Brain Sciences*, 30 (1), 1–61.

Gintis, H. (2008). Five principles for the unification of the behavioral sciences. Santa Fe Institute 39. [pdf file.]

Hiscock, P. (2006). Blunt and to the point: Changing technological strategies in Holocene Australia. In I. Lilley (ed.), *Archaeology of Oceania: Australia and the Pacific Islands*. Malden, MA: Blackwell, 69–95.

Kahneman, D. (2003). A perspective on judgment and choice: Mapping bounded rationality. *American Psychologist*, 58 (9), 697–720.

Kahneman, D., Slovic, P., and Tversky, A. (eds) (1982). *Judgment under Encertainty: Heuristics and Biases*. Cambridge: Cambridge University Press.

Keen, I. (2006). Constraints on the development of enduring inequalities in Late Holocene Australia. *Current Anthropology*, 47 (1), 7–38.

Odell, G. H. (1996). *Stone Tools: Theoretical Insights into Human Prehistory*. New York: Plenum Press.

Pettit, P. (1993). *The Common Mind: An Essay on Psychology, Society, and Politics*. Oxford: Oxford University Press.

Richerson, P. J., and Boyd, R. (2005). *Not by Genes Alone: How Culture Transformed Human Evolution*. Chicago: University of Chicago Press.

Robson, A., and Kaplan, H. (2003). The evolution of human life expectancy and intelligence in hunter-gatherer economies. *American Economic Review*, 93 (1), 150–169.

Ross, D. (2006). Evolutionary game theory and the normative theory of institutional design: Binmore and behavioral economics. *Politics, Philosophy and Economics*, 5 (1), 51–80.

Schelling, T. C. (1971). Dynamic models of segregation. *Journal of Mathematical Sociology*, 1, 143–186.

Smith, E. A., Borgerhoff Mulder, N., and Hill, K. (2001). Controversies in the evolutionary social sciences: A guide for the perplexed. *Trends in Ecology and Evolution*, 16 (3): 128–134.

Sperber, D. (1996). *Explaining Culture: A Naturalistic Approach*. Oxford: Blackwell.

Stanovich, K. (2004). *The Robot's Rebellion*. Chicago: University of Chicago Press.

Sterelny, K. (2003). *Thought in a Hostile World*. New York: Blackwell.

Sterelny, K. (2006). Cognitive load and human decision, or, three ways of rolling the rock up hill. In P. Carruthers, S. Laurence, and S. Stich (eds), *The Innate Mind*, Vol. 2: *Culture and Cognition*. Oxford: Oxford University Press, 218–233.

Sterelny, K. (2007). SNAFUS: An evolutionary perspective. *Biological Theory*, 2 (3), 317–328.

Tomasello, M. (1999). *The Cultural Origins of Human Cognition*. Cambridge: Harvard University Press.

Tooby, J., and Cosmides, L. (1992). The psychological foundations of culture. In J. Barkow, L. Cosmides, and J. Tooby, *The Adapted Mind*. Oxford, Oxford University Press, 19–136.

48

Animal Agency

HANS-JOHANN GLOCK

Prolegomena

Can non-human animals (henceforth simply 'animals') act intentionally? Can they act for a reason? If not, are they capable of acting at all, or are they restricted to mere mechanical behavior? The answers to these questions depend not just on empirical findings (whether observations in the field or experiments in the laboratory), but also on what one makes of philosophically contested concepts like reason, intention, agency, and related mental notions.

There are two opposing stances on animal minds. *Differentialists* maintain that there are crucial qualitative differences separating us from animals; *assimilationists* insist that the differences are merely quantitative and gradual. Differentialism tends to be more popular among philosophers than among ethologists (see chapter 49). But there are also differentialists within behavioral science. According to a well-known methodological principle – 'Morgan's canon' – we should only attribute a certain mental capacity to a creature if this is the *only* explanation of its behavioral repertoire. Yet it is more plausible to insist that we attribute a certain mental capacity to a creature only if this is the *best* explanation of its behavior, taking into account not just ontological parsimony but all the parameters by which theories are to be judged (explanatory power, simplicity, and so on). Weakening Morgan's canon in this way puts pate to a widespread malpractice in comparative psychology. It is common to account for the cognitive achievements of apes and cetaceans by invoking more or less far-fetched feats of associative learning, for the sole purpose of scotching the *prima facie* compelling suggestion that these animals engage in genuine planning or reasoning (see for instance Povinelli and Vonk 2006; compare Tomasello and Call 2006).

Turning from methodological to conceptual qualms, the most important variant of differentialism is *lingualism*. It denies on a priori grounds that animals without a language can have mental capacities at all, or at least the 'higher' mental capacities required for rational agency. This raises the question of whether there are conceptual connections between the possession of language on the one hand, and the capacity to act, to act for reasons, and to reason on the other. These issues ought to be approached from a *third-person perspective*. Our mental concepts capture neither genetic nor neurophysiological differences, but differences in the kinds of *behavioral* and *perceptual* capacities we human beings are interested in. As a result, the criterion for the possession of mental powers by a species is not the DNA, or even the brain of its members. These only come into play when one proceeds to explaining *why* these specimens possess the mental powers they do, namely by specifying the causes for such possession. They do not determine whether the animals possess such powers in the first place. That depends on what they are capable of doing in various circumstances.

Mental phenomena as defined by our mental concepts must be capable of being manifested in behavior. The moot question is whether certain mental features can only be manifested in *linguistic* behavior, and whether acting for a reason and reasoning are among these (see Glock 2009). In addressing that question, we need to consider not just extant species and their actual behavioral repertoire, but also what kind of behavior non-linguistic creatures are capable of in principle. For lingualism to be correct, even animals very much like us in their facial expressions, gestures, and non-linguistic behavioral patterns *must be* incapable of rational or intentional agency, simply because they lack linguistic competence.

Types of Rationality

Unlike problem-solving strategies which are innate or result from rigid stimulus–response patterns established through conditioning, intelligent behavior is plastic, responsive to altering circumstances, and therefore capable of tackling problems which the subject has never encountered before. Such intelligence is clearly a feature of some higher animals. It extends from problem-solving through trial and error, as with the Cappuchin monkeys in the trap tube task, to the kind of insight and foresight displayed by chimpanzees or Caledonian crows in the fashioning of tools (see Tomasello and Call 1997: 10–11 and ch. 3; Kacelnik 2006: 101–2). But are intelligent animals *ipso facto* rational? One aspect which distinguishes rationality from intelligence is that rationality suggests a capacity for *reasoning*. This difference is often glossed instead in terms of a distinction between two kinds of rationality: 'behavioral rationality' is a feature of behavioral patterns and capacities that lie open to observation, whereas 'process rationality' is a special kind of behavior generating process (see Hurley and Nudds 2006). But even the most rational performances need not be accompanied (and a fortiori need not be caused) by *conscious* processes of reasoning (Ryle 1949). What counts is not what crosses the mind of an agent *A*, but what *A* is capable of doing, say, by way of justifying her beliefs and actions.

It is more fruitful, therefore, to distinguish between *externalist* and *internalist* conceptions of rationality. Are *A*'s performances assessed exclusively by reference to external standards of which *A* may be entirely unaware? Or are they also assessed by reference to *A*'s own perspective, by reference to *A*'s beliefs, desires, intentions, and preferences? Externalist conceptions have gained favor in the wake of Darwinism. *A*'s behavior is rational in a Darwinist sense insofar as it maximizes *A*'s biological fitness. Animals are indisputably capable of Darwinist rationality. But Darwinist rationality does not correspond to our everyday notion. There is nothing irrational, for instance, about minimizing one's biological fitness through effective contraception. More importantly, Darwinist rationality does not require animals to possess higher mental faculties, or even to be intelligent.

For these reasons, we need to go beyond external conceptions of rationality. A first step in this direction is the conception of rationality which underlies 'expected utility theory.' According to this conception, *A*'s behavior is rational insofar as it maximizes *A*'s expected utility. This approach includes a subjective element, by making *A*'s rationality dependent on an efficient pursuit of *A*'s own *preferences*. At the same time, these preferences are imputed either by identifying arbitrary goals that *A*'s behavior seems to pursue consistently, or by ascribing to *A* substantive interests suitable for creatures of *A*'s kind, irrespective of whether *A* herself is even potentially aware of them.

It is precisely the possibility of ascribing a subjective perspective to an agent, however, that is crucial to the debate about animal rationality. By contrast to machines, higher animals have purposes *of their own*, which is to say that they pursue goals. And these goals may conflict with their objective needs. We can ask whether the animal has adopted a feasible, promising or optimal way of achieving its goals or of satisfying its desires, independently of whether achieving these goals or satisfying these desires is conducive to its biological fitness, its objective wellbeing, or the consistent maximization of arbitrary objectives.

Intentional Explanation

An agent is rational in the internalist sense if she can perform an action in order to attain a good, subjectively conceived – something she herself wants. In other words, the agent needs to be capable of acting *purposively* or *intentionally*, in pursuit of her own goals. Such actions are subject to 'intentional' or 'rational explanations,' explanations that refer to the agent's reasons – her beliefs, desires, intentions, goals, purposes. Now, in science no less than in everyday life, we apply such explanations not just to human behavior but also to the behavior of higher animals. In both cases we employ intentional verbs, and we explain the behavior by reference to the fact that *A* believes that *p*, desires *X*, wants to Φ, etc. But lingualists dismiss this practice as a misleading (if useful) *façon de parler*. Thus, according to Davidson, employing intentional explanations in the case of animals is just as anthropomorphic as employing them in the case of a heat-seeking missile (2001: 102). Davidson's analogy misses the mark, however. Attributing thoughts to animals is not just convenient, as he would have it, but entirely justified. It is based not on technological ignorance but on a biological insight, namely that animals have both wants and perceptual capacities. Admittedly, Davidson has produced a raft of independent arguments to the effect that animals can't have beliefs (believe that *p*) or desires (desire that *p* be the case). Yet these arguments have been found wanting; and there is the counterargument that animals must be capable of believing or knowing that *p*, since they are capable of *perceiving* that *p* (see Glock 2000 and Glock 2010).

Acting for a Reason

If acting for reasons simply means acting in a way that is subject to intentional explanation, then animals *can* act for reasons. But the idea has been construed in potentially more demanding ways. In fact, the very idea of acting for a reason can be spelled out in two different ways. First, there is an understanding of acting for a reason which can be labeled as psychologistic, psychological, internal, or subjectivist. It goes back at least to Hume, and at present it is epitomized by Davidson (1980). According to this subjectivist conception,

> [1] *A* is capable of acting for a reason iff *A*'s actions are to be explained by reference to mental states of *A* (beliefs and 'pro-attitudes' like desires and intentions).

Subjectivism insists that the beliefs and desires invoked in intentional explanations are *mental states* of the agent – states of desiring or wanting something and states of believing something.

By contrast, according to recent revisionists, the reasons for which agents act are not mental states of the agent herself. Instead, they are objective *facts* or *states of affairs* which, save for special cases, concern the agent's environment rather than her own mind. Insofar as the reasons for which an agent acts can be said to be beliefs and desires at all, they are not subjective states of believing or desiring, but *what is believed* or *what is desired* (Hornsby 1997; Hyman 1999; Dancy 2000; Stout 2005; Alvarez 2010). An agent *A* acts for a reason if *A* acts on account not of her own beliefs, but on account of facts or states of affairs, on account of how things are (from *A*'s perspective). Accordingly,

> [2] *A* is capable of acting for a reason iff *A* can act in the light of reasons, that is, in the light of facts (as *A* sees them).

The *objectivist* conception of reasons does not imply an *externalist* conception of rationality. Although *A*'s reasons for *Φ*-ing are facts, they are facts which make *Φ*-ing good or attractive in *A*'s eyes (either instrumentally or intrinsically), that is, from the agent's own perspective.

In spite of important differences, objectivists tend to agree on two points. First, *A*'s reason for *Φ*-ing is something that makes *Φ*-ing good or valuable in *A*'s eyes; secondly, what makes *Φ*-ing good or valuable in *A*'s eye is (by and large) not *A*'s *believing* something to be the case, but *what is believed* to be the case. My reason for *Φ*-ing is what I specify in response to the question 'Why are you *Φ*-ing?'; and this answer typically takes the form 'Because *p*' rather than 'Because I believe that *p*.' My reason for taking an umbrella is that it is raining, not that I believe that it is raining; for it is the weather rather than my own mental state that makes taking an umbrella good or bad in my eyes.

This is not the place to develop and defend a watertight version of objectivism. What matters for present purposes are two points: first, there are noteworthy reasons for adopting such an account; secondly, such an account *removes an important obstacle* to crediting animals with the capacity to act for reasons.

Acting in the Light of Reasons

The obstacle arises from the idea that rational agency requires that the agent be able to act *in the light of reasons*. The action makes sense to the agent (as the rational or a rational thing to do), given those reasons. And this implies that the agent is aware of those reasons.

At this point the contrast between subjectivism and objectivism makes a crucial difference. For subjectivism, the reasons in the light of which *A* acts are subjective states, antecedent to *A*'s action. In Davidson, for instance, *A*'s reason for *Φ*-ing is *A*'s mental state of believing that *p* will lead to *q*, in combination with her mental state of desiring that *q*.

Now, if reasons for action are subjective states of agents, acting in their light seems to require *A* to entertain thoughts about *A*'s own thoughts. More specifically, it appears to require *A* to think about, or represent, *A*'s own states of believing and desiring. To put it more grandly, animals would have to possess not just consciousness of their environment but *self-consciousness*, awareness of their own mental phenomena (states, processes, abilities, and so on). The same would hold if the reasons in the light of which *A* acts were psychological facts about *A*, for instance the fact that *A* believes that *p*, desires *X* or wants to *Φ*.

Such self-consciousness may be beyond the ken of animals. But the apparent obstacle does not even arise on the objectivist account of reasons for action. According to objectivism, reasons for action are facts, or at any rate things which are believed rather than subjective states of believing. This immediately removes the threat posed to the idea of animals acting in the light of reasons. For animals are capable of acting in the light of facts, in the light of how things are in their environment. This is just a corollary of their having cognitive capacities. In particular, animals are able to perceive, and hence to believe and know things.

According to some objectivists, reasons for action include not just facts the agent is aware of, but also goods or goals – things desired as well as things believed. Yet this does not pose a threat to the claim that animals can act in the light of reasons. That animals possess *conative* powers is at least as clear as that they possess cognitive powers. They have not just needs of the kind invoked in some externalist conceptions of rationality, but also wants, and they can pursue goods or goals and avoid things. In addition, higher animals have and adopt purposes or goals of their own, namely the goals they pursue, the ends for the sake of which they act (Hacker 2007: 130–140, 160–164). They can also evaluate facts – or, in a more realistic ethological idiom, features of their environment – in the sense of responding to them as good or bad (for instance attractive or threatening), and they can act accordingly.

A lingualist might insist nonetheless that animals cannot act *for* reasons, while conceding that there are reasons *why* they act. For instance, the elephant drinks from the well *because* it is thirsty. But on the lingualist's gloss of that statement, the 'because' refers not to something objective that makes drinking good from the elephant's perspective, but simply to an inner state leading to outward behavior. In that case, the alleged 'reasons why' animals act would simply be causes, rather than reasons as objectivists understand them. So this apparent compromise is at best open to subjectivists.

The upshot is that animals *are* capable of acting in the light of reasons, provided that these are construed as they should be: as objective features of the environment, assessable from the perspective of agents.

Reflecting on Reasons

Even without appealing to subjectivism, some lingualists deny that animals can act in the light of reasons, on the grounds that they cannot *reflect* on their reasons (see for instance Hacker 2007: 204, 236, 240; McDowell 1996: 70; Frankfurt 2004, 18–19; Brandom 2010).

Admittedly there is one mental power that does presuppose the power to reflect on reasons, namely the power to deliberate. But, as we shall see, it need not presuppose the ability to justify one's action verbally. Even more problematic is the idea that one can only act *for a reason*, in response to reasons, if one is able to *reflect* on reasons, at least if the latter requires the agent to entertain self-conscious thoughts about certain things (facts, goals) *being her reasons* (that is, thoughts of the form 'My reason for Φ-ing is that *p*'). Indeed, there is a positive argument for keeping the having of reasons separate from reflecting on reasons: *A* couldn't develop a capacity to reflect on *A*'s reasons if *A* didn't *have* reasons to begin with (MacIntyre 1999: 56). Lingualists could respond, however, that there is no distinction between a creature that can act for reasons and one that can reflect on these reasons. Without the capacity for reflection, and hence, they continue, without the gift of language, an agent cannot act for a reason. Having reasons and being able to reflect on them come as a package.

But how can this holistic response account for the intermediate stages that lie between the human infant, who can neither act for reasons nor reflect on them, and the adult, who can do both? Furthermore, how can lingualism do justice to the intentional explanation of animal behavior? Unlike machines or plants, animals can act for purposes, adopt purposes of their own, and adapt their behavior to circumstances in pursuit of these purposes. Yet it is unclear what this could amount to, if such animals could not act in the light of facts pertinent to achieving those purposes. For instance, we explain a well-known behavior among some chimpanzees by saying that they batter nuts with hard stones *in order to*, or *for the purpose of* cracking them. This implies that they act *on account of the fact* that nuts crack when treated in this way. Furthermore, great apes, at least, are capable of organizing their behavior in the light of what they perceive, remember, and so on, in such a way that they distinguish means from ends, notably by showing awareness of the fact that one and the same end can be achieved by different means and that one and the same means – for instance a tool – can serve different ends (Tomasello and Call 1997: 318; Hurley 2006: 148–149).

Reasoning and Deliberation

Nevertheless there may be a case for insisting that, in order to act for reasons in the fullest sense, it does not suffice to be *responsive* to reasons (something feasible for animals on an objectivist construal); the agent must also be capable of *operating* with reasons.

After all, the reasons of fully linguistic creatures are closely tied to *how they reasoned* or could have reasoned. And such deliberation or practical reasoning seems to be the prerogative of language users.

According to a plausible account, practical reasoning takes the following form (Kenny 1989: 43–45; see also chapter 31):

P_1 *X* is to be brought about
P_2 If I *Φ* then *X*
C So I'll *Φ*!

By contrast to the conclusions of theoretical reasoning, those of practical inferences are not assertions or beliefs, but resolves or expressions of intentions. This does not count in favor of lingualism, however. As regards context (problem), demeanour (say, head scratching) and result (problem solution), the behavior of chimpanzees, for instance, resembles that of human beings. They interrupt an activity, examine an obstacle, pursue a certain solution, discard one type of tool in favor of another, resume their activity in a purposeful and determined fashion. All of this is accompanied, moreover, by gestures and grimaces displaying displeasure, hesitation, resolve, and satisfaction. In short, it is perfectly possible for non-linguistic creatures to manifest not just intentions, but also choices, resolves or decisions.

A more serious difficulty for the idea of animal reasoning is that P_2 is an 'I thought,' which seems to require self-consciousness and thereby language. However, there are forms of self-awareness which do not presuppose consciousness of one's own mental phenomena (states, processes, and the like), let alone consciousness of a 'self,' and which do not require language. Great apes and dolphins, for instance, can recognize themselves – their own bodies – in mirrors and are also aware of their own status and role within complex social groups (Plotnik et al. 2006; Tomasello and Call 1997, Part II). The crucial point is that P_4 requires only such simple self-awareness, namely awareness of *one's own actions and of their consequences*. What is more, this kind of self-awareness is already implied by the very idea of intentional action. For behavior can only be explained by reference to reasons, if it is under the control of the agent, and such control clearly presupposes awareness of what one is doing. Similarly, one can ascribe wants and goals to an agent *A* only if *A* is capable of recognizing having attained what *A* wants. Yet this, again, implies self-awareness of a minimal kind. Nor should we be all that surprised by the fact that animals can be aware of what they are doing. This is a straightforward outgrowth of kinaesthetic knowledge and it is essential to the survival of higher animals, who need to adapt their behavior to changing circumstances in an intelligent manner.

Finally, great apes can choose *in a deliberate way*, that is, a way which is controlled and responsive to the situation. For instance chimpanzees choose tools for cracking nuts or for hunting insects in a deliberate and foresightful way, often without seeing the location in which the tool is to be used. Furthermore, as indicated above, this process closely resembles human instrumental reasoning in concrete situations. Therefore we can speak here of deliberation, if not reasoning. Some non-linguistic creatures can weigh the conflicting claims of objective features of the situation, including their own behavior, and act accordingly.

Animal Action

There is no reason for denying that some animals are capable of acting for reasons. The attempts to sustain this denial are either question-begging or fallacious, or they lead to conclusions such as that animals cannot do things intentionally or because they want to do them, or that they cannot adapt their behavior to their goals and circumstances, or even that they cannot perceive. And these conclusions are unpalatable or worse.

Nevertheless, let us grant, for the sake of argument, that animals cannot act in the light of reasons and that our practice of applying intentional explanations to their behavior can somehow be debunked. In that case we would have to conclude that animals cannot act for reasons at all. Would we also have to conclude that they cannot *act* at all, but merely display behavior? Were the behaviorists right to insist that, at least strictly speaking, all animal activity, however evolved and plastic, ultimately reduces to mechanical reactions?

There is only one point in favor of such a radical conclusion. We speak more readily of animal behavior than of acts which animals perform (Hacker 2007: 140). On the other hand, when we turn from highly general terms like 'action' and 'behavior' to specific action verbs, the picture is very different. Animals can do, and actually do, many of the things that we do. They forage and search, hunt and kill prey, eat, court, and mate, defend their off-spring, groom, and the like. Some of them also play, prepare and hide food, manufacture and use tools, form alliances, fight, make up, and so on. This way of describing and explaining animal activity is tried and tested. Nor should we concede that animals can act only in an attenuated sense. On the contrary, the kind of activity we share with higher animals is *not* a limiting case of action, but the *basic* and *paradigmatic* one. It is the kind of activity one can invoke to explain what an action is, or what it is to do something. As Goethe's *Faust* wisely reminds us, in the beginning was the deed rather than the word. Therefore, even if animals could not act for reasons, their behavior could still be purposive and flexible enough to qualify as agency.

See also: REASONS AND CAUSES (17); TRIGGERING AND STRUCTURING CAUSES (18); MOTIVATING REASONS (19); AGENCY, PATIENCY, AND PERSONHOOD (26); PRACTICAL REASONING (31); ACTION IN COGNITIVE ETHOLOGY (49); DAVIDSON (73).

References

Alvarez, M. (2010). *Kinds of Reasons: An Essay in the Philosophy of Action*. Oxford: Oxford University Press.

Brandom, R. (2010). Conceptual content and discursive practice. *Grazer Philosophische Studien*, 81, 13–36.

Dancy, J. (2000). *Practical Reality*. Oxford: Oxford University Press.

Davidson, D. (1980). *Essays on Actions and Events*. Oxford: Oxford University Press.

Davidson, D. (2001). *Subjective, Intersubjective, Objective*. Oxford: Oxford University Press.

Frankfurt, H. (2004). *The Reasons of Love*. Princeton: Princeton University Press.

Glock, H.-J. (2000). Animals, thoughts and concepts. *Synthese*, 123, 35–64.

Glock, H.-J. (2009). Can animals act for reasons? *Inquiry*, 52, 232–254.

Glock, H.-J. (2010). Can animals judge? *Dialectica*, 64, 11–34.
Hacker, P. M. S. (2007). *Human Nature: The Categorical Framework*. Oxford: Blackwell.
Hornsby, J. (1997). *Simple Mindedness*. Cambridge, MA: Harvard University Press.
Hurley, S. (2006). Making sense of animals. In Hurley and Nudds (eds), 139–171.
Hurley, S., and Nudds, M. (eds) (2006). *Rational Animals*. Oxford: Oxford University Press.
Hyman, J. (1999). How knowledge works. *Philosophical Quarterly*, 49, 433–451.
Kacelnik, A. (2006). Meanings of rationality. In Hurley and Nudds (eds), 87–106.
Kenny, A. J. P. (1989). *The Metaphysics of Mind*. Oxford: Oxford University Press.
MacIntyre, A. (1999). *Dependent Rational Animals*. London: Duckworth.
McDowell, J. (1996). *Mind and World*. Cambridge, MA: Harvard University Press.
Plotnik, J. M., de Waal, F. B. M., and Reiss, D. (2006). Self-recognition in an Asian elephant. *Proceedings of the National Academy of Sciences*, 103, 17053–17057.
Povinelli, D., and Vonk, J. (2006). We don't need a microscope to explore the chimpanzee's mind. In Hurley and Nudds (eds), 385–412.
Ryle, G. (1949). *The Concept of Mind*. London: Hutchinson.
Stout, R. (2005). *Action*. Dublin: Acumen Press.
Tomasello, M., and Call, J. (1997). *Primate Cognition*. Oxford: Oxford University Press.
Tomasello, M., and Call, J. (2006). Do chimpanzees know what others see – or only what they are looking at? In Hurley and Nudds (eds), 371–384.

49

Action in Cognitive Ethology

MARC BEKOFF

Introduction

Understanding the actions that animals perform during different contexts is central to learning about what animals know, desire, intend, believe, and feel. While philosophical discussions of action theory focus almost exclusively on humans, there is quite a lot of information stemming from cognitive ethological investigations of animals, which can inform discussion among people who do not spend much time watching other animals, or who focus on non-human primates to the exclusion of other groups. Cognitive ethologists are breaking new ground almost daily about the surprising cognitive abilities of a wide range of animals, and these data are essential for informing philosophical inquiries about the nature of animal minds – what is in them and how they process information. Because of the rapid accumulation of comparative data, there is less guesswork about what animals know, desire, intend, believe, and feel.

Cognitive ethology is the comparative, evolutionary, and ecological study of non-human animal minds, including thought processes, beliefs, rationality, information processing, emotions and feelings, and consciousness. Cognitive ethology traces its beginnings to the writings of Charles Darwin and some of his contemporaries and followers. Their approach incorporated appeals to evolutionary theory, interests in mental continuity (where it is argued that differences among species are differences of degree rather than of kind), concerns with individual, intraspecific (within species), and interspecific (between species) variation, strong interests in the worlds of the animals themselves, close associations with natural history, and attempts to learn more about the behavior of animals in conditions that are as close as possible to the natural environment where selection has occurred. In addition, cognitive ethologists are concerned with the diversity of solutions that living organisms have found for common problems; they emphasize broad taxonomic comparisons and do not focus on a few select representatives of limited taxa such as laboratory rats, pigeons, or non-human primates. People often inform their views on cognitive ethology and on the cognitive and emotional capacities of animals by appealing to studies of non-human primates, especially of the great apes, and ignore the fact that there are many other animals who also show interesting patterns of behavior, which lend themselves to cognitive analyses and explanations that broaden action theory. The rise of modern cognitive ethology is dated from the publication of Donald Griffin's *The Question of Animal Awareness* in 1976.

Cognitive ethology helps to broaden the perspective of cognitive studies in two ways. First, it helps to situate the study of cognition in an evolutionary framework. It should be a necessary condition for postulating a cognitive state in a human being that the existence of this state is at least consistent with evolutionary history. Although lip service is sometimes given to this constraint, talk of evolution in cognitive science is often metaphorical. Cognitive ethology has the potential to make cognitive science take evolution seriously. Second, because cognitive ethology sheds light on similarities and differences among closely and distantly related species, the sorts of studies undertaken within it contribute to making cognitive science more broadly comparative. Many people are more willing to countenance cognition in computers, or in aliens from space, than in rodents, amphibians, or insects. Even in cognitive studies there is a tendency to view cognition as 'essential' to humans, and as instantiated to various degrees – usually lesser – only in those species that are phylogenetically close to humans. With its view of cognition as a strategic evolutionary response to problems that might have been faced by a variety of diverse organisms, cognitive ethology can help to overcome this form of parochialism.

Cognitive ethology also is critical for learning about the reasons why animals perform certain actions in specific contexts – what they desire, intend, or believe. Behavioral studies usually start with the observation, description, and categorization of behavior patterns of animals. The result of this process is the development of an ethogram, or behavioral catalog, of these actions. Ethograms present information about an action's form or morphology. Descriptions can be based on visual information (what an action looks like), auditory characteristics (sonograms, or pictures of sounds), or chemical constituents (for example, pictorial output of chromatographic analyses of glandular deposits, urine, or feces). It is essential that great care be given to the development of an ethogram, for this is an inventory that others should be able to replicate without error. Permanent records of observations allow others to cross-check their observations and descriptions against original records. The number of the actions and the breadth of the categories that are identified in a behavioral study depend on the questions at hand; but generally it is better to split rather than lump together actions in initial stages, and then lump them together when questions of interest have been carefully laid out. Detailed analyses of what animals do are central to learning about what animals are thinking and feeling, and also for informing philosophical inquiries into what animals believe, desire, and intend, and if they have a theory of mind. There is no substitute for these sorts of studies, although they are extremely time-consuming and grating on one's patience.

Comparative cognitive ethology is an important extension of classical ethology, because it explicitly licenses hypotheses about the internal states of animals in the tradition of classical ethologists such as Nobel laureates Niko Tinbergen and Konrad Lorenz. However, although ethologists such as Lorenz and Tinbergen used phrases like 'intention movements,' they used them quite differently from the way they are used in the philosophical literature. The phrase 'intention movements' in the ethological literature refers to preparatory movements that might communicate what action individuals are likely to undertake next, and not necessarily to their beliefs and desires, although one might suppose that the individuals did indeed want to fly and believed that, if they moved their wings in a certain way, they would. This distinction is important because the use of such terms does not necessarily add a cognitive dimension to classical ethological notions, although it could.

In 1963 Niko Tinbergen published a classic essay, titled 'On aims and methods of ethology' and dedicated to his friend Konrad Lorenz. This essay is a landmark in the development of ethology. Here Tinbergen defines ethology as 'the biological study of behavior' and seeks to demonstrate the 'close affinity between Ethology and the rest of Biology' (p. 411). In his early work Tinbergen identified four overlapping areas with which ethological investigations should be concerned: evolution (phylogeny), adaptation (function), causation, and development (ontogeny). His framework also is useful for those interested in animal cognition. The methods for answering questions in each of these areas vary, but all begin with the careful observation and description of the behavior patterns exhibited by the animals under study. The information provided by these initial observations allows a researcher to exploit the animal's normal behavioral repertoire so as to answer questions about the evolution, function, causation, and development of the behavior patterns exhibited in various contexts.

The tractability of cognitive questions involves the application of a diverse set of comparative methods in order to draw inferences about cognitive states and capacities. Cognitive research may include staged social encounters, playback of recorded vocalizations, the presentation of stimuli in different modalities, observation of predator–prey interactions, observation of foraging behavior, application of neurobiological techniques, and studies of social and other sorts of learning. Computer analyses are also useful for those who want to learn what kind of information must be represented in an adequate computational model.

There are no large differences between methods used to study animal cognition and methods used to study other aspects of animal behavior. Differences lay not so much in what is done and how it is done, as in how data are explained. Thus Allen and Bekoff (1997) argue that the main distinction between cognitive ethology and classical ethology lies not in the types of data collected, but in the understanding of the conceptual resources that are appropriate for explaining those data.

Dale Jamieson and this author drew a useful distinction between 'weak cognitive ethology' (WCE) and 'strong cognitive ethology' (SCE). WCE is the most common form of cognitive ethology. It countenances the use of a cognitive vocabulary for the explanation of behavior, but not for its description. SCE underwrites a range of research programs in which both cognitive and affective vocabularies are willingly employed for purposes of interpretation and explanation.

Antipredatory Behavior in Western Evening Grosbeaks and its Relevance to Action Theory

The application of the cognitive ethological approach and its usefulness in the study of action is nicely shown in a study of antipredator behavior in western evening grosbeaks. The study was laborious: single frames of videotape had to be analyzed every twentieth of a second, so that information about the birds' behavior was not lost. Bekoff found that western evening grosbeaks modified their vigilance or scanning behavior in accordance with the way in which individuals were positioned with respect to one another, whether they were organized in a circle or in a line. Grosbeaks and other birds often trade off scanning for potential predators and feeding. In essence (and with over-simplification), some birds scan while others feed, and some birds feed when others scan. Thus it is hypothesized that individuals want to know what others are doing and to learn about others' behavior by trying to watch them.

Bekoff's study of grosbeaks showed that, when a flock contained four or more birds, there were large changes in scanning and other patterns of behavior that seemed to be related to ways in which grosbeaks attempted to gather information visually about what other flock members were doing. When birds were arranged in a circular array, so that they could see one another easily, after having been arranged in a line, which made the visual monitoring of flock members more difficult, birds who had difficulty in seeing one another (1) were more vigilant, (2) changed their head and body positions more often, (3) reacted to changes in group size more slowly, (4) showed less coordination in head movements, and (5) showed more variability in all measures. The differences in behavior between birds organized in circular arrays and birds organized in linear arrays were best explained in terms of individuals' attempts to learn, via visual monitoring, about what other flock members were doing. These results say something as to whether birds attempt to represent to themselves flock members, and as to how they would do it. It may be that individuals desire to know what other birds are doing; form beliefs about it, or about what others are likely to do in a given situation; and predicate their own behavior upon these beliefs.

As a result of this study, Bekoff argued that cognitive explanations were simpler and less cumbersome than non-cognitive rule-of-thumb explanations (for instance 'Scan this way if there is this number of birds in this geometric array' or 'Scan that way if there is that number of birds in that geometric array'). Non-cognitive rule-of-thumb explanations did not seem to account for the flexibility in animals' behavior as well, or as simply, as did explanations that appealed to cognitive capacities in the animals under study. And it should be emphasized that flexibility in action depending on the context individuals find themselves in is the rule rather than the exception among most species where individuals find themselves in groups that vary in size and composition.

Social Play Behavior and Action Theory

Social play is another behavior that lends itself nicely to cognitive inquiries that can inform action theory. The study of social play involves issues of communication, intention, role-playing, and cooperation, and the results of these types of research projects yield clues about the ability of animals to understand each other's intentions. Play is also a phenomenon that occurs in a wide range of species and affords the opportunity for a comparative investigation of cognitive abilities, extending the all-too-common narrow focus on primates, which dominates discussions of non-human cognition.

While we all recognize animal play when we see it, the study of play continues to challenge students of animal behavior. Researchers are still discovering new facts about this fascinating activity by asking questions about how and why animals play and, for example, how animal play may be related to evolution and to the development of fairness, justice, and social morality (Bekoff and Pierce 2009). Almost all mammals who have been studied engage in play, and so do many birds and, perhaps, fish, reptiles, and amphibians. While play is difficult to define and study, it is recognized as a distinctive and important category of behavior.

What is play? This deceptively simple question has troubled researchers for many years. A well-received definition of social play is the one I developed with John Byers: social play is an activity directed toward another individual in which actions from other contexts are used in modified forms and in altered sequences. Our definition centers on what animals *do* when they play, or on the structure of play. Our definition also highlights the fact that, when animals play, they use actions which are also used in activities such as predation (hunting), reproduction (mating), and aggression. Full-blown threatening and submitting occur only rarely, if ever, during play. During play actions may be changed in their form and intensity and combined in a wide variety of unpredictable sequences. Among polecats, coyotes, and American black bears, biting in play-fighting is inhibited by comparison with biting in real fighting. Clawing in bears is also inhibited and less intense (see the section on self-handicapping below). Also, play in bears is non-vocal, and biting and clawing are directed to more parts of the body of another individual during play than during aggression.

It is extremely difficult to describe or explain play behavior without using a cognitive vocabulary. One and the same bodily movement can represent fighting, preying, mating, or playing. The difference between a movement that is aggressive and one that is playful is naturally described in terms of one animal's intention and another animal's appreciation of the intention. There are also differences in the form and duration of the same basic actions, such as biting or hip-slamming one's playmate. Similarly, the cognitive vocabulary appears to provide the resources for explaining some play behavior. For example, suppose that we want to know why Zeke (a dog) permitted Jethro (another dog) to nip at his ears. One explanation may be that Zeke believes that Jethro is playing. This gives rise to further questions, such as whether Jethro believes that Zeke believes that Jethro is playing.

To learn about the dynamics of play, it is essential to pay attention to extremely subtle details, which are otherwise lost in superficial analyses. Dogs and other animals keep track of what is happening when they play, so we need to do this too when we study it.

By studying play we can learn about what may be going on in other individuals' minds, what they are thinking about, what they want, and what they are likely to do during a social encounter. Because of the intermingling of actions from various contexts in unpredictable sequences, it is important to ask questions such as 'How do animals know that they are playing?'; 'How do they communicate their desires or intentions to play or to continue to play?'; and 'How is the playing mood maintained?'

A detailed study of the structure of play signals and play sequences in canids (primarily young dogs, wolves, and coyotes) conducted by this author showed that the 'bow' – a gesture by which an animal crouches on its forepaws, elevates its hind end, and may wag its tail – is not only used to solicit play, but also (and very often) *immediately* before and *immediately* after an action which can be misinterpreted and disrupt ongoing social play. Bows occur almost exclusively in the context of social play. To gather these data, animals were videotaped while playing, and single frames were then analyzed, so as to reveal where the bows were performed during an ongoing play sequence. An earlier study established that the bow is a highly stereotyped, ritualized action, which is used as a social signal to solicit play: it stimulates recipients to engage in, or to continue to engage in, social play (see Figure 49.1 and details in the accompanying legend).

To illustrate how animals communicate their intentions and desires to play, consider domesticated dogs and their wild relatives. A dog typically asks another to play by bowing. Bows occur throughout play sequences, but most commonly they are performed at the beginning or towards the middle of playful encounters. Bows help to establish a 'play mood.' Play bows are always more stereotyped when they are performed at the beginning rather than in the middle of ongoing play sequences.

It is important for individuals to tell others that they want to play with them and not to fight with them, or eat them, or mate with them; and this message is sent by play-soliciting signals such as the bow. In canids and other mammals, actions such as biting, accompanied by rapid side-to-side shaking of the head, are used in aggressive interactions and also during predation, and could be misinterpreted when used in play. Bekoff hypothesized that, if bites accompanied by rapid side-to-side shaking of the head or other behavior patterns could be misread by the recipient and could result in a fight, for example, then the animal who performed the actions that could be misinterpreted might have to communicate to its partner that this action was performed in the context of play and was not meant to be taken as an aggressive or predatory move. On this view, bows would not occur randomly in play sequences: the play atmosphere would be reinforced and maintained by performing bows immediately before or after actions that could be misinterpreted.

To solve the problems that might be caused by confusing play with mating or fighting, many species have evolved signals such as the bow, which function to establish and maintain a play 'mood.' I discovered that infant domestic dogs, wolves, and coyotes used bows non-randomly, especially when biting accompanied by rapid side-to-side shaking of the head was performed. Youngsters were intentionally using bows with a purpose in mind. Bows are used right at the beginning of play, to tell another dogs 'I want to play with you,' and they are also used right before biting, being accompanied by a rapid side-to-side head shaking, as if to say 'I'm going to bite you hard but it's still in play,' and right after vigorous biting, as if to say 'I'm sorry I just bit you so hard but it was play.' Biting accompanied by rapid side-to-side shaking of the head is performed during serious aggressive and predatory encounters and can easily be misinterpreted if its meaning is not modified by a play signal. Bows essentially serve as punctuation, an exclamation point (!), to call attention to what the dog wants to tell his friend. Bows reduce the likelihood of aggression.

Play signals are what ethologists call 'honest signals.' There is little evidence that social play is a manipulative activity, and play signals are rarely used to deceive others. My own long-term studies of young dogs, coyotes, and wolves show that deceptive signaling is so rare that I cannot recall more than a few occurrences in thousands of play sequences. Cheaters are unlikely to be chosen as play partners; the others can simply refuse to play with them and choose others. Infant coyotes who mislead others into playing so as to dominate them have difficulty persuading other young coyotes to play with them. The message is clear: Don't bow if you don't want to play.

The results of Bekoff's study of different canids support the inference that bows provide information about other actions, which followed or preceded them, and about the goals, beliefs, and intentions of the players. When an animal (Jethro) performs a play bow to ask another animal (Zeke) to play, Jethro intends to play and, if Zeke responds in a playful manner, he believes that Zeke wants to play too and will abide by the rules of the game. When a play bow is used before a hard bite, it signals, say, Jethro's intention to play despite what he is going to do; and when Jethro performs a bow after

Figure 49.1 Dog (right) performing a bow to initiate play with his friend (left). To learn more about the structure of bows – an action which is critical for animals to be able to play with one another and for us to know that play is the name of the game – detailed film analyses were conducted of this action. Animals were photographed with a super-8 or 16-mm movie camera (film speed, 64 frames per second). Films were analyzed with a single-frame analyzer. Camera speed was checked prior to each analysis, to correct for possible error. Both duration and form were measured for bows that occurred at the beginning of a sequence (that is, the first act) and during a sequence. Duration was measured by counting the number of frames during which the individual remained crouched. The number of frames was then multiplied by 0.0156 second (= 1 frame) to convert to a measure of time. Means, standard deviations, and coefficients of variation were then calculated. Form was measured as declination of the shoulders relative to standing height on a grid system (= a in the figure). In order to standardize for individual differences in size as well as for changes in size with age, the height of the body at the shoulders was divided by 10, and a grid system of ten equal segments was used. Each grid unit was divided into fourths. Two observers independently took measures for each data point, and measurements were taken only when vertical displacement of the shoulders could be observed unambiguously. Inter-observer agreement was consistently between 90 and 95 percent. For each group of animals, data from different rearing conditions were lumped, because no significant differences were detected. In addition, data for the wolves and wolf-malamute hybrids were combined, because the two groups were indistinguishable. Photo from Bekoff (1977)

a hard bite he is telling Zeke that he still wants to play, and wants Zeke to forgive this transgression. The basic rules of social play are: ask first; be honest; mind your manners; and admit when you're wrong. Non-cognitive rules-of-thumb. 'Play this way if this happens' and 'Play that way if that happens' are far too rigid explanations for dealing with the flexible behavior that the animals show when they are playing.

The study of antipredatory behavior in western evening grosbeaks and the analysis of social play behavior in various canids show clearly that cognitive ethological investigations are essential for coming to terms with what animals do in certain contexts and why. We can learn much about intentions, beliefs, and desires, for example, by taking the time to study the actions that are performed in different situations. Then a richer understanding of philosophical theorizing will surely follow the resurgence of time-consuming studies of animal cognition.

See also: ACTION THEORY AND ONTOLOGY (1); PLURALISM ABOUT ACTION (12); THE EXPLANATORY ROLE OF CONSCIOUSNESS (24); WHAT A DIFFERENCE EMOTIONS MAKE (25); ANIMAL AGENCY (48).

References

Allen, C., and Bekoff, M. (1997). *Species of Mind: The Philosophy and Biology of Cognitive Ethology*. Cambridge, MA: MIT Press.

Bekoff, M. (1977). Social communication in canids: Evidence for the evolution of a stereotyped mammalian display. *Science*, 197, 1097–1099.

Bekoff, M., and Pierce, J. (2009). *Wild Justice: The Moral Lives of Animals*. Chicago: University of Chicago Press.

Tinbergen, N. (1963). On aims and methods of ethology. *Zeitschrift fur Tierpsychologie*, 20, 410–429.

Further reading

Bekoff, M. (1995). Play signals as punctuation: the structure of social play in canids. *Behaviour*, 132, 419–29.

Bekoff, M. (1995). Vigilance, flock size, and flock geometry: Information gathering by western evening grosbeaks (*Aves fringillidae*). *Ethology*, 99, 150–161.

Bekoff, M. (1995). Cognitive ethology and the explanation of nonhuman animal behavior. In J.-A. Meyer and H. Roitblat (eds), *Comparative Approaches to Cognitive Science*, Cambridge, MA: MIT Press, 119–150.

Bekoff, M. (1996). Cognitive ethology, vigilance, information gathering, and representation: Who might know what and why? *Behavioural Processes*, 35, 225–237.

Bekoff, M. (1998). Cognitive ethology: The comparative study of animal minds. In W. Bechtel and G. Graham (eds), *The Blackwell Companion to Cognitive Science*. Oxford: Blackwell, 371–379.

Bekoff, M. (2007). *The Emotional Lives of Animals: A Leading Scientist Explores Animal Joy, Sorrow, and Empathy – and Why They Matter*. Novato, CA: New World Library.

Griffin, D. R. (1992). *Animal Minds*. Chicago: University of Chicago Press.

Jamieson, D., and Bekoff, M. (1993). On aims and methods of cognitive ethology. *Philosophy of Science Association*, 2, 110–124.

50

Action in History and Social Science

DANIEL LITTLE

If we take the view that social outcomes and historical changes are ultimately the result of the actions of individuals within social relations and constraints, then we plainly need to have a nuanced and satisfactory framework of analysis within which to understand 'action.' Rational choice theory is one such framework. But social scientists and historians have made it plain that the origins, motives, dynamics, and meanings of individual actions are broader and more heterogeneous than these rational–intentional theories would suggest. Purposive, calculated action is an important part of the story of social action – but it is only a part.

Fundamentally, the concept of action comes down to 'persons intervening intentionally.' Persons commit actions. Persons have beliefs, desires, intentions, plans, and goals; they have reasons for what they do; they have emotions and aversions; they have habits. Persons also have freedom: they have the ability to choose to act or not to act, in typical circumstances.

This construction emphasizes the role of deliberation in action. Deliberation involves explicit consideration of one's goals, of the opportunities that are currently available within the environment of choice, and of the advantages and disadvantages of the various choices. Deliberation results in deliberate, planned choice. This represents the category of agency that is partially captured by rational choice theory: deliberate analysis of means and ends, and a calculating choice among possible actions. Planning is an extended version of this process, in which the actor attempts to orchestrate a series of actions and responses in such a way as to bring about a long-term goal (Bratman 1987).

All these components support the idea of the agent as a conscious, intentional intervener: the agent intervenes in the world in some way, in order to bring about an outcome that she desires or intends, on the basis of her beliefs about the causal relationships that exist between the intervention and the outcome. Purpose, beliefs, freedom to choose, and selected intervention fit together as an integrated ideal type of 'action.'

This construction fits together into the Aristotelian idea of purposive action, or rational–intentional action (Aristotle 1987). But consider a few variations of individual behavior, which seem to point in a different direction: behavior following a script, reflexive or instinctive behavior, impulsive behavior, self-destructive behavior, self-deceptive behavior, possessed behavior, coerced behavior. In each instance we lose an element that plays a key role in the purposive/intentional description of action above:

self-direction, intentionality, self-control, rational goals and purposes, and freedom. We might take these instances to describe cases of behavior that fall short of 'action'; or we might hold that there is a range of degrees of intentionality associated with action, from fully free and deliberative choice to programmed or impulsive behaviors. We return to these issues below.

Rational choice theory has been a particularly compelling basis for theory formation in several of the social sciences (Elster 1979, 1986). It is appealing because it is an *agent-centered* approach to social explanation: it explains the social outcome on the basis of an analysis of the beliefs, intentions, and circumstances of the individual agents who make up the social setting. What rational choice theory adds to this description is a specification of the decision-making processes which are attributed to the individual agent – typically, that the agent has a consistent set of preferences among accessible alternatives and that she chooses in such a way as to maximize the satisfaction of this set of preferences. (This is referred to as the 'preference satisfaction' model of choice.) Various objections have been offered against rational choice theory as a basis for social explanation – for example, that it overlooks social motivations, that it presupposes egoism, that it over-simplifies the logic of practical reasoning, or that it fails to correspond to typical human behavior. (See Green and Shapiro 1994 and Friedman 1996 for a developed set of critiques and responses.)

Two points are worth underlining here. First, rational choice theory has a major theoretical advantage precisely because it is an agent-centered framework. Rational choice theory is one possible way of articulating a set of hypotheses about how individuals reason and act. This is a major advantage in comparison to explanatory frameworks that essentially assume programmed behavior on the part of participants in a social event. Moreover, the assumption of preference-satisfaction lines up pretty well with a somewhat broader conception of human action in terms of goal-directedness and purposiveness. If we believe that individuals have goals and purposes which underlie their choices and actions, then it is an appealing simplification to represent their actions as the outcome of deliberation about goals, strategies, and circumstances. In other words, rational choice theory can be seen as a specification of a philosophical idea of human action that is at least as old as Aristotle: the idea of individuals as deliberative and purposive agents. And this is in fact a credible and empirically defensible theory of action.

But a second point is equally important: rational choice theory, with its model of utility maximization, is only one out of a range of possible specifications of the idea of deliberation and purposiveness. There are important alternative specifications that can be offered. For example we might say, along with Kant, that individuals possess a set of moral rules as well as a set of specific goals, and that they deliberate among possible choices of action on the basis of both considerations (Kant 1990; Gert 1970). How do the various possible actions conform to the moral rules? And how do they do from the point of view of accomplishing my goals? This process of reasoning is 'deontological' – that is, it cannot be subsumed under a simple model of maximizing rationality. It is, nonetheless, an intelligible interpretation of what rational human decision-making involves.

A less restrictive conception of human agency maintains that real human social behavior is a complex mix of commitments, loyalties, emotions, solidarities – as well as purposes and goals (Sen 1987; Scott 1976; McAdam 1999). So a theory of action that isolates 'goal-directedness' and its associated framework of utility maximizing is one that already overlooks a set of motivational factors that are crucial to explaining real social behavior.

So far we have focused on individual agency. What is involved in acting as a group? This is the central idea that Max Weber explores in his conception of social action: action which is oriented to the actions of other individuals (Weber 1947). What is the difference between a crowd of pedestrians crossing the street when the light changes and a group of students marching into a university building in an attempt to initiate a protest, or a business person 'dressing for success'? In each of the latter instances, the individual's action is constructed out of consideration for the behavior and intentions of other people.

Consider, first, group activity. How does a collection of individuals constitute a group? Group activity requires some level of collective intentions and purposes on the part of the participants – toward each other and toward the group itself. A group is more than an ensemble of individuals performing a similar set of actions (say, pedestrians or independent steel workers). Rather, we expect some indication that the individuals regard themselves as members of the group; that they embrace some conception of the action which the other members of the group propose to perform; and that they, individually, choose their plans of action out of consideration for this group or collective purpose. In a group's actions, the individuals who make up the group are oriented toward the group and its goals and purposes. In other words, groups are constituted by some form of group-oriented intentionality on the part of individual members, and group actions are performed by individuals who have adopted a set of beliefs and attitudes toward other members of the group and toward its collective purposes.

How about the other example – dressing for success? This also counts as a 'social action,' according to Weber's definition. The individual is choosing his wardrobe out of consideration for the tastes, judgments, and behaviors of other individuals. He expects to elicit more favorable responses from the people he engages with by wearing the red silk tie rather than the silver bolo tie. The behavior is adaptive and socially sensitive; if the tastes of the professional space change suddenly, the individual's wardrobe will be adjusted accordingly. And, if business is to be done in Albuquerque, then the bolo tie may be reconsidered.

Several philosophers have focused on the set of problems surrounding 'group intentions' (Gilbert 1989; Tuomela 1995; Giddens 1979). Gilbert and Tuomela argue that there is a level of group agency separate from the agency and thoughts of the individuals who make up the group. This is not a credible view; ultimately, groups have no properties that do not supervene upon the properties and states of mind of the individuals who make them up. As Weber insisted throughout his work, ultimately the social sciences need to be constrained by a reasonable principle of methodological individualism.

That said, there is still a crucial role for group-oriented thoughts and purposes at the level of at least some of the participants in a group. Without these group intentions at the individual level, we could not say that there is a group at all – only a collection of individually oriented individual actors. Individuals within a group must somehow represent their social space in a way that reflects group membership. And there must be some tangible process of communication and mobilization through which the group-oriented intentional states mentioned here are created in the various individuals.

Another aspect of social action is the category of social norms. We might define a norm as a socially embodied and individually perceived imperative that such-and-so an action must be performed in such-and-so a fashion. How do norms influence action? There seem to be only three possible answers, and each one is socially and psychologically possible:

1 The imperative may be internalized into the motivational space of the individual, so she chooses to act according to the imperative (or is habituated to acting in such a way).
2 There may be an effective and well-known system of sanctions that attach to violations of the norms, so the individual has an incentive to comply. These sanctions may be formal or informal. The sanction may be as benign as being laughed at for wearing a Hawaiian shirt to a black tie ball, or as severe as being beaten for making a Texas joke in a cowboy bar.
3 Or there may be benefits from conformity, which make the latter a choice that is in the actor's rational self-interest. (Every time one demonstrates that he can choose the right fork for dessert, the likelihood of being invited to another formal dinner increases.)

Each of these points would make sense of the fact that an individual conforms her behavior to the requirements of a norm and would help to answer the question: Why do individuals conform to norms?

Consider a specific kind of social action, cooperation. Why do people cooperate when it is not in their self-interest to do so? Standard rational choice theory implies that cooperation should be unstable in the face of free-riding. This was Mancur Olson's central conclusion in his classic book about collective action (Olson 1965). Roughly, his conclusion was that cooperation would be possible only if there were excludable side benefits for participants, selective coercion to enforce cooperation, or privatization of the gains of collective action. However, we know from many social contexts that individuals do in fact succeed in establishing cooperative relationships without any of these supporting conditions. So what are we missing when we consider social action from the narrow perspective of rational choice theory?

A part of the answer to this puzzle involves the role of norms in action. Here the criticism is that the rational–intentional approach, by attending solely to calculations of self-interest, is blind to the workings of normative frameworks; but in fact norms are powerful factors underlying behavior in most traditional contexts. According to this perspective, traditional societies are communities: tightly cohesive groups of persons sharing a distinctive set of values in stable, continuing relations to one another (Taylor 1976, 1982). The central threats to security and welfare are well known to such groups – excessive or deficient rainfall, attacks by bandits, predatory tax policies by the central government, and so on. And village societies have evolved schemes of shared values and cooperative practices and institutions that are well adapted to handle these problems of risk and welfare in ways which protect the subsistence needs of all villagers adequately in all but the most extreme circumstances. Theorists in this perspective thus maintain that traditions and norms are fundamental social factors and that individual behavior is almost always modulated through powerful traditional motivational constraints. (An important empirical defense of this perspective can be found in the work of Elinor Ostrom and her fellow researchers in their treatment of 'common property resource regimes': Ostrom 1990).

The account of action up to this point has focused on a particular cluster of features of action: purposiveness and choice, deliberation, planning, and improvisation. Here we turn to the idea of action as a performance – a series of behaviors meaningfully orchestrated by the actor out of consideration for an expected 'script.' Here we interpret actions as falling into scripts and roles created by the culture's history and constituting the actor's behaviors as a performance. The agent is postulated to possess a stock of mini-scripts and role expectations, which are then invoked into a 'syntax' of performance in specific social settings.

The anthropologist Victor Turner makes central use of this framework in constructing his ethnographies (1974). He refers to this approach as 'dramaturgical ethnography.' The idea here is that social groups – cultures – have created for themselves a set of schemes of ways of behaving which individuals internalize and play out as social settings arise. There are the roles of the doctor, the salesman, the librarian, the clown, and the general, and the individuals who assume these roles know the scripts. So, when they interact in social settings relevant to their roles, their behaviors reflect the role and the script. The scripts become part of the furniture of 'behavioral cognition' – the routines the players string together in ordinary and extraordinary social settings. And perhaps the script governs the social actor so deeply that her behavior no longer has its own individual meaning or intention.

There is an important parallel here with Erving Goffman's treatment of everyday behavior (Goffman 1974, 1980), and urban anthropologists and sociologists are often interested in providing micro-descriptions of social behaviors as well – for example Whyte (1993) or Liebow (1967). Goffman's central insight is this: It is apparent that there are patterns in the ordinary social interactions between individuals in various societies. Whether and how to greet an acquaintance or a stranger, how close people stand together, how loudly people speak, what subjects they turn to in idle social conversation, how conflict is handled – all of these topics, and more, seem to have specific and nuanced answers in various specific social environments. It seems likely enough that there are persistent differences at this level of social behavior across city, profession, gender, race, and class. And these embodied features of social practice are an important component of social action and behavior.

The school of ethnomethodology also attempts to provide this kind of detailed observation and description. This approach is illustrated, for example, by Harold Garfinkel's descriptions of the procedures embodied in the practices of professional accountants or lawyers (1967). A major objective of the method is to arrive at an interpretation of the rules that underlie everyday activity and thus constitute part of the normative basis of a given social order. Research from this perspective generally focuses on mundane forms of social activity – for instance psychiatrists evaluating patients' files, jurors deliberating on defendants' culpability, or coroners judging causes of death. The investigator then attempts to reconstruct an underlying set of rules and ad hoc procedures that may be taken to have guided the observed activity. The approach emphasizes the contextuality of social practice – the richness of unspoken shared understandings that guide and orient participants' actions in a given practice or activity.

So there are fairly tangible ways in which the behaviors of members in small social groups are in fact governed by scripts and roles. The dramaturgical interpretation makes sense here. The actions of these participants are not invented *de novo* in the moment; rather, they derive from earlier practice of the roles and, more intangibly, they carry out a certain conception of the behavior suited to a specific social role. We don't get actions here that derive from unadorned actors, who consider a range of choices and choose the best in the given circumstances.

But neither do we get the opposite extreme – robots playing out their scripts without intelligence or adaptation to circumstance. Individuals retain instead their own assessment of what is currently going on and of what deviations may be demanded from the script. The individual retains the ability to break with procedures when there is an imminent reason to do so; and this degree of autonomy extends throughout the complex of social interactions. So the routines and scripts guide rather than generate the behavior.

Hence the performative interpretation of social action is not inherently inconsistent with the idea of intelligent, purposive action. Instead, we can think of the actor in this case as being involved in a complicated series of behaviors that reflect both deliberation and internalized script. This interpretation is very analogous to Pierre Bourdieu's position on the subject of *habitus* in *Outline of a Theory of Practice* (Bourdieu 1977). Conduct that is guided by norms (in this case, scripts and roles) can nonetheless also be intelligent and strategic. Seen in this light, the dramaturgical interpretation supplements the purposive theory of action rather than replaces it.

Let us close by considering a debate that has much relevance to an agent-centered approach to historical explanation: the covering-law debate. A major source of debate in the philosophy of history since the 1950s has concerned the role of law-governed regularities in historical change. Carl Hempel maintained that historical explanation resembled scientific explanation in requiring an appeal to laws (Hempel 1942, 1965). This view derives from Hempel's idea that all scientific explanation is of this nature; so if there is such a thing as an explanation of historical events and trends, it, too, must take the form of a deductive–nomothetic argument. Numerous philosophers and historians have taken issue with this view in its application to historical explanation. Central among the critics are Patrick Gardiner (1952), William Dray (1957), and Alan Donagan (1966). Several chief concerns about the covering-law model arose in the course of this debate: that historical explanation involves interpretation of motives and meanings rather than derivations from natural laws; that historical events are unique and therefore not amenable to generalizing explanations; that working historians almost never explicitly refer to strong laws or regularities in their accounts; that, when generalizations are invoked in historical explanations, they are often trivial; and that human freedom in action makes law-governed derivations of historical outcomes impossible in principle. There is also the complication that most explanations in natural science invoke probabilistic laws rather than exceptionless regularities; but this does not make the covering-law model any more appropriate as a basis for understanding the logic of historical events.

The covering-law model is deeply unsatisfactory as a model of historical explanation. A more compelling approach relies on two ideas: the idea of social–causal mechanisms that can be investigated directly, and the idea of the purposiveness and intentionality of historical actors. If we want to explain why Roman warfare was usually seasonal, it suffices to observe that Roman armies were only poorly supported by logistical systems and were heavily dependent on food and shelter locally requisitioned, and to think through how intelligent commanders would design campaign plans in light of these constraints (Goldsworthy 1996). In other words, we can explain a historical outcome by investigating the background circumstances within which agents made their decisions about the action which led to that outcome; we can examine the systemic and causal interconnections that exist among these conditions; and we can offer interpretations of the actions of the major categories of actors who made up the historical moment in light of these circumstances. This account specifies an understanding of historical explanation which is both causal and interpretive; it gives a role to generalizations; but it finds that the historian's work is generally at the level of discovering the concrete causal and purposive pathways through which historical events unfold.

Karl Popper's critique of 'historicism' is a widely discussed contribution to the understanding of history in mid-twentieth century (Popper 1957), and one that is highly relevant to the question of laws in history. Popper characterizes historicism as

> an approach to the social sciences which assumes that historical prediction is their principal aim, and which assumes that this aim is attainable by discovering the 'rhythms' or the 'patterns,' the 'laws' or the 'trends' that underlie the evolution of history. (ibid., p. 3)

Historicists differ from naturalists, however, in that they believe that the laws which govern history are themselves historically changeable. So a given historical epoch has its own laws and generalizations – unlike the laws of nature, which are uniform across time and space. So historicism involves combining two ideas: prediction of historical change on the basis of a formulation of general laws or patterns; and a recognition that historical laws and patterns are themselves variable over time, in a reflection of human agency. Popper's central conclusion is that large predictions of historical or social outcomes are inherently unjustifiable. He finds that 'holistic' or 'utopian' historical predictions depend upon assumptions which simply cannot be justified; and he prefers instead 'piecemeal' predictions and interventions (ibid., p. 21).

What Popper calls 'historicism' amounts to the aspiration that there should be a comprehensive science of society which permits the prediction of whole future states of the social system, and also supports a re-engineering of the social system, if we choose. In other words, historicism in his description sounds quite a bit like social physics: the aspiration to find a theory that describes and predicts the total state of society. Popper rejects the feasibility or appropriateness of this vision of social knowledge, and he is right to do so. The social world is not amenable to this kind of general theoretical representation.

The social thinker who serves as Popper's example of this kind of holistic social theory is Karl Marx. According to Popper, Marx's *Capital* (1977 [1867]) was intended as a general theory of capitalist society, designed to provide a basis for predicting its future and its specific internal changes over time. Marx's theory of historical materialism ('History is a history of class conflict,' 'History is the unfolding of the contradictions between the forces and relations of production' (Marx and Engels 1970 [1845/49]; Marx and Engels 1974 [1848]) is Popper's central example of a holistic theory of history. And it is Marx's theory of revolution that provides a central example for Popper, under the category of utopian social engineering. Elsewhere I argue that Popper's representation of Marx's intentions is flawed (Little 1986); but his general point is correct. Sociology and economics cannot provide us with general theories that permit the prediction of large historical change.

Popper's critique of historicism, then, can be rephrased as a compelling critique of naturalism as a metatheory for the social and historical sciences. History and society are not law-governed systems for which we might eventually hope to find exact and comprehensive theories. Instead, they are the heterogeneous, plastic, and contingent compound of actions, structures, causal mechanisms, and conjunctures that elude systematization and prediction. And this conclusion brings us back to the centrality of agent-centered explanations of historical outcomes.

See also: COLLECTIVE ACTION (9); INTENTION (14); RATIONALITY (36); INTENTIONAL ACTION IN FOLK PSYCHOLOGY (45); THE PREDICTION OF ACTION (51); HUME (63); WEBER (67); RICŒUR (75).

References

Aristotle (1987). *The Nicomachean Ethics*. Buffalo, NY: Prometheus Books.

Bourdieu, P. (1977). *Outline of a Theory of Practice*. Cambridge: Cambridge University Press.

Bratman, M. (1987). *Intention, Plans, and Practical Reason*. Cambridge, MA: Harvard University Press.

Donagan, A. (1966). The Popper–Hempel theory reconsidered. In W. H. Dray (ed.), *Philosophical Analysis and History*. New York: Harper and Row, 127–159.

Dray, W. (1957). *Laws and Explanation in History*. London: Oxford University Press.

Elster, J. (1979). *Ulysses and the Sirens: Studies in Rationality and Irrationality*. Cambridge and New York: Cambridge University Press.

Elster, J. (ed.) (1986). *Rational Choice, Readings in Social and Political Theory*. Washington Square, NY: New York University Press.

Friedman, J. (1996). *The Rational Choice Controversy: Economic Models of Politics Reconsidered*. New Haven, CT: Yale University Press.

Gardiner, P. L. (1952). *The Nature of Historical Explanation*. London: Oxford University Press.

Garfinkel, H. (1967). *Studies in Ethnomethodology*. Englewood Cliffs, NJ: Prentice-Hall.

Gert, B. (1970). *The Moral Rules: A New Rational Foundation for Morality*, 1st edn. New York: Harper and Row.

Giddens, A. (1979). *Central Problems in Social Theory: Action, Structure and Contradiction in Social Analysis*. Berkeley: University of California Press.

Gilbert, M. (1989). *On Social Facts*. Princeton: Princeton University Press.

Goffman, E. (1974). *Frame Analysis: An Essay on the Organization of Experience*. New York: Harber and Row.

Goffman, E. (1980). *Behavior in Public Places: Notes on the Social Organization of Gatherings*. Westport, CT: Greenwood Press.

Goldsworthy, A. K. (1996). *The Roman Army at War, 100 BC–AD 200*, Oxford and New York: Clarendon Press and Oxford University Press (Oxford Classical Monographs series).

Green, D. P., and Shapiro, I. (1994). *Pathologies of Rational Choice Theory: A Critique of Applications in Political Science*. New Haven: Yale University Press.

Hempel, C. G. (1942). The function of general laws in history. *The Journal of Philosophy*, 39 (2), 35–48.

Hempel, C. G. (1965). *Aspects of Scientific Explanation, and Other Essays in the Philosophy of Science*. New York: Free Press.

Kant, I. (1990). *Foundations of the Metaphysics of Morals and What is Enlightenment*, 2nd rev. edn. New York: Macmillan (The Library of Liberal Arts).

Liebow, E. (1967). *Tally's Corner: A Study of Negro Streetcorner Men*. Boston: Little, Brown.

Little, D. (1986). *The Scientific Marx*. Minneapolis: University of Minnesota Press.

Marx, K. (1977). *Capital* Vol. 1 [1867]. New York: Vintage.

Marx, K., and Engels, F. (1974). The communist manifesto [1848]. In K. Marx, *The Revolutions of 1848: Political Writings*, Vol. 1, edited by D. Fernbach, 62–98.

Marx, K., and Engels, F. (1970). *The German Ideology* [1845/49], 3rd rev. edn. Moscow: Progress Publishers.

McAdam, D. (1999). *Political Process and the Development of Black Insurgency, 1930–1970*, 2nd edn. Chicago: University of Chicago Press.

Olson, M. (1965). *The Logic of Collective Action: Public Goods and the Theory of Groups*. Cambridge: Harvard University Press.

Ostrom, E. (1990). *Governing the Commons: The Evolution of Institutions for Collective Action*. Cambridge and New York: Cambridge University Press.

Popper, K. R. (1957). *The Poverty of Historicism*. Boston: Beacon Press.

Scott, J. C. (1976). *The Moral Economy of the Peasant: Rebellion and Subsistence in Southeast Asia*. New Haven: Yale University Press.

Sen, A. (1987). *On Ethics and Economics*. New York: Basil Blackwell.

Taylor, M. (1976). *Anarchy and Cooperation*. London: Wiley.

Taylor, M. (1982). *Community, Anarchy and Liberty*. Cambridge: Cambridge University Press.

Tuomela, R. (1995). *The Importance of Us: A Philosophical Study of Basic Social Notions*. Stanford: Stanford University Press.

Turner, V. (1974). *Dramas, Fields, and Metaphors: Symbolic Action in Human Society*. Ithaca, NY: Cornell University Press.

Weber, M. (1947). The definitions of sociology and of social action. In M. Weber, *The Theory of Social and Economic Organization*. New York: Oxford University Press, edited by A. M. Henderson and T. Parsons, 88–114.

Whyte, W. F. (1993). *Street Corner Society: The Social Structure of an Italian Slum*. Chicago: University of Chicago Press.

51

The Prediction of Action

NASSIM N. TALEB AND AVITAL PILPEL

Introduction

The philosophical motivation behind the interest in action is, traditionally, twofold. First, there is a metaphysical one, evinced by attempts to relate various theories of action to the mind–body problem, to the age-old problem of free will, and so on. Second, there is an ethical and legal motivation to this interest whatever view of action one adopts, it will relate to the problem of what legal and moral responsibility, if any, an agent has for her actions. (Unless otherwise noted, we mean here by 'action' intentional human action performed by an individual or a group.)

Both of these issues are dealt with elsewhere in the present volume. In Parts III and IV of the book, the contributors concentrate instead on scientific theories and on their prediction and explanation of action. They are concerned with fields like epistemology, neuroscience, or ethnology rather than with metaphysics or ethics. Of course, the science of action affects the philosophy of action, and vice versa: developments in neuroscience can challenge ideas of free will, while on the other hand libertarianism (in the incompatibilist sense, not in the political sense) might come up with convincing arguments as to why no scientific advance will ever eradicate it.

The particular scientific theories and their relationship to action have been dealt with in previous chapters. Here we wish to take a different track. Instead of arguing for a particular metaphysical or scientific view of action, we are going to make a general point about predicting action.

Classes of Uncertainty

In rational choice theory there are three types of decision-making.

The first one is decision-making under certainty, when *Y* knows the (single) state of the world, *S*1, and therefore what outcome o_{11}, o_{21}, ... o_{2n} will be the certain result of each of his possible choices, A_1, A_2, ... A_n.

The second type of decision-making is decision-making under known and computable probabilistic structures, sometimes called 'risk' (after Knight 1921 and Keynes

1937). Here Y knows not only the possible states of the world, S_1, S_2, ... S_j, ... S_m, but also the probability with which each of them will occur. This is, for example, the case in games of chance (*Y* knows what numbers are on the roulette wheel and also what the probability is of each one coming up.) For our purposes, it is of little importance how the very concept of probability is defined –if probability is seen as a logical relation between propositions, as Carnap (1950) attempted to construct it; as a shorthand predicate describing the dispositions of the chance system, as was proposed by Levi (1980); as an expression of the ratio of the systems' outcomes in the long run, as conceived by von Mises (1919); or anything else.

The third type of decision-making is decision-making in conditions of true uncertainty – which, in Knight's words, is the situation when

> The liability of opinion or estimate to error must be radically distinguished from probability or chance of either type, for there is no possibility of forming *in any way* groups of instances of sufficient homogeneity to make possible a quantitative determination of true probability. Business decisions, for example, deal with situations which are far too unique, generally speaking, for any sort of statistical tabulation to have any value for guidance. The conception of an objectively measurable probability or chance is simply inapplicable [...] [A]t the bottom of the uncertainty problem in economics [...] is the forward-looking character of the economic process itself. (Knight 1921)

In other words, there isn't even a reasonable probability value to give to the possible outcomes; 'there is no scientific basis to form any calculable probability whatever [...] [such as the] price of copper and the rate of interest twenty years hence' (Keynes 1937).

The very nature of (typical and/or important) economic decisions is that of one-time choices, which are forward-looking and whose very making influences the possible outcomes (future states of the world) the agent might encounter. This makes it usually impossible, as Knight (1921, quoted above) or Shackle (1979) note, to assign any reasonable a priori probability values to the likelihood of such outcomes, when the agent is deliberating what to do. (We are using the term 'likelihood' here untechnically, in the most general sense.) Assigning probability to an outcome requires repeatability and stability among the consequences of the event that might cause such outcome.

In particular, games are a case where both sides must make decisions under uncertainty, since it is precisely the fact that the opponent is a human being who makes free choices and can act as she wishes that makes it impossible to assign probabilities to her choice (see Von Neumann and Morgenstern 1944, or any of the numerous works on game theory, for instance Luce and Raiffa 1958).

The distinction between the three cases is not absolute: choice under certainty can be seen as a limiting case of choice under known probabilistic structures, with the probability $p = 1$ for one outcome and $p = 0$ for all the rest – although, as Levi (1980) points out, the analogy is not exact since *E*'s having probability 1 is not logically the same as *E*'s being certain to occur. Uncertainty, too, admits of degrees: one can be certain that the probability of an event is, say, between 0.2 and 0.8 and at the same time be uncertain about what the event is. By contrast, in complete uncertainty no probability value at all can be assigned – or, equivalently, the agent is in complete uncertainty, assigning no narrower range of probabilities to the event than [0,1] (see Levi 1980).

Our Argument

We argue that *X*'s action in situation *T* is – in a sense to be made clear presently – hard for *Y* to predict precisely in those situations where predicting *X*'s action is, for *Y*, a case of prediction under uncertainty; while it is comparatively easy when, as sometimes occurs, predicting *X*'s actions at *T* is, for *Y*, a case of prediction under a known and computable probabilistic structure (such as that discussed by von Neumann and Morgenstern 1944). This is the case whether *X* (or *Y*) are individuals or groups (say, economic agents involved in transactions, or voters in an election), or indeed when $X = Y$ (as in the case of an agent considering her own future actions.) To avoid a possible misunderstanding, we are not dealing with why prediction of *X*'s actions is often a case of prediction under uncertainty for *Y*. The libertarian and the (hard-determinist) neuroscientist will have very different answers. We are only saying that it is in those cases that predicting *X*'s action is (especially) difficult for *Y*.

We argue, further, that this distinction – between tractable probabilistic structure and unstable, more complicated uncertainty – is of great practical importance. It helps to explains why, in some cases, the rational choice and economics literature considers that it is easier to predict the action of entire groups than that of of individuals, or why others may know our actions better than we know them ourselves. It also explains why so many confident predictions fail: very often, the predictor falls into what we call the 'ludic fallacy' – that is, the creation of a crisp structure of games from which we can produce analytical responses which only hold in this artificial construct and break down outside of it. It leads to the mistake of confusing a situation of predicting under unstructured uncertainty with one of predicting under structured probability (as happens in games of chance – hence the fallacy's name).

Predicting Other People's Action

There is a well-known tension between free choice (or, more generally, free action or free will) and prediction. This state of affairs goes back to – but in fact is much older than – St Augustine, who wondered how free will is possible in a world where God has foreknowledge of all events (Augustine 1988).

The tension also applies to probability: if an all-knowing being made sure that one has exactly a 87.5 percent chance of having fried eggs and a 12.5 percent chance of having cornflakes for breakfast tomorrow, one would not choose any more 'freely' than if the all-knowing being decided 100 percent in favor of fried eggs. Indeed, for some modern thinkers the 'standard,' probability-centered view of economics is misguided due to its lack of concern for people's freedom to choose (Shackle 1979). As said above, it is for this reason that outcomes are considered cases of decision under true uncertainty, not under computable probabilistic structure. Computable probability structures with precisely known spaces of possible outcomes are commonly called 'risks' in rational choice theory: a typical example would be a casino where the possible outcomes and their associated probabilities are known in advance with precision. Other, more ambiguous situations are called 'uncertainties.'

Typically, when *Y* attempts to predict *X*'s actions and *X* is an individual agent, then *Y* is in a situation where (as in games) the prediction is impossible, since one is in a situation of uncertainty: *Y* has no way to assign any probability to *X*'s possible choices (the possible future actions he will decide to take), since *X* – from *Y*'s point of view – has freedom of choice in his actions. This situation is very common –when it comes to predicting individual actions, it probably constitutes the typical case – and it is what was called above the 'hard' case for the prediction of *X*'s actions.

To describe things by using the terminology of randomness, the reason why this situation is typically one of uncertainty and not of risk is that, in order to have a good idea of what *X*'s probabilities of actions are, *Y* needs to know *X*'s 'generator' – that is, the generating function that determines the mean, variance, and higher-level moments of his actions – what makes him tick, what is it in *X* that makes *X* evince a certain probability to choose one way and another probability to choose another way.

But, with human beings (for whatever reason: call it free will, neurochemical complexity or anything else), the generator is hidden, and there is no reason to believe that it is of a 'good' type. *X*'s generating process might not even have truly quantifiable properties, including such metrics used in statistical methods as the mean – let alone a variance; or these might change over time; and so on. Assume *Y* to be an external agent not cognizant of the generator of *X*, only observing the properties of *X* from the outside. Typically, for *Y* to reduce the situation to one of risk – as in games of chance – *X*'s generator must be known; must be of a 'good' type (with a finite mean); and must be stable. Usually, when Y attempts to predict *X*'s actions, none of these conditions holds (see Taleb 2007a, 2007b).

Nevertheless, *Y* can try to reduce this uncertainty: *Y* can learn about *X*'s psychological state, his character, his genetics, his environment, his social position, and so on, in an attempt to predict *X*'s actions. This is sometimes successful. It is not at all rare for *X*'s spouse, or psychologist, or co-workers to assign quite reasonable probabilities (or certainties) to *X*'s future actions – to 'know *X* better than *X* knows herself.' This means that *Y* has managed to reduce the situation to that of risk (or certainty); it means that *Y* is able, due to his knowledge of *X*, to assign (reliable) probabilities to *X*'s future actions. This is the 'easy' case.

It should be noted that, from *Y*'s point of view, *X* is not a free agent in the indeterminist sense of the term – *X* has no choice but to act as he does (either perform a certain action for sure, or choose between several actions with a given probability for each). At most, *X* can be a free actor in the compatilibist/'soft' determinist sense of (roughly) doing what one wants to do even if one could not help but want to do it.

The disagreement between different views about free will and determinism can be described as a disagreement about whether, and if so under what conditions, *Y* can ever actually turn the prediction of *X*'s actions into a case of prediction under risk instead of prediction under uncertainty: determinists say that in principle, indeed sometimes in practice, it could be done; indeterminists deny it.

Predicting One's Own Actions

It is important to consider what happens when $X = Y$ – when an agent attempts to predict his own future actions. As Levi (1990), Shackle (1979), and many others have noted, inasmuch as an agent succeeds in this task, that agent is no longer acting freely (making a genuine choice) in the future: if I determine now that I will have eggs for breakfast tomorrow, I can predict my exact future actions, but I will no longer be making a choice tomorrow about what to have for breakfast. Predicting one's own future actions is sometimes possible, but at a price. Note that I may predict something vague and general, like 'when I am older, I will get married,' but such a generality, by providing a high number of free factors (the timing of the wedding, the person to whom I will get married), does not really enter the category of prediction that we are dealing with.

Predicting Group Action

There is another way of reducing the uncertainty in the prediction of action that, it seems, is inherent to the human condition where people make choices. This is, namely, for Y to predict, not what an individual X will do, but what a group of individuals will do. Here the law of large numbers often comes to Y's aid. It is sometimes possible to employ it in order to predict the behavior of large groups of people – Republicans, or investors in the market – despite the fact that the actions of each individual in the group are unpredictable.

However, one must be very careful. For the law of large numbers to be applicable, the random generators of individuals in the group must be independent of each other. If independence does not hold – if agents do not make decisions in isolation but while considering the actions of other agents, if Republicans do not decide independently on each issue but also take into account what other Republicans are doing – then convergence to commonly tractable properties will not take place, making the law of large numbers of little applicability and use.

This behavior of the aggregate is qualitatively central. There is no exact definition of what constitutes a 'complex system,' except for a consensus across the interdisciplinary literature that the degree of interdependence or 'connectedness' of the elements is an essential determining property – one which thus prevents the analysis of any single of them in isolation. The difference is crucial: in an ordinary system the agents might not be predictable but the various idiosyncrasies will tend to compensate for each other, and the aggregate will appear more stable than any of its components, hence more predictable. However, this cancelling-out effect is lost when the agents start acting in locksteps, with contagions and feedback loops causing exacerbation of the properties. In such situations we have, in effect, a 'group mind' with its own single generator – a single individual (from the point of view of predicting its actions) – and, what is more, an 'individual' more prone than an actual person to have a 'bad' sort of generator, one that makes predicting its actions difficult or a case of prediction under uncertainty. This is due to the disproportionate effect which extreme individuals tend to have on a group's behavior, as is manifested in cascades, panics, and bubbles (Mackay and Tobias 1995).

The Danger of Prediction

To summarize: predicting *X*'s action is (relatively) easy when one has reason to believe *X*'s actions can be described under risk – with reliable probability functions. This is not impossible. But there are two risks involved here, and they are often involved.

The first is what Taleb and Pilpel (2007) called the non-observability of the generators of the random process, also described as the inverse problem. Upon observing a series of points, an infinity of generators from four qualitatively different classes can be ascribed to the data. In a way similar to Goodman's riddle of induction (Goodman 1983), the empirical data can justifiably lead to two completely opposite extrapolations. Indeed agents fall prey to choosing from the data what confirms (that is, does not disconfirm) their theories.

This risk is related to the ludic fallacy ('ludic' comes from the Latin noun *ludus*, 'game'), when the agents make a mistake by assuming that the outcomes they are facing resemble the structures of the games of chance when in fact they do not. The conventional economics and rational choice literature has traditionally assumed that people confront clear choices, in one period, with clear answers (even in some situations of unknown probabilities). The error is to believe that the passage from the 'ludic,' casino-like analysis can be generalized outside of it. Indeed people tend to overestimate their knowledge of the world – here they tend to overestimate, often ludicrously, the amount of knowledge they have about the 'random generator' of *X*, whose actions they are trying to predict. They tend to treat both other individuals and other groups as if those groups and individuals were as simple as games of chance – as if the behavior of Republicans, or of the market, or of individual strangers could, with a little shoehorning perhaps, be described in terms of probability functions no more complex, and as (or more) reliable, than that of a roulette wheel.

So the 'forcing' of a situation of prediction under uncertainty about *X*'s future actions into one of prediction under known probabilistic structures commits two main errors. First of all, as we said, it assigns probabilities to *X*'s known actions when there is no justification. What is more, and worse, it tends to ignore unknown and unimagined actions which *X* could take: the very fact of analyzing *X*'s possible actions in terms of risk means having a set of possible outcomes (*X*'s actions) among which the probability is distributed.

But there is an unknown risk that some actions have been forgotten or ignored – typically, the most extreme ones! So we are not just dealing with the underestimation of the magnitude of possible outcomes, but with the possible sources of randomness. And such sources of randomness about another's actions have a disproportionately high effect in real-life situations. Accordingly, the second problem is that of high-impact uncertainty or consequential low-probability events. Sometimes we may be able to predict an agent's action in ordinary circumstances where such prediction does not carry serious consequences, yet fail in those situations where prediction matters. We may be able to predict what a criminal can eat for breakfast, but miss out on whether or when he may commit a crime. We may be able to predict what the pilot would do at the weekend, but not if he will crash the plane. The point is serious, as (1) these less ordinary, low-probability events have a structure that is less computable than ordinary events; and (2) they represent the bulk of what is meaningful to predict (Taleb and Pilpel 2007). Indeed the role of these hard-to-predict high-impact outliers coming from human action is dominant in history, economic life, and politics. These may make the man-made social world functionally unpredictable.

See also: COLLECTIVE ACTION (9); AGENTS' KNOWLEDGE (30); RATIONALITY (36); FREE WILL AND DETERMINSIM (38); ACTION IN HISTORY AND SOCIAL SCIENCE (50); AUGUSTINE AND AQUINAS (56); WEBER (67).

References

Augustine of Hippo (1988). *The City of God. Against the Pagans*, translated by R. W. Dyson. Cambridge: Cambridge University Press.

Carnap, R. (1950). *Logical Foundations of Probability*. Chicago: University of Chicago Press.

Goodman, N. (1983). The new riddle of induction, 4th edn. In N. Goodman, *Fact, Fiction, and Forecast*. Cambridge, MA: Harvard University Press, 59–83.

Keynes, J. M. (1937). The general theory of employment. *Quarterly Journal of Economics*, 51 (2), 209–223. Knight, F. H. (1921). *Risk, Uncertainty, and Profit*. Boston: Hughton Mifflin.

Levi, I. (1980). *The Enterprise of Knowledge: An Essay on Knowledge, Credal Probability, and Chance*. Cambridge, MA: MIT Press.

Levi, I. (1990). *Hard Choices: Decision Making Under Unresolved Conflict*. Cambridge: Cambridge University Press.

Luce, R. D., and Raiffa, H. (1958). *Games and Decisions*. New York: Wiley.

Mackay, C. (1995). *Extraordinary Popular Delusions and the Madness of Crowds*, with an Introduction by A. Tobias. New York: Three Rivers Press.

Shackle, G. L. S. (1979). *Imagination and the Nature of Choice*. Edinburgh: Edinburgh University Press.

Taleb, N. N. (2007a). *The Black Swan: The Impact of the Highly Improbably*. New York: Random House and London: Penguin.

Taleb, N. N. (2007b). Black swans and the domains of statistics. *American Statistician*, 61 (3), 198–200.

Taleb, N. N., and Pilpel, A. (2007). Epistemology and risk management, *Risk and Regulation*, 13, 6–7.

Von Mises R. (1919). Grundlagen der Wahrscheinlichkeitsrechnung, *Mathematische Zeitschrift*, 5, 52–99.

Von Neumann, J., and Morgenstern, O. (1944). *Theory of Games and Economic Behavior*. Princeton: Princeton University Press.

Part IV

Prominent Figures

52

Indian Philosophers

ELISA FRESCHI

The present chapter has a double aim. On the one hand, I will try to show what Indian philosophers have to say on themes in contemporary western philosophy of action (from the nature of action to the role of intention). On the other, I shall also outline the Indian views from their own perspective, so as to familiarize readers with the context of the debates which gave rise to them.

Classical Indian philosophy (between around the second century BC and the eighteenth century AD) is usually divided into 'schools' or 'systems' (*darśana*, lit. 'vision'), each specializing in certain themes (linguistics, ontology, logic, and so on) and often borrowing from the others any additional notions it might need to use. For example the 'logic-epistemology' system (Nyāya) borrows physical categories from the 'ontology' one (Vaiśeṣika), and both borrow exegetical rules from the 'hermeneutics' school (Mīmāṃsā). These systems all agreed in their common attribution of a certain degree (at least) of authority to the 'sacred texts' (Veda). Jaina and Buddhist philosophers developed their own philosophies, which often clashed with those of the systems mentioned above, though cross-influences were certainly common.

Action as Evidence for the Existence of a Self: Effort, Mental Acts, Motion, and Cause

As stated above, Indian *darśana*s share commonly agreed terms and concepts. One of these is the notion of categories as actually existing classes in which reality can be organized. The most ancient ones are probably substance, quality (*guṇa*) and motion (*karman*), the latter being directly relevant for the present study. The Vaiśeṣika system – crystallized as such at an early stage (Frauwallner 1973 [1956]: 15) – does not distinguish sharply between motions and intentional actions. Both are described as motions of atoms (conceived of as the minutest particles of matter, unchangeable and eternal) and are implemented according to the same causal scheme. The difference between them lies only in the fact that the former are produced by *material* causes and the latter by *effort* (*prayatna*, understood not as bodily effort but as volition leading to the initiation of an activity). Effort is in turn determined by desire or aversion.

A similar causal scheme is adopted by Nyāya. As remote causes of desire and aversion, either non-knowledge (erroneous knowledge, leading to erroneous attachment to worldly things) or *dharma* and *adharma* (merit and demerit: qualities of the self resulting from its past actions) are mentioned. Nyāya authors add a 'connection with a recollection' (*smṛtyanubandha*; see below) as a determinant for the arousal of desire or aversion and, eventually, effort. Notably, effort is not in itself a motion. Rather, it is a quality of the self (*ātman*), deemed to be composed of a single atom. Hence its changes cannot be described as atomic motion, in contrast to the descriptions of modern neuroscience. By the same token, Nyāya and Vaiśeṣika thinkers do not consider psychic 'acts' such as consciousness and desire to be motions. This leads to the problematic assumption that cognition is a quality which needs an instrument (namely the sense faculties) and is related to a subject and an object – characteristics typically attributed only to motions. Mīmāṃsā and, to an even greater extent, Buddhist thinkers adopt a different position here.

Due to its specific link to intentional actions, *prayatna* plays an essential role in the Indian polemic about the existence of a self. In the *Nyāyasūtra* (the foundational text of the Nyāya system, around the second century AD) and the *Praśastapādabhāṣya* (which is the oldest extant commentary on the foundational text of the Vaiśeṣika system and dates from the sixth century AD) several logical reasons (*liṅga*) are listed through which a self can be inferred. One may, for instance, infer a self from the fact that one is aware of one's own cognitions, but not directly through one's own perceptions. In fact cognitive acts (from perception to the simplest mental acts) are thought of as being produced by sense faculties and by the interaction of the latter with the mental faculty (*manas*). To be *aware* of them, one needs to be a conscious self; until then they can only be carried out, so to speak, mechanically. The seat of awareness is thus not in the sense faculties themselves (not even in the mental one), and one has to postulate a self beyond them. Similarly, one can infer a self from the fact that one acts; for the faculties of motion are not responsible for the fact that one *undertakes* an activity. Rather, effort proves that there is an intentional subject beyond the bodily movements, in other words the self. Through motions, one can further infer the presence of other selves. This resembles the arguments from analogy for other minds later put forward by John Stuart Mill (1889) and by Bertrand Russell (1948): one sees bodily movements in other people which are similar to one's own and, knowing that a certain bodily movement corresponds to an effort of the self in one's own case, one deduces that things happen like this also in the case of other people.

Since effort is the necessary antecedent of any conscious action, those who try to deny the existence of a self often point to the similarity between the common motions of unconscious agents and those of allegedly conscious ones. These objectors maintain that, just like the former, the latter are merely results of a series of causes, with no intervention of a conscious agent determining the successive action. A typical example is the similarity between a lotus flower and a new-born baby. Just as the lotus opens and closes its petals, so the baby has physical and emotional reactions (which do not entail that s/he is a conscious self). Nyāya authors respond by claiming that one can infer, from an analogy with adults, that one's acts are caused by pleasure or pain, where these are further caused by a 'connection with a recollection.' Intentional actions are thus also attributed to new-born babies (who have not developed tastes and dislikes yet), and this leads to the further inference that the babies have anamnestic traces (*saṃskāras*)[1] of previous lives (see Preisendanz 1994: 335–348 and 305–319). In addition, no external object is in itself pleasant or painful; only once one has repeatedly experienced its ability to quench thirst, for example, can one rejoice at seeing a cup of tea. The role of recollection here, then, is not unsimilar to the one it plays in Plato's work, which resurfaces in modern doctrines of innate ideas.

In the later history of Nyāya, Bhāsarvajña (*c.* 860–920) states that motion (*karman*) is a sort of quality, for – like qualities – motions are momentary and inhere in a substance.

Action in the Context of Linguistic Use: Basic Acts, Effort, Production, Aim, and Reasons

It is not uncommon in India for concerns with language to develop into more general theories. Some scholars (notably Johannes Bronkhorst 1999: 34–35 and 109) have even claimed that the specificity of 'Indian thought' actually lies in the implicit postulate that language describes reality and that, consequently, analyzing language is the first step towards the description of reality. Issues such as causation, exhortation, and inducement have all been discussed through the use of linguistic instances.

Indian Grammarians – by which I mean adherents of the Vyākaraṇa school – distinguished between a certain activity, for instance cooking, and the numerous (more basic) acts which compose it – such as burning the wood, boiling the water, softening the rice and so on (see also chapter 2).

Mīmāṃsā authors are primarily concerned with the exegesis of the Veda, particularly its sacrificial prescriptions. Their standard example of a prescription is this: 'the one who is desirous of heaven should sacrifice with the New and Full Moon sacrifices.' Here Mīmāṃsā authors point out an active component, embedded in the verb and corresponding to the fact that one undertakes an activity in general. This component, they maintain, is expressed by the verbal ending, whereas the verbal root expresses the specific activity undertaken. So the verbal ending informs one about the sheer fact that an activity is being initiated, and one turns to the verbal root in order to name it. Śabara (possibly before the fifth century AD), who wrote the first extant commentary to the foundational text of the Mīmāṃsā system, first called this generic activity *bhāvanā* (lit. 'the causing to be'), an action noun from the causative form of the verb 'to be.' He thus defined an activity in general as the fact of bringing about ('causing to be') an aim (in the example mentioned above, heaven).

Kumārila (to be placed roughly in the period between the sixth century AD and the seventh), who is one of the foremost Indian philosophers and who commented on the work of Śabara, further characterized *bhāvanā* as the 'activity of an inciting [subject].' Accordingly, he did not classify the acts defined by verbs such as 'to be' as *bhāvanā*.

Maṇḍana Miśra, who lived shortly after Kumārila, denied this difference, maintaining instead that an active component (the *bhāvanā*) is in fact present in *all* acts. He further defined this component as effort (*prayatna*; see the section entitled 'Action as Evidence for the Existence of a Self'). Indeed, all mental activities are labeled by him *bhāvanā* and *karman*. Thus the latter acquires a wider meaning than in Nyāya. All subsequent Mīmāṃsā authors (as well as many Nyāya ones) discussed Maṇḍana's view that one undertakes an action either in order to pursue pleasure or to avoid pain (see Warren Quinn's definition of a reason to act as 'nothing more than something good in itself that it realizes or serves, or, short of that, something bad that it avoids,' 1993: 234). Maṇḍana's theory does not explain the ability of exhortations to incite actions, as was demonstrated by later Mīmāṃsā thinkers such as Kumārila's commentator Pārthasārathi Miśra (*c.* twelfth century AD). Still, Maṇḍana's account of the reasons why one undertakes an action remains valid, at least from the point of view of hard empiricists such as the Mīmāṃsā authors.

Following Maṇḍana, Someśvara Bhaṭṭa – another commentator of Kumārila, possibly from the twelfth century – again identified *bhāvanā* and effort. In consequence he explicitly denied the Nyāya-Vaiśeṣika idea that effort is a quality inherent in the self. Pārthasārathi, by contrast, defined the *bhāvanā* as an 'activity leading to the arousal of something else' (*anyotpādānukūlavyāpāra*). This division had a major impact on the successive generations of commentators, all of whom sided either with Pārthasārathi or with Someśvara. The former argued that the description of *bhāvanā* as effort fails to make sense of all the effortless actions, such as that of seating (see also chapters 3 and 68), while it also excludes the acts of unconscious agents. The latter replied that actions are primarily intentional, adding that acts such as that of 'the chariot going' can be metaphorically described in the same way.

Interestingly, both discussants agree on the fact that what merits most consideration is the initiation of the action (*pravṛtti*), while its actual realization does not matter much. Consequently both describe the process leading to action as threefold: (1) cognition; (2) wish (*icchā*); (3) effort. Nyāya authors, by contrast, add the actual performance of the action at the end. It is possible that Mīmāṃsā's reaction against the stress laid on the actual implementation of the action was caused by the objections of an anonymous thinker whose views have been reproduced in Maṇḍana's *Bhāvanāviveka* ('Discernment about the *bhāvanā*'). This interlocutor rebutted the whole theory of *bhāvanā* by saying that an action is nothing but a motion and that a motion is nothing but the sum of two qualities of things –namely the qualities of conjunction and disjunction. Against this view, Mīmāṃsā replied that 'action' must instead be understood as the effort of the person who initiates it, and not (merely) as its output (that is, as the motion of some things).

According to Mīmāṃsā authors, an aim is *necessarily* included in an action. So an aim cannot be the unintentional output of an action such as (according to a Mīmāṃsā example) touching the roots of a tree while going to a village. Instead, it is defined as something desired by the agent, independently of any prescription enjoining it. Prabhākara (a contemporary of Kumārila and the founder of the antagonist school of Prābhākara Mīmāṃsā) is usually credited with the theory that Vedic prescriptions have to be obeyed just insofar as they have been prescribed, independently of their result. This is true; still, Prabhākara does not deny the role of the aim within the description of human actions. Human beings become engaged in, for example, sacrifices having a certain aim already in view (though they need not act *merely* for the sake of it). The aim is thus necessarily included in the activity as one of its components, but not as its determinant. (See also chapter 66.)

The case of sacrificial activities also made Mīmāṃsā authors aware of the problem of the direct *result* (or effect) of an action which arises long after the action has ceased. For instance, heaven is attained after one's death and not immediately after sacrifices. The same discontinuity was also detected by Mīmāṃsā philosophers in activities such as studying: one learns something after a protracted study, which does not seem to bear any fruit for a long time. Yet how can an already extinguished action bear a result? That is to say, how can the causal link reach out to the result, if the action is long gone? Indian authors felt the need to postulate an invisible potency bridging the gap between action and result. Mīmāṃsā authors called this condition *apūrva* ('not [existing] before') and assumed that it is raised by the act and, in turn, itself raises the result.

Moral Actions

Introduction: Moral dilemmas

Bimal Krishna Matilal (2002: 36–70, esp. p. 38) explains the lack of ethical theories in Indian *philosophical* texts through their presence in different sorts of other texts, for instance normative and epic ones. In fact, one finds in the *Mahābhārata* interesting instances of moral dilemmas such as whether one should tell the truth to people who are likely to use it to harm innocent others (see Matilal 2002: 9 and 19–34). Of central significance is also the dialogue between God (in his Kṛṣṇa appearance) and the warrior Arjuna, depicted in the *Bhagavadgītā*. Arjuna and Kṛṣṇa stand before the battlefield at the outbreak of a 'just war,' yet Arjuna refuses to harm other people. Kṛṣṇa explains that he is only responsible for the *immediate* action he is about to undertake, and not for its results. On this conception, one is only involved in the result's moral consequences (in Indian terms, 'karmic fruits') if one craved for it, and not if one only engaged in the action for its own sake (for example because it was commanded by God). Accordingly, a warrior who does not crave for killing is not responsible for any deaths he causes in a just war. (See also chapter 41.) In fact, the idea of acting without identifying with the action or coveting its results is a pan-Indian theme. For different reasons (especially the idea that at the root of suffering lies our erroneous identification with an enduring self), Buddhists also stressed the need for actions which are free of desire and of ego.

A second context where moral reflections are developed is that of ritual. In the Veda, a malevolent sacrifice called *Śyena* is prescribed to those who want to harm their enemies. Nonetheless, the Veda also prescribes that 'no harm should be inflicted' (*na hiṃsyāt* – hence the well-known ideal of *ahiṃsā*, 'non-violence'). All Mīmāṃsā authors agree that the *Śyena* must not be performed (thinkers affiliated to other schools generally also follow Mīmāṃsā in these matters). This is because the Veda does not exhort one to crave for a certain result; it only prescribes the way to reach it. One is only to perform the *Śyena* if one desires to harm one's enemy, and the burden of the harm lies entirely with the one who desires it.

Buddhist views of action: Intention, moral consequences, basic acts and enduring actions

Non-philosophical Indian texts are replete with the suggestion that an unintentional (or even unconscious) bad action affects its doer. Jaina authors deal extensively with the difference between bodily acts and mental ones (said to be only 'half-acts'), concluding that the former are considerably more important than the latter. Hence one should avoid harming, regardless of whether or not is it intentional. This leads to the Jaina compromise-free *ahiṃsā*, which is considered to have greatly influenced M. K. Gandhi's thought. Buddhist theories of action, by contrast, are primarily intentional. For example, it is thought that one is not culpable of an offence if one unwillingly touches someone else's wife. *Mutatis mutandis*, if one offers gold while thinking that one is offering rice, one will only get the moral reward for a rice offer.

Toward the end of the first half of the first millennium AD, the great Buddhist philosopher Vasubandhu composed his *Abhidharmakośabhāṣya*, a chief text summarizing Buddhist theories of the previous centuries (and thus constituting the common background for further developments). The entire fourth chapter of this text is dedicated to action, defined as follows in the first verse and in the subsequent commentary thereon:

> It is volition *(cetanā)* and that which is produced through volition.
>
> The verse says that there are two types of action, volition (*cetanā*) and the action after having been willed (*cetayitvā*). [...] These two actions form three actions: bodily action, vocal action and mental action. (Vasubandhu, *Abhidharmakośabhāṣya*, § IV, v.1b)

While various scholars (such as Thomas 1917–8: 139)[2] have stressed the moral character of the theory of *karman* (or karma, as common in English usage) in Buddhist and Indian thought (see the section below on 'Free will and determinism'), the chief role of intention is due more to the fact that mental acts are considered to be actions, hence legitimately engendering effects. Indeed, *cetanā* has here been translated as 'volition,' not in a sense which could make it a synonym of 'will,' but rather as the mental act through which the will-power resolves to do something. So conceived, *cetanā* is an active aspect of thought (*citta*).

All actions relate to intention. They are either mental actions (pure *cetanā*) or physical or vocal actions initiated by a mental one. Deeds performed in haste (*sahasā*), without thinking (*abuddhipūrva*), or by mistake (*bhrānti*) do not count. Likewise, passions such as greed are only called 'paths to the action' insofar as a mental action has been set into motion by them. Greed, accordingly, bears no karmic fruit. One's inner *approval* of greed, however, is a mental action, with all the karmic entailments that this involves.

The presence of mental actions in the classification implies that the *bodily* performance of the act is not necessarily part of the definition of an action. Yet the performance of an act is significant insofar as it affects the agent's own volition (in addition to its consequences for other living beings). Carrying out a murder, for instance, requires that one's volition has been protracted for a long time. Complete action (such as that of killing an animal) is consequently described as being qualified by several antecedents and consequents:

1 the remote preparatory act (the intention *–āśaya–* to kill an animal)
2 the proximate preparatory act (getting up, going to the market, choosing the animal, bringing it home, beating it);
3 the principal act (*maula*, the slaughter of the animal);
4 the consequent act (one skins the animal, sells its flesh, rejoices because of the profit).

The preparatory act (akin to the western legal concept of 'premeditation') may in itself be harmful. In this example, one beats the animal before killing it. Similarly, one may steal a gun in order to commit a murder. Also, an absence of the consequent act may affect the principal act itself. For example, the merit of one's offering alms is almost effaced if one regrets it.

This analysis is interesting and doubtless insightful. Still, as remarked by Louis de la Vallée Poussin (1927: 127), it may nonetheless reduce to a complex casuistry. Consider the case of a person who kills someone while throwing stones, without the intention of killing but also without the specific aim of avoiding it. He is guilty of murder even though he was not consciously trying to kill a person. This is because he was at least aware that he was throwing stones at something (and the possible effect was obvious). This notion may be compared to the legal category of *dolus eventualis*.

A peculiar place in the aforementioned theory of action is that of the categories of *vijñapti*/*avijñapti*. A *vijñapti* is whatever act informs others of one's intention. All bodily acts are considered *vijñapti*s. A typical example of vocal *vijñapti* is one's making monastic vows as a monk (which most western thinkers would label as a 'speech act'; see chapter 8). A monk's vow to refrain from violence in all circumstances renders him morally different from normal people. Buddhists do not admit any difference in substance, attributing instead the difference to an *avijñapti*: an invisible action which endures well after one has made one's vows (compare the Mīmāṃsā notion of *apūrva* (see above, end of the section on 'Action in the Context of Linguistic Use'). Similarly, if one tells another to kill someone, he is guilty of a vocal *vijñapti*, whereas the actual killer is guilty of a bodily one. The first one becomes guilty of murder only at the time when the second one has performed it. Yet at that point the first person was not actually doing anything at all. One must therefore postulate that the murder has created an *avijñapti* connected to the person who has ordered it. So the *avijñapti* has to do with the consequences of one's actions and is not entirely under one's control. The principle of intentionality here adjusts to further needs.

Free will and determinism

Free will is limited, in Indian texts, by the idea of an uninterrupted and beginningless series of causes (and their effects) which lead to each present action; this is the 'theory of *karman*.' Some authors add the further limitation of God's omnipotence, and God is consequently identified as being the only autonomous agent (*svatantra*). In Buddhist texts, causal antecedents and effects of the action determine an action through the circle of dependent origination (*pratītyasamutpāda*), whose links are: ignorance (of truth); mental formations; consciousness (*vijñāna*); the combination of mind and body (*nāmarūpa*); the six sense organs; sense-contact (*sparśa*); feeling (*vedanā*); craving (*tṛṣṇā*);

clinging to things; becoming; birth; ageing, death and sorrow. These causal links are circular, and hence follow each other independently of the starting point. Their translated names appear odd to a western audience insofar as they are based on a non-substantialist account of reality. For this reason, 'acts' and 'substances' are linked in the same circle and deemed to be, equally, results of previous acts. It is also worth remembering in this connection that Buddhist philosophers consequently pushed this non-substantialism until the effects of the absence of any solid substance (such as the thing perceived or the person perceiving it) beyond the perceptual act. Likewise, heaven and hell are thought to be only the result of one's previous deeds. So understood, they are 'events' (such as that of suffering because of being beaten) rather than physical places. With this in mind, one can better understand the *Abhidharmakośa*'s claim that 'the variety of the world arises from action' (§ IV, v.1a in La Vallée Poussin 1983/90), for what we perceive as our environment is in fact also the result of previous acts.

Modern interpreters debate on the question of the amount of freedom which the cause–effect chain leaves for everyone. A passage of the Pāli Buddhist Canon quoted by La Vallée Poussin (1927: 135) suggests that 'whenever a monk has reasons to complain about a fellow monk he should reflect like this: "This venerable one, who has offended me, is indeed heir to his acts"' (and, hence, did not freely decide to offend). Thus, as noted by La Vallée Poussin, rigid determinism in Buddhist texts is only meant as a spiritual exercise whose aim is to prevent one from feeling anger against other beings. The issue is complicated by the Buddhist claim that the concept of 'person' (and, hence, of 'myself' and 'others') is only provisionally real. Nonetheless, Buddhist philosophers cannot have consistently developed their ethical theories without presupposing at least some degree of freedom for every living being (in Buddhist terms: for every stream of consciousness). Moreover, one of the foremost Buddhist philosophers, Dharmakīrti (middle of the sixth century AD to the seventh), has dealt with the issue of the dependent origination while arguing about the possibility of attaining *nirvāṇa* ('extinction,' the end of worldly existences). If the *pratītyasamutpāda* were, in fact, a concatenation of causes (each necessary and sufficient for the next one), then nobody could ever attain *nirvāṇa*. So, if the Buddha did just that, each link must be the antecedent of the successive one, but *not* its sufficient cause.

Concluding Remarks

To sum up, as far as the relation between action and the mental is concerned, Indian philosophers can be collocated on an ideal scale:

ACTION = MOTION:	ACTION = INITIATION OF THE ACTIVITY:	ACTION = MENTAL ACTION AND ITS OUTPUTS:
Vaiśeṣika (Sāṅkhya, Nyāya)	Mīmāṃsā	Buddhists

From the slightly different perspective of taking action to be tantamount to *intentional* action (be it mental or physical), action is sometimes included in the category of 'motion' and sometimes in that of 'quality,' as explicated in the diagram below:

Objector in *Bhāvanāviveka* and Bhāsarvajña:	Vaiśeṣika (Sāṅkhya, Nyāya):	Mīmāṃsā (especially Someśvara):	Buddhists:
• motions are reduced to qualities	• mental actions are qualities of the soul • bodily actions are motions	• action is above all effort (mental actions included)	• substances and qualities are reduced to actions

See also: ACTION THEORY AND ONTOLOGY (1); BASIC ACTIONS AND INDIVIDUATION (2); TRYING TO ACT (3); BODILY MOVEMENTS (4); SPEECH ACTS (8); COLLECTIVE ACTION (9); VOLITION AND THE WILL (13); INTENTION (14); REASONS AND CAUSES (17); AGENCY, PATIENCY, AND PERSONHOOD (26); MENTAL ACTS (27); FREE WILL AND DETERMINSIM (38); RESPONSIBILITY AND AUTONOMY (39); THE DOCTRINE OF DOUBLE EFFECT (41).

Notes

1 *Saṃskāras* has also been translated as 'dispositional tendencies' and thought to name qualities of the self. They are produced by strong impressions (such as when one first sees an elephant), repetition, or effort. Inhering in the self as traces of preceding events (though one is not aware of them), they are the most direct cause of memory. Thomas (1917/8: 139–145) equates them with Richard Semon's engramms.

2 Thomas' essay is generally insightful (especially up until p. 152). His acceptance of Semon's theory of the inheritance of acquired characters does not flaw his own thesis.

References

Bronkhorst, J. (1999). *Langage et réalité: Sur un épisode de la pensée indienne*. Turnhout: Brepols.

Frauwallner, E. (1973). *History of Indian Philosophy*, Vol. 2: *The Nature-Philosophical Schools and the Vaiśeṣika system. The System of the Jaina. The Materialism [1956]*, translated by V. M. Bedekar. Delhi: Motilal Banarsidass. [Page numbers given in the text refer to the original German edition.]

La Vallée Poussin, L. de (1927). *La Morale bouddhique* [*Buddhist Ethics*]. Paris: Bibliothèque Française de Philosophie.

La Vallée Poussin, L. de (1983/90). *The Abhidharmakośa of Vasubandhu* [1923/31], translated by L. M. Prouden, Berkeley, CA: Asian Humanities Press.

Matilal, B. K. (2002). *Ethics and Epics. Philosophy, Culture and Religion*, edited by J. Ganeri. New Delhi: Oxford University Press.

Mill, J. S. (1889). *An Examination of William Hamilton's Philosophy*. London: Longman.

Preisendanz, K. (1994). *Studien zu Nyāyasūtra III.1 mit dem Nyāyatattvāloka Vācaspati Miśras II* [*Studies on Nyāyasūtra III.1 with the commentary Nyāyatattvāloka of Vācaspati Miśra the Second*]. Stuttgart: Steiner.

Quinn, W. (1993). *Morality and Action*. Cambridge: Cambridge University Press.

Russell, B. (1948). *Human Knowledge: Its Scope and Limits*. London: Allen and Unwin.

Thomas, F. W. Indian (1917/8). Ideas of action and their interest for modern thinking. *Proceedings of the Aristotelian Society*, New Series, 18, 138–157.

Vasubandhu, *Abhidharmakośa* and *Abhidharmakośabhāṣya*: see La Vallée Poussin, L. de (1983/90).

Further reading

Doniger O'Flaherty, W. (ed.) (1980). *Karma and Rebirth in Classical Indian Traditions*. Berkeley, CA: University of California Press. [Especially W. Halbfass. Karma, *apūrva* and 'natural' causes: Observations on the growth and limits of the theory of *saṃsāra*, 268–302.]

Gyatso, T. (2005). Sex. In D. S. Lopez, Jr (ed.), *Critical Terms for the Study of Buddhism*. Chicago and London: University of Chicago Press, 271–290.

Ingalalli, R. I. (1992). *Knowledge of Action. Logico-Epistemological Analysis*. Delhi: Sri Satguru (especially §§ 4 and 5).

Marui, H. (1989). What prompts people to follow injunctions? An elucidation of the correlative structure of interpretations of *vidhi* and theories of action. *Acta Asiatica*, 57, 11–30.

Oetke, C. (1988). *'Ich' und das Ich. Analytische Untersuchungen zur buddhistisch–brahmanischen Ātmankontroverse*. Stuttgart: Steiner.

Potter, K. (ed.) (1977). *Encyclopedia of Indian Philosophies. Indian Metaphysics and Epistemology: The Tradition of Nyāya-Vaiśeṣika up to Gaṅgeśa*. Delhi: Motilal Banarsidass.

Reichenbach, B. R. (1989). Karma, causation and divine intervention. *Philosophy East and West*, 2, 135–149.

Siderits, M. *Buddhism as Philosophy*. Aldershot: Ashgate.

53

Plato

CHRISTINE J. THOMAS

Introduction

Though Plato (429–347 BC) does not develop a theory of action as such, he is rightly regarded as addressing a cluster of issues most often broached under the rubric 'the philosophy of action.' In particular, Plato's metaphysical commitments support a substantive – though not unproblematic – view of the types of changes that are a person's doings, as opposed to those changes that might merely happen to someone; and his psychology contains complex and rewarding efforts to identify the roles that beliefs, desires, and other mental states play in generating and explaining purposeful behaviors.[1]

Still, there are important respects in which Plato's efforts do not map straightforwardly onto the contemporary discussion. For Plato, the metaphysics of actions and of their correlated passions is as important to the individuation and explanation of action as the psychology of intentional agency. Like many contemporary theorists, Plato supposes that understanding observable human behaviors as actions requires appeals to the beliefs and desires from which those behaviors issued. Plato adds that such actions ultimately arise out of structured souls (or parts of souls), which are the proper subjects of psychic states or events. But what *makes* something a token action, for Plato, is also, importantly, its being an instance of an action type, where the latter is a genuine or fundamental being, a form (*eidos*). At *Sophist* 261e–263b, walking and running are characterized as actions (*praxeis*), and also placed among those beings (*ta onta*) designated by verbs (*rhêmata*).[2] We learn, moreover, that 'Theaetetus is walking' is true only if 'Theaetetus' is a sign for Theaetetus, 'walking' is a sign for the action of walking, and the action of walking is among the beings which are with respect to Theaetetus (*Sph.* 263a–b).[3] As we shall see, for Plato, the identification and full accounting of an action will require appeals to a variety of distinct types of causal or explanatory factors, including forms, souls, psychic motions and, at least in some cases, material conditions.

The Metaphysics of Action

The most fundamental realities or beings in Plato's ontology are the forms. In contrast to sensibles, forms are imperceptible and unchanging. Changing perceptibles depend for their features on their relations to forms. Simmias is tall, for example, because he participates in the form of tallness. Michelangelo's David is beautiful insofar as it has a share of beauty itself. Plato puts the point as follows: 'nothing else makes [*poiei*] something beautiful except the beautiful itself' (*Phd.* 100d5).

Actions or doings (*praxeis*), such as cutting something or burning something, are among the beings (*Cra.* 386e6–8).[4] Actions have their own natures, and any particular attempt at action must accord with the appropriate nature if it is to count as a token action of that type. According to Plato's *Cratylus*, if

> we choose to cut in accord with the nature of cutting and being cut and with the natural tool for cutting, we will succeed and cut correctly. If we attempt to cut contrary to nature, however, we will be in error and accomplish nothing. (*Cra.* 387a5–9)

A failure to instantiate the appropriate nature results in a failure to engage in the attempted action. And 'the same holds for the other actions' (*Cra.* 387b6).

For Plato, there is clearly an intimate relation between actions and their correlated passions.[5] He suggests that where there are doings there are corresponding affections:[6]

> SOCRATES: If someone does something, must there also be something affected by the doer?
>
> POLUS: I think so.
>
> SOCRATES: Is it affected by what the doer does to it, and by such a thing as the doer does to it? I'm saying this kind of thing: if something hits, must there be something that is being hit?
>
> POLUS: There must.
>
> [...]
>
> SOCRATES: And if something cuts, is it not the same account? For something is cut.
>
> POLUS: Yes.
>
> SOCRATES: And if the cut is large or deep or painful, the thing cut is cut with the kind of cut with which the cutter cuts?
>
> POLUS: Apparently. (*Grg.* 476b4–d2)[7]

When the actions are qualified, so too are the corresponding affections. If an agent cuts, a patient is cut; and, if the agent cuts deeply, then the patient is cut deeply.

Though there appears to be a necessary correlation of actions with affections, the exact nature of the relation is difficult to discern. If an action is simply identical to an affection, then we would predict the necessary correlation. If, on the other hand, a particular action and its correlated affection are distinct events or states, we ought to wonder about the force of the claim that the action *must* be accompanied by the affection. Moreover, if the action and affection are distinct, are they instances of the same nature or distinct natures? Though I am unsure of how to answer that question,[8] Plato seems to me to be committed to the distinctness of particular correlated actions and affections, since he is committed to the view that token actions and affections are asymmetrically related.

In the *Sophist*, what marks something as a being is its capacity either to do something (*poiein*) or to be affected (*pathein*: *Sph.* 247d8–e4, 248c4–5).[9] The most striking example in the passage is the case of a soul affecting some being in coming to know it. In that case, we are told,

> if knowing is doing something, then necessarily what is known has something done to it. When being is known by knowledge, according to this account, then insofar as it is known it is changed [*kineisthai*] by having something done to it. (*Sph.* 248d10–e4)[10]

There is no explicit ontological privileging of acting over being affected here, but it is crucial to the larger context of the dialogue that the object of knowledge is taken to be changed in coming to be known.[11] The cause of change in the being affected is the activity of the doer (in this case, the soul's knowing). Of course, the absence of a claim to symmetry in this case does not rule out the possibility that Plato would also countenance a symmetrical change in the soul when it comes to know, a change – if we are to preserve symmetry – he would have to regard as caused by the affection of the known being.[12] Even so, Plato elsewhere associates changes, presumably including actions and affections, with plurality and difference (*Ti.* 57d7–58a2). Moreover, metaphysical asymmetry is evident elsewhere.

In the *Euthyphro*, Socrates proposes that token actions of carrying, leading, loving, and seeing are cases of agents (for instance carriers, leaders, lovers, and seers) standing in interactive relations with patients (for instance carried things, led things, loved things, and seen things). The question arises, then, of how to understand the relations of agents to patients and of actions to affections. Socrates asks 'whether the carried thing is a carried thing because it is carried or because of something else' (*Euthphr.* 10b1–2). Euthyphro replies, 'because [it is carried]' (10b3). The patient, in this case, is affected because of the action of the agent. Moreover, Euthyphro later agrees that it is not because an object is a carried thing (that is, because it is affected) that it is carried (that is, someone acts to affect it). Affections in patients are due to actions of agents; actions of agents are not due to affections in patients.[13] The same asymmetric relation is said to hold in relations of leading, seeing, and loving. Socrates infers from the results that any patient which is affected is affected because of the actions of an agent, though agents do not act because of affections of patients (*Euthphr.* 10c3–4).[14]

Though the range of actions discussed in the various passages I have cited above is as diverse as the contexts at issue across the various dialogues, it is not unreasonable to suppose that Plato is committed quite generally to some kind of ontological dependence of token affections on token actions.[15] Actions produce affections, but affections do not produce actions. Affections are the result of alterations in a patient and are ontologically dependent on the actions of an agent.

But let us turn now to focus on the doers and their doings. Plato's metaphysics of actions and passions allows for inanimate agents. Fire, for example, can act on flesh to cut it or to burn it, thereby producing sensations of pain or heat (*Ti.* 61d–62a). But the soul is Plato's favored example of an agent capable of doing something by initiating change. Indeed, all motion or change in the sensible realm ultimately originates in soul (*Phdr.* 245c–246a; *Laws* 894b–896b).

Plato's position on the origin of change flows primarily from two commitments: (1) an infinite regress of change is impossible and (2) the cause of *F* must itself be *F*. In the case of change, then, there must be an original cause of change, and that cause of change must itself be changing. Plato posits soul as a regress-halting, self-moved mover. He identifies soul with

> the original principle of the generation and motion of all things past, present and future [...] it has been shown to be the cause of all change and motion in everything. (*Laws* 896a)[16]

Though the argument initially suggests an appeal to cosmic soul, Plato quickly extends the results so that individual souls are masters of individual bodies and produce bodily motions by means of their own psychic motions. The motions of a soul are said to include wish, true and false belief, joy, grief, fear, love, and hate (*Laws* 897a).

The details of how psychic motions produce (or are) actions will be discussed briefly in the final section of this chapter, but we can anticipate that souls initiate actions by means of beliefs, desires, and emotions. Moreover, the appeal to soul assists us in distinguishing between the case in which my hand moves as a result of, say, an earthquake and the case in which I act when I wave. In the former case, my hand moves, but its motion is caused by something external to me. I am merely a moved thing; I am affected. In the latter case, my hand's motion is also caused by something distinct from it, but the cause is internal to me; the cause is a principle of self-motion that moves my body from within (*Phdr.* 245e4–6). Moreover, my waving – the motion that counts as my doing something – is not simply internally caused; it is caused by the representational states (for instance beliefs, desires) of my soul.[17]

The Explanation of Action

The introduction of psychic motions not only provides a (mechanical) causal origin for action, but also plays a role in Plato's broader efforts to render actions intelligible or explicable. For a human soul is not simply a principle of motion; it is also intelligent. Since it is intelligent, the soul can direct the body (or even itself) to pursue what it believes is good, or at least what it somehow represents to itself as beneficial. Indeed Plato is attracted to the idea that all actions are for the sake of the good:

> It is in pursuit of the good that we both walk when we walk, thinking it is better, and on the other hand stand still when we stand still, for the sake of the same thing, the good [...] Then it is for the sake of the good that those who do these things do them all. (*Grg.* 468b1–8)

> [The good is] that, then, which every soul pursues and for its sake does all that it does. (*R.* 505d11–e1)

That actions are teleologically directed is a central feature of Plato's conception of human action (*Phd.* 97c–99c).

With the introduction of intelligent purposes, we are better situated to see how Plato might come to classify a particular motion as an action. Consider the case of Socrates walking across the room. The complete account of the action will make appeal to all of the relevant explanatory factors, where an explanatory factor – an *aition* – is 'that because of which something comes to be' (*Cra.* 413a4). The motions of Socrates' body when he walks are caused by the psychic motions that are his beliefs, emotions or desires. Those psychic motions aim, in some sense, at what Socrates takes to be good. Socrates' motion counts, then, as an action (and not merely an affection) because of its mechanical and teleological origins in Socrates' soul. Socrates' motion counts as the particular sort of action that it is, namely walking, insofar as the being that is named by the verb 'walks' is among the beings which are, with respect to Socrates.

Finally, there are also material conditions that must obtain for Socrates' motion to occur at all although those conditions are not always regarded as genuine explanatory factors by Plato. Socrates' bones are 'hard and separated by joints,' and are attached to 'sinews that are such as to contract and relax' (*Phd.* 98c–d). In the *Phaedo*, such material conditions are identified as necessary conditions for Socrates' bodily actions; but they are not themselves regarded as genuine 'causes.' In the *Timaeus*, however, material conditions are elevated to the status of auxiliary causes (*sunaitiai*). Intelligence acts on matter, but is constrained by the limits of material natures (*Ti.* 46c–e). So, although the complete explanatory account of Socrates' action will give preference to appeals to formal instantiation and to the motions and purposes of an intelligent soul, material natures determine certain features of the action, and therefore count as explanatory factors.[18] Moreover, material conditions must obtain if bodily action forms are to be instantiated and if psychic motions are to be effective in originating and directing bodily motion.

The Psychology of Action

Though there are developments and expansions of Plato's views of the metaphysics and explanation of action across the dialogues, the most dramatic revisions occur in the psychology of action.[19] The primary difference between the Socratic and the Platonic psychology of action has to do with the possibility of non-rational and akratic action. The Socratic model suggests that all desires issuing in action are desires for the good (*Meno* 77c–78b, *Grg.* 468b–d). Those desires align with an individual's beliefs about the good to produce actions. It is not possible, on this model, for an individual simultaneously to believe that one course of action is best and yet to act contrary to that belief (*Prt.* 352b–358e). If she believes that the action is of the best kind, her motivating desire for the good will lead her to act in accordance with that belief.

The Platonic model, on the other hand, countenances non-rational desires, in addition to rational ones, as sources of psychological conflict, and also as forces capable of motivating action. On the Platonic model, non-rational desires can (and do) motivate action, sometimes overcoming or corrupting rational desires and beliefs. Some actions are independent of reason, and some are contrary to reason. Determining how such actions fit into Plato's general framework of teleological explanation is a long-standing difficulty, one I will comment upon briefly below.

According to Plato, the sorts of psychic conflicts he wishes to accommodate require a soul that is itself complex. He argues that there are (at least) three distinct types of motivations, corresponding to three distinct parts of the soul (*R.* 436a–441c, 580d7–8).[20] Appetitive desires are bodily and seek the pleasures of food, drink, sex, and money. Spirited desires are associated with competitive action and incline toward honor, victory, power, and esteem. Finally, rational desires aim at truth, wisdom, goodness, and the wellbeing of the entire soul. In the virtuous person, the various parts are highly integrated and they function harmoniously under the guidance of reason. In the vicious individual, reason fails to occupy its natural place as ruler and psychic tension results. Since each of the parts is individually capable of motivating action,[21] actions that issue from the motivating conditions of appetite or spirit alone can be contrary to the desires and beliefs of the rational part.

In the course of characterizing psychic conflict, Plato reveals how he thinks of the psychic states or events that motivate action. Desires, emotions, and beliefs are sometimes characterized as actions, sometimes as affections. In the *Republic*, desires and aversions are vividly depicted as doings (*poêmata*) of the part of soul to which they belong (*R.* 439a–d). The desires of appetite, for example, are active impulses toward potential pleasures, and its aversions are motions away from potential pains. When sufficiently strong, the desires of one part of the soul can successfully 'draw,' 'push,' 'pull,' or 'drag' the whole soul toward its object. In cases of psychic conflict, the desires or aversions of one part of the soul can overcome the simultaneous and opposing motions of another part (*R.* 439b–d).

The psychological attitudes associated with the various parts of soul, even the non-rational parts, are also generally depicted as representational.[22] Desires are characterized as a kind of assent, aversions as dissent (*R.* 437b–c). Presumably the objects of desires, of aversions, and of emotional responses are apprehended or represented via at least some minimal conceptual characterization in order to elicit the particular psychic motions they elicit.[23] Whether or not beliefs or rational capacities belong to the non-rational parts of the soul,[24] the cognitive resources of appetite and spirit at least include perceptual contents or appearances, memory, and imagination (*R.* 602c–603b, *Ti.* 71a–e, *Phlb.* 32b–36c). Representational cognitions enable the soul to depict the objects of non-rational desires as, say, pleasant or honorable. Non-rational aversions might arise, then, out of representations that portray a certain course of action as painful or humiliating, evoking fear or shame (*Ti.* 71a–e).

Plato's *Philebus* develops an account of the nature of (at least some) desires according to which desires are for affections opposite to those currently being experienced. My desire for drink, for example, is a desire to experience the pleasure of replenishing the bodily lack I currently experience as the pain of thirst. This desire, according to Plato, depends crucially on memory, since memories of past pleasures associated with past replenishments 'direct my soul' toward the proper objects of my current desire, in this case drink (*Phlb.* 34a–35c). Finally, desires and aversions can be nourished by means of anticipatory pleasures and pains when sensory imagination 'paints' images in the soul to portray some unactualized state of affairs as appealing or unappealing (*Phlb.* 38e–40c).

The fact that desires, aversions and their associated psychic states have specific contents of their own ensures that those states can function as effective motivating conditions while also securing the capacity of the various parts of the soul to interact with one another. For, although the parts or motions of the soul are sometimes depicted as overcoming one another by sheer force or strength, they are also characterized as influencing one another by means of successful communicative exchanges (*R*. 442b–d, 554c–e, 589a–b; *Ti*. 69d–71e). Reason, spirit, and appetite can share information. Reason can issue threats or commands that are received by the non-rational parts, and it can also successfully persuade the other parts to cooperate. Of particular interest to Plato is the idea that intrapsychic interactions make it possible for reason to shape the content and strength of non-rational desires and aversions (*Ti*. 71a–c; *Laws* 644d–645b). Plato's psychology of action is committed to the view that neither the rational nor the non-rational motivations which lead to action are mere blind cravings or impulses. Rather they rely on representational, and sometimes malleable, psychological attitudes.[25]

I will close by briefly considering only two of the many fruitful questions Plato's views of action evoke. First, given his apparent denial that all desires are for the good (*R*. 437e-439a) and his commitment to the possibility of akratic action, how seriously does Plato take the claim that every action is for the sake of the good? Second, how thoroughgoing is Plato's commitment to the tripartition of soul? Both questions have received quite a bit of scholarly attention.[26] My own view is that Plato takes both commitments very seriously and that, in light of them, his account is put under pressure. As for the first question, I will suggest only that actions might count as aiming at the good in some sense, even when they issue from non-rational desires and aversions that have no reliable access to what is genuinely good. This is perhaps possible, if such desires and aversions represent their objects as having positive or negative value along some dimension (for instance pleasure/pain or honor/humiliation), even in the absence of all-things-considered judgments regarding the good – judgments available only to reason, the part of the soul capable of calculation and measurement.

The potentially problematic implications of tripartition strike me as more intractable. For a divided psyche challenges the view that persons and agents are genuine unities. Of course we can coherently say that a single soul might both desire and be averse to the same things in virtue of distinct parts of itself. But that strategy fails to address the issue of the unity of consciousness.[27] Who is it, exactly, that has cognitive access to both the desire and the aversion, and how is such co-consciousness possible? Moreover, is it accurate to say that I act, if only a single part of me causes my motion, while the other parts resist or are dragged in opposition to their own motions? Am I genuinely acting in that case, or am I merely affected? Which part, or parts, represent me most? Such questions become especially pressing when the issues of freedom and responsibility for action arise. Plato seems comfortable with the idea that non-rational agents (for instance young children) act, so reason and rational desires are not necessary for action. But he also suggests that at least some unity of the soul is a normative condition for action (*R*. 352c, 443d–e).[28] Moreover, his vivid image of the human soul as a complex compound – made up of a many-headed beast, a lion, and a human being, all encased within a human body – is evidence of Plato's inclination to depict embodied human agents as genuinely multiple, but also as identifying in some important sense with the uniquely human element, reason (*R*. 588–589).

At this point, however, the richness of Plato's account is evident in the challenges he faces. He attempts to develop a psychologically realistic account of human motivation and action by respecting the reality of psychic conflict, of psychic fragmentation and of the efficacy of non-rational desires. He strives to accomplish all of this while also appreciating that there are important normative differences between actions issuing from reason and a unified psyche and actions issuing from forceful, non-rational elements which might drag along a divided mind.

See also: ACTION THEORY AND ONTOLOGY (1); DESIRE AND PLEASURE (15); WHAT A DIFFERENCE EMOTIONS MAKE (25); AKRASIA AND IRRATIONALITY (35); MOTIVATIONAL INTERNALISM AND EXTERNALISM (37).

Notes

1 My discussion will draw more on the so-called middle and later dialogues than on the Socratic ('early') dialogues. This is due partly to the fact that the resources for uncovering Plato's metaphysics, explanation, and psychology of action are more developed in the middle and later dialogues. But, as will become evident, I also incline toward the view that, where there are topical points of contact across the dialogues, the possibility for continuity or for development without conflict is worth pursuing (with, of course, some exceptions).

2 The beings of the *Sophist* (and of the *Cratylus*) are treated here as Platonic forms.

3 The *Sophist* also characterizes sitting, learning, sleeping and flying as actions.

4 We might be inclined to apply the term 'activities' where I am translating *praxeis* as 'actions' or 'doings.'

5 According to Sedley (2003), important features of some actions' natures are determined by the natures of the proper objects of those actions.

6 Though this commitment might seem implausible for many cases of action, Plato is attracted to the idea that doing something (*prattein*) is akin to making something (*poiein*), where the latter is product-oriented.

7 Translations from the *Gorgias* are, with minor modifications, Irwin's in Plato (1979).

8 Sedley (2003) suggests that, for Plato, token actions and affections are distinct instances of the same nature. Aristotle lists actions, such as cutting and burning, and affections, such as being cut and being burned, as distinct categories of beings (*Categories* 2^a3–4). Yet Aristotle also suggests that the change which is an agent's particular action is one and the same change as the particular affection brought about in a patient (*Physics* iii 3). For discussion, see Charles (1984), Coope (2005), and Gill (1980).

9 I follow Brown (1998) in taking the mark of being passage to articulate a substantive criterion for being and not merely a formal point focused on subject and predicate terms. It will become clear, however, that I disagree with her view that forms count as beings in virtue of affecting other things without themselves being affected.

10 The translation is White's in Plato (1993).

11 Some commentators disagree with the view that forms admit of change in the *Sophist*. Vlastos (1981) argues that, although forms are affected in coming to be known, they are not thereby changed. Brown defends the view that, although something is changed in being affected, forms are neither changed nor affected in cases involving knowing. Rather forms produce affections in souls when souls come to know them.

12 The discussion of perceptual activities (e.g. seeing and hearing) at *Tht.* 156c–157c is thought by some to exhibit metaphysical symmetry across actions and affections, though the view outlined there is not one that belongs to Plato. See also *Ti.* 61c–68d, where a perceptual experience or affection (*pathos*) is produced when an external object acts on a perceiving subject.

13 I intend the phrase 'due to' to allow for a metaphysical reading of the 'because of' relation, though I cannot attempt to defend such a reading here. For a helpful discussion, see Evans (2009). Evans defends the view that, in the *Euthyphro*, the active fact of x's affecting y metaphysically grounds the distinct, passive fact of y's being x-affected, where the relation of metaphysical grounding is distinguished from that of mechanical causing. I agree with Evans that the relation of affecting to being affected, in the *Euthyphro*, is metaphysical and not simply logical or conceptual, and that the relation is asymmetrical. Given the broader range of cases and dialogues under consideration here, I would construe the possibilities for asymmetrical metaphysical relations more broadly, to allow for cases of mechanical causation, metaphysical grounding as Evans characterizes it, and other types of metaphysical dependence.

14 Contrast Aristotle, *Physics* 202^{a}3–7.

15 Not unreasonable, even if controversial. Whether or not Plato is right or even consistent in holding the views I attribute to him is a separate question.

16 Though see *Ti.* 47e–53c, *Laws* 896d–e, and *Plt.* 272b–274e for the idea that disorderly motions and, perhaps, evil must originate in something other than intelligence or rational soul.

17 As opposed to the inner motions associated with, say, a muscle spasm.

18 See Hankinson (1998) for the view that Socrates' preference for appeals to intelligent purposes arises out of his view that change is explicable and intelligible. Mechanistic accounts might explain how changes occur or what conditions must be in place for particular types of changes to arise; but they do not explain why they occur.

19 For recent discussions of the development of Plato's psychology of action, see Anagnastopoulos (2006), Bobonich (2002), Carone (2001), Lorenz (2006) and Penner (2006).

20 There is, of course, much debate about how to understand Plato's appeal to tripartition. I agree with Bobonich and Lorenz (2006) that Plato argues, in *R.* IV, for a composite, embodied soul with (at least) three agent-like parts. Cf. Price (1995 and 2009).

21 For defense of this claim, see Cooper (1997) and Lorenz (2006) and compare Anagnastopoulos (2006).

22 See Lorenz (2006) for defense.

23 According to Lorenz (2008: 49), appetite's desires and aversions, for example, 'go hand in hand with an awareness or representation of objects as pleasant [...] or painful.'

24 According to the *Timaeus*, appetite lacks belief, reasoning and understanding (77b5). The commitments of the *Republic* are less clear. Commentators who attribute beliefs or limited rational capacities to appetite and spirit in the *Republic* include Bobonich (2002), Irwin (1995), and Lorenz (2006).

25 See Lorenz (2006). See also Evans (2007 and 2008) for a defense of the view that, in the *Philebus*, Plato portrays pains and pleasures as being similar to beliefs, hopes, and fears in that they are psychological attitudes with representational contents.

26 For discussion of the first, see Anagnastopoulos (2006), Carone (2001), Penner (2006), and Lorenz (2008). Treatments of the second include Bobonich (2002), Lorenz (2006 and 2008), and Price (1995 and 2009).

27 See Bobonich (2002) and Price (2009).

28 Korsgaard (1999) emphasizes this aspect of Plato's conception of action.

References

Primary sources

Plato (1979). *Gorgias*, translated with notes and introduction by T. Irwin. Oxford: Clarendon Press.

Plato (1993). *Sophist*, translated with introduction by N. White. Indianapolis: Hackett Publishing Co.

Plato (1995). *Platonis Opera*, vol. 1, edited by E. A. Duke, W. F. Hicken, W. S. M. Nicoll, D. B. Robinson, and J. C. G. Strachan. New York: Oxford University Press.

Plato (1997). *Complete Works*, J. Cooper (ed). Indianapolis: Hackett Publishing Co.

Secondary sources

Anagnastopoulos, M. (2006). The divided soul and the desire for good in Plato's *Republic*. In G. Santas (ed.), *The Blackwell Guide to Plato's Republic*. Oxford: Blackwell Publishing, 166–188.

Bobonich, C. (2002). *Plato's Utopia Recast: His Later Ethics and Politics*. Oxford: Clarendon Press.

Brown, L. (1998). Innovation and continuity: The Battle of the Gods and Giants, *Sophist* 245–249. In J. Gentzler (ed.), *Method in Ancient Philosophy*. Oxford: Clarendon Press, 181–207.

Carone, G. (2001). *Akrasia* in the *Republic*: Does Plato change his mind? *Oxford Studies in Ancient Philosophy*, 20, 107–148.

Charles, D. (1984). *Aristotle's Philosophy of Action*. Ithaca: Cornell University Press.

Coope, U. (2005). Aristotle's account of agency in *Physics* III 3. *Proceedings of the Boston Area Colloquium in Ancient Philosophy*, 20, 201–221.

Cooper, J. (1997). Plato's theory of human motivation. In G. Fine (ed.), *Plato 2*. Oxford: Oxford University Press, 186–206.

Evans, M. (2007). Plato and the meaning of pain. *Apeiron*, 40, 71–94.

Evans, M. (2008). Plato on the possibility of hedonic mistakes. *Oxford Studies in Ancient Philosophy*, 35, 89–124.

Evans, M. (2009). Lessons of *Euthyphro* 10a–11b. Unpublished manuscript.

Gill, M. L. (1980). Aristotle's theory of causal action in *Physics* III.3. *Phronesis*, 25, 129–147.

Hankinson, R. J. (1998). *Cause and Explanation in Ancient Greek Thought*. Oxford: Clarendon Press.

Irwin, T. (1995). *Plato's Ethics*. Oxford: Oxford University Press.

Korsgaard, C. (1999). Self-constitution in the ethics of Plato and Kant. *Journal of Ethics*, 3, 1–29.

Lorenz, H. (2006). *The Brute Within: Appetitive Desire in Plato and Aristotle*. Oxford: Clarendon Press.

Lorenz, H. (2008). Plato on the soul. In G. Fine (ed.), *The Oxford Handbook of Plato*. Oxford: Oxford University Press, 243–266.

Penner, T. (2006). Plato's ethics: Early and middle dialogues. In M. L. Gill and P. Pellegrin (eds), *A Companion to Ancient Philosophy*. Oxford: Blackwell Publishing, 151–169.

Price, A. (1995). *Mental Conflict*. London: Routledge.

Price, A. (2009). Are Plato's soul-parts psychological subjects? *Ancient Philosophy*.

Sedley, D. (2003). *Plato's Cratylus*. Cambridge: Cambridge University Press, 1–15.

Vlastos, G. (1981). An ambiguity in the *Sophist*. In G. Vlastos, *Platonic Studies*, 2nd edn. Princeton: Princeton University Press.

54

Aristotle

URSULA COOPE

Modern discussions of action often focus on a distinctively human kind of purposive action. They ask: 'What is it to act for a reason?' One of the most striking things about Aristotle (384–322 BC) is that he does not seem concerned to give an answer to this question. He comes closest to discussing it in his accounts of voluntariness and of choice. In this chapter I shall look at each of these in turn. I shall argue that *voluntary action* is too broad a category, and *action stemming from choice* too narrow, to capture what modern philosophers have in mind when they inquire into human intentional action.

The Voluntary

Aristotle's account of the voluntary is found at *Nicomachean Ethics* III 1 and 5 and V 8, and at *Eudemian Ethics* II 6–9. I concentrate here on the account at *NE* III 1 and 5, though I make some references to Aristotle's remarks elsewhere. At *Nicomachean Ethics* III 1, Aristotle describes voluntary action as 'that of which the moving principle is within the agent himself, he being aware of the particular circumstances of the action' (1111ª22–4). He arrives at this definition by laying out the conditions under which something fails to be voluntary. These conditions are of two types:

1 an action is not voluntary if it is forced (1110ª1ff.); and
2 an action is not voluntary if it is done in ignorance of the particular circumstances of the action (1110ᵇ18ff.).

It will be helpful to consider these two kinds of case in more detail.

Voluntariness and force

Forced actions are actions to which the agent contributes nothing (1110ª1–4). Aristotle's only examples are of things that we *undergo* involuntarily (rather than of involuntary actions): being swept off course by the wind, or being carried from place to place by kidnappers. He goes on to consider examples of actions that we tend to regard as involuntary though the agent *does* contribute to them. A captain who throws his cargo overboard in a storm is, in a sense, forced to jettison his cargo. Aristotle denies that this action is, in the strict sense, involuntary. He points out that in such a case the captain jettisons the cargo on purpose, in order to save the ship. If he had decided not to jettison the cargo, we could criticize him for foolhardiness. Aristotle calls actions of this sort 'mixed': the agent does not have any choice over the circumstances he is in, but, given that he is in them, it is still open to him to act in one way or another. Though they are mixed, Aristotle says that such actions are more like voluntary than like involuntary actions, since they are subject to praise and blame (1110ª8ff.).

What exactly does it mean to say that the origin of an action is in the agent? Aristotle cannot simply mean that the action is a process that has its causal origin in the agent's body. As he himself points out, the processes of growing old and dying have their causal origin in the agent's body, but when we undergo these processes knowingly, we are not doing so voluntarily (*NE* V 8, 1135ª33ff.). Aristotle excludes such cases by claiming that, if an action is to be voluntary, it must be in the agent's power to perform it or not (1135ª32). It is not entirely clear, though, whether this is a condition on an action's having its origin in the agent or a separate condition on voluntary action. At *Eudemian Ethics* II 6, 1223ª7–9, he says something is in my power to do or not just in case it has its origin in me. This suggests that, according to the *Eudemian Ethics*, part of what it is for an action to have its origin in the agent is for the action to be something that it is in the agent's power to do or not. This is why, in the *Eudemian Ethics*, Aristotle is prepared to count an action as forced if it is done under unbearable pressure. Someone who is subjected to torture that it is beyond human nature to withstand, and who as a result gives away a secret, does so involuntarily: it was not in his power to act otherwise (1225ª22ff.).

Voluntariness and ignorance

The other way in which an action may fail to be voluntary is if the agent suffers from a certain kind of ignorance. The kind of ignorance that makes an action voluntary is ignorance of the particular circumstances of the action. Ignorance of right and wrong does not make the action involuntary (1110ᵇ30ff.). If I kill you by hitting you with a sword, thinking (mistakenly) that it is only a harmless stage sword, then I have killed you involuntarily. On the other hand, if my mistake is not about the particular circumstances, but merely about the morality of killing (if, for instance, I think it is a good thing to kill anyone I find annoying), then my action is voluntary.

To this basic account, Aristotle adds certain complications. First, he makes a distinction between two ways of not being voluntary: the involuntary and the non-voluntary. Actions that are done in ignorance of the particulars do not count as involuntary unless they are also regretted. If the agent, when he finds out what he has done, is glad about it, then his action counts as 'non-voluntary' (1110ᵇ18ff.).

Second, he distinguishes between an action done 'in ignorance' and an action done 'because of ignorance' (1110ᵇ24ff.). It is not clear exactly what this distinction amounts to. Aristotle says that someone who is drunk or in a rage acts in ignorance, but not *because of* his ignorance; rather, he acts because of his drunkenness or rage. Perhaps Aristotle is thinking here of cases in which the agent's ignorance is not an essential part of the explanation of his action; it is a mere side effect of something else in him (for instance his rage), and it is this other state that led him to act. Even if his rage had not caused temporary ignorance, it would nevertheless have led to his action. This kind of ignorance, then, does not render an action involuntary.

At *Nicomachean Ethics* III 5 Aristotle discusses voluntary states. One is in a state voluntarily if one has got into it voluntarily. Aristotle seems to count an agent as getting into a state voluntarily just in case being in that state is a foreseeable consequence of the agent's voluntary actions. For example, drunkenness is voluntary, provided that it has not been caused by trickery or force. On this view, negligent ignorance is also voluntary. Aristotle goes on to imply that actions that stem from this sort of voluntary state are themselves voluntary, even if they are done in ignorance of the particulars. This, he says, is why people are punished twice over for crimes they commit while drunk: once for the criminal action itself, and once for being in the drunken state (1113^b30ff.).

Voluntariness, intentionality, responsibility

This, then, is an outline of Aristotle's account of the voluntary. It leaves us with the question: what is Aristotle's account of the voluntary an account *of*?

If the interpretation I have given is right, voluntary action is not the same as intentional action. When a nurse, through negligent ignorance, administers the wrong drug, he does so voluntarily (on Aristotle's view), but clearly he does not do so intentionally. If getting drunk is a foreseeable consequence of my actions, then Aristotle holds that I have got drunk voluntarily – but it is quite possible that I have not intentionally made myself drunk.

Is Aristotle's account of voluntariness, then, an account of responsibility? This suggestion is in many ways attractive. One is responsible for what one does in a state of negligent ignorance. However, this suggestion is hard to square with Aristotle's claim, in *Nicomachean Ethics* (1111^a24–6, 1111^b8–9) that animals and young children act voluntarily. One would expect an account of responsibility to explain why adult humans can, whereas animals and infants cannot, be held accountable for their actions.

One response to this might be to argue that some of Aristotle's discussion of the voluntary is meant to apply specifically to *human* voluntary action. This was the view of the Aristotelian commentator Alexander of Aphrodisias (who was active in the late second and early third centuries AD). He claimed that 'being up to' the agent was not meant to be a general requirement on voluntary action: only for human voluntary action is it up to the agent whether or not to act as he does (Alexander of Aphrodisias, *On Fate*, 14, 183–184, in Sharples 1983). (See also chapter 55.)

However, this is unlikely to have been Aristotle's view. Although in the *Nicomachean Ethics* his examples of actions that are 'up to us' tend to be of human actions, he never suggests that there can be voluntary actions that fail to meet this condition. Moreover, elsewhere (at *Physics* 255^a5–10) he assumes that animals' actions can be up to them.

Aristotle does, at *Metaphysics* IX 2 and IX 5, describe a contrast between rational and non-rational powers that might seem to support Alexander's view. Rational powers, unlike non-rational powers, are powers for opposites. When something with a non-rational power is in circumstances that are appropriate for the exercise of that power, the power is necessarily exercised. (For example, fire's power to heat is necessarily exercised when a fire is near to something heatable.) This is not true of a rational power. A doctor has one power in virtue of his medical skill, and this is a power to heal and to harm. When the doctor is in the appropriate circumstances for the exercise of this power, he can either heal or harm. Which of these he does will depend on his desires. Non-human animals cannot have this kind of power for opposites. As they lack reason, they cannot have rational powers.

A more careful consideration of this distinction suggests, however, that it provides little support for Alexander's view. For there are many *human* voluntary actions that are certainly within our power to perform or not, but that do not stem from (what Aristotle would count as) a rational power. It is up to me whether or not I now stand up (if it mattered, this is something for which I could be held responsible), but there is no Aristotelian rational power that is exercised in my standing up or remaining seated.

If Aristotle's account of the voluntary does not tell us what it is to act for a reason, is there somewhere else where he explains this? A natural place to look for such an explanation is in his account of choice (*proairesis*).

Choice (*Proairesis*)

Aristotle's term *proairesis* has been variously translated as 'choice,' 'reasoned choice,' and 'decision.' I shall use 'choice,' although it will become clear that none of these translations fully captures what Aristotle means. He defines choice as deliberate desire of things in our own power (1113ᵃ11–12). Choice (*proairesis*), he says, is the origin of action (*praxis*; VI 2, 1139ᵃ31–33). By 'action' here he means, specifically, human action. He assumes that whatever is the origin of human action must itself be specifically human. Perception, for instance, could not be such an origin, because other animals too share in perception (VI 2, 1139ᵃ18–20).

This might suggest that, if we are looking for an account of human intentional action, we can find it in Aristotle's account of *praxis*: the kind of action that has its origin in choice. However, there are two arguments that have been thought to cast doubt on this suggestion:

1 Aristotle says that choice must always be the result of deliberation. Human intentional action, however, is not always preceded by deliberation. We sometimes act intentionally on the spur of the moment.
2 Aristotle says that the akratic person does not act in accord with his choice; but presumably the akratic person acts intentionally.

The first of these arguments can, I think, be answered, but the second cannot. On Aristotle's account, there is a type of akratic action that is both intentional and reason-involving but does not stem from a choice (*proairesis*).

Choice and deliberation

Aristotle defines choice as what is determined by deliberation (*NE* III 2, 1112ᵃ15–17); but what exactly does he mean by this? Is he implying that intentional actions that are done on the spur of the moment (and hence not preceded by an explicit reasoning process) are not chosen? Whatever one's view about the relation between choice and intentional action, this is problematic. For Aristotle implies that I only count as acting virtuously if my action is chosen (1105^{a}31–2), but surely he does not think that, whenever I act virtuously, my action is preceded by explicit reasoning. On the battlefield, the courageous person will often not have time to deliberate.

One way in which interpreters have tried to mitigate this problem has been to point out that deliberation can be carried out in advance of the action (Cooper 1975: 7–8). Thus, before I go to a party, I might deliberate about how much I will have to drink. If I then drink just that much at the party, I act on my choice, even though while at the party I am not engaged in deciding how much to drink. However, this kind of answer only helps with a limited range of cases. Often virtue requires us to act immediately, in response to situations we could not possibly have foreseen.

Another possible response is to argue that the deliberation need only be hypothetical. On this view, Aristotle is not committed to saying that every choice is preceded by a process of deliberation. Instead, he means only that any choice can be explained by a deliberative argument. To say that an agent acted on choice is to say that he acted for reasons that could be spelled out by such an argument (Cooper 1975: 9–10). However, this solution seems to let in too much. Aristotle thinks that someone who is acting akratically (that is, acting against his better judgment) is not acting in accordance with his choice. His akractic action can, however, be explained by a practical argument. For example, as Aristotle says (1147^{a}32–33), the akratic might take the chocolate because he regards everything sweet as pleasant (and hence, to be tasted) and notices that the chocolate is sweet.

A third possible response is to argue that Aristotle has a broader conception of deliberation than we have been assuming. Perhaps deliberation (for Aristotle) need not be an explicit process of reasoning. On this interpretation, deliberation simply is the reason-involving process of arriving at a choice. When a soldier recognizes that this is the moment to rush to the aid of his comrade, he is exercising his reasoning capacities, though he is probably not going through the steps of any kind of argument. He acts in the light of his general views about how one should live, together with his recognition of the relevant features of his situation. According to this interpretation, for one's choice (and hence one's action) to be determined by one's reason in this way just is for it to be determined by a process of deliberation. (For an interpretation along these lines, see Segvic 2009.)

Akratic action and choice

To act akratically is to act on one's desire for pleasure, contrary to what one knows to be best. For example, if I know that it would be better for me not to have another chocolate but I take one anyway, then I am acting akratically. According to Aristotle, when someone acts akratically, his action does not stem from a choice (1148^{a}13–17, 1150^{a}19–31, 1151^{a}1–14). This shows, I shall argue, that on Aristotle's view there are some human intentional actions that do not have their origin in choice: I act intentionally in taking the chocolate, but my action is not chosen. When Aristotle says that the origin of action (*praxis*) is choice, what he means by 'action' (*praxis*) cannot be, simply, human intentional action.

In making this claim, I assume that akratic action, for Aristotle, is an instance of human intentional action. Is this assumption right? Aristotle says that a certain kind of akratic person (the weak akratic) suffers from a temporary failure of knowledge when he acts, and is, in this respect, like someone who is asleep, mad, or drunk (1147^{a}10–15). This might suggest that someone who is acting akratically, like a sleep-walker or someone who is very drunk, is not at all aware of what he is doing. However, Aristotle cannot think that the person who acts akratically is quite like someone who is floundering about in a state of complete drunkenness. In acting akratically, one acts on a certain non-rational desire. To act in this way, one must see the desired object as good, or at least as pleasant. Moreover, as I said above, Aristotle thinks that the akratic's action can be explained by a kind of practical argument (for example, 'pleasant things should be tasted; this is pleasant; this should be tasted'). If his action can be explained in this way, the akratic person must have *some* kind of awareness of what he is doing.

This still leaves open the possibility that the weak akratic, though he acts intentionally, does so in an animal-like way. He makes use of his lower cognitive capacities (for instance he uses a cognitive capacity he shares with animals: the capacity to see something as pleasant), but he is temporarily unable to access his *reasoning* capacities. Some interpreters have argued that, on Aristotle's view, the akratic's reasoning powers are temporarily disabled by his appetitive desire, leaving him with the use only of the cognitive powers he shares with animals (Lorenz 2006: 197). However, this too is unlikely to be quite what Aristotle had in mind. For he says that the akratic person can calculate how to get the object of his desire (1142^{b}18–19). The capacity for calculation is a reasoning power and is distinctively human.

Exactly what the akratic's failure of knowledge consists in is a matter of considerable dispute. On one interpretation, Aristotle holds that 'clear-eyed akrasia' is possible: the akratic can be fully aware, at the time of action, that what he is doing is wrong. (See, for example, Broadie 1991, ch. 5). The challenge for this interpretation is to explain in what sense the akratic either lacks or fails to use his knowledge. On an alternative interpretation, Aristotle holds that, when the akratic acts, he is unaware that he ought to act otherwise. This could be because he is temporarily unable to access his knowledge about particular facts (for example, his knowledge that 'tasting this would be unhealthy') and hence is unable to draw the conclusion that what he is doing is wrong (for example, unable to draw the conclusion 'don't taste this'; see Price 2006). The challenge for this interpretation is to explain why the akratic's action nevertheless counts as voluntary.

According to both these interpretations, Aristotle holds that the akratic person voluntarily pursues an object of his desire, knowing that he is pursuing that object. Even if he is temporarily unaware that chocolate is unhealthy, he is fully aware that he is trying to get some chocolate and that he wants the chocolate because it tastes good. Moreover, he may even use his reason in pursuit of this object (in working out how best to set about getting the chocolate).

The fact that the akratic may calculate how best to get the object of his desire brings out one reason why neither 'choice' nor 'decision' fully captures the meaning of *proairesis*. Suppose the calculating akratic sets out for the bus stop, having considered various options and concluded that catching a bus to the shops is the most efficient way for him to acquire some chocolate. We would ordinarily say that he has decided or chosen to catch the bus in order to go to the shops and get some chocolate. But Aristotle has to deny that his action of catching the bus stems from a *proairesis*.

Why does Aristotle insist that the akratic is not acting from *proairesis* (or 'choice' as we have been translating it)? One possible answer is that the akratic person's reasoning is confined to figuring out how to *attain* the object of his desire. He does not use his reason to decide whether to have this desire in the first place; the appetitive desire simply comes upon him. A problem for this answer is that Aristotle claims quite generally that we do not deliberate about ends ($1112^{b}11$–12), and this suggests that even the virtuous person does not deliberate about the *ultimate* object of his desires. Anyone who gives this answer, then, needs to spell out the sense in which the virtuous person does, and the akratic person does not, use reason in determining what to pursue.

Another possible answer is that choice (*proairesis*) essentially involves a *rational* desire: the fact that one's desire has been formed in response to means–end reasoning does not make it a rational desire, unless one's desire for the end is itself rational. But if this is right, what exactly does it mean to insist that the desire for the end must be *rational*? One possibility is that the desire must involve a judgment that the end is good (or perhaps good overall). On this view, someone who acts akratically does not *judge* that the object of his desire is good: perhaps he judges that it is good in some limited way (for instance, that it is pleasant) or perhaps, though it appears good to him, he does not *judge* that it is good.

A third possibility is that something is only a *choice* (in the sense of *proairesis*) if it is made in the light of the agent's overall views about how best to live his life. Someone who lacked a moral character at all (for instance a young person whose character had not yet been formed) would not have such an overall view, and for this reason would not count as making a choice. The akratic person has an overall view (for he makes the right choice) but when he acts akratically he does not act 'in the light of' this view. Hence, this action is not 'chosen.' Of course, a defense of this interpretation would need to explain more fully what is meant by 'acting in the light of' one's overall view.

Conclusion

Aristotle's discussions of voluntary action and of choice include much that is of interest to the modern philosopher of action. But in neither do we find an attempt to answer one of the central questions of modern philosophy: *what is it to act for a reason?* Aristotle does not think that providing an account of human intentional action is fundamental to his project. This in itself is interesting. Is the absence of such an account a flaw in Aristotle's philosophy? Does it, for instance, impede his understanding of akrasia or of human responsibility? Or does it provide him with insights to which we, with our different presuppositions, have become blind?

See also: VOLITION AND THE WILL (13); INTENTION (14); DESIRE AND PLEASURE (15); TELEOLOGICAL EXPLANATION (16); AGENTS' KNOWLEDGE (30); PRACTICAL REASONING (31); DELIBARATION AND DECISION (32); MOTIVATIONAL STRENGTH (33); AKRASIA AND IRRATIONALITY

(35); RESPONSIBILITY AND AUTONOMY (39); VIRTUOUS ACTION (40); THE DOCTRINE OF DOUBLE EFFECT (41); STOICS, EPICUREANS, AND ARISTOTELIANS (55); ANSCOMBE (74).

References

Primary sources

Aristotle (1894). *Ethica Nicomachea*, edited by L. Bywater. Oxford: Oxford University Press.

Aristotle (1951). *Physica*, edited with commentary by W. D. Ross. Oxford: Oxford University Press.

Aristotle (1957). *Metaphysica*, edited by W. Jaeger. London: Oxford University Press.

Aristotle (1991). *Ethica Eudemia*, edited by R. R. Walzer and J. M. Mingay. Oxford: Oxford University Press.

Alexander of Aphrodisias (1983). *On Fate*. Edited and translated with commentary by R. W. Sharples. London: Duckworth.

Secondary sources

Broadie, S. (1991). *Ethics with Aristotle*. New York: Oxford University Press.

Cooper, J. M. (1975). *Reason and Human Good in Aristotle*. Cambridge, MA: Harvard University Press.

Lorenz, H. (2006). *The Brute Within. Appetitive Desire in Plato and Aristotle*. Oxford: Clarendon Press.

Price, A. W. (2006). Akrasia and self-control. In R. Kraut (ed.), *The Blackwell Guide to Aristotle's Nicomachean Ethics*. Malden, MA and Oxford: Blackwell Publishing, 234–253.

Segvic, H. (2009). Deliberation and choice in Aristotle. In M. Burnyeat (ed.), *From Protagoras to Aristotle. Essays in Ancient Moral Philosophy*. Princeton, NJ: Princeton University Press, 144–171.

Further reading

Anscombe, G. E. M. (1981). Thought and action in Aristotle. What is practical truth? In G. E. M. Anscombe, *From Parmenides to Wittgenstein. The Collected Papers of G. E. M Anscombe*, Vol. 1. Minneapolis: University of Minnesota Press, 66–77.

Charles, D. (2007). Aristotle's weak *akrates*: In what does her ignorance consist? In P. Destrée and C. Bobonich (eds), *Akrasia in Greek Philosophy: From Socrates to Plotinus*. Leiden: Brill, 193–214.

Irwin, T. H. (1992). Who discovered the will? In James E. Tomberlin (ed.), *Philosophical Perspectives*, Vol. 6: *Ethics*. Ridgeview: Atascadero, 453–473.

Price, A. W. (2003). Aristotle, the Stoics and the will. In T. Pink and M. W. F. Stone (eds), *The Will and Human Action: From Antiquity to the Present Day*. London: Routledge, 29–52.

55

Stoics, Epicureans, and Aristotelians

T. H. IRWIN

The Hellenistic Debates

Explicit discussion of questions about the nature of rational action, human freedom, and their relation to causal determination begins in the philosophers of the Hellenistic schools after the death of Aristotle (384–322 BC). Epicurus (341–271 BC) and the major Stoic philosophers – Zeno (334–262 BC), Cleanthes (331–232 BC), and Chrysippus (*c.*280–*c.*206 BC) – maintain opposite views about the compatibility of determinism with freedom. Alexander of Aphrodisias, a later Aristotelian (*fl.* AD 200) criticizes the Stoics from the point of view – as he supposes – of Aristotle.

These philosophers examine the distinctive features of human action and the connexion between action and responsibility. None of them allows action without responsibility. Hence different conceptions of action and of responsibility influence each other. This mutual influence is especially clear in Epicurus and the Stoics, but it is also present in Aristotle and Alexander.

Our sources for Hellenistic philosophy are fragmentary; many of the works of Epicurus and all the works of the early Stoics have perished, and we have to fill the gaps from references in later writers. It is difficult, therefore, to be sure how far one philosopher is aware of the views of another. It is especially difficult to know how far Epicureans and Stoics were aware of Aristotle's views. Nonetheless, it is philosophically instructive and historically plausible to present them as engaging with one another's views. To introduce this debate, we may begin with Aristotle.

Action, Reason, and Assent

When Aristotle discusses action (*praxis*), he sometimes takes it to be peculiar to rational agents; this is why he remarks that non-rational animals perceive but do not act, and this is why sense-perception is not the origin of any action (*Nicomachean Ethics* (hereafter *NE*) 1139^{a}18–20). Similarly, the Stoics allow goal-directed movement (*energein*) to non-rational animals, but they confine action (*prattein*) to rational agents (Alexander, *On Fate*, 205.28; 206.5). When he restricts the scope of action in this way, Aristotle probably means that animals do not engage in action because they lack universal apprehension, and have only experience and memory of particulars (*NE* 1147^{b}3–5).

The Stoics offer a fuller account of rational action. In their view, rational agents act on assent (*sunkatathesis*). Appearance (*phantasia*) and assent are the passive and the active conditions for belief.

> For having an appearance happens without our wanting it, and our being in this condition does not depend on the subject being affected, but on the thing causing the appearance [...] whereas assenting to this motion depends on the subject receiving the appearance. (Sextus Empiricus, *Adversus Mathematicos* viii 397: Sextus reports the Stoic view)

> Zeno [...] said some new things about the senses themselves, which he said were composed out of a sort of impact presented from outside – which he called *phantasia*, and let us call it appearance [*visus*] and retain this word, since we will have to use it often in the rest of the discussion – to these things that appear and are, so to speak, received by the senses he adds assent of our minds, which he wants to be placed in us and voluntary [*quam esse vult in nobis positam et voluntariam*]. (Cicero, *Academica* i 40)

Assent is not simply a further appearance directed to the initial appearance. It also involves an assessment of the appearance; this is why it belongs to rational animals.

Aristotle also claims that human beings differ from animals in being appropriately subject to praise and blame for their actions. Let us say that they are thereby responsible for their actions. What makes them subject to these reactions? We might answer that they act voluntarily (*hekousiôs*). But this does not seem to be an adequate answer; for animals also act voluntarily (*NE* 1111^{b}8–9), but are not responsible for their actions, in Aristotle's view.

Aristotle's view about conditions for responsibility is difficult to discern, because he introduces a number of conditions without saying how they are connected and how far they can be ascribed to all voluntary agents, or only to responsible agents.

> [I]n such actions he has within him the origin of moving the limbs that are the instruments; but if the origin of the actions is in him, it is also up to him to do them or not to do them. (*NE* 1110^{a}15–18)

> For when acting is up to us, so is not acting, and when No is up to us, so is Yes. [...] If this is not so, we must dispute what has been said, and we must deny that a human being is an origin, begetting actions as he begets children. But if [...] we cannot refer back to other origins apart from those that are up to us, those things that have their origin in us are themselves up to us and voluntary. (*NE* 1113^{b}7–21)

In summary, if an agent is responsible, then

1 he is the 'origin' (or 'principle'; *archê*) of his actions;
2 the origin of his actions is in him;
3 it is up to him (*ep'autô(i)*) to do or not to do what he does.

(Further questions arise; see chapter 54 on Aristotle.)

Are these features of the actions of responsible agents necessary or sufficient for being a rational agent? Might there be rational agents who are not responsible for their actions? We might make progress with these questions if we could say what Aristotle's three conditions mean. In particular, we may wonder how they are connected to the truth or falsity of determinism.

Alexander: Aristotle as an Indeterminist

Some students of Aristotle in antiquity interpret him as an indeterminist. Alexander's discussion in his *On Fate* shows us how one might argue from the three Aristotelian conditions to an indeterminist conclusion.

Alexander observes that Aristotle allows voluntary action to non-rational animals, and he infers that in human beings voluntary action cannot be sufficient for responsibility. We are responsible if and only if we meet the further three Aristotelian conditions, which are conditions for responsibility, but not for voluntariness.

If we are responsible, it is up to us to do what we do. For when we act rationally we act on deliberation; when we deliberate about which of two possible actions we should choose, we believe we can do either of these actions; we are responsible for our action only if our belief is true. But if determinism is true, an unbroken chain of sufficient conditions leads to my action from events that happened thousands of years ago. Hence my action is made inevitable by past events; hence it is not really up to me to act differently.

Similarly, insofar as we are rational and responsible, we are origins of actions:

> For to be rational is nothing other than to be an origin of actions. For as the being of different things is in different things [...] so the being of man is in being rational, which is equivalent to having in oneself an origin of choosing something and not choosing it. [...] So that the one who does away with this does away with the human being. (Alexander, *On Fate* 184.15–20)

If our reasoning, deliberation, and rational assent have an external cause, we are not the origins of our actions.

> For a human being is an origin and cause of the actions that come about through him, and this is being a human being – to have the origin of acting in him [...] This is why each of the other things follows the causes that are its external circumstances, but a human being does not, because his being consists in having an origin and cause in him, so as not to follow the external circumstances at all events. (Ibid., 185.15–21)

Determinism implies that there always are external causes, and hence that the origin is not really in us. Alexander infers that Aristotelian conditions for rational and responsible agency conflict with determinism. He does not separate rational from responsible agency, and hence he does not concede that bare rational agency is compatible with determinism. In his view, genuine rational agency requires deliberation in order to control action, and in a deterministic world it would not control action.

It is difficult to find explicit support in Aristotle for Alexander's arguments. (See chapter 54.) But we might nonetheless suppose that Alexander is right on philosophical grounds, even if not on exegetical grounds. For, if the Aristotelian conditions would be false in a deterministic world, is Aristotle not committed to the acceptance of indeterminism, whether he sees it or not?

This question will clarify the discussions of responsibility by Epicureans and Stoics. Epicurus argues (without explicit reference to Aristotle) that the Aristotelian conditions are false in a deterministic world. The Stoics reply that the Aristotelian conditions are compatible with determinism. Epicureans and Stoics agree that the conditions for responsibility are not to be distinguished from the conditions for rational agency. But they take different views about the relevance of determinism to these conditions.

Epicurus: Determinism Excludes Freedom

Epicurus believes that conditions for responsibility are included in the conditions for rational agency, and that rational agency requires the falsity of determinism. He opposes a philosophical doctrine of 'fate' (*heimarmenê*) that prevents us from acting so as to change our lives. He asserts that the popular belief in gods who reward and punish us after our deaths produces pointless fear and anxiety; but he takes the belief in fate to be even worse.

> It would be better to follow the story about gods than to be enslaved to the fate of the natural philosophers. For the one indicates a hope of changing the mind [*paraitêseôs*] of the gods by honouring them, but the other has necessity whose mind cannot be changed [*aparaitêton*]. (Epicurus, *Letter to Menoeceus*, in Diogenes Laertius, *Lives of the Philosophers*, x 134 = Long–Sedley 20A (hereafter LS). The Greek words in brackets are variously rendered by translators)

If we have to deal with the traditional gods, we can change their minds by honouring them, and so, to this degree, it is up to us whether we are punished or not. But since we cannot change the mind of necessity, it follows that, if it is necessary for us to die in a car crash, it is not up to us not to die in a car crash.

What kind of fate or necessity implies that nothing is up to us? Epicurus describes the position of his opponents by referring to their unacceptable conclusion rather than to their premisses. If they claim that everything that happens is necessary, independently of our choices and actions, they draw the conclusion Epicurus rejects. According to this position, we suffer from an illusion if we suppose that our choices make a difference to what happens. Though I may suppose that the intentional content of my choice – for instance, my choice to illuminate the room by raising my arm to switch on the light – makes a difference to whether my arm rises or not, I am mistaken.

Some types of materialism support this conclusion. According to eliminative materialism, there are no mental events or properties. According to epiphenomenal materialism, there are mental events and properties, but they make no difference to what happens because they are causally inert. But these do not seem to be the doctrines that Epicurus attacks for claiming that nothing is up to us. When he speaks of fate and necessity, he seems to have in mind some doctrine of causal necessitation and determination. He seems to suppose that this doctrine leads to the unacceptable conclusion that would also follow from eliminative or epiphenomenal materialism. Hence he avoids the unacceptable conclusion by rejecting determinism and introducing events without causes:

> Epicurus thinks the necessity of fate is avoided by a swerve of an atom [...] He is compelled to admit, in fact if not in words, that this swerve happens without a cause. [...] He introduced this view because he was afraid that if an atom were always carried along by natural and necessary weight, nothing would be free for us. (Cicero, *On Fate* 22–23 = LS 20, E)

If Epicurus' solution introduces indeterminism, he probably takes determinism to be the position that requires the denial of freedom.

The details of Epicurus' views on the atomic swerve are uncertain and may have already been obscure to ancient readers. If Cicero is right, the swerve is an uncaused motion of atoms that introduces a break in the sequence of sufficient causal conditions. It is uncertain how often Epicurus takes swerves to occur, and whether they occur both outside the minds of rational agents and inside them. We can perhaps understand what he says, or needs to say, about atomic motion if we understand why he takes determinism to be incompatible with freedom.

Epicurus takes causation to imply necessitation. He might, therefore, argue as follows:

[1] If *A* causes *B*, *A* necessitates *B* – that is, necessarily [If *A*, then *B*].
[2] If *A* necessitates *B*, *A* makes *B* necessary.
[3] If *B* is necessary, it is not up to us whether *B* happens or not.
[4] Hence if my raising my arm has a cause prior to my choice, it is not up to me whether I raise my arm or not.

According to determinism, every event has causes that go back to the distant past. Hence determinism seems to imply that nothing is up to us.

This argument is open to question at [2], which seems to assume that the necessity of a conditional (*necessitas consequentiae*, as in [1]) also makes the consequent necessary (*necessitas consequentis*). This assumption is false; if *A* necessitates *B*, but *A* is contingent, *B* may still be contingent. Aristotle points out this error (*De interpretatione* 19[a]23–38).

Epicurus might reply, however, that his argument does not rely on this false assumption, but on a true claim about the necessity of the past.

[1] If *A* causes *B*, *A* necessitates *B* – that is, necessarily [If *A*, then *B*].
[2a] The past is now necessary – in other words I cannot do anything now to change the past.
[3a] Hence, if *A* is past, and if *A* causes *B*, *B* is now necessary.

From these premisses [3] and [4] follow, and determinism still excludes freedom.

Though Epicurus does not state this argument explicitly, it offers a reasonable account of what he has in mind when he claims that fate and necessity exclude freedom.

Epicurus: Argument against Determinism

If Epicurus argues successfully for the incompatibility between freedom and determinism, has he any reason to believe that we should reject determinism in order to retain freedom, instead of denying freedom?

Some of his remarks suggest that he believes that the determinist position is self-refuting. He remarks that a determinist cannot criticize those who reject his position.

> The one who says that everything comes about in accord with necessity has nothing to criticize in the one who asserts that not everything comes about in accord with necessity; for he [*sc.* the determinist] says that this very assertion also comes about in accord with necessity. (Epicurus, *Vatican Sayings* 40 = LS 20, D; my translation)

Since the determinist position rejects freedom, it rejects the possibility of praise and blame, so that a determinist cannot criticize others for their actions and beliefs; in particular, he cannot criticize them for their disbelief in determinism. In that case, he cannot consistently tell us that we ought to believe determinism. If he cannot consistently tell us this, and we do not believe it in any case, we have no reason to accept determinism.

Epicurus offers a fuller version of his argument to show that determinism is self-defeating. He presents a debate with a determinist opponent who believes that all events in the universe, including our thoughts, choices, and actions, are necessitated.

> [1] We rebuke, oppose, and reform one another on the assumption that we have the cause in ourselves also, not merely in our initial constitution and in the random necessity of things that surround and enter us. [2] For suppose that someone were to claim that rebuking and being rebuked themselves have the very same random necessity of whatever happens to be present to oneself at a time. [...] still, he would be leaving intact this very behaviour that, in our own case, produces the preconception of the cause. [...] [3] And even if he goes on to infinity saying that this action of his is in turn necessitated, [...] he still leaves in himself the cause of having argued correctly, and in his opponent the cause of having argued incorrectly. (Epicurus, *On Nature*, in Arrighetti 34.27–30 = LS 20, C2–6. Numbers are added; the translation is mine. This argument is preserved in a fragmentary condition, and at some points the text depends on conjecture)

In [1] Epicurus asserts that attitudes and actions connected with responsibility presuppose that we have the cause of our actions in ourselves. In [2] he answers an opponent by saying that the opponent's belief in necessity fails to undermine the belief that we sometimes have the cause in ourselves. In [3] he defends this answer by extending the scope of his argument, from action to rational belief. He suggests that, if his opponents claim to have argued correctly, their claim counts against their deterministic thesis.

The argument relies on claims about internal causation ('the cause in us') in both [1] and [3]. If we suppose that we hold beliefs for reasons, we assume internal causation; for we assume that some states of ours (our recognition of the reasons) cause other states of ours (our beliefs). But determinism casts doubt on this assumption. Since determinists believe that every event has causally determining and necessitating conditions in the distant past, they hold that my recognition of reasons, my beliefs, my choices, and my actions all have their causes in the distant past. But – Epicurus insists – if the causes are in the distant past (before I was ever born), the causes are not internal to me.

If, then, determinists claim to believe their deterministic thesis for good reasons, they refute themselves. For if they believe for good reasons, their beliefs have internal causes; but if determinism is true, their beliefs have external, not internal, causes. Hence they must admit that they do not believe their thesis for good reasons, and that no one else who believed it could believe it for good reasons. But if they admit that, we need not take it seriously.

Epicurus argues therefore, that rational agency and rational belief require internal causation, and hence require indeterminism. If this argument is sound, Aristotle is committed to indeterminism, whether or not he recognizes it. The argument is sound, however, only if Epicurus' conception of causation is correct. He believes that, if events outside me causally determine my internal states, none of my internal states causes other internal states; this is why the causes of my beliefs are not in me, if determinism is true.

What account of causation would justify this belief? We might argue that causation is causal determination, the existence of sufficient conditions. If I want to water the lawn, I put the sprinkler in the right place, connect one end of the hose to the sprinkler, connect the other end to a tap, and turn the tap on. My turning the tap on is now sufficient to water the lawn, because it initiates a series of events that ends in the lawn being watered. And so this earliest sufficient condition seems to cause the watering of the lawn. Since the earliest sufficient condition is sufficient for the later conditions, it causes the watering of the lawn and they do not; they are simply part of the causal sequence. If this is Epicurus' view, he hols that, if some earlier event (such as the turning on of the tap) necessitates a later event (the watering of the lawn), none of the intermediate events in the deterministic sequence that ends with the later event can cause the later event.

If Epicurus' indeterminism rests on this account of causation as causal determination and on his belief that rational action requires internal causation, he requires frequent undetermined events, and therefore frequent atomic swerves. Suppose, for instance, that an atomic swerve happened ten thousand years ago, but none has happened since then. In that case, my raising my arm now has a long, though not infinite, series of external causes, and so (according to Epicurus) cannot be internally caused. If, then, it is to be internally caused by a rational choice of mine, that rational choice itself cannot be caused, and hence must be preceded by a swerve. Since rational belief, action, and responsibility require internal causation, they require radical indeterminism.

Stoics: Fate without Fatalism

Our survey of Epicurus' arguments shows that the self-defeating conclusion from determinism depends on assumptions about causation and necessitation. His argument succeeds only if either (1) these assumptions are plausible in their own right, or (2) determinists are committed to them. The Stoics deny both (1) and (2). Since they are determinists who believe that we are responsible for our actions insofar as we are rational agents, they are compatibilists about responsibility and determinism. If they agreed with Epicurus' views about causation and causal determination, they could not consistently maintain compatibilism. They have a good reason, therefore, to present a different account of causation.

The Stoics express their determinism as a belief in 'fate.' They agree that there is a sequence of causes going back from (e.g.) my raising my arm now to its cause, to the cause of that cause, and so on. In this order every event has some cause that is sufficient for its occurrence. The Stoics say that they can maintain fate, but still escape necessity (see Cicero, *On Fate* 41, quoted below). Epicurus argues that those who believe in fate are committed to the belief that everything is necessary and that nothing is up to us. The Stoics distinguish fate from necessity in order to show that a doctrine of fate does not lead, as Epicurus alleges, to the denial of freedom.

The Stoics explain the implications of their determinism in different ways, to counter different incompatibilist objections. First, they consider an incompatibilist argument from past determination:

[1] If my action is fated, then it will happen whatever else I do.
[2] If it will happen whatever else I do, I cannot do anything about it.
[3] Hence, if my action is fated, I cannot do anything about it.

If I say that it is not up to me to change tomorrow's weather, or that I cannot do anything about it, I mean that, whatever I do or fail to do, the weather is going to be whatever it is going to be. According to the incompatibilist, determinists are committed to a similar conclusion about my actions.

The Stoics reply that [1] is false, and so the argument fails. They argue against [1] by considering the 'lazy argument' (see Cicero, *On Fate* 28 = LS 55, S):

[1a] Either it is fated that I will pass the examination tomorrow or it is fated that I will fail it.
[1b] If it is fated that I will pass (fail), then I will pass (fail) whether I study or not.
[1c] Hence there is no point in my studying, since it will make no difference whether I study or not.

If this argument were sound, then it would follow that, if something is fated, then it will happen no matter what I do, and so I cannot do anything about it.

The Stoics, however, argue that [1b] is false. To say that something is fated is to recognize a series of causes, each of which is sufficient for its effect, beginning in the distant past and continuing without interruption into the future. But the existence of the series does not make the different causes in the series unnecessary. Similarly, if you bowl at a row of ten pins, and you hit the middle pins hard enough so that they hit the next two, they hit the next two, and so on until all ten fall over, it does not follow that by hitting the middle pins you would make the outer ones fall over even if the intermediate ones were not hit. If a sequence of causes, including your studying or failing to study, will inevitably result either in your passing or in your failing the examination, your studying or failing to study is still necessary for your passing or failing.

This is what the Stoics mean by saying that some events are 'co-fated.' They mean that, if the laws of nature and the past are what they are, then certain intermediate events are fated if the outcome is fated. If it is fated that you will drive to London tomorrow, even though you have no fuel in your car today, it is co-fated that there will be fuel in your car tomorrow.

This argument about co-fated events is part of a reply to incompatibilism. It shows that, even if everything is fated, I can still do something about what happens. But the question is whether the ability that the Stoics allow is of the sort that I need for freedom and responsibility. The doctrine of co-fated events covers too many cases. Admittedly, my choice is necessary if the fated event is to occur; but I also need paper to write on if I am to pass the exam. We do not believe that the paper is free just because it plays some essential role in the causal process. The paper does not control its place in the causal process.

If the reply to the 'lazy argument' fails to vindicate freedom, not every kind of causal contribution implies freedom. The Stoics need to show that our causal role – unlike the role of the paper – in a co-fated event allows us to be free.

Stoic Causes

The Stoics distinguish the cause of an event from the antecedent conditions that are necessary for the cause.

> And if something is cause and producer, that is always also that because of which (*di'ho*); but if something is that because of which, it is not always also the cause. For many things concur towards one end, because of which the end comes about, but they are not all causes. For Medea would not have killed her children if she had not been angry; nor would she have been angry if she had not become envious; nor this if she had not fallen in love; nor this if Jason had not sailed to Colchis; nor this if the Argo had not been fitted out; nor this if the logs had not been cut down from Mount Pelion. For in all these cases the because of which is found, but they are not all found to be causes of the child-killing, but only Medea. (Clement of Alexandria, *Stromata* 97)

The events all the way back to the felling of the trees on Mount Pelion are 'antecedent' conditions of Medea's killing her children, but they are not the cause of it. The Stoics sometimes express the same distinction by distinguishing types of causes, so that the felling of the trees may be counted as an 'antecedent cause'; but only Medea's choice is the 'principal cause.'

What is the basis of this distinction? If we want to explain why Medea killed her children in precisely these circumstances (when Jason had abandoned her for another woman), it does not seem enough to say that she had saved her husband and he had abandoned her. Since many mothers would not kill their children in these circumstances, we have not explained the killing simply by referring to these provocations. We have to refer to Medea's character and to her view of her situation. Features of her are the principal cause insofar as they explain why the killing of the children (as opposed to some less extreme reaction) was the outcome in that situation. Since her character and outlook have this explanatory role, the Stoics take them to be the principal cause.

Determinism, therefore, asserts that every event has a series of antecedent causes, each of which is sufficient for its successor. This series of causes constitutes fate. The Stoics agree that this series of antecedent causes determines the outcome. But they deny that it is the principal cause of the outcome.

> Chrysippus [...] both rejected necessity and wanted nothing to happen without previous causes; and so he distinguishes kinds of causes, so that he can both escape necessity and hold on to fate. [...] He says: 'Someone who has pushed a roller gives it an origin of motion, but he has not given it the capacity to roll. So also something seen when it confronts us will indeed imprint and, so to speak, seal its character in the mind; but our assent will be in our power, and, as we said about the roller, once it is struck from outside for the rest it will be moved by its own force and nature.' (Cicero, *On Fate* 41–3 = LS 62, C)

Even if our action is determined by a series of antecedent causes, the principal cause is nonetheless in us.

Assent as Principal Cause

According to the Stoics, the principal cause of a rational agent's action is the agent's assent. The existence of an external object is a necessary condition, and the appearance caused by the object is an antecedent cause; but neither of these is the principal cause. The incompatibilist would be right, if the past and the laws of nature determined our actions irrespective of what we assent to and choose. But this is not the role of the past and the laws of nature. Past events determine my actions only because they lead to the assent and choice that is the principal cause of my action. Since my assent plays a crucial causal role in the production of my action, I am responsible for the action.

Why does this causal role matter? The mere fact that we are the principal causes of something cannot by itself make us morally responsible for it, since plants, animals, and other non-responsible agents can also be principal causes. The Stoics, however, argue that, since assent is the principal cause, we are responsible. Since the general evaluative outlook that causes assent is itself open to alteration by deliberation and reflexion, it is appropriate to praise and blame agents who act on assent.

This link between assent and responsibility depends on the rational character of assent and of praise and blame. The Stoics assume that our assent is open to influence from rational assessment, and that praise and blame are forms of rational assessment, because they point out reasons for and against an action, that should weigh with an agent who considers whether to assent to an appearance that suggests doing the action. If praise and blame were not concerned with reasons but were simply expressions of favorable and aversive reactions, or if assent were not influenced by reasons but were simply influenced by causal processes immune to reasons, the Stoics would have no ground for their claim that actions caused by acts of assent are proper objects of praise and blame. Since, however, they have good reason to believe that praise, blame, reasons, and assent are linked in the ways they claim, they reasonably infer that we are justly held responsible for the actions we assent to.

A Stoic Defense of Compatibilism

How far do the Stoics answer the incompatibilist arguments of Alexander and Epicurus? We can summarize some of the discussion as follows:

1 They use their doctrine of causes to answer Epicurus' charge that determinism implies that we can do nothing about what happens to us.
2 They accept Aristotle's claims that the origin is in us and that we are the origins of our actions – but only if these claims apply to principal causes, not to antecedent causes.
3 Given their conception of the principal cause, they can also agree that it is up to us to do or not to do whatever we choose.
4 Since assent is the principal cause, we can speak of moral responsibility. Since the general evaluative outlook that causes assent is responsive to deliberation and reflexion, it is appropriate to praise and blame agents who act on assent. While Alexander is right to insist on the distinctive connexion between human agency and responsibility, we need not, in the Stoics' view, accept an indeterminist account of this connexion.

The Stoic arguments do not close debates about responsibility and determinism, but they make a reasonable case for a compatibilist interpretation of the Aristotelian conditions for responsibility.

See also: REASONS AND CAUSES (17); MENTAL ACTS (27); PRACTICAL REASONING (31); DELIBERATION AND DECISION (32); FREE WILL AND DETERMINISM (38); RESPONSIBILITY AND AUTONOMY (39); SCIENTIFIC CHALLENGES TO FREE WILL (44); ARISTOTLE (54).

References: primary sources

Alexander of Aphrodisias, *On Fate* (1983). Edited and translated, with notes, by R. W. Sharples. London: Duckwortth.

Aristotle, *Categories and De interpretatione* (1963). Edited and translated with notes by J. L. Ackrill. Oxford: Oxford University Press.

Aristotle, *Nicomachean Ethics*, 2nd edn (1999). Translated by T. H. Irwin. Indianapolis: Hackett.

Cicero, *On Academic Scepticism* (= *Academica*) (2006). Translated, with notes, by C. Brittain. Indianapolis: Hackett.

Cicero, *On Fate* (1991). Edited and translated, with notes, by R. W. Sharples. Warminster: Aris and Phillips.

Clement of Alexandria, *Stromata*, 2nd edn (1970). Edited by O. Stählin and L. Fruechtel. Berlin: Akademie Verlag.

Diogenes Laertius, *Lives of the Philosophers* (1937). Edited and translated by R. D. Hicks. London: Heinemann.

Epicurus, *Opere*, 2nd edn (1973). Edited and translated into Italian, with commentary, by G. Arrighetti. Turin: Einaudi. [Contains *Vatican Sayings*.]

Inwood, B., and Gerson, L. P., *Hellenistic Philosophy: Introductory Readings*, 2nd edn (1997). Indianapolis: Hackett. [A useful collection of translated extracts (longer and more continuous than those in Long–Sedley).]

Long, A. A., and Sedley, D. N., *The Hellenistic Philosophers*, 2 vols (1987). Cambridge: Cambridge University Press. [Vol. 1: English translations and commentary of selected texts; Vol. 2: The texts (Greek and Latin); referred to throughout chapter as LS.]

Sextus Empiricus, *Against the Logicians* (2005). Translated by R. Bett. Cambridge: Cambridge University Press. [Contains *Adversus Mathematicos* VIII.]

Further reading: secondary literature

Annas, J. (1992). *Hellenistic Philosophy of Mind*. Berkeley: University of California Press.

Bobzien, S. (1998). *Determinism, Fate, and Stoic Philosophy*. Oxford: Oxford University Press.

Brennan, T. (2005). *The Stoic Life*. Oxford: Oxford University Press.

Furley, D. J. (1967). *Two Studies in the Greek Atomists*. Princeton: Princeton University Press.

Inwood, B., *Ethics and Human Action in Early Stoicism* (1985). Oxford: Oxford University Press.

Irwin, T. H., *The Development of Ethics*, Vol. 1. Oxford: Oxford University Press, 2007. [See esp. chs 8 and 10–12.]

Malcolm, N. (1967). The conceivability of mechanism. *Philosophical Review* 76, 97–104.

Meyer, S. S. (1998). Moral responsibility: Aristotle and after. In S. E. Everson (ed.), *Ethics: Companions to Ancient Thought*. Cambridge: Cambridge Unicersity Press, ch. 9.

Sedley, D. N. (1983). Epicurus' refutation of determinism. In *Suzetesis: Studi sull' epicureismo greco e romano offerti a Marcello Gigante*, 2 vols. Naples: Biblioteca della Parola del Passato, 11–51. [A thought-provoking account of Epicurus, partly inspired by Malcolm (above).]

Sorabji, R. R. K. (1980). *Necessity, Cause, and Blame*. London: Duckworth.

56

Augustine and Aquinas

STEPHEN BOULTER

St Augustine (354–430)

St Augustine's theory of action is never developed and presented at length for its own sake. It is only while pursuing strictly theological matters that Augustine has occasion to comment on aspects of action theory, and then he does it only to shed light on his primary concerns. It is perhaps not surprising, then, that philosophical commentators have tended to find his work on action a rather unsystematic amalgamation of often suggestive but conflicting ideas. His most significant works for our purposes are *De civitate Dei* (*On the City of God*), *De libero arbitrio* (*On Free Choice*), and *De duabus animabus* (*On the Two Souls*).

Augustine's distinctive contribution to action theory is best captured in two theses, both of which are essential components of his theory of voluntary action and responsibility. Augustine's theory of voluntary action is itself taken largely from the classical tradition. Along with Aristotle, Augustine maintains that properly human action is always undertaken in pursuit of an end, which can be either the attainment of a perceived good or the avoidance of a perceived evil (1954b: *De libero arbitrio*, 1.30). Moreover, Augustine (usually) maintains that a voluntary action is one performed by an agent in the absence of compulsion and of relevant ignorance (1954a: *De duabus animabus*, 14). Any agent who meets these criteria knowingly performs an action while simultaneously being able to do otherwise; and this, according to Augustine, is to act voluntarily. To this classical theory Augustine adds an insistence upon the twofold freedom of will. According to him, human freedom consists in (1) having the power to will or to refrain from willing; and (2), once this power has been exercised, choosing to act in this or in that fashion. (1) can be called freedom of will, (2) can be called freedom of choice. Augustine's second contribution pertains to action explanation and is altogether more striking. Relying, again, on the classical tradition, Augustine maintains that it is always possible in principle to explain an agent's good actions, but that it is impossible in principle to explain an agent's evil actions. Both theses are crucial components of Augustine's theodicy. A word on each is in order; but it is best to begin with some remarks on Augustine's understanding of will.

Given the manner in which Augustine expresses his views, it is not surprising that many have taken him to posit a distinct faculty in the soul called the 'Will,' the acts of which are called 'volitions.' No doubt Ryle had Augustine in mind when he gave his account of the 'traditional dogma' according to which the mind or soul functions in three 'irreducible modes' – the cognitive mode associated with thought, the emotional mode associated with feelings, and the conative mode associated with the will. What Ryle takes great exception to is precisely what many have taken Augustine to have postulated – namely a 'Faculty, immaterial organ, or Ministry, corresponding to the theory's description of the "Will," and, accordingly, that there occur processes, or operations, corresponding to what it calls "volitions"' (Ryle 1984: 63).

It is true that Augustine is not always the most careful or consistent of writers; and it is true that much of what he says could be taken to imply the existence of such a faculty psychology, for he does say that voluntary actions stem from a kind of 'movement of the soul' (*animi motus*) inevitably putting volition in the reader's mind (1954a: *De duabus animabus*, 14). Moreover, he does describe the workings of the soul in terms of *memoria*, *intelligentia*, and *voluntas*. Nonetheless, while Augustine would no doubt insist that there are acts of the soul properly described as volitions, he explicitly denies the faculty psychology often attributed to him. At *De trinitate* (*On the Trinity*) X, 11.18 he writes:

> Since [...] these three, memory, understanding and will, are not three lives but one life, nor three minds but one mind, it follows certainly that neither are they three substances but one substance [...] And hence these three are one, in that they are one life, one mind, one essence; and whatever else they are severally called in respect of themselves, they are called also together not plurally but in the singular number.

The point, as Bourke emphasizes (1985: 68), is that the diversity of functions in the soul does not reflect a diversity in the structure of the soul. The whole soul remembers, the whole soul understands, and the whole soul wills. This is no idle point for Augustine, since he uses this account of the soul to throw light on Trinitarian theology. Nonetheless his point is often lost, particularly by theologians of a Thomistic stripe, because Aquinas attributes distinct functions or operations only to substances or parts of substances.

To return to Augustine's distinctive theses: as noted above, Augustine's interest in action and action explanation per se stems from his theological concern to exonerate God of any responsibility for the moral evils perpetrated by human beings. Central to Augustine's theodicy is the claim that human beings are alone responsible for their evil deeds, because these are voluntary in the sense sketched above. Of course, God created human beings with free will knowing that evil would result, but the idea is that, on balance, a world with free agents and the evil which this unavoidably produces is better than a world without free agency – and God is morally bound to create the best of all possible worlds. But even if one were to accept the general outlines of this theodicy, the free will defense raises some tricky issues. For one, the question immediately arises as to why God did not make human beings morally perfect, or, at the very least, less prone to sin. Surely this would have limited the evil produced by human free agency. Augustine's answer is that our current liability to sin is in fact the punishment meted out for the Fall of Adam. This punishment consists in our willing to do deliberately what we know to be wrong (something that the classical tradition, with its more optimistic view of human nature, thought impossible). Our 'wretchedness' consists in our own disobedience to our better nature – a fitting and just retribution for Adam's original disobedience of God (1972: *De civitate Dei*, XIV, 15). But this only takes Augustine so far. For, even if one agrees to waive objections regarding the coherence of inherited guilt, the original question re-emerges in the form of a dilemma. Was Adam, the first man for whose sins we are now punished, created morally perfect? If not, then it would seem that Adam was not responsible, or at least not solely responsible, for his disobedience; in which case our current punishment would be unjust. On the other hand, if Adam was created morally perfect, then how could he have sinned at all? A morally perfect Adam surely would not have succumbed to temptation in the Garden. Now Augustine's theodicy prevents him from accepting the first horn of the dilemma, because God's punishment must always be just. So he is left with his central question regarding action: how is it possible for a morally perfect agent to sin?

Again, Augustine turns to the classical tradition for help. He adopts the classical view that one explains an action by reference to the motive of the agent, the motive always being some good envisaged by the agent. This point is familiar to all from Davidson's example of the person drinking a can of paint. If we are to explain the drinking of the paint, we have to find some account of the action which makes it intelligible, and we do this by identifying some point to the action from the agent's perspective. If we cannot find such a point, then the action remains unintelligible and unexplained. Augustine applies this general account of action explanation to his theologically motivated question, with surprising results. He does not conclude that agents never knowingly perform evil actions, as a Socrates was wont to do. Rather he concludes that, while it is always possible to explain an agent's good actions, it is impossible in principle to explain an agent's evil actions, because such actions lack any good at which the agent might aim. He concludes that, while evil actions have a cause in the choice of the agent, there is no cause or explanation of the agent's choice. He writes:

> If you try to find the efficient cause of this evil choice, there is none to be found. For nothing causes an evil will, since it is the evil will itself which causes the evil act; and that means that the evil choice is the efficient cause of the evil act, whereas there is no cause of an evil choice; since if anything exists, it either has, or has not a will. If it has, that will is either good or bad; and if it is good, will anyone be fool enough to say that a good will causes an evil will? If it does, it follows that a good will is the cause of sin; and a more absurd conclusion cannot be imagined. Now if whatever is supposed to cause the evil will itself had an evil will, then I go on to ask what caused *that* evil will, and thus, to set a limit to these questions, I look for the cause of the first evil will. (Ibid., XII, 6)

Augustine, employing the classical theory, of course fails to find a cause for the first evil will, and so concludes that:

> [...] one should not try to find an efficient cause for a wrong choice. It is not a matter of efficiency, but of deficiency; the evil will is itself not effective [*efficiens*] but defective [*deficiens*]. For to defect from him who is the Supreme Existence, to something of less reality, this is to begin to have an evil will. To try to discover the causes of such defection [...] is like trying to see darkness or to hear silence. (Ibid., XII, 7)

This asymmetry in action explanation suits Augustine from a theological point of view. If God is the ultimate cause of all that exists, then God is the ultimate cause of our actions as well. This result is fine with respect to our good actions; but Augustine cannot attribute responsibility to God for our evil actions if his punishment of us is to remain just. But if there is no cause of the choice of an evil will, then the causal chain stops with human agents and does not extend further to God. If there is no cause of an evil will, then a fortiori God cannot be the cause of moral evil. It is surely here that libertarian views of agency find their initial motivation.

St Thomas Aquinas (1225–1274)

Although he was first and foremost a theologian, like Augustine, Aquinas offers a much more complete theory of action from a philosophical point of view, of which only the briefest of overviews can be offered here. The completeness of his treatment of action arises from the centrality of action to Aquinas' theological and philosophical projects. First, Aquinas maintains that human happiness and wellbeing are to be gained through human action (1997b: *Summa theologica*, I–II, q. 6). And, since his main theological authority taught that there is no reason for humans to philosophize except to gain happiness (Augustine 1972: *De civitate Dei*, XIX, 1), Aquinas naturally takes it to befall both a philosopher and a theologian to understand action fully, the better to facilitate the achievement of human wellbeing. Second, an understanding of action is central to Aquinas' strictly philosophical project inasmuch as his standard method in epistemology turns on the close connections that obtain between the necessary conditions of our understanding *x*, the essence of *x*, and the activities of *x*. This second point deserves some elaboration.

Aquinas, like Aristotle, maintains that many of the questions we pose regarding any particular object can be answered by reference to the nature of the object in question. The assumption is that, if one knows the what-ness of *x*, *x*'s essence or nature, then one is in a position to explain why *x* has the properties it has. But how does one identify the essence of *x*? Aquinas' answer is that, while a thing's nature is not immediately accessible to us, its actions are, and these reflect the nature of the thing in question. A thing's nature, essence, or substantial form, says Aquinas, determines its activity. '[N]ote that activity flows from actuality, so that the way an agent acts is determined by the way it has actual existence'; thus 'what things do reflects what they are' (1965: *Quaestiones disputatae de potentia*, 3.1–3). Again, 'everything acts in accordance with the sort of thing it is' (1997b: *Summa theologica*, I–II, q. 55, a.2). This gives Aquinas a methodological rule: in any effort to understand a particular object, 'we proceed from [...] *acts* to *faculties*, and from *faculties* to *essence*' (1994: *Commentary on Aristotle's De anima*, Book II, Lecture VI). It is thus vital to Aquinas' larger project that he has a clear understanding of the nature of action, for on this rests the possibility of rendering the workings of the world intelligible to ourselves. Aquinas quite systematically applies this rule to the study of everything in the inanimate world, to the philosophy of mind, and even to political institutions.

The following is a basic sketch of Aquinas' general theory of action. Aquinas takes properly human actions – that is, those undertaken from a deliberate will and a process of practical reasoning – to provide the focal sense of the term 'action.' But he develops a theory of action that applies to non-human animals and inanimate objects as well.

He begins by defining action as a kind of change in particulars. In general, a change is taken to be an actualization of something that exists potentially, and an action is the actualization, from an agent, of such a potentiality existing in something external to the agent (1998: *In Aristotelis libros Physicorum* 3.5). In this most general sense, an action is an agent's bringing about of a change in an object capable of undergoing that change. Actions, then, fall into two general categories: an *external* action is one in which the agent brings about a change in a body distinct from that of the agent (as when a source of light illuminates another body), while an *internal* action is one in which the agent brings about a change in another part of itself (as when a light source is glowing). External actions Aquinas calls 'actions proper,' while internal actions he prefers to call 'activities' (1987: *Quaestiones disputatae de veritate*, 8.6).

Behind this general picture of action stands the view that an object's properties (or forms, in Aquinas' terminology) both qualify the object and bestow upon it certain dispositional powers. In virtue of being, say, red, an object is both colored and able to affect other objects in particular ways, for instance to produce a visual stimulus of a particular variety in a suitably situated visual system. It is in virtue of these dispositional powers that an agent is able to bring about a change in something else (of course such a change happens only if the agent comes into contact with another object whose own properties bestow upon it the dispositional power of being able to be affected in the relevant manner). Identifying these linked pairs of dispositional abilities and liabilities and grounding them in the properties of the respective objects is part of the task of the natural sciences.

With this general picture of action in place, Aquinas then distinguishes different kinds of actions by focusing on the different ways in which these dispositional powers arise in the various kinds of agents. Aquinas distinguishes between (1) the actions of inanimate objects (agents which move by nature but do not move themselves); (2) the actions of non-human animals (agents which move themselves but are not masters of their actions); and finally (3) the actions of human beings (agents who, under the appropriate circumstances, both move themselves and are masters of their actions). To draw these distinctions in a principled way, Aquinas again relies on the point that what something is determines its activities. But now he goes on to say that *the way in which* an agent acquires the form or property through which it derives its operative powers determines the way in which the agent is active (1997a: *Summa contra gentiles*, 2.47). He writes:

> from forms which are in agents but not from them, there issues activity of which its agent is not master. But if there could be agents acting through a form they themselves produced, then such agents would also be masters of the consequent activity. (Ibid)

He then points out that inanimate natural objects do not produce the form or properties by which they are active, these being produced entirely by external forces. A piece of copper, say, plays no part in its acquisition of the properties in virtue of which it enjoys its characteristic range of dispositional powers. By contrast, non-human animals do move themselves inasmuch as they move their limbs in accordance with their desires. But the form by which they act is received via sense perception, and then evaluated by 'an instinctive judgment of nature.' So while non-human animals do move themselves, they do not control their actions as human do because they are not in control of the acquisition of the form through which they act. For purposes of illustration, imagine a rabbit's instinctive behavioral response to seeing a hawk-shaped shadow. The visual stimulus is produced in the rabbit by factors external to the rabbit, and the rabbit's subsequent instinctive flight behavior is triggered immediately, without any deliberation on the part of the rabbit. While this sort of action can be performed by human beings, this is not how we act in the normal course of things. According to Aquinas, properly human actions fall into a distinct category because the forms by which human beings act are not received from external forces but are genuinely produced by us. Key to this claim is the idea that human beings act in accordance with their beliefs and desires. But beliefs are not merely the reports of sense-experience – experiences that fall within the cognitive life of the higher animals. Properly human cognition involves understanding, not merely sensing, objects in the external world. But the forms through which we understand are not produced by the external world impinging on our sense organs. Although sensory experience is a necessary condition of our understanding things in the external world, it is not sufficient. Concepts, the ingredients of propositions and beliefs, are produced by the agent's intellect via a process of abstraction performed on data derived from sensory experience. Thus there is a sense in which human agents produce the form through which they gain their operative power, and this is the metaphysical ground of human freedom.

See also: VOLITION AND THE WILL (13); TELEOLOGICAL EXPLANATION (16); MENTAL CAUSATION AND EPIPHENOMENALISM (23); PRACTICAL REASONING (31); DELIBERATION AND DECISION (32); FREE WILL AND DETERMINISM (38); RESPONSIBILITY AND AUTONOMY (39); ARISTOTLE (54); RYLE (69).

References

Primary sources

Aquinas, T. (1965). *Quaestiones disputatae de potentia (On the Power of God)*. Tuarini: Marietti.

Aquinas, T. (1987). *Quaestiones disputatae de veritate (Disputed Questions on Truth)*, in *Opera Omnia*, Vol. 22. Rome: Leonine.

Aquinas, T. (1994). *Commentary on Aristotle's De anima*, translated by K. Foster and S. Humphries. Notre Dame: Dumb Ox Books.

Aquinas, T. (1997a). *Summa contra Gentiles*, translated by L. Shapcote and revised by A. C. Pegis. In *Basic Writings of Aquinas*, edited by A. C. Pegis, Vol. 2. Indianapolis: Hackett, 3–224.

Aquinas, T. (1997b) *Summa Theologica*, translated by L. Shapcote and revised by A. C. Pegis. In *Basic Writings of Aquinas*, edited by A. C. Pegis, Vol. 2. Indianapolis: Hackett, 225–1121.

Aquinas, T. (1998). *In Aristotelis libros Physicorum (Commentary on Aristotle's Physics)*, translated by R. Blackwell, R. Spath, and W. E. Thirlkel. Notre Dame: Dumb Ox Books.

Augustine (1954a). *De duabus animabus conta Manichaeos (On the Two Souls)*. In *Augustini (Aurelii) Opera*. Turnhout: Corpus Christianorum Series Latina.

Augustine (1954b). *De libero arbitrio (On Free Choice)*. In *Augustini (Aurelii) Opera*. Turnhout: Corpus Christianorum Series Latina.

Augustine (1954c). *De trinitate (On the Trinity)*, in *Augustini (Aurelii) Opera*. Turnhout: Corpus Christianorum Series Latina.

Augustine (1972). *De civitate Dei contra paganos* (*City of God*), translated by H. Betterson. London: Penguin.
Bourke, V. J. (1985). *The Essential Augustine*. Indianapolis: Hackett Publishing.

Secondary sources

Ryle, G. (1984) *The Concept of Mind*. Chicago: University of Chicago Press.

Further reading

Boulter, S. (2009). Aquinas on action and action explanation. In Sandis (ed.) (2009), 257–275.
Brock, S. (1998). *Action and Conduct: Thomas Aquinas and the Theory of Action*. Edinburgh: T. and T. Clark.
Brown, R. (1978). The first evil will must be incomprehensible: A critique of Augustine. *Journal of the American Academy of Religion*, 46, 315–329.
Chappell, T. (1995). *Aristotle and Augustine on Freedom: Two Theories of Freedom, Voluntary Action and Akrasia*. Houndmills: Macmillan.
Kirwan, C. (1991). *Augustine*. London: Routledge.
Sandis, C. (ed.) (2009) *New Essays on the Explanation of Action* (Basingstoke: Palgrave Macmillan).

57

Duns Scotus

THOMAS WILLIAMS

The Category of Action

Action is one of the ten Aristotelian categories. Duns Scotus (1266–1308) holds that the division of contingent being into the categories is both *sufficient* and *immediate*: sufficient in the sense that there are no other categories, and immediate in the sense that no two or more of the categories fall under some still more generic category (King 2003: 28). In arguing for the distinctness and irreducibility of action as a category, Scotus focuses on why action (along with its correlative category, passion) is not to be subsumed under the category of relation. One might suppose that there is nothing more to the action of, say, heating than the relation between the active power that causes heat and the passive recipient of that heat; but that would be a mistake. For one thing, even in the case of heating more is required for there to be an action than merely the relation between the agent and patient: there must also be something that actualizes the active power. More crucially, there are some actions that do not involve any relation. When an action remains within the agent, there is no relation to any passion, because the agent does not *cause* any passion (Scotus 1997/8: *Questions on the Metaphysics of Aristotle* V, questions 5–6, n. 97).

An action that remains within the agent is called an *immanent* action; one that 'passes through' or 'goes out from' the agent is called a *transeunt* action. Transeunt actions produce something – some form – in a patient; this form is called the *terminus* of the action. The terminus of an immanent action, by contrast, is not a form produced by the action, but the *object* with which the action is concerned. The paradigmatic cases of immanent actions are acts of intellect and will. Immanent actions are said to be 'elicited' by the powers that perform them.

Self-Motion and the Metaphysics of Freedom

The centerpiece of Scotus' theory of active causal powers is laid out in two closely connected questions in Book IX of the *Questions on the Metaphysics*. Critical attention has focused on question 15, in which Scotus draws his crucial distinction between nature and will; but a full understanding of this distinction requires that we begin with question 14, in which Scotus argues for the possibility of self-motion.

There was formidable authority in favor of the proposition that nothing can move itself. Aristotle was generally read as denying the possibility of self-motion, most explicitly in *Physics* VII: 'It is manifest that everything that is moved is moved by another.' Thomas Aquinas had adopted the slogan *omne quod movetur ab alio movetur* and put it to use in his metaphysics and natural theology; and both Godfrey of Fontaines and Siger of Brabant had denied the possibility of self-motion. Scotus rejects this widespread consensus, however, and argues that something can act upon, and thereby move, itself. In essence, his argument is that the primary object of an active power is not some particular passive thing, but any passive thing that falls under some relevant general description. The primary object of the active power to heat, for example, is not some particular heatable thing, but whatever can be heated. And it is possible for something to fall under the general description that marks off the primary object of an active power of that thing itself. In such a case, the thing will be an object of its own active power; in other words, it will be able to move itself (*Questions*, IX, q. 14, n. 24). This argument, Scotus notes, does not show that just anything can act upon itself in just any way. A thing can act upon itself only by way of an *equivocal* action – an action whose product is not the same in kind as the active power that produced it – and only if the thing has the capacity to receive the product of that kind of action.

The examples of self-motion that Scotus considers in question 14 are all of transeunt actions (broadly construed: when a thing acts on itself, the action does not 'go out from' the agent in the most obvious sense, but Scotus has in mind cases in which the action produces some form as its terminus). Nonetheless, the general possibility of self-motion that he establishes there is clearly meant to apply in question 15, which is primarily concerned with immanent actions. In question 15 Scotus asks whether Aristotle's distinction between rational powers, which are powers for opposites, and irrational powers, which are for only one of a pair of opposites, was drawn correctly (*bene assignata*). He answers that it was, and goes on to explain, first, how it ought to be understood and, second, what its cause is.

By a 'power for opposites,' Scotus clarifies, we mean a power for opposite *actions*, not merely for opposite *effects* or *products*. The sun can soften wax and harden mud, but that is not the kind of 'opposite' Scotus has in mind. At issue is a power that is sufficient for eliciting both an act and its negation (as would be the case if the sun had the power either to soften wax or not soften it) or for eliciting opposite acts (as would be the case if the sun had the power either to soften wax or to harden it). Aristotle, according to Scotus, had explained this difference by appealing to the difference between a natural form and an understood form. A natural form can act in only one determinate way: the form of fire heats and can only heat. But on the basis of an understood form one can act in opposite ways: by having the form of fire in my understanding I can know both fire and non-fire. Scotus argues, on several grounds, that this difference is an inadequate basis for the distinction between rational and irrational powers. Instead, the fundamental distinction in the domain of active powers has to do with the differing ways in which these powers elicit their acts. There are only two possible ways of eliciting acts:

> Either a power is by its very nature (*ex se*) determined to acting in such a way that, as far as it is up to that power, it cannot not act when it is not impeded by something extrinsic to it; or else it is not by its very nature determined, but can do this act or the opposite act and can also act or not act. The first power is commonly called 'nature' and the second is called 'will.' (*Questions*, IX, q. 14, n. 22)

The division into nature and will is the most basic division of active powers. And what is the cause of this division? Scotus says that there is no cause: it is a brute fact that will is a power for opposites and nature is not. Just as that which is hot heats, and there is no further explanation for why it heats, so too there is no further explanation for why it heats *determinately*; nor is there any further explanation for the fact that a will does not will determinately. Moreover, the will's mode of acting is so distinct from the mode of acting proper to every other active power that 'it appears altogether ridiculous to apply universal propositions concerning active principles to the will, simply because they have no exception in any active principle other than will' (ibid., n. 44).

One would expect, given general Aristotelian metaphysical principles, that what is in itself indeterminate would require some extrinsic cause to determine it. Scotus argues, however, that this is not so. There are two kinds of indeterminacy:

> There is a certain indeterminacy of insufficiency, in other words, an indeterminacy of potentiality and deficient actuality, as matter that does not have a form is indeterminate with respect to doing the action of that form; and there is another indeterminacy of superabundant sufficiency, which derives from an unlimitedness of actuality, whether altogether or in some particular respect. (Ibid., n. 31)

Something that is indeterminate in the first way does not act unless it is determined to some form by something else; but something that is indeterminate in the second way can determine itself. If there were no such thing as the indeterminacy of superabundant sufficiency, Scotus argues, it would be impossible for God to act, since God is 'supremely undetermined to any action whatsoever' (ibid., n. 32).

Scotus seems at this point to have wandered rather far from the Aristotelian distinction he had allegedly set out to defend. How does the distinction between nature and will map on to the original distinction between a rational power – which in Aristotle appeared to mean the intellect, not the will – and irrational powers? Scotus says that we can speak of intellect and will either in terms of their own proper acts or in terms of the acts of inferior powers on which they exercise some causality: 'the intellect by presenting [objects] and directing, the will by inclining and commanding' (n. 36). The first way of considering intellect and will is more fundamental (and obviously so, says Scotus); and intellect, so considered, gets classified as nature. It is beside the point that the intellect is capable of cognizing opposites, since in a given case of intellectual cognition the intellect necessarily elicits whatever cognition it in fact elicits. (Here we see clearly how Scotus' distinction between rational and irrational powers depends on the notion of synchronic contingency: a rational power has, and an irrational power lacks, the ability to act otherwise *at the very moment of acting*; see MacDonald 1995.) The second way of considering intellect and will appears to be 'quasi-accidental' (n. 37), but it is nonetheless the way in which Aristotle considers the intellect in drawing his distinction between rational and irrational powers. For, although the intellect's own act is not undetermined in itself, that act is required for the act of the will, which *is* undetermined. So Aristotle can call the intellect a rational power in this derivative sense.

The Relationship between Intellect and Will

Scotus is emphatic in the *Questions on Aristotle's Metaphysics* that the will's mode of acting is irreducible and basic; the will is by its very nature (*ex se*) such as to be able to act or not act, and to do this or that. In particular, Scotus emphasizes that the will's freedom does not derive from its relation to the intellect. This emphasis puts Scotus squarely in the broad voluntarist tradition. But our reading of Scotus' account of the will as a rational power leaves us with two further questions. First, exactly how does Scotus understand the relationship between intellect and will? The general voluntarist stance leaves room for different views, and it appears that Scotus adopted different views at different points in his career. The second question is why, if indeed the will's mode of acting admits of no more basic explanation, Scotus appears to offer an explanation for it in terms of the two 'affections' of the will. I will take up these two questions in turn.

First, I shall look at the development of Scotus' views of the relationship between intellect and will. (In tracing this development I accept the chronology defended in Dumont 2001.) In his earliest engagement with the issue, the Oxford *Lectura*, Book II, distinction 25, Scotus attempts to steer a middle position between, on the one hand, the intellectualism of Thomas Aquinas and Godfrey of Fontaines, and, on the other hand, the voluntarism of Henry of Ghent. He understands Aquinas and Godfrey as having held that the object is the sole efficient cause of volition: Aquinas meaning the object as it exists in the intellect and Godfrey the object as it exists in the imagination. Scotus argues both against the general view that the object is the sole cause of volition and against the particular versions of that thesis defended by Aquinas and Godfrey. He then turns to the view of Henry of Ghent, calling it 'extreme.' Henry held that the will is the sole efficient cause of its own action and the cognized object is only a *sine qua non* condition. Scotus deploys several arguments against Henry's view, drawing some of them from Godfrey. Scotus then sets out his own middle view, according to which the will and the object, together, make up the total efficient cause of the act of will. The will and intellect concur in the same way in which male and female concur in the production of offspring (according to the biology of the day): neither depends on the other for its causal power, but both are required for the production of the effect: one as 'the more principal and perfect agent' and the other as a less perfect agent. The will is the 'more principal' agent because it is responsible for the freedom and contingency of the volition, but the intellect is nonetheless required. As Scotus realizes, it might seem that this position is not so different from Henry's view that the intellect is merely a *sine qua non* condition. But Scotus argues that, if the intellect is merely a *sine qua non* condition, *liberum arbitrium* (generally translated as 'free choice' or 'free judgment') does not include both intellect and will, and so it would be blind. One must therefore ascribe some efficient-causal role to the intellect in producing the act of willing.

In the later *Reportatio* of Scotus' lectures in Paris, however, Scotus adopts the very view that he had earlier described as 'extreme': the view that the will is the total cause of its act, and the intellect's presentation of an object is merely a *sine qua non* condition. The *Reportatio* largely recapitulates the arguments from the *Lectura* against the position of Aquinas and Godfrey, but it does not present Henry of Ghent's position and argue against it, as the *Lectura* had – after all, now Scotus is adopting that very position as his own. Recent scholarship has wondered how Scotus came to adopt a position that he had regarded as 'extreme' only a few years before. Stephen Dumont has suggested a historical factor at work: it is all but certain that at Paris Scotus began his lectures under the regency of Gonsalvus of Spain, who

> was actually in the process of mounting a defense of Henry's voluntarism against Godfrey and his followers. [...] At Paris Scotus took up the defense of his master's position, a position against which he had previously argued at Oxford. (Dumont 2001: 776–777)

For my part, I should hesitate to appeal to such purely external factors in accounting for the development in Scotus' views, and I do wonder how we are to square Dumont's explanation with the undoubted fact that, at Oxford, Scotus had taught a view contrary to that of his supposed teacher, William of Ware. Fortunately, philosophical explanations present themselves.

First of all, we should not lean too heavily on the word 'extreme.' As Scotus uses the word here, an 'extreme' view need not be one that is crazy or 'way out there'; it is merely a view that lies at either end of a spectrum of possible views. (It would be very odd indeed for Scotus to stigmatize as crazy a view that had been defended by such Franciscan luminaries as William de la Mare, Roger Marston, Peter Falco, and William of Ware.) As Dumont himself has shown, Scotus structures his *Lectura* discussion in such a way that his view will be the moderate alternative that is left after the two views at either end of the spectrum – one attributing all causality to the intellect, the other attributing all causality to the will – are rejected. We already see in the *Lectura* discussion that Scotus has his suspicions that his *via media* is going to collapse into Henry's view, and it requires no great effort of philosophical imagination to suppose that, as he reflected on his position, he found that it did in fact so collapse. His *Lectura* argument against Henry's position – that without some causal role for the intellect, *liberum arbitrium* would be blind – is already an odd one for Scotus to make, since the shift in philosophical discussion from talking about *liberum arbitrium* to talking about the freedom of the will was already well underway. Scotus does not ordinarily talk in terms of *liberum arbitrium*, and he may well have come to realize that his invocation of it was not only philosophically retrograde but question-begging, since the requirement that there be some causal role for the intellect is built into the notion of *liberum arbitrium*. Furthermore, even in the *Lectura* it is not clear what the efficient-causal role of the intellect could come to. Unlike in the case of the production of offspring, in which the mother does exercise a non-derived efficient-causal role, though a subordinate one, the intellect's causal contribution seems to be determined entirely by the will. It's not that the intellect does not exercise a non-derived causality in *presenting* the object; the intellect does not derive its power to cognize potential objects of will from the will. But it *is* up to the will whether the intellect's presentation of an object results in an act of will: the intellect's presentation of an object is an efficient-causal dead end if the will does not will the object presented. This line of thought very quickly leads to the *Reportatio* position that the intellect's presentation of the object is merely a *sine qua non* condition for an act of will whose total efficient cause is the will itself.

The Two Affections of the Will

I turn now to the second question: why, if the will's mode of acting admits of no more basic explanation, does Scotus appear to offer an explanation for it in terms of the two 'affections' of the will? Scotus gets the idea of two affections or fundamental inclinations in the will from Anselm, who had identified an affection for the advantageous (*affectio commodi*) and affection for justice (*affectio iustitiae*) in the course of explaining the primal sin of the angels in *On the Fall of the Devil*. It is clear that Anselm intends the two affections as an *explanation* of the will's freedom; and readers of Scotus have assumed that he, too, means to explain the will's freedom by appeal to the two affections. Interpretations have differed, however, about how that explanation is supposed to work. According to the most common interpretation, the affection for the advantageous is an inclination to pursue what is beneficial for oneself, and the affection for justice is an inclination to love things (including other people) in accordance with their intrinsic worth. Now Scotus is quite emphatic that the will cannot have (or be) only an affection for the advantageous, because, if it were, it would operate deterministically and would therefore be a natural, not a rational power. But the standard interpretation leaves it wholly mysterious how the affection for justice helps matters, because it is not at all clear why a disposition to love things in accordance with their intrinsic worth would operate any less deterministically than the affection for the advantageous; and a will with two deterministic inclinations is no freer than a will with only one.

An alternative interpretation emphasizes that Scotus identifies the affection for the advantageous with intellectual appetite: the will's disposition to choose what the intellect presents to it as perfective. On this interpretation, Scotus thinks of the affection for the advantageous as being exactly what Thomas Aquinas had claimed the will to be, and he rejects Aquinas' account of the will because it does not provide for genuine freedom in the will. The affection for justice, then, is the will's capacity to choose in accordance with what is morally right. Such choices must be free if they are to be genuinely morally praiseworthy, and the affection for justice is what provides such freedom. But, as the proponent of this interpretation has acknowledged, this account of the affection for justice would seem to provide for freedom only on those occasions on which the will is faced with a choice between happiness and morality; it does not offer the untrammeled or ubiquitous freedom that Scotus consistently ascribes to the will (Williams 2003: 348–349).

What both interpretations miss is that Scotus' use of the two affections is not intended as an explanation of the will's mode of acting. For Scotus, the two affections are not (as they were for Anselm) two mutually exclusive dispositions that *belong to* the will; the two affections are not really distinct from each other or from the will itself. The affection for the advantageous is no aspect or part of the will; it *is* the will *qua* intellectual appetite. And the affection for justice is not an aspect or part of the will; it *is* the will *qua* free rational power. So the will's possessing an affection for justice does not *explain* the will's freedom. The will's mode of acting – its being a will as opposed to a nature, a rational power as opposed to an irrational power – remains unexplained.

See also: ACTION THEORY AND ONTOLOGY (1); VOLITION AND THE WILL (13); MENTAL ACTS (27); AGENT CAUSATION (28); FREE WILL AND DETERMINISM (38); ARISTOTLE (54); AUGUSTINE AND AQUINAS (56); REID (62).

References

Primary sources

John Duns Scotus (1968). *Reportatio in librum secundum Sententiarum* [*Reportatio on the Second Book of the Sentences*] [1639. Lyon: Laurentius Durand.] Photoreprint, Hildesheim: Georg Olms.

John Duns Scotus (1993). *Lectura in librum secundum Sententiarum, distinctiones 7–44 (Lectura on the Second Book of the Sentences, Distinctions 7–44)*. Vatican City: Vatican Polyglot Press. 1993.

John Duns Scotus (1997). *Quaestiones super libros Metaphysicorum Aristotelis, libri VI–IX (Questions on Aristotle's Metaphysics, Books VI–IX)*. Saint Bonaventure, NY: Franciscan Institute Publications.

Secondary sources

Dumont, S. D. (2001). Did Scotus change his mind on the will? In J. A. Aertsen, K. Emery, Jr, and A. Speer (eds), *After the Condemnation of 1277: Philosophy and Theology at the University of Paris in the Last Quarter of the Thirteenth Century*. Berlin: Walter de Gruyter, 719–794.

King, P. (2003). Scotus on metaphysics. In Thomas Williams (ed.), *The Cambridge Companion to Duns Scotus*. Cambridge: Cambridge University Press, 15–68.

MacDonald, S. (1995). Synchronic contingency, instants of nature, and libertarian freedom: Comments on 'The Background to Scotus's Theory of Will.' *Modern Schoolman*, 72, 169–174.

Williams, T. (2003). From meta-ethics to action theory. In Thomas Williams (ed.), *The Cambridge Companion to Duns Scotus*. Cambridge: Cambridge University Press, 332–351.

Further reading

Dumont, S. D. (1995). The origin of Scotus's theory of synchronic contingency. *Modern Schoolman*, 72, 149–167.

John Duns Scotus (1998). *Duns Scotus on the Will and Morality*, edited and translated by A. B. Wolter. Washington, DC: Catholic University of America Press.

Kent, B. D. (1995). *Virtues of the Will: The Transformation of Ethics in the Late Thirteenth Century*. Washington, DC: Catholic University of America Press.

58

Thomas Hobbes

THOMAS PINK

Introduction

Thomas Hobbes (1588–1679) produced a profoundly original account of human action and of its freedom. His most extended development of this theory was in *The Questions Concerning Liberty, Necessity and Chance*, published in London in 1656 – his dialogue with John Bramhall, a defender of a late scholastic account of action and freedom greatly influenced by the doctrines of Francisco Suarez.

Hobbes' theory of action has transformed and dominated subsequent English-language action theory. But his theory of freedom has been much less influential. Modern English-language compatibilism is an attempt somehow to preserve within the framework of a broadly Hobbesean action theory the intuition that freedom is a power of agents to determine for themselves how they should act. But Hobbes thought that his metaphysics of action ruled out the very possibility of freedom existing as such a power of self-determination.

Hobbes' Target

Blame, it seems, is no ordinary criticism. To blame someone for what they do is not just to point out a fault in them. We can do that without blaming them for the fault. Blame adds something more; the thought that not only is there a fault, but the fault's existence is *their* fault – the responsibility of the person blamed. Blame involves the idea of a special or moral responsibility. In blame, we are putting the faulty action down to them. And if the fault can be put down to them as their fault, this implies that they must have had the power to determine its occurrence for themselves. Ordinary morality, then, assumes that we have the power to determine for ourselves how we act, and may consequently be responsible and to blame for any fault or wrong which thereby arises.

This power to determine things for ourselves is naturally conceived by us as *freedom*. Freedom is a two-way kind of power – a power to do *A* or to refrain: a power of control that leaves it up to us – within our control – which of these alternatives we do. And this power of control over what we do is one which we definitely think of ourselves as possessing. Within certain limits imposed by our intelligence, knowledge and physical capacity, it is, we suppose, up to us – within our power – to determine how we act. It is up to us what we do, so that we are free to act otherwise. This two-way power extends to our agency as a whole – and to our decisions to act, as well as to the acts decided upon. So we naturally believe in some kind of freedom specifically of decision – specifically of the will understood as a capacity for decision and intention-formation.

Moreover, we naturally place a libertarian gloss on this power of freedom. Suppose that causal determinism is true, and your every action was already predetermined, well before your birth, by prior causes falling all along outside your control. Given these prior causes, you must act as they determine you to. Can how you act still be within your control – something for you to determine? Many of us share the intuition that freedom is incompatible with causal determinism – that if such prior causes have already determined what we will do, then what we do can no longer be determined by us. So we commonly conceive of freedom in incompatibilist terms – as something removed by causal determinism. But we still believe in our actual possession of the power of freedom, despite its being so removable. Hence our natural libertarianism.

Francisco Suarez shared this libertarian view of freedom, and thought that the existence of the power of freedom can be known from experience:

> Second we can argue from experience. For it is evident to us from experience that it is within our power to do a given thing or to refrain from doing it; and we use reason, discourse, and deliberation in order to incline ourselves towards the one rather than the other. That is why choice is place in our control. (Suarez 1994: 291)

The power of freedom, in Suarez's view, is causal – but its bearer is an agent, it is a two-way power to cause or not, and it is entirely contingent which way the agent will exercise it. So there are in fact two kinds of cause: the free causes, which are human agents who can produce a variety of effects without being necessitated to produce a given one and who determine for themselves which effects they produce; and necessary causes, the occurrence of which necessitates the production of one specific effect.

The human action through which freedom is exercised is, in Suarez's view, a distinctive mode of exercising rationality. It is not the theoretical exercise of rationality that occurs in forming beliefs, but rather it is the exercise of a practical capacity to apply certain kinds of belief – beliefs about how to act. And this capacity is located in the will, understood as a psychological capacity to take decisions and to form intentions. The function of the will is precisely to determine action in accordance with the agent's prior deliberation and belief about how to act. The will is a rational appetite – a locus of reason-responsive motivations whose function is to respond to and execute our deliberations about how to act. We have a theory of action that is *practical reason-based*. Intentional action occurs as a distinctively practical mode of exercising rationality. And so freedom itself is a power exercised over, and dependent on, the exercise of a capacity for rationality. As Bramhall puts it:

> Reason is the root, the fountain, the original of true Liberty, which judgeth and representeth to the will, whether this or that be convenient, whether this or that be more convenient. (Bramhall in Hobbes and Bramhall 1656: 30)

For scholastic action theorists, human action in fact divides into two elements. There is the primary instance of action, where the practical reason-based model applies directly. These are *actus eliciti*: 'elicted acts' of the will itself – acts of choice or decision. Then there are the actions decided upon that involve capacities outside the will itself, including capacities located in bodily organs, for instance limb motion. These are *actus imperati* – 'commanded acts,' external to the will itself but motivated or 'commanded' by it. These latter actions are actions only derivatively, through being motivated objects and effects of the primary cases of action, the elicited actions of the will itself.

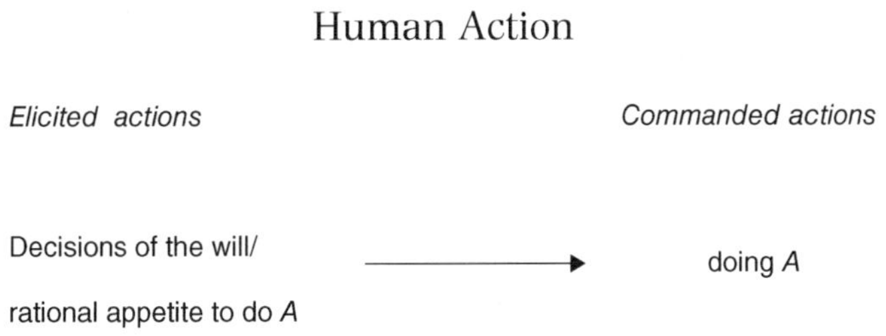

Human Action

Elicited actions | *Commanded actions*

Decisions of the will/ rational appetite to do *A* → doing *A*

Figure 58.1 Elicited actions and commanded actions

The intellectual nature – the capacity for rationality – that we, as humans, possess involves a radical psychological distinction between us and the lower animals, which lack any capacity for rationality. This distinction shows up in the nature of agency itself, and in the constitution of the mind. Since the intentional actions that we perform occur as a mode of exercising rationality, strictly speaking no such actions are performed by animals. Animal action is only a passion-driven analogue of human action, not another case of a distinctively practical mode of exercising reason.

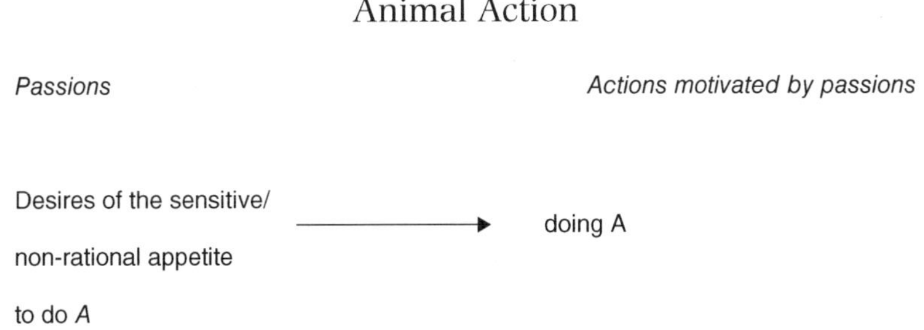

Figure 58.2 Passions and actions motivated by them

And, since reason has a metaphysical dignity that places it above matter and material embodiment, our capacity to respond to reason – both theoretically, in belief, and practically, in action – is exercised independently of any bodily organ. The faculties of intellect and will are immaterial and survive bodily death. So humans possess immaterial capacities or faculties wholly absent from animal minds.

Hobbes' assault on this whole scholastic theory of self-determination centres on the gulf it places between human and animal psychology. To an important extent, Hobbes removes the distinctively rational or intellectual part of scholastic psychology, to leave, at least in broad outline, the part shared with the animals. There are no longer any immaterial faculties of intellect and will. We are left instead with sense and sensorily based belief, and with desire or passion. The theory of human rationality, of human action, and of our capacity to determine action is then reconstructed so as to fit into this reduced psychology – a psychology which leaves human psychology continuous with, indeed only a slightly more developed version of, the psychology of the lower animals, and human action a phenomenon no different from animal action. And with the rational faculties of intellect and will departs also the distinctive power of freedom that they supported. There are no free causes, operating immaterially and apart from any bodily organ, but only necessary ones, operating within a wholly material world.

Hobbes does not deny that humans have a distinctive capacity for rationality. But it ceases to be a capacity separating the very constitution of our mind from that of animals. Since the psychological states possessed by humans are just those possessed by animals, reason involves something importantly extra-mental – not a further part of the mind, but the use of a tool, language, which some minds, human minds, use to express what they contain. Human reasoning is simply a form of thinking that uses and is concerned with language:

> Out of all which we may define, (that is to say determine,) what that is, which is meant by this word Reason, when wee reckon it amongst the Faculties of the mind. For REASON, in this sense, is nothing but Reckoning (that is, Adding and Subtracting) of the Consequences of generall names agreed upon, for the marking and signifying of our thoughts; I say marking them, when we reckon by ourselves; and signifying, when we demonstrate, or approve our reckonings to other men. (Hobbes 1651: 18)

There are no longer distinctively reason-involving motivations. All motivations are mere passions – and, as such, far from being cases of action themselves, they are merely passive antecedent causes of action. The will is simply the last appetite or passion in deliberating – the passion that finally determines how we act. Action is then identified by Hobbes with what he calls *voluntariness* – by which he means the occurrence of action caused and motivated by a prior pro-attitude toward its performance. So action can no longer be understood in terms of some distinctive mode of exercising rationality, but becomes identified with the only element of scholastic action theory that survives – the category of 'commanded' actions, actions motivated by prior appetites for or pro-attitudes toward their performance.

The only power that is exercised in action is not a power possessed and exercised by the agent to determine his actions for himself; it is instead a power of voluntariness – a power attaching to passive appetites or desires to cause us to act as desired. Indeed, the very notion of a power of *self*-determination is viewed by Hobbes as viciously regressive: 'And if a man determine himself, the question will still remain what determined him to determine himself in that manner' (Hobbes 1656: 26).

The scholastic claim that there are elicited acts of the will itself is confused, even unintelligible. The claim is confused on three counts. First, it involves a distinction of supposedly 'rational' motivations from 'non-rational' motivations or passions that is empty and has never been satisfactorily explained by its scholastic defenders:

> For I do not fear it will be thought too hot for my fingers, to shew the vanity of words such as these, Intellectual appetite, conformity of the appetite to the object, rational will, elective power of the rational will; nor understand I how reason can be the root of true liberty, if the Bishop (as he saith in the beginning) had the liberty to write this discourse. I understand how objects, and the conveniences and inconveniences of them, may be represented to a man by the help of his senses; but how reason representeth anything to the will, I [do not] understand ... (Ibid., pp. 35–36)

The idea of a freedom or agency of will is as absurd as the idea of a freedom or agency of passion, since the former reduces to the latter: 'nor can a man more determine his will than any other appetite; that is, more than he can determine when he shall be hungry and when not' (ibid., p. 25).

Second, given the unintelligibility of a practical mode of exercising rationality, the only consistent and intelligible model of agency is that which identifies action with voluntariness. Intentional action is action that is the effect of a desire or motivation to perform it. But that model cannot apply to passions or motivations. For passions are not themselves voluntary: 'I acknowledge this liberty, that I can do if I will, but to say, I can will if I will, I take to be an absurd speech' (ibid., p. 29). 'Can any man but a schoolman think that the will is voluntary? But yet the will is the cause of voluntary actions' (ibid., p. 256).

Third, since the will is the locus of a power to act, its role is to explain and give rise to our actions, but it cannot be supposed to perform actions itself – any more than our power or capacity to dance can itself be supposed to go in for dancing itself. The very idea of actions of the will is a kind of category mistake:

> Secondly, you may observe, that actus elicitus, is exemplified by these words, to will, to elect, to choose, which are all one, and so to will here is made an act of the will; and indeed, as the will is a faculty or power of a man's soul, so to will is an act of it, according to that power. But as it is absurdly said, that to dance is an act allowed or drawn by fair means out of the ability to dance; so it is also to say, that to will is an act allowed or drawn out of the power to will, which power is commonly called, the will. (Ibid., pp. 217–218)
>
> And where he [Bramhall] sayes our wills are in our power, he sees not that he speaks absurdly; for he ought to say, the will is the power. (Ibid., p. 40)

Freedom survives, not as a two-way power of the agent over his action, but as Hobbesian liberty – not itself a power, but an absence of obstacles to power, such as to the force of passions or indeed to any force:

> As if it were not Freedome enough for a man to do what he will, unless his will also have power over his Will, and that his will be not the power itself, but must have another power within it to do all voluntary acts. (Ibid., p. 38)

> Liberty is the absence of all impediments to action, that are not contained in the nature, and in the intrinsecal quality of the agent. (Ibid., p. 285)

In fact liberty is no more peculiar to rational humans than is this passive voluntariness – which can be found as much in animal action as in human. Indeed liberty extends even wider – to streams and rivers, or to anything with force that might go in for some action. Given a lack of external obstruction to that force, we find liberty:

> [H]ow reason representeth anything to the will, I understand no more than the Bishop understands there may be liberty in children, in beasts, and inanimate creatures. For he seemeth to wonder how children may be left at liberty; how beasts imprisoned may be set at liberty; and how a river may have a free course. (Ibid., 35–36)

Hobbes clearly understands liberty in a way that renders it consistent with causal determinism. Moreover, Hobbes regards the truth of causal determinism as established, not by reference to experience, but on a priori grounds. Thus he argues that all things that begin at some time to exist must have an (efficient) cause:

> Also the fixt point, that a man cannot imagine anything to begin without a cause, can no other way be made known but by trying how he can imagine it. But if he try, he shall find as much reason (if there be no cause of the thing) to conceive it should begin at one time as another, that is, he hath equall reason to think, it should begin at all times, which is impossible. And therefore he must think there was some special cause, why it began then rather than sooner or later, or else that it began never, but was Eternal. (Ibid., p. 302)

And the efficient causal relation is one of determination and necessitation for Hobbes. Hobbes puts forward the following a priori argument. All causes must be sufficient to produce their effect. But, if they are sufficient, the effect must follow. So the idea of a free cause is incoherent: if the free cause is enough for each of a variety of possible effects, it must produce each, which is impossible:

> But the Bishop defineth Contingents thus, 'All things which may be done and may not be done, may happen or may not happen by reason of the indeterminacy or accidental concurrence of the causes' by which definition contingent is nothing, or it is the same that I say it is. For there is nothing can be done and not be done, nothing can happen and not happen by reason of the indetermination or accidental concurrence of the causes. It may be done or not done for aught he knows, and happen or not happen for any determination he perceaveth; and that is my definition. But that the indetermination can make it happen or not happen is absurd; for indetermination maketh it equally to happen or not to happen; and therefore both; which is a contradiction. Therefore indetermination doth nothing, and whatsoever causes do, is necessary. (Ibid., p. 184)

It is important that Hobbes makes no appeal to experience to establish the truth of causal determinism. For in fact the appeals to experience tend to come from his opponents. It is Suarez and his followers who appeal to experience to establish the existence of a causal power constitutive of libertarian freedom. Hobbes dismisses these appeals on the basis of what he takes to be the complete absurdity of such a power's existence.

Belief in such a power is a philosophical confusion, and reflects not the representation within experience of such a power – there is no such representation – but the failure of experience to represent the real necessary causes of our actions, causes that philosophy can tell a priori must be present, and operative through our passions:

> Commonly when we see and know the strength that moves us, we acknowledge necessity, but when we see not, or mark not the force that moves us, we then think there is none, and that it is not causes but liberty that produceth the action. (Ibid., p. 265)

Notice that though freedom or liberty is explained by Hobbes in terms that leave it consistent with causal determinism, his view is not that of standard modern English-language compatibilism. For modern compatibilism does take freedom to be a power – but a power immediately of passive motivations within the agent to cause him to act voluntarily, as he is motivated to. Modern English-language compatibilism identifies freedom, which we initially and naturally understand as a power of the agent to determine his action, in terms of a power to determine action attaching to passive motivations within the agent but distinct from him. In other words, freedom is identified with Hobbesian voluntariness.

But Hobbes did not think it sensible to understand freedom in this way. For he took seriously the fact that his opponents, when they conceived of freedom as a power, conceived of it as a power of the agent to determine for himself what he did. But as we have seen, for Hobbes there could be no such power. Any determination of action is by prior passion – it is the determination of one motion in matter by another distinct from it, which determining motion is itself determined by another in its turn. The incoherent idea of a self-determining power of freedom is never instanced. Rather, Hobbes concluded, we should understand how we really use the idea of liberty, in the political sphere and more generally: not to denote a power, but rather to denote an absence of various kinds of obstacles to powers, such as when an absence of binding laws leaves us at liberty or free. So, in relation to action, all that can contribute to freedom is not the presence of any power, but the absence of obstacles to the operation of power – the power that attaches to motions of the will, which are left free to determine what he agent does: 'true Liberty, which doth not consist in determining itself, but in doing what the Will is determined unto' (ibid., p. 26).

Nor, properly understood, does our ethical practice of blaming or holding responsible presuppose a power of freedom in the agent blamed. According to Hobbes, blame is no more than a form of disapproval; and, so understood, it is far from presupposing any power of self-determination in the person blamed. Why do we blame people? 'I answer because they please us not. I might ask him, whether blaming be any thing else but saying the thing blamed is ill or imperfect' (ibid., p. 39). Blame merely asserts a fault or imperfection. And there can be imperfection or fault without any power in the thing that is imperfect to produce or remove that fault. In which case agents can be blameworthy for evil or fault in what they do whether or not it was within their power not to do it:

> I answer, they are to be blamed though their wills be not in their power. Is not good good and evill evill though they be not in our power? And shall I not call them so? And is that

> not praise and blame? But it seems that the Bishop takes blame not for the dispraise of a thing, but for a praetext and colour of malice and revenge against him that he blameth. (Ibid., p. 40)

Hobbes excluded the idea of liberty or freedom as a power of self-determination with the same ruthlessness from his ethical theory as he excluded it from his metaphysics of action and of the self.

See also: VOLITION AND THE WILL (13); DESIRE AND PLEASURE (15); RATIONALITY (36); FREE WILL AND DETERMINISM (38); RESPONSIBILITY AND AUTONOMY (39); ANIMAL AGENCY (48).

References: primary sources

Hobbes, T. (1651). *Leviathan*. London.

Hobbes, T., and Bramhall, J. (1656). *The Questions Concerning Liberty, Necessity and Chance, clearly stated between Dr Bramhall Bishop of Derry, and Thomas Hobbes of Malmesbury*. London.

Suarez, F. (1994). *On Efficient Causality: Metaphysical Disputations 17, 18 and 19*. New Haven: Yale University Press.

Further reading: secondary sources

Leijenhorst, C. (2002). *The Mechanisation of Aristotelianism: The Late Aristotelian Setting of Thomas Hobbes' Natural Philosophy*. Leiden: Brill.

Pettit, P. (2008). *Made with Words: Hobbes on Language, Mind and Politics*. Princeton: Princeton University Press.

Pink, T. (2004). Suarez, Hobbes and the scholastic tradition in action theory. In T. Pink and M. W. F. Stone (eds), *The Will and Human Action: From Antiquity to the Present Day*. London: Routledge, 127–153.

59

Descartes

PAUL HOFFMAN

The primary historical contribution of René Descartes (1596–1650) to the theory of action would appear to be that he expanded the range of action by freeing the concept of efficient causation from that of final causation. If to act entails being an efficient cause, and if efficient causes are, or at least can be, independent of final causes, then acting is independent of final causation. Yet at the same time Descartes is widely thought to hold views that limit the range of action considerably. Many contemporary commentators attribute to him the view that bodies are entirely passive and incapable of acting, and Jaegwon Kim has argued that immaterial substances are incapable of causing effects outside of themselves. If these views are correct, there is not much action in the Cartesian universe, and indeed there is no causal interaction between substances.

In this essay I want to explore a few broad themes concerning Descartes' theory of action. First, I will examine the relation of efficient causation to final causation. In so doing I will try to defend further the view held by me and others that Descartes does think bodies act. Second, I will offer a defense of Descartes' account of mental causation against Kim's deployment of the pairing problem.

Efficient and Final Causation

Thomas Aquinas, the most prominent among Descartes' scholastic–Aristotelian predecessors, held that final causation is the most fundamental of the four causes, so that there can be no efficient cause where there is no final cause. This means that, in order for an agent to act, it must be aiming at something as an end. It does not mean that an agent must always achieve its end, but it does mean that, in order to do anything, for example spilling wine on your shirt, I must be aiming at something – for example, pouring wine in your glass. An agent is said to aim at something in the most proper sense when it has cognition of the end as an end. So, among created beings, only those with an intellect are agents in the proper sense, because they are aimed at their end by themselves. Animals were thought to be capable of cognition of ends, for example food, but not as ends; in consequence they would not be aimed at their end by themselves, but rather by God. They were held to be aimed at their ends in the same way an arrow is aimed at its end – namely, by something else. Plants – which, again like arrows, have no cognition of an end – were also thought to be aimed at an end, for example producing fruit, by God. As long as things of a given kind have a tendency to a certain outcome, which they do if they achieve that outcome for the most part, then they are aimed at that outcome as an end (Aquinas 2000: *Summa theologica*, Ia–IIae, q.1 a.2 (= *quaestio* 1, articulus 2); see also Hoffman 2009a).[1]

Descartes famously asserts that physics should proceed without recourse to final causes. His two principal arguments for this view are widely diverse. One is epistemological. The motions of bodies depend on God's will, but God's purposes are inscrutable to us (Descartes 1897/1913, Vol. 7: 55, 374–375). Thus we should restrict our search to the efficient causes of the motions of bodies (ibid., Vol. 8A: 15–16). The other argument is metaphysical. Descartes argues that nothing aims at its own destruction (ibid., p. 63). Thus he rejects the Aristotelian view that the motions of bodies have natural endpoints, for in that case the motion would be aiming to cease when it reaches a particular location (ibid., Vol. 9: 40). So he rejects the views that fire travels upward because it is aiming at its natural resting place near the heavens and that things composed of earth fall toward the center of the earth because that is their natural place. A third argument is that natural appetites or inclinations presuppose understanding (ibid., Vol. 3: 213), and so to attribute them to bodies is to attribute minds to those bodies. He argues that he cannot conceive how gravity could carry bodies toward the center of the earth unless it had knowledge of the center (ibid., Vol. 7: 442).

When one considers these arguments carefully, it is not actually evident that they amount to rejecting the Aristotelian principle that efficient causation presupposes final causation. Descartes does not deny purposes to God; and there is no indication, in spite of his identification of God's intellect and will, that he thinks God does anything without a purpose.[2] Thus if God is taken to be the sole cause of the motion of bodies, then Descartes could be interpreted as subscribing to the view that all efficient causation involves an act of will. On this interpretation Descartes could consistently endorse the view that efficient causation presupposes final causation. Indeed he would be narrowing the range of efficient causes to beings who possess wills. So to deny that we should search for final causes in physics because God's will is inscrutable is not necessarily to deny that there are underlying final causes.

The second argument does amount to a rejection of final causes under the common understanding of that notion. According to that common understanding, the end or final cause is an endpoint. It is the point at which the action ceases. On Descartes' view, even if the motion of a body has a final cause in the sense of having a purpose that is inaccessible to us, it nevertheless still does not have a final cause in the sense of aiming at an endpoint where it ceases. So Descartes has freed the notion of efficient causation from final causation in this important sense: an efficient cause need not be aiming at an endpoint at which it will cease acting. In other words, something can act without that action having a natural completion.

But in fact this is not really an innovation. Aquinas did not think that all ends were necessarily endpoints. He distinguished between changes, which do have natural endpoints, and activities, which do not (for example, our thinking and the sun's shining were conceived of as activities), and activities were recognized as perfectly good ends (Aquinas 2000: *Summa contra gentiles*, Book 3a, ch. 2). So it is not a requirement of the scholastic–Aristotelian notion of a final cause that it be an endpoint. Thus we cannot infer from the fact that Descartes has reconceived the motion of bodies so that it does not have a natural endpoint – in other words, from the fact that he has reconceived of the motion of bodies as an activity as opposed to a change – that he thinks that the motion of bodies does not have a final cause in the sense of having an end toward which it is aimed.

Now even though Descartes states that he rejects natural inclinations and appetites in the physical world because they presuppose understanding, he does not deny tendencies to bodies. He holds generally that things, insofar as they are simple and undivided, persist in the same state, unless something external changes them. So a square will remain square, a body at rest will stay at rest, a moving body will continue moving, unless an external cause changes them (Descartes 1897/1913, Vol. 8A: 62). He argues further that moving bodies tend to move in a straight line, because this is the only motion that can be defined in an instant (ibid., Vol. 9: 44–45).

There are various ways, though none explicitly articulated by Descartes, by which his rejection of natural inclinations and appetites can be reconciled with his acceptance of the tendency of bodies to persist in the same state. First, he might be objecting to the view of various philosophers that there are different kind of bodies which have different inclinations and appetites, in contrast to his own view that all bodies have the same tendency to remain in the same state. Second, he might be objecting to inclinations and appetites which have an endpoint. That is, he might think that an inclination to move to particular a place requires knowledge of that place, whereas an inclination or tendency to move in a straight line does not. Third, he might be objecting to inclinations and tendencies which are considered natural in the sense that they belong to a thing's nature. In contrast, it might be argued, the tendency he recognizes of bodies to remain in the same state is not part of, nor is it a consequence of, their nature, but rather follows from God's immutability in sustaining them from moment to moment.

There is decisive evidence that, even if Descartes does not think this tendency to remain in the same state is a part of, or a consequence of, the nature of body, he does think it exists in bodies. Indeed he thinks that the tendency is grounded in a force located in these bodies:

> He [Father J. Lacombe] is right in saying that it was a big mistake to accept the principle that no body moves of itself. For it is certain that a body, once it has begun to move, has in itself for that reason alone the force to continue to move, just as, once it is stationary in a certain place, it has for that reason alone the force to continue to remain there. But as for the principle of movement which he imagines to be different in each body, this is altogether imaginary. (Descartes 1897/1913, Vol. 3: 213)

Given that Descartes locates this force, and the resulting tendency to remain in the same state, in bodies, it seems correct to assert that Cartesian bodies are aimed toward a certain end (though not an endpoint), namely, remaining in that state. Indeed, since that tendency arises from an internal state – Descartes says that a body remains in that state *quantum in se est* ('insofar as it is in itself' 'by its own force,' or 'from its own nature' – see below; ibid., Vol. 8A: 62) – bodies are appropriately characterized as striving to remain in that state:

> When I say that the globules of the second element strive [*conari*] to move away from the centres around which they revolve, it should not be thought that I am implying that they have some thought from which this striving [*conatus*] proceeds. I mean merely that they are positioned and pushed into motion in such a way that they will in fact travel in that direction, unless they are prevented by some other cause. (Ibid., p. 108)

Since the Cartesian theory of motion includes the thesis that bodies in motion strive to preserve the same state of travelling in a straight line, his account of motion is no more independent of final causes, in the broader sense which includes ends that are not endpoints, than the account of his scholastic–Aristotelian predecessors. There is one important difference, however. According to his scholastic–Aristotelian predecessors, something tends to something only if things of its kind achieve it for the most part. Descartes has a much weaker account: for Descartes, bodies that are moving tend to move in a straight line even if they rarely if ever do move in straight lines, because the Cartesian world is a plenum and bodies are typically knocked off course by collisions with other bodies (ibid., Vol. 11: 43–4; Vol. 8A: 63). But Descartes' account seems correct. It seems correct to say that a body is striving to travel in a certain direction provided that it would, due to an internal force, continue in that direction were it not for the influence of external causes.

In suggesting above that Descartes does not think that the tendency of bodies to remain in the same state is a part or a consequence of their nature, I am going against the important argument of Michael Della Rocca, my fellow defender of the view that Descartes does attribute forces to bodies and does think that bodies are causes. I think the textual evidence cited by Della Rocca is problematic (Della Rocca 1999: 66). The first passage is one in which Descartes is reciting the scholastic–Aristotelian view he rejects: 'It is in the very nature of motion to come to an end, or to tend towards a state of rest.' Della Rocca asserts that 'Descartes here seems to be treating as equivalent the notion of what motion tends to do and the notion of what it does by its very nature.' But, at best, we can infer from this passage that Descartes thought his opponents were guilty of that identification, not that he himself is endorsing it. The second passage is one in which Descartes rejects the scholastic–Aristotelian view: 'Nothing can by its own nature be carried towards its opposite, or towards its own destruction.' Contrary to Della Rocca's reading, this passage does not provide grounds for inferring that Descartes treats as equivalent what a thing does by its own nature and what it tends to do. The fact that something cannot have certain tendencies according to its nature does not show that all of its tendencies are things that it does by its own nature. The final piece of textual evidence cited by Della Rocca does provide genuine support for his interpretation, He appeals to I. Bernard Cohen's analysis of the phrase *quantum in se est*, used by Descartes in setting out his laws of motion. Cohen makes a convincing case that the phrase is plausibly understood to mean 'from its own nature' (Cohen 1964). However, while I agree that this is a highly plausible interpretation of what Descartes meant, I do not see that there is conclusive evidence that this is what he meant (see n. 5). And indeed Della Rocca himself points out the leading problem with interpreting Descartes as he does. The problem is that it is hard to see how the nature of body could be constituted by extension and also involve the tendency to remain in the same state. Della Rocca's response to the problem is to say that Descartes may have been using the term 'nature' in different senses which he did not completely reconcile (Della Rocca 1999: 69).

It seems to me more charitable to interpret Descartes as denying that bodies persist in the same state according to their nature, even if, as is clear from the letter to Mersenne quoted above, there is something internal to them, namely, a force, which plays a causal role in their persisting in the same state. But even this might seem problematic. Commentators have wondered how force could be internal to bodies, because it is hard to see how it could be even a mode of extension, that is, a way of being extended. I myself do no find this so problematic. First, I am not sure that it is significantly more problematic to suppose that striving to move and striving to remain at rest are modes of extension than to suppose that motion and rest are modes of extension. That is, if one is willing to grant that motion is a way of being extended, why should it be any worse to grant that striving to continue to move is also a way of being extended? Second, even if striving to continue to move is not a way of being extended, it does not necessarily follow that it could not be internal to body.[3] Duration is not a mode of extension, but Descartes thinks it is an attribute of bodies nevertheless (Descartes 1897/1913, Vol. 8A: 30).[4] I don't see why striving to continue in the same state could not also be an attribute of bodies, even though, like the duration of bodies, its presence in bodies depends on the continued action of God.[5] This is not to identify this striving with duration, as Martial Gueroult advocates, but merely to put it in the same category as duration (Gueroult 1980: 197).

Daniel Garber has argued that force cannot be an attribute like duration because, unlike duration, it does not exist in body in an unchanging way. Therefore it must be a mode of body, and hence a mode of extension, which, Garber and others claim, it cannot be (Garber 1992: 296–297). But I do not agree that Descartes has to hold that striving to persist in the same state exists in bodies in a variable way. It is true that Descartes sometimes identifies a body's force with its quantity of motion, so that there is a notion of force that is variable (Descartes 1897/1913, Vol. 8A: 66–67). But I think it is important to distinguish a body's striving to persist in its present state from both its force of resisting the action of another body and its quantity of motion (which amounts to a body's speed times its size) – that is, its force of acting on another body. It seems plausible to me to suppose that Descartes thinks a thing's striving to persist in its present state does not exist in it in a variable way. Nevertheless, since its present state can vary, the forces – namely its force of acting on another body and of resisting the action of another body – that result from its striving to persist in its present state can vary. Now Garber would object that such variable forces – forces which result from a thing's unchanging striving to persist in its present state and the present state that it is in – are not modes of extension and that Descartes is committed to the view that all of a body's variable features must be modes of extension (Garber 1992: 296–267). But my response is that, if these variable forces are not modes of extension, they are close enough for us not to worry about it. I think it is in no way problematic to amend Descartes' view to be this: all variable features of a body are modes of extension or arise from its present modes of extension and its unchanging attributes.

In this section I have argued that, contrary to what might appear at first glance, it is far from clear that Descartes did in fact conceive of efficient causation as independent of final causation – that is, it is far from clear that he thought that things, in acting, need not be aimed at, or striving for, an end. It is true that he conceived of motion or moving bodies as not aiming at or striving for endpoints at which the motion would cease; but this is different from conceiving of motion or moving bodies as not aimed at or striving for an end. Moreover, I have defended the view that we should understand a body's striving to persist in its present state to be an unchanging attribute of body, distinct from its nature.

Descartes' Account of Mental Causation

Jaegwon Kim has argued that we cannot solve the problem of mental causation – the problem of explaining how psychological properties/events can be the cause of physical properties/events or of psychological properties/events belonging to numerically distinct psychological beings – by positing immaterial substances. This is because immaterial substances fall prey to the pairing problem. The pairing problem is as follows: given two simultaneous causes (to use Kim's example, two guns being fired) and two simultaneous effects (two people being killed), what pairs one cause with one effect and the other cause with the other effect? Kim argues that, in order for this problem to be solved, the causes and effects must be spatially located. But, since immaterial substances are not spatially located, we could never pair simultaneous psychological properties/events of two immaterial substances with simultaneous effects belonging to distinct beings, whether those other beings are physical or immaterial (Kim 2005, Ch. 3).

I think there is much to be said in defense of Descartes against this objection. First, it seems to me that, if Kim's argument succeeds in undermining immaterial substances, it equally undermines material substances. Here is why. Kim considers the reply to his argument that, if each immaterial substance stood in some relation *R* to a particular body, then immaterial substances could be located spatially. But he argues there is no good candidate relation *R*. Causation is ruled out because to say that an immaterial substance causally interacts with a particular body and therefore can inherit its spatial location presupposes that the pairing problem has already been solved, and thus it begs the question (Kim 2005: 89). Kim also rejects the hypothesis that there is some primitive notion of union by which immaterial substances are united to particular bodies. He says that such talk of a union is a mere label (pp. 77–78). My response is that, if Kim wants to admit the existence of material substances, he has to concede that there is some primitive relation *R* which qualities such as shape and size bear to those material substances. Philosophers have tended to say that shape and size exist in substance; but, as Berkeley argued convincingly, this relation cannot be a spatial one (Berkeley 1979: 33–35). So either we follow Berkeley and Hume in rejecting material substances or we are forced to accept that there is some primitive non-spatial relation between a material substance and its qualities. Now if we read Descartes as endorsing the hylomorphic account of the relation between mind and body – that mind is related to body as form is to matter, and thus can be said to exist in the body – then we can reply to Kim on Descartes' behalf that his account of the relation between mind and body is the same as, or at least sufficiently similar to, the relation that qualities bear to material substances, so that immaterial and material substances stand or fall together. And if minds exist in bodies, then we can attribute a spatial location to them and thereby solve the pairing problem.

Kim further objects, however, that if a mind exists in a body, then it has to exist in some particular place within it, which he thinks is problematic (Kim 2005: 88–89). But this seems wrong. Shape and size exist in body, but they don't exist in some particular place within it. Rather it seems that the shape of a body exists in the whole body, as does its size. Descartes, endorsing the language of his Aristotelian–scholastic predecessors in describing the relation of substantial form to matter, says that the mind exists whole in the whole body. He also endorses their view that a substantial form exists whole in each part of the body, which is obviously not true of shape or size, which are perhaps better described as existing part in each part of the body (Descartes 1897/1913, Vol. 7: 442; Vol. 11: 351).

Now I certainly do not want to assert that the hylomorphic account of the relation between form and matter is unproblematic. One might well be troubled by the notion of something's existing whole in the whole and whole in each of the parts, and one might further be troubled by the notion that a form can stand in such a relation to a material thing and still be considered immaterial and non-extended. But it seems to me that much more work needs to be done to show that such a view should be cast aside and that it can be cast aside in way that does not also jeopardize material substances.

There is another important way in which Descartes can claim to solve the pairing problem. The pairing problem arises only on a Humean conception of causation according to which cause and effect are distinct non-simultaneous events – a conception that is utterly foreign to the Aristotelian conception of causation endorsed by Descartes. I have argued elsewhere that Descartes is committed to the Aristotelian doctrine of the identity of action and passion – an agent's action is one and the same thing as the passion undergone by the patient (Hoffman 2009b, chs 7–9). It is not the case that there are two distinct non-simultaneous events when one substance acts on another. My lifting the vase is not numerically distinct from the vase's being lifted; they are one and the same event. On this Aristotelian conception, the action of the agent, since it is the same as the effect, namely the passion in the patient, already comes paired. Now this is not to say that the Aristotelian doctrine of the identity of action and passion is unproblematic; but I would assert that it is no more – and, in my view, less – problematic than the Humean conception of causation.[6]

See also: VOLITION AND THE WILL (13); TELEOLOGICAL EXPLANATION (16); MENTAL CAUSATION AND EPIPHENOMENALISM (23); AGENCY, PATIENCY, AND PERSONHOOD (26); AUGUSTINE AND AQUINAS (56); BERKELEY (61).

Notes

1 Jeffrey McDonough has noted, in correspondence with me, that someone might object that 'things could achieve a certain outcome for the most part, and yet not be aimed at that end – an elephant (say) might regularly kill the grass it walks on, but not have that as an end.' I think Aquinas would grant that there are exceptions of this sort. But, in order for them to arise, there must be some other outcome that is aimed at, and the process of moving toward

that end must have as a typical side effect the outcome that is not aimed at. So a more precise statement, which includes the exceptions, would be this: as long as things of a given kind have a tendency to a certain outcome, which they have if they achieve that outcome for the most part, they are aimed at some outcome as an end.

2 Here I disagree with Tad Schmaltz (2008: 62), who makes the opposite assertion. To say, as Descartes does, that God's choices are not impelled by God's idea of the good simply does not imply that God has no purpose in making choices. God can act for a reason without being impelled by that reason. In general, the liberty of indifference is not incompatible with acting for a purpose.

3 It is worth noting that, while Descartes asserts in a letter to Regius that 'in corporeal things, every action and passion consists of local motion alone' (1897/1913, Vol. 3: 454), in *The World* he asserts that a body's tendency ('*inclination*') to move in a straight line is an action that differs from its motion (ibid., Vol. 11: 44).

4 Here I am using the term 'attribute' as Descartes sometimes does to refer to features of a thing that exist in it in an unchanging way, and not to its nature or essence.

5 Della Rocca holds that this striving to continue in the same state is part of a body's nature, but not in the sense of the term 'nature' according to which extension is the nature of body. I agree that this striving is not part of a thing's nature in the sense in which extension is the nature of body, and I hold that it is instead an attribute of body that exists in it in an unchanging way. So the difference between us is that I am not confident that there is some other appropriate sense of 'nature' according to which this striving would count as belonging to a body's nature. It is also important to note that Cohen's paper does not support Della Rocca's interpretation over mine. Cohen suggests that the phrase *quantum in se est* is as plausibly translated as 'by its own force' as 'from its own nature' or 'naturally,' and for his purposes there is no significant difference in the use of these different interpretations. But the dispute between Della Rocca and me amounts to a dispute over which of Cohen's approved translations is better. If 'by its own force' is as adequate a rendering as 'from its own nature' or 'naturally,' then Descartes' use of the phrase *quantum in se est* does not favor Della Rocca's interpretation over mine (see Cohen 1964: 147–148).

6 I would like to thank Jaegwon Kim, Jeffrey McDonough, Michael Della Rocca, and Alan Code for helpful discussion.

References

Primary sources

Aquinas, T. (2000). *Summa contra gentiles*. Available at: [http://www.corpusthomisticum.org/iopera.html].

Aquinas, T. (2000). *Summa theologica*. Available at: [http://www.corpusthomisticum.org/iopera.html].

Berkeley, G. (1979). *Three Dialogues between Hylas and Philonous*, edited by R. M. Adams. Indianapolis: Hackett Publishing Company.

Descartes, R. (1897/1913). *Oeuvres de Descartes*, Vols 1–12 and Supplement, edited by Charles Adam and Paul Tannery. Paris: Leopold Cerf.

Secondary sources

Cohen, I. B. (1964). '*Quantum in se est*': Newton's concept of inertia in relation to Descartes and Lucretius. *Notes and Records of the Royal Society of London*, 19, 131–155.

Della Rocca, M. (1999). 'If a body meet a body': Descartes on body–body causation. In R. J. Gennaro and C. Huenemann (eds), *New Essays on the Rationalists*. Oxford: Oxford University Press, 48–81.

Garber, D. (1992). *Descartes' Metaphysical Physics*. Chicago: University of Chicago Press.

Gueroult, M. (1980). The metaphysics and physics of force in Descartes. In S. Gaukroger (ed.), *Descartes: Philosophy, Mathematics and Physics*. Sussex: Harvester Press Limited, 196–229.

Hoffman, P. (2009a). Does efficient causation presuppose final causation? Aquinas vs. early modern mechanism. In S. Newlands and L. M. Jorgensen (eds), *Metaphysics and the Good: Themes from the Philosophy of Robert Merrihew Adams*. Oxford: Oxford University Press, 295–312.

Hoffman, P. (2009b). *Essays on Descartes*. New York: Oxford University Press.

Kim, J. (2005). *Physicalism, or Something Near Enough*. Princeton: Princeton University Press.

Schmaltz, T. (2008). *Descartes on Causation*. New York: Oxford University Press.

60

Locke

MATTHEW STUART

The philosophy of action of John Locke (1632–1704) is rich and underexplored territory. It is also a somewhat complicated terrain. The main text is the chapter 'Of Power' (2.21) in his *Essay Concerning Human Understanding* (Locke 1975); but there are also important discussions about agency, freedom and volition in his correspondence. Locke revised 2.21 more heavily than any other chapter in the *Essay*, and in some cases the revisions represent real changes of mind on fundamental points. Four editions of the *Essay* appeared during Locke's lifetime, and he left instructions regarding the fifth edition. The biggest changes in 2.21 come between the first edition and the second, but there are notable alterations in the fourth and fifth editions as well.

Locke is a volitionist. He holds that the will is a mental faculty distinct from the understanding. It consists of the powers to begin, continue, forbear, and end actions (2.21.5). The exercise of this faculty he calls volition or willing. The actions at which volitions are directed fall under two headings: thinking and motion (2.21.8). Locke conceives of volitions themselves as actions of the former sort (2.21.15). Thus, although he takes an action to be voluntary just in case it is produced by a volition (2.21.5), he cannot use production by a volition as the criterion for an episode's being an action – or else he would face a regress. He offers no general criterion for an episode's being an action, but he suggests that bodily motions are actions only if they involve the beginning of motion rather than the transfer of motion (2.21.4). He seems to presume that, when we move our bodies in ordinary ways, we are beginning motions rather than merely transferring them.

In the first edition of the *Essay*, Locke says that the will is the 'Power the Mind has to prefer the Consideration of any *Idea*, to the not considering it; or to prefer the Motion of any part of the Body, to its Rest' (2.21.5). Two different conceptions of volition lurk beneath this formulation, the difference turning on an ambiguity in the meaning of 'prefer.' To prefer an action can be a matter of wanting it to happen. This seems to be what Locke has in mind when he says that preferring an action is 'nothing but the *being pleased*' with it (2.21.28). If we are to think of volitions in this way, it is best to conceive of them as episodic, occurrent wantings rather than mere dispositional states, since volitions are supposed to be what explains the triggering of thoughts and bodily motions. The *Oxford English Dictionary* tells us that in the seventeenth century 'prefer' was also used to mean 'to forward, advance, promote (a result); to assist in bringing about.' If willing an action is preferring it in this sense, then willing is not a matter of having a positive attitude toward an action, but one of trying to bring it about.

Locke may be thinking about volition as an occurrent wanting when he remarks on the case of a man who falls when a bridge breaks under him. He says that the man has a volition because he 'preferrs his not falling to falling' (2.21.9). Yet it seems wrong to say that the man who is already falling *tries* not to fall, unless we suppose that he has some confused or instinctive belief that it may be in his power to stop his fall. On the other hand, Locke also says that he uses the word 'preference' in characterizing volition specifically to avoid a meaning that is too close to 'desire' (2.21.33). This, together with his view that willing is itself a kind of action (a case of *doing* something rather than merely feeling something), suggests that he is often thinking of volition as a 'preferring' understood in the second sense.

In the second and later editions of the *Essay*, Locke distances himself from the suggestion that willing is a matter of wanting; instead he characterizes volition in terms of commanding or ordering the performance of an action (2.21.5, 28). He warns against confounding will with desire, and one imagines that he is speaking partly about himself when he says that even men who thought themselves clear writers and thinkers have put one for the other (2.21.30). In the second and later editions we also find Locke articulating more clearly an important difference between desire and volition: desires can be directed at faraway things or events, but volitions target only one's own thoughts and bodily motions (2.21.30). He also notes that will and desire can be at odds with one another. He illustrates the point with a nice example: 'A Man, whom I cannot deny, may oblige me to use persuasions to another, which at the same time I am speaking I may wish may not prevail upon him' (2.21.30).

Locke holds that a person is free to the extent that he 'has a power to think, or not to think; to move, or not to move, according to the preference or direction of his own mind' (2.21.8). To act freely, one must think or move as one wills to do; but mere voluntariness does not suffice for freedom. It is also necessary that one could have done otherwise. An act is free only if one would have forborne it, had one willed to forbear it; a forbearance is free only if one would have performed the action, had one willed to do so. He invites us to consider the following situation:

> [S]uppose a Man be carried, whilst fast asleep, into a Room, where is a Person he longs to see and speak with; and be there locked fast in, beyond his Power to get out: he awakes, and is glad to find himself in so desirable Company, which he stays willingly in, *i.e.* preferrs his stay to going away. (2.21.10)

The man in the locked room stays there voluntarily, but Locke says that he is not free in this regard because he could not leave if he wanted to.

Locke's term for unfree is 'necessary.' To say that events are under necessity is not to say that they are governed by deterministic causal laws, or that things could not have been otherwise, but just that they are not free actions. The behavior of inanimate objects is all 'under our *Idea* of *Necessary*' (2.21.9) simply because inanimate objects cannot think, and consequently do not will. The main point that Locke is making with his falling man example is that even the behavior of a man who is capable of volitions will be 'under our *Idea* of *Necessary*' when that behavior is insensitive to the contents of his willings. One upshot of the case of the man in the locked room – and of the similar case of the 'Paralytick' who prefers sitting still to moving – is that '*Voluntary* [...] *is not opposed to Necessary; but to Involuntary*' (2.21.11).

Locke's examples of the man in the locked room and of the complacent paralytic raise the question of what it is *voluntarily not to do* something. The volitionist need not say that voluntarily remaining in a room involves an episode of willing directed at not-moving. Instead, he could give negative actions a deflationary treatment. He could say that voluntarily remaining in a room is a matter of deciding not to leave, and then of not-leaving because of that decision (Moore 1979); or of performing some positive action in favor of leaving (Brand 1971); or of something else. However, Locke does seem to treat not-doings as being objects of volition as much as doings are. He says that we can prefer forbearances (2.21.7), command them (2.21.5), and produce them (2.21.8). He says that our volitions can produce silence and rest (2.21.21). One could refuse to take this at face value, but there is nothing in his text to suggest that negative actions should be given a deflationary treatment.

If we do take at face value Locke's talk of willing such not-doings as staying and resting, there is a problem about what sort of connection has to obtain between the willing and the not-doing for the volition to count as a success. Locke generally employs causal language when describing the relation between successful volitions and their objects: we produce motions, begin them, cause them. It is easy to see why one might think that there must be a causal connection between a volition and its target for the volition to count as a success. In the case of a positive action such as an arm raising, we would not say that the volition to raise the arm was a success if the arm rose only because some other mechanism coincidentally intervened. The trouble is that, if a volition to stay must cause the absence of motion in one's body in order to be successful, then we are threatened with the result that few – if any – such volitions would ever succeed. For it is not clear that it is ever possible to single out an event as the cause of something's *not* happening. The occurrence of any particular volition is unlikely to be a necessary condition (or even, to adopt the terminology of Mackie 1965, an INUS condition, that is, an insufficient but non-redundant part of an unnecessary but sufficient condition) of a man's not leaving a room. Suppose the man does will to stay in the room. What confidence can we have that, if he had not so willed, his body would have gone through the motions of trying to leave? Might he not have stared vacantly into space instead? Or fallen asleep? Or gotten distracted by a chess problem that he has been trying to solve?

Usually it is agents that Locke speaks of as being free or not. When occasionally he speaks of acts as being free or not, this is to be understood as an indirect way of talking about the freedom or unfreedom of the agents who perform them. The freedom of an agent is not an all-or-nothing affair. To be free is to be free with respect to some action under some set of circumstances. Each of us is simultaneously free with respect to some actions and unfree with respect to others. Locke disdains all talk of freedom of the will as involving a category mistake. The will is a faculty, not a little agent, so to ask whether man's will is free is as insignificant as to ask 'whether his Sleep be Swift, or his Vertue square' (2.21.14).

Locke allows that it does make sense to ask whether a man is free to will, but he thinks that the answer to that question is 'No.' The answer is 'No' because we cannot forbear willing one way or the other on an action once it is proposed to our thoughts. Why Locke thinks this is a matter of debate. He says:

> The reason whereof is very manifest: For it being unavoidable that the Action depending on his Will, should exist, or not exist; and its existence, or not existence, following perfectly the determination, and preference of his Will, he cannot avoid willing the existence, or not existence, of that Action. (2.21.23)

Vere Chappell follows Leibniz, and says that Locke is neglecting the possibility that a contemplated action might fail to exist, not because the agent decides against performing it, but because he puts off deciding whether to perform it (Chappell 1994; Leibniz 1981). Samuel Rickless defends Locke against this charge by arguing that he eventually saw the need to restrict drastically the principle that we cannot forbear willing on actions once they are proposed to our thoughts, so that it applies not to actions generally, but only to those that involve stoppings of processes – and only those stoppings that are proposed to be carried out immediately (Rickless 2000). A more thoroughgoing defense of Locke is possible if we ascribe to him the view (defended in Ginet 1990) that all volitions concern only what is to be done in the next instant. To one who thinks of willing as something like trying, this view of the objects of volition has considerable appeal. For, although one can decide, plan, or intend now to do something later, one cannot *try* now to do something later. If Locke thinks that we can will only actions and forbearances in the next instant, then he may say that to put off deciding whether to φ is to will not to φ now, while also resolving to take up again later the question of whether to φ. To do this is to will on the only question in relation to φ-ing upon which one might have willed.

Locke is frequently described as being a compatibilist (Chappell 1998; Jolley 1999; Yaffe 2000), though at least one author has portrayed him as a libertarian incompatibilist (Schouls 1992). His account of free action does seem to make it compatible with determinism, though he does not trumpet the fact. Also, the evidence of his commitment to determinism is not strong, and there is reason to think that he despairs of a solution to the free will problem. In a 1693 letter, Locke confides to his friend William Molyneux that

> I cannot make freedom in man consistent with both omnipotence and omniscience in God, though I am as fully perswaded of both as of any truths I most firmly assent to. (Locke 1979, #1592)

His concern seems to be that, if God knows now (or timelessly) that an agent will φ tomorrow, then there is a sense in which the agent cannot forbear φ-ing tomorrow, and so one in which his φ-ing cannot be free. A similar worry can be raised about determinism. For if it is determined that an agent will φ tomorrow, then there is a sense in which the agent cannot forbear φ-ing tomorrow, and so one in which he cannot qualify as free with respect to φ-ing. One might expect a thoroughgoing compatibilist to insist that in both of these contexts there is an important sense in which the agent can forbear φ-ing. Instead we find Locke confessing to Molyneux that, ‘if it be possible for God to make a free agent, then man is free, though I see not the way of it’ (Locke 1979, #1592). Causal determinism and theological determinism do raise different problems, and Locke may be a compatibilist who cannot see his way around the problem of divine foreknowledge. On the other hand, he may not regard himself as having solved either of these problems.

In the first edition of the *Essay*, Locke contends that each of us always decides to do what seems likeliest to bring himself the most good. This theory of motivation is hedonistic and egoistic. He identifies the good with what is apt to increase pleasure or diminish pain (2.20.2), and says that no one would 'willingly put into his own draught any bitter Ingredient, or leave out anything in his Power, that could add to its sweetness, but only by a wrong judgement' (2.21.40). Thus Locke commits himself to saying that even one who appears to make great sacrifices for others does so only because she judges that her own life would contain less pleasure if she did anything else. However, he does allow that we are prone to several kinds of error about what will bring us pleasure. We give disproportionate weight to present pains and pleasures over future ones, take too little account of pleasure when it is leavened with pain, and are always vulnerable to making errors about the likely consequences of our actions.

In the second edition, Locke offers a different account of motivation. The new account is still hedonistic and egoistic, but now he says that what determines us to will as we do is always one sort of uneasiness or another. Not all of his arguments in support of it are models of clarity (2.21.36–37), but one strong advantage of the new view is that it accommodates cases of weakness of will. On his view as presented in the first edition, Locke had to insist that every time one gives in to temptation or addiction one makes at least a short-lived error of judgment about which course of action is the likeliest one to bring one the greatest pleasure overall. On his later view, he can allow that people sometimes choose to do what they know not to be in their own best interest:

> [L]et a Drunkard see, that his Health decays, his Estate wastes; Discredit and Diseases, and the want of all things, even of his beloved Drink, attends him in the course he follows: yet the returns of *uneasiness* to miss his Companions; the habitual thirst after his Cups, at the usual time, drives him to the Tavern, though he has in his view the loss of health and plenty, and perhaps of the joys of another life: the least of which is no inconsiderable good, but such as he confesses, is far greater, than the tickling of his palate with a glass of Wine, or the idle chat of a soaking Club. 'Tis not for want of viewing the greater good: for he sees, and acknowledges it ... (2.21.35)

Locke goes on to argue that, if we were really motivated only by the prospect of securing future goods, then we should expect nearly everyone to live blameless lives. For even if worldly pleasures seem a nearer and more certain prospect than heavenly bliss, the greater potential payoff of heavenly bliss plainly outweighs them (2.21.38).

Another change in the second edition is the addition of a number of passages about our ability to suspend acting on our desires. He also adds the observations that this ability is 'the source of all liberty' (2.21.47) and the 'hinge on which turns the liberty of intellectual Beings' (2.21.52). What exactly this suspension is supposed to involve, how it relates to Locke's account of freedom, and whether it is consistent with his denial that we can forbear willing on actions once they are proposed to our thoughts, are all disputed questions.

Vere Chappell speaks of Locke as having a 'doctrine of suspension' (Chappell 1998), but this may exaggerate the theoretical content and status of what is intended as a commonplace observation. That we can suspend the prosecution of our desires in order to deliberate is, Locke says, 'evident in Experience' and something that 'every one dayly may Experiment in himself' (2.21.47). He thinks that we frequently find ourselves pushed in different directions by different uneasinesses. Usually we simply do whatever the strongest of these uneasinesses prompts us to do, without stopping to think about it. At times, however, our desire for perfect happiness prompts us to put off acting on these other competing uneasinesses, in order to assess what will really contribute best to our wellbeing. Such deliberation can change the relative strengths of our competing desires, and so can lead us to act in ways we otherwise would not have acted.

Chappell argues that Locke's 'doctrine of suspension' is incompatible with his earlier claim that we cannot forbear willing on an action once it is proposed to our thoughts (Chappell 1998). This would be a problem, because the claim about our inability to forbear willing, and the consequent repudiation of freedom with regard to willing, is retained in the later editions. Chappell presumes that it is Locke's view that, when one suspends the prosecution of several competing desires, one is not willing on any of the actions toward which those desires prompt us. However, another way to think about suspension is that it involves forbearing to act in accord with those desires for at least the next instant and intending to continue this forbearance until one has thought more about which of the prospective actions is best. This would mean that suspending the prosecution of our desires is not an alternative to willing on the actions proposed to our thoughts, but rather involves willing on them.

See also: VOLITION AND THE WILL (13); AGENCY, PATIENCY, AND PERSONHOOD (26); MOTIVATIONAL STRENGTH (33); FREE WILL AND DETERMINISM (38).

References

Primary sources

Leibniz, G. (1981). *New Essays on Human Understanding*, translated and edited by P. Remnant and J. Bennett. Cambridge: Cambridge University Press.

Locke, J. (1975). *An Essay Concerning Human Understanding*, edited by P. Nidditch. Oxford: Oxford University Press. [Cited by book, chapter, section and, where necessary, edition.]

Locke, J. (1979). *The Correspondence of John Locke*, edited by E. DeBeer. Oxford: Oxford University Press.

Secondary sources

Brand, M. (1971). The language of not doing. *American Philosophical Quarterly*, 8, 45–53.

Chappell, V. (1998). Locke on the suspension of desire. *Locke Newsletter*, 29, 23–38.

Chappell, V. (1994). Locke on freedom of the will. In G. A. J. Rogers (ed.), *Locke's Philosophy: Content and Context*. Oxford: Oxford University Press, 101–121.

Ginet, C. (1990). *On Action*. Cambridge: Cambridge University Press.

Jolley, N. (1999). *Locke: His Philosophical Thought*. Oxford: Oxford University Press.

Mackie, J. (1965). Causes and conditions. *American Philosophical Quarterly*, 2, 245–264.

Moore, R. (1979). Refraining. *Philosophical Studies*, 36, 407–424.

Rickless, S. (2000). Locke on the freedom to will. *Locke Newsletter*, 31, 43–67.

Schouls, Peter (1992). *Reasoned Freedom*. Ithaca: Cornell University Press.

Yaffe, G. (2000). *Liberty Worth the Name: Locke on Free Agency*. Princeton: Princeton University Press.

61

Berkeley

TOM STONEHAM

Introduction

If we are to understand the account of action put forth by George Berkeley (1685–1753), we should begin by being clear about what a Berkeleian idealist really believes (for more details, see Stoneham 2009 for more details). This can be summed up in two theses:

[ONT] Everything which exists is either a mind or an object of perception.
[MET] Objects of perception exist when and only when, and in virtue of, being perceived by some mind.

What is 'an object of perception'? Given [MET], the Berkeleian thinks it perfectly reasonable to call these 'ideas,' but notes that it can be misleading to substitute 'idea' in [ONT], for the term carries an implication to the effect that ideas are mental items, whereas the Berkeleian thinks that ordinary, perceivable physical objects consist of collections of ideas – so ideas are no more mental than tables and trees. As Berkeley says, he is not for changing things into ideas but ideas into things (*DHP* 3, 244). The key Berkeleian thought is that it is a mistake to take something's being independent of its being perceived by some mind as a criterion of objective reality (note that here the polysemous word 'objective' is being understood as contrasting with being a property of the subject: the Berkeleian thinks that your fear is real, but subjective in this sense, whereas the tiger you are afraid of is real and not subjective). Consequently the Berkeleian commitment to [ONT] is dualist in nature, though it is not a form of substance dualism. As Berkeley puts it:

> *Spirits* and *ideas* are things so wholly different, that when we say, *they exist, they are known*, or the like, these words must not be thought to signify any thing common to both natures. (*PHK* 142)

To avoid this dualist consequence, a Berkeleian idealist would have to allow that minds – that is, the perceiving subjects – can also be objects of perception. But, given the very general arguments for [MET], this would create considerable problems. So for present purposes I will assume that the Berkeleian, like Berkeley himself, is committed to a form of dualism between minds, that is, perceiving subjects, and ideas, that is, the objects they perceive, which make up the world they inhabit. This commitment has the immediate consequence that the subject is distinct from her body, for the latter is an object of perception.

What consequences does this consequence have for the philosophy of action? Well, if the Berkeleian idealist is to allow that we can act upon the physical world, the world of objects of perception, and we typically do so by moving our bodies, then she will have to see those actions as composed of two distinct elements: a mental one and a physical one.[1] There is plenty of scope for disagreement about what each element is, about the relation between them, and about whether we identify the action with one, with the other, or with their union (Hornsby 1980: 52), but all the resulting views will have the bipartite structure characteristic of a traditional volitional theory of action. If I raise my arm, then there must be two events: one mental, which we can call a 'volition,' and one physical, which in this case will be my arm rising. Furthermore, the volition must bring about, either causally or in some other way, the arm movement. (For a sophisticated recent presentation of a volitional theory, see O'Shaughnessy 2008, Ch. 11.)

The most common objection to volitional theories of action is that it is simply false that every action of mine is preceded by a volition. And if there are actions which are not preceded by volitions, they are not caused by volitions, so there are actions which are not physical events caused by volitions. Most of the examples given to show that there is a problem with identifying a volition for every action can be dealt with by seeing the problematic actions as foreseen or foreseeable elements of more complex actions, for which there is a volition. Consider this version of the problem from a textbook in the philosophy of mind:

> Suppose, however, that you are at the bank; the cashier passes over a familiar slip of paper, saying 'sign here, please' and you oblige. Now your signing is certainly an action. But is it, in the typical case, preceded by any conscious mental event of which you are even dimly aware? Does introspection or reflection really reveal an internal 'act of will'? Surely you will normally sign 'straight off' without deliberation, without consciously setting yourself to perform the task, without mental or physical effort. (Smith and Jones 1986: 125)

One option would be to deny that the volition must always be conscious. Cases of conscious willing of actions allow us to understand the nature of a volition, but philosophical argument might give us a reason to think that volitions occur even in cases where we are not consciously aware of them. Unfortunately, that response is not available to the Berkeleian, who takes introspection to reveal decisively whether certain events, such as perceivings, are voluntary imaginings or involuntary perceptions. Instead we should note that the complex action of going into the bank to withdraw some cash probably was something one consciously set oneself to perform. And, in so doing, either one expected to be asked to sign something or one did not. If one had that expectation, then the willing of the complex action suffices to cause the specific action of signing. If, in contrast, one lacked that expectation, then it is highly unlikely that one would just sign 'straight off'; rather one would look at what one was being asked to sign and decide whether or not to sign it.

Occasionalism versus Realism

If a volitional theory holds that the volition *causes* the bodily movement, then some scholars have denied that Berkeley holds a volitional theory, for they have denied that our volitions have any causal powers. Rather, God causes our bodily movements on the occasion of our volitions. This is occasionalism about action, and the contrasting view that we do in fact cause our bodily movements can be called realism.

The textual facts are that in his notebooks Berkeley wrote: 'We move our Legs our selves. 'tis we that will their movement. Herein I differ from Malbranch.' (*PC* 548), but nothing in the published works is as unequivocal as this in distancing Berkeley from an occasionalist account of physical action. At this point, some scholars argue that Berkeley's proof of the existence of God, which is surely quite fundamental for him, requires all our ideas of sense to be caused by God, ruling out some being caused by finite spirits (see for example Bracken 1974: 117). Others argue that considerations of 'commonsense and theology' (Ayers 1970: 96; see also Jolley 1990: 234–238) make such occasionalism about action unacceptable to Berkeley.

This is a clear case where the correct interpretive method is to attribute to Berkeley the view which maximizes the coherence and cogency of his philosophical system as a whole.[2] And here I think two considerations favor the claim that we do in fact act on the world ourselves: Berkeley's theodicy and his account of other minds. At *PHK* 153, Berkeley claims that, among the benefits which counterbalance the presence of apparent evils in the world, making it plausible that they bring a greater good, is 'the nature of human freedom.' Now, presumably freedom is limited to what we can do, and if that is in turn limited to willing and we rely on God to make the physical changes, then human freedom would not be impaired if God decided not to bring about the evil acts we will. So appeal to human freedom could have no role in Berkeley's theodicy. Furthermore, when considering the related but slightly different question of whether his view makes God the author of our sins, he first notes that physical events, such as killings, are not intrinsically sinful, but only so relative to a specific motive. While this allows even an occasionalist to get out of the objection, Berkeley immediately follows it by saying:

> Lastly, I have no where said that God is the only agent who produces all the motions in bodies. It is true, I have denied there are any other agents beside spirits: but this is very consistent with allowing to thinking rational beings, in the production of motions, the use of limited powers, ultimately indeed derived from God, but immediately under the direction of their own wills, which is sufficient to entitle them to all the guilt of their actions. (*DHP* 3, 237)

This move allows Berkeley to get out of the objections that not only is God the author of sins, but also that he is directly responsible for the suffering which those sinful willings bring about. So, while Berkeley carefully avoids committing himself to the realist account of action at this point, he has powerful reasons to accept it.[3]

On the question of our knowledge of other minds, some care is needed. Consider these three sentences from consecutive sections of the *Principles*:

> But though there be some things which convince us, humane agents are concerned in producing them; yet it is evident to every one, that those things which are called the works of Nature, that is, the far greater part of the ideas or sensations perceived by us, are not produced by, or dependent on the wills of men. (*PHK* 146)

> There is not any one mark that denotes a man, or effect produced by him, which doth not more strongly evince the being of that spirit who is the Author of Nature. (*PHK* 147)

> Hence it is plain, we do not see a man, if by man is meant that which lives, moves, perceives, and thinks as we do: but only such a certain collection of ideas, as directs us to think there is a distinct principle of thought and motion like to our selves, accompanying and represented by it. (*PHK* 148)

The first states quite clearly that the objects of perception can be divided into two exclusive groups – the works of nature and the works of human (and presumably other finite) agents – and, furthermore, that it is the works of nature which reveal to us the existence of God. But the second says that we find evidence of the existence of God in the works of man – in fact these give better evidence of God than of man. The third tells us what it is about the works of man that gives us reason to believe in other minds. I think this third passage provides the ground for arbitrating between the other two and for concluding that the second is a mistake on Berkeley's part: he is trying to emphasize how strong and immediate the proof of God is on his system, and he ends up saying something more than he should.[4]

Consider those objects of perception which we take as evidence of another finite spirit, for example a handshake and an utterance of 'Good morning.' Is this or is this not part of Divine Providence, an event in the world which leads me to believe in the existence of a benign God? If it is, then it can be explained in terms of God's purposes, and we are in no position to infer a 'distinct principle of thought and motion like ourselves.' And if we can infer a distinct principle, then we cannot regard the event as part of Divine Providence (or at least not directly; for, if the event evinces human free will, then we can see the existence of that free will as part of Providence). It seems, then, that the second quotation above just must be a mistake on Berkeley's part. And if that is so, if we can divide the objects of experience into two exclusive groups, those which evince Divine nature and those which evince human nature, then the main reason for the occasionalist interpretation of Berkeley's views on action has been undermined.[5]

Affecting Other Minds

Berkeley is certain that everything we do, we do by moving our bodies (or limbs, as he incorrectly says, overlooking his own examples of moving our eyes, and also actions such as speaking). This is presumably one of the things experience teaches us,[6] though we often describe our actions in terms of the events which are consequent upon the bodily motion. So, in order to kill someone, I may have to hold, aim, and fire the gun with my hand; and we still describe that as a killing of that person, which is not a bodily motion of mine. But, for Berkeley, this is loose talk: while I may have known that my action would result in the other person's death, that death is not something I caused, and thus not something I did. This is because ideas do not cause other ideas, but merely stand in regular, discoverable, but contingent relations to each other. So Berkeley goes one step further than saying that we only do things *by* moving our bodies and claims that all we ever do is move our bodies, the non-causal laws of nature taking over after that.[7]

In a famous passage, Berkeley seems to draw the conclusion that, since we only move our limbs, we do not affect the experiences of others:

> For it is evident that in affecting other persons, the will of man hath no other object, than barely the motion of the limbs of his body; but that such a motion should be attended by, or excite any idea in the mind of another, depends wholly on the will of the CREATOR. (*PHK* 147)

However, we should not read too much into this particular sentence because, as it stands, it just has to be a mistake on Berkeley's part. The problem is that the claim made here requires us to distinguish the motions of someone's limbs from 'any idea in the mind of another': but when you perceive my arm moving, whether or not that is an action of mine, it is a motion of my limbs which is an idea in your mind. The only way we could make this sentence consistent with Berkeleian idealism would be to deny that we ever perceive the motion of anyone else's limbs. Sensitive to this problem, Ayers (1970: 96) interprets it thus, calling it a 'curious view':

> For it is evident that in affecting other persons, the will of man hath no other object, than barely the motion of the limbs of his body *as perceived by himself*; but that such a motion should be attended by, or excite any idea in the mind of another, depends wholly on the will of the CREATOR.

While this is certainly a legitimate re-interpretation and it fits with the rest of *PHK* 147, as we noted above, it creates problems for Berkeley's account of our knowledge of other finite minds and it does not fit so well with *PHK* 146 and 148. Furthermore, it restricts our field of action even further than the existing restriction to the motions of our limbs. There is an alternative re-interpretation which does not have this consequence, allowing that we may move our limbs even when that motion is perceived by another:[8]

> For it is evident that in affecting other persons, the will of man hath no other object, than barely the motion of the limbs of his body; but that such a motion should be attended by, or excite any *other* idea in the mind of another, depends wholly on the will of the CREATOR.

However, the resulting account of the scope of human action faces a serious philosophical problem (Taylor 1985: 219–220): it appears to commit Berkeley to the existence of some form of telepathy, that is, it appears to give us the power to cause ideas in the minds of others *directly*. (Note that the alternative is that we cannot cause ideas in the minds of others *at all*, which may seem equally unpalatable.)

This objection only has any force if we take telepathy to be inherently implausible or, more precisely, if we take it to be implausible that ordinary humans possess telepathic powers. Now it is certainly implausible that we have a totally general power of telepathy, an ability to directly cause others to have ideas of any sort in any context.

But this is not the claim the Berkeleian makes. All he is committed to saying is that we can directly cause other people to perceive our limbs moving. Is this an implausible telepathic power?

Let us begin to answer this question by considering what is going on according to the materialist. On his account, I indirectly cause other people to have perceptual experiences of my limbs' movement by moving my limbs in a manner and in a physical context where the motion of my limbs, an effect of my volition, causes the others to have perceptual experiences. The motion of my limbs is both the effect of my volition and the cause of their experience. If the Berkeleian's claim is that we can directly cause those experiences without moving our limbs, it would certainly be implausible. But the implausibility here derives from thinking of the perceptual experiences as mental events which can be caused in different ways, which is something that Berkeley denies.

According to Berkeley, to have a perceptual experience is to have an object – he calls it an idea – before the mind. These ideas are the elements of the real physical world: tables, trees, and bodies with limbs are just collections of them. So, if another person perceives my limbs moving, they have some ideas, and these ideas are part of the collection which is my limb. Thus, while the materialist thinks of the perceptual experience as an effect of the limb moving, the idealist thinks of it as someone standing in a relation to that very limb which is moving (Stoneham 2006). So what do I have to do in order to directly cause someone else to have a perceptual experience of my limb moving? I have to move my limb in such a way as to make the other person perceptually related to it. I am affecting the other's mind by affecting the relations in which it stands, and not by affecting its intrinsic properties.

Another way of putting the point is this. Suppose I form the volition to raise my arm (something I know I have the power to do). The effect of this volition will be my arm rising. My arm rising is just a series of ideas. Some of these ideas are perceived by me, and some are perceived by others. So, by directly causing my arm to rise, I have directly caused other people to perceive certain ideas.

My body just is a collection of ideas, each of which is necessarily perceived by some mind. So if I move my body, I am thereby causing a change in the sum total of ideas perceived. If you see me move my arm, I am affecting the ideas you have. Similarly, it would seem, if I see my own arm move. Acting on the world just is changing people's perceptions. But those perceptions are perceptions of how the world really is; so by changing people's perceptions I am also changing the way the world is, with all the consequences that may follow from this according to the laws of nature.

Solitary Actions

Suppose I am on my own in my study, with no other (finite) minds to perceive what I do – not a dog or a mouse or a fly is there with me – and I perform an action, perhaps taking my pen from my pocket and placing it on my desk. What is the difference, for Berkeley, between actually doing this and merely imagining it? In both cases I have certain ideas before my mind, and in both cases those ideas are under my voluntary control. Of course, in one case I perceive the pen and my hand moving whereas in the other I do not, but the crucial mark of the distinction between perceiving and imagining is, for Berkeley, that only the latter is under voluntary control. So in the case of perceiving my own voluntary actions it is not possible to distinguish perception from imagination in this way.

In the example just given, the answer is simple: if I have actually performed the action rather than imagined it, then the pen will be on the table. This means that, if I look again, I will see it, and if I forget ever taking it out of my pocket and start searching for it, it will be on the table, not in my pocket. But what of an even more inconsequential action? What if I simply shift slightly in my seat, then carry on reading? What is the difference between doing that and merely imagining it?

We need to see that this question has two aspects, which can come apart. One is: How can I tell that I actually moved rather than merely imagined it? The other is: What is it that constitutes this difference? The latter question can be dealt with quite easily by noting that every physical event has *some* physical effects. The shifting in my seat will have changed the distribution of weight on the chair legs and the floorboards and disturbed some air particles, all of which have tiny but in principle detectable consequences for these objects. Furthermore, my change of posture will have eased my muscles a bit and reduced stiffness, which has consequences for the way I will feel later. But all these things could happen without my being aware of them, so they do not help me to differentiate between when I am acting and when I am merely imagining.

In fact, our imaginings are rarely as vivid as our perceivings, and we are particularly poor at imagining proprioceptive sensations, so imagining moving is not at all like actually moving. However, that there are some fairly reliable, if contingent, signs of the difference may solve the problem in practice, though not to the satisfaction of a philosopher. It is only in abnormal circumstances that one would need to seek evidence in the content of an experience to tell whether it was an imagining or not; perceiving my own solitary and inconsequential actions is not abnormal, but part of everyday life.

It is not easy to give a solution to this problem, so long as Berkeley holds that:

1 when I imagine something I have those ideas before my mind;
2 there is no distinction in kind between ideas of imagination and ideas of perception, such as one being private and the other public; but
3 only ideas of perception are part of the real world (Stoneham 2002: 181–186).

These three claims force Berkeley into trying to find a difference between perception and imagination as ways of having ideas, and the problem of solitary action undermines the simple appeal to voluntariness or to the cause of those ideas. Personally I now think (*pace* Stoneham 2002: 192–199) that no such difference can be found; so the only way forward for the Berkeleian is to drop one of the propositions (1)–(3). In his early notebooks, Berkeley toyed with dropping (3) (see *PC* 473–474), and some interpreters have argued that his ideas of perception are public (for instance Hight 2009). Perhaps we could drop (1), denying that imagining is actually having ideas before the mind and claiming that it is more like thinking about having ideas. Whatever it is, some aspect of Berkeley's system has to give to accommodate our solitary actions.

Conclusion

It is sometimes thought that any attempt by Berkeley to produce a theory of action will be hopelessly flawed. I have tried to show that this is not the case, that he can give a theory which answers many objections. But the theory may still be ultimately flawed, if he cannot deal with the problem of solitary action.

See also: BODILY MOVEMENTS (4); VOLITION AND THE WILL (13); MENTAL CAUSATION AND EPIPHENOMENALISM (23); AGENCY, PATIENCY, AND PERSONHOOD (26); MENTAL ACTS (27).

Notes

1 This distinction is not restricted to dualists, as Berkeley was aware; for the monist materialist Alciphron accepts it too: 'I grant that there is such a principle [of thought and action], and that it is not the object of sense itself but inferred from appearances which are perceived by sense' (*A*, IV, 4).

2 Berkeley planned and allegedly drafted a second part of the *Principles*, which was to cover topics in the philosophy of mind (among others); but it was lost. So we are in effect working with an incomplete corpus.

3 It is worth noting that, if one is responding to an objection by showing one has a variety of solutions available, it is rhetorically most effective to place the one which is strongest, and which one favors, last.

4 To be precise, I am not claiming it is an oversight or a simple error, but a philosophical misjudgment. Berkeley appears deliberately to leave his published comments on action neutral between realism and occasionalism. One explanation for this is that he did not want to give up the doctrine of *PHK* 147, but he could not see how to reconcile it with realism and yet continued to think that there must be some way of doing so. This would also go some way towards explaining why he never rewrote the lost Part 2 of the *Principles*.

5 In fact, I think the argument from divine language for the existence of God, in *Alciphron*, gives Berkeley a way to accept the doctrine of *PHK* 147. For most human intentions are not merely to perform bodily movements, but to bring about certain effects, which are consequent upon those movements. In other words, we continually exploit the cause–effect/sign–signified relations which constitute the laws of nature: most of our actions are speech acts in the divine language. The paradigm of such exploitation is the creation of an artefact such as a watch. So, while a watch does 'denote a man' as creator, it also gives us evidence of the laws of nature which that man must have exploited in order to make the watch, and thus it 'evinces' the author of nature.

6 Developing technologies which control computers by measuring localized electrical activity in the cortex suggest that an alternative is conceivable, though one might argue that someone using such a device is 'moving' her brain just like someone using a keyboard is moving his fingers.

7 In fact, the non-causal nature of the relation between my squeezing the trigger and the other person dying does not rule out the latter as an act of mine without some other assumptions, specifically that every event has a cause and only spirits are causes. These assumptions require that some other mind causes John's death, so it is their action not mine.

8 To be clear, I suspect that Ayers' re-interpretation is the historically correct account of Berkeley's intentions at the time of writing *PHK* 147, for it is the one interpretation which

best supports the main claim of that section. But the main claim of that section is also hard to make consistent with the overall position of Berkeleian idealism, as I argued above. The proposal here is that this other re-interpretation of the problematic sentence is the one which would maximize consistency and thus is the one that Berkeley should accept, forcing him to weaken the main claim of *PHK* 147 (which is not philosophically fundamental, though it may have been close to Berkeley's heart for theological reasons).

References

Primary sources and their abbreviations

There are many editions of Berkeley's major works and, since there is no significant scholarly dispute about the texts, any edition will do for the student. The standard scholarly edition is *The Works of George Berkeley* (9 vols), edited by T. Jessop and A. Luce, 1948–1957, London: Thomas Nelson. The material relevant for the present chapter is in Vols 1–3 (1948–1950) of this edition.

PC Berkeley's early notebooks [1707–1708], sometimes called *Philosophical Commentaries.* Referred to by the numbering in Jessop and Luce, Vol. 1.

PHK *Principles of Human Knowledge* [1710]. Referred to by original paragraph numbers, which are reprinted in all editions, including Jessop and Luce, Vol. 3.

DHP *Three Dialogues between Hylas and Philosonous* [1713]. Referred to by dialogue number and page in Jessop and Luce, Vol. 2. These page numbers are reprinted in the margins of most modern editions.

A *Alciphron, or the Minute Philosopher* [1732]. Referred to by dialogue number and section number of the 1752 edition, which is reprinted in Jessop and Luce, Vol. 3.

Secondary sources

Ayers, M. (1970). Perception and action. In G. Vesey (ed.), *Knowledge and Necessity*. London: Macmillan, 91–106.

Bracken, H. (1974). *Berkeley*. London: Macmillan.

Jolley, N. (1990). Berkeley and Malebranche on causality and volition. In J. A. Cover and M. Kulstad (eds), *Central Themes in Early Modern Philosophy*, Indianapolis: Hackett, 227–244.

Hight, M. (2009). The myth of privacy. Unpublished manuscript.

Hornsby, J. (1980). *Actions*. London: Routledge.

O'Shaughnessy, B. (2008). *The Will*, 2nd edn. Cambridge: Cambridge University Press.

Smith, P., and Jones, O. (1986). *The Philosophy of Mind.* Cambridge: Cambridge University Press.

Stoneham, T. (2002). *Berkeley's World.* Oxford: Oxford University Press.

Stoneham, T. (2006). Berkeley's '*esse* is *percipi*' and Collier's 'simple' argument. *History of Philosophy Quarterly*, 23: 211–224.

Stoneham, T. (2009). Berkeley: Arguments for idealism. In R. Le Poidevin, P. Simons, A. McGonigal, and R. Cameron (eds), *Routledge Companion to Metaphysics*, London: Routledge, 119–130.

Taylor, C. (1985). Action and inaction in Berkeley. In J. Foster and H. Robinson (eds), *Essays on Berkeley*. Oxford: Clarendon Press, 211–226.

62

Thomas Reid

MARIA ALVAREZ

Introduction

Thomas Reid (1710–1796) is regarded as the founder of the Scottish school of 'commonsense' philosophy. In 1737 he became a minister at the parish of New Marchar, leaving it in 1752, when he was appointed professor of philosophy at King's College, Aberdeen. He was professor of moral philosophy at the University of Glasgow from 1764 until 1789, when he retired to devote himself to his philosophical writing.

Among his most significant published works are: *An Inquiry into the Human Mind on the Principles of Common Sense* (1764); the *Essays on the Intellectual Powers of Man* (1785); and the *Essays on the Active Powers of Man* (1788). I shall focus on the last one, in which Reid develops his views on active power, agency, and moral liberty. (All the quotations from Reid are taken from the 1969 edition of that work which, confusingly, bears the title *Essays on the Active Powers of the Human Mind.*)

Reid had much influence on his contemporaries, both at home and abroad, but he was increasingly neglected during the nineteenth century, until the second half of the twentieth century saw a revival of interest in his philosophy, particularly in his epistemology and his views on human agency and moral liberty. The latter are certainly worth exploring; they offer astute criticisms and subtle, albeit not unproblematic, alternatives to a number of arguments and positions that are still prevalent in philosophical debates. Besides, his style is clear and direct, his arguments are straightforward and his writings are full of insight and – well – common sense.

It will not be possible to do justice to the complexity of Reid's views here, but I shall try to provide an overview of the main features of his account of agency and liberty and then briefly discuss some difficulties which affect the former.

Active Powers

In the *Essays on the Active Powers of Man* Reid defends the concept of 'active power' and develops his accounts of human agency and liberty around this concept. He claims that 'power is a thing so much of its own kind, and so simple in its nature' (Reid 1969: 5) that it cannot be defined. And he agrees with Hume that we have no sense impression of power. Nonetheless, he argues, our idea of power *is* derived from experience, though, admittedly, not *directly* so: 'our conception of power is relative to its exertions or effects' (ibid., p. 10; see also p. 36), which are the operations of the mind, and of which we are conscious. Our idea of power, then, is inferred from our consciousness of its operations.

Although Reid mounts a determined defense of the concept of power, he has a fairly restricted notion of 'active power.' First, he argues that the phrase 'active power' is to be contrasted with 'speculative power' and not with 'passive power.' For, he says, the capacity to undergo change, as opposed to the capacity to produce it, is not a power; and, although Locke uses the phrase, passive power is a 'powerless power, and a contradiction in terms' (ibid., p. 23). Second, he denies that matter has any causal powers: he accepted the Humean doctrine that we perceive only constant conjunction of events and not efficient causation, and the doctrine taught by 'eminent natural philosophers' that 'matter is a substance altogether inert, and merely passive' (ibid., p. 41). Reid recognizes that this goes against common usage (we attribute causal powers to substances) and that those same scientists ascribed to matter 'the powers of corpuscular attraction, magnetism, electricity, gravitation, and others' (ibid.). His response is that the words 'cause,' 'agency,' 'active power,' and so on are ambiguous. The proper meaning of 'cause,' he holds, is 'efficient cause,' and that of 'power' is 'active power' (as characterized below). But, he says, there is another 'lax' sense of the words 'cause' and 'power,' authorized by custom and used in 'Physics'; in this sense we may say that inanimate things or laws of nature have powers or are causes. But talk about the powers of physical bodies in this sense merely describes the laws and regularities in accordance with which the real – that is, efficient – causes of observable changes in nature, of which we are ignorant, produce these changes. (For a discussion of why this is an unsatisfactory response, see Madden 1982, esp. 329ff.). Indeed, Reid says, if 'all the phenomena that fall within the reach of our senses, were accounted for from the general laws of nature,' that would not reveal 'the efficient cause of any one phenomenon in nature' (Reid 1969: 46).

As well as denying that matter has causal powers, Reid holds that all active powers are so-called 'two-way powers': 'power to produce any effect implies power not to produce it' (ibid., p. 35); otherwise it is not power but necessity. And this, he says, implies or strongly suggests (he fluctuates between the two) that only creatures endowed with understanding and will can have active powers. The reason for this is that 'we can conceive of no way in which power may be determined to one of these rather than the other, in a being that has no will' (ibid.) and, he adds, will requires a degree of understanding, for it requires an object of which one must have some conception.

Active Powers, Human Agency, and Liberty

So what, in Reid's view, is the relation between active powers and agency? He says:

> The name of a *cause* and of an *agent*, is properly given to that being only, which, by its active power, produces some change in itself, or in some other being. The change, whether

it be of thought, of will, or of motion, is the *effect*. Active power, therefore, is a quality in the cause, which enables it to produce the effect. And the exertion of that active power in producing the effect, is called *action, agency, efficiency*. (Reid 1969: 268)

Thus to act is to exert active power to produce a change. Active power is exerted at will, the change produced is the effect, and the agent, who has the power (a quality), is the cause.

Reid goes on to say that 'human active power' has two kinds of 'immediate effects': 'We can give certain motions to our own bodies; and we can give a certain direction to our own thoughts' (ibid., p. 49). Any other effects we might bring about, which may be varied and significant, are 'remote' and brought about 'by moving first our own body as an instrument' (ibid.).

It is important to understand how Reid thinks that we 'give motions' to our bodies. First, Reid accepted the essentially dualist conception of agency, widespread among seventeenth and eighteenth-century philosophers, that the body is causally moved by the mind; a conception encouraged by the doctrine, mistakenly believed to be scientific, that matter is inert. Thus, for Reid, an agent who, for instance, freely raises his arm does so by first exerting his power to determine his will, thus causing a volition that his arm rise. Such a volition, characterized as 'the determination of the mind to do, or not to do something which we conceive to be in our power' (ibid, p. 58), in turn causes the arm to rise. And the rising of the arm so caused is the action. However, Reid says that

we know not even how those immediate effects of our power are produced by our willing them. We perceive not any necessary connection between the volition and exertion on our part, and the motion of our body that follows them. (Ibid., p. 50)

According to Reid, experience teaches us that there is an 'established harmony' between our willing certain motions of our bodies and the occurrence of these motions. The willing, Reid says, is 'an act of the mind,' but

whether this act of the mind have any physical effect upon the nerves and muscles, or whether it be only an occasion of their being acted upon by some other efficient, according to the established laws of nature, is hid from us. (Ibid.)

And he adds:

it is possible therefore, for any thing we know, that what we call the immediate effects of our power, may not be so in the strictest sense. Between the will to produce the effect and the production of it, there may be agents or instruments of which we are ignorant. (Ibid.)

The conclusion is obvious: this 'may leave some doubt, whether we be, in the strictest sense, the efficient cause of the voluntary motions of our own body' (ibid., p. 51), or whether we are, as Malebranche held, only 'occasional causes' (ibid.). And, he adds, 'I see no good reason why the dispute about efficient and occasional causes, may not be applied to the power of directing our thoughts' (ibid., p. 52).

This dispute, however, Reid takes to be both impossible to settle and of no significance, for he says that what matters for 'the moral estimation of our actions' (ibid.,

p. 51) is whether we had the power to determine our wills to bring about an event, and not whether we were the efficient, or merely the occasional, cause of that event:

> The man who knows that such an event depends upon his will, and who deliberately wills to produce it, is, in the strictest moral sense, the cause of the event; and it is justly imputed to him, whatever physical causes may have concurred in its production. (Ibid., p. 51)

Thus having active power to cause a volition to cause a particular event is both necessary and sufficient for moral responsibility for that event.

But does an agent not cause all of his volitions? According to Reid, he does not. For the will can be determined by 'principles of action' such as appetites, passions, and affections. When the will is so determined, the resulting action is voluntary because it depends on the agent's will, but it is free only if, and to the extent that, the agent could have determined his will otherwise:

> By the *liberty* of a moral agent, I understand, a power over the determinations of his own will.
>
> If, in any action, he had the power to will what he did, or not to will it, in that action he is free. But if, in every voluntary action, the determination of his will be the necessary consequence of something involuntary in the state of his mind, or of something in his external circumstances, he is not free: he has not what I call the liberty of a moral agent, but is subject to necessity. (Ibid., p. 259)

Reid further explains that moral liberty requires the agent to have not only the power to will or not to will what he did, together with some conception of what he wills, but also 'some degree of practical judgment or reason,' that is, 'the judgment to discern one determination preferable to another' (ibid., p. 259), since otherwise active power 'would be given in vain' (ibid., p. 260).

So Reid is an incompatibilist libertarian. He holds that moral responsibility requires what is sometimes called 'liberty of indifference': that the agent could have willed otherwise; and the fourth of the *Essays on the Active Powers* is devoted to explaining his notion of moral liberty and to defending the claim that we have such liberty with an array of arguments, many of them of great power and ingenuity.

Particularly interesting in this context is Reid's treatment of motives. He says that every motive is addressed either 'to the animal or to the rational part of our nature' (ibid., p. 288). The first kind, 'animal motives,' are appetites and passions which we share with animals, and whose 'influence is immediately upon the will' (ibid., p. 289). The second kind, 'rational motives,' influence our judgment by presenting an action as our duty or as something conducive to our good, directly or instrumentally.

Against his opponents, Reid denies that motives are the causal determinants of actions. In general, Reid says, the influence of motives is like that of advice or exhortation, 'which leaves a man still at liberty' (ibid., p. 283): they may be compared to 'advocates pleading the opposite sides of a cause at the bar' (ibid., p. 288), where 'the sentence is in the power of the judge, not of the advocate.' Reid challenges the necessitarian claim that every action is caused by the strongest motive, pointing out that its truth cannot be determined 'unless some measure of the strength of motives can be found distinct from their prevalence' (ibid).

He offers his own account of the strength of motives. Concerning animal motives, he suggests that their strength is judged 'by the conscious effort that is necessary to resist them' (ibid., p. 289); while the strongest rational motive 'is that which it is most our duty and our real happiness to follow' (ibid., p. 291). He adds that, in 'the grand and the important competition of contrary motives,' which is between the animal and the rational, we may ask which is the strongest motive. If we use the test for animal motives, he says, then the animal motive tends to be stronger (for it requires more effort to resist). But if we use the rational test, then 'it is evident, that the rational motive is always the strongest.' And, he concludes, whichever test we use, it seems false that the strongest motive always prevails:

> In every wise and virtuous action, the motive that prevails is the strongest, according to the rational test, but commonly the weakest according to the animal. In every foolish, and in every vicious action, the motive that prevails is commonly the strongest according to the animal test, but always the weakest according to the rational. (Ibid.)

To be sure, Reid's explanations and arguments will fail to convince many; nonetheless, anyone interested in these topics will certainly profit from paying careful attention to them.

For now, though, I shall leave behind Reid's defense of moral liberty and turn to his account of agent causation, which strikes me as being at once very attractive and deeply problematic. I shall argue that, although the difficulties are serious, they are rooted in Reid's allegiance to doctrines that are independent of, and in fact inimical to, the concept of agent causation that he sought to defend.

Agent Causation and Volitionism

Reid's account of human agency has several unwelcome consequences. First, it engenders skepticism about physical agency. For, as we saw, Reid thinks that, although we certainly cause volitions that our bodies move, when the willed motions occur, it is not certain that they are indeed caused by our volitions, since all we perceive is constant conjunction between the latter and the motions. This means that we cannot be sure that it is we who move our bodies.

Reid recognizes that his account has this skeptical implication. As we saw, he tries to deflect the issue by asserting that what matters is that we are the efficient causes of our volitions, and hence morally accountable for our actions. But, while this may or may not be a satisfactory response to skepticism about free will and moral responsibility, it is certainly not a satisfactory response to 'physical' agency skepticism. For, in the first place, as Reid himself might have put it, it is more certain that we can causally affect the physical world through our agency than it is that any particular theory of action is true. And secondly, if we set out to give an account of the nature of human agency as involving the power to cause changes 'in bodies,' it is self-defeating to conclude that there may be no such power.

A second difficulty concerns the much-disputed issue of whether Reid's notion of agent causation involves an infinite regress.

The charge that volitionist theories generate a vicious regress is a familiar one. Briefly, and in its most basic form, the objection goes as follows. If what makes an event voluntary is that it is caused by a volition, and if volitions themselves are voluntary events, then every volition needs to be caused by a prior volition, *ad infinitum*. (And if volitions are not voluntary, in what sense are the resulting actions voluntary?) Reid himself acknowledges and dismisses the objection (1969: 263), and in general his advocates have endeavored to show that Reid's volitionism escapes the objection. But does it?

I am not convinced that it does – not for anti-libertarian reasons, but because I think Reid's conception of volitions and their roles is untenable. Reid holds that:

1 volitions, that is, determinations of the will, are caused by agents;
2 we cause volitions through an exertion of our active power;
3 every exertion of active power requires a determination of the will (remember that the latter was his main ground for holding that only creatures with a will can have active power).

And this seems to suggest that the causing of every volition by an agent requires a prior determination of the will – in other words a prior volition. In short, the combination of the doctrines that agents cause events by causing volitions and that volitions are themselves events which agents cause does seem to generate a regress (see Alvarez 2000).

Reid and his defenders argue that this objection rests on a misunderstanding; for, they hold, Reid did not think that, in order to cause a volition, an agent needs to determine his will to do so, in other words to cause a prior volition (see Rowe 1991 and O'Connor, 1994: 613ff. O'Connor claims that the regress of volitions arises only if one mistakenly thinks that an exertion of active power *is* itself a type of volition. But in fact the regress arises from the view, held by Reid, that an exertion of active power *requires* a volition.) It's clear that Reid did not *explicitly* hold that every volition requires a prior volition, for he says that he does not, and in fact it requires very little reflection to see that this view generates a regress. However, the question is whether his other views commit him to it. And the views outlined in (1)–(3) above seem to. Besides, if we accept Reid's explicit rejection of the view, then the question arises: if an agent can cause a volition without the need for a prior volition to do so, why cannot he cause other events without the need for a prior volition to do so? The answer cannot be that, without a prior volition, the causing of those events would not be an exertion of active power, because *pari passu* we should conclude that, without a prior volition, the causing of the volition would not be an exertion of active power. So, either volitions are required for all exertions of active power, or they are required for none. And if they *are* required, then either we abandon the view that volitions are caused by agents through an exertion of active power, or we end up with an infinite regress.

Thus it seems that Reid's account of agency does face some serious problems. I shall conclude by exploring whether this means that his concept of agent causation is irremediably doomed.

Conclusion: Agent Causation

I have argued that the problems identified in Reid's account arise from his endorsing two dubious doctrines: that matter is inert and must be moved by mind; and that we cause changes in matter (and mind) by causing volitions. If we abandon those doctrines, however, it is possible to develop a broadly Reidian agent-causal account of human agency that avoids those problems. For, arguably, what is essential to an agent-causal account of human agency is the idea that agents can and do cause events at will – and that the causal relation between agents and those events is not reducible to event causation (see Alvarez and Hyman 1998).

First, we can accept that agents do things at will, and indeed will to do things, without accepting that these 'willings' or 'volitions' are events caused by agents and events which cause other events. And if we remove such volitions from the picture, we are left with the idea that agency involves a direct causal relation between agents and the mental or physical changes they bring about at will. On this view, an action is the causing of an event or change, but is not itself an event (for the causing of an event is not itself an event) and, a fortiori, an action is not an event caused by the agent. So agent causation involves a causal relation not between an agent and his actions but between the agent and the *results* of his actions – which include those motions of his body that he causes when he moves it.

The resulting conception of agent causation involves the capacity to move one's body at will directly, not by means of volitions. This may prompt the question: if not by means of volitions, how do we move our bodies? But it is possible that this question is motivated by the conception of matter mentioned above and endorsed by Reid. For, if matter is 'a substance altogether inert, and merely passive,' then it seems that our bodies cannot move themselves and need to be moved by something else. But, if we reject that conception of matter, the question of how we move our bodies takes on a different complexion. If we think of the human body as animated or, what is the same, of ourselves as essentially embodied agents, our active power to move our bodies can be seen for what it is: the power of embodied creatures to move at will. As Reid argued, human beings have the power to move their bodies at will. This power need not and should not be understood as involving a sort of causal transaction between a mental event (a volition) and a physical entity (one's body). Our active power to move our bodies is the power we have to move them *directly* and *at will*, and thereby to cause changes in the world, including our bodies, at will.

I have tried to diagnose the roots of some problems in Reid's account of agency and to suggest ways of overcoming them. I hope in this way to have shown that Reid's writings are not, at their core, obsolete or superseded, but rather repay the attention they are increasingly beginning to receive – indeed, that they establish him as one of the eighteenth century's richest and most rewarding philosophers of action.

See also: ACTION THEORY AND ONTOLOGY (1); VOLITION AND THE WILL (13); REASONS AND CAUSES (17); AGENT CAUSATION (28); MOTIVATIONAL STRENGTH (33); FREE WILL AND DETERMINISM (38); RESPONSIBILITY AND AUTONOMY (39); HUME (63); CHISHOLM (71).

References

Primary sources

Reid, T. (1969). *Essays on the Active Powers of the Human Mind* [1788], edited by B. A. Brody. Cambridge, MA: MIT Press. [NOTE The original title is *Essay on the Active Powers of Man.*]

Secondary sources

Alvarez, M. (2000). Reid, agent causation and volitionism. *Reid Studies*, 4, 69–87.
Alvarez, M., and Hyman, J. (1998). Agents and their actions. *Philosophy*, 73, 219–245.
Madden, E. H. (1982). Commonsense and Agency Theory. *Review of Metaphysics*, 36, 319–341.
O'Connor, T. (1994). Thomas Reid on free agency. *Journal of the History of Philosophy*, 32/4, 605–622.
Rowe, W. L. (1991). *Thomas Reid on Freedom and Morality*. Ithaca: Cornell University Press.

Further reading

Cuneo, T., and Van Woudenberg, R. (eds) (2004). *The Cambridge Companion to Thomas Reid*. New York: Cambridge University Press.
Haldane, J., and Stephen, R. (eds) (2003). *The Philosophy of Thomas Reid*. Oxford: Blackwell.
Lehrer, K. (1989). *Thomas Reid*. London: Routledge.
O'Connor, T. (2000). *Persons and Causes: The Metaphysics of Free Will*. New York: Oxford University Press.
Yaffe, G. (2004). *Manifest Activity: Thomas Reid's Theory of Action*. New York: Oxford University Press.

63

Hume

ANNETTE C. BAIER

David Hume (1711–1776) does not deny that human beings have purposes, make plans, and act, nor that their actions make a difference in the world, but often, he thinks, this is not the difference they aimed to make. And he sees our intentions and voluntary actions as themselves the causal outcome of situations, passions, and characters that we did not choose. We have 'the liberty of spontaneity' when the causes of our decisions and actions are our own desires and beliefs, but there are always external causes for those desires and beliefs. We are acted upon as well as actors, and free will, if this is thought to require absence of determining causes, is an illusion. We confuse our ignorance of the determining causes of our decisions with the absence of such causes. Hume's philosophy of action, then, can be called skeptical. In taking such a line he followed Hobbes and Spinoza and reacted particularly against religious versions of the notion of active powers in us, such as those proposed by Cumberland and Clarke, and later by Reid – which take us to have God-like free will and a vocation toward God-like actions. Hume was brought up in the Church of Scotland, which believed in original sin and in predestination – either 'election' to salvation or consignment to eternal damnation. He seems to have retained the doctrine of predestination in its secular version. But he had no room for the notion of original sin (Gill 2006), any more than he had for divine vocations. His pious mother was from an Episcopalian family, and she may have influenced him against Calvinist extremes. We do not know just how he arrived at the views he expresses in his writings, but trials for heresy like that of the deist and pantheist William Dudgeon by the Chirnside presbytery (see Russell 2008, chapter 4), must have warned him against outspoken irreligion and convinced him of the evils that dogmatic religion was wreaking. In his own careful examination of the human motives for action in his *History of England*, superstition, religious enthusiasm, and bigoted zeal are given their due as forces that have led to foolish and cruel actions. But they also had some accidentally good outcomes, including relative religious toleration (Dees 2004).

Few other philosophers of action have also been historians capable of giving us not just a theoretical account of what goes into human action but also a careful examination of what went into the actions of their country's governors, other public officials, and rebels against them. At the end of his two volumes on medieval English history, Hume wrote that going back so far in history is useful to its readers by making them appreciate their own better situation, especially as regards government and liberty. History also, he said, instructs us in 'the great mixture of accident, which commonly concurs with a small ingredient of wisdom and foresight, in erecting the complicated fabric of the most perfect government' (*H.* 3, 23, 525). He was referring here not to any ideal commonwealth, but to the constitution of Britain in his time, which was, he thought, as perfect a 'plan of liberty' as any other nation had enjoyed. It was by no means perfect, but it was very good compared with the situation in the fifteenth century, let alone earlier. Hume thought that the Whigs of his day were making too much of the supposed ancient liberties of the English, and in particular of Magna Carta – which he regarded as a concession wrenched by the barons from a particularly corrupt king, John, and not as an advancement in the cause of general liberty. What did advance that cause was mainly the unplanned results of the Stuart Restoration, the fears of reverting to civil war and to the tyranny of a Cromwell, and, later, the popular distrust of the Catholic James II, which led to the 'Glorious Revolution' of 1688. It was religious quarrels and fears that eventually led to a state of relative toleration and liberty, although the latter were not explicit aims of those whose actions brought them about. James II was willing to tolerate all brands of Christianity as long as his Catholicism was accepted, just as the Independents, under Cromwell, were willing to tolerate all Protestants.

> The catholics, pretending to an infallible guide, had justified, on that principle, their doctrine and practice of persecution: the presbyterians, imagining that such clear and certain tenets, as they themselves adopted, could be rejected only from a criminal and pertinacious obstinacy, had hitherto gratified, to the full, their bigotted zeal, in a like doctrine and practice. The independents, from the extremity of the same zeal, were led into the milder principles of toleration. Their mind, set afloat in the wide sea of inspiration, could confine itself within no certain limits, and the same variations, which the enthusiast indulged himself, he was apt, by a natural train of thinking, to permit in others. (*H.* 5, 57, 443)

The good constitutional changes came about by accident as much as by wise design. Hume is a skeptical historian as well as a skeptical philosopher.

Hume's first discussion of 'the influencing motives of the will' is found in Part 3 of Book 2 of his *A Treatise of Human Nature*, where he begins by defining the will as 'the internal impression we feel and are conscious of, when we knowingly give rise to any new motion of our body, or new perception of our mind.' The crucial term here is 'knowingly,' rather than 'voluntarily.' It is the indicative, not the imperative mood, that is appropriate, and Hume's definition leaves no room for any doctrine of double effect, which would distinguish what we intended from what we knew we were bringing about. Of course we can welcome some results of our action more than others, even when we knew that the latter would come about. We know what we are about to do because we know what our passions incline us to do – and our passions, directed as they are by our beliefs about how those passions can be best satisfied or, in cases like resentment, can be best expressed, along with our characters and in some cases with our moral sentiments, cause our intentions and intentional actions. (A vacillating or forgetful person may fail to carry out some of her intentions, and of course there can be changes of mind, sometimes because of moral reflection: see Baier 1995.) Hume does not exactly subscribe to a 'belief + desire' analysis of motivation, since desires are only among the passions and sentiments which lead to action, and for him a main role for belief is to cause passions, as well as to instruct us on how to satisfy them.

Hume devotes two sections to persuading us that we have, at best, 'the liberty of spontaneity' when the immediate causes of our actions are within our own minds and hearts, and never 'the liberty of indifference,' claimed by those who, like Descartes, take us to have God-like free will. He stresses that his own deflationary account of causation and of causal necessity should reassure us that there is nothing threatening to our usual view of ourselves and to our responsibility for our actions in his claim that the latter are caused by our characters, and hence by our lasting passions and beliefs. In Section 3 of Part 2 of the same book he goes on to look at the role of reason, and he follows Hobbes in finding it to be a servant to our passions. Then he looks at the occasional conflict within us between 'violent' desires for close tempting goods and our 'calmer,' more reason-informed preferences for remoter but greater goods. Although violence is not the same as strength, still 'when we wou'd govern a man, and push him into any action, 'twill commonly be better policy to work upon the violent than the calm passions' (*T.* 2.3.4.1). He looks at causes of violence in passions, and at the effect on them of the distance in space and time between us and the objects of our passions. Desire cannot be for what is past, but admiration can be increased by the antiquity of its object. Distance from us has greater effect in time than that in space. 'Ancient busts and inscriptions are more valued than Japan tables' (*T.* 2.3.8.3). We venerate the past and 'are not apt to think our posterity will excel us, or equal our ancestors' (*T.* 2.3.8.11). This veneration for the past makes us spend efforts to get to know past history, so it affects our love of truth. We are more likely, he says, to make efforts to get to know the history of ancient Greece, the source of those valued busts and inscriptions, than to take a long journey to find out what Japan is like. Often Hume is expressing his own predilections in these musings, rather than his researched findings about human nature. He is also repeating Malebranche. Ancestor worship is a known phenomenon, and Hume comes back to it in Section 5 of his *Natural History of Religion.* (Hume was proud of his family, but certainly did not worship his covenanting Home ancestors.) One thing he finds to increase both the strength and the violence of a desire is its satisfaction being forbidden. Another is the teasing veiling of the attractions of an object of desire, or repeated postponements in satisfying the desire. Little of this fairly elaborate psychology of desire is repeated in Hume's *Dissertation on the Passions*; he may have decided that these observations were more revealing of his own nature than confirmed generalizations in a science of man. (What was forbidden to him? Who teased him with veils and postponements? We know very little about Hume's youth and the formation of his ruling passions, including his animus against religion.)

He repeats his arguments against indeterminism in Section 8 his *Enquiry Concerning Human Understanding,* after having, in Section 7, added an argument against Locke's view that we experience the causal power of our own wills. All we experience, he claims, is a fairly constant conjunction between what we come to intend and what we do, and a more constant conjunction between what we most want and what we intend. In Section 8 he emphasizes the 'great uniformity among the actions of men, in all ages [...] the same motives always produce the same actions, the same events follow from the same causes' (*EHU* 8.1.7). He claims that we depend on this in our daily lives. 'A manufacturer reckons upon the labour of his servants for the execution of any work, as much as upon the tools he employs' (*EHU* 8.1.17). Another example he gives is that of his 'honest and opulent' friend, whom he trusts not to stab him and steal his silver. Were he in fact to do so, Hume would be as surprised as if the walls of his house were to collapse in an earthquake. Such sudden unexpected events do sometimes occur, but they do not alter the general reliability of houses or people. What Hume goes on to do, in the second part of Section 8, is to repeat his arguments in the *Treatise* about the compatibility of his 'doctrine of necessity' with the human practices of praise, blame, and punishment. He says that these practices would make no sense if human actions, themselves 'temporary and perishing,' were not caused by lasting passions and character traits in agents. To this he adds a final jab at the religious, who believe both that we have free will and that we will be judged by an omnipotent creator, who could have prevented our wrong actions. The sort of cause of our actions that would make it unfair to punish human misdeeds, he argues, would be a will behind our will, an 'ultimate Author of all our volitions.' If God knew what we were going to do before we did it, and still did not intervene to stop it, then His will is the will which knowingly does what happens, and we are mere puppets. Hume's own view does not make us puppets, but the religious have a nasty choice:

> Human actions, therefore, either can have no moral turpitude at all, as proceeding from so good a cause; or if they have any turpitude, they must involve our Creator in the same guilt, since he is acknowledged to be their ultimate cause and author. (*EHU* 8.2.9)

Hume's discussion of the problem of evil, in Part 10 of his *Dialogues on Natural Religion*, has his character Philo invoke Epicurus' generalization of this dilemma for the religious, about God's responsibility for evil:

> Is God willing to prevent evil, but not able? Then he is impotent. Is he able but not willing? Then he is malevolent. Is he both able and willing? Whence then is evil?' (*D* 198)

Hume is at his most devilishly clever in turning back against the theists the charge that his own determinist secular views are a danger to morality and moral responsibility.

Hume sees our nature as continuous with that of other animals, and so there are sections in the *Treatise* which deal with reason in animals, pride and love in animals, sympathy and desire in animals. None is specifically devoted to animal action, but Hume takes animals to act – and to act predictably, just as we do. What is distinctive to us is not so much our basic motivation as our capacity for language, moral praise and blame, social organization, long-term planning, and also the form taken by our animal 'curiosity,' which embraces not just history and science but also religion – a response, Hume thinks, to our anxiety about the future and our ignorance of some of the causes affecting our fate. We are the talkative, cultural, political, moralizing and religious animals, and so our actions can be done from motives unlike those of even the higher apes. We build cathedrals and parliament buildings, as well as ordinary dwellings. But there is nothing more God-like, or freer, or more creative, in what we do than in what a mother cat does for her kittens, or in what a dog does for his master, or in what a bird does when it carefully builds its nest. Unlike other animals, we have divided the labor, so we have specialists – architects, builders, plumbers. Badgers and birds have to be their own architects and builders.

Unlike other animals, we may worry about what we do and about why we do it. We try to produce theories explaining it and we preach sermons denouncing it. We have the capacity to reflect on what we are doing; so now we worry about the effects of our voluntary actions on our environment – we have become the polluting and the worrying animal. In Hume's day such worries were in the future. His and his contemporaries' concerns were more about unruly political behavior, or about people's tendency to kill each other in wars and to burn each other at the stake. Hume's portrayal of human actions is more of a satire than of a panegyric, and by the end of his life he was pessimistic about our prospects. The greatest praise he gives for human achievements is for wise legislators like Alfred and Henry II of England, for scientists like Newton, and for poets like Milton. Hume disagreed with Newton's religious views as much as he did with Milton's, but he respected the achievements of both, just as the Christianity of Alfred and Henry did not stop him from appreciating their wisdom as legislators. So there are aspects of human action that can give us pride in our species. Poetic genius, scientific genius, wisdom in legislation – all these are possible for us, even though, on the other side of the ledger, our religious persecutions put us 'below the infernal spirits in wickedness, and below the brutes in folly' (*H.* 3, 37, 437), and some of our religious antics are rather like 'the playsome whimsies of monkeys in human shape' (*Diss.* 15, 6). When considering slavery and the Roman games, Hume expressed sympathy with Caligula's wish that humanity had but one neck, so one might with one blow put an end to such a 'race of monsters' (*Ess.* 386). He does not often give expression to such misanthropic sentiments, but he did spend a lot of his own life as a man of letters accumulating, in his *History of England*, a sorry record of atrocities. He is not just a skeptical philosopher of human action, he is sometimes a cynical one. What we and our ancestors have done is so terrible that, if our posterity is unlikely to do better, the future is bleak. On his diagnosis, it is 'faction' and religious divisions that motivate most of the worst human behavior, so he searches for a cure for these ills in his essays on politics and in his writings on religion. He does not believe that we are bound to be religious. It is a 'secondary,' not a 'primary' principle in us, and he finds its root causes to be anxiety about our fate, along with curiosity about ultimate causes. Such inevitable forces could take other forms than that of religious devotion – for instance environmental activism, cosmology, and astro-physics. Hume never assumes the role of prophet and, although he thinks that the English constitution has improved over time, he does not expect later generations to become wiser and less prone to quarrel than in the past. 'Flux and reflux' between barbarity and civilization is the most we can hope for. Hume considered his own times to be fairly civilized by comparison with earlier periods in English history, but at the end of his life he denounced the 'barbarians' who were stirring up riots on the banks of the Thames.

The actions that interested Hume were not only those staples of twentieth century action-theorists, cleaning the house and painting it, or pumping its water supply, but also riot and revolution, enacting a new law, abolishing the Star Chamber, refusing the crown of England, and some small acts that had large consequences, such as Henry II expressing anger in a way that led to the assassination of Becket, or Charles I preventing a ship of emigrants for America from leaving, and thus keeping in England Cromwell, who was to lead the revolt against him. Such actions, many of them on the public stage, captured his attention; and I shall end by looking at his account of some of the actions of Henry II, one of the few leaders who received treatment in more than one chapter in Hume's *History of England.* (Others are Elizabeth and Cromwell.)

Henry II was a monarch whom Hume admired greatly, in part for his attempts to contain the power of the church, in part for his legal reforms, which separated crimes against the person from crimes against the king's peace and against property. Before these reforms, murder was treated as theft of manpower or woman power, and the fine was smaller if the victim was female. Murder could also be a disturbance of the king's peace. Henry made murder a capital offence, regardless of the sex or rank of the victim. Henry had an open and affectionate nature, but, after his friendship with Becket came to its sorry end, he found himself in danger from 'the thunders of the Vatican,' so two years after Becket's murder he put on a fake show of repentance at Becket's tomb, and had his bare back whipped by priests. It was an uncharacteristic gesture of hypocrisy, but it did improve relations with the church. Clearly this was no spontaneous impulsive act of remorse for the angry outburst in which he had dispatched his knights to kill Becket, for that would have occurred (and some such act of penitence did occur) as soon as he heard of Becket's death. It was instead a carefully calculated act. He put up with the pain and humiliation of it for the sake of his country and for the success of his own policies. Here is what Hume says about it. Faced with dangerous discontent in England and Scotland, Henry returned from 'baffling' his French enemies in Normandy, determined

> by his presence to overawe the malcontents, or by his courage and conduct to subdue them: and knowing the influence of superstition over the minds of the people, he hastened to Canterbury, in order to make his atonement to the ashes of Thomas a Becket, and tender his submissions to a dead enemy. (*H.* 1, Ch 9, p. 355)

Then after walking barefoot and prostrating himself before Becket's shrine, he fasted and prayed for a night and day before having his bare back whipped by monks.

> Next day he received absolution, and departing for London, got soon after the agreeable intelligence of a great victory which his general had obtained over the Scots, and which, being gained on the very day of his absolution, was regarded as his final reconciliation with Heaven and with Thomas a Becket. (Ibid.)

This sardonic account makes it clear that, although Henry's main aim was to improve relations with the church and the people, he was not entirely free of the superstition he knew they shared. Hume calls his penance a 'hypocritical devotion towards a man, whose violence and ingratitude had so long disquieted his government' (ibid.). The submission to Becket's remains was hypocritical; but not the desire for reconciliation with Heaven, or at least with its worldly representatives. Henry was 'the greatest prince of his time for wisdom, virtue and abilities' (*H.* 1, Ch 9, p. 370); but, although he tried to restrain ecclesiastical privileges, he was a believing Christian. Hume brings out the calculated nature of the king's act of spectacular penance, and it is a good case of a long-term purpose requiring a humbling act, which did not come easily to a powerful king. Henry did not stand on ceremony – he had abolished the expensive custom of yearly re-coronation repeated three times; still, to be whipped by monks was to humble his kingly pride. This was an act motivated by peculiarly human motives – long-term ambition for his kingship, love of his country, concession to popular superstitions, and in particular to the recent sainthood of Becket, who, as Hume sourly remarks, had sacrificed his life for the privileges of the clergy which Henry had tried to curtail. The blood of the martyrs may be the seed of the church, but Becket's blood was shed for the privileges of the princes of the church. (This passage in Hume may have been what put his works put on the Index, once the *History* was translated into Italian; see Mazza 2007.) The hostility between Henry and Becket may also have been the momentous result of a small impulsive act of Henry's. Becket was a proud man, and Henry had made him look foolish, as Chancellor, when he brought him to agree that it would be a fine act of Christian charity to give a coat to a shivering beggar, then seized Becket's fine scarlet cloak lined with ermine and gave it to the beggar (*H.* 1, 8, 308). Henry was affectionate and impulsive (Hume calls him 'affable'), and did not guard his speech or actions in the company of those he trusted. For all his superior wisdom, he misjudged Becket when he made him look foolish and then expected his loyalty as head of the church; he also misjudged his loyal knights when he expressed his anger with Becket in their presence.

Few action theorists do better than Hume at understanding the complexities of human motivation and how character is expressed in action – but then few have seen this as part of their task.

See also: DESIRE AND PLEASURE (15); HUMEANISM ABOUT MOTIVATION (20); WHAT A DIFFERENCE EMOTIONS MAKE (25); FREE WILL AND DETERMINISM (38); VIRTUOUS ACTION (40); ACTION IN HISTORY AND SOCIAL SCIENCE (50); LOCKE (60); REID (62).

References

Primary sources with their abbreviations

T. Hume, D. (2007). *A Treatise of Human Nature*, edited by D. and M. Norton. Oxford: Clarendon Press. [Referred to by book number, part number, section number, and paragraph number.]

Diss. Hume, D. (2007). *A Dissertation on the Passions; The Natural History of Religion*, edited by T. L. Beauchamp. Oxford: Clarendon Press. [Referred to by section number and paragraph number.]

D Hume, D. (1947). *Dialogues on Natural Religion*, edited by N. K. Smith. Edinburgh, London, Melbourne, Toronto: Thomas Nelson and Sons. [Referred to by page number.]

EHU Hume, D. (2000). *Enquiry Concerning Human Understanding*, edited by T. L. Beauchamp. Oxford: Clarendon Press. [Referred to by section number, part number, and paragraph number.]

Ess. Hume, D. (1985). *Essays Moral Political and Literary*, edited by E. F. Millar. Indianopolis: Liberty Classics. [Referred to by page number.]

H. Hume, D. (1983). *The History of England*, 6 volumes. Indianopolis: Liberty Classics. [Referred to by volume number, chapter number, and page number.]

Secondary sources

Baier, A. C. (1995). Moral sentiments and the difference they make. *Proceedings of the Aristotelian Society (Suppl.)* 69 (ed. Jonathan Wolff), 15–30.

Dees, R. (2004). *Trust and Toleration.* London: Routledge.

Gill, M. (2006). *The British Moralists on Human Nature, and the Birth of Secular Ethics.* Cambridge: Cambridge University Press.

Mazza, E. (2007). Hume on the index: Religion and the early history of England. *Modern Schoolman*, 84, 353–373.

Russell, P. (2008). *The Riddle of Hume's Treatise: Skepticism, Naturalism, and Irreligion.* Oxford: Oxford University Press.

64

Kant

ERIC WATKINS

The theory of action of Immanuel Kant (1724–1804) forms a central component of his metaphysical and ethical views, and several of its most distinctive features are fully intelligible only when seen against the background of his larger critical project. In the bulk of this chapter I explain the basic features of Kant's theory of human action by showing how it draws on his more general account of action and causality and how it is similar in fundamental ways to his explanation of the actions of inanimate bodies. I also sketch Kant's distinctive account of moral action and indicate how it can solve several traditional difficulties associated with the problem of free will and determinism. At the end of the chapter, I argue that Kant's theory of action can neatly avoid one problem that contemporary proponents of agent causation have faced.

Kant does not provide an explicit definition of action (*Handlung*) in any of his major critical publications. However, in the so-called L_2 transcripts of his metaphysics lectures, most likely held in 1790–1791, he makes remarks that amount to a succinct, yet still informative general definition of action:

> Action is the determination of the power [*Kraft*] of a substance as a cause of an accident [*accidentis*]. Causality [*causalitas*] is the property of a substance insofar as it is considered as a cause of an accident. (Kant 1902–, Vol. 28: 564–565)

According to this definition, the concept of action essentially involves the concepts of substance and causality. Specifically, an action occurs if and only if a substance causes an accident by means of a determination of its power (*Kraft*). For an action is a determination of the substance's power by means of which it causes its effect.

This definition provides a helpful broader framework for a series of remarks Kant makes about action in the *Critique of Pure Reason*, which might otherwise appear to be puzzling. In the context of the Second Analogy of Experience, for example, where Kant is attempting to counter Hume's deflationary empiricist account of causality, he notes:

> This causality leads to the concept of action, this to the concept of power [*Kraft*], and thereby to the concept of substance. (A204/B249)

> Where there is action, consequently activity and power [*Kraft*], there is also substance. (A204/B250)

> Action already signifies the relation of the subject of causality to the effect. (A205/B250)

What is striking about both Kant's explicit definition in his metaphysics transcripts and these remarks from the Second Analogy is how general they are. The concept of action is not limited to human cases, but rather applies to any kind of substance and to any instance of causality (Willaschek 1992: 38–39, 251).

Accordingly, to grasp Kant's conception of human action properly, it is necessary to understand the central features of his general model of causality. Though there has been considerable scholarly disagreement about its basic structure as well as about its myriad details, my own preferred understanding of it in its simplest version is that a substance causes an effect when it acts according to its own nature, powers, and circumstances so as to determine the (change of) state of a substance (Watkins 2005: 230–297). This model contrasts starkly with event-based models of causality, according to which one event simply causes another, without requiring any further ontological commitments. Though Kant's basic model (which invokes substances, actions, natures, powers, and circumstances) is metaphysically more robust than the simplest event-based models, he not only is open to, but also emphasizes, even more complicated cases. In the Third Analogy of Experience, for example, Kant maintains that at least *two* substances stand in mutual interaction by *jointly* acting according to their natures, powers, and circumstances in the determination of their simultaneous (changes of) state.

Kant's basic model of causality is able to account for two central claims of the Second Analogy: (1) his assertion of a necessary connection between cause and effect (of which Hume failed to find an impression in the world); and (2) his claim that all events in the sensible world occur according to universal laws of nature.

Necessary connections can be explained on the basis of the natures that substances have. For if substances have natures, insofar as they necessarily act in accordance with their natures, the effects they bring about follow necessarily. (It is to be noted that this kind of necessity is hypothetical insofar as it depends on the natures of things.) In the *Metaphysical Foundations of Natural Science*, Kant distinguishes between the nature and the essence of a thing (1902–, Vol. 4: 468), the former being the inner principle of all that belongs to the *existence* of a thing and the latter being the inner principle of all that belongs to the *possibility* of a thing. (Since the essence of a thing concerns what must be the case for a thing to be at all possible, it involves an absolute necessity.) As a result, even within the nature of a thing there can be both essential (or necessary) and contingent (though still explanatorily basic) properties. This distinction will be important below. The main point for present purposes is that, by positing natures that substances act in accordance with, Kant's model has sufficient resources to account for the possibility of necessary connections in the world.

Kant's model of causality can also account for his claim that all events occur according to universal laws of nature. If a substance acts according to its nature and its nature is general in the sense that a substance never exists without it (since the nature in question is an internal principle that belongs to the very existence of the substance, regardless of what other substances exist), then a substance will always act in the same way in the same circumstances, causing the same events. Another way to think about this point is to note that the laws of nature are laws that derive from the general natures of the substances that are causally active in bringing about events in the world in accordance with these natures. A model of causality that involves natures in this way is thus in a position to explain why events would occur in accordance with universal laws of nature.

In developing this general model of causality, Kant clearly has in mind the way it applies to physical bodies in Newtonian science. In the *Metaphysical Foundations of Natural Science*, for example, Kant argues that bodies are spatial substances endowed both with mass and with attractive and repulsive forces, which necessarily act in accordance with the laws of mechanics in the communication of motion. Thus, when one body either repels or attracts another, it acts by exercising its causal powers (its force of repulsion or attraction) in accordance with its nature (its elasticity or its mass) and its circumstances (its position and state of motion, or its distance from the other body). It also obeys the laws of mechanics insofar as, for instance, any change of state in one body must have an external cause in another body and the action of the one body is equal (and opposite) to the action of the other body.

It is important to note that on this model the cause of the acceleration or deceleration of a body is not an event (such as the motion of the one body), but rather a substance (the body itself). More specifically, it is in virtue of the *action* of the substance, the exercise of its causal powers, that the substance can be a cause. In fact, the exercise of a causal power cannot be an event (a change from one determinate state to another); it is, rather, what makes such an event possible in the first place. Kant refers to it instead as 'a uniform continuous action' (A208/B254). The difference is particularly manifest in the case of gravity: all bodies act *continuously* on all other bodies according to *uniform* laws. There are no discrete changes in their actions (which we could observe), as there are in their effects. Nor, for that matter, does Kant think that any of the circumstances in accordance with which a substance acts is, properly speaking, the cause, though we may talk in this way in certain contexts, for the sake of brevity. Thus the motion of one billiard ball is not the cause of the motion of another billiard ball with which it comes into contact (even if one can establish a strict correlation between these motions); it is rather the exercise of their repulsive powers (according to their degree of elasticity). This is perfectly consistent with holding that the causal powers are exercised *in accordance with* such events (as relevant circumstances) in bringing about such an effect, and that regularities involving them can be stated.

Armed with this general account of action and causality as well as with a sense of how it applies to the case of bodies, we can now turn to the basic structure of Kant's explanation of *human* action. A human being acts if and only if it is a substance that exercises its causal powers according to its nature and circumstances. It was common at the time to refer to the causal powers of human beings as faculties (*Vermögen*), and Kant does not depart significantly from this practice (but see 1902–, Vol. 29: 823–824). Though he distinguishes numerous particular faculties – wit, fantasy, memory, and so on – his most fundamental division is into three faculties: cognition, feeling, and desire. And the actions of each of these faculties can be divided into higher and lower kinds, which results in intellectual or sensible cognitions, (dis-)satisfactions or (dis-) pleasures, and motives or impulses. Now the faculty which is crucial for *intentional* human action is that of desire, which is defined as 'the faculty of the soul for becoming cause of the actuality of the object through the representation of the object itself' (ibid., p. 1012; see also p. 894). Insofar as the nature of the soul is rational and the faculty of desire is exercised in accordance with it (through a representation of the goodness of its object), this faculty is called the will – although Kant does on occasion appear to define the will in other ways. However, Kant attributes a range of propensities and predispositions to human nature in addition to rationality. For example, in *Religion within the Boundaries of Mere Reason* (1793), he discusses animality, which includes the propensities for self-preservation, propagation, and community with other beings (Kant 1902–, Vol. 6: 27). Moreover, different human beings can have these propensities and dispositions to different degrees, and hence they can have different characters. Kant's account of intentional human action can thus be summarized at this point as follows: to say that a human being acts is to say that a substance whose nature involves rationality and a range of propensities and predispositions exercises its faculty of desire (or determines its will) according to its specific character and circumstances so as to bring about in the world an object which it represents as good.

Note that this account of human action is still very general and, as such, must be applicable both to the empirical actions of human beings and to *freely* chosen *moral* actions. While Kant discusses the empirical actions of human beings in detail in his treatments of empirical psychology and anthropology, we can focus here simply on how the empirical actions of human beings are consistent with the conditions specified by the Second Analogy, namely that they must involve necessity and must follow according to uniform laws of nature, just as all other events in nature do. Indeed, Kant expresses a clear commitment to these conditions as applied to human action:

> if we could investigate all the appearances of his power of willing [*Willkür*] down to the ground, then there would not be a single human action that we could not predict with certainty, and cognize as necessary from its preceding conditions. (A549–550/B577–578; cf. also Kant 1902–, Vol. 8: 17)

Now, as Frierson has shown (2005: 1–33), Kant maintains that, in certain circumstances, certain intellectual (higher) or sensible (lower) cognitions are followed by corresponding feelings of (higher) (dis-)satisfaction or (lower) (dis-)pleasure, which in turn are followed by corresponding (higher) motives or (lower) impulses, according to the empirical characters of human beings and the psychological laws which govern them. As a result, cognitions and feelings are the antecedent circumstances, and our actions follow with necessity according to uniform (psychological) laws, just as Kant's Second Analogy requires.

Kant's account of freely chosen moral actions involves a number of particularly difficult issues. According to his argument in the Third Antinomy in the *Critique of Pure Reason*, freedom and determinism are inconsistent unless one draws a distinction between the knowable realm of spatio-temporal appearances and the unknowable but still conceivable realm of non-spatio-temporal things in themselves, since that distinction allows one to maintain determinism with respect to the world of appearances, while still being open to the possibility of freedom for things in themselves. Considerable scholarly and philosophical controversy has arisen over the way in which one is to understand this distinction and the larger doctrine of transcendental idealism, of which it is a foundational element. However, one can largely, if not entirely, avoid some of the most controversial features of Kant's position in sketching a picture of the possibility of the occurrence of freely chosen moral action at the level of things in themselves.

Kant's basic idea is that a human being acts morally if the soul, as a thing in itself whose nature includes rationality, freely adopts a maxim (a subjective principle) which subordinates happiness to the moral law (as expressed by the 'categorical imperative') in accordance with its character or, as he puts it, 'conformably with the conditions of the subject' (Kant 1902–, Vol. 4: 421). As with Kant's general model of causality, we have a substance (the soul) that exercises its causal powers (its will) according to its nature (its rationality and character) and circumstances (being faced with the choice between happiness and the moral law).

Needless to say, there are several elements of this picture that require further spelling out. One crucial element is freedom. On the one hand, Kant sometimes defines freedom negatively, as independence from sensible causes (such as appearances in general and impulses in particular). This kind of freedom, which he calls practical freedom, is assured by moral action's being located at the non-empirical level of things in themselves, because things in themselves are not determined by appearances. On the other hand, he asserts freedom in a positive sense as well – in which case the soul is not only free from external determinations but also, in virtue of its practical rationality, responsible for 'absolutely beginning a state' (A445/B473) (and then it is spontaneous) and for giving itself a law, namely the moral law (and then its principle is autonomous). A second crucial element is that the empirical actions of human beings depend on the non-empirical actions (or adoption of a maxim) of the free agents. Kant sometimes expresses this point by saying that a person's empirical character is caused by that person's intelligible character (A539/B567). The intelligible character, by contrast, is basic.

While this description of moral action would require considerable filling out, one can see, at least in bare outline, how one could use it to navigate a number of difficult problems that arise in attempting to explain free will and determinism (Watkins 2005: 301–361). First, it provides clear guidance on whether moral actions are determined by laws of nature, in which case freedom appears to be threatened, or whether they occur independently of such laws, in which case they might seem to be random. Because the agent is an atemporal thing in itself, its actions will not be determined by the laws that govern appearances. (Admittedly, not everyone is immediately comfortable with the notion of an atemporal action, but one might reasonably be more optimistic about making progress in this respect than about tackling the difficulties that come with other possible responses.) At the same time, moral action is not random for that reason, because the agent does act according to his character or nature.

Second, the modal problem posed by the fact that a free action is supposed to be both determined (insofar as it is necessary according to natural laws) and contingent (insofar as the agent could have done otherwise) can be solved, because the laws of nature that necessarily determine an agent's empirical action derive (at least in part) from the agent's empirical character or nature, which is, in turn, caused (at least in part) by the agent's intelligible character, which is basic. As a result, Kant can maintain that while, given the laws of nature, all the appearances follow with necessity from them, these very laws depend ultimately upon the natures of things in themselves. Given that certain things in themselves, namely rational souls, could have characters that are not necessary, the empirical laws of nature that depend on them could have been otherwise. This claim is consistent with maintaining that the laws of nature which do not pertain to specifically human actions are necessary, since the natures on which they are based might include only necessary properties.

Third, there are problems posed by regress and location: any human action *qua* event is caused by a previous event (such as a desire), which is caused in turn by another previous event, and this goes on either *ad infinitum* (but then a regress ensues) or until one identifies an uncaused event which clearly lies outside the agent's control (but then agency is outside the agent's control). Such problems can be solved too, because human actions do not depend causally solely on events that might lead, via a potentially infinite series of events, beyond an agent's control. They depend instead, at least in part, on agents, which are to be conceived of as substances endowed with rationality and a will. The rejection of an exclusively event-based model of action – and thus of the belief–desire model of human action, which presupposes such a model – in favor of an agent-causal theory provides the means to block the regress through the agent and its nature and to locate the source of an action in an appropriate place, with the agent rather than with a potentially never-ending series of events.

Moreover, Kant's account has one important advantage over many contemporary theories of agent causation. The scenario with which contemporary advocates of agent causation begin is that events in the world not involving humans directly are governed by event causation. Then they introduce some notion of an agent and explain how such an agent is distinct from an event or set of events (for instance in terms of the agents' being 'things' that 'endure' as compared to events whose temporal duration is instantaneous or at least indexed to a specific datable time). The final step is then to explain how such an agent could act freely – where freedom is typically understood in incompatibilist terms – though not necessarily, as Markosian has argued (1999: 257–277). For an excellent instance of this kind of approach, see O'Connor (2000).

However, such advocates of agent causation then encounter the challenge of reconciling event causation, which obtains throughout most of the world, and agent causation, which occurs only in the case of human beings. What happens if one event would, in the normal course of things, cause another event, but an agent cause intervenes so as to cause some other event? Is a 'normal' event no longer sufficient to bring about its effect? How, or by what means, could an agent be in a position to preclude one 'normal' event from having its 'normal' effect? While these questions are not necessarily unanswerable, the advantage that Kant's account enjoys is obvious and real. At the empirical level there is no fundamental difference between human action and the action of bodies, given that in both cases substances bring about events in accordance with their natures, causal powers, and circumstances, which will include other substances, their natures, and their causal powers. Human action involves a different kind of substance: an agent, with a different nature: rationality, and different causal powers: faculties; but the fundamental philosophical account is essentially the same. As a result, explaining how a human being interacts with a billiard ball is not fundamentally different from explaining how two billiard balls interact. This is not to say that Kant's account of human action solves all problems associated with free will and determinism, or that his theory is without problems of its own. For example, the crucial relations that Kant maintains between the noumenal character of agents and the phenomenal actions that are grounded on them, as well as Kant's agnosticism about this point, present immediate problems. However, his overall account does provide an independent and distinctive perspective on an especially important set of contemporary problems.

See also: VOLITION AND THE WILL (13); REASONS AND CAUSES (17); AGENT CAUSATION (28); MOTIVATIONAL STRENGTH (33); FREE WILL AND DETERMINISM (38); RESPONSIBILITY AND AUTONOMY (39); HUME (63).

References

Primary sources

Kant, I. (1902–). *Gesammelte Schriften*, 29 vols. Berlin: De Gruyter.

Secondary sources

Frierson, P. (2005). Kant's empirical account of human action. *Philosopher's Imprint*, 5, 7, 1–33.

Markosian, N. (1999). A compatibilist version of the theory of agent causation. *Pacific Philosophical Quarterly*, 80, 257–277.

O'Connor, T. (2000). *Persons and Causes: The Metaphysics of Free Will*. New York: Oxford University Press.

Watkins, E. (2005). *Kant and the Metaphysics of Causality*. New York: Cambridge University Press.

Willaschek, M. (1992). *Praktische Vernunft: Handlungstheorie und Moralbegründung bei Kant*. [*Practical Reason: Action Theory and Moral Justification in Kant*]. Stuttgart: Verlag J. B. Metzler.

65

Nietzsche

BRIAN LEITER

Introduction

Friedrich Nietzsche (1844–1900) holds that people lack freedom of the will in any sense which would be sufficient for ascriptions of moral responsibility; that the conscious experience we have of willing is actually epiphenomenal with respect to the actions which follow that experience; and that our actions largely arise through non-conscious psycho-physical processes of which we are only dimly aware, and hence over which we exercise little or no conscious control. At the same time Nietzsche, always a master of rhetoric, engages in a 'persuasive definition' (Stevenson 1938) of the language of 'freedom' and 'free will,' to associate the positive valence of these terms with a certain Nietzschean ideal of the person, unrelated to traditional notions of free will.

Denial of Free Will and Moral Responsibility

Nietzsche's skepticism about freedom and responsibility is a pervasive theme throughout the corpus of his writings. In a relatively early work, *Daybreak*, he wrote:

> Do I have to add that the wise Oedipus was right that we really are not responsible for our dreams – but just as little for our waking life, and that the doctrine of freedom of will has human pride and feeling of power for its father and mother? (*D* 128)

Belief in freedom of the will is to be explained by the motivations we have for accepting it, not by its reality: we are as little responsible for what we do in real life as we are for what we do in our dreams. The same idea recurs in one of his very last works:

> Formerly man was given a 'free will' as his dowry from a higher order: today we have taken his will away altogether, in the sense that we no longer admit the will as a faculty. The old word 'will' now serves only to denote a resultant, a kind of individual reaction, which follows necessarily upon a number of partly contradictory, partly harmonious stimuli: the will no longer 'acts' or 'moves.' (*A* 14)

Denial of the causality of what we experience as 'the will' is central to Nietzsche's skepticism about free will and moral responsibility. If the faculty of the will 'no longer 'acts' or 'moves'' (*A* 14) – if it is no longer causal – then there remains no conceptual space even for the compatabilist idea that the right kind of causal determination of the will is compatible with responsibility for our actions. (There is also no need for the idea of an 'unfree will': since the will is epiphenomenal, its freedom or causal determination is irrelevant.) If, as Zarathustra puts it, 'thought is one thing, the deed is another, and the image of the deed still another: the wheel of causality does not roll between them' (Z I, 'On the pale criminal'; compare *D* 124 for the same point), then there is no room for moral responsibility: I may well identify with my 'thoughts' or my will, but if they do not *cause* my actions, how could I possibly be responsible for them?

In the central discussion of free will and responsibility in his *Genealogy of Morality*, Nietzsche writes:

> For just as common people separate the lightning from its flash and take the latter as a *doing*, as an effect of a subject called lightening, so popular morality also separates strength from the expressions of strength as if there were behind the strong an indifferent substratum that is free to express strength – or not to. But there is no such substratum [...] [T]he suppressed, hiddenly glowing affects of revenge and hate exploit this belief [in the subject] and basically even uphold no other belief more ardently than this one, that *the strong is free* to be weak, and the bird of prey to be a lamb: – they thereby gain for themselves the right to hold the bird of prey *accountable*. (*GM* I: 13)

The 'will' that was denied as a faculty in the other passages is now here dubbed a 'substratum,' which stands behind the act and chooses to perform it – or not. But there is no such faculty choosing to manifest strength or weakness: there just is the *doing*, and no doer who bears the responsibility for it. The discussion of 'The four great errors' in *The Twilight of the Idols* is to the same effect. As he concludes there,

> Today we no longer have any pity for the concept of 'free will': we know only too well what it really is – the foulest of all theologians' artifices, aimed at making mankind 'responsible' in their sense [...] [T]he doctrine of the will has been invented essentially for the purpose of punishment, that is, because one wanted to impute guilt. (*TI* 7)

Once again, denial that the will is a causal faculty is juxtaposed with a psychological explanation of why people would nonetheless be motivated to believe in freedom and responsibility. Once we abandon this 'error of free will,' we should also abandon the reactive concepts whose intelligibility depends on it – concepts like 'guilt.' Zarathustra describes well the required revision of our thinking about freedom and responsibility that results: "Enemy' you shall say, but not 'villain'; 'sick' you shall say, but not 'scoundrel'; 'fool' you shall say, but not 'sinner'' (Z I: 'On the Pale criminal'). The abandoned concepts – that of villain, scoundrel, and sinner – are all ones that require freedom and responsibility that would license blame, while the substitute concepts (enemy, sick, and fool) merely describe a person's condition or status, without supposing anything about the agent's responsibility for being in that condition.

Against the Causality of the Will

Nietzsche offers two arguments against the causality of the will – or, more precisely, against the causal efficacy of what we *experience* as willing. We may call one 'the phenomenology of thoughts argument,' the other, 'the doctrine of types argument' (see Leiter 2007).

Nietzsche observes that 'the feeling of *will* suffices for' a person 'to assume cause and effect' (*GS* 127). But he claims that this feeling *misleads* us: the phenomenology of 'willing' an action, the experience we have which leads us (causally) to conceive of ourselves as exercising our will (to say 'I will'), is not causally connected to the resulting action in a way that would underwrite ascriptions of moral responsibility. Nietzsche's central account in *BGE* 19 breaks the experience of willing into three components: the feelings or experiences associated with bodily movement (hereafter 'the bodily qualia'); the 'commandeering thought' whose propositional content (and temporal priority) seems to connect it with the bodily movements; and the metafeeling of power or pleasure that emerges from a conscious identification with the commandeering thought (which explains why we identify with the thought rather than with the bodily movement). We *feel* as though we are exercising free will when we *identify* with the commandeering thought (e.g. 'I want to get up'), which we feel is superior to, and being obeyed by, the bodily qualia (the feelings of the body moving as we get up); and we so identify because of the feelings of pleasure and power that arise from what Nietzsche calls the 'affect of superiority' that flows from this identification. That this experience is misleading as to the causation of action – at least if that causation is to underwrite moral responsibility – follows from another bit of phenomenology, namely that 'a thought comes when 'it' wants, and not when 'I' want' (*BGE* 17). From the fact that there is thinking it does not follow that *I*, some subject or agent, am doing the thinking, and so it does not follow that I exist. Although the explicit target in this particular passage is the Cartesian 'I,' the surrounding context makes it clear that the real target is the will.

What does it mean to say that a thought comes when 'it' wants, not when 'I' want? Nietzsche's point is that our 'thoughts' appear in consciousness without our having willed them. Of course, Nietzsche is engaged in an attack on the existence of will, so he can't believe that there is any sense in which I could genuinely will a thought into existence. Yet he cannot presuppose that contention here without begging the question. Thus we must take the talk of willing here to refer to the *experience of willing*, which, Nietzsche concedes, is real enough.

Nietzsche's phenomenological point then comes to this: a 'thought' that appears in consciousness is *not* preceded by the phenomenology of willing that Nietzsche has described – that is, there is no 'commandeering thought' preceding the conscious thought to which the metafeeling (the affect of superiority) attaches. (Even if there were such a commandeering thought in some instance, this would just create a regress, since not every commandeering thought will be preceded by the experience of willing.) Since we do not experience our thoughts as willed in the way we experience some actions as willed, it follows that no thought comes when 'I will it,' because the experience to which the 'I will' attaches is absent.

Nietzsche cleverly points out that the criterion of willing, which agents themselves treat as reliable guides to a causal relationship – namely, the phenomenology described above – is in fact completely absent in the case of thoughts (or at least in the case of the thought that starts an inferential chain of thinking which involves the experience of willing). As an introspective matter, it seems that Nietzsche is plainly correct about this point. But if we do not experience our thoughts as willed, then it follows that the actions which result from our experience of willing (which includes those thoughts) are not caused in a way sufficient to underwrite ascriptions of moral responsibility, unless Nietzsche were a compatibilist – which, we have already seen, he is not.

The phenomenology of thoughts argument is not, however, the only consideration influencing Nietzsche's skepticism about free will and moral responsibility. Influenced, in part, by Schopenhauer's views about the immutability of character and developments in nineteenth-century physiology, especially as popularized by the so-called 'German materialists' of the 1850s and '60s, Nietzsche holds that persons are constituted by certain, largely immutable, psychological and physiological characteristics (call them 'type-facts'), which play a decisive role in explaining much of their behavior and their moral beliefs. Thus Nietzsche accepts what we may call a 'doctrine of types' (Leiter 1998), according to which 'Each person has a fixed psycho-physical constitution, which defines him as a particular *type* of person' (1998: 230).

In consequence, claims Nietzsche, the 'morality' that a philosopher embraces simply bears 'decisive witness to *who he is*,' that is, to the 'innermost drives of his nature' (*BGE* 6). Nietzsche explains that 'moralities are [...] merely a sign language of the affects' (ibid., p. 187), and he observes elsewhere that '[a]nswers to the questions about the *value* of existence [...] may always be considered first of all as the symptoms of certain bodies' (*GS* P: 2). '[O]ur moral judgments and evaluations [...] are only images and fantasies based on a physiological process unknown to us' (*D* 119), so that 'it is always necessary to draw forth [...] the *physiological* phenomenon behind the moral predispositions and prejudices' (ibid., p. 542). A 'morality of sympathy,' he claims, is 'just another expression of [...] physiological overexcitability' (*TI* IX: 37). Nietzsche sums up well the idea in the preface to the *Genealogy of Morality*: 'our thoughts, values, every 'yes,' 'no,' 'if' and 'but' grow from us with the same inevitability as fruits borne on the tree – all related and each with an affinity to each, and evidence of one will, one health, one earth, one sun' (*GM*: 2).

The doctrine of types is central to Nietzsche's second argument against the causality of the will in the chapter 'The four great errors,' in *Twilight of the Idols*. The first error, that 'of confusing cause and effect,' can be summarized as follows: given two regularly correlated effects E1 and E2 and their mutual 'deep cause,' we confuse cause and effect when we construe E1 as the cause of E2, missing altogether the existence of the deep cause. We may call this error 'Cornarism,' after the example Nietzsche uses:

> Everybody knows the book of the famous Cornaro in which he recommends his slender diet as a recipe for a long and happy life [...] The worthy Italian thought his diet was the *cause* of his long life, whereas the precondition for a long life, the extraordinary slowness of his metabolism, the consumption of so little, was the cause of his slender diet. He was not free to eat little *or* much; his frugality was not a matter of 'free will': he became sick when he ate more. (*TI* VI: 1)

What explains Cornaro's slender diet *and* his long life is the same underlying fact about his metabolism. Cornaro's mistake was to prescribe his diet to all and sundry, without regard for how individuals differed metabolically – metabolism being the relevant type-fact in this context.

Quite generally, Nietzsche saddles morality and religion with Cornarism. According to him, the basic 'formula on which every religion and morality is founded is: 'Do this and that, refrain from that and that – then you will be happy! Otherwise ...'' Cornaro recommended a slender diet for a long life; morality and religion prescribe and proscribe certain forms of conduct for a happy life. But, says Nietzsche,

> [A] well turned-out human being [...] *must* perform certain actions and shrinks instinctively from other actions; he carries the order, which he represents physiologically, into his relations with other human beings and things. (*TI* VI: 2)

So morality and religion are guilty of Cornarism: the conduct they prescribe and proscribe in order to *cause* a 'happy life' are, in fact, *effects* of something else, namely the physiological order represented by a particular agent – one who (as Nietzsche says) '*must* perform certain actions,' just as Cornaro *must* eat a slender diet (he is 'not free to eat little *or* much'). That one performs certain actions *and* that one has a happy life are themselves, both, effects of the physiological order – conclusions that follow if we grant Nietzsche the doctrine of types.

This brings us to the next central 'error,' that of 'false causality,' the mistake of thinking that we know what causation is because of our introspective confidence in what we take to be the causal powers of our own mental life. Nietzsche explains:

> We believed ourselves to be causal in the act of willing [...] Nor did one doubt that all the antecedents of an act, its causes, were to be sought in consciousness and would be found there once sought – as 'motives': else one would not have been free and responsible for it. Finally, who would have denied that a thought is caused? That the 'I' causes the thought? (*TI* VI: 3)

The argument from the phenomenology of thoughts licenses precisely such a denial, and Nietzsche soon makes clear that his view remains unchanged:

> The 'inner world' is full of phantoms [...]: the will is one of them. The will no longer moves anything, hence does not explain anything either – it merely accompanies events; it can also be absent. The so-called *motive*: another error. Merely a surface phenomenon of consciousness – something alongside the deed that is more likely to cover up the antecedents of the deeds than to represent them [...] What follows from this? There are no [conscious] mental causes at all. (*TI* VI: 3)

Skepticism about the causal efficacy of conscious motives is a recurring theme. As he writes in *Daybreak*, 'we are accustomed to exclude all [the] unconscious [*unbewusst*] processes from the accounting and to reflect on the preparation for an act only to the extent that it is conscious' (*D* 129) – a view which Nietzsche deems to be mistaken. Indeed, the theme of the 'ridiculous overestimation and misunderstanding of consciousness' (*GS* 11) is a recurring one: '[B]y far the greatest part of our spirit's activity,' says Nietzsche, 'remains unconscious and unfelt' (*GS* 333). To be sure, there is a somewhat suspect overreaching in these passages: are we to believe that no conscious belief is part of the causal explanation of *any* action? Nietzsche does not need to defend this radical thesis, for what he is interested in debunking is the causal nexus between the conscious experience of will and actions of moral significance, that is, the actions to which moral praise and blame might be ascribed.

If morally significant actions and the conscious mental states that precede them are themselves the product of type-facts (according to the doctrine of types), then it follows that *the conscious mental states* that precede the action and whose propositional contents would make them appear to be causally connected to the action are, in fact, epiphenomenal, either as tokens or as types: that is, they are either causally inert with respect to the action or causally effective only in virtue of other type-facts about the person.

How does it follow from these errors about causation that 'free will' is also an error? The error of confusing cause and effect is a *general* error, which afflicts morality because morality is based on a mistaken picture of agency: we think that certain moral prescriptions will bring about certain consequences for those who follow them, yet the ability and disposition to act on the prescriptions, and the enjoyment of the consequences, are possible only for certain types of persons. The exercise of free will plays no role.

The error of false causality is an error because we wrongly infer that we know what causation is from our experience of the will's being causal; but the will is not, in fact, causal, which follows from the doctrine of types. But, on any account of free will and moral responsibility, the will must be causal (even if not *causa sui*), in order for agents to have it and to be morally responsible for their actions. Therefore, if the error of false causality is a genuine error, then it follows that there is no free will. Only this second error implicates the phenomenology of willing, since it claims that we are in error when we think we know what causation is, on the basis of our *experience* of the will. And the argument says that we are in error here because our experience of the will misleads us as to the causal powers of the will: 'there are no mental causes at all' (*TI* VI: 3).

The Genesis of Action

If the experience of willing does not, according to Nietzsche, illuminate how actions are brought about, what, then, really explains our actions? Nietzsche's account has a startling resonance with recent work in empirical psychology. Daniel Wegner, for example, wants to establish Nietzsche's claim that the phenomenology of willing systematically misleads us as to the causation of our actions, drawing in part on Libet's work on the electrical activity of the brain before the experience of willing (Wegner 2002: 50–55). And, in the place of the 'illusion of conscious will' (as he calls it), Wegner proposes a different model, according to which the experience of willing and the action are products of unconscious causes, yet the chain of causation does not run between the experience of willing and the action; rather, in Nietzschean terms, some type-fact about persons explains both the experience *and* the action (ibid., pp. 68, 98).

Wegner's discussion resonates with Nietzsche's detailed remarks in his famed discussion of 'self-mastery' (*D* 109). There Nietzsche was concerned to answer the question of the 'ultimate motive for 'self-mastery." He explains it as follows:

> *[T]hat* one *wants* to combat the vehemence of a drive at all [...] does not stand within our own power; nor does the choice of any particular method; nor does the success or failure of this method. What is clearly the case is that in this entire procedure our intellect is only the blind instrument of *another drive*, which is a *rival* of the drive whose vehemence is tormenting us [...] While 'we' believe we are complaining about the vehemence of a drive, at bottom it is one drive *which is complaining about the other*; that is to say: for us to become aware that we are suffering from the *vehemence* of a drive presupposes the existence of another equally vehement or even more vehement drive, and that a *struggle* is in prospect in which our intellect is going to have to take sides.

Although the intellect can 'take sides' (*Partei nehmen*), this does not mean that the intellect determines which side prevails: on the contrary, the intellect is a mere spectator upon the struggle. Thus the fact that one masters oneself is *not* a product of 'free will,' but rather an effect of the underlying type-facts characteristic of that person: it depends, namely, on which of his various drives happens to be strongest. There is, as it were, no conscious 'self' who contributes anything toward 'self-mastering'; and the latter is merely an effect of the interplay of certain unconscious drives, drives over which the conscious self exercises no control. The 'person' is an arena in which the struggle of drives (type-facts) is played out; how they play out determines what the person believes, what he values, what he becomes. But, *qua* conscious self or 'agent,' the person takes no active part in the process. As Nietzsche puts it elsewhere: 'The will to overcome an affect is, in the end, itself only the will of another, or several other, affects' (*BGE* 117). The will, in other words, or the experience of willing (in self-mastery), is itself the product of various unconscious drives or affects.

A 'Persuasive (Re)Definition' of Free Will

Recent commentators (for instance Gemes 2009 and Poellner 2009) have been impressed by Nietzsche's occasional positive use of the language of 'freedom' and 'free will.' Nietzsche's usages, however, are naturally assimilated to what Stevenson (1938) dubbed 'persuasive definitions': attempts to revise the meaning of a term to which a positive valence already attaches. The passages at issue are few and far between (compare *GS* 347; *GM* II: 2; *GM* III: 10; *TI* IX: 38); some are ironic (see for example the slightly ludicrous figure of the *souverain Individuum* at *GM* II: 2, who never appears again in the corpus and is described as a product of good animal breeding who is 'free' (in quotes) because he can make promises and remember that he has made them); and some present, as Poellner puts it, a 'substantive ideal' of the self (2009: 152), unconnected to any recognizable philosophical claim about freedom. Nietzsche certainly celebrates the 'higher type' of person, who has a certain pattern of coherent drives; but this is a fortuitous natural fact about certain persons, not an achievement of autonomous agency.

Typical of Nietzche's persuasive definitions of freedom is this passage:

> [W]ar educates for freedom. For what is freedom? That one has the will to assume responsibility for oneself. That one maintains the distance which separates us. That one becomes more indifferent to difficulties, hardships, privation, even to life itself. That one is prepared

> to sacrifice human beings for one's cause, not excluding oneself. Freedom means that the manly instincts which delight in war and victory dominate over other instincts, for example, over those of 'happiness.' The human being who has *become free* – and much more the *spirit* who has become free – spits on the contemptible type of wellbeing dreamed of by shopkeepers, Christians, cows, females, Englishmen, and other democrats. The free man is a *warrior*.

This bracing statement of a 'noble' ideal of the person, equally plainly, has nothing to do with any notion of freedom, free will, or moral responsibility that has engaged any philosopher in the entire tradition of western philosophy. That should not surprise, since Nietzsche's aims are polemical and rhetorical: a persuasive definition of a concept like freedom, which enjoys such authority in western culture, is one way to cause an affective response in some readers, which might lead to a transformation of their consciousness. But such a transformation is, itself, a causal process in which free choice is irrelevant, but evaluative (which, for Nietzsche, involves emotional) excitation is key to it (Leiter 2002: 91–101, 157–158).

See also: VOLITION AND THE WILL (13); REASONS AND CAUSES (17); MOTIVATING REASONS (19); ACTION EXPLANATION AND THE UNCONSCIOUS (22); MENTAL CAUSATION AND EPIPHENOMENALISM (23); THE EXPLANATORY ROLE OF CONSCIOUSNESS (24); AGENTS' KNOWLEDGE (30); FREE WILL AND DETERMINISM (38); RESPONSIBILITY AND AUTONOMY (39); SCIENTIFIC CHALLENGES TO FREE WILL (44).

References

Primary sources and their abbreviations

I have followed the major translations by Clark and Swensen, Hollingdale, and Kaufmann, with some of my own modifications. These are based on the 1980 edition of Nietzsche's works by G. Colli and M. Montinari: *Sämtliche Werke: Kritische Studienausgable*, Vols. 1–15. Berlin: de Gruyter.

A *The Antichrist*.
BGE *Beyond Good and Evil*
D *Daybreak*
GS *The Gay Science*
GM *On the Genealogy of Morality*
Z *Thus Spoke Zarathustra*
TI *Twilight of the Idols*

Roman numerals refer to chapters or major divisions, Arabic numerals to sections within the former.

Secondary sources

Gemes, K. (2009). Nietzsche on free will, autonomy, and the sovereign individual. In K. Gemes and S. May (eds), *Nietzsche on Freedom and Autonomy*. Oxford: Oxford University Press, 33–50.

Gemes, K., and May, S. (eds) (2009). *Nietzsche on Freedom and Autonomy*. Oxford: Oxford University Press.

Leiter, B. (1998). The paradox of fatalism and self-creation in Nietzsche. In C. Janaway (ed.), *Willing and Nothingness: Schopenhauer as Nietzsche's Educator*. Oxford: Oxford University Press, 217–255.

Leiter, B. (2002). *Nietzsche on Morality*. London: Routledge. [See esp. Chapter 3.]

Leiter, B. (2007). Nietzsche's theory of the will. *Philosophers' Imprint*, 7, 1–15. [Reprinted in Gemes and May (eds) (2009).]

Poellner, P. (2009). *Nietzschean freedom*. In Gemes and May (eds), 151–180.

Stevenson, C. L. (1938). Persuasive definitions. *Mind*, 47, 331–350.

Wegner, D. M. (2002). *The Illusion of Conscious Will*. Cambridge, MA: Harvard University Press.

66

Hegel

MICHAEL QUANTE

Introduction

Underlying neither the spell of scientistically guided philosophizing nor the spell of a one-sided metaethical perspective on our ethical practice, G. W. F. Hegel (1770–1830) develops the outlines of an integrative philosophy of action within the framework of a conception of social institutions and practices which can meet the requirements of the phenomenon of human agency.

The model of agency as the objectivization of a purpose is a main feature of Hegel's thought; for he defines reason, which is clearly the fundamental principle of his philosophical system, as 'purposive activity' (Hegel 1977, § 22). But, despite the fact that both the concept of action and various basic elements of a Hegelian philosophy of action are introduced and elaborated in central passages of Hegel's *Phenomenology of Spirit* and in his *Elements of the Philosophy of Right*, scholarship has devoted remarkably little attention to this aspect of his philosophy. Unlike Hegel's theory of the will or his conception of labor, his concept of action only rarely takes center stage in interpretations of his works; a systematic account integrating issues of (now) contemporary philosophy of action can likewise be found only sporadically (exceptions are Pippin 2008 and Quante 2004).

This can be explained through the fact that the theorems in Hegel's mature system are intricately linked to his *Science of Logic* and to the systematic philosophical aims and claims formulated therein. Thus Hegel's concept of action and his philosophy of action are located in a categorial framework that defies comprehension by today's readers in more than one way. It is therefore indispensable to approach inductively an explication of Hegel's contribution to contemporary philosophy of action and not to take the overall framework of his speculative–dialectical justificatory strategy as a leitmotif of the reconstruction.

If one concentrates further on the texts that Hegel himself wrote and if one brackets the transcripts of lectures that have been highly influential in the reception of his thought, the central elements of Hegel's philosophy of action are to be found in his *Phenomenology of Spirit* (hereafter *PhS*) and in his *Elements of the Philosophy of Right* (hereafter *PR*). However, since these two works pursue different philosophical aims and since no uniform agreement as to their relation with one another can be found in Hegelian scholarship, these two contexts in which Hegel develops his philosophy of action shall be dealt with separately here. This is apt insofar as Hegel's critique of a conception of the mental – which would nowadays be classified as scientistic or naturalistic – is a prominent topic in the *PhS* (see Quante 2008), but plays only an implicit role in the context of his *PR*. On the other hand, both conceptions of human agency developed by Hegel in these two works are not only compatible with each other, but complement each other and are mutually dependent in central aspects (cf. Pippin 2008, Ch. 6). This holds particularly for Hegel's claim that human actions are constituted by intersubjective recognitive relations and are thus genuine social entities. The analysis of this aspect of Hegel's philosophy of action with respect to its elaboration in the *PR* is not meant to deny that the claim concerning the social constitution of agency is already crucial to the *PhS* (see Pippin 2008, Part II and Part III, and Quante 2009). But, as the arguments for this claim are more comprehensible against the framework of the theory of will developed by Hegel in the *PR* than in the context of the richer but conceptually less stringent reflections in the *PhS*, this trait of Hegel's philosophy of action is sketched on the basis of the *PR*.

Hegel's Critique of a Scientistic Philosophy of Action in the *Phenomenology of Spirit*

In his *Phenomenology*, Hegel refers to the stance of a scientific worldview as the stance of 'observing reason.' On the way to the *telos* of self-knowledge, which is immanent to reason, this observing reason reflects on itself and tries to capture the essence of human reason, which according to Hegel is an autonomous individuality with regard to its own epistemic and methodological standards (see Quante 2008). The observing reason's various attempts to make human individuality the object of observing reason steer reason toward the phenomenon of agency, in which individual subjectivity manifests itself. Observing reason conceives agency as a contraposition between the private, unobservable internality of intention and the observable externality of the action. What is specific to agency is that the observable action is interpreted by the acting individual in the light of his own intention. The observing reason, which seeks to compass not only behavior but also individual agency, therefore has to integrate this reflexive self-thematization of the observable and external agency, through internal and private intention, as a constitutive element. Neglecting its own practical constitution, the observing reason thereby encounters the antithesis as well as the unsolvable interleaving of theoretical and practical reason, by which human agency is distinguished from mere behavior:

> The antithesis which this observation encounters has the form of the antithesis of the practical and the theoretical, both falling within the practical aspect itself – the antithesis of individuality making itself actual in its 'doing' ('doing' in its most general sense), and individuality as being at the same time reflected out of this 'doing' into itself and making this its object. Observation accepts this antithesis in the same inverted relationship which characterizes it in the sphere of appearance. It regards as the *unessential outer* the *deed* itself

> and the performance, whether it be that of speech or a more durable reality; but it is the being-within-self of the individuality which is for it the *essential inner*. (Hegel 1977, § 319)

This model of agency provided by observing reason rests on the assumption that the internal is essential to agency, whereas the observable deed is only an inessential, external sign of it. It presupposes that 'inner' and 'outer' are two ontologically independent spheres whose interrelation is, in line with the explanatory strategies of the observing reason, to be interpreted as lawlike causal relations.

By way of very complex reflections, Hegel demonstrates that this basic model is inadequate for representing the essence of human agency – and mainly for two reasons. First, the antithesis between inner and outer is an invalid hypostatization of two aspects of the human mind that do not stand in a causal relation to each other. According to Hegel, the relation between these two aspects is to be interpreted in a categorially different way, namely expressivistically (see Taylor 1975 and 1983; Pippin 2008). Second, the interpretation of the connection between inner and outer is not to be made according to the model of causal laws; the connection should be understood as a social practice of rule-following which comprises ascriptions and interpretations of actions in the context of explanations, apologies, justifications, and so on. While Hegel neither denies the existence of causal relations between mental episodes and physical events nor deems the search for them to be in principle impossible, he does argue for the claim that the point of human agency is not visible within the perspective of observing reason, which is oriented towards nomological causal explanations. For this reason, both in the *PhS* and in the *PR*, Hegel turns to the social practice of ascribing actions as the actual locus from which human agency can be explicated philosophically.

Hegel's Philosophy of Action: The 'Morality' Chapter of the *Philosophy of Right*

Hegel introduces the concept of action in the chapter on 'Morality' of his *PR* – a concept embedded in a comprehensive theory of the will, which includes not only individual mental episodes but also the structure of social institutions (Quante and Schweikard 2009). Michelet (1828) was the first to attempt a reconstruction of this chapter as a philosophy of action (see Quante 2004). The context of Hegel's philosophy of action is thus our manifold practice of ascribing responsibility, interwoven with ethical and legal questions. Since Hegel approaches the phenomenon of human agency from the perspective of the practice of ascribing responsibility, and hence does so *post festum*, some 'classical' questions of contemporary philosophy of action such as mental causation, or the mind–body relationship, play only a minor role, and those regarding freedom of will, determinism, and agent causality do not provide adequate points of departure for a philosophical explication of agency (Pippin 2008, chs 4–6; Wolff 1992).

Whereas the agent's individual perspective on his own doings is not paramount within the sphere of the 'abstract right,' it is crucial for the moral assessment of actions. In explaining, justifying, excusing, and criticizing an action from the moral standpoint, the key question is whether the agent's specific perspective on his own deeds can (or should) be recognized. This is a question that usually cannot be answered at the level of causal explanations, but refers to the rules and social institutions of a social community. Actions, in contrast to mere behavior, are connected to a claim to rationality that can be justified or called into question. In accordance with this principled difference between action and behavior, Hegel identifies three characteristics of human agency:

> The expression of the will as *subjective* or *moral* is action. Action contains the following determinations: (α) it must be known by me in its externality as mine; (β) its essential relation [*Beziehung*] to the concept is one of obligation; and (γ) it has an essential relation [*Beziehung*] to the will of others. (Hegel 1991, § 113)

Our conception of responsibility and agency unarguably also contains causal elements, which is why the causal aspect also plays a role in (1) Hegel's explication of the structure of agency. But, on his account, (2) the analysis of the structure of intention, by which actions are distinguished from mere behavior, comes to the fore; intentions are crucial to the ascription and imputation of actions. Furthermore, we can identify (3) presuppositions regarding the structure of the agent within the structure of agency and our practice of ascription. Above all, however, Hegel takes these contexts as (4) revealing the genuine social constitution of human agency; for only in already presupposed social contexts can the specific structures of agency be realized. These four central features of Hegel's philosophy of action, which are encapsulated in the three 'determinations' of agency, will now be developed starting from § 113 of the *PR*.

The structure of the action

In the first section of the 'Morality' chapter of the *PR*, Hegel distinguishes between action and deed (§§ 115–118). This distinction is unclear; for, on the one hand, he uses it to distinguish between the event-aspect and the description-aspect of the action, on the other, 'action' and 'deed' are two ways of describing an action. In terms of the first distinction, the deed has traits and stands in causal relations that need neither to be known nor to be intended by the agent. *Qua* action, an action is only ascribed – and this is due to the specific perspective of morality – when the specific intention of the agent is part of the act description. In terms of the second distinction, 'action' and 'deed' represent two interpretations of the doing in question, whereby the former takes the agent's knowledge and intention as criteria and the latter employs a social criterion that comprises both social standards and aspects such as factual consequences.

The structure of intention

The first determination of an action emphasizes that my action 'must be known by me as mine in its externality.' Hegel has given a detailed analysis of this claim in a previous paragraph (§ 110). As purposive behavior – in other words behavior that is to be understood teleologically and not to be given a causal explanation – the process that passes from the subjective, inner, or undeveloped form to the objective, outer, or developed realization must have a content. In contrast to merely biological processes, such a realization of a purpose is only present in the specific form of agency if the agent is conscious of this process in a first-personal, propositional way. This also constitutes the specific structure of intention:

> The content is determined for me as *mine* in such a way that, in its identity, it *contains* my subjectivity *for me* not only as my *inner end*, but also in so far as this end has achieved *external objectivity*. (Hegel, 1991, § 110)

A human being can, at least by default, only understand his own behavior as his action (and explain, justify, or apologize for it upon request or critique) if he can interpret the result achieved by performing the action in such a way that the result in question can count as an execution and realization of the intention he had tried to realize by performing the action. The process of action – which Hegel conceives of as the 'translation' of the inner purpose into the outer objectivity – is accompanied by the intention-in-action, that is to say, by specific knowing and willing. That an agent can understand his doing as such a realization counts as a validity claim which must be ready to endure in the social space of reasons and withstand possibly conflicting interpretations. This objectivization is to be distinguished from the realization of the intention in a material act – an event which Hegel terms *Vergegenständlichung*. The external objectivity Hegel refers to in this context means primarily the acceptance of the agent's interpretation of what he has done as an intentional action. This claim is intersubjectively answerable and criticizable, and it can be recognized or overridden. Hegel decidedly defends the thesis that the action, viewed as an externally objectivized purpose, is not an incorrigible product of a private, inner intention, but essentially constituted in the social space as a phenomenon of validity (Pippin 2004).

The structure of the agent

The second determination of action (cf. *PR*, § 133, β) assigns the concept of action to the sphere of the logic of essence, – in other words, to the second part of Hegel's *Science of Logic*. This sphere is characterized by categories whose semantic content presupposes the possibility of failure and therefore implies that success is an ought. Actions are self-determined realizations of purposes and as such they are at the same time objectivizations of reason, so that they are generally subjected to the standard of rationality. In consequence, actions are interpretable and subject to rules. According to Hegel, the concept of reason implies, furthermore, that agency cannot be limited to the selective execution of singular intentions, but – in the case of beings who persist through longer periods of time and enact a complex structure of needs, drives, and desires – requires plans of action. Such plans allow the agent to order his possibly conflicting preferences in a rational scheme and to stabilize his preference structure over time. This is important, Hegel continues, from the agent's point of view – for in this way his own wellbeing is rendered realizable through temporally extended phases – but also from a wider perspective: the transtemporally stabilizing function of plans of action is important for the possibility of lasting cooperation, since only such stability can ground the reliability of the agent in the social space.

Hegel elaborates on this aspect of our concept of action in two ways. First he employs the theory of judgment he had developed in his *Science of Logic* in order to explain that a self-determining reason can only realize itself by means of more complex judgments and intentions; in the *PR*, this elaboration of the concept of action is represented in the development of 'purpose' (an intention that is selective regarding its semantic content) to 'intention' (a complex intention in whose semantic content the single action is intended as a token of a type of act or as a case of applying a rule). Second, Hegel points out *ex negativo* that there is this dimension to our concept of action, which can be understood as a necessary transgression from the singular, isolated action to the action within a network of action plans and in the network of a system of the agent's preferences. In the third section of the 'Morality' chapter Hegel discusses various strategies of excuse, whereby he rejects a pattern of excuse in which the agent is reduced to a momentary singular impulse that is taken to have determined the content of his intention; and he remarks that our concept of agency and our notion of a responsible person do not allow for such a minimal conception:

> The nature of a human being consists precisely in the fact that he is essentially universal in character, not an abstraction of the moment and a single fragment of knowledge. (*PR*, § 132)

At this stage, Hegel forestalls crucial insights of the theory of action plans (or the 'planning theory of intentions'), which is being developed nowadays first and foremost by Michael Bratman (2007). Hegel does not just derive this dimension of human agency from his metaphysics of subjectivity, grounded as the latter is on the theory of judgment developed in the *Science of Logic*, but he anchors this aspect of his philosophy of action in our practice of excuse and critique of actions (which is why this aspect of Hegel's philosophy of action is not dependent on his metaphysics of subjectivity).

The structure of agency

The aspect of Hegel's philosophy of action that is systematically most up to date is his thesis concerning the social constitution of agency. This thesis is implicit in the third determination, according to which agency displays an essential reference to the will of other agents. In the context of a philosophy of action that is focused on causal relations and scientistic insofar as it is trapped in the image of inner and outer, this thesis must seem absurd, or at least extremely implausible. But, with this third determination, Hegel expresses nothing more than his insight that actions are not to be conceived just as bodily movements caused by mental episodes in the right way, but have to be conceptualized as realizations of purposes interpreted in social space and endowed with specific validity claims by the agent. As such, actions are dependent on recognition by others; for it is only through recognition and by means of its objectivization into social space that the non-arbitrariness of the individual claim can be successful.

In the *PR*, the arguments Hegel presents for the indispensability of the social dimension of human agency boil down to the point that agency, as the expression of a self-determining reason, can only be understood as following some rule. But – and this is the systematically crucial point of Hegel's critique of conscience and of the Kantian and Fichtean justification of morality – this cannot be accounted for as an achievement of individual reason. In this way, Hegel argues, the difference between being justified in following a rule and being justified in being an exception becomes unstable, because the autonomous individual subject could at any time alter the rules of its agency. In Hegel's view, this form of moral solipsism – which he criticizes as the vanity and evil of the subjectivity that takes itself to be absolute – can only be overcome (or not arise in the first place) if agency is from the very start conceived of as a social practice of ascription and of justification of actions. A more precise analysis of the arguments with which Hegel justifies his concept of action in the *PR* shows that they do not suffice for a complete justification (for a detailed analysis, see Quante 2004: 73–91). In order to provide a complete image of Hegel's philosophy of action, one has to take into account the theory of recognition, as it is developed in the *PhS* (as Pippin 2008, Ch. 6, rightly points out). In the end, this aspect of Hegel's philosophy of action is dependent on the plausibility of the thesis concerning the intersubjective constitution of self-consciousness, which Hegel expresses through the formula of the '"I" that is "We" and "We" that is "I"' (*PhS*, § 177; for a reconstruction and defense of this thesis, see Quante 2009).

Hegel's Philosophy of Action in the Contemporary Systematic Context

Hegel's concept of action takes center stage in his practical philosophy; his comprehensive philosophy of action is furthermore central to his entire philosophy of spirit and is the foundation of his philosophical system. As can be seen especially in the context of his critique of a scientistically oriented philosophy of mind, such as the one developed in the *PhS*, the basic elements of his philosophy of action are grounded in a social–externalist conception of the mental which, without rejecting the phenomenal differentiation between inner and outer *tout court*, nevertheless does not transform it into a dichotomy between a private, inner sphere of mental episodes and a publicly accessible, observable sphere of external behavior. Moreover, Hegel's analysis of the structure of philosophical explanations, which was expounded in the *Science of Logic*, allows him to claim that teleological explanations are irreducible to causal explanations without committing him to the thesis that there are no relations of cause and effect between the mental episodes and the actions of an agent. Hegel thereby overcomes or circumvents the jejune dispute between intentionalists and causalists in the philosophy of action. For him it is crucial that the concept of causation is not scientistically curtailed, and that it should not be overlooked that causal explanations do not usually get to the heart of human agency, for this heart is located in our normative practice.

Setting the course this way within the general structure of his philosophy enables Hegel to develop a philosophy of action that is free both from scientistic restrictions and from misguided philosophical rejections of such restrictions. At the same time he can capture human agency within his complex practical philosophy, in which deontological, consequentialist, and virtue-ethicist aspects constitute integral elements of his theory of the will, as a reconstruction of our practices of ascription.

See also: ACTION THEORY AND ONTOLOGY (1); REFRAINING, OMMITTING, AND NEGATIVE ACTS (7); VOLITION AND THE WILL (13); INTENTION (14); FREE WILL AND DETERMINISM (38); RESPONSIBILITY AND AUTONOMY (39); THE DOCTRINE OF DOUBLE EFFECT (41); ANSCOMBE (74).

References

Primary sources

PhS Hegel, G. W. F. (1977). *Phenomenology of Spirit* [1807], translated by A. V. Miller. Oxford: Oxford University Press.

PR Hegel, G. W. F. (1991). *Elements of the Philosophy of Right* [1820], translated by H. B. Nisbet, edited by A. Wood. Cambridge: Cambridge University Press.

Secondary sources

Bratman, M. E. (2007). *Structures of Agency*. Oxford: Oxford University Press.

Michelet, K. L. (1828). *Das System der philosophischen Moral und das christliche Moralprinzip*. Berlin: Schlesinger'sche Buch- und Musikhandlung.

Pippin, R. B. (2004). Hegels Praktischer Rationalismus: Rationales Handeln als Sittlichkeit. In C. Halbig, M. Quante and L. Siep (eds), *Hegels Erbe*. Frankfurt am Main: Suhrkamp Verlag, 295–323.

Pippin, R. B. (2008). *Hegel's Practical Philosophy*. Cambridge: Cambridge University Press.

Quante, M. (2004). *Hegel's Concept of Action*. Cambridge: Cambridge University Press.

Quante, M. (2008). 'Reason ... apprehended irrationally': Hegel's critique of observing reason. In D. Moyar and M. Quante (eds), *Hegel's Phenomenology of Spirit*. Cambridge: Cambridge University Press, 91–111.

Quante, M. (2009). 'Der reine Begriff des Anerkennens.' Überlegungen zur Grammatik der Anerkennungsrelation in Hegels *Phänomenologie des Geistes*. In H.-C. Schmidt am Busch and C.F. Zurn (eds), *Anerkennung*. Berlin: Akademie Verlag, 91–106.

Quante, M., and Schweikard, D. (2009). Leading a universal life: The systematic relevance of Hegel's social philosophy. In *History of the Human Sciences* 22 (1), 58–78.

Taylor, C. (1975). *Hegel*. Cambridge: Cambridge University Press.

Taylor, C. (1983). Hegel and the philosophy of action. In L. S. Stepelevich and D. Lamb (eds), *Hegel's Philosophy of Action*. Atlantic Highlands: Humanities Press, 1–18.

Wolff, M. (1992). *Das Körper-Seele Problem: Kommentar zu Hegel, Enzyklopädie (1830), § 389*. Frankfurt am Main: Klostermann.

Further reading

Alessio, M. (1996). *Azione ed eticità in Hegel*. Milano: Guerini.

Bernstein, J. (1996). Confession and forgiveness: Hegel's poetic of action. In R. Eldridge (ed.), *Beyond Representation: Philosophy and Poetic Imagination*. Cambridge: Cambridge University Press, 34–65.

Derbolav, J. (1975). Hegels Theorie der Handlung. In M. Riedel (ed.), *Materialien zu Hegels Rechtsphilosophie*, Vol. 2. Frankfurt am Main: Suhrkamp Verlag, 201–216.

Giusti, M. (1987). Bemerkungen zu Hegels Begriff der Handlung. *Hegel Studien*, 22, 51–71.

Jermann, C. (1987). Die Moralität. In C. Jermann (ed.), *Anspruch und Leistung von Hegels Rechtsphilosophie*. Stuttgart-Bad Cannstatt: Frommann Holzboog, 101–144.

Menegoni, F. (1993). *Sogetto e Struttura dell'agire in Hegel*. Trento: Verifiche.

Menegoni, F. (1997). Elemente zu einer Handlungstheorie in der 'Moralität' (§§ 104–128). In L. Siep (ed.), *G. W. F. Hegel: 'Grundlinien der Philosophie des Rechts.'* Berlin: Akademie Verlag, 125–146.

Moyar, D. (2004). Die Verwirklichung meiner Autorität: Hegels komplementäre Modelle von Individuen und Institutionen. In C. Halbig, M. Quante, and L. Siep (eds), *Hegels Erbe*. Frankfurt am Main: Suhrkamp Verlag, 209–253.

Moyar, D. (2008). Self-completing alienation: Hegel's argument for transparent conditions of free agency. In Moyar and Quante (eds), 150–172.

Moyar, D., and Quante, M. (eds) (2008). *Hegel's Phenomenology of Spirit*. Cambridge: Cambridge University Press.

Peperzak, A. T. (2001). *Modern Freedom*. Dordrecht: Kluwer Academic Publishers.

Pinkard, T. (1994). *Hegel's Phenomenology: The Sociality of Reason*. Cambridge: Cambridge University Press.

Pippin, R.B. (2004). Taking responsibility: Hegel on agency. In B. Merker, G. Mohr, and M. Quante (eds), *Subjektivität und Anerkennung*. Paderborn: Mentis Verlag, 67–80.

Pippin, R.B. (2008). The 'logic of experience' as 'absolute knowledge' in Hegel's *Phenomenology of Spirit*. In Moyar and Quante (eds), 210–227.

Rózsa, E. (2007). *Hegels Konzeption praktischer Individualität*. Paderborn: Mentis Verlag.

Schmidt am Busch, H.-C. (2002). *Hegels Begriff der Arbeit*. Berlin: Akademie Verlag.

Siep, L. (1992). *Praktische Philosophie im Deutschen Idealismus*. Frankfurt am Main: Suhrkamp Verlag.

Siep, L. (2000). *Der Weg der Phänomenologie des Geistes: Ein einführender Kommentar zu Hegels Differenzschrift und Phänomenologie des Geistes*. Frankfurt am Main: Suhrkamp Verlag.

Siep, L. (2008). Practical reason and spirit in Hegel's *Phenomenology of Spirit*. In Moyar and Quante (eds), 173–191.

Speight, A. (2001). *Hegel, Literature and the Problem of Agency*. Cambridge: Cambridge University Press.

Stepelevich, L. S., and Lamb, D. (eds) (1983). *Hegel's Philosophy of Action*. Atlantic Highlands: Humanities Press.

67

Weber

KIERAN ALLEN

Introduction

Today Max Weber (1864–1920) stands at the apex of the canon of classical sociology. Yet in the immediate aftermath of his death in 1920, his influence was 'fragmentary and patchy' (Mommsen 1989: 170). His ascent to the sociological cannon owed much to Talcott Parsons, the leading theoretician of American sociology during the Cold War. Parsons' major theoretical work, *The Structure of Social Action*, which was published in 1937, characterized Weber as someone who fought 'against the positivist tendencies of Marxian historical materialism' (Parsons 1949: 721) and as a precursor to Parsons' own 'voluntaristic action' theory. The category of social action was thus promoted as the key to understanding society.

Weber's sociology is based on a methodological individualism which seeks to break down collectivities such as classes or nations in order to see them as the outcome of social actions of individual persons. He wrote as follows:

> If I have become a sociologist (according to my letter of accreditation) it is mainly to exorcise the spectre of collective conceptions which still lingers among us. In other words, sociology itself can only proceed from the action of one or more separate individuals and must therefore adopt strictly individualistic methods. (Quoted in Razzell 1977)

Weber's targets were holistic and naturalistic interpretations of society. In the former camp belonged contemporaries such as Roscher and Knies, who saw the nations as organic wholes animated by particular cultural spirits. Marxism also belonged in this camp, because it drew on a totality of relationships within a particular mode of production and it saw the individual as being formed in and through society. In the latter camp belonged Auguste Comte, the founder of positivism, who, inspired by the success of the natural sciences, sought to discover universal social laws.

Against these approaches, Weber argued that the primary subject matter of sociology was social action. Action occurs when 'the acting individual attaches a subjective meaning to his behavior – be it overt or covert, omission or acquiescence' (Weber 1978a: 4). In other words the individual interprets, chooses, and evaluates what she are doing, according to her own distinct mental life. Action is social when the meaning given by the individual 'takes account of the behavior of others and is thereby orientated in its course' (ibid.).

Values and motives play a major role in Weber's sociology. People envisage desired outcomes. They select means to achieve these outcomes, and this sequence becomes the cause of their actions. This led Weber to invert the explanations offered by other social scientists. Whereas they assumed that motives offered by individuals were rationalizations for underlying structural causes, Weber focused on the motives themselves.

This also had implications for his methodology. Influenced by Kantianism, he claimed that reality is a chaotic mass of sense experiences which our perceptions actively structure.

> Empirical reality becomes 'culture' to us because and insofar as we relate it to value ideas. It includes those segments and only those segments of reality, which have become significant to us because of their value relevance. (Weber 1949: 76)

But if this is the case how does one arbitrate between these values? How does one know which value system provides a closer approximation of the truth?

Here an element of relativism appears in Weber's work. If utilitarianism saw economic interests and Durkheim saw morality as the key ingredient for social integration, Weber placed power centre stage. He assumed that 'violent action is obviously absolutely primordial' (Weber 1978b: 904) and defined the state as an institution which upheld a claim to the monopoly of the legitimate use of violence. Consistent with this realist account of power and violence, he boldly embraced the claims of German nationalism. At the start of his career he argued that there was an eternal struggle designed to improve national character, and that the standard of value adopted by a German social scientist had to be a German standard (Weber 1989: 198). In other words, social science had a role to play in augmenting national power.

This was by no means a youthful excess, because a consistent theme in Weber's writing was that values were unamenable to rational scientific investigation. In *The Meaning of Ethical Neutrality in Sociology and Economics*, which was written 1917, he claimed that

> It is really a question not only of alternatives between values but of an irreconcilable death struggle like that between 'God' and 'the Devil.' Between these, neither relativization nor compromise is possible. (Weber 1949: 17–18)

A year later, in a speech delivered at Munich University and later printed as *Science as a Vocation*, he noted: ' "Scientific" pleading (between the different stands) is meaningless in principle because the various value spheres of the world stand in irreconcilable conflict with each another' (Weber 1948: 147).

Weber, therefore, made two seemingly antagonistic assumptions. First, that social scientists should primarily focus on social action, which was guided by values and motives set by individual actors. Second, that these values could not be subject to scientific investigation because they arose from primordial power struggles.

Verstehen Method

Weber did not feel, however, that these assumptions ruled out a scientific approach.

Instead a number of complex methodological principles were adduced to deal with this tension. The first was the famous *Verstehen* method. Following the wider German idealist tradition, Weber denied that the discovery of general laws added anything to our understanding of why humans acted as they did. Even if there was strictly statistical evidence to show that all people who had been placed in a particular situation invariably reacted in a certain way, this only showed that their actions were calculable. But such a demonstration, he argued, would 'contribute absolutely nothing to the project of 'understanding' 'why' this reaction ever occurred and, moreover, 'why' it invariably occurs in the same way' (Weber 1975: 129).

The *Verstehen* method, by contrast, allowed us to capture the inner sense in which individuals subjectively interpreted and chose what they were doing. According to Weber, the *Verstehen* method means

> to identify a concrete 'motive' or complex of motives 'reproducible in inner experience,' a motive to which we can attribute the conduct in question with a degree of precision that is dependent upon our source material. In other words because of its susceptibility to a meaningful *interpretation* [...] individual conduct is in principle intrinsically less 'irrational' than the individual natural event. (Weber 1975: 125)

Or, to put it differently, the behavior of someone you truly know is far more predictable than the weather.

Weber's aim was to rid the *Verstehen* method of a lazy, intuitive approach, which assumed a natural empathy between individuals. He wanted to lend it scientific rigor instead.

A Value-Free Sociology

The precondition was that social scientists had to be 'value-free.' They had to put aside their own values when engaged in research, so that it was clear 'exactly at which point the scientific investigator becomes silent and the evaluating and acting person begins to speak' (Weber 1949: 60). Weber also believed that there was an unbridgeable gap between the world of 'what is' and the world of 'what should be.' Empirical research could not lead to any conclusions about values, because 'to *judge* the *validity* of such values is a matter of *faith*' (Weber 1949: 55).

Against holistic approaches, Weber argued that the social scientists had to study unique events and phenomena. But this demanded some form of selection, as the items for study had to be hewn out from an infinite number of possible alternatives. He acknowledged that this selection occurred on the basis of the value system of the researcher; because there could be no

> absolutely 'objective' analysis of culture – or [...] 'social phenomena' independent of special and one 'sided' viewpoints according to which – expressly or tacitly, consciously

> or unconsciously – they are selected, analyzed and organized for expository purposes. (Weber 1949: 72)

One has to distinguish, therefore, between *value freedom* and *value relevance. Value freedom* represented a severe injunction to put aside all value judgments when one engaged in the process of analysis. However, *value relevance* implied that particular research problems are chosen by researcher, because of his or her own value related interests. Weber went somewhat further and suggested that these same interests also 'give purely empirical scientific work its direction' (Weber 1949: 22). In other words, the researcher's values – which are not amenable to rational argument – influence the way in which investigators go about providing answers to the problems they choose.

Weber appears to be on very slippery ice here, and much of his writing on methodology is torturously complex, as he tries to navigate between the traditional German idealist emphasis on the active mind structuring reality and the requirements of modern research. One way he tries to solve this conundrum is by drawing a distinction between ends and means.

Social action, he claims, is oriented to particular ends. We desire something for its own sake, or as a means to something that is more desirable. The social scientist has little to say about those ends other than to suggest whether they are internally consistent and feasible in terms of the present society, or whether they represent 'absolutist' ends. Social scientists could also assess the way people use the scarce means at their disposal to achieve their ends. They could then 'scientifically' draw out the implications of the pursuit of certain values and illustrate to people what means would be required to achieve them. They could do this even while being opposed to the value system of those they studied.

Economic Methods and Ideal Types

Weber added one more element to his attempt to marry a subjective focus on values with a desire for objective methodological rigor in the study of social action. It is the *ideal type*, which Weber believed was 'heuristically indispensable' for sociological and historical research (Burger 1976). To understand it, we need to return to the Austrian marginalist school of economics, which influenced Weber considerably.

The Austrian school sought to eliminate all discussion of particular national cultures from the discourse of economics by starting from an 'economic man,' who existed as an isolated unit. The marginalists placed this imaginary man in particular situations of scarcity or in situations where there were different balances between supply and demand. From these scenarios they devised general laws of economy, which could be stated with quite mathematical precision.

Weber summarized the underlying philosophy of the marginalist school by claiming that it examined what course a

> given type of human action would take if it were strictly rational, unaffected by errors or emotional factors and if, furthermore, it were completely and unequivocally directed to a single end, the maximization of economic advantage. (Weber 1978a: 9)

Weber wanted to import this method into the wider field of social science, in order to impose an intellectual discipline on the researcher who was using the *Verstehen* method.

The sociologist, he argued, had to follow the economist in constructing an ideal type, which highlighted certain aspects of reality. The ideal type was not meant as a description, but was a

> one sided accentuation of one or more points of view and a 'synthesis' of a great many diffuse, discrete [...] *concrete individual* phenomena, which are arranged according to these one-sidedly emphasized viewpoints into a unified *analytical* construct. (Weber 1949: 90)

This was therefore a model, or a thought experiment based on pure elements, which represented people's motives and culture.

Weber was keen to stress that ideal types are only explanatory devices, which helped to bring out the significance and meanings that humans bestow upon their actions. The criterion of their success was whether they revealed 'concrete culture phenomena in their interdependence, their causal conditions and their significance' (Weber 1949: 92). They did not represent actual forces that existed in reality.

Marxism, for example, operated with a number of ideal types, such as historically specific relations of production, as explanatory variables; but, according to Weber, it failed to see that these were only some among many possible ideal types. Its fatal flaw was to assert that its own models existed in reality. By contrast, Weber argued that anyone who could 'perceive the fundamental ideas of modern epistemology which ultimately derive from Kant' would have no difficulty accepting that they were 'primarily analytic instruments for the intellectual mastery of empirical data and can only be that' (Weber 1949: 106).

The ideal types were related to the four main categories of social action. These were:

- *Traditional action*, which was a form of ingrained habit – one acts because this was always done;
- *Affective action*, which was based on emotional feeling – one acts out of love for, say, a brother or sister;
- *Value rational action*, where actions were undertaken for some ethical or religious ideal and there was no consideration of their prospect of success – one acted for God, or for 'the cause';
- *Instrumentally rational action*, which was based on rational calculation about the specific means of achieving definite ends – one acted because that was the most effective means of achieving a specific goal.

Weber believed that the first two forms of social action were very 'close to the borderline of what can justifiably be called meaningful orientated action' (Weber 1978a: 25). The main dichotomy in his writings is between actions launched by absolutist, utopian goals and actions carried out by a calculating version of the 'economic man.' Instrumental rationality became the dominant mode of action in modern society – even if it was occasionally upset by charismatic movements, which arose with value rational action.

Conclusion

Weber's examination of instrumental social action drew on the methodology of marginalist economics. His writings repeatedly used economic examples, and his own methodology borrowed from the 'economic principle,' which assumed that actors have full knowledge of their future needs and of the resources available to them (Ringer 1997: 97). In his refutation of Rudolf Stammler, he claimed that the standards of marginal utility theory should be used as 'a way of determining how (an actor's) actual conduct 'measures up' (Weber 1977: 111). Just like the 'economic man,' many modern social actors in a highly rationalized society have perfect knowledge of their ends and calculate precisely how to use the scarce resources available to them. These ends are pure choices that individuals decide on. But once these ends are chosen, the individuals who chose them will behave like a sober bourgeois who calculates his profit and loss accounts.

Weber is aware that this is a pure idea – a utopia. However, just as conventional economics proceeded from this model, he agues that social scientists must start by attributing a 'right rationality' to the actor and then examine where this would take them. Only after they have done this, could social scientists build in a calculation for incorrect assessments made by the social actors or for other deviations from the norm of rationality (Ringer 1997: 98).

All of this raises some problems. The cornerstone of Weber's entire approach is that values are arbitrary entities which are chosen by individuals and so they cannot be subjected to scientific analysis. Researchers can only accept the values of those they study as an irrational given for which there is no explanation. However, one can equally ask: why should inquiries be restricted in this fashion? Why assert that one can only examine the effects of values – but cannot analyze how these values arose? As Hirst puts it,

> the effect of [...] the unquestionable priority of human freedom [...] is to limit the explanatory power of discourse, to close and to silence areas of problems and avenues of theorization. (Hirst 1976: 62)

More generally, the primacy Weber placed on motives as causal factors in social action is also questionable. Individuals can make mistakes and lie to themselves and others about their motives. Their motives can be confused, vague and contradictory. They may also be rationalizations for the pressures which society places upon them. Many women stayed at home in the 1950s, for example, because they accepted a popular mythology about 'maternal deprivation.' Some black people in apartheid South Africa enlisted in the Hammer regiment, which upheld a system that oppressed them. In all societies, individuals have held values which militate against their own direct interests. Why, therefore, should we rule out inquiries into conflicts between values and interests?

There are also practical problems about Weber's methods. Even if we were to assume that an individual's values existed prior to, and independently of, society, how can we be sure that we have understood them? What if that individual is living in a different culture from our own? Weber's own immersion in the imperial culture of his day casts considerable doubts on his capacity to engage in *Verstehen*. He states, for example, that 'our ability to share the feeling of primitive men is not very much greater' than our ability to know 'the subjective state of mind of an animal' (quoted in Parkin 1982: 23). In an extraordinary passage on Chinese culture, he claimed that 'the power of logos, of defining and reasoning was not accessible to the Chinese' (Weber 1951: 125).

Weber's argument that ideal types are purely analytic devices, with no relationship to reality, also means that he cannot show causal links. The ideal types become instead entirely formal categories, around which large segments of history are grouped. So ancient Egypt and socialism are linked together under the term bureaucracy. Or the ideal type of 'charisma' connects revolutionary leaders and Hindu shamans. The overall effect is that Weber substitutes the drawing up of typologies for real explanations of how societies change (Lukács 1972: 386–398). This method can sometimes illuminate interesting connections. However, there is also a profound agnosticism attached to the whole procedure, as Weber asserted that alternative, equally valid ideal types could also have been used. A focus on underlying structures of society is replaced by a desire to 'set up typologies and arrange historical phenomena in this typology' (Lukács 1980: 612).

Behind all of Weber's relativism there is, therefore, a status quo bias. If values cannot be critiqued, then the dominant values of the present system emerge unscathed from serious challenge. Moreover, Weber's calculating rational man, who pursues randomly chosen values, is by no means a neutral figure. His very individualism, his assertion that his choices cannot be subjected to rational inquiry, his notion of a profit and loss account between ends and means – all suggest that he acts according to the abstractly 'formulated psychology of the calculating individual agent of capitalism' (Lukács 1980: 613).

In brief, Max Weber's concept of social action has helped to create a sociology that is less critical of contemporary power structures and of the discourses that sustain it than it should be.

See also: COLLECTIVE ACTION (9); HABITUAL ACTIONS (10); VOLITION AND THE WILL (13); RATIONALITY (36); ACTON IN HISTORY AND SOCIAL SCIENCE (50); THE PREDICTION OF ACTION (51); KANT (64).

References

Primary sources

Weber, M. (1948). Science as a vocation. In H. Gerth and C. W. Mills (eds), *From Max Weber*. London: Routledge/Kegan Paul.

Weber, M. (1949). *The Methodology of the Social Sciences*. New York: Free Press.

Weber, M. (1951). *The Religion of China*. New York: Free Press.

Weber, M. (1975). *Roscher and Knies: The Logical Problems of Historical Economics*. New York: Free Press.

Weber, M. (1977). *Critique of Stammler*. New York: Free Press.

Weber, M. (1978a). *Economy and Society*, Vol. 1. Berkeley, CA: California University Press.

Weber, M. (1978b). *Economy and Society*, Vol. 2. Berkeley, CA: California University Press).

Weber, M. (1989). The nation state and economic policy (Freiburg address). In K. Tribe, *Reading Weber*. London: Routledge, 188–209.

Secondary sources

Burger, T. (1976). *Max Weber's Theory of Concept Formation: History, Laws and Ideal Types*. Durham: Duke University Press.

Hirst, P. (1976). *Social Evolution and Sociological categories*. London: Allen and Unwin.

Lukács, G. (1972). Max Weber and German sociology. *Economy and Society*, 1, 377–398.

Lukács, G. (1980). *The Destruction of Reason*. London: Merlin Press.

Mommsen, W. (1989). *The Political and Social Theory of Max Weber*. Cambridge: Polity.

Parkin, F. (1982). *Max Weber*. Chichester: Ellis Horwood.

Parsons, T. (1949). *The Structure of Social Action*. Glencoe: Free Press.

Razzell, P. (1977). 'The Protestant ethic and the spirit of capitalism: A natural scientific critique. *British Journal of Sociology*, 28 (1), 17–37.

Ringer, F. (1997). *Max Weber's Methodology: The Unification of Cultural and Social Sciences*. Harvard: Harvard University Press.

68

Wittgenstein

SEVERIN SCHROEDER

The contributions of Ludwig Wittgenstein (1889–1951) to the philosophy of action consist mainly in his discussions of the concepts of a voluntary action and of a reason. In both cases he rejects the prevalent causal accounts.

Voluntary Action

In asking: 'what is left over if I subtract the fact that my arm goes up from the fact that I raise my arm?' (*PI*, § 621), Wittgenstein is bringing out how tempting it is to think of voluntariness as a psychological occurrence that needs to be present on top of the physical movements involved in an action. For, after all, the same physical movements could be voluntary or involuntary. Hence the traditional philosophical account of voluntary action (versions of which were held by Descartes, the British empiricists, William James, and Bertrand Russell) is this: for a bodily movement to be voluntary, it must be *caused by an act of will*; without such a cause, the same movement would be involuntary. Wittgenstein was to criticize this view as an instance of the common philosophical tendency to construe all words as names of objects, events, or occurrences (cf. *PI*, § 1; Schroeder 2006: 128–134 and 181–135). In this case, words used to characterize an action as voluntary (like 'will' and its cognates) are uncritically taken to denote some mental occurrence. Wittgenstein offers three objections to the traditional causal account of voluntariness:

1 The acts of will postulated by the theory do not exist. If we take an impartial look at what goes on in our minds whenever we move our body voluntarily, no suitable mental events causing the movements come to light. However, the elusiveness of acts of will tends to be obscured by philosophers' selective attention when they focus on only a few, especially favorable, examples – such as this one: 'I deliberate whether to lift a certain heavyish weight, decide to do it, I then apply my force to it and lift it' (*BB* 150). Here we have some occurrences that could, without absurdity, be thought to constitute willing: some anticipatory thinking of the action, an act of resolve, a sensation of bodily effort. And now we take our ideas about voluntary action from this

kind of example and assume lightly that those ideas must apply to all cases of willing (*BB* 150). But of course not all cases are like that. We frequently do things without any such preliminaries. Ordinary speech, for instance, is often entirely unpremeditated and effortless, yet not, for that matter, involuntary.

2 Willing is thought to be a mental occurrence, but a mental occurrence must be either voluntary or involuntary. This leads to a fatal dilemma: if the mental act of willing is itself subject to the will, in order to be proper willing it would have to be willed. But then we are launched on an infinite regress: for the event of willing to be voluntary it has to be caused by an earlier event of willing; but that earlier event, too, in order to be voluntary, would have to be caused by yet an earlier event of willing, and so on *ad infinitum* – which is absurd (cf. Ryle 1949: 67). So it seems more promising to deny that willing itself could be subject to the will: 'I can't will willing' (*PI*, § 613). But that sounds odd as well. For now it would appear that 'willing too is merely an experience [...] It comes when it comes, and I cannot bring it about' (*PI*, § 611). But now the whole idea of voluntariness, of being in control of one's actions, seems to be lost. That must be wrong too (*PI*, § 612). The dilemma shows that the whole question (whether or not willing can be willed) is misbegotten. Willing is not the sort of thing of which it makes sense to ask whether it is voluntary or involuntary. 'Willing' is neither the name of an action, nor that of a passive experience. It is not the name of a mental occurrence of any kind.

3 According to the traditional account, a voluntary bodily action is a bodily movement caused by a mental act. Thus, on this theory, I *bring it about* that, say, my arm rises. But in fact, Wittgenstein objects, I don't (*PI*, § 614). I don't do anything else as a means to effect the rising of my arm. In particular, it cannot be said that I contract certain muscles in order for my arm to go up, for I don't even know which muscles need to be contracted for the arm to go up. (It is rather the other way round: I could raise my arm in order to bring about the contraction of whatever muscles are involved in the process.) Nor do I bring about bodily movements by acts of wishing or deciding. Wishing that something may happen is actually incompatible with doing it voluntarily (*PI*, § 616). The word 'wish,' like 'hope,' implies that one is not fully in control of what will happen. If I wish my arm to rise and, lo! it does – it wouldn't be my own action and I'd be very surprised (*Z*, § 586b). A decision to raise my arm, on the other hand, is of course likely to lead to my raising my arm; but it does not just cause my arm to go up. Again, I'd be rather surprised if it did. It would not be my own doing (*PI*, § 627). A decision to do something occurs *before* the action and cannot be regarded as part of it. Hence it cannot figure in the analysis of the concept of a voluntary action.

The traditional causal account of voluntary action must be rejected. Words like 'voluntary' or 'willing' do not stand for some distinctive mental occurrence that must precede and cause a movement for it to be voluntary. How, then, is the word 'voluntary' used? According to Wittgenstein, we should not expect the answer to be an exciting revelation. The concept is a familiar one, so its philosophical elucidation can only be a reminder of what in practice we are all familiar with. 'Voluntary movement is marked by the absence of surprise' (*PI*, § 628). I am not a third-person observer to my own behavior: I cannot look on with interest to see what will happen next, and then perhaps be surprised by it. Voluntary movements are characterized by a special surrounding of intention, learning, trying (*Z*, § 577); one can be ordered to do them (*Z*, § 588), and one can carry them out in different ways, instantiating familiar patterns of expressive behavior: readily, reluctantly, hesitatingly, cheerfully, carefully, or carelessly (*Z*, § 594).

Reasons and Causes

Wittgenstein's principal claim about reasons is that they must be distinguished from causes, for one can give the reasons for one's actions with authority, whereas one's statement of the causes of one's actions can only ever be a fallible hypothesis (*BB* 15). In the early 1930s, he considers the following example:

> Let us suppose a train driver sees a red signal flashing and brings the train to a stop. In response to the question: 'Why did you stop?' he answers perhaps: 'Because there is the signal 'Stop!'' One wrongly regards this statement as the statement of a *cause* whereas it is the statement of a *reason*. The cause may have been that he was long accustomed to reacting to the red signal in such-and-such a way or that in his nervous system permanent connections of pathways developed such that the action follows the stimulus in the manner of a reflex, or yet something else. The cause need not be known to him. By contrast, the reason is what he states it is. (*VW* 110–112, translation changed; cf. *PLP* 121)

In the discussion of this example Wittgenstein makes three points to set reasons apart from causes:

1 A reason, in this case, is a *rule* that justifies the action. It is not a hypothesis as to what happened, which might be falsified through further observations. The driver, in this example, 'could have also given this rule if he had not gone by it,' and it would have been equally correct (*VW* 110–112). – The rule in this case is: 'When a red signal is flashing trains must stop.' However, what the driver gave as his reason was not exactly this rule, although he referred to it by speaking of 'the signal 'Stop!'' Rather, he made the empirical claim that that signal was flashing at that moment. By itself, the semantic rule doesn't provide a reason to do anything; it needs to be combined with the observation that its antecedent is fulfilled at the time. Of course, it may not be necessary to point that out when one's interlocutor is already aware of it. In such a case, the reason explicitly stated may indeed be nothing more than a rule.

However, this point cannot be generalized, since, obviously, not all reasons involve semantic conventions or rules. Often, giving one's reason involves citing a causal regularity instead (e.g. 'Whisky gives me a headache').

2 A reason given in answer to the question 'Why did you do that?' is comparable to an answer to the question 'How did you get here?' It is

> the specification of the route one has taken, hence the description of a *singular* process, not the specification of a cause which always involves a whole host of observations. For this reason we say too that we know the reason for our action with certainty [...] but not the cause of an act. (*VW* 424; cf. *BB* 15)

Indeed, there is nothing hypothetical about describing the route one has taken, say: 'It occurred to me that *p*, and then I did *X*.' But for one thing, not all causal judgments are hypothetical and in need of confirmation by repeated observations (*PI*, § 169; *CE* 408). For another thing, mere succession of a thought and an action that could be justified by that thought is not sufficient to make the content of that thought the person's reason for acting. For example, looking at half a bottle of wine, it may occur to me that, since it's been opened, it won't keep, and then I proceed to drink it all up. Yet it's easy to imagine a context in which that thought would not in fact have contained my reason for drinking the wine (perhaps I'm well aware that I would have drunk two glasses regardless of whether it meant finishing up a bottle or not).

So far, then, it would appear that a causal construal of the relation between reason and action cannot be ruled out. However, *pace* Donald Davidson, a causal link cannot be the criterion for something's being the reason that is operative, for (as Davidson himself was forced to admit) the thought of a reason may (not just precede, but) trigger an action without being or containing the agent's reason for it. The thought may, for example, just serve as a reminder which leads the agent to act, but for a different reason. Moreover, although the occurrence of the thought that the wine in an open bottle won't keep may *cause* me to act, what could be invoked as a *reason*, as a justification of my action, is not the *occurrence* of the thought, but the *content* of the thought: that the wine in an open bottle won't keep. As Wittgenstein explained to Waismann:

> The attending to the rule can indeed be the cause for the rule being followed. [...] [But] the cause of an action can never be referred to, to justify the action. I may justify a calculation by appealing to the laws of arithmetic, but not by appealing to my attending to these laws. The one is a *justification*, the other a causal *explanation*. (*PLP* 123)

In any case, as Wittgenstein was to realize later, it is not always true that giving one's reason is like describing the route one has taken. Not all reasons are brought to mind before the action. In general, knowledge, beliefs, interests, and preferences can inform our actions without having to be brought to consciousness prior to their behavioral manifestations. There are countless things I believe without ever wasting a thought on them (for example that the chair I'm sitting down on is sufficiently stable to support me: *PI*, § 575) – which, however, I may bring up when asked to give reasons for some of my past behavior. 'The reason may be nothing more than just the one he gives when asked' (*AL* 5; cf. *PI*, § 479). And that, in fact, is the point to stress in order to account for the grammatical difference between reasons and causes:

3 Agents have first-person authority about their reasons for their actions: What they sincerely claim to be their reason *is* what we call their reason (*VW* 30f., 110f.).

With certain qualifications, such first-person authority applies even to reasons given for one's *past* actions. Elsewhere Wittgenstein considers the remarkable confidence with which we are able retrospectively to state our intentions (that is, one kind of reason for our behavior), especially what we meant to express by our words or what we were going to say (*PI*, §§ 633–663). The following points emerge:

(a) One knows what one was going to say or wanted to say, and yet one does not read it off from some mental process which took place then and which one remembers (*PI*, § 637).

(b) My words do not report what happened on that occasion, they are a *conditional* statement about the past. 'They say, for example, that I *should have* given a particular answer then, if I had been asked' (*PI*, § 684).

(c) My utterance is a *reaction* to what I remember of the situation (*PI*, §§ 648, 657, 659). That is to say, remembering the context, the situation, and a certain amount of details, I will now say: 'I wanted to φ'; or, 'I did it because *p*.'

(d) This is the language-game: We ask people for their reasons, and under certain conditions the explanations they give, even if retrospective, enjoy a privileged status. The conditions are as follows. First, the agent's claim as to his reason must be sincere and not conflict with what he expressed (by words or deeds, including the action in question) at other times. Second, the reason cannot have been a fact of which the agent was not aware, nor a supposed fact which the agent did not believe to (or knew not to) obtain. If these conditions are taken to be fulfilled, an agent's avowed reasons will be accepted. More than that, they will, as a matter of fact, *be* the agent's reasons, for the concept of an agent's reason is the precipitate of this language-game, together with the considerations given by those conditions.

The point of such a concept is easy to see. An agent's proffered reason will give us an insight into his character. It tells us what considerations he regards as justifying the action in question (at least in a weak sense of 'justify': as making the action understandable from the agent's point of view), or would so regard, given the information and interests he had at the time. Assuming that people's general views and dispositions remain fairly stable over short periods of time, we can generally trust people to be reliable in expressing subsequently what they *would* have been able to say at the time of action. Anyway, the justificatory aspect of explanations in terms of reasons is of paramount importance to us. By asking people to give reasons for their behavior, we challenge them to justify it; to tell us (if they can) why it wasn't a bad (or silly) thing. The question of when this justification was (or would have been) thought of for the first time may be quite irrelevant.

Wittgenstein's principal claim, that we can always be wrong about the causes of our actions but not about our reasons, is most persuasive where reasons and causes are logically independent. Thus the train driver's stated reason for stopping (that the stop signal was flashing) is independent of any causal explanation of:

[i] what made the agent become the kind of person who responds to such reasons;

[ii] physiological processes involved *in* the action, rather than causing the action.

However, there are some causal explanations of a different kind whose falsity would seem difficult to reconcile with the truth of an agent's sincere statement of his reasons. Where the reason given is that a certain event occurred (e.g. the flashing of a signal), it seems plausible to hold that it also implies a causal explanation:

[iii] what perceptible event occasioned the agent to act.

Thus, from the driver's professed reason it is natural to draw the causal explanation that the flashing of a red signal *caused* him to stop the train. Wittgenstein, at any rate, believed that, although we are more interested in explaining human behavior in terms of reasons, it may also be susceptible of corresponding causal explanations. Hence, although signals and linguistic utterances are primarily taken to give people reasons to respond to them, we can also regard language as a mechanism:

> It is clear that language is used for occasioning [*veranlassen*] people to take actions. It is used for purposes like a mechanism and it *is* a mechanism. (*VW* 100f.; cf. *PLP* 122f., *PI*, § 495)

In the present example, Wittgenstein suggests, as a parallel causal account, that perhaps the driver's 'action [of braking] follows the stimulus [of the flashing light] in the manner of a reflex' (*VW* 112f.).

Now the following problem arises: How can our fallibility about causal explanations be reconciled with our first-person authority about our reasons in cases where our reason seems to imply a certain causal explanation? In other words, if I may be wrong in thinking that a certain perceived event *caused* me to act, how can I be safe from error in declaring the occurrence of the event to be my *reason* for acting? Let us consider separately the two ways in which the causal statement may be false:

1 the event in question did not in fact occur;
2 the event occurred, but did not in fact cause the action.

Ad (1): Suppose the driver was mistaken in his impression that there was a red signal. Would it still be correct to say that the reason why he stopped was that a red light was flashing? Jonathan Dancy thinks so. He argues that explanations such as 'His reason for doing it was that *p*' are not factive: they report the considerations the agent regarded as justifying the action, without committing the speaker to the truth of those considerations. For 'a thing believed that is not the case can still explain an action' (Dancy 2000: 134). Dancy concedes, however, that there may be something like a conversational implicature to the effect that if the speaker simply reports the agent's reason he is naturally taken to endorse it. Hence, if we regard an agent's professed reason as false, we will normally distance ourselves from it by inserting an expression like 'he believed that.' So in the error case we may prefer to say:

[A] The driver stopped because *he believed that* a red signal had flashed.

Yet it would be wrong to understand this to mean that the driver's reason was the fact that he had a certain belief. Rather, the reason – what the agent thought to justify his action – was the content of the belief (cf. *PLP* 123, quoted above). Hence, [A] is plausibly construed 'appositionally' (Dancy 2000, 128f.):

[B] The driver stopped because, as he believed, a red signal had flashed.

His reason was indeed that a red signal had flashed, even though this was something he wrongly believed.

Ad (2): Post-hypnotic suggestion provides some clear examples of this kind. Wittgenstein considers the following case. (It should be noted that in this passage he uses the word '*Motiv*,' translated as 'motive,' for 'what somebody specifies as a reason for his action': *VW* 424f.)

> The experimental subject, who has under hypnosis been given a particular task to execute, e.g. to put up his umbrella, does precisely this – but has no inkling why he does what he does; asked to account for it, he may well invent a motive [...] and believe in it perfectly sincerely; all the same he is deluded. (*VW* 424f.)

Suppose that, when asked for his reason, the person says that the sky looked so grey, he thought it might start to rain any moment. In that case, the corresponding *causal* explanation – that the grey sky caused him to open his umbrella – is false. For what caused his behavior was obviously not the sky, but the preceding hypnosis. And yet, Wittgenstein suggests, the reason may be accepted as correct.

What the experimental subject is deluded about is the *cause* of his action, not its reason (*VW* 424f.). For the reason (what here Wittgenstein calls a 'motive') is what a person could sincerely have offered as a justification of his action at the time. What is peculiar about this case is that, because the person did not act of his own free will, we are not much *interested* in his reason. What he gave us was indeed *his reason* – but what he did was not really *his action*; it was, in fact, the hypnotist's doing, and so we might be more interested in the hypnotist's reason for it.

Related to this, but somewhat less pathological, are certain cases of self-deception. I may, for example, sincerely give as a reason for my telling someone off his lack of politeness. Yet a careful observer who knows me sufficiently well realizes that the occasion was fairly trivial and that I would never have lost my temper so much, had it not been for the fact that I felt jealous of the person I told off, perhaps without being clear about it myself. Here, again, a reason sincerely offered by the agent is not contradicted, but to some extent devalued by a causal explanation. The *reason* for my action was indeed the one I gave. But, since my behavior was less under my control than I believed, my behavior could not be fully accounted for by my reason. Part of it (the inappropriate vehemence of my outburst) could only be explained causally: by my being carried away by an emotion I hadn't yet fully taken stock of.

See also: TRYING TO ACT (3); BODILY MOVEMENTS (4); VOLITION AND THE WILL (13); INTENTION (14); REASONS AND CAUSES (17); MOTIVATING REASONS (19); DESCARTES (59); RYLE (69); VON WRIGHT (72); DAVIDSON (73); ANSCOMBE (74).

References

Primary sources and their abbreviations: Ludwig Wittgenstein

AL *Wittgenstein's Lectures, Cambridge, 1932–1935*, edited by A. Ambrose (1979). Oxford: Blackwell.

BB *The Blue and Brown Books* (1958). Oxford: Blackwell.

CE Cause and effect: Intuitive awareness (1993). In J. Klagge and A. Nordmann (eds), *Philosophical Occasions 1912–1951*. Indianapolis: Hackett, 370–426.

PI *Philosophical Investigations*, edited by P. M. S. Hacker and J. Schulte, translated by G. E. M. Anscombe, P. M. S. Hacker, and J. Schulte (2009). Oxford: Wiley–Blackwell.

PLP *The Principles of Linguistic Philosophy*, by F. Waismann, based on Wittgenstein's dictations, edited by R. Harré (1965). London: Macmillan.

VW *The Voices of Wittgenstein. The Vienna Circle*. by Ludwig Wittgenstein and Friedrich Waismann, edited by Gordon Baker (2003). London: Routledge.

Z *Zettel*, edsited by G. E. M. Anscombe and G. H. von Wright, translated by G. E. M. Anscombe (1967). Oxford: Blackwell.

Secondary sources

Dancy, J. (2000). *Practical Reality*. Oxford: Oxford University Press.

Ryle, G. (1949). *The Concept of Mind*. London: Hutchinson.

Schroeder, S. (2006). *Wittgenstein: The Way Out of the Fly-Bottle*. Cambridge: Polity.

69

Ryle

JULIA TANNEY

The Normativity of Action Concepts

We characterize human action as *voluntary, involuntary, intentional, unintentional, motivated, unmotivated, rational, irrational, performed for such a reason, for no reason,* and so on. These distinctions provide the logical space for the application of appraisal concepts or normative judgments such as, for example, *responsible, blameworthy, innocent, praiseworthy, good, bad, right,* and *wrong.*

What is it about humans in particular that makes them candidates for such normative judgments, which are only partially (and by an uncomfortable extension) applicable to animals and not at all to plant life and other biological systems? And how do we reconcile the distinctive human freedom presupposed by our use of normative concepts with our commitment to the view that mental phenomena are, like everything else, governed by laws of nature – which leave no room for normativity?

The correct answer, for Ryle (1900–1976), is that the conflict is illusory: laws of nature do not threaten freedom. And the two kinds of explanations, normative and causal, are different answers to different questions, not competing answers to the same question. An incorrect answer, which leads to unnecessary perplexities, is that human beings have cognitive, motivational, and emotive faculties which are causally implicated in the sort of behavior – action – that is apt for normative assessment.

Ryle's discussion in the *Concept of Mind* focuses on the 'will' as the relevant faculty and on volitions as the relevant force, though intentions, reasons, and motives, wrongly construed, are also within the target. It is clear that desires and pro-attitudes – indeed anything conceived of as mental thrusts – are equally within range, *whether or not these 'thrusts' are reconciled with the physical world.* Or so I claim. Ryle directed his wrath against the para-mechanical hypotheses of Cartesian or substance dualism; but it is clear that his fundamental gripe (shared with Wittgenstein) was against philosophical positions which resulted from mistaking conceptual questions for causal ones or which proffered mechanical or causal answers to puzzles that arise only because we have failed to notice, among other things, the indefinite variability in the ways mental predicates are (correctly) applied.

This puts his work squarely in opposition to present mainstream philosophy of mind, as well as to action theory and moral psychology. Mainstream philosophy of mind includes those, following Davidson, who construe actions as causal effects of belief–desire pairs, reasons, or intentions. It includes ethicists who dispute whether the faculty of judgment is sufficient to cause actions that are candidates for moral assessment, or whether this faculty needs assistance from the faculty of motivation. It includes functionalists who take mental predicates to pick out causally efficacious inner states, which may or may not be identical to, emergent from, or supervenient upon neural states. It includes anyone whose metaphysical account of action, reason, belief, desire, and so on rests on the (mistaken) assumption that the expressions ('action,' 'reason'...) and their cognates pick out states, events, or properties in the first place; for it is this assumption about the way language works that invites philosophical attempts to reconcile what seem to be mysterious referents with the world of natural law. In the discussion that follows, I shall put my own gloss on Ryle's arguments, to underline the relevance of his criticism for action theory and philosophy of mind today.

The Difficulties

Consider four arguments against invoking hidden mental operations or processes (volitions, intentions, motives, or reasons) to account for actions that merit appraisal or the application of intelligence predicates.

1 We do not describe our conduct in terms the philosophical theories indicate we should, nor, even if we accept the theory, would we know how. Save for the odd occasions in which we *resolve* to do something because of its difficulty or unpleasantness do we mention our having willed. We only occasionally deliberate about our choices; in these circumstances it may make sense to say that an act of judgment or formation of intention occurs. But, although most of what we do can be described as intentional (as opposed to unintentional or accidental) or understandable in the light of particular reasons, only for very few of our performances can we identify similar moments in their history. If all intentional actions, or actions understandable in the light of certain reasons, are to be construed as the upshots of operations or processes, by what sort of predicate should these processes be described?

> Can they be sudden or gradual, strong or weak, difficult or easy, enjoyable or disagreeable? Can they be accelerated, decelerated, interrupted, or suspended? Can people be efficient or inefficient at them? Can we take lessons in executing them? Are they fatiguing or distracting? [...] At which moment was the boy going through a volition [or forming an intention or being moved by reasons or motivated by desire or principles] to take a high dive? When he set his foot on the ladder? When he took his first deep breath? When he counted off 'One, two, three – Go' but did not go? Very, very shortly before he sprang? What would his own answer be to those questions? (Ryle 2009: 51–52)

And what would be the answer of one sufficiently *au fait* with the relevant theories of action and moral motivation?

> If ordinary men never report the occurrence of these acts, for all that, according to the theory, they should be encountered vastly more frequently than headaches, or feelings

> of boredom; if ordinary vocabulary has no non-academic name for them [as in cases of 'volitions' or 'willings']; if we do not know how to settle simple questions about their duration or strength [as is the case for 'intendings,' or the processes that guarantee we have acted for reasons or from motives], then it is fair to conclude that their existence is not asserted on empirical grounds. (Ibid., p. 52)

On the contrary, says Ryle with irritation, the acceptance of these hidden operations or causal factors rests not on their discovery, but on their postulation.
2 One cannot witness the causal factors that are alleged to render another's actions rational, subject to blame and praise, and so on. We can only infer their existence from certain actions; namely those which we already have reason to believe are rational, say, rather than irrational. The view that some mental causal factor accounts for the difference between free, rational action and automatic bits of behavior (for example) presupposes

> that one person could in principle never recognize the difference between the rational and the irrational utterances issuing from other human bodies, since he could never get access to the postulated immaterial causes of some of their utterances. (10)

'The onlooker, be he teacher, critic, biographer or friend, can never assure himself that his comments have any vestige of truth.' And yet,

> it was just because we do in fact all know how to make such comments, make them with general correctness and correct them when they turn out to be confused or mistaken, that philosophers found it necessary to construct their theories of the nature and place of minds. Finding mental-conduct concepts being regularly and effectively used, they properly sought to fix their logical geography. But the account officially recommended would entail that there could be no regular or effective use of these mental-conduct concepts in our descriptions of, and prescriptions for, other people's minds. (Ibid., p. 5)

> The curious conclusion results that though volitions [or, we might add: intentions, reasons, motives, and so on, construed as causal processes] were called in to explain our appraisals of actions, this explanation is just what they fail to provide. If we had no other antecedent grounds for applying appraisal-concepts to the actions of others, we should have no reasons at all for inferring from those actions to the volitions [etc.] alleged to give rise to them. (Ibid., p. 53)

Ryle points out that the agent herself cannot be said to know that her actions are the results of mental operations. Although he cites the 'mysteriousness' of the connection between the alleged operations and the movements they cause as that which threatens the practice of granting the agent presumptive authority over the voluntariness (and so on) of her doings, we can (bringing his ideas up to date) note that the possibility of *causal deviance* has the same consequence. Even if I form the intention to buy Nyons olives at the Uzès market, for all I know my intention, understood here as a causal factor, may have had some other action as its effect and the purchasing of olives some other event for its cause.
3 I am said to act from lofty intentions, disreputable motives, and good or bad reasons. Are the mental processes or operations that are supposed causally to constitute

rational, intentional, or motivated actions themselves rational, intentional, or motivated? A vicious regress awaits the one who answers 'Yes'; but those who claim that adjectives such as 'voluntary' or 'involuntary' do not qualify such processes should be embarrassed to explain how intentions, motives, and reasons are subject to normative judgments.

4 The mysteriousness of mental–physical causation is endemic to the view: it is not of an unsolved but soluble type, like the causes of global warming. The episodes which are supposed to constitute the careers of minds, Ryle says,

> are assumed to have one sort of existence, while those constituting the careers of bodies have another sort; and no bridge-status is allowed [...] Minds, as the whole legend describe them, are what must exist if there is to be a causal explanation of the intelligent behaviour of human bodies; and minds, as the legend describes them, live on a floor of existence defined as being outside the causal system to which bodies belong. (Ibid., p. 53)

The mysteriousness of mental causation will not simply disappear by a rejection of the 'official doctrine,' with its postulated 'ghost in the machine'; for it will be inherited by anyone who believes both that mental 'properties' must make a *causal* difference and that physics is a closed causal system. Just as mind–body interaction was a problem for substance dualism, so does the problem of mental causation continue to upset varieties of both reductive and non-reductive physicalism.

None of this is to deny, of course, that we sometimes deliberate, act in the light of certain reasons, and form intentions. But, aside from the considerations adduced above, another reason why these familiar activities cannot be identified with the mental thrusts that are supposed to ripen behavior for normative assessment is that they are themselves activities which can be performed rationally, judiciously, intelligently, and so on. So, according to the theory, these higher order activities would need mental thrusts of their own.

A Diagnosis of the Error

Given the difficulties with the view, why suppose that voluntary, rational, intentional, or motivated action is the causal upshot of (hidden) mental operations or processes? Ryle suggests that we have misconstrued the question, 'What makes a bodily movement voluntary [intentional, rational, etc.]?' as one demanding a causal answer instead of one that can be answered by looking at our ordinary, everyday practice of ascribing mental conduct verbs or intelligence predicates to certain overt behaviors and not to others.

The mistake is exacerbated by failing to recognize different elasticities of significance and thus differences in logical force attending the use of expressions such as 'voluntary,' 'involuntary,' 'intentional,' and 'unintentional.' Ryle's task as a conceptual cartographer is to examine these differences across a wide range of uses: *The Concept of Mind* is a sustained study of the logical force of mental predicates. Here we can review and adapt just one of his findings.

Outside philosophy, adjectives such as 'voluntary' and 'involuntary' are normally reserved for actions which ought not to have been committed, when we are trying to assess responsibility in order to establish blame or innocence. Philosophy, for reasons suggested below, has extended their use to apply to all actions. Some evidence for the fact that the concept has been extended can be seen by reflecting on the oddness of the question 'Are you doing this voluntarily?' asked of someone who is, in normal circumstances, (say) eating her evening meal, giving a lecture, or typing a report. ('Normal,' here, indicates that the circumstances surrounding these activities suggest no pressure, coercion, hypnosis, lack of skill, or other special story that would illuminate a contrast with 'voluntary.')

In extending the terms so that all actions are voluntary or involuntary, we will elide a key use: the sense in which an action is involuntary when someone could not have helped it because she was lacking the requisite competence, training, skill, or know-how, or voluntary insofar as she could have helped it because she had the competence or skill but failed to exercise it on this occasion. (Note that 'voluntary' is being used here, not in a sense in which it contrasts with compulsion or coercion, but in another sense, which overlaps somewhat with 'intentional.' I shall adapt Ryle's argument to cover both uses.) Let us consider an example.

My drinking the most expensive wine in the collection of my absent host (as of this writing valued at €1,172) was involuntary (unintentional) on this understanding, because I did not have the competence to ascertain its value just from reading *Gruaud Larose 1928* on the label. Your drinking it would have been voluntary (intentional) on this understanding, because you had the competence to know its value but did not exercise it.

On the ordinary use, and in ordinary circumstances, to question whether one's putting one's napkin on one's lap, picking up one's fork, and putting peas in one's mouth at mealtime is voluntary or intentional is distinctly odd. Though the sentence is understandable insofar as other circumstances may be imagined in which the point of the sentence is clear (for example after hypnosis), its application, or the way in which it is supposed to be used on this occasion, is not. (See *Philosophical Investigations* § 500ff.) But, in the philosophically extended use, going through the above activities of eating the evening meal are considered voluntary or intentional actions since they are clearly not involuntary or unintentional.

It is this philosophical extension that helps to support the idea that there are hidden, causally efficacious operations (volitions or intentions) which constitute voluntary or intentional behavior. How? As the concept is ordinarily used, we know full well how to determine whether an action was voluntary or intentional. Even if you were to claim innocence about this particular choice of wine, the fact that you are a member of the Wine Society, that you keep a locked cellar book, visit various *domaines* in France picking up wine along the way, and spend a few minutes every day checking auction prices counts in favor of the judgment that you had the competence to tell that the bottle of 1928 *Gruaud La Rose* was a very special wine indeed and worth a lot of money. I just wanted some red wine; this particular bottle was damp, dirty and therefore not worth keeping. These considerations count in favor of the judgment that I did not have the competence in question. You, however, had the competence, but failed to exercise it on this occasion; this is why your action was voluntary or intentional.

Now extend this use of 'voluntary' to the case of eating an evening meal. Did you have the competence to do otherwise and fail to exercise it? What does this question mean in the case of perfectly normal, expected behavior? We ought to reject the question on the grounds that it is an illegitimate extension of 'voluntary' ('intentional'). Failing to recognize this, and being convinced that the actions involved in eating a meal are not involuntary or unintentional, and being unsure how to answer the question by normal means, we may incline toward the idea that what makes it voluntary or intentional is the existence of some hidden postulated mental occurrence; a *volition* or *intention*.

A motivation for this philosophical extension of the term, Ryle suggests, is the fear that, as the sciences advance, we will discover laws of nature that govern what we do in such a way as to render our normative, appraisal predicates inapplicable. So we carve out a special place (the mind) or special properties (mental ones) to ensure that appraisal concepts will always have their place. But the fear is misguided, since it is based on a misunderstanding of the force of 'govern.' The laws of physics, biology, chemistry, and so on govern what we do in the sense that they set limits. The game of football would not be as we know it unless the laws of gravity, mass, motion, acceleration, and so forth were in play. (J. K. Rowling's Quidditch would be governed by different laws.) Once the ball is kicked, the angle and force of the kick calibrated, the wind speed and direction taken into account, it can in principle be explained and predicted whether the ball would go into the net (on the assumption that it is not interfered with by another player, there is no earthquake, and so on). Far from natural laws being a threat to our freedom, they are necessary for us to exercise it as we do. But these laws do not govern in the sense that they order or command what we will do. It is consistent with physical, chemical, and biological laws that the centre forward passes the ball to the right midfielder instead of the left midfielder. Or that he decides to run with the ball instead.

Why would anyone think otherwise? If one is already in the grip of the picture to be disputed – that what makes an action rational is the upshot of a special causal story – one will be obliged to explain how the decision to run with the ball can be part of a causal chain affecting the brain, which in turn gives messages to the muscles through nerve-fibres in the leg and foot. One is inclined to invent mental thrusts such as 'volitions' or 'motivational pulls,' or to extend the concepts we have by suggesting that 'intention' or 'reason' plays the requisite causal role. But one is still left with the obvious problem, not yet solved, of how to make sense of the gap between person-predicates and physical ones. The problem of bridge-status, in the form of bridge-laws, comes back to haunt and with it comes skepticism about the genuine causal power and thus the 'reality' of the mental.

Conceptual Cartography

Why should we care about what 'armchair philosophy' has to say? What good are 'intuitions'? Indeed what is the point of conceptual analysis, especially when history has shown that, if they exist at all, definitional analyses in the form of necessary and sufficient conditions can be found for none of the concepts that interest philosophers? And, given the evident bankruptcy of analytic philosophy, what accounts for certain philosophers' refusal to pay attention to what the sciences can contribute? Indeed why should one care about how we *talk* about reasons,

> rationality, and action, when it is the *phenomena* we are interested in: far from being interested in words, it is the *nature* of actions, reasons, and rationality that ought to concern us. The interdisciplinary work of the cognitive sciences, which combine conceptual philosophy with the empirical work of psychologists, anthropologists, linguists, and so on, is best placed to answer these questions.

This common and depressing refrain makes many mistaken assumptions. Like most early analytic philosophers (with the exception of Quine), Ryle agreed that philosophy is a priori conceptual investigation. But this is not, as some critics have maintained, to deny that philosophers of mind, for example, are interested in mental phenomena. A conceptual investigation sheds light on the nature of the relevant phenomena, but it is only by investigating expressions as they are (variously) employed that philosophers can elucidate the relevant concepts. The philosopher engaging in conceptual investigation is not using her intuitions, conceptual or modal. She is using, among other things, her linguistic and philosophical competence to reflect upon the various uses of the relevant expressions, and she is tracing and attempting to untangle their logical threads as they are so used.

Ryle's conceptual cartography is not a search for essential properties of that which the concept is taken to signify; for concepts do not signify anything. The fact that we tend to use abstract nouns to talk about that which is conveyed by various words should not mislead us. In spite of how Plato, Hegel, Russell, and Moore described their task, they did not execute it by investigating supra-mundane entities. When we investigate pleasure, we do not, any more than Aristotle did, 'stare hard' at an entity or 'essence' designated by this abstract noun: we consider, as a first step, what we are saying when we talk about someone (say) who enjoys sunbathing, or finds Kilian's *White Cristal* divine.

Nor does Ryle consider conceptual analysis to be the search for rules of meaning conceived of as (circumstance-independent) conditions, necessary and sufficient for the expressions' application; for, as Ryle makes clear, the inflections of meaning or elasticities of significance enjoyed by most, if not all, of our ordinary expressions will ensure that there are rarely, if ever, such context-free conditions. Most words, phrases, and sentences of natural languages have a capacity to express an indefinite variety of ideas; this capacity is one of the factors that makes original thought possible. Unlike ambiguous or 'pun' words, the various ideas expressed by a sentence in its different uses are intimately connected with one another: they are (like Wittgenstein's family resemblances, we might add) inflections that are offshoots of the same root. To say that most words, phrases, sentences, and grammatical constructions enjoy this 'systematic ambiguity' is to say that their logical threads or powers may change with the circumstances of their use. These powers involve the kinds of inferences we can make, the kinds of explanations and predictions they can be used to give, the kinds of expressions with which they are incompatible, compatible, or inconsistent and consistent. This sort of capacity for expressing an indefinite variety of ideas is inherited by translations and paraphrases of the expression. There is no such thing, for Ryle, as the meaning of a sentence that is independent of its context of use; and there are indefinitely many ways in which the sentence may be (correctly) employed. These, of course, will include uses that have yet to be considered, in which decisions will have to be made about how the concept should be extended. But, in considering these extensions, special care must be taken to ensure that such changes do not undermine the use of the expression in those circumstances in which the sentence already fulfills its explanatory role.

A philosophical investigation of reasons and action involves tracing the logical threads of a set of interlocking concepts such as 'voluntary,' 'intentional,' 'responsibility,' 'freedom,' 'innocent,' 'blameworthy,' and so on. The idea is that, like the problem of mental causation illustrated above, philosophical puzzles such as the mind–body problem, or free will and determinism, will start to dissolve as we unpick the threads of these interlocking concepts. In doing so we may note, as we have done above, that the force of an expression in one context has been illicitly imported into another, creating a puzzle or an anomaly which, for its solution, seems to generate additional problems. In the case considered here, the 'solution' that causes difficulties is the postulation of a cognitive mechanism.

A more thorough philosophical investigation will reveal that the sentences under investigation do not always function to describe or to report states of affairs; can only sometimes be assessed for truth or falsity; and can only with great risk of misunderstanding be said to attribute a quality, property, or relation to an object which is signified by the grammatical subject. A study of the general nature of action, reasons, rationality, and the will is a topic for conceptual elucidation of the kind illustrated here, and not a topic for science, because such an investigation reveals that there is no *thing* – object, event, property, or relation – which is the referent of the relevant expressions and whose nature is to be decided by an empirical investigation. Nor, for that matter, is it to be decided by a metaphysical one. To suppose otherwise is to commit a category mistake.[1]

See also: BODILY MOVEMENTS (4); HABITUAL ACTIONS (10); VOLITION AND THE WILL (13); INTENTION (14); REASONS AND CAUSES (17); MENTAL CAUSATION AND EPIPHENOMENALISM (23); DESCARTES (59); WITTGENSTEIN (68).

Note

1 Thanks to David Corfield, John Flower, Peter Hacker, Constantine Sandis, Sean Sayers, and Robin Taylor for helpful discussion and suggestions.

References: primary sources

Ryle, G. (2009). *The Concept of Mind*. London: Routledge.

Further reading

Ryle, G. (1954). *Dilemmas. The Tarner Lectures 1953*. Cambridge: Cambridge University Press.

Ryle, G. (2009), *Collected Papers*, Vols 1–2. London: Routledge.

Tanney, J. (2009). Re-thinking Ryle: Critical introduction to *The Concept of Mind*. London: Routledge.

Tanney, J. (2009). Prefaces to Ryle's *Collected Papers*, Vols 1–2. London: Routledge.

Tanney, J. (2007 and 2009). Ryle. In *Stanford Encyclopedia of Philosophy*. Accessed at: http://plato.stanford.edu/entries/ryle/.

70

Sartre

KATHERINE J. MORRIS

Introduction

Jean-Paul Sartre (1905–1980), the great twentieth-century French phenomenologist and existential philosopher, sets out his conception of human action in the course of his discussion of human freedom. Up to a point, Sartre can be seen as playing a variation, in his own inimitable style, on the theme that the reasons for an action cannot be causes of the action. The idea that reasons *are* causes is virtually a commonplace among post-Davidson Anglo-American analytic action theorists; but Sartre's arguments are left untouched by the usual 'refutations' of the idea that reasons cannot be causes. Hence his account of action presents an interesting challenge to much modern analytic action theory.

More widely, Sartre's account of action is framed by a background picture of perception, the perceived world, and the human body which is arguably at odds with the one that frames much modern analytic action theory. From this perspective Sartre's account of action presents a broader challenge to analytic action theory.

Background: Phenomenology and Existential Philosophy

Phenomenology as a method of philosophizing was developed by Edmund Husserl around the beginning of the twentieth century and was taken by others, including Martin Heidegger and Maurice Merleau-Ponty as well as Sartre, in a more 'existential' direction. For historical reasons too obscure and complex to detail here, phenomenology, as a movement within 'continental' philosophy, has largely been ignored by Anglo-American 'analytic' philosophers, including those studying action.

Phenomenology, as we might expect, is the *logos* or study of 'phenomena.' Readers who wish to understand this methodology and its history in greater depth may wish to read Moran (2000); for our purposes, the following three points are of particular significance:

1 Phenomena may be characterized as 'appearances.' However, we must not read 'appearances' as a foil for 'reality' in this context. The subject matter of phenomenology is, precisely, 'human *reality*,' and Sartre's monumental work

Being and Nothingness (hereafter *BN*) is subtitled *A Phenomenological Essay on Ontology*. Since Anglo-American philosophers tend to use the term 'phenomenology' to refer to a description of how things seem *as opposed to* how they really are, this is a potential source of serious misunderstanding.

2 What characterizes 'existential' approaches to phenomenology is their recognition that no single aspect of human reality can be fully understood in isolation from the whole. The whole, in Heidegger's famous phrase, is 'being-in-the-world.' In the present context, this means that any account of action presupposes – minimally – an account of perception, of the perceived world (the life-world or *Lebenswelt*), and of the human body. This outlook is antithetical to the specialization that characterizes many modern Anglo-American philosophy departments.

3 Descriptions of phenomena must be *unprejudiced*. Phenomenology emerged at a time in European history when, in Husserl's view, particular intellectual prejudices were so prevalent that they constituted a 'crisis': hence his 1935 lecture 'Philosophy and the crisis of European man,' which formed part of the basis of his great (though unfinished) work *The Crisis of European Sciences and Transcendental Phenomenology*. Nazism was only one manifestation of the crisis in question. What concerned Husserl was the danger posed to European culture by the growing predominance, in domains to which it was not appropriate, of a scientific rationality narrowly interpreted as a technical and technological rationality: a frame of mind that was reductive, atomistic, objectivist, and scientistic. One might well think that European culture has not yet averted this crisis. Nor have Anglo-American philosophy departments.

I begin by outlining Sartre's account of action; I then contextualize it within Sartre's descriptions of the life-world and of the human body. Critical assessment focuses on uncovering the assumptions which are implicit in much analytic action theory.

Sartre's Account of Action

Sartre's starting point will at least be familiar territory for Anglo-American philosophers: 'an action is on principle *intentional*'; it is the intentional realization of a conscious project (*BN* 433). Sartre connects the intentionality of action with reasons, and he uses this basic feature of action to argue both against determinism and against libertarianism.

To a first approximation, what is at issue in Sartre's view is whether actions are always done for *reasons* or whether some actions (the 'free' ones) are done for no reason. The libertarians – 'partisans of the liberty of indifference,' Sartre calls them, referring to the familiar scholastic doctrine and citing the novelist André Gide as a contemporary exponent – take as their paradigm of free action an action performed for *no reason at all*, or performed in conditions where the reasons for each of two opposed available actions are finely balanced. Sartre dismisses this libertarianism briskly: '[t]o speak of an act without a reason [*motif*] is to speak of an act which would lack the intentional structure of every act' (*BN* 436–437) – that is, of something that is not an act at all.

Thus far, Sartre is entirely on the side of the determinists; but he takes them to task for having an inadequate conception of reasons. An adequate conception, he argues, ultimately undermines determinism. We could say that the misconception in question is that of conceiving of reasons *as causes*, which would align Sartre with an established tradition in action theory (see Atwell 1980). While this is perfectly correct, Sartre's arguments really are unique to him.

To appreciate these arguments, we need to say more about the word 'reason.' I mean this to cover both what Sartre calls *motifs* and what he calls *mobiles*. These two terms are notoriously difficult to translate (and Sartre sometimes uses *motif* to cover both); I will leave them untranslated in what follows. To put it (too) crudely, they refer, respectively, to whatever it is about the world on the one hand, and about the agent on the other, that makes it intelligible that the agent did what he did. By 'making intelligible' I don't mean merely 'revealing what the agent actually saw in the action'; I also mean to contrast Sartre's account with the determinist's – which, he argues, actually leaves human action *inherently* mysterious (that is, unintelligible; see below).

Sartre sets out the determinist's construction of *motifs* and *mobiles* as follows: 'Generally by *motif* we mean the reason for the act; that is, the ensemble of rational considerations which justify it,' for example the sorts of reasons which the government might give for converting government bonds – say, the state of the national debt (*BN* 445–446). 'The *mobile*, on the contrary, is generally considered as a subjective fact. It is the ensemble of the desires, emotions, and passions which urge me to accomplish a certain act' (ibid.). An act is 'rational' or 'passionate' according to whether *motifs* or *mobiles* predominate, but in 'the everyday case [...] they exist side by side' (*BN* 447).

Sartre sees at least three problems with this construction:

1 It presupposes that the reasons for an action are 'factual': *motifs* are objectively factual states of affairs, *mobiles* are 'subjective facts.' Against this, Sartre argues, first, that '[n]o factual state whatever it may be [...] is capable of motivating any act whatsoever' (*BN* 435), and, second, that *mobiles* are 'haunted' by non-existent ends (*BN* 88).
2 On the determinist's picture, moreover, the *motif* and the *mobile* are externally related to each other (*BN* 447). Sartre argues that, on the contrary, *motif* and *mobile* are internally related. (The important concept of an internal relation is explored below.)
3 Additionally, for the determinist, *motif* and *mobile* are externally – because causally – related to the action; and this, together with the external relation between *motif* and *mobile*, leaves actions inherently mysterious: their story might as well read '*A*, *B* and then – hey presto! – *C*.' For Sartre, *motif* and *mobile* are internally related to the action, and seeing things in this way immediately dispels the mystery.

So consider an 'everyday case': I come home from work, tired after a long day of teaching; what I really need, I think to myself, is a Negroni. I fetch out a cocktail glass, fill it with ice, and reach for the Campari in my drinks cabinet, only to discover that *I'm out of Campari*. So – here is the action on which we will focus – I go off to the shop to purchase some Campari. The determinist might identify the *motif* here as the factual non-presence of Campari in my drinks cabinet, the *mobile* as my desire for a Negroni (together perhaps with such beliefs as that Campari is an ingredient of Negronis and that the shop sells Campari); these objective and subjective facts somehow join forces and push me off to the shop.

Sartre's story will be different: the *motif* here is the *absence* of Campari, an instance of those concrete nothingnesses which Sartre calls *négatités*. Absences can in no way be deduced from factual non-presences: '[n]o factual state can determine consciousness to apprehend it as a *négatité* or as a lack' (*BN* 435–436). Pernod, for instance, is not present in my drinks cabinet but it is not thereby *absent* (cf. *BN* 10f.). Unlike the mere non-presence of Pernod, I *encounter* the absence of Campari.

What, then, of the *mobile*? We can say, no doubt, that it consists in my desire for a Negroni (or perhaps in a desire for some Campari as a means to that end); but, Sartre argues, a desire cannot be understood as a 'subjective fact.' '[H]ow can we explain desire if we insist on viewing it as a psychic state; that is, as a being whose nature is to be what it is? [...] Desire is a lack of being. It is haunted in its inmost being by the being of which it is desire' (*BN* 87–88). My desire for a Negroni is 'haunted in its inmost being' by *a Negroni*; but not by a present, existent Negroni ('not even in the capacity of a representation,' Sartre might add; cf. *BN* xxvii), for then it would not be *desire*, but by a Negroni as a not-yet-existent future presence. It is only in the light of this not-yet-existent end which 'haunts' the *motif* that Campari is revealed as an absence.

The *mobile* and its end are *already implicit* in our description of the *motif*, since a factual state (the non-presence of Campari) can 'act in the capacity of a *motif*' – be an absence – only if it is 'discovered by a *mobile*' (*BN* 472). Thus *motif* and *mobile* are internally related. Someone with a different *mobile* would not encounter the same *motif* in the world as I. (The temptation to write '*ceteris paribus*' is misguided, for reasons we will come to.)

Moreover, *motif*, *mobile*, and end are internally related to action. *Motifs* are not motivationally neutral properties of the world. The *négatité* the perception of which I might express as 'Damn! No Campari' makes demands on me. Thus to perceive the drinks cabinet as having the property of 'lacking Campari' is to project the action of going to the shop for Campari. Nor must we make this 'projecting of the action' into yet a further subjective fact – a 'volition,' or an 'intention' – which would then itself cause the action. To a first approximation, to project the action *is* to act. Of course, I may not succeed: my body could be struck by a sudden paralysis (Hornsby 1980), or I could get hit by a car on the way to the shop, or the shop could be out of Campari; the success of my action, the coincidence between the action projected and the action performed, is, as Davidson (1980: 59) has happily put it, 'up to nature.' But, given that the world possesses the property 'Campari is lacking here,' my going to get Campari is utterly intelligible.

This is not the whole of Sartre's argument against determinism. He also argues that the end which haunts my *mobile* is integrated into a wider end, and ultimately into what he calls my fundamental project. Since I choose my fundamental project, and can change it, the element of 'could have done otherwise,' which is widely seen as so important to freedom, is preserved. There is no need to pursue this difficult doctrine here, since we have everything we need in order to understand Sartre's basic account of action.

Some Wider Background

Any account of action, the existentialist philosophers will urge, presupposes (at least) a conception of perception, of the perceived world, and of the human body.

Action, on Sartre's conception, is motivated by properties of things which are revealed to perception as 'potentialities, absences, instrumentalities': 'the nail is 'to be pounded in' this way or that, the hammer is 'to be held by the handle'' (*BN* 322). (Note that all of these properties may act as *motifs*, despite Sartre's official stress on absences in that capacity.) Hence perception and action are internally related: perception 'can be revealed only in and through projects of action' (*BN* 321).

Moreover, 'sense perception is in no way to be distinguished from the practical organization of existents into a *world*' (*BN* 321). What Sartre refers to as 'the system of seen objects' is *oriented*; there is a field of vision in which objects appear as 'thises' against a ground (*BN* 316), and '[i]t is necessary that the book appear to me on the right or on the left side of the table.' Additionally, objects always appear 'all at once – it is the cube, the inkwell, the cup which I see,' but at the same time always 'in a particular perspective' (*BN* 317).

These orientations, orderings, and perspectivity refer to a centre of the field, and that centre is my *body*. The place of objects within such a 'complex of instrumentality' 'is not defined by purely spatial coordinates but in relation to axes of practical reference' (*BN* 321). These 'axes of practical reference' – 'up' and 'down,' 'nearer' and 'further,' 'left' and 'right,' and so on – are centred on the body. This is not the body as an object in the world, not the body as it is *known*, but the 'lived body' or body-subject – in the words of Merleau-Ponty, 'a system of possible actions [...] with its phenomenal 'place' defined by its task and situation' (1962: 250).

In the background of this conception of human beings and of the life-world, one may find both Heidegger and an equally important, though often neglected, influence on Sartre: the Gestalt psychologists, especially (here at least) Kurt Lewin (see Morris 2008, Ch. 6). It is noteworthy that Gestalt psychology emerged in Europe in parallel with phenomenology, and partly in response to the same 'crisis': the empiricist psychologists (both behaviorists and introspectionists) against whom Gestalists defined their position were in the grip of the very intellectual prejudices identified by Husserl.

The 'real space of the world' – the life-world in which human beings perform actions – is, Sartre says, 'hodological' (*BN* 308), a term which Sartre takes from Lewin. This term derives from the ancient Greek *hodos*, meaning 'way' or 'path.' Thus

> the world of our desires, our needs and of our activities [...] [is] all furrowed with strait and narrow paths leading to such and such determinate ends [...] [H]ere and there [...] there are pitfalls and traps. (Sartre 1962: 61)

According to Lewin (1935), objects within our environment are not motivationally neutral; they have positive or negative 'valences' (*Aufforderungscharakters*, rendered more literally by the Gestalt-influenced psychologist J. J. Gibson as 'affordances'). Sartre is more likely to use the less technical-sounding language of Guillaume (who mediated his understanding of Gestalt psychology), for instance 'attraction,' 'exigence,' 'solicitation' (Guillaume 1937: 132). An object's valence 'usually derives from the fact that the object is a means to the satisfaction of a need' (Lewin 1935: 78) or – as Sartre would stress – of a desire: 'the hodological field [is] maintained by desire' (Sartre 1992: 350).

Valences and needs or desires are therefore internally related: as Guillaume puts it, 'there is a *reciprocity* between the feelings of the subject and certain affective properties of objects in the phenomenal field' (1937: 132, italics added). Sartrean *motifs* may be seen as valences which only appear in the world through *mobiles* and their associated ends. And these valences 'make demands' or 'solicit' actions from a 'lived body,' which is both the centre of its perceptive-cum-instrumental field and that by which there is such a field.

Assessment: Internal Relations

The concept of an internal relation plays a key role in phenomenology in general, where it functions as a bulwark against what is often called atomism, and in Sartre's account of action in particular. The phrase 'internal relation' has a long history; it is certainly not unique to the phenomenologists. Even in Anglo-American action theory, it was, not so long ago, common to argue that reasons and actions are, in some sense, internally related, and to use this as the basis of an argument to the conclusion that reasons cannot be causes, since causal relations are, in some sense, external. In more recent work on analytic action theory, however, the view generally seems to be that this line of argument has been refuted, largely by Donald Davidson. Davidson (1980; see especially the first essay, first published in 1963) construes internal relations as logical ones, and argues that logical relations can hold only between linguistic expressions. From this perspective, a reason and an action can be described in such a way that there is *no* logical relation between the two descriptions and, conversely, a cause and an effect can be described in such a way that there *is* a logical relation between the two descriptions; thus it cannot be claimed either that the reason/action relation is internal or that the cause/effect relation is external.

Whatever Anglo-American action theorists may mean, or may have meant, by the phrase 'internal relation,' this is not what Sartre meant. Internal relations are not logical relations between linguistic expressions; they are *ontological* relations between *phenomena*. One paradigm used both by Sartre and by Merleau-Ponty is the relation between the color and the texture of a carpet: the carpet hasn't got two externally related qualities, woolliness and redness: the carpet is a *woolly red* (Sartre 1965: 276; compare Merleau-Ponty 1962: 5). The color of the carpet would not be what it is, were the carpet of a different texture. Another paradigm is the relation between the two aspects of an ambiguous picture, say, the well-known picture that can be seen either as a black vase on a white background or as two white profiles facing each other on a black background: that very vase would not be there, were there not those very two profiles, and conversely. There is clearly no claim here that the *concepts* of woolliness and redness, or the *concepts* of a picture of a vase and of a picture of a profile, are logically related!

Nor is the claim that woolliness and redness, *in general*, or pictured profiles and pictured vases, *in general*, are internally related. Thus there is no claim here that any perception of the absence of Campari is internally related to the desire for a Negroni – it might be that my aperitif of choice is a Campari and white wine; indeed one might say that the absence I experience, in the story above, is the absence of Campari-*qua*-Negroni-ingredient. (Hence one can say, without *ceteris paribus*, that someone with a different *mobile* would not encounter the same *motif* in the world as I.) Nor is it even that every perception of the absence of Campari which appears in the light of a desire for a Negroni is internally related to my action of going to the shop for Campari now – I might know that the shop is closed, in which case I encounter a barrier to the fulfilment of my desire. (There is also the very different case in which I am planning to shop on my way home from work and, anticipating my desire for a Negroni when I get back, I look in the drinks cabinet, discover I'm out of Campari, and write 'Campari' on my shopping list.) Internal relations relate phenomena in all their particularity, so fully to understand an action requires a good deal of contextualization.

It may be that this conception of internal relations is equally problematic; what is clear is that Davidson's arguments against a very different conception don't touch it.

Assessment: Human Beings and the Human World

Sartre's determinist clearly, and many analytically oriented action theorists arguably, hold, explicitly or implicitly, a conception of human beings and of the world which is very different from the conception sketched earlier.

First, the accounts of analytic philosophers often leave no room for intrinsically motivating properties. Some analytic philosophers in the grip of empiricism may even see these as philosophically objectionable – perhaps properties 'of a very strange sort, utterly different from anything else in the universe' (Mackie 1977: 38) – and will attempt to explain them away in terms that echo those of the determinist addressed by Sartre. Thus they tend to treat perception and action as externally related.

Second, their accounts seem to allot no role whatsoever to non-existents: those absences and lacks which we encounter in the world. Perhaps they worry that to allow *négatités* into their account would invite something like Ayer's accusation that Sartre used the word 'nothing' to name 'something insubstantial and mysterious,' like the 'nobody' whom the Red King's eyes lacked the acuity to spot (Ayer 1945: 19). But Sartre is certainly not claiming that *négatités exist* – that is the whole point! Only those who suppose that the *real* is limited to the *existent* will find it strange to say that non-existents are part of reality, to be met with in the world.

Third, consider a question that occupies many analytic action theorists: 'What is the relation between actions and bodily movements?' Various answers are canvassed: the action is identical to the bodily movement; or it causes it; or the movement is part of the action. But if bodily movements are events, then all these ways of relating actions to bodily movements will transform actions into events as well – understood as nodes in the causal nexus (Hornsby 1980; Davidson 1980). (This is not, of course, to say that every way of relating actions and bodily movements treats actions as events.) Concomitantly, to speak of bodily movements is to speak of the body as an object rather than as a subject, as known rather than as lived; and if actions are supposed to be related to bodily movements in any of these ways, then these accounts of action treat the human body as an object and not as a subject (see Morris 1988).

If this is right, then many analytic approaches to action both impoverish our perceptual experience of the lived world and treat our relations to our own bodies as curiously external. This isn't, obviously, an *argument* against the analytic philosopher's conception of human beings and their world, nor an argument in favor of Sartre's. But the methodology of phenomenology encourages us to reflect as follows: if we find ourselves, as philosophers, unable to acknowledge what we experience as human beings, we ought to ask ourselves what pictures, what preconceptions – some would say: what intellectual prejudices – stand in our way of so doing.

See also: TRYING TO ACT (3); BODILY MOVEMENTS (4); INTENTION (14); REASONS AND CAUSES (17); WHAT A DIFFERENCE EMOTIONS MAKE (25); FREE WILL AND DETERMINISM (38); RESPONSIBILITY AND AUTONOMY (39); DAVIDSON (73).

References

Primary sources

Sartre, J.-P. (1962). *Sketch for a Theory of the Emotions* [1943], translated by P. Mairet. London: Methuen.

Sartre, J.-P. (1965). *The Psychology of the Imagination* [1940], translator unnamed. New York: Citadel Press.

Sartre, J.-P. (1986). *Being and Nothingness* [1943], translated by H. E. Barnes. London: Routledge.

Sartre, J.-P. (1992). *Notebooks for an Ethics* [1983], translated by D. Pellauer. Chicago and London: University of Chicago Press.

Secondary sources

Atwell, J. E. (1980). 'Sartre and action theory.' In H. A. Silverman and F. A. Elliston (eds), *Jean-Paul Sartre: Contemporary Approaches to his Philosophy*. Pittsburgh: Duquesne University Press, 63–104.

Ayer, A. J. (1945). Novelist-philosophers, V: Jean-Paul Sartre. *Horizon* 12, 12–26.

Davidson, D. (1980). *Essays on Actions and Events*. Oxford: Oxford University Press.

Guillaume, P. (1937). *La Psychologie de la forme* [*Gestalt psychology*]. Paris: Flammarion. [All translations mine.]

Hornsby, J. (1980). *Actions*. London: Routledge and Kegan Paul.

Lewin, K. (1935). *A Dynamic Theory of Personality: Selected Papers*, translated by D. K. Adams and K. E. Zener. New York: McGraw-Hill.

Mackie, J. (1977). *Ethics*. Harmondsworth and New York: Penguin Books Ltd.

Merleau-Ponty, M. (1962). *Phenomenology of Perception* [1945], translated by C. Smith. London and Henley: Routledge and Kegan Paul.

Moran, D. (2000). *Introduction to Phenomenology*. London and New York: Routledge.

Morris, K. J. (1988). Actions and the body: Hornsby vs. Sartre. *Philosophy and Phenomenological Research*, 68 (3), 473–488.

Morris, K. J. (2008), *Sartre*. Oxford: Blackwell (Great Minds Series).

71

Chisholm

MICHAEL J. ZIMMERMAN

Roderick M. Chisholm (1916–1999) made groundbreaking contributions to many areas of philosophy. He did pioneering work in epistemology, metaphysics, ontology, the philosophy of mind, the philosophy of language, value theory, and ethics – as well as in the philosophy of action.

Chisholm employed a distinctive method to tackle philosophical problems. First he would pose a series of puzzles in order to set in high relief the problem or problems that he wished to address; then he would introduce a small number of primitive terms that expressed concepts he believed would be readily understood by others; then he would propose analyses of further concepts in terms of the ones he had introduced; and finally he would put these analyses to work in solving the puzzles with which he had begun. He hoped thereby to improve our understanding of certain concepts which he took to be of fundamental philosophical importance. He placed a premium on precision and clarity and was scornful of those who remained content with, let alone courted, mystery and obscurity. Furthermore, he endeavored to preserve as much of our 'pre-analytic data' as rigorous reflection on the issues would permit: he believed that we are entitled to our commonsense opinions unless and until we are given good reason to reject them. There is some disagreement regarding how successful Chisholm was in elucidating the issues he addressed, but it is generally acknowledged that his method is well suited to exposing flaws not only in the philosophical views held by others but also in the views that he himself advocated. Indeed, Chisholm welcomed the sort of scrutiny of his views that his method made possible, and he was his own best critic. As a result, these views were in constant flux. Some he subjected to a series of modifications and refinements; others he threw entirely overboard. This makes it difficult to provide an overview of 'Chisholm's philosophy of *X*,' for any subject-matter *X*, including that of human action. I will therefore concentrate on the most thorough treatment of action provided by Chisholm, which is to be found in Chapter II of his [20]. To appreciate fully what he attempted to achieve in that work, though, we must begin with an earlier piece.

Background

There are a number of core issues in action theory, each of which Chisholm addressed. They may be listed as follows:

1 the nature of action (that is, what exactly it is to perform an act);
2 the nature of intentional action;
3 the nature of free action;
4 the nature of omission;
5 the individuation of acts (that is, what determines whether some act x is the same as, or is distinct from, some act y);
6 what it is to perform one act by performing another.

Although issue (1) is the most fundamental, Chisholm's initial foray into action theory in his [1] and [2] concerned issue (3).

In his [2], Chisholm raised the question of how we could ever be morally responsible for our acts. He assumed that moral responsibility requires us to have been able to avoid acting as we did, but he was unsure how this condition could ever be satisfactorily met. He posed the following dilemma (which he revisited in his [7], [9], and [13]):

[a] Either our choices have sufficient causal conditions or they do not.
[b] If they do, then they are not avoidable, in which case they are not free choices – they are not in our control – and so we are not morally responsible for them or their consequences.
[c] If they do not, then they occur fortuitously, in which case, although they may be avoidable, once again they are not in our control, and so, once again, we are not morally responsible for them or their consequences.
[d] Thus we are not morally responsible for any of our choices or their consequences.

Chisholm said that he felt certain that the conclusion of this argument is false, but he declared himself unsure about which premise or premises to reject. (He did not question the underlying assumption that moral responsibility requires avoidability.)

Chisholm recognized that some philosophers of a so-called 'compatibilist' bent would deny premise [b] of the foregoing argument on the basis of an account of avoidability according to which to say that an agent could have done otherwise is merely to say that she (or he) would have done otherwise if she had so chosen (or if she had tried, or if she had reflected further, or something along these lines), which is of course consistent with there having been a sufficient causal condition of her not having so chosen (or tried, and so on). But he rejected such an account on the grounds that it overlooks the possibility that the agent may not have been able to avoid choosing (or trying, and so on) as she did. (This was a criticism that he elaborated upon in a number of subsequent writings, including his [7], [8], [12], [13], and [20].) Right from the beginning, then, Chisholm was inclined towards incompatibilism – that is, to the view that freedom of choice and action, and hence moral responsibility, is incompatible with there being a sufficient causal condition of one's choice or act. Indeed, this was a view he came to endorse wholeheartedly and never relinquished.

What Chisholm did come to question, though, was premise [c] of the argument. He did so on the basis of attributing to agents the power to control choices and acts that lack sufficient causal conditions. Although at first Chisholm feared that such a power was 'impossible to conceive' ([2], p. 159), he quickly arrived at the view that it provided the best solution to the dilemma. In his [7], he held that, when acting freely, an agent is the 'immanent cause' of her own acts; he took such causation of an event by an *agent*, which he sometimes referred to simply as 'agent causation,' to be quite distinct from what he called 'transeunt causation' or 'event causation' – that is, the causing of an event by another *event*. He acknowledged that events or states, including the agent's own desires, might contribute causally to her behavior (in that she would not have behaved as she did, had not these events or states occurred); but no state or event, and no combination of states or events, can constitute a sufficient causal condition of a free act. The agent's behavior, then, will not be necessitated by any state or event (although her desires may incline her to act as she does), and thus the condition of avoidability will be satisfied. But, given that she is the cause of her own acts, her behavior will not occur fortuitously, and hence it is something for which she may be morally responsible after all. Chisholm summarized his position in the following memorable passage ([7], section 11):

> If we are responsible [...] then we have a prerogative which some would attribute only to God: each of us, when we act, is a prime mover unmoved. In doing what we do, we cause certain events to happen, and nothing – or no one – causes us to cause those events to happen.

In developing his account of how it is possible for us to be morally responsible for our acts, Chisholm was prompted to inquire into the nature of action as such. Thus he turned from issue (3) to issue (1). He noted immediately that being the cause of certain events is not sufficient to render one's behavior an instance of genuine action. Action, he claimed in his [5] and in all subsequent works ([7], [9]–[11], [13], [14], [17], [18], [20]–[22], [24], [25], and [30]) in which he discussed the matter, is essentially purposeful. Whenever someone acts, she undertakes or endeavors to make something happen, to bring something about; she acts with the intention of achieving some end or goal. Chisholm made it clear, however, that this does not mean that all action is intentional, since it is obvious that we sometimes act unintentionally, in that the intention with which we act may not be satisfied; that is, the end we seek may not be realized. He took great pains to explain what it is that renders an act intentional (issue (2)). In the course of doing this he also addressed issue (6), noting that there are some things which we bring about directly, namely those events (presumably, certain cerebral events) which we cause immediately, by virtue of the exercise of our causal powers; other things (such as the movement of a finger or the firing of a gun) we bring about only indirectly, insofar as they are the effects of events that we bring about directly. In this context Chisholm also discussed the distinction between basic and non-basic action. A basic act is, roughly, one which, like every act, is undertaken as a means to some further end, but nothing is undertaken as a means to it; a non-basic act is one which is such that some other act is undertaken as a means to it. For example, shooting a gun will typically be a non-basic act, insofar as moving one's finger (or something of the sort) will be undertaken as a means to it; one shoots the gun *by* moving one's finger. But, typically, nothing will be undertaken as a means to moving one's finger, and so this will be a basic act (see chapter 2).

Chisholm's Theory of Action

Let me turn now to a more detailed (though still sketchy) presentation of Chisholm's most thorough discussion of action: the one provided in his [20], in which he not only elaborates on the proposals mentioned above regarding issues (1), (2), (3), and (6), but also addresses issues (4) and (5). In this discussion he is concerned to find solutions to the following puzzles.

[i] How can anyone ever be morally responsible for an act? Such an act must be avoidable, and yet physiology indicates that whatever an agent accomplishes, for instance the movement of a finger, is something for which there is a sufficient causal condition (of which some cerebral event is a part).

[ii] Moving one's finger is often taken to be a basic act. But how can this be correct, if the finger's movement is caused only indirectly, by way of some cerebral event?

[iii] Suppose that a patient wakes up in a hospital bed and discovers that she is paralyzed. She cannot even move a finger. How can she discover this unless there is something else that she usually does for the purpose of moving her finger? But then it seems, once again, that moving one's finger is not a basic act after all.

[iv] Suppose that, in the course of a physical examination, a patient is told to move certain muscles and, in order to comply, she raises her arm. How can she move her muscles by raising her arm if it is the muscle motion that causes her arm to rise?

[v] Oedipus' father was identical with Laius. Oedipus intentionally killed Laius but did not intentionally kill his father. How can this be?

To resolve these and other puzzles, Chisholm begins by asking what it means to say that an act is avoidable in the manner required (as he believes) for moral responsibility. He notes that to say that an agent 'could have done otherwise' in the relevant sense is not to say that everything she did was something she could have refrained from doing, or that acting otherwise was morally or legally permissible, or that she had a general ability to do otherwise, or that she knew how to do otherwise, or that it was epistemically possible (that is, consistent with everything that was known at the time) that she do otherwise, or merely that she would have done otherwise if she had so chosen (since, as noted above, this is consistent with her being such that she could not have chosen otherwise), or merely that it was physically possible (that is, consistent with the laws of nature) that she do otherwise (since this is consistent with there having been a sufficient causal condition of her not doing otherwise), or merely that it was causally possible that she do otherwise (since the behavior of sub-atomic particles may lack sufficient causal conditions and so not be causally necessitated, and yet it would not follow that these particles could have behaved otherwise in the relevant sense). In order to clarify the relevant sense of 'could have done otherwise' and to elucidate other issues in the theory of action, Chisholm introduces six primitive concepts that he thinks we will readily understand and on the basis of which he offers analyses of several further important concepts. These primitive concepts are those of: a state of affairs (of which a proposition is one type and an event is another) – for example, the obtaining state of affairs of there being horses and the non-obtaining state of affairs of there being unicorns; consideration, which consists in entertaining or thinking about some state of affairs – as when one entertains the thought that there are horses or the thought that there are unicorns; acceptance, which consists in believing something – as when one accepts or believes that there are horses but not that there are unicorns; physical necessity, which has to do with whether some state of affairs is, or is implied by, some law of nature; causal contribution, which has to do with some state or event being the causal consequence of something else, which contributes to its occurrence; and undertaking, which he takes to lie at the heart of all genuine agency, in that, whenever one acts, one undertakes something – that is, there is something that one endeavors to achieve, even if one is not always successful in one's endeavors. Among the analyses he proposes are the following (all of which are stated here only roughly; there is no space to render and discuss them in detail):

(A) There occurs a sufficient causal condition of p = df. for some q, it is physically necessary that, if q occurs, then p occurs.

(B) S is free to undertake p = df. there occurs no sufficient causal condition either of S undertaking p or of S not undertaking p.

(C) p is directly within S's power = df. for some q, S is free to undertake q and S-undertaking-q would either be identical with, or contribute causally to, p.

(D) p is within S's power = df. p is a member of a series such that the first is directly within S's power and each of the others (if any) is such that its predecessor is a sufficient causal condition of its being directly within her power.

The last of these analyses captures Chisholm's conception of 'could have done otherwise.' Roughly, an agent could have performed some act other than the one which she did perform, just in case it was causally possible for her to undertake some event q distinct from the event p, which she did in fact undertake and, had she undertaken q instead of p, she would either have performed the act in question or have enabled herself to do so. Because it was causally possible for the agent to undertake q instead of p, her undertaking p was not causally necessitated; that is, there was no sufficient causal condition of her undertaking p. (Since sub-atomic particles cannot undertake anything, they cannot do otherwise, in the relevant sense, even if their behavior lacks sufficient causal conditions.) This does not mean, however, that nothing contributed causally to her undertaking p, since many of the conditions under which the undertaking occurred (including the desires the agent had and the options she faced) may have been necessary for it to have occurred.

When he first endorsed the idea of an agent as a prime mover unmoved, Chisholm offered no analysis of the type of causation at issue. As noted above, he took agent causation to be a species of causation quite distinct from that of event causation. But in his [20] he reverses himself on this matter and claims that agent causation can be analyzed in terms of event causation (and other concepts) after all. (This is a claim he upheld many years later when he returned to the issue in his [30].) He offers the following account of what it is for an agent to contribute causally to an event:

(E) *S* contributes causally to *p* = df. for some *q*, *S* undertakes *q* and either
  (i) *S*-undertaking-*q* is identical with *p*, or
  (ii) *S*-undertaking-*q* contributes causally to *p*.

The first clause expresses the idea that an agent contributes causally to her own undertakings; the second, that she contributes causally to the effects of her undertakings. Chisholm in fact adds a third clause, which is supposed to capture the idea that an agent also contributes causally to her own causal contributions. For technical reasons that cannot be discussed here, the clause does not quite succeed in capturing this idea, which is one he introduced as an assumption in some of his earlier work (including his [9], [10], [13], and [17]–[19]). He did not mention it when he first endorsed the idea of agent causation in [7] – where he said, as quoted above, that in doing what we do we cause certain events to happen, but nothing or no one causes us to do so. But he soon came to the view that, on the contrary, when we cause certain events to happen, there is indeed something or someone who causes us to do so, namely we ourselves. And he evidently came to this view because he recognized that, if it is unacceptable to hold that the mere absence of a sufficient causal condition of an act is enough to render that act something that is in the agent's control, since the act may occur wholly fortuitously, then simply adding that the agent contributes causally to her act will not ensure that it lies within her control, if her so doing is compatible with that very causal contribution occurring fortuitously. The control needed for morally responsible agency thus requires not only that the agent should contribute causally to her act, but also that she should contribute causally to her own causal contributions.

Next, Chisholm gives a brief account of omission. He proposes:

(F) *S* deliberately omits undertaking *p* = df. *S* considers undertaking *p* but does not undertake it.

He then goes on to give an extensive account of intentional action, one that builds on his treatment of this topic in earlier works ([3]–[6], [9]–[11], [13], [14], [17], and [18]). The highlights of this account are as follows. Chisholm notes that to say that *S* undertakes *p* is to say that she acts with the intention of bringing about, that is, of contributing causally to, *p*. This does not mean that *S* consciously entertains, or considers, *p* (although she may of course do so), or that *S* desires *p* (although again she may), or that *p* occurs (since *S* may be unsuccessful in achieving what she undertakes). Furthermore, when *S* undertakes *p*, this may or may not be with some further end in mind. Regarding such further ends, Chisholm proposes:

(G) *S* undertakes *p* for the purpose of bringing about *q* = df. *S* undertakes both
  (i) *p* and
  (ii) *S*-undertaking-*p* contributing causally to *q*.

The second clause is designed to allow for the possibility that *p* is not itself intended as a means to *q*, since *q* may occur prior to *p*. (Consider a case in which one aims to hit a target with a certain arrow, for the purpose of having the arrow traverse the space between oneself and the target.) Chisholm notes that something may be undertaken *merely* as a means to some other end, or it may be undertaken both as a means to some other end and for its own sake. He suggests:

(H) *p* is for *S* a mere means to something else = df. for some *q*,
  (i) *S* undertakes *p* for the purpose of bringing about *q*, and
  (ii) there is nothing that *S* undertakes for the purpose of bringing about *p*.

(I) *p* is an ultimate end for *S* = df.
  (i) *S* undertakes *p*, and
  (ii) it is not the case that *p* is for *S* a mere means to something else.

Chisholm then goes on to give an account of the steps one may take in order to achieve some end. He distinguishes between what he calls preliminary steps and (final) attempts thus:

(J) *S* undertakes *p* as a preliminary step toward bringing about *q* = df. *S* undertakes *p* for the purpose of bringing it about that someone (whether *S* or someone else) brings about *q*.

(K) *S* makes an attempt to bring about *p* = df. *S* undertakes *p* and does not undertake anything as a preliminary step toward *p*.

Finally, and perhaps most importantly, Chisholm observes that succeeding in bringing about what one undertakes to bring about does not necessarily mean that one has acted intentionally. For some successes may be inadvertent, as when a would-be assassin is driving to his intended victim's house and accidentally runs over a pedestrian, only to discover that the pedestrian is his intended victim. A distinction is to be drawn between being successful and being completely successful. Chisholm proposes:

(L) *S* is completely successful in his endeavor to bring about *p* = df.
  (i) *S* makes an attempt to bring about *p*, and
  (ii) everything *S* then undertakes for the purpose of bringing about *p* contributes causally to *p*.

If one is completely successful in one's endeavor, then one has acted intentionally.

Chisholm turns next to the question of what it is to perform one act by performing another. Sometimes we undertake certain things by undertaking others. The former are thus undertaken only indirectly; whether the latter are undertaken directly depends on whether they are in turn undertaken by way of something else being undertaken. In any case, some things must be undertaken directly if anything is to be undertaken at all. This is what basic action consists in. Chisholm says:

(M) *S* brings about *p* as a basic act = df.
  (i) *S*-undertaking-*p* contributes causally to *p*, and
  (ii) there is nothing that *S* undertakes for the purpose of bringing about *p*.

Chisholm notes, further, that we must take care to distinguish between those things that are directly undertaken and those things that are directly brought about:

(N) *S* brings about *p* directly = df.
  (i) *S* contributes causally to *p*, and
  (ii) there is nothing, *q*, such that *S* contributes causally to *q* and *q* contributes causally to *p*.

Each of analyses M and N provides for a different sense in which one may do something indirectly *by* doing another directly.

It is surprising that, despite the care that Chisholm takes to develop his account of action, nowhere in his [20] does he say precisely what he takes either acting or an act to be. Regarding the former issue, there are two possibilities. He might say that to act is simply to undertake something, or he might say that to act is to bring about something, that is, to contribute causally to something by virtue of some undertaking. In favor of the former is the fact that Chisholm holds all undertakings, whether efficacious or not, to involve the exercise of an agent's agent-causal powers, and it seems odd to say that there can be agent causation without agency. In favor of the latter is analysis M above, which requires that an undertaking be efficacious in order for a basic act to occur, and it seems odd to say that there can be action without basic action. As for what Chisholm takes an act to be, it is unclear whether analysis M is to be construed as implying that it is *p* that is a basic act or as implying that it is the bringing about of *p* that is a basic act. In either case, it might seem that, when it comes to issue (5), Chisholm is committed by his ontological presuppositions to the view that acts are to be individuated very finely indeed. For he holds (as in his [15], [16], and [21]–[23]) that acts are events and that events are a species of states of affairs, and he claims ([20], p. 118) that a state of affairs *p* is identical with a state of affairs *q* if and only if *p* entails and is entailed by *q*, where:

(O) *p* entails *q* = df. *p* is necessarily such that
  (i) if it obtains then *q* obtains, and
  (ii) whoever accepts it accepts *q*.

On this view, the state of affairs which is Smith flipping a switch is distinct from that which is Smith turning on a light, which in turn is distinct from that which is Smith illuminating a room. Indeed, the first of these states of affairs is even distinct from that state of affairs which is Smith intentionally flipping a switch. Nonetheless, there is some evidence that Chisholm would resist the idea that acts are to be so finely individuated, since in his [22] he suggested that an agent's act is to be identified with that conjunctive state of affairs consisting of her undertaking *together with* everything to which the undertaking contributes causally. (In still later writings, [26]–[33], in which he discussed the metaphysics of events, Chisholm abandoned entirely the view that acts constitute a subspecies of states of affairs in favor of the view that they are contingent entities, which exist only when they occur.)

On the basis of analyses A–O, Chisholm offers the following solutions to the puzzles that he posed.

[i] The movement of one's finger may be caused by some cerebral event; but, as long as one is the cause of (that is, contributes causally to) the latter, one is also the

cause of the former, and, as long as the latter is avoidable, so is the former. (See analyses D and E.)

[ii] Even if what one brings about directly is some cerebral event, one's bringing it about does not constitute a basic act if (as is typically the case) one does not undertake to bring it about; whereas moving one's finger is a basic act if (as is typically the case) there is nothing one undertakes for the purpose of bringing it about. (See analyses M and N.)

[iii] When someone discovers that she has lost the ability to perform some basic act, she has not undertaken something else for the purpose of bringing about her performing that act. She has simply undertaken to perform the act and failed. (See analysis M.)

[iv] Even though the motion of some muscles causes a person's arm to go up, she will have moved these muscles by raising her arm if, even though she did not endeavor to make her muscles move as a consequence of her arm's going up, she did endeavor to make them move as a consequence of her *undertaking* to make her arm go up. (See analysis G.)

[v] That state of affairs which is Oedipus killing Laius is distinct from that which is Oedipus killing his father. (See analysis O.) Hence it is perfectly possible for Oedipus to undertake the former without undertaking the latter, and hence to accomplish the former intentionally and yet not accomplish the latter intentionally. (See analysis L.)

Remaining Questions

As noted at the outset, the precision that Chisholm both sought and achieved by virtue of his method makes it possible to examine his proposals in detail and thereby to make real progress with the problems he addressed. There is no space here, however, to engage in such examination of the theory of action laid out in the last section; that is an exercise I will leave to the reader. Instead, let me simply raise three general worries concerning some assumptions underlying Chisholm's theory.

First, Chisholm's assumption that moral responsibility requires avoidability needs support. Although he never entertained doubts about this assumption in any of his writings, it is a thesis that was famously attacked in Frankfurt (1969) and which remains a topic of intense debate to this day.

Second, Chisholm's rejection of compatibilism also needs further support. Even if his argument against the compatibilist-friendly analysis of 'She could have done otherwise' in terms of 'She would have done otherwise if she had so chosen (or tried, and so on)' is sound, this leaves open the possibility that the former is to be understood in some other way which is consistent with the view that a person could have done otherwise even if there was a sufficient causal condition of her acting as she did.

Finally and perhaps most importantly, in taking agent causation to lie at the heart of all human agency, Chisholm appears not to have sufficiently appreciated the difference between issues (1) and (3). He originally invoked the concept of a special kind of agent causation in order to account for freedom of action. Perhaps he was correct in doing so; perhaps not. (One reason to think that he was not correct in doing so is that, in the absence of any positive characterization of agent causation beyond the claim that it is indeterministic and involves undertaking, it is not clear how it could help to provide the sort of control necessary for responsibility.) But, even if he was correct in doing so, that is, even if *free* action requires such causation, why think that *all* action does? (Chisholm was not alone in making this transition. See, in particular, Reid (1969) and Taylor (1966).) It is surely a pre-analytic datum that people sometimes engage in genuine agency, and there is little reason to think that we should reject this datum, were it to turn out that determinism is true. If so, it would seem to be a mistake to assume that all agency is essentially indeterministic. Perhaps we cannot be *morally responsible* for any of our acts that have a sufficient causal condition; nonetheless, they would appear to remain our *acts*.

See also: ACTION THEORY AND ONTOLOGY (1); BASIC ACTIONS AND INDIVIDUATION (2); TRYING TO ACT (3); REFRAINING, OMITTING, AND NEGATIVE ACTS (7); INTENTION (14); REASONS AND CAUSES (17); DEVIANT CAUSAL CHAINS (21); AGENCY, PATIENCY, AND PERSONHOOD (26); AGENT CAUSATION (28); FREE WILL AND DETERMINISM (38); RESPONSIBILITY AND AUTONOMY (39); REID (62); KANT (64).

References

Primary sources

[1] Chisholm, R. M. (1948). Review of S. Hook and M. R. Konvitz (eds), *Freedom and Experience*. *Philosophical Review*, 57, 613–619.

[2] Chisholm, R. M. (1958). Responsibility and avoidability. In S. Hook (ed.), *Determinism and Freedom in the Age of Modern Science*. New York: New York University Press, 145–146.

[3] Chisholm, R. M. (1959). Review of *Intention*, by G. E. M. Anscombe. *Philosophical Review*, 68, 110–115.

[4] Chisholm, R. M., and Taylor, R. (1960). Making things to have happened. *Analysis*, 20, 73–78.

[5] Chisholm, R. M. (1961). What Is It to Act upon a Proposition? *Analysis*, 22, 1–6.

[6] Chisholm, R. M. (1964). The descriptive element in the concept of action. *Journal of Philosophy*, 61, 613–625.

[7] Chisholm, R. M. (1964). *Human Freedom and the Self*. Lawrence: University of Kansas Press.

[8] Chisholm, R. M. (1964). J. L. Austin's Philosophical Papers. *Mind*, 73, 1–26.

[9] Chisholm, R. M. (1966). Freedom and Action. In K. Lehrer (ed.), *Freedom and Determinism*. New York: Random House, 11–44.

[10] Chisholm, R. M. (1967). Comments on D. Davidson's 'The logical form of action sentences.' In N. Rescher (ed.), *The Logic of Decision and Action*. Pittsburgh: University of Pittsburgh Press, 113–114.

[11] Chisholm, R. M. (1967a). Comments on von Wright's 'The Logic of Action.' In N. Rescher (ed.), *The Logic of Decision and Action*. Pittsburgh: University of Pittsburgh Press, 137–139.

[12] Chisholm, R. M. (1967b). He could have done otherwise. *Journal of Philosophy*, 64, 409–418.

[13] Chisholm, R. M. (1969). Some puzzles about agency. In Karel Lambert (ed.), *The Logical Way of Doing Things*. New Haven: Yale University Press, 199–217.

[14] Chisholm, R. M. (1970a). The structure of intention. *Journal of Philosophy*, 67, 633–647.

[15] Chisholm, R. M. (1970b). Events and propositions. *Nous* 4, 15–24.

[16] Chisholm, R. M. (1971a). States of affairs again. *Nous* 5, 179–189.

[17] Chisholm, R. M. (1971b). Reflections on human agency. *Idealistic Studies*, 1, 33–46.

[18] Chisholm, R. M. (1971c). On the logic of intentional action. In R. Binkley, R. Bronaugh, and A. Marras (eds), *Agent, Action and Reason*. Toronto: University of Toronto Press, 38–69.

[19] Chisholm, R. M. (1971d). Reply. In R. Binkley, R. Bronaugh, and A. Marras (eds), *Agent, Action and Reason*. Toronto: University of Toronto Press, 76–80.

[20] Chisholm, R. M. (1976a). *Person and Object*. La Salle: Open Court.

[21] Chisholm, R. M. (1976b). The agent as cause. In M. Brand and D. Walton (eds), *Action Theory*. Dordrecht: D. Reidel, 199–211.

[22] Chisholm, R. M. (1979). Objects and persons: Revision and replies. In E. Sosa (ed.), *Essays on the Philosophy of Roderick M. Chisholm*. Amsterdam: Rodopi, 317–388.

[23] Chisholm, R. M. (1981). *The First Person*. Minneapolis: University of Minnesota Press.

[24] Chisholm, R. M. (1985). Self-profile. In R. Bogdan (ed.), *Roderick M. Chisholm*. Dordrecht: Reidel, 3–77.

[25] Chisholm, R. M. (1985). Replies. In R. Bogdan (ed.), *Roderick M. Chisholm*. Dordrecht: Reidel, 195–216.

[26] Chisholm, R. M. (1985–86). On the positive and negative states of things. *Grazer Philosophische Studien*, 25/26, 97–106.

[27] Chisholm, R. M. (1989). *On Metaphysics*. Minneapolis: University of Minnesota Press.

[28] Chisholm, R. M. (1990). Events without times. *Nous*, 24, 413–428.

[29] Chisholm, R. M. (1992). The basic ontological categories. In K. Mulligan (ed.), *Language, Truth, and Ontology*. Dordrecht: Kluwer, 1–13.

[30] Chisholm, R. M. (1995). Agents, causes, and events. In T. O'Connor (ed.), *Agents, Causes, and Events*. Oxford: Oxford University Press, 95–100.

[31] Chisholm, R. M. (1996). *A Realistic Theory of Categories*. Cambridge: Cambridge University Press.

[32] Chisholm, R. M. (1997). Reply to Dean W. Zimmerman. In L. Hahn (ed.), *The Philosophy of Roderick M. Chisholm*. La Salle: Open Court, 101–105.

[33] Chisholm, R. M. (1997). Reply to Johannes L. Brandl. In L. Hahn (ed.), *The Philosophy of Roderick M. Chisholm*. La Salle: Open Court, 478–479.

Secondary sources

Frankfurt, H. G. (1969). Alternate possibilities and moral responsibility. *Journal of Philosophy*, 66, 829–839.

Reid, T. (1969). *Essays on the Active Powers of the Human Mind* [1788]. Cambridge, MA: MIT Press.

Taylor, R. (1966). *Action and Purpose*. Englewood Cliffs: Prentice-Hall.

Further reading

Bogdan, R. (ed.) (1985). *Roderick M. Chisholm*. Dordrecht: Reidel.

Hahn, L. (ed.) (1997). *The Philosophy of Roderick M. Chisholm*. La Salle: Open Court.

Lehrer, K. (ed.) (1975). *Analysis and Metaphysics: Essays in Honor of R. M. Chisholm*. Dordrecht: Reidel.

O'Connor, T. (2000). *Persons and Causes: The Metaphysics of Free Will*. New York: Oxford University Press. [Especially ch. 3.]

Sosa, E. (ed.) (1979). *Essays on the Philosophy of Roderick M. Chisholm*. Amsterdam: Rodopi.

72

von Wright

FREDERICK STOUTLAND

Georg Henrik von Wright (1916–2003) wrote a great deal about the philosophy of action, and his writings ranged from a formal logic of action embedded in a logic of change to a general account of the nature of action, which was written in the style of analytical philosophy while drawing on the later Wittgenstein and on the hermeneutic tradition. I will only discuss here his general account, and I will focus on his distinction between behavior 'explained teleologically as action [and behavior] explained causally as movement,' a distinction he grounded in 'two ways of conceptualizing behavior' (Hahn and Schilpp 1989: 808). My aim is to illuminate aspects of von Wright's view that remain significant for contemporary philosophy of action.

von Wright on Causality

von Wright's notion of behavior 'explained causally as movement' (as a body's moving) presumes his conception of causality, which he called 'Humean,' since he regarded causality as a matter of general laws, which he took to have modal force: *c* causes *e* only if, whenever *c* occurs, *e necessarily* occurs. Although von Wright granted that the term 'cause' was legitimately used in other ways too, he objected to 'the use of the technical term 'causal explanation' for explanations that do not conform to the covering law model' (von Wright 1971: 193). In denying that *R* is a cause he always had this conception in mind; and, since such a conception blurs the distinction between causal *explanation*, which connects facts, and causal *efficacy*, which relates particular events (because, if *c*'s causally explaining *e* entails that *c* is necessarily followed by *e*, then *c* is causally efficacious of *e*), he denied both that *R* figured in a covering law explanation and that it was causally efficacious.

Explanation is *intensional* in that whether *c explains e* depends on how they are described. Proponents of the covering law model tend to disregard this because, although a necessary connection between *c* and *e* depends on how they are described, that connection entails that *c* is causally *efficacious* of *e*, and intensionality is irrelevant to this fact. von Wright, however, took seriously the intensionality of covering law explanations, and hence he held that phenomena can be causally explained only if they are described or conceptualized in an appropriate way. That way, the one involving covering laws, is not, he argued, the only legitimate way and, in crucial respects, not the most fundamental one – points to which I return below.

Actions, Events, and Intentionality; Results and Consequences

Acts, von Wright wrote (1963: 35), are not 'a kind or species of events. But many acts may [...] be described as the bringing about or *effecting* ('at will') of a change [...]' I take that to mean that acting requires an agent's intentionally bringing about one or more events. For example, opening the window is intentionally bringing about the opening of the window (an event) by turning the handle (an action), which is intentionally bringing about the turning of the handle (an event) by moving one's hand (an action), which is the origin of one's acting. However, there need be no bodily movements additional to moving one's hand with the intention of bringing about some event: given the appropriate circumstances, that movement *is* turning the handle and opening the window. That is to say, in acting in a particular way, an agent does different kinds of things, depending on the circumstances in which she acts – things which we can call her *actions*.

The claim that acting is intentionally bringing about an event does not involve the further claim that all actions are intentional. Intentionally bringing about the opening of a window is intentionally opening a window, but in so acting one unintentionally brings about the cooling of the room. Every acting is both an intentional and a non-intentional bringing about of events, and hence is intentional under some descriptions and not intentional under others (or it is the performance of some actions that are intentional and some that are not). But acting is *essentially* intentional in that it *must* be intentional under *some* description; bringing about events unintentionally (inadvertently, in ignorance, and so on) is therefore a lesser, derivative form of acting.

von Wright carefully distinguished *acts* from the *events* brought about in acting. He called the event that must occur in order for it to be said that an agent has performed a certain action the *result* of that action. (In what follows, I shall put this technical use of 'result' in italics.) Thus the window's opening is the *result* of an agent's opening it – and the criterion for judging that he has done so. But an action *A* is not the cause (in von Wright's sense) of its own *result*; the cause of the latter is the *result* of the action that is the bringing about of *A*'s *result*. The cause of the window's opening is not an agent's opening it but the handle's turning, which is the *result* of her turning the handle – the act whereby the agent brings about its opening. To assert that the window is opening *because* Gwen is opening it rules out its opening by itself or by someone else. But, *given* that Gwen is opening it, it follows *logically* that it is opening, and hence her opening it is not a substantive – hence not a causal – explanation of its opening.

The *result* of an action causes numerous events, which von Wright (1971: 87) called its 'consequences.' The *result* of Gwen's opening the window is its opening, whose consequences include fresh air coming in, the room getting cool, mosquitoes flying in, and so on. These consequences are, in turn, the *results* of other of her actions – her bringing in fresh air, cooling the room, letting in the mosquitoes – because they are all brought about by her acting intentionally under a description. The events she brings about intentionally are *results* of her intentional actions; those she brings about non-intentionally are *results* of her non-intentional actions. There is no causal difference between her intentionally and her non-intentionally bringing about an event, since in either case the event is a consequence of, hence something caused by the *result* of, the action whereby she brings it about – ultimately by the movements of her limbs, which are the *result* of her moving them. The difference between her bringing about an event *with* the intention or *without* the intention of bringing it about is teleological, not causal.

Typically, the actions an agent performs in acting are sequentially structured, one action being done in order to do another, in order to do another, and so on: Gwen turns the handle with the intention to open the window with the intention to freshen the air. Such actions are intentional, if completed, and the first two at least are explained teleologically, as done in order to do (or to intend to do) something. Their completion presumes causation (since bringing about an event is causal), which obtains not between the actions, but between events that are *results* of the actions. This is also true of an agent's non-intentional actions: someone's inadvertently cooling the room does not cause other actions she performs. Although a non-intentional action is the *agent's* action – *her* bringing about an event – only because its origin is in her intentionally moving her limbs, it is not explained teleologically as being done in order to do something.

The events an agent brings about non-intentionally are not sequentially structured parts of his intentional acting; while belonging to some causal chain or other, they are random relative to the agent's acting. This is not so for events that an agent brings about intentionally. The handle does not turn randomly but intentionally, its turning being directed toward opening the window, which is directed toward letting in fresh air. These are events that are explained teleologically; they are, von Wright said, 'vested' with intentionality. While their occurrence presumes causal relations to other events, their explanation is that an agent intentionally brings them about.

These same events could also be explained causally. Fresh air coming in is caused by the window's opening, caused by the handle's turning, caused by muscle contractions, caused by neural impulses from the brain, and so on. But they can be explained in this way only if they are described in non-intentional terms as instances of physical event types suitable for inclusion in a law of nature, or as elements in a causal structure modeled by scientific theories. Thus described, they belong to the conceptual frame of the natural sciences, where there are causal chains and structures but no agents who act intentionally (von Wright 1971: 124).

Practical Inference and the Logical Connection Argument

The 'standard' causalist account of action regards von Wright's distinction between teleological and causal explanation as being essentially one between the *kinds* of causes involved. On this account, intentionally bringing about an event differs from merely bringing about an event in that, in the former case, an agent's intentions (or desires) and beliefs cause the event in the right way, whereas in the latter they do not. This is the claim von Wright criticized through his version of the 'logical connection argument,' which focused on the agent's bodily movements, because his analysis of an agent's acting as intentionally bringing about an event does not apply to them. If it did, an agent's bodily movements would be caused by the event that is the result of the action that she performs with the intention to move her body. But there is no such action: intentionally moving one's body, described as such, is a basic action, hence not done by doing something with the intention to move it. Although moving one's leg is not a basic action if one moves it by lifting it with one's arms, the normal case is that one moves one's limbs not *by* doing something, but one simply moves them.

We can explain an agent's moving her limbs *teleologically*. The explanation of Gwen's moving her hand, for example, is that she does so with the intention to turn the handle and open the window. But we cannot claim that she does something with the intention to move her hand, nor that her hand's movement is caused by her moving it, since an action does not cause its result. We have to take her intentionally moving her hand as the origin of her acting and explain it, not in terms of her intentionally bringing about its movement, but in terms of the actions she intends to be doing in moving it.

von Wright denied that the latter is a causal explanation either of her moving her hand or of that movement of her hand that is the *result* – the criterion – of her having moved it. To claim that her body moves because she intentionally moves it does rule out its moving randomly – because of a tic, electric shock, or because others move it; but that is not a causal explanation of its moving. von Wright's view is that a causal explanation of an agent's bodily movements requires that we conceptualize or describe them as non-intentional events governed by causal laws. Instead of conceptualizing the agent as intentionally moving her body, we must conceive of her bodily movements as intermediary between neural events internal to her body and external events caused by her bodily movements. That an agent's intentions and beliefs are no part of this chain is the point of his logical connection argument.

I shall only summarize the argument's main thrust, which von Wright (1971: 107; 1983) put in the form of a practical inference. Its premises are that an agent intends to open a window and believes he cannot do so unless he turns the handle; its conclusion is that he 'sets himself' to turn the handle, that is, moves his body with the intention to do so. von Wright argued that, if this expressed a *causal* explanation, the conclusion would follow from the premises only if we added a causal law that covers the agent's intention and belief and connects them with the conclusion. But the argument, he claimed, is valid as it stands (given ability, no impediments, and other conditions), and hence it does not express a causal explanation. An agent who intends to open a window and believes he must now turn the handle to do so will necessarily set himself to turn the handle; if he does nothing or something other than turning the handle, it follows logically that he didn't intend to open the window, that he didn't believe that he must turn the handle to do so, or that the conditions – on ability and so on – did not obtain.

von Wright defended this account by noting that, if a practical inference is to serve in explanation (rather than in deliberation), we must begin with its conclusion – that an agent sets herself to act in a certain way. But we cannot simply take for granted *what* the agent sets herself to do in moving her body. We cannot, for instance, take for granted that Gwen is setting herself to turn the handle to open the window. Perhaps she is moving her hand with the intention to close the window or to turn off the lights. Perhaps she is not intentionally moving her hand, but her elbow (her hand is sore) in order to open the window that way. The point is that what the practical inference can explain is not her moving her body in some particular way, but what she intends to do in moving it. But in order to discern that we must know her intention and what she thinks necessary to realize it, which is precisely what the premises of the inference specify. Establishing those premises, however, is not independent of observing what she is doing on this occasion. This means that we have a (hermeneutic) circle: establishing what an agent is intentionally doing is not independent of establishing the intention and the belief with which she is doing it, and vice versa (von Wright 1971: 117).

The conclusion of the practical inference is not that, given the premises, the agent must be moving his body in some particular way. Its conclusion is that, however he is moving his body, it must be understood as his setting himself to act in a certain way – as his beginning to act with a certain intention. If he intends to open the window and believes he must turn the handle in order to do so, then, whatever the movements of his body, he is moving it in order to turn the handle – even if he uses his teeth, or his elbow. The point of the practical inference is to situate his moving his body and the movements that are its *result* in the conceptual frame of action, thereby enabling their teleological explanation, which is what enables understanding them as his acting in the first place. To understand them as non-intentional movements caused by muscle contractions and by neural processes is to situate them in a different conceptual frame, where there are causal chains but no intentional agents. (For a related but different view of practical inference, see chapter 74.)

This version of the logical connection argument is not undermined by Davidsonian objections. It does not assume the confused claim that conceptual connections between intentions and actions rule out causal relations between events, since von Wright thought that intentions (and beliefs) are not events but *states* of agents, and hence that their role is not to produce actions but to *explain* them. His version of the argument holds, first, that, if an explanation is causal, it must involve covering laws, and, second, that if the explanatory premises alone conceptually necessitate the conclusion, then thed explanation does not involve such laws. The second claim is unobjectionable, but I agree with Davidson's objection to the first – the claim that causation must involve covering laws. That is not a devastating objection, however, since von Wright granted that there are legitimate senses of 'cause' which do not assume covering laws – which means that, on this point, his difference with Davidson is largely terminological.

Two Kinds of Explanation and Their Compatibility and Congruence

von Wright's view of the relation between the two conceptual frames is complex. He holds that events which are intentional *as results* of actions can also be described or conceptualized *as* non-intentional events in the frame of natural science, and hence can be explained in terms of either frame. Since events are explained only *as* described or conceptualized, the two kinds of explanation have different *explananda*, and consequently are compatible (von Wright 1971: 124).

Nor is either kind dispensable. Even if an event can be conceptualized as part of a causal chain extending indefinitely into the past, it may not have occurred unless an agent intentionally brought it about. We think, for instance, that the window would not have opened, had Gwen not opened it. Should we discover, however, that it would have opened anyway, because a timing mechanism caused it to open at that very moment, we would probably conclude that she didn't open it, but only turned the handle with the intention to open it. Should we also discover that the handle would have turned anyway because of some hidden mechanism, we might conclude that her acting was only her moving her hand with the intention to turn the handle. But, should we discover that some event caused her hand to move at that very moment, so that it would have moved even if she had not moved it, we cannot conclude that her acting was only her doing something with the intention to move her hand: since moving her hand is a basic action, there is no such action. We might conclude that she was not acting at all; but, von Wright argued, we should, under certain conditions, conclude that she was acting in moving her hand even if her hand would have moved anyway. Her moving her hand could be explained in action terms as done with the intention to turn the handle and open the window. The two kinds of explanation are thus compatible and neither is superfluous (von Wright 1971: 125f; 1973: 122f).

von Wright's compatibilism follows:

> Determinism is compatible with action *in the sense that* every change in the world which results from the action of an agent, i.e., is imputed to agency, might also have resulted from another change which is its causally sufficient condition. (von Wright 1973: 133)

The previous paragraph shows why he thinks that determinism is no threat to intentional agency. But he adds a further consideration, namely that the explanation of events in terms of their causes is *secondary* to their explanation as the results of intentional actions. He has two arguments for this. The first appeals to his 'interventionist conception of causality,' according to which establishing a causally necessary connection between events requires intervening experimentally in a situation by (to put it roughly) bringing about *c* and noting whether *e* results. Intervening in that way assumes that *e* would not occur on that occasion unless we brought about *c*, that is, unless we acted, which means that 'the concept of cause [is] secondary to the concept of human action.' (1973: 136)

The second argument appeals to his account of a 'congruence' between actions and bodily movements. When an agent acts intentionally, various movements of her body occur that enable her to act in that way and that are legitimate targets for neuroscientific explanation. Acting, that is to say, assumes a *congruence* between the way an agent moves her body in order to act and the way her body moves because of neural processes. Such congruence need not obtain: an agent's body might move as if she were acting even if she's not; and she may set out to act in a certain way, but the movements of her body sufficient for her so to act may fail to occur. If this sort of thing happened too often, there would be no congruence and hence no intentional acting.

von Wright thought that congruence is a 'problem' only if we fail to be clear about it, and hence he rejected any substantive explanation of it (von Wright 1998: 3). His resolution rests on his claim that the intentional bodily movements which are the *result* of an agent's intentionally moving her body differ only conceptually from the intentionless movements which occur because of neural processes. Those are the *same* movements, differently described and explained, and hence there can be no substantive explanation of their congruence. If an agent moves her hand in order to turn the handle to open the window, then a neuroscientific explanation of the movements of her hand involved in her moving it *could not fail to be* an explanation of the movements that are the *result* of her intentionally moving it, because the movements that are the *result* of her moving her hand are (under one description) the movements explained in neuroscience (under a different description).

If an agent acts intentionally in a certain way, therefore, the bodily movements he makes in acting that way are *necessarily* congruent with those explained by neural processes, because a neuroscientific explanation of those bodily movements is adequate only if those movements are the (differently described) *results* of his intentionally moving his body. This means that neuroscientific explanations are, in this respect, less fundamental than teleological explanations of action, in that the latter determine what the former must explain. The reason is that, when an agent acts, his body moves in all sorts of ways, which are not relevant to his acting. To determine which movements neuroscience must explain if its explanation is to be relevant to the agent's acting, we must determine what the agent's acting is, hence which of his movements are intentional under a description. It is those movements, the ones that are the *results* of his intentionally moving his body, that we aim to explain neuroscientifically (Stoutland 2005 and 2009).

The Determinants of Action

My discussion so far has concerned the internal structure of an agent's acting, which typically has a final end the agent intends and would specify if she were asked what she is doing. (I say 'typically' because this point, like many I have made, does not, as von Wright insisted, cover every kind of action.) Thus, although Gwen is moving her hand, turning the handle, and opening the window, she performs those actions in order to let in fresh air: that is what she is doing in this acting. The explanation of her moving her hand, turning the handle, and opening the window is internal to the teleological structure of what she is doing, whereas explanation of the latter requires considerations *external* to the actions she performs in an acting, which von Wright called its 'determinants.' These are reasons why she is letting in fresh air (or acting with that intention), not (except very indirectly) reasons why she is turning the handle or opening the window.

Determinants of an action may be either internal or external to an agent. *Internal* determinants are an agent's volitional and cognitive attitudes, whose contents are reasons that explain the action as a means to some end, external to the action itself. *External* determinants, von Wright asserted, are a much more common class of reasons for action. They involve the agent's 'participation in an institutionalized practice' that underlies, on the one hand, symbolic challenges to which an agent responds (like an order, a request, a question, a traffic light), and, on the other, actions done because of one's roles or duties, or in order to conform to various institutionalized rules (von Wright 1981).

von Wright regarded such determinants of action as being very diverse, and he refused to systematize them. He contended that the relation between an action and its determinant is neither logical nor causal (in his sense), but *sui generis*.

> It links the action as fact to other facts of either an internal (intention and beliefs) or external (symbolic challenges) nature. What makes the linking possible is a relation of *adequacy*. Thanks to it the determinant is a *reason* for action of the type which this individual action exemplifies [...]. (von Wright 1981: 65)

But this does not entail that the determinant is the agent's own reason for an individual action: to be that requires understanding – making sense of – the action in terms of the type, which is a fallible understanding. It can be the self-understanding of the agent or the understanding of an outside observer, and, if they disagree, there is no a priori way of telling which, if any, is right. But, 'in the *absence of reasons against* acting on them, they are the reasons why we act' (von Wright 1981: 65).

von Wright discussed many other features of reasons for action: ability and incapacity, impediments, omissions, compulsion, temptation, compelling and disjunctive reasons, internalization, preferences, desires, and more. His discussions are subtle, thought-provoking, deeply original, very instructive, and impossible to summarize. One reads them to be free from philosophical orthodoxy and dogmatism, to get clear about the problems involved, to avoid futile projects and dead ends, and to be stimulated to pursue new lines of thought.

See also: ACTION THEORY AND ONTOLOGY (1); BASIC ACTIONS AND INDIVIDUATION (2); BODILY MOVEMENTS (4); TELEOLOGICAL EXPLANATION (16); REASONS AND CAUSES (17); PRACTICAL REASONING (31); FREE WILL AND DETERMINISM (38); ANSCOMBE (74).

References

Primary sources

von Wright, G. H. (1963). *Norm and Action: A Logical Inquiry*. London: Routledge and Kegan Paul.
von Wright, G. H. (1971). *Explanation and Understanding*. London: Routledge and Kegan Paul.
von Wright, G. H. (1973). *Causality and Determinism*. New York: Columbia University Press.
von Wright, G. H. (1981). *Freedom and Determination*. Helsinki: Acta Philosophica Fennica.
von Wright, G. H. (1983). On so-called practical inference. In G. H. von Wright, *Practical Reason*. Oxford: Basil Blackwell, 18–35.
von Wright, G. H. (1998). *In the Shadow of Descartes: Essays in the Philosophy of Mind*. Dordrecht: Kluwer Academic Publishers.

Secondary sources

Hahn L., and Schilpp, P. A. (eds) (1989). *The Philosophy of G. H. von Wright*. La Salle, IL: Open Court (The Library of Living Philosophers).
Stoutland, F. (2005). The problem of congruence. In I. Niiniluoto and R. Vilkko (eds), *Philosophical Essays in Memoriam: Georg Henrik von Wright*. Helsinki: Acta Philosophica Fennica, Vol. 77, 127–150.
Stoutland, F. (2009). von Wright's compatibilism. In F. Stoutland (ed.), *Philosophical Probings: Essays on von Wright's Later Work*. Copenhagen: Automatic Press/VIP, 61–82.

Further reading

von Wright, G. H. (1968). *An Essay in Deontic Logic and the General Theory of Action.* Amsterdam: North-Holland Publishing Co.

von Wright, G. H. (1993). *The Tree of Knowledge and Other Essays.* Leiden: Brill.

73

Davidson

RALF STOECKER

The philosophical career of Donald Davidson (1917–2003) started with action theory, and modern action theory more or less started with Davidson. In 1963 he published his very first scholarly philosophical article, 'Actions, reasons and causes' (*ARC*), which almost immediately defined the standard for contributions to action theory. When Davidson wrote *ARC*, philosophy of action was strongly influenced by the insight of Wittgenstein, Ryle, Anscombe, and others, who maintained that one should not be misled by the linguistic similarities between our mentalistic and materialistic vocabulary into a quasi-mechanistic picture of thought and action. Some of these authors expressed their view by saying that the reasons on which we act are never the *causes* of our actions. Davidson's aim in *ARC* was to demonstrate that this claim was unfounded by defending a causal theory of both action and its explanation. *ARC* not only initiated an upheaval toward causalism, it also laid the foundation for what was to become the standard conception of agency in the philosophy of mind and action, namely the *belief–desire model* of motivation (see chapter 20).

According to Davidson, actions are events that may be explained through their *rationalization*. Rationalizations, in turn, combine two characteristics: first, they reveal something – a feature – of the action that appealed to the agent. Although these features may take different forms, they are always based on the assumption that the agent has (1) a certain inclination for a kind of action – what Davidson called a 'pro attitude,' while most philosophers today simply call it a 'want' or 'desire' – and (2) the belief that the event in question is an action of the favored kind. Davidson refers to this pair of attitudes as the 'primary reason' of the action. Every rationalization is based on a primary reason, although we only rarely refer to either one of these basic attitudes explicitly and almost never mention both. Nonetheless, in order to explain an action, it is also necessary that these reasons *causally explain* its occurrence.

These are, then, the three core elements of Davidson's conception of agency:

1 actions are events which are explainable by recourse to a pair of attitudes;
2 these qualify as its primary reason; and
3 they also explain the event *causally*.

Discussing them will also provide an introduction into the other elements of Davidson's action theory.

Claim (1) is *prima facie* plausible, since when we act something usually happens. Davidson has two further reasons for this claim. First, it adheres with his causalism (claim (3), to be discussed later). Second, it is supported by his general ontology.

In his work, Davidson has pursued two lines of consideration to answer ontological questions, both of which were strongly influenced by his teacher W. V. O. Quine. First, he subscribed to what he once called 'the method of truth in metaphysics' (*ITI* 199–214): In order to learn what kinds of entities there really are, we have to focus on the logical form of the sentences that apparently refer to these entities. (See also chapter 6.) The distinction between *logical* form and *surface* form goes back to Davidson's truth conditional semantics. According to this theory, the competence of understanding a language is to be construed as knowledge of the conditions under which the sentences of the language are true, on the basis of knowing how the structure of those sentences contributes to their truth conditions. This in turn combines the ability to detect a logical form beneath the irregular surface structure of the sentences and the mastery of a theory of truth for these logical forms. Davidson was convinced that the logical form of natural languages need not exceed the means of first-order predicate calculus, so his semantics has the immediate metaphysical consequence that we may read off from their quantificational structure the ontological commitments of the sentences under consideration (which may occasionally turn out to be quite different from what we think they are).

Good examples are action sentences which typically contain no action nouns and yet, according to Davidson, must be taken as quantifications over actions. At this point the second line of consideration comes into play: entities have to behave in an ontologically orderly fashion. In particular, they have to be answerable to questions of identity and difference. Events, according to Davidson, fulfill this condition, whereas other candidates, such as states of affairs, fail to do so. Since we are bound to admit actions into our ontology, we had therefore better assume that they are events.

Davidson has defended a robust or 'coarse-grained' understanding of events and consequently also of actions, in contrast to 'fine-grained' proposals like the property-exemplification account by Alvin Goldman and Jaegwon Kim. Events are independent particulars individuated by their causes and effects (*EAE* 163–203) as well as by their spatio-temporal location (*EAE* 305–311). Moreover, according to Davidson, actions are always *bodily movements*. It is easy to overlook this fact because, as with other entities, there are numerous different ways of referring to one and the same action, some of which relate the action to its consequences (thus creating the impression that some actions include more than mere bodily movement). Typical examples are acts of killing. Their temporal location provoked an extensive debate in the '70s and '80s (the so-called 'time-of-a-killing problem'; see chapter 2). Davidson, who was one of the first to discuss this problem (*EAE* 55 ff.), argued that the view that the killing of *B* by *A* has not occurred until *B* is dead is misled by the surface grammar of the respective sentences (*EAE* 299–301).

There is another problem with claim (1), though, which has not received much attention by Davidson: if actions are events, then there are no *negative actions*. Yet it is almost a truism that part of what we do is letting things happen or omitting something, so that it appears somewhat forced to deny that these are instances of agency.

According to claim (2), it is essential for actions that they occur for *reasons*, where reasons are basically understood as something mental. This view does not rule out the possibility of non-mental external reasons, but it denies that actions could be performed merely for such reasons. Moreover, it gives priority to a certain class of mental phenomena: beliefs and pro-attitudes, thereby running counter to the traditional preference for *volitions* and the *will*. In *ARC*, this was also meant to downplay the importance of *intentions* in acting as mere 'syncategorematic' expressions (*EAE* 8). Davidson later changed his position on this matter, since it did not fit with the phenomenon of *pure intending* (*EAE* 83–102) – that is, with intentions about the future (which we may have regardless of whether or not we finally act upon them).

Davidson's later account of intention is closely connected to his view on *practical reasoning*. On this view, it is essential for practical deliberations that some of their premises are *prima facie* evaluative judgments. These latter can consequently only entail other *prima facie* judgments, at most judgments about what is best all things considered. Our actions, by contrast, are determined by unconditional judgments about what we regard simply as the best, *sans phrase* or *all out*. Hence there is always a step from the results of practical reasoning to the mental antecedents of actions – namely *intention*. If an analog step is taken in practical deliberation concerned with the future, its result is a pure intending.

Davidson's understanding of practical reasoning also provides him with an answer to another classic difficulty in action theory, the problem of *weakness of will* (*EAE* 21–42). An agent displays weakness of will whenever her all-out judgment (that is, her intention) differs from her all-things-considered judgment. The agent thus does what she thinks is the best to do, even though at the same time, in her practical deliberation, she comes to the conclusion that, all things considered, it would be better to do something else. Weakness of will is thereby neither impossible nor the result of blunt inconsistency, but rather a weakness with regard to the propensity to be led from an all-things-considered judgment to an all-out judgment. Davidson characterizes this weakness as a lack of the *virtue of continence* – namely a local deviation from the *principle of continence*, which demands to act continently and is a constitutive element of rationality and hence of agency.

Given the central role that intentional attitudes like believes, desires, and intentions play in Davidson's account of action, we would do well to examine his understanding of such mental phenomena. Again, it is crucial to start with considerations of logical form (see also chapter 6). Providing with logical forms sentences that ascribe intentional attitudes is notoriously difficult, as it is not clear how to express the contribution of the so-called content sentence to the truth value of the whole sentence, which is apparently not only sensitive to the truth value of the content sentence and the entities it refers to, but also to its meaning (if not to its wording). To consider a famous example: 'Oedipus thought that Jocasta was sexy' was presumably true, while 'Oedipus thought that his mother was sexy' was false, although Jocasta was Oedipus mother, and hence 'Jocasta was sexy' and 'Oedipus' mother was sexy' are equivalent.

Davidson initially discussed this problem of the *semantic opacity* or *intensionality* of content sentences in relation to indirect speech (*ITI* 93–108), and only later turned to intentional attitude ascriptions (*SIO* 53–67). His solution is particularly radical: the problem arises because what at the surface appears to be one sentence turns out to consist of two sentences, which are logically unconnected yet related via an indexical (deictic) element in one of them pointing to the other one. In the example 'Oedipus thought that Jocasta was sexy,' the whole expression has the form: 'Oedipus thought *that* (i.e. the following:) Jocasta was sexy.' Only the former sentence is *asserted*, the latter is merely a sample used to make the assertion. As a specimen, it cannot always be substituted by another, even by an equivalent specimen like 'Oedipus' mother is sexy.'

This so-called *paratactic analysis* also helps to solve another problem for Davidson's action theory: the apparent inconsistency between his coarse-grained understanding of actions and his claim (2) that primary reasons are characteristic for actions. Suppose that the reason why Oedipus married Jocasta was that he wanted to marry a sexy woman. If Oedipus' action of marrying Jocasta was identical with his action of marrying his mother, we seem to be forced into the counterintuitive conclusion that the reason why he married his mother was that he wanted to marry a sexy woman. The same point can be made with respect to intentionality: Oedipus intentionally married *Jocasta*, but he certainly did not marry *his mother* intentionally. In order to account for this difference, Davidson originally fell back on a formulation proposed by Anscombe: actions are intentional only *under a description*. Yet it is only within the framework of his paratactic analysis that this formulation receives a clear meaning. When we say that Oedipus intentionally married Jocasta, we say something like: '*That* was intentional of Oedipus: he married Jocasta.' We thereby express two things: first, that Oedipus has married Jocasta; and, second, that he did it because he wanted to do something so described. Since he did not want to do something describable as marrying his mother, his marrying of his mother, although an action, wasn't intentional under that specific description.

An account of the logical form of intentional attitude ascriptions can only be the first step toward an adequate understanding of these attitudes; we still wish to know how to account for this specific practice of ascribing one's own utterances to another person. Here Davidson's account displays another non-standard feature. He denies something that many philosophers treat almost like a truism, namely that the content of a person's intentional attitude is something to be found *in* the person, in other words something that is *present to her mind* (for instance some sort of *mental representation*), which explains why the agent acts the way she does. Given such an account, we would have to assume that the sentences we use in order to ascribe propositional content to a person have to stand in a specific relationship to the actual content she has in her mind. According to Davidson, however, when we say what people believe, want, and so on, the utterances we use to ascribe these states are merely *our* tools (*SIO* 15–67). They do not correspond to anything that actually plays a role in the psychological process in the person who has the attitudes. Davidson's analogy is the use of numbers in order to ascribe temperature or weight to something. If a lake is 20° C warm, we should better not assume that the number 20 is to be found somewhere in the lake. Analogously, we should not expect to find anything like the sentence 'Jocasta is sexy' in Oedipus.

The analogy to measurement also demonstrates that, while intentional contents are not something present to the agent's mind, they can nonetheless explain what the agent does. This relates to another branch of Davidson's philosophy of language: his account of the *interpretation of speech acts*. According to Davidson, the interpretation of speech acts forms a special part of our understanding of actions, both of them belonging to a single, unified explanatory attitude (*POR* 152; compare *ITI* 161). Following Quine, Davidson begins his account by considering the situation of *radical interpretation*, where an interpreter tries to make sense of the utterances of a person totally alien to her. According to Davidson, the radical interpreter by and by will discover that the speaker holds certain sentences to be true depending on the circumstances of the utterance. This evidence will allow her to develop an interpretive theory for the speaker on the basis of two core elements: on the one hand, a theory that assigns truth conditions to all possible utterances of the speaker; and, on the other, the concept of belief, which allows for those occasional situations in which the speaker holds a sentence to be true even though the respective truth conditions are not met (*ITI* 170).

The ability to say what a sentences means and what the speaker believes, however, does not merely allow the interpreter to understand *what* the speaker says, but also *why* he said it. Since radical interpretation is based on causal relationships between the speaker's utterances and his environment, the interpretation of language discovers a certain propensity or disposition of a speaker that has to do with the way the world is. This is already an account of the role that *content sentences* play: they state the truth conditions of the sentences a speaker is disposed to utter.

Radical interpretation is not restricted to understanding speakers' making assertions, though. According to Davidson, the basic attitude of the speaker that allows for an understanding of our intentional vocabulary as a whole is evaluative: it is his attitude of *preferring a sentence to be true*. Since communication is not merely a means for mirroring the world, but is essentially geared toward changing the world, radical interpretation eventually leads to what Davidson has called 'a unified theory of meaning and action.' This traces back every speech act to three interpretative dimensions: a theory of truth for the agent; a desire; and an appropriate belief.

A speaker's ability to react to an unlimited number of finely discriminated situations (corresponding to sentences with different truth conditions) also allows for numerous non-linguistic reactions to these situations. The truth conditions of the language that the interpreter ascribes to the agent consequently provide her with a scale for measuring the agent's attitudes. This lies at the core of Davidson's measurement analogy.

That people are able to interpret others is an empirical fact, strongly dependent on certain similarities between interpreter and agent (*SIO* 107–121). The two must basically agree on what is salient in the world (*TLH* 61); only then can the interpreter achieve the *triangulation* required for communication. She may thus base her interpretation on the assumption that certain features of the world, which she notices, will also be the features that the agent will (even counterfactually) be disposed to react on. Otherwise, as a matter of fact, the intentional stance will not work: the beings under consideration would have no intentional attitudes; they would not be agents (*POR* 37).

Davidson's account of the explanatory character of the intentional vocabulary and of its strong dependency on linguistic interpretation has a number of prominent theoretical consequences. It leads to his well-known claim that *speechless animals* cannot think or act (*ITI* 155–170, *SIO* 95–105). Another surprising consequence bears on ontology: not only intentional contents, but also the intentional states themselves should not be taken ontologically seriously; they do not really exist (*SIO* 60). Talk of beliefs, desires, and the like only mentions a special aspect under which an interpreter ascribes one of her sentences to the agent, which is similar to ascribing a number to an object as its height, length, or width. This ontological consequence is striking – not only because it deviates from the surface ontology of language, but also because it conflicts with two prominent theses that are usually regarded as being central to Davidson's theory: that intentional attitudes are token identical with something physical; and that reasons are causes. The first thesis is a misunderstanding, though; Davidson has never claimed that beliefs, desires, and the like are instances of the token-identity theory, which forms part of his anomalous monism. The second thesis is not Davidson's either, although he occasionally spoke that way; as early as *ARC* he had already made it clear that reasons could not be causes, since they are not events (*EAE* 12 ff.).

If reasons are not causes, though, the question is how claim (3) above (that action explanations are causal explanations) could be true. In *ARC* Davidson defended this claim through two considerations directed primarily against the critics of the early '60s. First, in contrast to the critics' proposal, the treatment of action explanations as causal makes clear why they are explanatory at all. Second, the most prominent argument against causalism, the *logical connection argument*, fails. Davidson also addressed the tension between (3) and a principle that he himself occasionally defended: the 'principle of the nomological character of causality' (*EAE* 149–162, *TLH* 201–219). According to this principle, causal relations need to be backed up by causal laws. Yet action explanations do not refer to laws; they work instead by showing that the relation between reasons and action is an instance of a practical reasoning. So how could they be causal?

Davidson's reaction to this difficulty is threefold. First he denies any possibility of turning the quasi-logical relation between reasons and actions into a strict law that could cover a causal relation. This is a direct consequence of the *impossibility of strict psychophysical laws*, which underlies his anomalous monism (*EAE* 207–225; *THL* 204). The ascription of intentional attitudes is necessarily bound to the constraints of radical interpretation, in particular to the consistency demand that facilitates the construction of a truth theory, to the so-called principle of charity, and presumably also to the demands of practical rationality (for instance to the principle of continence). These are what Davidson called 'strong constitutive elements' of the psychological vocabulary. For every psycho-physical regularity, however, counterfactual situations are conceivable in which these constraints force an interpreter to revise her attitude ascription in such a way that the regularity under consideration no longer holds. Hence we should never expect from a psycho-physical law that it supports counterfactuals in a way required for a strict law. Strict laws must be purely physical laws.

Second, however, according to his coarse-grained understanding of events, causes and effects admit of various descriptions. It is therefore possible that two successive events instantiate a law when they are described in one way, while under a different description they don't. This is obvious from almost all the everyday singular causal statements we know; we have no chance of backing them up by a strict law without changing the terminology. Hence there can be mental causality without psycho-physical laws. Still, reasons are not events, and so they cannot be mental causes.

Third, we have to distinguish between causal relations and causal explanations. Not every singular causal statement qualifies as a causal explanation. More importantly, causal explanations need not be singular causal statements either, for they need not mention causes. They might instead be *dispositional explanations*, which are causal, though not because they specify a causally efficacious event. Dispositional explanations point to the characteristic feature of an object which consists in the fact that, if something happens to the object, it will probably cause something else to happen – which one would not expect to happen in objects that do not have this feature. If the wing of an airplane is elastic, we can expect that, when it is bent, the bending causes it to return to its original shape (*SIO* 216), while if it is brittle and it is bent the bending will cause it to break.

According to Davidson, action explanations by intentional attitudes are causal explanations of this latter kind. 'A desire for Abel's death is (no doubt among other things) a disposition to be caused to cause Abel's death given appropriate beliefs, the opportunity, etc.' (*POR* 95). When we learn that Cain wanted to kill Abel, while Abel had no desire to kill Cain, we do not discover what event out in the fields caused Cain to hit his brother. Still, we understand that it was to be expected that some event would make him kill Abel, while it was not to be expected that anything would occur which would cause Abel to hit Cain. The unified theory of meaning and action provides causal explanations by ascribing suitably subtle causal dispositions.

In contrast to other causal dispositions, however, we could not expect – even in principle – to refine these dispositions in a way which could transform them into strict correlations. So, while we may try to refine the conditions of brittleness until finally we are sure that, under certain circumstances, brittle things always break, due to the strong constitutive elements that ground radical interpretation it would be impossible to refine our intentional vocabulary analogously.

This impossibility has two immediate action-theoretical consequences. First, according to Davidson, it shows that our *freedom to act* is a causal power (*EAE* 80–81), so that possible worries about the incompatibility of his account with our freedom are baseless. Second, it frustrates any attempt to solve the so-called *problem of wayward causal chains* (that is, cases where a person's behavior is caused by intentions it accords with, and yet is not intentional under any relevant description; see chapter 21). This problem is not specific to action explanations (a brittle bridge may be torn down by the authorities because it is brittle, and yet its breakdown is not an instantiation of its brittleness). What seems particular to action explanations, however, is the impossibility to refine the respective disposition.

Davidson construes intentionality and agency as features of a specific kind of interaction between beings with linguistic capabilities. We might therefore question whether he could do justice to the *subjective* aspects of thinking and acting. Davidson addresses these difficulties as the *problem of first-person authority* (*SIO* 1–67). His surprising conclusion is that his externalism actually provides the very key for an adequate understanding of subjectivity. Our first-person authority is not due to any special epistemic capacity we have regarding our own minds, but is rather the reverse of our abilities as interpreters of everybody else. To put it slightly metaphorically, since it is essential for an interpreter to measure others in relation to herself, there is something trivial and futile about having her interpret herself; that would be like trying to measure a measuring stick with that very stick. In this meagre sense, she is endowed with first-person authority.[1]

See also: ACTION THEORY AND ONTOLOGY (1); BASIC ACTIONS AND INDIVIDUATION (2); BODILY MOVEMENTS (4); THE CAUSAL THEORY OF ACTION (5); ADVERBS OF ACTION AND LOGICAL FORM (6); REASONS AND CAUSES (17); HUMEANISM ABOUT MOTIVATION (20); DEVIANT CAUSAL CHAINS (21); AKRASIA AND IRRATIONALITY (35); WITTGENSTEIN (68); RYLE (69); ANSCOMBE (74).

Note

1 I want to thank Thomas Spitzley, Constantine Sandis, and the members of the European Action Group (funded by the Leverhulme Trust) for their valuable criticisms and remarks.

References: primary sources and their abbreviations

All references in this essay are to Davidson's *Collected Essays*, Vols 1–5, Oxford: Clarendon Press:

EAE Vol. 1: *Essays on Actions and Events* (2001) [1980].
ITI Vol. 2: *Inquiries into Truth and Interpretation* (2001) [1984].
SIO Vol. 3: *Subjective, Intersubjective, Objective* (2001) [2001].
POR Vol 4: *Problems of Rationality* (2004) [2001].
TLH Vol. 5: *Truth, Language, and History* (2005) [2001].

Further reading

Davidson, D. (1999). Intellectual autobiography. In L. Hahn (ed.), *The Philosophy of Donald Davidson*. Chicago: Open Court, 1–70.

Joseph, M. (2004). *Donald Davidson*. Acumen: Chesham

Lepore, E. (2004). An interview with Donald Davidson. In D. Davidson, *Collected Essays*, Vol. 4: *Problems of Rationality*. Oxford: Clarendon Press, 231–263.

Lepore, E., and McLaughlin, B. (eds) (1985). *Actions and Events. Perspectives on the Philosophy of Donald Davidson*. Oxford: Basil Blackwell.

Stoecker, R. (ed.) (1993). *Reflecting Davidson*. De Gruyter: Berlin.

Vermazen, B., and Hintikka, M. (eds) (1985). *Essays on Davidson, Actions and Events*. Oxford: Oxford University Press.

74

Anscombe

ROGER TEICHMANN

The monograph *Intention* by Elizabeth Anscombe (1919–2001) is an extraordinarily rich text, covering a host of issues in a mere ninety-four pages. It grew out of a series of lectures given at Oxford University in 1957, in which year it was also published.

At the start of the book, Anscombe introduces her subject under three heads:

1 expression of intention for the future ('I'm going to buy some milk');
2 intentional action (my buying of some milk);
3 intention in acting, or intention 'with which' (to buy some milk).

The structure of the book corresponds to these themes in this order. There are certain advantages to this division and ordering. For example, it will turn out that the picture of intentions as inner states that cause actions is radically defective; and, by postponing any direct discussion of phrases like 'the intention to φ' till we get to (3), Anscombe allows us to proceed unhampered by that picture. She is thus able to take such expressions of intention as 'I'm going to buy some milk' at face value, that is, as being about future actions, not about present mental states.

What, then, distinguishes 'I'm going to buy some milk' from 'I'm going to be sick'? Anscombe considers, but rejects, the thought that the latter is a 'prediction' while the former is not. Both statements are predictions, if that means statements about the future that can turn out true or false. The clue, she says, lies in the difference in the sorts of reasons or grounds that are given for each statement. Such reasons are given in response to the question 'Why?' – as 'Why are you going to buy some milk?' or alternatively 'Why are you going to be sick?' (where this means either 'Why do you think you are going to be sick?' or 'What is it that's causing your nausea?'). And intentional actions 'are the actions to which a certain sense of the question 'Why?' is given application' (*I* 9). The actions to which the question 'Why?' is given application may be past, present, or future actions. Our task is to elucidate the relevant sense of 'Why?'

Anscombe carries out this task partly by delineating the conditions under which 'Why?' is refused application, and partly by stating what sorts of answer can be given when the question does have application. Application of the question is refused by means of answers like 'I didn't know I was doing X,' and also 'I knew I was doing X, but only because I observed that I was' (with reference, for example, to making a squeaking noise with my shoes as I walked). The issue implicit here is that of practical knowledge or the lack of it, to which issue we will turn in a moment. Positive answers to 'Why?' are categorized by Anscombe as follows: 'the answer may (a) simply mention past history, (b) give an interpretation of the action, or (c) mention something future' (*I* 24). Anscombe should probably have said 'further' rather than 'future' in (c), since the sorts of answer to 'Why?' she discusses include some that give wider descriptions of a present action without adverting to the future – for instance 'Why are you putting an X in that box?' – 'I'm voting for Bloggs' (or 'To vote for Bloggs'). Construed thus generally, (c)-type answers give 'further intentions,' and figure importantly in practical deliberation and practical inference.

Both (a)-type answers and (b)-type answers (purport to) give what Anscombe calls 'motives,' the former giving backward-looking motives, the latter, interpretative motives (or 'motives-in-general'). An example of a backward-looking motive is the motive of revenge: 'Why did you kill him?' – 'Because he killed my brother.' An example of an interpretative motive is the motive of patriotism: 'Why are you singing?' – 'It is my country's national anthem.' Neither sort of case can be reduced to a 'further intention.' If you answer 'Why did you kill him?' by saying 'So as to have my revenge,' your answer does not show you to be aiming at some independently specifiable outcome or action-description. For the concept of revenge is explained via such reasons as 'Because he killed my brother,' not vice versa (compare *I* 20). To avenge a deed is, roughly, to harm someone *because* they have harmed you or yours. Though Anscombe does not point this out, the existence of genuinely backward-looking motives generates *prima facie* problems for various philosophical theories. These include utilitarianism, which typically construes all rational deliberation as reliant on forward-looking reasons, and also those theories which define intentional actions as actions caused by intentions – since an act of revenge, for example, is certainly intentional, but is not done *with* any independently specifiable intention, and a fortiori is not caused by any such intention. (That is to say, 'Because he killed my brother' does not give such an intention; asked 'Why are you shooting?' you could of course state a further intention: 'So as to kill him.')

However, more than one kind of answer to 'Why did you do that?' can mention past history, and some answers cite causes rather than reasons (in the sense of 'reasons' we have been trying to pin down). 'As e.g. when we give a ready answer to the question 'Why did you knock the cup off the table?' – 'I saw such-and-such and it *made me jump*'' (*I* 16). Anscombe labels such causes as seeing a face at the window 'mental causes.' These cannot be distinguished from backward-looking motives by alleging that the effect of a mental cause is always involuntary, for it is not; Anscombe illustrates this with: 'The martial music excites me, that is why I march up and down.' Nor are mental causes known to the subject only indirectly, by induction or from general knowledge. They are known directly – a fact, by the way, which shows the inadequacy of a Humean conception of causation, insofar as that conception insists that knowledge of causation is never direct. Anscombe suggests that the difference between backward-looking motives and mental causes has to do with the ideas of good and of harm, which are involved in the former but not in the latter.

The distinction between reasons and causes is not a hard and fast one, and there are borderline or complex cases (*I* 23–24). Nevertheless the distinction is real, and Davidsonian theories of 'reasons as causes' would be rejected by Anscombe. One way in which the difference typically shows up is in the fact that a person can say straight off what her reasons are, but not what causes an event has – mental causes being a notable exception. And in fact a person will typically be able to say straight off what action she is performing. What is the nature of this ability?

In a famous example, Anscombe imagines someone going out with a shopping-list and returning with a bag whose contents do not correspond to what's on the list. This mismatch does not show that the list is at fault. For

> if the list and the things that the man actually buys do not agree, and if this and this alone constitutes a *mistake*, then the mistake is not in the list but in the man's performance. (*I* 56)

By contrast, a detective whose job it was to record what the shopper bought would produce a list that was in error, given a mismatch between list and bought items. This phenomenon has been dubbed a difference in 'direction of fit,' a phrase which nowhere occurs in *Intention*, and accounts of which usually differ significantly from what Anscombe says on the topic. For Anscombe, the shopping-list example illustrates the difference between *practical knowledge* and *contemplative knowledge*. Knowing what you are about (practical knowledge) is not a case of correctly assessing facts that are prior to, and independent of, the knowledge. A statement of intention is like a shopping-list, and to that extent it is also like an order (as Anscombe says, the shopping-list could in fact embody an order, if given to the man by his wife); but, whereas an order is not false if it doesn't get obeyed, a statement of intention that doesn't get carried out is properly called false. For a statement of intention does *tell* others, e.g. where you will be, and in general what to expect of you. Hence such statements, when they do get carried out, and so come true, count as expressing knowledge. Nevertheless, where there is a discrepancy between what a person does and what he said he meant to do, and if this and this alone constitutes a mistake, then the mistake is not in the statement of intention but in the person's performance.

Connected with this is the following: you do not justify a statement of intention by giving grounds for believing it true, but by giving reasons for doing the thing in question. (For example, 'I'm going to the shops.' – 'Why?' – 'To buy some milk.') The epistemic ungroundedness of statements of intention is linked by Anscombe with the ungroundedness of the knowledge a person has of the positions of his limbs. Both kinds of knowledge are non-observational, and with both there is room for intelligible error: you may fail to do what you set out to do, and you may think your leg is bent when in fact it is straight. By contrast, there is no room for intelligible error about the locations of your pains. If you say your hand hurts and not your foot, but keep rubbing the foot, limping, etc., then it would be 'difficult to guess what you could mean' (*I* 14).

The claim that some kind of statement is or would be *unintelligible* (especially if no appropriate explanations were forthcoming) is very often philosophically significant, for Anscombe, and there are several points in *Intention* where she argues for such a claim, and draws substantive conclusions from her arguments. She thus relies on considerations to do with meaning and use that will be obscure to readers not acquainted with the Wittgenstein of the *Philosophical Investigations* (which, of course, she had translated into English). For Wittgenstein, and for Anscombe, a person's authority as to what he means, or as to whether he means anything, is defeasible. And a word or expression is not to be thought of as carrying its meaning around with it from context to context.

To return to the question of knowledge: Anscombe marks the difference she has in mind by saying that you *can say* where your pains are, not that you *know* where they are – but that you do *know* what you are, or will be, doing. It doesn't follow from this that you know what you intend, since with statements of the form 'I intend to φ' there appears to be little or no room for intelligible error. (Or rather, any error here would be pathological, and would not constitute a *mistake*; perhaps subconscious intentions are a case in point.) This seems to show that 'I am going to buy some milk' and 'I intend to buy some milk' are not exactly equivalent; nor is Anscombe committed to saying that they are. Rather she is reminding us that the first is as much an expression of intention as the second, and that the first does not 'rest on' the second in any way. Note also that we need not follow Anscombe and Wittgenstein in their strictures on the use of 'know' in order to agree with Anscombe that practical knowledge and knowledge of the positions of one's limbs differ importantly from 'knowledge of' (or ability to say) where one's pains are.

The question 'Why are you doing X?' uses a particular description of what the person is doing – say, pushing a handle up and down. Of a given action many descriptions will be true, and the agent will be unaware of the truth of many of these descriptions. Thus, an action is never intentional *simplement* – it is only intentional under certain descriptions, namely those that could occur in a 'Why?' question that would not be refused application. And the action will generally be unintentional under many other descriptions. The notion of an action's being intentional under a description has been influential, as has the more general notion of an action's having many descriptions. The latter notion has come to play a role in discussions of the 'ontological status' of actions, something Anscombe showed little interest in. Her interest in this second notion related to its bearing on the first notion, one that she perceived was crucial in any investigation of intention, as also of responsibility. For example, we can ask, 'Under which descriptions of an action is an agent responsible for having done it?' All the descriptions? All those he knew (or believed with good reason) to be true of the action? All those he ought to have known to be true of the action? Or all those under which his action was in fact intentional? These are issues that Anscombe tackles elsewhere in her philosophy. In a famous passage from 'Modern moral philosophy,' written at about the same time as *Intention*, she expresses the view that ethics requires an adequate philosophy of mind thus:

> is it not clear that there are several concepts that need investigating simply as part of the philosophy of psychology and – as I should recommend – *banishing ethics totally* from our minds? Namely – to begin with: 'action,' 'intention,' 'pleasure,' 'wanting.' (*MMP* 188)

We should remember that her interest in the topic of intention was tied to, and possibly inspired by, her interest in concrete ethical issues, such as President Truman's responsibility for dropping the atom bomb.

'Why are you doing that?' is a question that can be iterated, each answer giving a wider description of the action, the action being intentional under all these descriptions. Anscombe's colorful example here is of a man pushing a handle, to pump a pump, to get poisoned water into a water tank, to poison the inhabitants of the house, to make a political revolution possible, and so on. (See *I* 37–49.) Each answer gives a means for achieving the end given by the next answer, except for the final answer, which gives the person's overall end or goal. The series corresponds, in reverse order, to the premises and conclusion of a practical syllogism. Anscombe discusses practical syllogisms and practical reasoning in *Intention* and also in 'Practical inference,' and in both pieces she stresses that the end a person has, expressible as 'I want such-and-such,' does not occur as a premise in a practical argument. A premise of the form 'I want such-and-such' *can* occur in a practical argument, in the rather special case where the agent is considering some want of his as just one of the facts of the case – as in the practical argument which includes the premise 'I want to kill my parents' and which (with some other premises) yields the conclusion 'So I'll consult NN, the psychiatrist' (Anscombe acknowledges Anselm Müller as the originator of this example). But 'I want to kill my parents' does not here express the person's end or goal. Of this case Anscombe says that '[t]he decision, if I reach it on these grounds [i.e. in the light of these premises], *shews* that I *want* to get rid of the trouble' (*PI* 115–116). In general, it is the practical decision you reach on the basis of known premises that *shows* what it is you want. The premises do not themselves contain a specification of the overall goal, and the same set of premises can be used by people with different goals. Indeed, a given set of premises and conclusion – a structure of propositions, typically bound together by conditionality ('If *p*, then *q*') – can be used by somebody engaged in practical reasoning and also by somebody else engaged in theoretical reasoning. The difference between the two modes of reasoning resides in the different 'uses' to which the structure is put (*PI* 133–134, 139).

A practical conclusion shows what it is that the agent wants. What, then, is wanting? As elsewhere in her philosophy of mind, Anscombe rejects the empiricist model of the mental state as quasi-sensation, that is, as occurrent episode of consciousness, known authoritatively to the subject by introspection and reportable by him on that basis. Wants are no more 'inner states,' in this sense, than are intentions. 'The primitive sign of wanting is *trying to get*,' she writes (*I* 68), and this is a conceptual truth. There are limits on what can count as trying to get which impose limits on the range of wantable things: thus you cannot try to achieve something that you believe you cannot achieve. No action, such as flapping your arms, counts as trying to get to the moon unaided, if you believe that no action could ever get you to the moon unaided. And there are other limits on the range of wantable things. Though you can wish the past had been different, you cannot want it to be different (assuming the impossibility of backwards causation): see *I* 67.

Are the limits mentioned so far the only limits? Can a person want anything, so long as he believes it to be attainable? Anscombe remarks:

> It will be instructive to anyone who thinks this to approach someone and say: 'I want a saucer of mud' or 'I want a twig of mountain ash.' He is likely to be asked what for [...] (*I* 70)

She goes on to show that an expression of a want will only make sense if the person can ultimately give a *desirability characterization* – that is, a description of the thing wanted that supplies a final, because adequate and sufficient, answer to 'What do you want that for?' – which, like 'Why are you doing that?,' has the form of an iterable question. Examples of desirability characterizations are: 'X would be good for my health' and (for some X) 'X would be fun.' The further question 'But why do you want what's good for your health?' is frivolous or uncomprehending. Sometimes there is some reason *against* doing the thing which would benefit your health (for example 'It will cause Smith's death'), and in this way a consideration can *undermine* the answer 'X would be good for my health.' But this does not impugn the status of the answer as a desirability characterization. Though Anscombe does not go into the question further in *Intention*, it seems clear that the range of possible desirability characterizations is determined in large part by what is normal and natural for human beings. It is our form of life that determines the intelligibility of reasons for wanting, of reasons for action, and of action itself. The limits thus imposed upon what can be intelligibly wanted or aimed at indicate that any out-and-out subjectivism in ethics is untenable.

Anscombe follows Aristotle and Aquinas in thinking that practical reasoning aims at the good in the same way in which theoretical reasoning aims at the true. With this view goes the thesis that anything that is (sanely) desired is desired under the aspect of the good – *quidquid appetitur, appetitur sub specie boni*. A rational agent always desires a thing in the belief that it is somehow good, a belief which can of course be mistaken. A thing may be instrumentally good only, in other words good as a means to something good; but ultimate ends will be deemed by the agent to be good *simpliciter*. This view leads Anscombe to assimilate 'What do you want that for?' – the final answer to which gives a desirability characterization – and 'What is the good of that?' (see *I* 78).

If there are many final goods, there appears to be a problem with the ordering of goods, and therefore (potentially) with the notion that practical reason should be capable always of discerning a best, or equal best, course of action. Anscombe asks:

> But may not someone be criticizable for pursuing a certain end, thus characterizable as a sort of good of his, where and when it is quite inappropriate for him to do so, or by means inimical to other ends which he ought to have? (*PI* 147)

And she answers, 'This can be made out only if man has a last end which governs all.' It is clear that Anscombe did think that 'this could be made out,' and hence that man does have a final end. What that end is must be a factual matter, not decidable by a priori philosophy.

See also: BODILY MOVEMENTS (4); INTENTION (14); DESIRE AND PLEASURE (15); TELEOLOGICAL EXPLANATION (16); REASONS AND CAUSES (17); AGENTS' KNOWLEDGE (30); PRACTICAL REASONING (31); DELIBERATION AND DECISION (32); ARISTOTLE (54); WITTGENSTEIN (68); DAVIDSON (73).

References: primary sources

I Anscombe, G. E. M. (2000). *Intention*, 2nd edn [1963]. Cambridge, MA: Harvard University Press.

PI Anscombe, G. E. M. (2005). Practical inference. In G. E. M. Anscombe, *Human Life, Action and Ethics: Essays by G. E. M. Anscombe*, edited by M. Geach and L. Gormally. Exeter, UK and Charlottesville, VA: Imprint Academic, 109–147.

MMP Anscombe, G. E. M. (2005). Modern moral philosophy. In G. E. M. Anscombe, *Human Life, Action and Ethics: Essays by G. E. M. Anscombe*, edited by M. Geach and L. Gormally. Exeter, UK and Charlottesville, VA: Imprint Academic, 169–194.

75

Ricœur

ANNA C. ZIELINSKA

Introduction

Paul Ricœur (1913–2005) is mostly known for his work on hermeneutics and phenomenology. But he was also close, for quite a long time, to the structuralist tradition which became notorious through works of Ferdinand Saussure, Roman Jakobson, and Algirdas Greimas.[1] He thus had a double heritage, philosophical and linguistic, which in all likelihood made him more open to the so-called analytical tradition in philosophy (his fellow French philosophers saw him as the most 'transatlantic' among them).[2] He did not, however, live this duality as something natural, torn as he was between linguists who considered linguistic communication as an unproblematic 'given' and philosophers who regarded the very fact of communicating as a fundamental mystery. He eventually conceded that there is indeed a mystery in the fact that we communicate, but that it is not definitive and can be transgressed. At one point he described his work as an attempt to 'understand the discourse as a transgression of the monadic incommunicability' (Ricœur 2004: 53). The urge to leave the naturalistic framework and adopt the transcendental perspective is here motivated by the will to put the theory of discourse in the 'space of the game, both logical and phenomenological, which is not the one of nature' (ibid.). This denaturalized conception of discourse was subsequently refined, but its role remained central throughout Ricœur's work.

The present chapter focuses on the way Ricœur dealt with the problem of action, which became increasingly important to him from the end of the seventies. Ricœur was the first French reader of Anscombe and Davidson. His interest in them arose primarily because they were both working on action discourse within a broadly Aristotelian tradition. One of his major books, *Oneself as Another*, contains both an original contribution to the philosophy of action and an interesting criticism of the most discussed questions of the discipline as he encountered it. In what follows, I shall try to reconstruct a part of it; however, it is an image, and not an idea, that is going to give the tone to my investigation. My starting point is Ricœur's own remark at the beginning of his discussion of the Anglo-Saxon philosophy of action:

> Anscombe's book *Intention* provides in this regard the most elegant example of what I shall call, without any pejorative overtone, a conceptual impressionism, to distinguish it from the somewhat cubist version found in Donald Davidson's theory. (Ricœur 1992: 67)

Preliminaries: Thinking about Language

One of the major notions in Ricœur's work is that of *interpretation* (which gave him several reasons to think about Freud's psychoanalytic theory).[3] Ricœur wished to 'preserve the fullness, the diversity and the irreductibility of the various *uses* of language' (Ricœur 1983: 175), thus distancing himself from those analytic philosophers who maintained that well-formed languages 'are alone capable of evaluating the meaning-claims and truth claims of all non 'logical' uses of language' (ibid., p. 176). His second aim was to '*gather together* the diverse forms and modes of the game of storytelling' (*le jeu de raconter*), guided by the claim of '*functional* unity' among fiction and non-fiction. The temporal character of this unity manifests itself as a 'common feature of human experience' which allows the author to consider 'fiction, history and time' as 'one single problem' (ibid.). Ricœur's contribution to the philosophy of language thus seems to consist in the shift from *proposition to text* as a basic unit of language itself.

An interest in text is, of course, fundamental to Ricœur's hermeneutics, which first of all deals with the 'rules required for the interpretation of the written documents of our culture' (1991: 144), and consists of an *Auslegung* (explanation) rather than a *Verstehen* (understanding). The latter requires a deeper understanding of the entire context, whereas the former limits itself to a narrow class of signs 'fixed by writing':

> Sensible action is an object for science only under the condition of a kind of objectification that is equivalent to the fixation of a discourse by writing. This trait presupposes a simple way to help us at this stage of our analysis. In the same way that interlocution is overcome in writing, interaction is overcome in numerous situations in which we treat action as a fixed text. (Ricœur 1991: 150)

Ricœur invokes a well-known distinction between understanding on a pre-scientific level (which he relates to Anscombe's 'knowing how') and understanding on a deeper level, which he calls 'interpretation.' He next suggests that the 'sensible action' (*action sensée*) 'may become an object of science, without losing its character of meaningfulness through a kind of objectification similar to the 'fixation' that occurs in writing' (ibid., p. 151). This announcement sets our present framework: we should not conceive of the philosophy of action as the study of disembodied action, but rather as a study of the *significance* of action. This meaningfulness is neither deep nor hidden; it belongs to the public sphere of the narrative.

Philosophical anthropology is thus a place where the theories of text and action meet through the notion of discourse. This is 'realized temporally and in the present,' has an identified speaker, 'is always about something,' and has 'an other, another person, an interlocutor to whom it is addressed' (ibid., 145–146). Discourse assures the stability of this common space between language and interacting people; a space called 'action.'

Oneself as Agent

Ricœur began to work on *Oneself as Another* during the Gifford Lectures he delivered at the University of Edinburgh in February 1986, shortly after the publication of the last volume of his *Time and Narrative* (1985).[4] He used this occasion not only to distance himself from Heidegger, but also – more importantly – to clarify his disagreement with the Cartesian conception of the self as transparent. The resulting book constitutes a dialogue between his original (albeit Husserl-influenced) thought and several major themes in the contemporary analytical tradition.

When Ricœur talks of the 'theory of action,' he refers to the ostensibly autonomous field of study recently established by English-speaking philosophers, treating the philosophy of language as a mere working *tool* (ancient Greek *organon*) within action theory. As far as Ricœur is concerned, this subject matter differs from that of selfhood, which engages moral responsibility and requires a broader context of study (see also chapter 66). Thus it is not action but *personhood* that constitutes the primitive notion of any 'philosophy of action.' The problem of personal identity is first raised through this double attribution. Among English-speaking philosophers, it was Peter Strawson who proposed the most elaborate theory of the agent, through his idea of 'mutual dependence.'

Within Ricœur's framework, the problem of action arises in a way which further relates to a number of other issues. In response to the centrality of Anscombe's question, 'Which action?' (an intersection between 'What?' and 'Why?'), Ricœur sets up a series of questions we might ask about action – who does what, why, how, where, and when – awarding the first question, the one about the agent ('Who?'), a privileged place. Ricœur's aim is to show that, once all the other questions are answered, 'Who?' becomes more powerful than ever. By contrast, Anglo-Saxon philosophers on the one hand and Heidegger and Arendt on the other do not recognize this primacy. Their preclusion of the question 'Who,' Ricœur observes, opens their respective theories of action to the possibility of being myopically reduced to mere theories of events.

Ricœur is nevertheless far from being straightforwardly opposed to either Anscombe and Davidson, let alone the Anglo-Saxon tradition as a whole. He admires their capacity to eliminate numerous pseudo-concepts such as kinaesthetic sensations, 'which would allow us to know as an internal event our production of voluntary motions,' where the alleged internal observation 'is constructed after the model of external observation' (Ricœur 1992: 62). Moreover, he greets Davidson's anomological theory of mental causation with much enthusiasm. Indeed, Volume 1 of his own *Time and Narrative* contains an analogous conception of the singular causal explanation of historical events,[5] and he is even more open to von Wright's quasi-causal model of action as described in *Explanation and Understanding* (Ricœur 1992: 110).

Mistaken Dichotomies

Once action is granted an autonomous ontology, it becomes indeed natural to impose on it a number of distinctions that may subsequently become the subject of sophisticated philosophical discussion (see the reasons–causes and action–event distinctions). Ricœur recognizes the ambition of these distinctions as belonging to philosophy proper: 'the argument claims to be logical and not psychological, in that it is the logical force of the motivational connection that prevents classifying the motive as a cause' (1992: 63). He sees the opposition between reason and cause as 'strictly parallel with the opposition between action and event' (ibid., p. 64). Reasons and actions are said to belong to one language game, cause and event to another, and these should not be confused. Ricœur rejects this dichotomy, seeing no reason to take the two categories as granted; questions such as 'what made you do this?' cannot be relevantly answered without mixing purportedly separate language games. He claims that the clear-cut distinction made between reasons and causes was only possible because the place of the agent was left obscured: if we kept in mind the initial idea, that both mental and physical predicates apply to the same person, we would not be able to distinguish these two questions. With this in mind, Ricœur proposes a category of 'wanting,' which includes relevant features of reason and causal explanations while also allowing the agent the ability to make clear the point of his action.

Dichotomies of this kind are less pervasive (if not silenced) in Anscombe's work and explicitly combated in Davidson's. Ricœur contrasts both with other philosophers of action, such as A. I. Melden or Stuart Hampshire. In *Intention*, Ricœur notes,

> we observe the *esprit de finesse* of this analysis, which will erode the clear-cut dichotomies of the preceding analysis and, paradoxically, will open the way for the *esprit de géométrie* characterizing a theory of action diametrically opposed to the preceding one. (Ibid., p. 69)

This remark is an allusion to Pascal's idea that

> all geometers would then be intuitive if they had clear sight, for they do not reason wrongly from principles known to them. And intuitive minds would be geometric if they could bend their thinking to the principles of geometry to which they are unaccustomed. (Pascal 2005: 207)

In our context, it seems that, although able to have both *esprits*, Anscombe somehow does not manage to make them work simultaneously.

Ricœur's own ambition is to propose an alternative conception of motivation which (1) rejects the above-mentioned dichotomies and (2) satisfies what he calls 'phenomenological intuition' (1992: 77). The sharpness of the distinction between reason and cause is only plausible if we ignore both the passive aspect involved in the notion of desire and the grammar of several crucial intentional notions (emotion, affection, and so on) whose explanation is essentially causal. The explication sought for is teleological, yet this teleology is only dependent upon a self-imposed order. Consequently, the event to be explained is not hidden, for what is being related is a (chosen) system and its laws. This is what can be called the normative part of the investigation, whereas Ricœur's originality lies in his capacity to make it inseparable from the descriptive one (which provides us with a description of reasons). He correlates the essential features of the causal explanation of action with the reason-structured descriptions, and then concludes (somewhat provokingly) that '[t]he epistemology of teleological causality is thus the explanation of the insurmountable nature of ordinary language' (ibid., p. 79). This statement is not to be understood as the end of an investigation, but as its starting point, since it opens new perspectives for a more attentive study of the 'intentionto.' (For Ricœur, Davidson's main mistake is to have misunderstood the substantive role played by the 'intention to,' as compared to other uses of the term 'intention.')

The temporary dimension associated with 'intentions to' and with the pragmatic aspects of judgments presuppose a fundamental entity, namely the agent, and Ricœur is, unsurprisingly, reticent about its quasi-absence in Davidson's version of the story (Ricœur 1992: 80–81). Ricœur thereby questions the relevance of the whole ontological project advanced by Davidson, in which events, and not persons, are credited with the status of substances. The phenomenologist, by contrast, seeks 'a different ontology, one in harmony with the phenomenology of intention and with the epistemology of teleological causality' (ibid., p. 86).

Intention

The continental tradition has had a long-time interest in the problem of intention. It is therefore not surprising that Ricœur found Anscombe's choice of focus appealing. While aware that her Wittgensteinian take on the notion was quite different, he also noted that the Aristotelian roots of her work were also shared by Husserl – namely Aristotle's medieval commentators, read both by Anscombe and by Husserl's master, Brentano. What Ricœur viewed as Anscombe's 'piecemeal' approach (1992: 68) he took to be relevant only to a part of the problem of intention. Undertaking an analysis of several grammatical problems related to intention expressions (in order to understand better the appealing character of Anscombe's proposals), he was subsequently able to make clear the chief points of disagreement.

The notion of 'intention to' (do something) occupies a privileged place in the phenomenological study of intentionality, admitting the purported transparency of consciousness to itself. Yet, Ricœur remarks, both the privileged place and the transparency are rejected by Anscombe, chiefly because this sort of intention is not (immediately) verifiable through behavior and thus much better known to the agent than anyone else. Anscombe concentrates on an adverbial form of the notion of intention, 'intentionally,' which refers to phenomena that are altogether different from those associated with the 'intention to.' Ricœur, for his part, distinguishes three distinct kinds of intention-related expressions: to act intentionally, to act with a certain intention, and have an 'intention to.'

Past actions are said to be done (un)intentionally, which links the adverbial form of the term to descriptions (and explanations) of past actions. Likewise, when we say that we act or acted with a certain intention, we refer to our past or present actions (we never say 'I am going to act with the intention of doing so and so'). Intention talk about the future differs in an important way from other uses, since it is 'the only one that is amenable to analysis solely on the basis of its expression.' The two other uses, by contrast, are 'secondary qualifications of an action that can be observed by everyone' (Ricœur 1992: 68). This 'expression' (*déclaration*) presupposes a priority of the agent who, at this point, has complete control over his own intentions: if she does not express them, they will remain entirely unknown. The superficial grammatical study of this problem seems insufficient, given that predictions of the future look exactly like the expressions of 'intention to,' and are thereby not capable of giving an account of any specific personal engagement of the agent (like promissory utterances such as 'I am going to help you,' and unlike warnings such as 'I am going to be sick').

The future-related intentions in Ricœur's sense are inexistent in Anscombe's analysis: Anscombe braces her field of study through the well-known criterion of the application of 'a certain sense of the question 'Why?'' (Anscombe 2000, § 5). Such analysis of the variety of contexts in which we can ask this question encourages a piecemeal approach which is – here – quite satisfactory. This also renders plausible the moving apart of agent and analysis of intention (which is coherent with Anscombe's former presuppositions concerning the agent-independent character of action). Ricœur further remarks that her choice of the word 'wanting' over the expression 'I want' contributes to the project of eliminating the agent:

> what is eliminated is the one who, in intending, places this intention on the path of promising, even if the firm intention lacks the conventional and public framework of explicit promising. (1992: 73)

By implication, the problem of personal identity (of whether the person who does the intending and the one who later comes to act upon it are one and the same) disappears too.[6] This leads Ricœur to examine Derek Parfit's *Reasons and Persons* and to propose a novel criticism of his ideas.[7]

Ricœur understands Anscombe's and Davidson's project as one of eliminating a number of 'mysterious' inner entities from their ontology (and he is thereby surprised by Davidson's admission of mental events). He thus recognizes Anscombe's attack on the conception of pure intention (in section 32 of *Intention*) as a 'seeing eye in the middle of the acting,' since the conception belongs to the paradigm of representation.[8] Be that as it may; Ricœur maintains that it would be sufficient to modify our understanding of this 'pure act of intending' and that it would be necessary to preserve at least a part of it if we wish to give a complete account of embodied intention having a concrete spatio-temporal dimension. In order to prepare the ground for such a conception, he introduces the notion of *veracity* (different from the truth – *vérité* – of descriptions), as a part of a wider issue of *attestation*. This enables him to set criteria of correctness (for intentions) that might be known only by the person who has them (her 'shared confession' does not therefore amount to a public description: Ricœur 1992: 72–73). This specific notion of attestation (involving the notions of sincerity, lying, illusion, and so on) allows for an inner and reflexive side of intention, with no commitment to the Cartesian conception of the self.

Action as a Story about the Agent

As noted above, Ricœur chose a non-naturalist and transcendental perspective, in which the text becomes the place where our humanity deploys itself. He accordingly assigns a crucial role to the notion of narrativity in the formation of the identity of a character (in the sense of a character in a novel). The roots of this conception lie in Aristotle's *Poetics*, where action receives a privileged place not in virtue of its intrinsic properties, but (only) because it constitutes a useful means for transmitting views about the agent. Action so understood is an instrument, or a mere point of convergence. In Aristotle's *Poetics*, it is *praxis* and life, not people, that are central to the tragedy genre as a genre.[9] Ricœur retains the double meaning of the word 'tragedy,' referring both to literary genre and to the archetypical dilemma in ethics where one has to choose between two equally bad courses of action. In ethics, from his agent-focused perspective, Ricœur is open to the tragic dimension of action, which, as he sees it, is by no means manageable through the philosophical apparatus. This dimension reduces the force of any ethics of obligation; our understanding of ethical issues needs to be much richer than most moral systems might suggest (leaving room for the lack of a preferable solution). This understanding goes beyond the first understanding of the term 'tragedy' and, unlike it, offers no hope of *catharsis*. It invites the action, in its narrative complexity, to move '[f]rom tragic *phronein* to practical *phronesis*: this will be the maxim that can shelter moral conviction from the ruinous alternatives of univocity or arbitrariness' (Ricœur 1992: 249).[10]

The second source of influence on Ricœur's conception of narrativity in relation to action is the Russian literary critic Vladimir Propp, whose influence on the French structuralists was crucial. Just as Propp wanted to identify basic components of narrative structure of Russian folk tales, Ricœur aimed to identify action through its narrative (*récit*).[11] Narrative contains the essence of action, which has no independent ontology.

Narrative also contains a number of dichotomies; but they differ greatly from those of action theory. The first appears to oppose patient and agent: those who endure given processes and those who make them happen (see also chapter 26).[12] In parallel, Ricœur evokes Greimas' idea of the *actant* – a type of character having a metalinguistic (as opposed to concrete) status[13] – that has the ambition 'to subordinate the anthropomorphic representation of the agent to the position of the operator of actions along the narrative course' (1992: 145). In this framework, all action is *inter*action,[14] and a character's identity is correlated with the notion of action. Such identity is by no means reductive and constitutes an antidote to Parfit's conception of it. Nonetheless, it is far from being classical: the identity of the story makes, according to Ricœur, the identity of the character (ibid., p. 148). The effect of contingency disappears in this kind of narrative model: any 'it could have been otherwise' is 'inverted' into 'it must have been like that'; a new kind of necessity is 'produced at the very core of the event' (ibid., p. 142) from a backwards perspective. The narrative perspective, as it incorporates the temporal dimension, contains what is called a 'dynamic identity' of characters. These include both identity proper and diversity. Like Aristotle,[15] Ricœur sees the person as an open project, to be understood better through (the general context of) passing time.

Ricœur maintains that narrative cannot be ethically neutral and that, if it is to constitute the foundation for thinking about the action and the self, an 'objective' theory of action is an illusion. Consequently, for Ricœur, 'the dialectic between *episteme* and *doxa* will never be completed. What he seeks therefore is a space between 'mere' opinion and science [of action]' (van den Hengel 2002: 88). Yet Ricœur's idea of individual action as (only) a derivation from interactions involves no commitment to any 'profound' subjectivism.

See also: ACTION THEORY AND ONTOLOGY (1); SPEECH ACTS (8); PLURALISM ABOUT ACTION (12); INTENTION (14); REASONS AND CAUSES (17); AGENCY, PATIENCY, AND PERSONHOOD (26); ARISTOTLE (54); HEGEL (66); VON WRIGHT (72); DAVIDSON (73); ANSCOMBE (74).

Notes

1. This tradition had its own 'linguistic turn' (it took place around 1950–1960, being marked by the rediscovery of Saussure's writings by young structuralists).
2. The expression was coined by François Wahl in 1989 (Dosse 1997: 619).
3. See Ricœur 1965.
4. This corresponds to an extremely difficult period in Ricœur's life. Weeks after the lectures in 1986 his son Olivier committed suicide, and Mircea Eliade, one of his closest friends, died around the same time too.
5. It is not, however, clear that Ricœur perceives the difference between the two kinds of studied phenomena (history and the psycho-physical mental sphere).
6. Ricœur distinguishes here two kinds of identity, which he calls *ipséïté* (selfhood) and *mêmeté* (sameness). This allows him to put forward a 'dialectic of the *self* and the *other than self*' (1992: 3).
7. See the fifth study in Ricœur 1992, 'Personal identity and narrative identity.'
8. This expression is not Ricœur's, and should be understood as opposing the idea of a 'paradigm of action' (*paradigme actionnel*), as developed by Denis Vernant.
9. 'Tragedy is essentially an imitation [*mimesis*] not of persons but of action and life': Aristotle, as quoted by Ricœur (1992: 157).
10. The chapter on tragedy from *Oneself as Another* is dedicated to the memory of Ricœur's son Olivier.
11. He finds a number of similarities between his position and the notion of 'the narrative unity of a life,' present in MacIntyre's *After Virtue*, only to notice that this narrativity does not have to be naively unified (for we do not have a mastery of the beginning and of the end of our lives). This is why stories – narratives of action – always include arbitrarily imposed limits and viewpoints.
12. Ricœur here quotes Claude Bermond's *Logique du récit* (Paris: Seuil, 1973).
13. See Greimas 1966: 75.
14. This interactional dimension is also present in Ricœur's reading of speech-act theories: he thinks that the analyses they offer us are interesting, yet limited to a purely linguistic sphere of dialogical exchanges (see e.g. the second study in Ricœur 1992). What is needed, according to Ricœur, is an account of how different speech acts lie at the origin of a genuine dynamic co-alteration of speaker and interlocutor. Not only words, but the whole of action must be analyzed in order to enrich our response to the initial question (the 'who?' of what is going on).
15. For details, see Léandri 1997: 45–55.

References

Primary sources

Ricœur, P. (1965). *De l'interprétation. Essai sur Freud*. Paris: Seuil.

Ricœur, P. (1983). On interpretation. In A. Montefiore, *Philosophy in France Today*. Cambridge: Cambridge University Press, 175–197.

Ricœur, P. (1991). *From Text to Action*, translated by K. Blamey and J. B. Thompson *Du texte à l'action. Essais d'hermeneutique II* [1986]. Evanston, IL: Northwestern University Press.

Ricœur, P. (1992). *Oneself as Another*, translated by K. Blamey [*Soi-même comme un autre*, 1990]. Chicago: University of Chicago Press.

Ricœur, P. (2004). Discours et communication [1973]. In *Paul Ricœur. Cahiers de l'Herne*. Paris: Herne, 51–67.

Secondary sources

Anscombe, G. E. M. (2000). *Intention*, 2nd edn [1963]. Cambridge, MA: Harvard University Press.
Dosse, F. (1997). *Paul Ricœur: Les sens d'une vie*. Paris: Editions de la Découverte.
Greimas, A. J. (1966). *Sémantique structurale*. Paris: Larousse.
Van den Hengel, J. (2002). Can there be a science of action? In R. A. Cohen and J. L. Marsh (eds), *Ricœur as Another. The Ethics of Subjectivity*, Albany: SUNY Press, 72–92.
Léandri, A. (1997). L'action et la vérité. In J.-Y. Château (ed.) *La Vérité pratique*. Paris: Vrin.
Pascal, B. (2005). *Pensées*, translated by R. Ariew Indianapolis: Hackett.

Index

87370731R00363

Made in the USA
Columbia, SC
12 January 2018